TABLE OF CONTENTS

PREFACE

The fourth edition of *Personal Finance for Canadians* follows the same basic structure as previous editions but with substantial updating and revision to reflect recent changes in our economic and financial environment: inflation, revisions to the *Income Tax Act*, and changes in practices and policies of firms.

CHANGES IN THE FOURTH EDITION

In Part I, Chapter 1 has been strengthened by further reference to psychological factors that affect financial management, a new sample financial plan, and updated problems; and Chapter 2 by recent information about income tax changes and tax credits.

In response to recent changes in automobile insurance, Part II includes a revised and expanded discussion of this aspect of general insurance. Current information about RRSPs and about the effects of pension reform was added to the chapter on retirement income. To better illustrate the present value of a series of annuity payments and the gradual withdrawal of capital to extinguish a fund, two additional examples are included in Chapter 8. New information and current examples have been added to the chapters on saving and investing.

Particular attention has been given to restructuring and rewriting chapters in Part III. New graphs and tables illustrate the use of consumer credit and substantial revision with new information about types of consumer loans update the following chapter on consumer loans. New material on credit card costs and identification of current issues related to credit cards and credit contracts enhance the discussion of vendor credit.

Partially restructured, the chapter on mortgages has an expanded section on mortgage features and options. A new look at the content of Chapters 16 and 17 indicated a need to separate the discussion of credit reporting and debt collection, matters of particular concern to creditors, from possible solutions overcommitted debtors might employ. Therefore, Chapter 16 focuses on remedies creditors may use and Chapter 17 has been renamed "Strategies for Overcommitted Debtors."

There are fewer tables and contracts in the Appendix and, with the exception of a few very long ones, most are placed in the chapter where they are needed.

THESIS

Beginning with the first edition, the thesis of this book has been that, under dynamic conditions, memorizing many details has limited long-term value, and that the best preparation for taking control of personal financial affairs is a thorough understanding of basic principles, concepts, and vocabulary. With these skills, a person will be able to adjust to changing situations, recognizing the ways in which a new practice or financial instrument relates to previous ones, and to evaluate its usefulness. Although there is much readily available information about financial matters, many people fail to make maximum use of it. Either they do not know where to find it, or they do not know how to understand and use it. The purpose of this book is to assist readers in comprehending and making use of the constant flow of financial information. A competent financial manager should be able to ask meaningful questions before completing a transaction, but to do so requires knowledge of basic vocabulary and principles.

ORGANIZATION AND APPROACH

The chapter format is unchanged from previous editions: each begins with educational objectives to guide the learner, followed by a brief introduction and many examples, case studies, tables, figures, and contracts to illustrate the subject matter. A set of problems which offer opportunities to apply the material studied in the chapter to a variety of situations and a list of references complete each chapter. Instead of a glossary, the index indicates where to find definitions of new terms.

The topics included in this text, chosen to provide beginners with a comprehensive introduction to the field of personal finance, vary in depth of coverage. This was determined to some extent by the availability of other source material to the reader. For instance, there are many publications that discuss income tax and specific investments but few that explain, in any detail, either consumer credit or general insurance. Consequently, income tax, a very complex subject with frequent changes in regulations, is not treated in depth in this book but, instead, an overview of the tax system is presented to guide readers in the use of more specific or technical publications. Readers are referred to the suggestions for further reading offered at the end of each chapter.

Part I explains how to make financial plans for spending and saving, and the functions of wills in planning for the distribution of an estate after death. Tax planning is included as an integral part of financial management. Part II, Financial Security, involves identifying economic risks that threaten individuals and selecting appropriate ways to minimize risk. Insurance on personal possessions or on the life of a breadwinner is an important way to reduce risk. Increasing savings through investing is fundamental to enhancing wealth, and thus, financial security. Finally, credit, an integral part of our way of life, is examined in some depth in Part III. The complexities of obtaining consumer credit, credit reporting, collecting practices, and overindebtedness are thoroughly discussed, and attention is given to the many financial aspects of a home purchase in the chapter on mortgages.

The dilemma faced by authors of books on personal finance is how to handle the ever-changing nature of the information. Some respond by keeping their books very general, others by producing revised editions annually. The solution chosen here is to present reasonably complete information available at the time of writing while making it clear to the reader how necessary it is to keep up-to-date and be aware of changing conditions.

In spite of great care, it is difficult to ensure that there are no errors in this text and, therefore, it would be helpful to hear from anyone who finds mistakes.

K.H.B.

ACKNOWLEDGEMENTS

The preparation of this book required the generous help and cooperation of quite a number of people. In addition to those who assisted with previous editions, particular credit is due to the following persons who made contributions to this edition. Patricia Liptrap, an experienced credit counsellor, made significant suggestions for improvements to the chapters on consumer credit. Ilona Dobos worked tirelessly as a research assistant, searching out needed information and checking tables, figures, and manuscript drafts. Sue Wakefield persuaded officials at various financial institutions to provide sample contracts and other useful information. Donald Mcclure, senior account manager at Canada Trust did a most thorough review of the chapter on mortgages, and Paul Mustin, a manager at The Cooperators insurance company, checked the material on automobile insurance. Craig Hurl, of the Index Section of the Toronto Stock Exchange, kindly produced graphs of the TSE index.

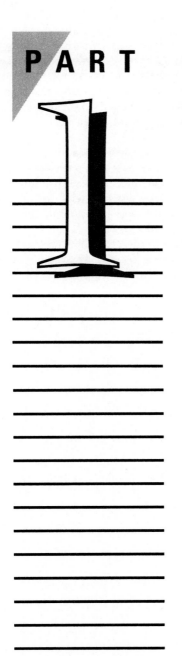

PART

FINANCIAL PLANNING

Contemporary interest in financial planning has generated not only increasing numbers of books and articles on the subject but a developing profession dedicated to helping people solve their financial problems. But what is financial planning? It has been interpreted to mean various things, including tax planning, development of an investment strategy, determination of life insurance needs, or a comprehensive financial appraisal. Although analyzing or forecasting almost any personal financial activity has been labelled financial planning, the results may differ in scope from a very specific tax plan to a complete strategy covering all personal financial affairs.

In Chapter 1 the general process of making financial plans is explained, including why future cash flow projections must be based on identification of future goals and knowledge of present resources. Related to most financial planning is the need for an understanding of basic tax concepts, as outlined in Chapter 2. More discussion of income tax will follow in later chapters that deal with retirement income, savings, and investments.

Financial planning is not only important in directing the management of resources during our lives but also in preparing for the disposition of our estate after death. Therefore, this section includes the chapter on wills and planning for the distribution of estates.

1

FINANCIAL PLANNING

1. To explain how financial planning can improve the use of economic resources.

2. To examine reasons for taking a lifetime perspective in personal financial planning.

3. To explain the basic principles of financial planning.

4. To analyze the functions of these types of records in the financial planning process: net worth statements, expenditure records, and budgets.

5. To evaluate various methods of controlling expenditures, and to identify obstacles to successful control.

6. To evaluate a net worth statement.

7. To distinguish between income and wealth.

8. To examine the status of the new financial planning industry.

9. To identify behaviours with a psychological or social origin that may interfere with successful implementation of a financial plan.

10. To demonstrate how a financial plan can influence decisions about spending, income tax, insurance, and investments.

INTRODUCTION

Money means a great deal to most of us. A minority are obsessed with it, some try to disregard it as much as possible, but most of us fall between these extremes. We depend on money to get the goods and services we want, but also as an indicator of our material success. Perhaps because it is so important, our emotional relationship with money, shaped by cultural and family influences, is not something we want to talk about. Nonetheless, the way we spend our money is a reflection of our most important values. The emotions of greed, fear, anger, pride, and guilt may all play a part in our financial activities.

Financial behaviour, like other types of behaviour, is determined by personality as well as influences from our social and economic environments. Whether you are a tight-wad or a free-spender, whether you see money as basic to your self-esteem and security, or whether you use money to control and dominate others is a result of your psychological make-up. In your social environment, established norms dictate many aspects of behaviour, such as what you consider essential for an acceptable lifestyle. In an economic context, you are constrained because your desires and wants usually exceed your resources and force you to make choices.

Most personal finance literature has either an economic or psychological orientation. Economists and family economists explain financial institutions and practices and how to make rational choices among competing demands. Psychologists are less likely to address the subject, but when they do, they examine reasons for our financial behaviour. Journalists may choose to write from an economic or psychological perspective. Sociologists, who study groups of people and societies, do not usually examine personal financial activities. A more interdisciplinary approach to money management would be a worthwhile goal.

While this text is written from an economic perspective, it is recognized that powerful psychological and social influences must not be ignored. You may have a clear understanding of financial planning at the cognitive level, but be unable to implement your plan successfully because of conflicting underlying forces in your personality or social environment. To help you to better understand your own financial behaviour you are referred to the publications on the psychology of money listed at the end of this chapter.

Why do the people who say they are in favour of financial plans far outnumber those who actually make plans? The reasons are many and varied. While the idea of being in control of money and financial affairs is widely appealing, many people may feel overwhelmed by the process and intimidated by their perceptions of its restrictiveness. They are fearful that it may prove too constricting on their lifestyle, they believe they don't have enough money to make any plans, are hesitant to make commitments to the future, are reluctant to spend the time, or are unaware of how to make plans. However we rationalize it, most of us procrastinate and feel guilty about it. This chapter explains how to make financial plans and suggests that psychological aspects of money and behaviour play a very significant part in their implementation.

How do you make financial decisions? Do you decide on impulse? Do you leave things to chance? Do you make decisions by default or, do you make deliberate financial choices in the context of an overall plan? It is said that there are two types of financial plans: those you make and those forced on you by circumstances. The way financial matters are handled can have a significant impact on the quality of your life. Decisions guided by a financial plan increase the probability of your goals being achieved. If, instead, you make hasty *ad hoc* choices, isolated from any long-term strategy, the best use of your resources may be impossible.

You can increase your wealth, achieve financial security, and gain economic independence if definite goals are identified and strategies to achieve them are developed. To do so, you must be clear about your objectives, be prepared to make plans, and be willing to give close attention to your financial affairs. Some people feel that careful financial planning exacts too high a personal cost and prefer to let their affairs take care of themselves. Perhaps they are unaware that neglect of financial management can be costly. Generally, we put a great deal of time, effort, and money into developing skills needed to earn money, but very little into its management after we get it.

As most topics in financial planning are interrelated, it is impossible to avoid mention in this chapter of some terms and concepts that will be explained fully later. For this reason, it may be worthwhile to review Chapter 1 after reading the rest of the book.

NEED FOR FINANCIAL PLANS

WHAT IS A FINANCIAL PLAN?

A *financial plan*, as any other kind of plan, begins with goals that indicate what is to be achieved. After available resources are identified and assessed they are allocated to the desired objectives. Finally, a strategy is developed to ensure that goals are reached. Although the procedure for making a plan is straightforward, implementing it is quite another matter, especially if some change in behaviour is required.

Financial plans come in many degrees of completeness and complexity. A small plan might be devised to control spending on entertainment and recreation; such a plan would include specific goals, a set limit for this category, and some ways to ensure that you do not overspend. Or, at the other extreme, a very comprehensive financial plan can include all aspects of a person's financial affairs, starting with financial objectives and including current spending and saving projections, investment strategies, income tax plans, estate plans, and schemes for financing specific goals including retirement. In most cases, people make financial plans that fall somewhere between these two extremes of complexity. An example of a financial plan is included later in this chapter.

WHY PLAN FINANCIAL AFFAIRS?

Planning makes it possible for you to live within your income, save money for short-term and long-term goals, and reduce financial worries and stresses in the household. Do you hope to purchase expensive goods, take a big trip, buy a house, send your children to university, or just make ends meet? Do you want to achieve financial independence and have a comfortable retirement? Do you wish to leave your dependents well provided for if something should happen to you? A financial plan will help you to take control of your finances and attain these goals.

There are both non-economic and economic reasons for making financial plans. Taking control of your finances can eliminate anxieties, abolish guilt, raise self-confidence, and increase satisfaction. In addition to feeling much better about yourself and your finances, there are a number of economic goals that can be accomplished by planning:

(a)   balancing cash flows,
(b)   accumulating funds for special goals,
(c)   adjusting lifetime earnings to expenses,
(d)   meeting the needs of dependents in case of death or disability,
(e)   minimizing income taxes,
(f)   maximizing investment return.

BALANCE CASH FLOWS   Everyone faces the necessity of ensuring that current income is adequate to cover expenses, a task otherwise known as making ends meet. Those with financial plans are in a better position to balance receipts and expenditures because of their overall view of the situation. Some non-planners go through cycles of feast and famine, spending money when they have it and doing without when it is gone. Others have sufficient margin between income and expenses so the problem does not arise. Taking control of current cash flows leads to peace of mind and greater probability of achieving other financial goals.

FUNDS FOR GOALS   We all have dreams of things we would like to do or possessions we would like to buy, but know the cost is too much to handle from current income. We have a choice: to wait until we have saved enough or, to do it now and pay later. There are costs and benefits to each option. Would it be better to submit to the discipline of waiting and saving, or to pay the extra costs of using credit? The alternatives must be weighed before making a choice. If the expenditure can be postponed, there is much to be said for selecting a savings target and gradually accumulating the needed funds. In this way, interest can be earned while waiting instead of being paid to someone else as a credit charge. Good money managers try to receive interest, not pay it. In the case of a house, it is usually worthwhile to save before buying because a large down payment substantially reduces interest costs. The key point is that more goals will be reached if there is a plan for achieving them.

LIFETIME PERSPECTIVE   A planner has a long time horizon, looking ahead to future years and not just this month or year. For instance, most people can expect the relation between their income and expenses to vary over their life span: generally, living expenses will be more stable than employment earnings. Living costs tend to rise somewhat as our expectations increase and definitely expand when children join the family. Earnings, on the other hand, may be very small or nonexistent for a student, take a jump with labour force involvement, increase gradually with experience, and reach a peak just before terminating at retirement.

In the early stages of family formation, it is not unusual to find expenses exceeding income and a consequent dependence on consumer credit. In middle age, as the children leave home and earnings are reaching a peak, opportunities to save may be particularly good. At retirement, there may be income from deferred earnings in the form of pensions, but often this is inadequate to support the accustomed lifestyle. At this stage, investment income can make life much more comfortable. In summary, an important planning task is to develop a way of distributing resources to support a fairly stable consumption level throughout the life span. A lifetime perspective on income and expenses is suggested in the diagram in Figure 1.1.

NEEDS OF DEPENDENTS   If you have dependents you will want to consider the economic consequences of your untimely death. Should death occur tomorrow, would there be enough money to support the dependents for as long as needed? Young families, who usually lack enough wealth to cope with such situations, buy life insurance to fill the gap. Another aspect of planning is to make a will to ensure that funds will be distributed as intended after death.

MINIMIZE INCOME TAX   The income tax system, which has become very complex, includes some opportunities to minimize our tax bill, but the responsibility is ours to know and take advantage of all the possibilities. By tax filing

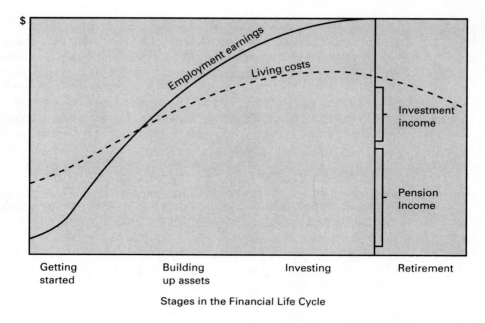

Figure 1.1   INCOME AND LIVING COSTS: AVERAGE LIFETIME PROFILE

time in April, it is usually too late to implement most tax-saving strategies. Plans must be made well in advance.

MAXIMIZE INVESTMENT INCOME   Some people who are good savers have no idea how to go about investing. They find the subject of investments so overwhelming that they leave too much money in low-yielding securities. If increasing wealth is a goal, it is necessary not only to save but also to invest prudently.

WHEN TO START PLANNING

Planning is best not postponed on the assumption that there will be more money in the future. Start right now to make the best use of what you have. You can achieve financial independence if you are determined to do so. It will mean taking deliberate control of your own financial affairs, rather than delaying decisions, letting things drift, and becoming a victim of circumstances. Many opportunities have been missed by those who considered financial matters beyond their control. Numerous people have retired with insufficient funds for a comfortable life because they did not save and invest during their working years.

REACHING FINANCIAL INDEPENDENCE

The way to financial independence is to spend less than you earn and to invest the savings. As your wealth gradually grows you will be able to achieve more of your financial goals and perhaps retire earlier. The key is to increase your wealth steadily so that eventually investment income can replace or augment your employment income. Naturally, it helps to have a high income but many highly-paid people spend their money as quickly as they get it. The sooner you begin to plan, save, and invest, the more time the money will have to grow.

LIFE CYCLE DIFFERENCES

Although there are individual differences, most of us will go through a series of phases in our lifetimes, called stages in the life cycle by sociologists. In terms of financial management they could be designated:

(a) getting started (to mid-thirties),
(b) building up assets (mid-thirties to fifties)
(c) investing (fifties to retirement),
(d) retirement.

Financial planning is dynamic. Expect your plans to change as you move through the life cycle.

GETTING STARTED   Students are concerned with educational and living costs and obtaining a job in a chosen field. Money saved from summer employment may be invested in secure, short-term deposits to generate as much interest as possible. Careful spending plans can be helpful in ensuring that funds will last until the end of term. Perhaps you have noticed that for some students the money ends before the term does. There are others who manage to put themselves through college or university and still have a nest egg at the end of it all. Why the difference? Could it be planning?

After graduation, high priority will be given to advancing careers, saving for an emergency fund, perhaps buying a house, and starting a modest investment portfolio. If you are raising a family, life insurance may be needed to cover the risk that you might die while supporting dependents. The funds available to do all these things will usually come from earnings, since there has not been time to build up wealth to generate investment income.

BUILDING UP ASSETS   The middle years are the time to concentrate on paying off the mortgage on the house, increasing saving and investments, and giving some thought to retirement planning.

INVESTING   In middle age most people have the best opportunity to save and acquire a variety of assets. Obligations to children usually diminish, the house becomes mortgage-free, and income will be at or near its peak. This is the time to give a high priority to increasing assets for an adequate retirement income.

RETIREMENT   After retirement, your opportunities to increase wealth will be much diminished. Your attention will be focused on sound management of the assets previously acquired and changing the mix of assets to emphasize income rather than growth.

From this review of changes in financial management as one moves through the life cycle, it will be apparent that long-term planning is essential. For instance, a small investment left to grow for many years will take advantage of the time effects of compounding, but those who wait until age 55 to start saving for retirement will have to save more to compensate for the shorter time for growth. Since we all want to achieve financial independence we must be willing to pay the price in time, effort, and self-discipline.

THE FINANCIAL PLANNING PROCESS

Financial planning is the name currently in vogue for a time-honoured process, often known as budgeting. A word here about terminology—the word budget, which has a strict technical meaning, is often misused in informal speaking and writing. A *budget* is a plan for using financial resources; it is a projection for the future. It is not a record of what was spent last year. Very often "budget" is used in a popular way to imply thrift, scrimping, or lower quality. This book adheres to the technical definition of a budget.

The basic principles of management apply just as much to handling financial affairs as to any other kind of activity. In this section, a general overview of the process will be followed by more detailed discussion of each component. The time span to use for financial planning is entirely personal, but for simplicity we will assume that the plan is for one year. During that time, most kinds of expenses and income will have occurred at least once.

The first principle of financial management—as with any other type of management—is that goals must be identified before they can be achieved. Because it is usual to have more objectives than financial resources, priorities must be attached to goals to reflect their relative importance. The second principle is that an analysis of present financial resources is basic to future planning. Assemble all records of income and expenses for the past year, as well as a list of your assets and debts.

The third principle is that successful planning requires that future cash flows be balanced. Refer to past spending records as a basis for estimating the cost of accomplishing objectives. Draw up a plan or forecast for a specific period, perhaps a year, which includes a statement of anticipated financial resources and their allocation; this plan is called a budget.

Fourth, strategies for the implementation and control of a plan are essential. Plans are intended to direct some action, to manage changes as they occur. The fifth and final principle is that effective financial management requires ongoing evaluation of plans and implementation strategies to keep the plan relevant and effective. A summary of the process is shown in Figure 1.2.

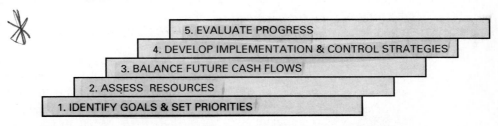

5. EVALUATE PROGRESS
4. DEVELOP IMPLEMENTATION & CONTROL STRATEGIES
3. BALANCE FUTURE CASH FLOWS
2. ASSESS RESOURCES
1. IDENTIFY GOALS & SET PRIORITIES

Figure 1.2   STEPS IN THE FINANCIAL PLANNING PROCESS

IDENTIFY VALUES, GOALS, PRIORITIES

What is meant by a financial goal and how does it differ from a personal goal? Personal goals tend to be more global and depend on a range of other resources as well as financial ones; a personal goal to have a happy, satisfying lifestyle will require other resources in addition to money and may be accomplished through a number of intermediate goals. The desire to buy a house would be a goal with a financial component, contributing to the larger personal goal of obtaining a certain lifestyle. In this book the focus tends to be on the financial aspects of goals, sometimes referred to as financial goals.

Three major areas in which many people have goals with financial elements are: (i) level of living, (ii) financial security, and (iii) estate planning. In allocating financial resources, each individual creates his or her own balance among desires for comforts and amenities at present, developing a reserve of funds to be used in emergencies and in retirement, and amassing an estate to bequeath to others.

Establishing financial goals is a very personal matter. A counsellor or advisor can ask questions to help you identify goals and the priorities placed on them, but cannot and should not attempt to decide what your goals are. Once the goals and their attached priorities are made explicit, a financial adviser can assist you to learn the management process necessary to reach the goals.

CONFLICTS IN GOALS AND VALUES

Unfortunately, it is a common family problem that people sharing economic resources do not always share financial goals. For example, the wife may want to save as much as possible for a down payment on a house, while her husband has a strong need to pursue an expensive hobby or other recreation. She places a high value on living in their own home and building up equity in it, but he considers this less important than present enjoyment. With limited resources, this couple will have difficulty in reaching both goals. There will be problems in their interpersonal relationships until the difference in values is settled. Recognition that a difference in values is at the root of their problem is an essential first step in resolving these difficulties but unfortunately some families miss this point.

Financial management sounds easy, but it can be difficult to accomplish because conflicts in attitudes, beliefs, and values continually intrude. One might think that a person who lives alone and who does not have to share resources or cooperate with others in determining goals would have no problems. Not so. Single individuals often experience financial difficulties because of a lack of clarity in goals, unresolved conflicts in priorities, lack of self-discipline, and poor methods of control. Nevertheless, the greater the number of individuals involved in the financial management of a common set of resources, the greater the potential for conflict. You may wish to do further reading about clarifying values and handling interpersonal conflicts; here we wish to emphasize that attitudes, values, and motivation are probably the most important components in the financial management process. Books, courses, and financial advisers can tell you how to manage your money, but only you can decide whether to act.

ASSESS RESOURCES

Once you are clear about goals and priorities, the next step is to take an inventory of resources—those you have or can expect to receive—that may be used to achieve these goals. There are two components to this resource assessment: (i) an inventory of assets called a net worth statement, and (ii) an income statement. The distinction between these two is important. A net worth statement shows the *stock* of assets and the amount of liabilities at a specific time. Income, which is not a stock but a *flow* of resources over a period of time, is usually expressed as an amount per week, per month or per year. An analogy may help to clarify this point. Think of income as the rate that water flows into a pond, and net worth as the amount of water in the pond (Figure 1.3). Those people who do not let some water stay in their ponds will find that their net worth fails to grow.

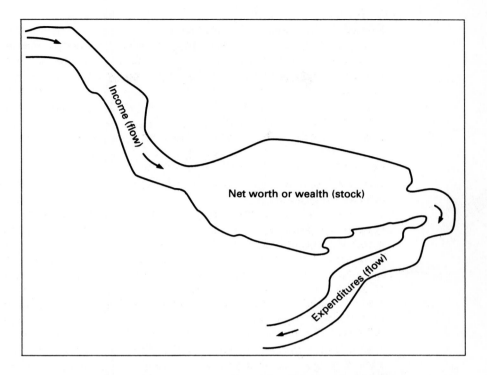

Figure 1.3   ECONOMIC RESOURCES OF THE HOUSEHOLD: FLOWS AND STOCK

NET WORTH

An essential requirement for financial planning is knowledge of exactly what is owned and what is owed. Begin by making a list of all assets and liabilities, or a *net worth statement*. Subtract liabilities from assets to find actual *net worth*, or wealth. Those who make a wealth inventory are usually surprised by what they find. They may have more assets than they thought, or more debts than imagined, or find that assets are not sufficiently diversified.

MEASURE OF ECONOMIC PROGRESS   If one goal is to increase wealth for financial security and independence, there must be some way to measure progress. A series of annual net worth statements will reveal the rate at which wealth is growing, and indicate whether changes should be made in saving or investing practices. Think of a net worth statement as a snapshot of wealth on a given day; since it may be larger or smaller at another time, it should always be dated.

Net Worth Statement   When making a net worth statement, list all assets at their current value and the total amounts presently outstanding on all existing liabilities, as shown in Table 1.1. Assets, such as a house or car that are not fully paid for, are listed at their present market value in the asset column, and the amount owing listed under liabilities. Total each column and find the difference between the two. If assets exceed liabilities there is a positive net worth. Many people start their working lives with a negative net worth, but expect a growing positive net worth as middle age nears. In summary:

$$\text{net worth} = \text{total assets} - \text{total liabilities}$$

Use the sample net worth statement in Table 1.1 as a guide in preparing your own. A couple is advised to make individual net worth statements as well as a joint one. Since Canadians submit individual tax returns, it will be helpful for tax planning to be able to analyze the assets of each person separately. For instance, a family might decide that the spouse with the lower income will own those assets that generate the most income. For later analysis, calculate what proportion of the total is represented by each asset.

What to Include   What to include in a net worth statement will depend on the intended purpose. Be consistent in the choice of items in annual net worth statements used to measure economic progress, ensuring comparable results from year to year. You may decide that household furnishings and clothing are fairly constant and can be excluded. On the other hand, if there is a need to monitor the growth in personal household capital goods, specific items may be shown each year. When an estate is being settled, a very detailed net worth statement may be required which will include all the personal possessions of the deceased. For loan applications, the credit manager might ask enough questions to estimate the borrower's net worth, with emphasis mainly on liquid assets and real property. When preparing a net worth statement for retirement planning, the emphasis will be on assets that have income-producing potential.

Uses for Net Worth Statements   What uses are there for net worth statements, other than to measure economic progress, obtain a loan, or settle an estate? Much benefit can be gained from an analysis of assets and debts to determine if the asset mix is appropriate and whether the debt/asset ratio is satisfactory. When making plans for retirement, it is necessary to know what wealth will be available to generate future investment income. Should there be a need to draw on net worth in a time of crisis, it will be helpful to have a clear idea of what the resources are. Whenever the need for life insurance is analyzed, the net worth statement must be examined to see if there is a gap between the resources the dependents would need and what the family already has.

Table 1.1 NET WORTH STATEMENT

ASSETS	Self or Joint Amount	% of total	Spouse Amount	% of total
Liquid Assets				
Cash, bank accounts	1200			
Canada Savings Bonds	3000			
Term deposits	1500			
Life insurance (cash surrender value)	500			
(a) **Total Liquid Assets**	6200			
Other Financial Assets				
Stocks and bonds	2500			
GICs	1500			
RRSPs	7500			
Pension plan credits				
(b) **Total Other Financial Assets**	11500			
Real Estate				
Home	135,000			
Other Real Estate				
(c) **Total Real Estate**	135,000			
Personal Property				
Vehicles	13000			
Furnishings, jewellery	9500			
(d) **Total Personal Property**	22500			
(e) **Business Equity**				
(f) TOTAL ASSETS Add subtotals (a), (b), (c), (d), (e)	$ 166,200		$	

LIABILITIES

	Self or Joint Amount	% of total	Spouse Amount	% of total
SHORT-TERM DEBT				
Loans, Instalment contracts	10 000			
Credit card debts	450			
Life insurance loans	—			
LONG-TERM DEBT				
Mortgages	110,000			
Other debts	—			
Total Liabilities	120,450			
Total Assets (f)	166,200			
Assets − Liabilities = NET WORTH	$		$	
COMBINED NET WORTH OF SELF AND SPOUSE		$		

Date *January 31st, 1990*

ANALYZE NET WORTH   Once made, a net worth statement should be analyzed, not just filed. Use Table 1.2 and the following questions as a guide for evaluating net worth.

(a) *Has net worth grown faster than inflation in the past year?*
     If not, assets have been losing purchasing power. Look for a minimum long-term growth of about two to three percent after inflation. For instance, if net worth increased eight percent in a year when inflation was five percent, there would be a net change of three percent after inflation, also known as the *real rate of return*. Next, check if all the growth has been in the value of your home. If so, this may be overshadowing a lack of growth in other assets.

(b) *What is the ratio of liquid assets to total assets?*
     In order to answer this question, you need to know that *liquid assets* are those which can be converted to cash readily without loss of principal, such as bank deposits or Canada Savings Bonds. Too much or too little liquidity can be unwise, as will be discussed in the chapter on investments. Some liquid assets, perhaps the equivalent of three months' wages, may be reserved for emergencies. However, since liquid assets tend to earn less than other investments, an over-emphasis would mean a loss of potential income. Many people have too large a proportion of their assets in liquid form.

(c) *What is the ratio of short-term debt to liquid assets?*
     A high ratio creates a precarious position if anything happens to income. Is the ratio appropriate for your stage in the life cycle? Normally, the debt/income ratio will decrease with age.

(d) *What is the ratio of investment assets to investment debt?*
     After purchasing a house with a large mortgage, this ratio may be low, but with time, it should increase.

(e) *What is the ratio of short-term to long-term liabilities?*
     It is best that short-term debt not be greater than long-term debt. Is most of the debt for long-term borrowing to acquire assets, or short-term for living expenses? Borrowing to buy assets such as property makes sense, but too much dependence on credit for living costs will be a drain on resources and impede the growth of wealth.

(f) *How diversified are the assets?*
     Add up all the assets that are deposits, bonds, or other loans, also referred to as debt securities. These assets are usually low risk, and

Table 1.2 ANALYSIS OF NET WORTH

1. ANNUAL GROWTH IN NET WORTH

Present net worth	$ 45 750
Previous net worth (year ago)	$ 42 525
Change in net worth (+ or −)	$ 3 225
Percentage change in net worth	7.6 %
Inflation rate for same period	5.1 %
Net change after inflation	2.5 %

2. LIQUIDITY

Total liquid assets	$ 6 200
Total assets	$ 166 200
Liquid assets/total assets ratio	0.04

3. DEBT RATIOS

Liquid assets	$ 6 200
Total short-term debt	$ 10 450
Short-term debt/liquid asset ratio	0.59 1.69
Total assets in property, and other investments	$ 146,500
Total debts for property and other investments	$ 110,000
Investment asset/debt ratio	1.33
Total short-term debt	$ 10 450
Total long-term debt	$ 110,000
Short-term/long-term debt ratio	0.10

4. DIVERSITY

Deposits and Other Loans (Debt securities)

Total liquid assets	$ 6 200
Total GICs	$ 1 500
Total RRSPs	$ 7500
Bonds other than CSBs	$ —
Other loans (you are the lender)	$ —
Total debt securities	$ 15 200

Ownership (Equities)

Total stocks	$ 2 500
Total equity in property	$ 25 000
Total business equity	$ —
Total equity securities	$ 27 500
Ratio of debt securities to equity securities	0.55

pay interest income. Compare this total with those assets for which you are the owner, such as property or stocks, called equity securities. What is the ratio of debt securities to equity securities? Are the various kinds of risks balanced? What might happen to the purchasing power of assets if we have a period of high inflation? Generally, debt securities lose purchasing power in periods of inflation and equity securities are more likely to appreciate. How much is exposed to market risk, as in a business or the stock market?

INCOME

The second task in assessing financial resources is to examine past income in preparation for predicting the amount expected to be received during the planning period. Use Table 1.3 to record income for the last calendar year. Income tax records can be helpful for this. Enter gross income before any deductions, not take-home pay. All deductions, including income tax, will be shown in the expenditure record.

OTHER RESOURCES USED   Include in the income statement any other resources used last year to cover living expenses, such as savings, credit, or gifts.

EXPENDITURES

ESTIMATE LIVING COSTS   Before making plans for next year, it is best to have the most complete information possible about current living costs. Those who have been keeping records will have a great advantage here. Otherwise, make the best and most detailed estimates possible of costs for the past year, using Table 1.4 as a guide. Try to reconstruct the outward cash flow, using cheque stubs, receipts, and any records available. Anyone who feels overwhelmed by the detail required for Table 1.4 can skip to the end and use the summary part only. This may be quicker but you will recognize that these estimates may not be as accurate.

Note that in Table 1.4 a check mark is to be put beside all expenses considered to be fixed. It is helpful in planning to distinguish between *flexible expenses* (which can be altered if needed) and *fixed expenses* (which are difficult to change in the short term). In the long run, of course, all expenses can be altered. Whenever quick adjustments are required, it will probably have to be in the flexible expenses. Enter expenses by week or month as convenient, then convert all to annual amounts.

Table 1.3 ESTIMATED ANNUAL INCOME

Source	Self	Spouse
Employment		
Gross income from employment	56 900	25 000
Other (bonuses, etc.)		
(a) Total Employment Income	56 900	25 000
Government Payments		
Unemployment Insurance		
Family Allowance	388	
Workers' Compensation		
Pensions (Veteran's, CPP, Old Age Security, other)		
Welfare, family benefits		
(b) Total Government Payments	388	
Investment		
Interest and dividends	450	
Rent (net income)		
Capital gains/profit		
Annuities		
Other		
(c) Total Investment Income	450	
Other Income		
(d) Total Other Income		
TOTAL ANNUAL INCOME [(a) + (b) + (c) + (d)]	$ 57 738	$ 25 000
TOTAL FAMILY INCOME	$ 82 738	
Other Resources Used		
Savings spent		
Money borrowed		
Gifts received		
Total Other Resources	$	$

Date *January 31st, 1990*

Table 1.4   ESTIMATED ANNUAL EXPENSES

Expense Item	Per wk.	Per mo.	Per yr.	Check fixed expenses
Deductions from Pay				
Income tax (include with taxes and security at end)		88.55	1062.60	✓
Canada Pension Plan	————	109.27	1311.24	✓
Unemployment Insurance	————	24.00	288	✓
Parking	————	367.26	4407.12	✓
Company pension	————	35	420	✓
Association/union dues	————	0	0	✓
Health insurance	————	10.00	120.00	✓
Group life insurance	————	10.00	120.00	✓
Long term disability insurance	————	12.51	150.12	✓
Dental plan	————	0	0	✓
Extended health insurance	————	10	120.00	✓
Other	————			
Total deductions	————		7999.08	
Food				
Groceries	180	————	9360	
Eating out	————	30.00	360	
Total food	————		9720	
Housing				
Rent or mortgage	————	929	11148	✓
Real estate taxes	————	125	1500	✓
Hydro, water	————	60	720	✓
Heat	————	75	900	✓
Telephone	————	40	480	
Cable TV	————	30	360	✓
Household operation and household help	————			
Home maintenance	————	58.33	700	
Purchase of furniture and appliances	————		1000	
Home insurance	————		300	✓
Total housing	————		17108	
Medical				
Insurance premiums	————	————	230.00	✓
Dental	————	————	120.00	✓
Drugs	————	10.00	120.00	✓
Optical (annual average)	————	————	50	✓
Other	————	————		
Total medical	————	————	400.00	

Table 1.4 ESTIMATED ANNUAL EXPENSES (continued)

Expense Item	Per wk.	Per mo.	Per yr.	Check fixed expenses
Transportation				
Car/vehicle purchase or payments		260.00	3120.00	✓
Vehicle insurance		42.50	510.00	✓
Operation (including gas, oil, licence, parking)			1200.00	✓
Vehicle maintenance			500.00	✓
Travel and public transportation				
Total transportation		302.50	5330.00	
Personal Needs				
Pocket money		100.00	1200.00	
Personal care (toiletries, hair cuts, etc.)		45.00	540.00	
Total personal needs		145.00	2740.00	
Gifts and Donations				
Gifts			1500.00	
Charitable donations		53.33	640.00	
Religious contributions		190.00	2288	
Total gifts and donations			4428	
Clothing				
Wife			450.00	
Husband			400.00	
Other family members			600.00	
Laundry and cleaning			100.00	
Total clothing			1550.00	
Recreation and Entertainment				
Hobbies			1500.00	
Liquor, beer, tobacco				
Books, subscriptions, records, tapes, etc.			520	
Other: _____				
Total recreation			2020	
Security and Taxes				
Life insurance		98	1176.00	✓
Annuities, RRSPs		50	600.00	
Regular savings		300	3600.00	
Income tax			18904.60	✓
Total security and taxes			23280.60	

Table 1.4   ESTIMATED ANNUAL EXPENSES (continued)

Expense Item	Per wk.	Per mo.	Per yr.	Check fixed expenses
Other Expenses				
Total other expenses			*800.00*	
Debt Repayment				
_____		*3120*		
Total debt repayment		$ *3120* *(included in transportation)*		

Summary of Expenses

Expense item	Per yr.
1. Deductions	*7999.08*
2. Food	*9720*
3. Housing	*17180*
4. Medical	*400*
5. Transportation	*5330*
6. Personal needs	*2740*
7. Gifts and donations	*4428*
8. Clothing	*1550*
9. Recreation and entertainment	*2020*
10. Security and taxes	*23280.60*
11. Debt repayment	
12. Other	*800.00*
TOTAL EXPENSES	$ *72172*
TOTAL FIXED EXPENSES	$ *48737.68*
TOTAL SAVINGS	$ *3600* *4.4* % of income

ANALYZE EXPENSE RECORD   Review the expense record to discover whether there is consistency between the way money has been spent and the statement of goals and priorities. Quite often we say one thing but do another. Identify spending categories that may need better methods of control. Is debt repayment too large a proportion of expenses? Will next year's expenses be about the same as the last, or are changes expected?

SAVING   What proportion of income was saved last year? Is this satisfactory or could it be increased? A discussion of savings strategies may be found in Chapter 9.

BALANCE FUTURE CASH FLOWS

INCOME
Based on the data assembled, estimate the amount of income expected for next year. If there is any uncertainty about receiving some income, do not include it. There will be fewer unpleasant surprises if you are conservative in predicting income, but generous in estimating expenses. Enter the amounts in Table 1.5.

IRREGULAR INCOME   When income is irregular it is harder to make a forecast, unless there are adequate records from past years. Make the best estimate possible of next year's income, but be restrained. Since expenses are likely to be more regular than income, divide total expenses by 12 and allocate this amount for monthly living expenses and savings.

OTHER RESOURCES TO BE USED
If it is expected that there will not be enough income to cover expenses, list the other resources that will be used, such as savings, borrowed funds, and

Table 1.5   THE BUDGET

Planning period from *January 1st, 1990* to *December 31st, 1990*

AVAILABLE RESOURCES
Income		$ *82 738*
Savings		
Borrowing		
TOTAL RESOURCES AVAILABLE		$ *82 738*

ALLOCATION OF RESOURCES
Savings
Emergency funds	*1000.00*	
Short-term goals	*1400.00*	
Long-term goals		
Total savings	*2400.00*	

Expenses
Total expenses	*72172*	
TOTAL SAVINGS AND EXPENSES	*74572*	$ *74572*
Difference between total resources and total savings and expenses		$ *8166*

gifts from others. Such resources may be needed by students, the unemployed, or the retired if they have insufficient income to support living costs. At other times in the life cycle, it should be possible to add to savings rather than use them. It has been observed that those who have been good savers all their lives are often reluctant to use these assets to support their lifestyle when they are old. They have saved for a rainy day and they are concerned that things may be worse in the future.

SAVINGS

First, plan savings for the year; don't just hope that some money will be left over. How much must be saved to meet various long-term and short-term objectives? For instance, if there is to be a large purchase made in four years, determine how much must be saved each year. Is there enough in the emergency fund? What part of the savings is going towards a retirement fund? Keeping in mind goals and annual resources, decide how much would be realistic to save for the year. This subject is explored in more detail in Chapter 9.

LIVING EXPENSES

How much does it cost to run a household, to clothe and feed family members, to take an annual holiday? How much will be needed for those desired expensive items, or the down payment on a house? Past records of expenditures will be helpful in predicting regular costs.

Whenever there is a lack of adequate records or the expectation that next year will be very different from the last, it may be difficult to make realistic projections. Allow for flexibility in your plan. Make another table like the summary part of Table 1.4 and enter predicted expenses in Table 1.5.

PERSONAL ALLOWANCES   Designate a sum of money for each individual in the family to use without having to give account to others. This will simplify record-keeping and also enhance family harmony. Obviously, some agreement will have to be reached about the general nature of the expenditures to be covered by these personal allowances.

BALANCE INCOME AND EXPENSES

Will the financial resources that are expected to be available during the budget period cover predicted saving and spending? Use Table 1.5 as a guide for comparing total budget figures. It is not unusual at this stage to find that there is not enough money for everything and that adjustments are needed. To balance the budget, you have the choice of increasing resources, reducing wants, or doing some of both. This balancing step is a critical one in financial management because goals, priorities, and the total expected financial situation for a year (or other period) are being taken into consideration. A calm look at the overall plans will lead to more careful, rational allocation of resources than hasty *ad hoc* decisions made while shopping.

When trying to make a budget balance, review estimates to ensure that they are as accurate as possible. Has uncertain income been included? Are the expenditure estimates inflated? What has been included that is not essential or important? Could better use be made of the money?

DEVELOP IMPLEMENTATION AND CONTROL STRATEGIES

A critical part of the planning process is controlling the plan. Many splendid budgets have been prepared and filed away by their creators who thought the task was finished. In fact, a plan for any type of activity is ineffective until it is put into action. Once the saving and spending estimates have been made to balance with expected resources, consider how the plan can be made to work.

Several key ideas about controlling a financial plan may be summarized in the following four generalizations:

(a) All those handling the money share a commitment to the plan.
(b) The control system is compatible with an individual's personality and habits.
(c) Controlling a plan requires that someone know where the money is going.
(d) The funds for major groups of expenditures are segregated in some way to prevent overspending.

SHARED COMMITMENT

Each person in the household who will be spending some of the funds must not only be informed about the budget but also be committed to it. Any plan not supported by both spouses will be doomed at the outset. For instance, the aftermath of a family argument may result in one person using money to punish the other by running up large bills on a spending spree. Such a family relations problem must be dealt with before any budget can be effective. Ideally, all those in the spending unit will work together in preparing the financial plan, taking time to resolve conflicts in values as they arise.

A SYSTEM TO SUIT YOUR PERSONALITY

It is impossible to prescribe a system of control for another's financial affairs; we can only suggest possible alternatives. People differ too widely in their styles of handling money and in their willingness to maintain written records. Consider your own habits and personality, and develop ways to ensure that your money will be spent or saved as planned. If money "burns holes in your pockets," something will have to be done to curb your impulsiveness.

Know Where the Money is Going

This involves some kind of record-keeping, but keep the system simple enough that it does not become onerous and thus neglected. Decide how much detail is needed or wanted and proceed accordingly. Often the act of recording expenditures in itself serves as a control on spending because having to write down what you spent tends to encourage reflection on your financial habits.

Control the Allocations

There are several ways this can be done. The simplest is to operate strictly on a cash basis, putting the allocated amounts in envelopes, purses, or sugar bowls. During a specific period, spending is restricted to the sum in each container. It is not a practical system for many people because of the danger of theft and loss, and the inconvenience of handling complex affairs this way. However, this concrete approach is useful, on a restricted basis, for people who have difficulty with abstract thinking. At the opposite extreme is the completely abstract method of control by double entry bookkeeping, which can be very effective if you are committed to the system.

A possible compromise is to establish several levels of control by opening a number of savings and chequing accounts. For example, you could have one account for long-term savings, one for short-term goals, one for irregular expenditures, and one for regular living expenses. These accounts serve the same function as envelopes or the sugar bowls mentioned above. Decide which groupings of expenditures can be handled by the same account and deposit the planned amount each time a pay cheque is received. To make certain that this system will work, cheques must be written on the appropriate account and cheque records kept up to date. If there is a joint account, each user must inform the other of deposits and withdrawals.

Actions or Events That Jeopardize Plans

Unexpected Expenses   As many will attest, unexpected expenses occur just about every month, so you may as well plan for them. Add such a category to the budget to prevent frustration when the unforeseen occurs. Accept that it is virtually impossible to plan spending exactly to the last dollar, but with experience it is easier to know approximately how much to allow for the unexpected.

USE OF CREDIT   How will the use of credit cards affect the control system? If purchases are charged as a convenience and the total bill paid monthly, these can be treated in the same way as other bills. However, some people need to consider whether they are susceptible to the impulse buying that credit cards encourage. If so, restrictions on having or carrying credit cards may need to be developed. If charge account balances are growing because only a portion is paid each month, consider the costly credit charges and also whether you have a tendency to overspend. Behaviour must be examined to decide if any changes are necessary.

IRREGULAR EXPENSES   Everyone has irregular large bills that cannot be paid from the monthly allocation without planning for them. Using last year's records as a guide, find the annual total of expenses such as insurance, taxes, auto licence and maintenance, and income tax. Divide the total by the number of pay days and deposit the appropriate amount in the account earmarked for these bills.

UNREALISTIC PLAN   If plans never seem to materialize, it could be due to unrealistic assumptions and plans, not an inadequate control system. It is predictable that the first time a budget is made, lack of experience and inaccurate records may result in poor plans. However, do not give up, but expect to make more adjustments to the plans. Remember that you can change the plan at any time. As time goes on, your plans will become more realistic.

A budget may be most needed just when predictions are most difficult to make. For instance, when there is a change in living arrangements or in household composition, or a drop in income, it is evident that things are going to be different but it is hard to know how different. A couple establishing a new household, will have no past records to refer to. They will have to make the best estimates they can for a few months, then review them and make a better plan. Likewise, the arrival of a child will add to costs, but new parents lack data to make forecasts.

INFLEXIBLE PLANS   Do not consider plans to be unchangeable. A plan is a device to help achieve goals, not a strait jacket. Any time it becomes inappropriate for some reason, it may be revised. Consider plans to be your servants, not your masters.

TOO MUCH PRECISION EXPECTED   Decide how precise financial plans and records must be to achieve the desired goals, and proceed accordingly. Do not make the mistake of embarking on a first financial plan with unrealistic notions of how much record-keeping will be done and how precisely the actual expenses must match the budgeted amount. Governments sometimes have an item called a balancing difference that is in the millions of dollars!

USING A FINANCIAL PLAN TO REFORM BEHAVIOUR   Feeling guilty about the way you are now spending money, you might want to make a plan on the assumption that certain vices will be cut out. How successful will that plan be? Reforming yourself may be a good idea, but it would be best to separate that from financial planning. We need to accept the fact that changing behaviour, even our own, is difficult. Anyone who intends to change their spending habits, their record-keeping practices, or their savings goal, must plan for a series of small changes, not a large one. As success with each small change is achieved, there will be motivation to undertake another modification. Attempts to make too big a change usually result in failure.

EVALUATE PROGRESS

Since the purpose in making a budget is to have a blueprint to guide financial decisions, there must be a mechanism for measuring progress. Periodically, compare what is happening with the plan. Are goals being met? If what is happening does not correspond very well with the plan, ask why. Was the plan unrealistic because it was based on wrong assumptions or on incomplete data? Is the problem with the methods of control? Do not expect too perfect a match between the actual and the budgeted amounts for each category of spending. Rather, look for a balance in overall cash flow, and check if any particular category is out of line.

Develop some system to simplify comparisons between the amounts budgeted and actual cash flow, and check on this often enough to prevent things getting out of control. An annual review of changes in net worth should be adequate but allocations for saving and living expenses need a closer watch, perhaps monthly or at least quarterly. Successful monitoring and review of budgets requires a system of records.

FINANCIAL RECORDS

CASH FLOW CONTROL WORKSHEET   There are three steps in this record-keeping task: (i) collecting the data, (ii) summarizing or finding monthly and annual totals, and (iii) analyzing the results. Some may get stuck at the first step because there is no system for recording what was spent. It may help to begin by concentrating on the regular, fixed expenses that are usually well known, or are recorded in cheque books. Once all the information on the fixed expenses has been obtained, the flexible expenses can be added.

Develop a method that suits you and provides enough information for your purposes. Do not attempt too ambitious a scheme, which may become neglected because it is too time-consuming. Some people use a ledger book, or ruled loose-leaf pages, with columns for all the expense categories. Enter each expense, as it occurs, under the appropriate column. The monthly summary can be obtained by adding each column. Others carry a small notebook to record expenditures as they occur, and later transfer the information to a ledger.

Analyze the results by comparing the actual monthly totals with the budgeted amounts. This can be done on another summary sheet that has space for 12 months.

A microcomputer can be used for record-keeping. A number of commercial software programs have been developed for this purpose, but they do not eliminate the chore of keeping records. The computer, however, does facilitate summarizing and analyzing the data. If you find the computer more fun than working with pencil and paper, use it for your record-keeping.

REASONS FOR NOT MAKING PLANS

Although almost anyone will tell you that it is a good idea to make a financial plan, few people actually do much planning. Why the discrepancy? If plans are considered to be such good things, there must be reasons for their rarity. Making and using a financial plan requires motivation, knowledge, time, effort, and finally, discipline and persistence. Planning is easily postponed in favour of more interesting or more pressing activities. This chapter, as well as other sections of this book, are intended to increase your motivation to take control of personal financial affairs and to show how it may be done, but it will be up to you to provide the other necessary components.

Those who think everyone ought to do some financial planning but do very little themselves, may ask themselves why they do not plan. What obstacles are preventing them from taking greater control of their finances? Is it lack of motivation or lack of a reason for getting involved? Is it not knowing how to get started? Or, is it a general distaste for financial matters? Once the reason for not doing more planning has been identified, steps can be taken to improve matters. The choices are to learn how and then get started on the process, to delegate planning to someone else in the family, or to hire assistance.

A variety of reasons have been advanced for not making financial plans. Some people say that their income and expenses are too unpredictable to plan anything; others feel that plans are much too confining, or that planning takes all the fun out of spending. Discouragement with a plan that did not work effectively may be the result of unrealistic estimates, or inadequate methods of controlling the plan. It would be better to try again than to abandon all plans.

A PLAN THAT WORKS FOR THEM

Iona and Peter belong to the ranks of people who don't like to keep a regular account of their expenses and who prefer to plan their budget in their heads. However, now that their children have reached university age, they find that they need to maintain a reserve fund to cover some of the boys' expenses. Also, they want to be able to finance the family's hobbies of cycling and cross country skiing, both of which are becoming more expensive with each new high-technology development. To find the least demanding and tiresome method of financial planning, they attended a one-day workshop that also included planning for retirement.

After brief deliberation, they decided that the best method for them was to create a budget around their current spending habits. To start, they needed to estimate their expenses for the next year. This involved figuring out how much will be spent on three major categories: (i) the house (mortgage, electricity, taxes, insurance, telephone, water softener, landscaping, repairs and maintenance), (ii) personal/discretionary (groceries, drugstore, cosmetics, clothing, medical, non-essentials for the house, gifts, books, ski and bicycle accessories, race fees, boots), and (iii) savings and investment (RRSPs, mutual funds, Canada Savings Bonds, savings account).

Their pay cheques, with combined earnings of $83 000 per year, are deposited into their personal chequing account. Automatic monthly transfers of funds have been arranged for RRSPs, investments, life insurance, mortgage payments, and to the savings account. To avoid recording detailed grocery expenditures, a sum of $850 per month is set aside for this purpose, or $180 for a week.

Once a month Ilona and Peter spend a few hours recording the cash flows of the previous month. They use a transaction log to record all deposits, automatic monthly transfers, cheques, cash withdrawals (automatic teller), and any other transactions. From Visa statements and cheque book records they are able to categorize all expenses according to their two major categories: personal/discretionary and house. Next, the amounts for each category are totalled and entered on the budget monthly page and also on a year-to-date statement.

Like everyone else, they find that there are times when there has been overspending in one or more categories. They are able to bring the budget in line over the next several months by spending less in each category or skipping a category (for example, no new cycling shorts and jerseys, videos are rented instead of going to the movies).

By choosing a budget method that suits their personalities, Ilona and Peter have been able to gain control over their expenses without drastically changing their lifestyles and without feeling bound by too stringent a system. In their case, flexibility and the ease of administration were the key factors that made their financial planning successful.

In summary,

(a) Inflow/Outflow

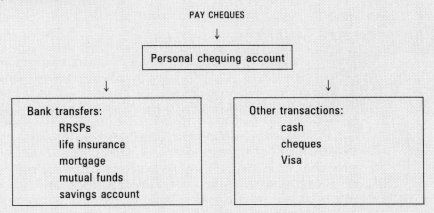

(b) Monthly Budget Control Sequence and Records

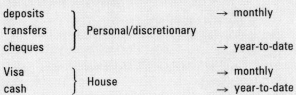

(c) Categories and Items

HOUSE	PERSONAL/DISCRETIONARY	SAVINGS/INVESTMENT
mortgage	groceries	RRSPs
electricity	clothes	mutual funds
taxes	car	Canada Savings Bonds
insurance	cosmetics	savings account
telephone	gifts	
water softener	ski & bicycle accessories	

HOUSE	PERSONAL/DISCRETIONARY	SAVINGS/INVESTMENT
landscaping	race fees	
repairs	books	
maintenance	magazines	
furnishings	medical	
	entertainment	
	donations	
	miscellaneous	

PROFESSIONAL FINANCIAL ADVISERS

Professional advice on personal financial affairs has long been available to certain segments of society. The wealthy pay investment counsellors for advice on investments and tax planning. The overindebted go to publicly-supported credit counsellors, who suggest ways of coping with too much debt. Where do the rest of us go for advice? There is no shortage of those who want to advise us—to invest in term deposits, guaranteed investment certificates, Canada Savings Bonds, mortgages, real estate, stocks, bonds, mutual funds or to buy insurance. Each advisor has a special interest in promoting ways to invest our spare cash, and each is knowledgeable in a special area. Since many of these sales people depend on sales commissions, we are uncertain whether their advice is unbiased.

The various kinds of financial advisers may be categorized as:

(a) investment counsellors,
(b) credit counsellors,
(c) officers and sales persons of financial institutions (e.g., bankers, trust company officers, life insurance agents, brokers, mutual funds agents),
(d) financial planners,
  – fee-only
  – commissions only (may be the same as (c), above)
  – mixture of commission and fees.

INVESTMENT COUNSELLORS

For years, professional counsellors have advised the wealthy how to handle their finances, with special attention to minimizing income tax and maximizing investment return. Many will invest funds and handle all the day-to-day decisions for clients, although some investment counsellors are not interested in clients with less than $200 000 or even $500 000. For ongoing investment services, the management fee may be based on a percentage of assets. Clearly, the assistance of these investment counsellors is beyond the reach of most families.

CREDIT COUNSELLORS

At the other end of the financial spectrum are the overindebted, who do not necessarily have low incomes, although many do. In times of debt crises, they turn to credit counsellors for help in reducing the pressure from creditors and debt collectors. Every effort is made to find ways to help families and individuals cope with the crisis situation, or to offer information and assistance to those not yet overindebted. This service, now available in most major communities, is free to clients. There is more about credit counselling in Chapter 17.

FINANCIAL ADVICE FOR THE MAJORITY

The majority of citizens, who are neither very wealthy nor overindebted, have lacked independent financial counsellors to turn to for help. If they wanted to know more about financial management, they had to read books, take courses, or consult those selling various financial products. The high cost of providing advice meant that independent financial advisers were not available for the vast middle class.

By the 1980s, both the availability of microcomputers and greater family affluence (largely the result of two-earner households) caused the situation to change. As the sums of money families handled increased and the services and products offered by financial institutions became ever more complex, the demand for information and help with financial management grew. This need was recognized by publishers who rapidly expanded the numbers of books and articles on personal finance, and by companies selling such products as mutual funds, stocks, life insurance, annuities, and RRSPs. The offer of some financial planning became a new marketing tool for a variety of companies. Large financial institutions, such as banks and trust companies, began to offer financial planning without charge, to entice customers. Computers made the planning process quicker and cheaper.

FINANCIAL PLANNERS

Financial planners may be categorized in three groups, based on the source of their remuneration. Many of those who call themselves financial planners sell financial products, such as mutual funds, guaranteed investment certificates, life insurance, bonds, and stocks, and gain their incomes from sales commissions. A much smaller number are fee-only planners who depend solely on client fees and sell no financial products. The third group are planners who combine characteristics of the other two: they charge fees for financial planning and commissions on the products sold.

A big issue is the potential conflict of interest when a financial adviser does not charge for advice but gains his or her income from product commissions. It would be natural for such a planner to find that a client's solutions included some of the products he or she is particularly well informed about and is licensed to sell.

Financial planning, one of the most rapidly growing businesses in the United States and Canada, may soon become an accepted profession, but in the meantime, efforts are being made to reduce the confusion resulting from its rapid expansion. It has been a largely unregulated activity, under review by securities branches in several provinces where discussions are going on about establishing standards for education, liability insurance coverage and ethics. In the summer of 1989, Quebec became the first province to pass legislation linking the use of the term "financial planner" with specific educational criteria and mandatory registration. Other provinces are expected to take similar action soon. Until then, anyone can call himself/herself a financial planner, financial consultant, or financial adviser.

The Canadian Association of Financial Planners, founded in 1983, is anxious to solve the problems of educational requirements and certification. Meanwhile, a number of competing groups are offering educational programs in financial planning. Those who successfully complete these programs are given a special designation such as certified financial planner or chartered financial planner, and may add the appropriate initials to their business cards. All this activity seems to indicate the emergence of a new profession that will eventually become standardized and regulated.

COMPUTER PROGRAMS FOR FINANCIAL PLANNERS   Since it may take a financial planner up to 40 hours to create a comprehensive financial plan for a family, which may cost as much as $3000-$4000, a way was needed to deliver financial planning to clients more cheaply. The solution was found in computers. Software programs have been developed that will use the data provided by a client to generate a financial plan fairly inexpensively. The programs vary widely in the extent to which they make adjustments for personal habits and preferences, and the assumptions being used. The expansion of financial planning coincided with the availability of microcomputers and suitable programs, and most financial planners now depend heavily on computers.

CHOOSING A FINANCIAL ADVISER
It is wise to make some inquiries before entrusting your financial affairs to an unknown adviser.

(a) Find out how the financial planner is paid. Is it from fees only, fees and commissions, or commissions only?

(b) Inquire about the planner's qualifications. What educational background, experience, and licences does the person have?

(c) Does this planner have certain areas of specialization?

(d) What sort of planning is being offered? Is it to be a very detailed, comprehensive plan, or the solution to a specific problem? Will there be a written report with recommendations? Does the planner have a sample plan to show you?

(e) Will the planner provide an analysis of the costs and benefits of the various alternatives suggested?

(f) What will the cost of the plan be?

SUMMARY

We have examined reasons why individuals should take control of their own financial affairs, rather than let them drift. Those who take control will increase their chances of reaching their financial goals and improving their quality of life. Although money is not everything, it has become the means of achieving many desires. The process of planning and managing finances begins with specifying definite goals, followed by an assessment of the resources available to reach them. With this information, a plan can be made for the next year or other time period. To ensure that the plan becomes reality, means must be designed to implement the plan and control spending behaviour. Periodic review of the process will reveal whether progress is satisfactory.

Financial planning requires some record-keeping. In this chapter we have presented sample forms for net worth, the analysis of net worth, assessment of income, summary of expenditures, and a budget for the next year.

Financial planning is an emerging profession. Financial planners offer advice on personal financial affairs, sometimes for a fee and sometimes not. Those who do not charge fees for their advice depend for compensation on commissions from the sale of financial products, such as mutual funds, life insurance, stocks, bonds, annuities, and RRSPs.

PROBLEMS

1.

WHERE DOES ALL THE MONEY GO?

J an and Dave, a couple in their early thirties, have recently purchased a new house in Vegreville, Alberta. The purchase price of $145 000 was a little more than they anticipated, but they love the life in this small town, from which Dave is able to commute to his office in Edmonton where he works as a sales manager for a scientific supply company. Jan, an elementary school teacher, is just getting back into the work force now that eight-year old Brent and six-year old Karen both attend school. Since she is working as a substitute teacher until a full-time position becomes available, her income is quite uncertain and irregular.

With a down payment of $49 000 from the sale of their old home, the mortgage of $96 000, to be paid off in 25 years, costs them $1093.44 a month. In the excitement of buying the new house, they forgot to allow for legal bills, moving costs, and the need for new draperies so they had to get a personal loan of $3000, with a two-year term. Recently, they purchased a new car for Jan, which cost $12 500, financed with a loan of $10 000, costing $333 a month.

They have $1500 in Canada Savings bonds (a gift from Jan's grandmother), $355 in Jan's savings account, and about $456 in their joint chequing account. Last year they received about $125 in interest from Canada Savings Bonds. Except for a pension plan refund put into a RRSP a few years ago when Dave transferred from another company, and now worth about $3755, their only major asset is their home.

When they married, Jan and Dave each bought a $100 000 life insurance policy. If they were to cash in these policies, each would have a cash surrender value of $2000.

They rely on a line of credit from the bank for emergencies, but apart from this have very little flexibility if Dave should be off work for any length of time. He does have insurance coverage at work which would pay about half of his usual wages if he should become disabled longer than three months. During the three-month waiting period, there would be a small unemployment insurance benefit and a few days' sick leave with pay.

Dave's benefits at work include the use of a leased car, and an expense account for lunches and the occasional dinner. He also has comprehensive dental, drug, and vision care plans, and some group life insurance coverage.

Fortunately, there seems to be little need for maintenance work on their new house, but Jan and Dave would like to start fixing up the basement. They are hoping that

Jan will get full-time work soon so that they will be able to clear some debts and be able to start on the basement.

Dave feels that with his relatively high income of $55 000 a year, including commissions, they should not have the money worries they are currently experiencing and should be in a better position to invest some funds in RRSPs to save for the future and take advantage of the tax saving, but at the moment he does not see how he can afford to do so.

Jan confesses that before the children came along they became used to spending quite freely since both were earning good wages. Now, with no established management pattern, the money just seems to disappear.

Following is the list Jan and Dave made of their monthly income and expenses. They do not keep records, so these are their best estimates. The income figures are net of deductions at the source such as, income tax, Canada Pension and Unemployment Insurance premiums, and registered pension plan contributions.

Income	Per month
Dave's salary	$2909
Jan's average salary	600
Family allowance	62
TOTAL	$3571

Short-term debt repayment	
Bank loan for car	$333
Bank loan	142
TOTAL	$475

Expenses	
Mortgage	$1093
Heating	95
Electricity and water	85
Telephone	30
Home insurance	20
Property taxes	120
Food	600
Entertainment	100
Clothes	200
Babysitter	30
Books, magazines, records	30
Gifts	100
Life insurance	110

Transportation (Jan's car)	200
Miscellaneous	200
TOTAL	$3013

(a) Make a net worth statement for this couple. Analyze their net worth position and make a list of issues you would raise in a discussion with them if you were their financial counsellor.

(b) Make a summary cash flow statement for Jan and Dave, noting which expenditures are fixed and which flexible. Analyze their cash flow situation. Are there some expense categories that seem to be missing?

(c) Evaluate the financial security of this couple. How well prepared are they for a financial emergency?

(d) Do you think this couple ought to be saving more? What do you suggest? What future difficulties do you foresee for them if they continue as at present?

(e) Evaluate the financial management strategies of this couple in terms of the basic steps of financial planning. If they are really motivated to make a change, where might they begin?

2. Decide whether you AGREE or DISAGREE with each of the following statements:

(a) Making a financial plan and sticking to it is easier if some rewards are built into the system.

(b) A budget takes all the fun out of spending.

(c) Financial planning makes more sense for those with a good income; for those who are poor, planning is impossible.

(d) If you and your spouse cannot agree on some financial goals, perhaps the solution is to handle your money separately instead of pooling it.

(e) If your financial affairs have been stable for some years and you have reached a comfortable agreement with your spouse about who pays for what and how much to spend on various things, your need for detailed budget analysis may be less than for a couple recently married.

(f) Students can't really make spending plans because they have no regular income.

(g) If your income is very irregular, your spending must necessarily be adjusted to the fluctuations of your income.

(h) It is impossible to make a budget work because of all the unexpected expenses that occur.

(i) The reason there is more belief in the value of budgets than in actually making them is the amount of paperwork involved.

3. Explain the difference between these pairs of terms:

    (a) budget and expenditure record,
    (b) assets and liabilities,
    (c) net worth and income,
    (d) credit counsellor and financial planner,
    (e) cash flow control worksheet and net worth analysis,
    (f) budget and methods of control.

4. Julie was taught that responsible financial management required that a record be kept of every penny she spent. She has continued to do this throughout her life. She keeps this in a running diary without any expenditure categories, and does not total the figures or do any analysis. What value does this record-keeping probably have for Julie? What is your opinion of its usefulness?

5. How important is it to have an emergency fund when you do not know if you will ever need it, and you feel that you could always borrow in a pinch?

6. Suggest reasons why people get into a position where their income does not cover expenses.

7. How did your parents teach you how to handle money? Will you do things differently with your children?

8. Some people say that the only way to teach children responsibility in handling money is to give them an allowance. What is your opinion?

9. Mark and Janet, who always ran out of money before the next pay day arrived, become so frustrated with the frequent crises that they decided to seek help from a financial counsellor. As the interview progressed, it became apparent that Mark was in a job that involved much entertaining of clients. Somehow this had led to more and more partying until he felt he needed quite a bit of money to pay his share when out with others.

    Janet was working full-time, but they both intended that she stop soon to have a family. Her complaint was that there was no way they could make the payments on the mortgage and the car loan, and support Mark's social life on his salary alone. She had wanted a cheaper house and a smaller car, but Mark felt the need to keep up a fairly expensive lifestyle. She blames Mark for spending more money than they can afford and making it impossible to save, and he says that, if she would be more patient, he will soon be earning more.

    What would you say to this couple if you were their counsellor?

REFERENCES
Books

AMLING, FREDERICK, and WILLIAM G. DROMS. *The Dow Jones-Irwin Guide to Personal Financial Planning*. Second Edition. Homewood, Illinois: Dow Jones-Irwin, 1986, 549 pp. Although written for American readers, much of the discussion of financial planning, life insurance, retirement planning, and investments is relevant for Canadians.

ANDERSON, BRIAN, and CHRISTOPHER SNYDER. *It's Your Money*. Sixth Edition. Toronto: Methuen, 1989, 264 pp. A reference for the general reader that includes financial planning, budgets, income tax, disability insurance, savings, investments, retirement planning, credit, wills, and estates.

BELAND, PAUL, and ISAAC CRONIN. *Money Myths and Realities*. New York: Carroll and Graf, 1986, 205 pp. Popular book that attempts to dispel widely-held myths about money.

BIRCH, RICHARD. *The Family Financial Planning Book, A Step-by-Step Moneyguide for Canadian Families*. Toronto: Key Porter, 1987, 216 pp. An easy-to-read guide to taking control of your personal finances that discusses budgets, income tax, insurance, RRSPs, mortgages, and investments.

CHILTON, DAVID. *The Wealthy Barber, The Common Sense Guide to Successful Financial Planning*. Toronto: Stoddart, 1989, 201 pp. In a chatty style, a financial planner advises how to organize your personal finances.

COHEN, DIAN. *Money*. Scarborough, Ontario: Prentice-Hall Canada, 1987, 270 pp. An economist suggests strategies for coping with personal finances in the context of changing economic conditions. Topics include financial plans, buying a home, insurance, income tax, retirement, estate planning, and investments.

COTE, JEAN-MARC, and DONALD DAY. *Personal Financial Planning in Canada*. Toronto: Allyn and Bacon, 1987, 464 pp. A comprehensive personal finance text that includes financial planning, income tax, annuities, pensions, investments, credit, mortgages, and wills with particular attention to the banking and insurance industries.

DRACHE, ARTHUR B. C., and PEGGY WATERTON. *Dollars and Sense, The Complete Canadian Financial Planner*. Toronto: Grosvenor House, 1987, 207 pp. An overview of a range of financial topics, including budgets, credit, investing, taxes, insurance, retirement planning, estates, and effects of changes in family status.

FORMAN, NORM. *Mind Over Money, Curing Your Financial Headaches with Moneysanity*. Toronto: Doubleday Canada, 1987, 248 pp. A psychologist examines the effects money has on behaviour, looking at the origin of money problems and suggesting therapies to help us to better understand ourselves.

GOHEEN, DUNCAN. *Planning for Financial Independence, Choose Your Lifestyle, Secure*

Your Future. Vancouver: International Self-Counsel Press, 1988, 111 pp. Detailed guidance for making a financial plan, including the necessary charts and tables.

GOLDBERG, HERB, and ROBERT T. LEWIS. *Money Madness, The Psychology of Saving, Spending, Loving and Hating Money.* New York: William Morrow, 1978, 264 pp. Two psychologists explain, in non-technical terms, how to become disentangled from our self-destructive money behaviours.

KNIGHT, JAMES. *For the Love of Money, Human Behaviour and Money.* Philadelphia: Lippincott, 1968, 184 pp. Addresses psychological meanings of money, including its uses and misuses, children and money, and family ties and money.

LINDGREN, HENRY CLAY. *Great Expectations, The Psychology of Money.* Los Altos, CA: William Kaufmann, 1980, 246 pp. A classic, but non-technical book, that explores how money motivates our behaviour.

MACINNIS, LYMAN. *Get Smart! Make Your Money Count in the 1990s.* Second Edition. Scarborough, Ontario: Prentice-Hall Canada, 1989, 317 pp. A book for the general reader that includes financial planning, income tax principles, but gives major attention to investing in the stock market.

PAPE, GORDON. *Building Wealth, Achieving Your Financial Goals.* Scarborough, Ontario: Prentice-Hall Canada, 1988, 246 pp. An easy-to-read guide for the novice financial manager and investor that considers interest rates, credit cards, mortgages, RRSPs, mutual funds, and the stock market.

TURNER, MARY, DANIEL LEROSSIGNOL, CLAUDE RINFRET, and RICHARD DAW. *Canadian Guide to Personal Financial Management.* Fourth Edition. Scarborough, Ontario: Prentice-Hall Canada, 1989, 231 pp. Accountants provide guidance on a broad range of topics, including planning finances, estimating insurance needs, managing risk, and determining investment needs. Instructions and the necessary forms for making plans are provided.

WEINSTEIN, BOB. *Money Hang-ups.* New York: Wiley, 1982, 157 pp. A financial journalist examines our attitudes towards money and their origins, and suggests coping strategies.

WYATT, ELAINE. *The Money Companion, How to Manage Your Money and Achieve Financial Freedom.* Markham, Ontario: Penguin Books, 1989, 203 pp. A guide to personal financial management that focuses on planning, investment strategy and retirement needs.

WYLIE, BETTY JANE, and LYNNE MACFARLANE. *Everywoman's Money Book.* Fourth Edition. Toronto: Key Porter, 1989, 223 pp. A journalist and a stock broker have collaborated on this wide-ranging treatment of a variety of personal finance topics, including women and credit, the budget, insurance, retirement, children and money.

Articles

"Achieving Your Goals," *The Financial Post Moneywise*, December 1989, 28-35. Offers suggestions for reviewing your financial management.

HIRSHORN, SUSAN. "And Baby Makes Three," *Canadian Consumer*, 17, No. 11, 1987, 6-10. Discusses the effect of a new child on the family budget.

TOWNSON, MONICA. "The Professional Plan," *Canadian Consumer*, 16, No. 11, 1986, 12-15. Offers guidance in selecting a financial planner.

Periodicals

Canadian Consumer. Monthly. Canadian Consumer Inc., Box 9300, Ottawa, Ontario, K1G 3T9. In recent years, the personal finance articles have been concentrated in the November issue, "Personal Money Guide."

The Financial Post Annual Moneyplanner. Annual. The Financial Post Company, 777 Bay Street, Toronto, Ontario, M5G 2E4. Usually contains articles on financial planning, income tax, insurance, investing, and retirement planning.

2 INTRODUCTION TO PERSONAL INCOME TAX

OBJECTIVES

1. To explain how the following elements fit into the basic structure of the Canadian personal income tax system: gross income, deductions (exemptions), taxable income, tax rates, and tax credits.

2. To distinguish between the following pairs of concepts:
   (a) gross income and net income,
   (b) average tax rate and marginal tax rate,
   (c) progressive tax rate and marginal tax rate,
   (d) wealth and capital gain,
   (e) before-tax and after-tax dollars,
   (f) tax-exempt income and tax-sheltered income,
   (g) tax avoidance and tax evasion,
   (h) income exemption and tax credit,
   (i) capital gain and taxable capital gain,
   (j) refundable and non-refundable tax credit,
   (k) RRSP and RESP,
   (l) tax avoidance and tax deferment.

3. To outline some approaches to tax planning, including income deferment, income splitting, and transfer of tax credits.

4. To explain the principle of attribution.

INTRODUCTION

In the late 1980s the federal government made major revisions to the income tax system, reducing the kinds of deductions, increasing tax credits, changing tax rates, and shifting taxation from income to expenditures. To keep up-to-date with the details of our ever-changing tax rules, you are advised to refer to the financial press and the frequently published books on the subject.

This chapter provides an overview of the income tax system, rather than an in-depth treatment of a very large and complex topic. Some basic terminology and a simplified framework showing the relationships among a few key concepts will set the stage for future reading and should facilitate your understanding of the many articles and books on the subject. In addition to the discussion in this chapter, some mention of income tax will be found in relation to other topics, especially investments.

THE PERSONAL INCOME TAX SYSTEM

THE TAX BURDEN

Personal income tax, one of the several taxes collected by the various levels of government and one of which most of us are very aware, has become an increasing burden. The $79 billion Canadians paid to federal and provincial governments in 1988 is, on a per capita basis, about $3062 for each man, woman, and child. Since 1944, our income tax burden has been steadily increasing, as shown by the per capita data in Figure 2.1. Note that these data have been adjusted for the effects of inflation by converting all values to 1981 dollars using the consumer price index. Thus it is possible to see the trend in the tax burden while holding population growth and inflation constant.

Although income tax was introduced in 1917 as a temporary measure to pay the costs of World War I, it has been continued to meet governments' ever increasing need for funds. Since we have become accustomed to a wide variety of government-provided services and a quite comprehensive income security program, large amounts of public funds are required to support these programs. Therefore, it is not surprising to observe that we are allocating increasing shares of personal income to tax payments. The situation is not quite as bad as it appears; during the past 40 years the incomes of most Canadians have risen substantially in real terms (i.e., after accounting for inflation), making it somewhat easier to support the tax burden.

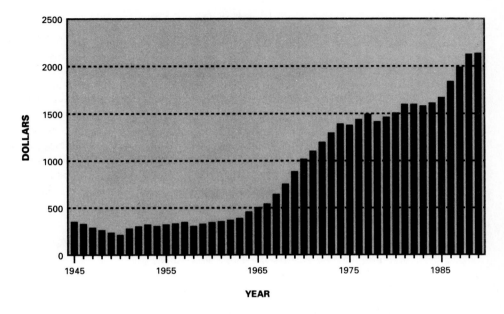

Figure 2.1 INCOME TAX PER CAPITA (1981 $), CANADA, 1945-1989
Sources: *Canadian Economic Observer, Historical Statistical Supplement, 1989/90.* Ottawa: Statistics Canada, 1990 (Catalogue number 11-210), Tables 1.5, 3.2, 11.1; and Leacey, F.H., editor, *Historical Statistics of Canada,* Second Edition. Ottawa: Statistics Canada, 1983 (Catalogue number 11-516), Series K8-18. Reproduced and edited with the permission of the Minister of Supply and Services Canada.

WHO PAYS INCOME TAX?

All Canadian residents, with incomes above a certain level, are taxed on their Canadian income as well as any received from outside the country. Each of us must file an individual income tax return; spouses cannot file a joint return as in the United States.

PROVINCIAL INCOME TAX

Although the provinces as well as the federal government levy income taxes, all except Quebec have arranged for Revenue Canada to collect the tax for them, making it simpler for taxpayers who need to complete only one combined tax return. Quebec residents file separate provincial returns. Provincial tax rates, expressed as a percentage of federal tax payable, change from time to time. The 1990 rates are shown on the next page.

1990 Provincial Tax Rates

British Columbia	51.5%	Nova Scotia	56.5%
Alberta	46.5	Prince Edward Island	56.0
Saskatchewan	50.0	Newfoundland	60.0
Manitoba	52.0	Yukon	45.0
Ontario	53.0	Northwest Territories	43.0
New Brunswick	60.0		

After calculating the amount of your federal tax you must add on the provincial tax. For example, if your federal tax were $2000 and you lived in New Brunswick, you would add 2000 × .60 = $1200, making your combined tax a total of $3200.

HOW MUCH TAX TO PAY

Stripped of detail, the process of calculating the amount of federal income tax payable can be summarized in three steps:

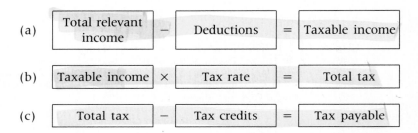

(a) Total relevant income − Deductions = Taxable income

(b) Taxable income × Tax rate = Total tax

(c) Total tax − Tax credits = Tax payable

If you analyze the articles on income tax in the financial press, you will find that most of the content has to do with these three issues:

(a) What is counted as relevant income for tax purposes.
(b) Which deductions can be used to reduce taxable income.
(c) How to make use of tax credits.

Each of these will be examined in turn.

WHAT IS INCOME?

Income can be quite difficult to define. In economic terms, *income* is a flow of economic resources over a specified time period. Income is referred to as a rate per hour, per day, per week, per month, or per year. The *Income Tax Act*, for the purposes of taxation, uses a legislative concept of income and does not necessarily define income in the way economists do. Therefore, we find that some income is presently subject to income tax, and some is not. As an illustration, an abbreviated list of some forms of income which are taxable and some which are not is given here:

Income Subject to Tax	Income Exempt from Tax

Income from employment
- wages, salaries
- net income from self-employment
- value of employment benefits

Pensions and social security
- Canada/Quebec Pension benefits
- Old Age Security Pensions
- Unemployment Insurance benefits
- employment-related retirement pensions
- annuity income bought with RRSP funds

Income support payments
- Guaranteed Income Supplement
- Spouse's Allowance
- Workers' Compensation
- welfare

Investment income
- interest
- dividends
- rent
- net profit
- withdrawals from RRSPs

EMPLOYMENT BENEFITS   With some exceptions, such as employers' contributions to plans for employee pensions or group insurance, the value of benefits resulting from employment is included in income. Some of the taxable benefits include employee loans, personal use of a company car, medical care plans, and travel benefits.

GROSS AND NET INCOME   When a reference is made to *gross income* it means all the income assigned to an individual before anything has been subtracted. Wage rates are usually quoted as gross income. *Net income* is less precise; it indicates that something has been subtracted. Any use of the term should be accompanied by information about what the income is net of; for instance, it may be net of deductions by the employer or net of income tax.

CAPITAL GAIN OR LOSS

In addition to taxing income, there may be tax on a change in wealth. Previous taxes on estates, inheritances, and gifts have been discontinued but currently there is taxation of some capital gain. *Capital gain* is not income but a change in wealth, or the windfall accruing to an owner because property or possessions have increased in value. In simple terms, capital gain is the difference between original cost and selling price. The income tax literature makes a distinction between capital gain and *taxable capital gain* because only a portion of any capital gain (e.g., three-quarters) is considered to be taxable.

Always associated with the opportunity to make a capital gain is the possibility of having a capital loss. Therefore, for tax purposes, capital losses are subtracted from capital gain, to get *net taxable capital gain*.

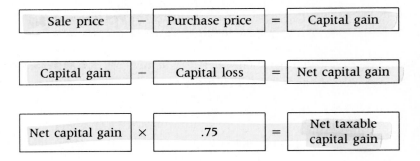

PRIMARY RESIDENCE   Capital gain realized on the sale of your home is not subject to tax, but there are limits on this: you (and your spouse) can have only one primary residence at any one time.

CAPITAL GAIN EXEMPTIONS   Since 1985 there has been a lifetime exemption for each taxpayer of $100 000 net capital gain. (There is a larger exemption for qualified farm property or shares in a small business corporation.) That means that during your lifetime you can receive a total of $100 000 in capital gain (net of capital losses) without paying tax. The tax department will keep a record of the amounts you have claimed, and you should do likewise.

The calculation of capital gains and losses has become quite complex in recent years; consult books on income tax if you wish to have more information.

NON-TAXABLE CHANGES IN WEALTH   If you receive an inheritance, win a lottery, or make a gain from gambling, these increases in your wealth are not subject to income tax. In the case of an inheritance, any taxes owing on the estate of the deceased will have been paid before the estate was distributed.

deductions to have less taxable income

DEDUCTIONS FROM INCOME

Once income and the changes in wealth that are subject to tax have been identified and listed, the next step is to examine deductions that may be used to reduce taxable income. The exact nature and amounts of deductions allowed may change whenever the federal government amends *The Income Tax Act*. Deductions from income may be classified in three categories, with the specific examples changing from time to time.

(a) *Contributions to retirement pension plans and Unemployment Insurance*
  – registered pension plan (RPP)
  – registered retirement savings plans (RRSP)
  – Unemployment Insurance premiums (UI)

(b) *Specified expenditures* (some within limits) associated with:
  – earning a living
    • union and professional dues
    • moving expenses
    • child care
  – investing
    • interest on money borrowed to invest
    • rent of safety deposit box
    • accounting fees
    • investment counsel fees
  – family support
    • alimony

(c) *Capital gains exemption*
  – net capital gains, within limits

CONTRIBUTIONS TO RETIREMENT AND UNEMPLOYMENT PROGRAMS

Encouraging Canadians to save for their retirement has been a matter of public policy implemented through the income tax system. Therefore, contributions to employer-sponsored registered pension plans (RPP) and registered retirement saving plans (RRSP) have been exempt from tax, within limits. Since money goes into these plans tax-free and any return generated within the tax shelter is not taxed, they are *tax-sheltered funds*. However, whenever they are withdrawn or turned into retirement pensions, they come out of the shelter and become fully taxable. A major reason for putting money in a tax shelter is to defer taxes until a time, such as retirement, when you expect to have a lower marginal rate.

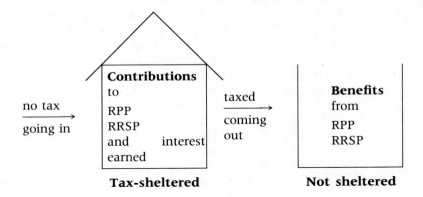

Tax-sheltered   **Not sheltered**

SPECIFIED EXPENDITURES   Within limits, a few types of expenditures are exempt from tax, including some associated with earning a living, investing, and family support.

EXEMPTIONS AND DEDUCTIONS   You may be confused about whether there is a difference between an exemption and a deduction, both of which serve to reduce taxable income. Technically, there may be a difference but in practice the two terms are often used interchangeably.

TAX RATES

Our income tax system is *progressive*, which means that as taxable income increases, the tax rate increases. You will recall that taxable income is income after subtracting certain deductions. The federal tax diagram below illustrates the progressive nature of tax rates.

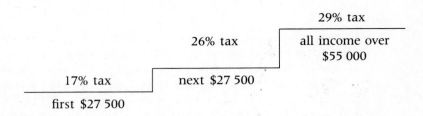

This means that taxable income of $27 500 or less is taxed at 17 percent. If you have more taxable income than this, the next $27 500 is taxed at 26 percent, and anything beyond $55 000 at 29 percent.

The highest rate you pay on taxable income is referred to as your *marginal tax rate*, a concept that is basic to understanding the significance of tax shelters and to choosing investment alternatives. For example, if you paid 26 percent as your highest federal tax rate, that would be your federal marginal rate and each extra dollar of taxable income you receive will be taxed at this rate. Obviously, if taxable income increases sufficiently, there will be a move onto the next step to the higher marginal tax rate of 29 percent.

To find your combined federal and provincial marginal tax rate, multiply the federal rate by the provincial rate and add this amount to the federal rate. Assume, for example, that you have a federal marginal tax rate of 26 percent and that you live in Manitoba where the provincial rate is 54 percent of federal tax. Your combined marginal tax rate would be 26 + (.54 × 26) = 40 percent.

Average tax rate is the percentage of gross income that is paid in income tax. Generally, this concept is less useful in tax planning than the marginal tax rate, although occasionally there may be a need to know what proportion of income was paid in taxes.

TAX CREDITS

After calculating total federal income tax, determine your eligibility for certain tax reductions, called *tax credits*. A tax credit is subtracted after total tax has been determined. Because deductions tend to be of greater benefit to those with higher incomes, many income deductions were replaced with tax credits in the tax reform of 1988. To illustrate how tax credits make the tax burden more equitable, under the previous rules a person with a marginal tax rate of 54% would save $540 for each $1000 deduction while one with a marginal rate of 32% would save only $320. However, if both persons were eligible for the same tax credit they would have an identical benefit, unrelated to income.

Some deductions that were changed to tax credits are: the basic personal amount, the age amount, the married amount, the amount for dependents, contributions to Canada or Quebec Pension Plan and Unemployment Insurance, educational costs, medical expenses, pension income, and charitable donations.

As most tax credits are not refundable, they are not useful unless you have some taxable income. If, for example, you calculated that your federal tax was $5000 and your tax credits $1000, your federal tax would be reduced to $4000. If, on the other hand, your taxable income were so low that you owed no tax, a tax credit would be of no use.

Some tax credits, such as the basic personal amount and the married amount, are partially indexed or adjusted for part of the annual change in the consumer price index. If the price index rose more then three per cent in the previous year, these amounts would be increased by the difference between the inflation rate and three per cent. For instance, an annual inflation rate of 5.5% would mean an increase of 2.5% in certain tax credits.

INDEXATION OF PENSIONS

Marina's CPP retirement pension, which was $450 a month last year, will be revised in January to take account of the inflation rate. Since prices rose an average of five percent last year, her pension will be increased by five percent: $450 + (450 × .05) = $472.50. This is an example of full indexation.

Unfortunately for her, the pension from her previous employment was only partially indexed. Adjustments were made for inflation greater than 3 percent. The pension of $750 a month was adjusted as follows: $750 + (750 × [.05 − .03]) = $765.

REFUNDABLE TAX CREDITS   The child tax credit is *refundable*. This means that a person with children but no taxable income can claim a child tax credit that will be paid to them twice a year by cheque. Those who have taxable income can use their child tax credit to reduce taxes. The amount of the child tax credit decreases as income rises, to a point where it disappears. The intent is to help low-income families with children.

The other refundable tax credit is the sales tax credit. The credit for each adult is reduced by family net income so that it benefits low income families only.

NON-REFUNDABLE TAX CREDITS   Most tax credits are in this category. A partial list follows:

Basic personal amount	Age amount
Married amount	Dependent children
Pension income	Disability
Tuition fees	Medical expenses
Charitable donations	Donations to political parties
Dividends	
Canada or Quebec Pension contributions	
Unemployment Insurance contributions	

The specifics of each of these tax credits, subject to change from time to time, will not be discussed here. Instead, you are referred to current income tax books. Because of its significance for investment planning, the dividend tax credit will be explained in detail in the chapter on stocks and mutual funds.

TAX PLANNING

The aim of personal tax planning is to pay no more taxes than necessary at present and whenever possible to defer tax to a future time when your marginal rate may be lower. Effective tax planning cannot be done each April, just as you are completing your tax return, but should be an ongoing process started months ahead. Most tax planning possibilities may be classified as either: (i) tax avoidance, or (ii) tax deferment. A few examples to be discussed here include avoiding tax by income splitting and transfer of deductions or credits, and deferring tax with registered retirement savings plans or registered educational savings plans.

TAX AVOIDANCE

Arranging one's affairs to minimize income tax is considered perfectly acceptable and is called *tax avoidance*. Many Canadians pay more tax than necessary through ignorance of the tax rules and failing to report deductions or tax credits for which they are eligible. This is quite understandable given the increasing complexity of our income tax system. The solution is either to become knowledgeable yourself by following the financial press, or to obtain advice from a tax accountant.

Deliberate *tax evasion*, on the other hand, is more than tax avoidance, it is a violation of the law. Our system depends on voluntary compliance which is encouraged by unannounced audits of a sample of taxpayers each year, involving an examination of records, receipts, cancelled cheques, bank statements, etc. It is in your own interest to keep your records in good order. Less complex than a tax audit is a tax reassessment. Revenue Canada may conduct a reassessment of your taxes for any year within the past three, which may involve a request for more information to support your claims.

INCOME SPLITTING   A family unit that is pooling income and expenses may have some members who earn a great deal more than others; nevertheless, each must file individual tax returns. An aim in tax planning is to shift some of the income from high earners to low earners with lower marginal tax rates and thus reduce the family's total income tax. This is a complicated matter for which professional advice is best.

A basic principle to be considered when contemplating intrafamilial transfers of funds is that of *attribution*. Under income tax legislation, reported income must be identified with a specific earner. In most cases, the person who earned the income also received it. However, if one person (A) earns revenue but arranges that it be received by another (B), such income is generally *attributed* to the earner (A) who is liable for the tax on it. Attribution rules are designed to discourage income splitting.

ATTRIBUTION OF INCOME

Keith, who has a higher income than his wife, wants to reduce the family's income tax burden. He thought that if he gave Sarah $20 000 in Canada Savings Bonds she would receive the interest of about $2000 and report this revenue on her income tax return. By reducing his income and increasing hers he hoped to minimize family tax.

Unfortunately, Keith did not understand the attribution rules that apply to any loans or transfers of property to a spouse. The $2000 in interest will be attributed to Keith and taxed as his income. However, if Keith pays the tax but Sarah keeps the $2000 and invests it, any yield she gets will not be attributed back to her husband. Generally, there is no attribution of income earned on attributed income. Therefore, it may be to their advantage to make this transfer if they take a long-term perspective because over time Sarah will have a growing asset. The bookkeeping will be simplified if they keep the principal of $2000 in a separate account from the yield this sum generates.

With professional advice some income splitting can be achieved, for instance, attribution rules do not generally apply to business income earned by a spouse or child from funds lent or transferred to them. Funds may be contributed to a spouse's RRSP, about which more will be said in Chapter 7. As a gift, the higher income spouse may pay the income tax of the lower income spouse as a way of transferring funds. Or, if one spouse has more income than the other, the higher income one can pay as many of the family expenses as possible, leaving the other to invest his or her personal income to eventually generate revenue for the lower income spouse. A spouse or child may be paid an income for work performed in the family's unincorporated business.

If family allowance cheques are put into an account or investment for the child, the income earned will not be attributed back to the parent. This is an effective way of income splitting and building an asset for the child.

TRANSFER OF TAX CREDITS　　If your spouse cannot use all the eligible tax credits, they can be transferred to you. For instance, if one spouse is eligible for but cannot use certain tax credits, such as the age amount, pension income amount, or tuition fees, they may be transferred to the other spouse.

TAX DEFERMENT

With careful planning, you may be able to defer income tax by arranging for some income not to come into your hands until a later time when you expect to have a lower marginal tax rate.

REGISTERED RETIREMENT SAVINGS PLANS　　RRSPs are good examples of tax deferment. While you are earning wages you can shift some funds into a tax shelter or RRSP without paying any tax and the money will grow, sheltered from tax, until you deregister the plan. Of course, when you take the funds out of the RRSP you will pay income tax, but at a lower rate if you choose a year when you have less income. Even if your marginal tax rate is not expected to be lower in the future, funds in a tax shelter will grow faster than unsheltered funds. This point is illustrated in an example in Chapter 7.

　　Whenever you have income not needed currently, give some thought to possibilities for deferring it. Situations to consider are pension plan refunds when you change jobs and retirement allowances. Possibly these may be transferred directly from your employer to your RRSP.

REGISTERED EDUCATION SAVINGS PLANS　　To create a fund to support a child's post-secondary education and to defer tax on investment income, you might enrol in a RESP. The money put into a RESP is not tax deductible, but the interest earned while it is in the plan is tax-sheltered. If the child participates in post-secondary education, the money will be paid to the child and taxed in his or her hands, presumably at a lower marginal rate than the parents'. There is a disadvantage in this plan, in that if the child does not continue past the secondary level of education, and no other children in the family continue either, the interest earned in the fund may be forfeited; the invested capital would be refunded to the parents. However, some plans permit the funds to be paid to almost any designate attending a post-secondary educational program.

BEFORE-TAX AND AFTER-TAX DOLLARS

Articles on tax planning or investing often mention the terms before-tax and after-tax dollars. It is important to make a distinction between funds on which income tax has already been paid, or *after-tax dollars*, and money received on which no tax has been paid, or *before tax dollars*. The following example illustrates the difference.

SHOULD SHE USE A TAX SHELTER?

Sarah has $1000, before tax, to invest and she is wondering whether to put the money in an RRSP or to simply buy a guaranteed investment certificate without the restrictions of a tax shelter. Her combined federal and provincial marginal tax rate is 39 percent, and the interest rate on the certificate is 9 percent. When she worked out the return over five years for each alternative, her results were as follows:

Alternative 1: put $1000 in tax shelter

Amount invested	$1000 before tax
Compound interest @ 9%	540 not taxed
Total value after 5 years	1540 before tax

Whenever she takes the money out of the tax shelter, these before-tax dollars will become subject to income tax. If taken out when her marginal rate is 39 percent she would pay $600 in taxes and have $940 left. However, if she can leave the funds in the tax shelter until some time when her income is less, the tax will be lower.

Alternative 2: invest $1000 not tax-sheltered

Amount available	$1000.00 before tax
Income tax payable	390.00
Amount to invest	610.00 after tax

Year 1

Interest @ 9%	54.90 before tax
Income tax on interest @ 39%	22.41
Interest 56.90 − 22.41	33.49 after tax

Year 2

Interest on $643.49 (610 + 33.49)	57.91 before tax
Tax on interest (.39 × 57.91)	22.59
Interest (57.91 − 22.59)	35.32 after tax

Year 3

Interest on $678.81	61.09 before tax
Tax on interest	23.83
Interest	37.26 after tax

Year 4

Interest on $716.07	64.45 before tax
Tax on interest	25.13
Interest	39.32 after tax

Year 5

Interest on $775.39	67.98 before tax
Tax on interest	26.51
Interest	41.47 after tax
Total value of investment	816.86 after tax

Comparison of the Alternatives

	Alternative 1	Alternative 2
Amount invested	$1000	$610
Total interest earned	540	306
Income tax paid	nil	485
Asset value after 5 years	1540	817
Income tax due if taken out of shelter	600	nil
After-tax value	940	817

SUMMARY

This chapter provides a framework for understanding personal income tax because the income tax literature is full of details which can be confusing if the basic structure is not clearly understood. Some principles discussed in this chapter were: (i) the distinction between income that is taxable and income that is not, (ii) the reduction of taxable income by certain exemptions or deductions, (iii) the progressive nature of tax rates, and (iv) the function of tax credits in reducing tax payable and (v) the attribution of income.

Tax planning should be a year-around activity because many significant steps cannot be taken at the last minute. It is important to pay attention to marginal tax rate, or the rate on the last dollar of income, and to distinguish between before-tax and after-tax dollars. Much tax planning is either identifying ways to avoid income tax or ways to defer tax until a time when marginal tax rate will be lower. In addition to taxing income, some increases in wealth or capital gain are subject to taxation.

PROBLEMS

1. If you received any of the following, should they be reported as income on your tax return?

    (a) an inheritance from your grandfather's estate.
    (b) a lottery winning.
    (c) the old age security pension.
    (d) capital gain from selling your principal residence.
    (e) Unemployment Insurance benefits.

2. If you have dependent children, can you claim a deduction for them, a tax credit, or both? Explain.

3. Decide whether you AGREE or DISAGREE with each of the following statements:

    (a) The money put into a tax shelter would be classed as after-tax dollars.
    (b) The proportion of taxable income on which tax is paid is called the marginal tax rate.
    (c) To find your taxable income, you would deduct from gross income any applicable tax credits.
    (d) Capital gain is a change in wealth rather than income.
    (e) Persons over the age of 65 are allowed special tax credits.
    (f) On a per capita basis, the federal income tax burden has not changed significantly over the past 25 years.
    (g) Spouses have a choice whether to file individual or joint income tax forms.
    (h) You can earn $1000 of interest income without paying tax on it.
    (i) Capital loss is deducted from capital gain before determining net taxable capital gain.
    (j) RRSPs are tax shelters because the funds put in are not taxed, even though the income gained while in the shelter is taxed.

4. Jean, who lives in Manitoba, has determined that she owes $8997 in federal income tax. How much provincial tax does she owe? Find the current tax rate for Manitoba, or use the 1990 rates given in this chapter.

5. Assume that you have a mortgage at 11 percent and also have $6000 that can be used either to reduce the mortgage or to invest at 9 percent. Should you (i) reduce your mortgage by $6000 and borrow money to invest, or (ii) simply invest the money?

The mortgage company will not charge a penalty if you decide to reduce your mortgage. Your combined federal and provincial marginal tax rate is 39 percent. If you borrow money to invest, the interest will be a tax deduction, but the interest paid on your mortgage is not deductible.

6. Obtain a current income tax form and complete it for Vivian who lives in Vancouver, is aged 45, employed full-time, and has no dependents. She has never before reported any capital gains. The information she provides is as follows:

Employment income	$34 540
Interest income	1 875
Net capital gain from selling property (not her home)	9 600
Contributions to	
Unemployment Insurance	570
Canada Pension Plan	450
RRSP	1 500
registered pension plan	2 000
professional dues	350
Charitable donations	950
Rent on safety deposit box	15
Accountant's fee	150
Donation to the federal Liberal party	250

(a) Find Vivian's
   – taxable income
   – federal tax
   – provincial tax
(b) What is her federal marginal tax rate?
(c) Does Vivian have any tax credits? If so, which?

7. What is a significant difference between an RRSP and an RESP?

8. Suggest some ways of reducing a family's income tax. Would they be considered tax avoidance or tax evasion?

REFERENCES
Books

ANDERSON, BRIAN, and CHRISTOPHER SNYDER. *It's Your Money*. Sixth Edition. Toronto: Methuen, 1989, 264 pp. A reference for the general reader which includes financial planning, budgets, income tax, disability insurance, savings, investments, retirement planning, credit, wills, and estates.

BEACH, WAYNE, and LYLE R. HEPBURN. *Are You Paying Too Much Tax?* Toronto: McGraw-Hill Ryerson, annual, 206 pp. A tax planning guide for the general reader that includes a discussion of capital gains, RRSPs, and investment income.

BIRCH, RICHARD. *The Canadian Price Waterhouse Personal Tax Advisor.* Toronto: McClelland-Bantam, 1989, 199 pp. A non-technical guide prepared by tax accountants that outlines how the tax system works and explains the basics of personal income tax, including RRSPs.

COSTELLO, BRIAN. *Your Money and How to Keep It.* Fifth Edition. Toronto: Stoddart, 1990, 248 pp. Particular emphasis on investments and income tax.

DELOITE, HASKINGS, SELLS. *How to Reduce the Tax You Pay.* Revised Edition. Toronto: Key Porter Books, 1989, 245 pp. A non-technical guide, prepared by tax accountants, that explains the basics of personal income tax.

DRACHE, ARTHUR B. C., editor. *Canada Tax Planning Service.* Toronto: Richard De Boo Publishers, subscription service. A detailed professional reference that is kept up-to-date by regular mailings of replacement pages. Four-volume looseleaf set.

DRACHE, ARTHUR B. C., editor. *The Canadian Taxpayer.* Toronto: Richard De Boo Publishers, bimonthly. A newsletter with up-to-date income tax information. Includes articles on tax cases, relevant political events, recent changes to regulations and other tax planning topics of interest.

FISHER, S. BRIAN and PAUL B. HICKEY, editors. *The Canadian Personal Tax Planning Guide, 1989-90.* Don Mills, Ontario: Richard De Boo, 1989, 203 pp. A comprehensive and non-technical guide to personal income tax, written by accountants for the general reader.

GRENBY, MIKE. *Mike Grenby's Tax Tips, How to Pay Less Tax This Year*, annual. Vancouver: International Self-Counsel Press. A quick reference on how to reduce your income tax.

HOGG, R. D. *Preparing Your Income Tax Returns.* Toronto: CCH Canadian, annual, 589 pp. A complete and technical guide to income tax preparation.

HUOT, RENE. *Canadian Income Tax Desktop Reference, 1989-90 Edition.* Toronto: Richard De Boo Publishers, 81 Curlew Drive, Don Mills, Ontario, 1989, A comprehensive professional reference that includes personal, corporate and Quebec taxation rules. Is referenced to the *Income Tax Act.*

JACKS, EVELYN. *Jacks on Tax Savings.* Toronto: McGraw-Hill Ryerson, annual, 228 pp. Explains the current tax rules and demonstrates how to prepare a tax return.

MACINNIS, LYMAN. *Get Smart! Make Your Money Count in the 1990s.* Second Edition. Scarborough, Ontario: Prentice-Hall Canada, 1989, 317 pp. A book for the general reader that includes financial planning, income tax principles, but gives major attention to investing in the stock market.

TURNER, MARY, DANIEL LEROSSIGNOL, CLAUDE RINFRET, and RICHARD DAW.

Canadian Guide to Personal Financial Management. Fourth Edition. Scarborough, Ontario: Prentice-Hall Canada, 1989, 231 pp. Accountants provide guidance on a broad range of topics, including planning finances, estimating insurance needs, managing risk, and determining investment needs. Instructions and the necessary forms for making plans are provided.

WYATT, ELAINE. *The Money Companion, How to Manage Your Money and Achieve Financial Freedom.* Markham, Ontario: Penguin Books, 1989, 203 pp. A guide to personal financial management that focuses on planning, investment strategy and retirement needs.

ZIMMER, HENRY B. *The Revised and Expanded Canadian Tax and Investment Guide.* Edmonton: Hurtig, annual, 315 pp. Very comprehensive treatment of income tax and investment.

Articles

"Easing Your Tax Load," *The Financial Post Moneywise*, December 1989, 87-98. Offers a variety of suggestions for reducing income tax.

MCLEOD, BILL. "Picking a Course," *Canadian Consumer.* 19, No. 11, 1989, 30-33. Suggests strategies for funding education costs, including the use of RESPs.

Periodicals

Financial Times. Weekly. Suite 500, 920 Yonge Street, Toronto, Ontario, M2W 3L5. Provides current information on a range of business and economic topics.

Report on Business. Daily. A section of *The Globe and Mail.* Important source of information on the financial markets.

The Financial Post. Daily and weekly. The Financial Post Company, 777 Bay Street, Toronto, Ontario, M5G 2E4. Up-to-date information on business, economics, income tax, and investments.

3 WILLS: PLANNING FOR THE DISTRIBUTION OF ASSETS

OBJECTIVES

1. To explain how wills fit into comprehensive financial planning.

2. To differentiate among the responsibilities involved in:
   (a) drawing a will,
   (b) witnessing a will,
   (c) acting as executor of an estate.

3. To compare the effects on the settling of an estate of:
   (a) the existence of a valid will,
   (b) no will.

4. To identify assets that are not distributed by a will.

5. To explain the purpose of probate.

6. To explain the distribution of an estate in the case of an intestacy.

7. To evaluate the legal position of dependents who are not provided for in the will.

8. To distinguish between the following pairs of terms:
   (a) testator and testatrix,
   (b) executor and administrator,
   (c) bequest (or legacy) and beneficiary (or legatee),
   (d) codicil and holograph will,
   (e) joint tenancy and tenancy in common.

9. To explain these terms: letters of administration, letters probate, preferential share, testamentary trust, power of attorney.

10. To explain how the transfer of ownership of assets underlies most of the formalities associated with wills and the settling of estates.

INTRODUCTION

The general discussion of financial planning in Chapter 1 focused on the maximization of resources during one's lifetime. Persons with assets also need to make provision for the distribution of their estate after death, but estate planning is often postponed because there is no sense of urgency. Unfortunately, those who procrastinate until it is too late and die without having made a will leave no legal statement of their wishes for the disposition of their possessions and assets, often creating difficulties for the surviving family members. However, our society is prepared for these situations for, as we shall see, provincial laws direct how such estates shall be distributed.

A will provides an orderly procedure for changing the ownership of assets after a death, indicating which assets should be transferred to which people. When a person dies without a will, the assets are distributed according to the law of the province, which may or may not coincide with the desires of the deceased. A comprehensive financial plan includes a will to ensure the orderly transfer of assets at death.

Some of the general procedures and terminology associated with wills and estates are introduced in this chapter. Although they may seem confusing at first, there is a logic in the process which, once identified, makes it quite understandable. After death, the person named to act in your place—the executor—gets the power to do so from the will. Often the will is submitted to a special court to verify that it is valid. Then the executor proceeds to make a list of the assets of the deceased, pay the bills, and finally distribute the estate according to the will. Much of the legal formality is concerned with the transfer of ownership of assets from the deceased to other people.

NEED FOR A WILL

WHAT IS A WILL?

A *will* is a legal document that gives someone the power to act as your financial representative after your death and directs how your assets should be distributed. The person named in the will to act as your agent is called an *executor* if a man, or an *executrix* if a woman. A will has no effect or power during your lifetime; while you are alive you can change your will as often as you wish, give away the possessions listed in your will, or write new wills. A will takes effect on the death of the *testator*, or the one who signed the will. A woman who makes a will is a *testatrix*.

WHO NEEDS A WILL?

Most adults should have a will for two reasons: it ensures that their estate is distributed according to their wishes, and by naming an executor, the handling of the estate is simplified. Most people have a larger estate than they realize because they tend to forget about those assets that do not form part of their estate until they die, such as the proceeds from life insurance, the lump-sum death benefit from the Canada Pension Plan, group life insurance plans in connection with their employment, registered retirement savings plans, and credits in company pension plans. All of these assets become part of the estate at death, even though some may not be accessible at present.

LEGAL CAPACITY TO MAKE A WILL
To make a valid will, the testator must be:

(a) of the age of majority (17 in Newfoundland; 18 in Alberta, Manitoba, Ontario, Quebec, Prince Edward Island, and Saskatchewan; 19 in New Brunswick, the Northwest Territories, Nova Scotia, British Columbia, and the Yukon). A person is permitted to make a legal will before the age of majority if he or she is married or a member of the military.

(b) of sound mind, i.e., he or she must understand what is being done. People who are mentally unfit may not meet this requirement. This is a particular concern with those who may have some degree of senility, or anyone who is undergoing psychiatric treatment. If the will is contested (i.e., disputed before a court) after their death, and it can be shown that the person signing it was not of sound mind, the will may very well be considered invalid.

(c) free of undue influence by another person. A will should not be signed under conditions of coercion or persuasion, or there may be a basis for contesting it.

DRAWING UP A WILL

HOW TO BEGIN
First, take stock of possessions, assets, and any other moneys that would form part of your estate. Next, decide how you want to allocate this estate. If you take this list to a lawyer along with the name of your executor, a will can be drafted for you. The lawyer's role is to translate your wishes into legal language and suggest ways to allow for various contingencies that you may not have considered, such as naming an alternate executor, including a common disaster clause if husband and wife should be killed in a common accident, and allowing for children yet unborn.

It is not essential that a will be drawn up by a lawyer. The law does not require any special format, or legal words, or typing. You can write a will in your own words or use a standard form bought at a stationery store. However, if you are not experienced in writing wills, you may not make your intentions perfectly clear by your choice of words, and you may forget important clauses. Lawyers charge nominal fees to draw up wills and it is worthwhile to have their assistance.

What to Include in a Will

A will usually includes statements about the following matters:

(a) the domicile of the testator.

(b) that previous wills made by the testator are revoked.

(c) direction to pay funeral expenses, debts, and taxes before distributing the estate.

(d) possible specific bequests (or legacies) of certain possessions or moneys to be given to named persons.

(e) a clause to dispose of the residue of the estate, e.g., one or more persons who may be named as *residual legatees* to receive any balance remaining after debts, taxes, and specific bequests.

(f) the appointment of an executor and possibly an alternate executor.

(g) the naming of a guardian if there are minor children.

(h) possibly, a common disaster clause to cover a situation such as the death of a couple as a result of one event.

A person who benefits from a will is called a *beneficiary*, and an asset or possession left to this person is called a *bequest* (or *legacy*) or, if real property, a *devise*.

Guardians for Children

Designating a guardian for children is often done in a will, but the testator does not have the final word on this decision. After the death of parents the court appoints a guardian for the children; in many cases the guardian named in the will is appointed by the court if that person is agreeable and able to act. Not being bound by the terms of a will, the court has the flexibility to make the most appropriate decision about guardianship at the time of death.

Can the Family be Disinherited?

There is no legal requirement that a person leave his or her estate to family members, contrary to the hopes of some children. However, if a spouse or children who were financially dependent on the deceased at the time of death are disinherited, these survivors may have a basis to contest the will under provincial legislation that protects such dependents. If they can show that they have financial needs, the court may award them a share of the estate. The relevant acts are:

Alberta, Newfoundland	*Family Relief Act*
British Columbia	*Wills Variation Act*
Manitoba, New Brunswick, Nova Scotia	*Testator's Family Maintenance Act*
Ontario	*Succession Law Reform Act*
Prince Edward Island	*Dependents of a Deceased Person Relief Act*
Saskatchewan	*Dependents' Relief Act*
Northwest Territories, Yukon	*Dependents' Relief Act*

Recent changes in family law acts regarding the division of family property (after family break-up or death) can have an effect on the spouse's share of an estate. For instance, under *The Ontario Family Law Act* of 1986, a spouse may choose between the provisions under the will or a half share of the net family property calculated according to this act. That means that the surviving spouse may compare the amount that would be received if the will were followed to one-half of the net family property and choose the larger benefit. Certain property of the deceased, such as a prior inheritance, may be excluded from net family property.

Since this legislation has implications for wills written previously, they should be reviewed. For instance, a will that leaves an estate in trust for a spouse during that person's lifetime, with the balance going to a third party after the spouse's death, may be put aside if the spouse elects to take one-half of the net family property.

SIGNING AND WITNESSING A WILL

A will must be signed at its end almost simultaneously by the testator and two witnesses; all three must be present together. By their signatures, the witnesses attest that they watched the testator sign this will, but they need not read the will or know the contents. It is advisable that a spouse or a person who is to benefit from a will should not be a witness in order to avoid the possibility of a later accusation of undue influence on the testator. Check provincial legislation on this point.

A person named in a will as executor may also be a beneficiary, and very often is one. For instance, if a man names his wife as executrix and leaves his estate to her, this should present no difficulty; however, it would be preferable that she not be a witness.

How to Choose an Executor

When selecting an executor, consider the person's age, willingness to handle your business, and capability of doing so. It is wise to appoint an executor who may be expected to survive you. Often close relatives are appointed executors, but in cases of large and complex estates, a trust company may be appointed sole executor or joint executor with a family member. If, for instance, the testator considers that the management of the estate may be a burden for the survivor, the spouse may be appointed a *co-executor* with a trust company. This would allow the spouse to be involved in settling the estate and be aware of what is being done without taking the sole responsibility. However, trust companies are not very interested in small estates because of the limited revenue generated.

An executor named in a will is not bound to accept this appointment and may decline if unable or disinclined; therefore, it is wise to determine your nominee's preference in advance. The executor need not see the will, but it would be helpful to know where it is kept. Several executors may be named to act jointly, but for small estates it can be an unnecessary complication to require the signatures of several people in order to implement each action. However, it is wise to name an *alternative executor* who would act if the one originally selected is unwilling or unable to act, or has predeceased the testator.

Where to Keep a Will

A will should be kept in a safe spot, but where the survivors can find it. The main alternatives are to leave it with a trust company or lawyer to keep in their vaults, or put it in your safety deposit box. There is only one signed copy of a will, but the unsigned duplicate could be kept at home with other personal papers.

Disposing of Small Personal Possessions

People often change their minds about which relative should receive the grandfather clock or the antique rocker, but it may be inconvenient and expensive to have a new will drawn to accommodate each change. One solution is to attach a memorandum to the will listing such possessions and who should receive each. The list can easily be changed because it is not part of the will, and if there is harmony in the family, the executor is likely to follow these instructions. However, it must be remembered that such a memorandum carries no legal weight and if the will were contested, such a list might not be followed. It is wise to make reference to the memorandum in the will.

Instructions About Funeral Arrangements

These instructions do not need to be included in a will because after death the body belongs to the next of kin, who decide on its disposition. Nevertheless, in most cases relatives try to follow the wishes of the deceased. Such instructions can be filed with the will if desired, but it is important that others know about such instructions or they may not be found until it is too late to act on them.

MARRIAGE AND WILLS

Usually a will made prior to marriage is void unless the spouse elects in writing to uphold it after the testator's death. To avoid having to make a will on your wedding day, you may write a *will in contemplation of marriage* that takes effect after the marriage. It states that it was written in contemplation of marriage and names the expected spouse.

REVOKING OR ALTERING A WILL

While you are alive you can alter your will or make new ones as often as you wish because the document has no power until after your death. You may cancel or *revoke* your will by (i) destroying it, (ii) writing a new will which expressly states that previous wills are revoked, or (iii) getting married. If you want to change your will after it has been drafted but not yet signed, alterations may be made as long as each change is signed and witnessed. If you should decide to alter an existing will without writing a new one, you could add a codicil. A *codicil* is a postscript to a will although it is really a separate document. It must contain a reference to the will to which it is appended and must be dated, signed, and witnessed.

Some lawyers feel that it is better to rewrite a will than to add a codicil. However, in cases where there was no question about mental capacity at the time the original will was signed but there is such a question at the time a change is to be made, it might be better to add a codicil. It would be preferable for the codicil to fail than for the entire will to fail.

THE HOLOGRAPH WILL

A will entirely in the handwriting of the testator, dated and signed, but not witnessed, is called a *holograph* will and is valid in some provinces, such as Ontario (if the will was written since 1978), Quebec, and Saskatchewan. Holograph wills are not valid in British Columbia, Nova Scotia, and Prince Edward Island, which require that the testator's signature be witnessed. An example of a holograph will is shown in Figure 3.1.

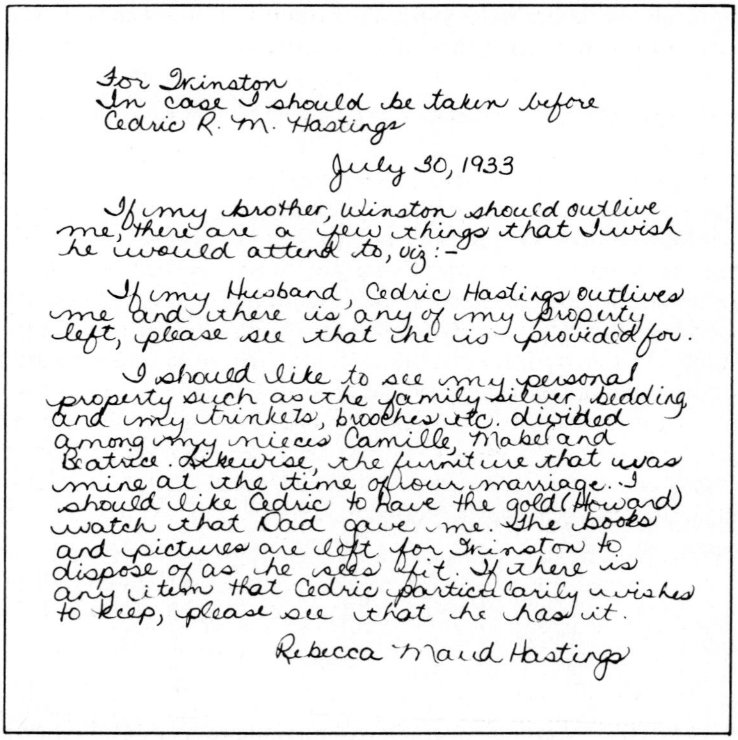

For Winston
In case I should be taken before
Cedric R. M. Hastings

July 30, 1933

If my brother, Winston should outlive me, there are a few things that I wish he would attend to, viz :—

If my Husband, Cedric Hastings outlives me and there is any of my property left, please see that he is provided for.

I should like to see my personal property such as the family silver, bedding and my trinkets, brooches etc. divided among my nieces Camille, Mabel and Beatrice. Likewise, the furniture that was mine at the time of our marriage. I should like Cedric to have the gold (Howard) watch that Dad gave me. The books and pictures are left for Winston to dispose of as he sees fit. If there is any item that Cedric particularly wishes to keep, please see that he has it.

Rebecca Maud Hastings

Figure 3.1   MRS. HASTINGS' HOLOGRAPH WILL

SETTLING AN ESTATE WITH A WILL

FINDING THE WILL

After a death the first and obvious step in settling the estate is to find the will. It must be the most recent will, if there are several. A thorough search of the deceased's home, safety deposit boxes, and appropriate lawyers' offices must be conducted before concluding that there is no will.

DUTIES OF THE EXECUTOR

A will usually names one or more persons to act as executors or as the personal financial representatives of the deceased. The executor is charged with a variety of duties which may be categorized as:

(a)   proving the validity of the will,

(b) assembling and administering the assets of the estate in trust,

(c) distributing the estate to the heirs.

If no executor was named, if the named executor is deceased, unable, or unwilling to act, or if the deceased died without a will, someone with a financial interest in the estate must apply to the Surrogate Court for *Letters of Administration* which appoint an administrator to act for the deceased. The *Surrogate Court* is the provincial court that arbitrates matters relating to wills and the settling of estates. Once appointed, an *administrator* has the same duties and responsibilities as an executor. The only difference between an executor, named by a will, and an administrator, given authority by the Surrogate Court, is in the manner of their appointment and the possible requirement to post a bond. A bond, equivalent to the value of the estate, can be posted by paying a fee to a bonding company to insure that the administrator is trustworthy in carrying out his or her duties. Bonding, of course, represents an additional cost to the estate. It is apparent that the process of having an administrator appointed means additional steps before the settling of the estate can begin.

PROVING THE WILL

In order to validate a will, it is submitted to the Surrogate Court for *probate*, a process whereby the Court approves the authenticity of the will and confirms the appointment of the executor. The executor receives from the Court a document called *Letters Probate*, which is a legal statement confirming the will and the executor. In the subsequent steps of assembling the assets and paying the taxes, the Letters Probate are used to support the authority of the executor to conduct these transactions.

Some wills are not probated, especially when the estate is small and uncomplicated. The legal transfer of ownership of assets from the name of the deceased to the names of the heirs, the crucial task in settling an estate, may sometimes be accomplished without probate. However, the financial institutions involved require adequate documentation if there are no Letters Probate.

ADMINISTERING THE ESTATE IN TRUST

After the testator's death, the property included in the will comes under the authority and control of the executor, whose duty it is to implement the provisions of the will. An executor usually engages a lawyer, and delegates to this person certain tasks in fulfilling the legal formalities involved with the estate. The final responsibility, however, still rests with the executor. The extent of the executor's task depends on the complexity of the deceased's estate and whether or not it was left in good order.

ASSEMBLING THE ASSETS   Once the executor's or administrator's authority to proceed has been established, the next task is to compile an inventory of the deceased's assets and liabilities. In the process of doing so, the executor informs all financial institutions holding these assets of the testator's death. The executor opens a trust account into which funds belonging to the deceased may be deposited temporarily. This account is needed to handle the business of the estate, including the payment of bills and the final distribution to beneficiaries.

PAYING THE DEBTS   Once the financial institutions holding accounts in the name of the deceased are given proof that the person has died and that the executor is empowered by the will to act, funds are usually released. During the time the estate is being settled the assets may be generating income in the form of interest, dividends, rent, and profit. For income tax purposes, the executor must keep a record of the income received by the estate during the time it was held in trust.

Before the estate can be distributed, all debts must be paid, with taxes and funeral expenses taking first priority. There are no longer any succession duties or estate taxes in Canada, although some people seem to be unaware of this. When the duties and taxes existed, all assets were frozen until the taxes had been assessed. Should the debts of the deceased exceed the assets, some scheme must be devised to distribute what there is among the creditors, perhaps on a *pro rata* basis.

The executor has to pay any income tax due on (i) any income the deceased received during that part of the year from January first until the date of death, and (ii) any income generated by the estate between the date of death and the date of distribution. An executor should contact the local office of Revenue Canada Taxation for instructions about income tax for deceased persons and estates. Essentially, the first task is to complete an income tax return for the portion of the year that the deceased was alive. The executor must pay whatever income tax is owing from the estate funds being held in trust. Just before distributing the estate, another income tax return must be completed reporting any estate income and paying the appropriate tax. This process is summarized in Figure 3.2.

RECORDING THE ACCOUNTS   The executor is responsible for maintaining a record of accounts showing all receipts and disbursements, but this task may be delegated to a lawyer. Beneficiaries with questions may wish to see the accounts, and if there is concern about the misuse of funds, the court may require that the accounts be submitted, a process known as *passing the accounts*.

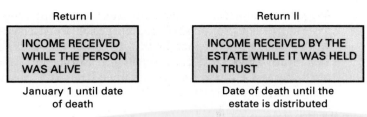

Figure 3.2   INCOME TAX RETURNS FOR DECEASED PERSONS

DISTRIBUTING THE ESTATE

When the executor has paid the deceased's debts, filed an income tax return, and paid the legal fees, the estate may be distributed to the beneficiaries according to the will. In some instances it may be necessary to sell certain assets in order to pay debts and make the distribution; other assets may be transferred to new owners. Whether all assets must be converted into cash or whether some may be transferred in their present form depends on the instructions in the will and the wishes of the beneficiaries.

In some cases, it may be necessary to sell property in order to divide the estate so that it may be distributed to several people. For instance, if the chief asset in the estate was a house and there were three beneficiaries, the house could be sold and the proceeds divided, or one of the heirs could buy the house by paying the other beneficiaries their shares. In other cases where a division of the asset is not necessary, the ownership of the property may be transferred.

The demands on the executor at this stage depend on the complexity of the deceased's estate. The means of transferring various forms of property involve legal formalities for which the assistance of a lawyer is valuable.

FEES FOR SETTLING AN ESTATE   Settling an estate involves two sets of fees: one for the services of a lawyer and one for the executor. Lawyers prepare applications for probate, and there is usually a Surrogate Court tariff setting the fee for an estate of average complexity, plus disbursements, e.g., $5 per $1000.

Executors are responsible for all the other work regarding the settling of the estate and are entitled to fees based on the complexity of the estate and the time and effort expended. This fee is usually around four to five percent of the value of the estate. If the executrix wants the lawyer to do her work, the lawyer charges the executrix who pays the lawyer from the moneys due to her as executrix. If several executors are involved, the fee is divided among them. Frequently, family members act as executors without taking any fees from the estate.

Legal fees depend on the amount of work the lawyer has to do for the estate. Fees may be established by the time spent or as a percentage of the assets. The executor should discuss the fee schedule with the lawyer before work on the estate begins. Legal fees can be reduced if the executor decides to do some tasks, such as assembling the assets and paying debts. These fees are paid from estate funds held in trust before the distribution of the estate.

SETTLING AN ESTATE WITHOUT A WILL

It is not uncommon to discover that there is no will; many people who are fond of talking about their wills and their plans for disposing of their possessions have never made a will at all. It is something we tend to postpone, thinking that a will is not an urgent matter. Also, we are reluctant to contemplate our mortality. However, before concluding that no will was left, a thorough search must be made of all possible places.

If the relatives think that a will existed at some time, but it cannot be found, the will is presumed to have been revoked unless contrary evidence can be discovered. Should a will be found subsequent to the distribution of the estate, it may be very difficult or impossible to make any alteration in the distribution.

NAMING THE ADMINISTRATOR

If you die without a will, known as dying *intestate*, someone with a financial interest in your estate must apply to court to be appointed administrator. If family members do not do so, a creditor, such as the funeral director, may press for action. The application includes an inventory of the estate's assets and debts, a list of close relatives, and an affidavit stating that the deceased left no will. As previously mentioned, the applicant also may be asked to *post a bond of indemnity* with the court so that the estate would be protected should the administrator be dishonest. If the administrator absconds with the assets or dissipates the estate and fails to render a true accounting to the court, the bond of indemnity is there to be called upon to protect the financial interests of the beneficiaries. A fee also must be paid to the Surrogate Court. After Letters of Administration are received, steps can be initiated to settle the estate.

WILL BUT NO EXECUTOR   If there is a will but no executor prepared to act, it is necessary to apply to court for the appointment of an administrator and Letters of Administration. In such a case, the situation is referred to as an *administration with will annexed*.

Table 3.1 PROVINCIAL LEGISLATION REGARDING INTESTATE SUCCESSION

Although legislation governing intestate succession varies from province to proivce, there are a number of aspects which are the same in all 10 jurisdictions. Similarities will be outlined first with differences listed below.

(i) General Rules for Intestate Succession   *die w/out will*

If the deceased left	the estate goes
spouse, no children	all to the spouse
spouse and 1 child*	preferential share to spouse; excess split 50/50 between spouse and child
spouse and 2 or more children*	preferential share to spouse; excess split 1/3 to spouse and 2/3 shared equally among children
no spouse, but children	all to children, shared equally
no spouse or children	all to parents
no spouse, children or parents	all to brothers and sisters

(ii) Intestate Succession and Variations from General Rules

Province	Relevant Legislation	Variations from General Rules
Alberta	*Intestate Succession Act*	— spouse's preferential share is $40 000
British Columbia	*Estate Administration Act* (Pt. 7)	— spouse's preferential share is $65 000
Manitoba	*Devolution of Estates Act*	— spouse's preferential share is $50 000 — spouse gets 1/2 excess regardless of number of children
New Brunswick	*Devolution of Estates Act*	— no preferential share to spouse
Newfoundland	*Intestate Succession Act*	— no preferential share to spouse
Nova Scotia	*Intestate Succession Act*	— spouse's preferential share is $50 000
Ontario	*Succession Law Reform Act*	— spouse's preferential share is $75 000
Prince Edward Island	*Probate Act* (Pt. 4)	— no preferential share to spouse
Quebec	*Civil Code of Quebec*	— no preferential share to spouse — spouse gets 1/3 of estate; children get 2/3
Saskatchewan	*Intestate Succession Act*	— spouse's preferential share is $10 000

*predeceased children are "represented" by their surviving children.

THE ADMINISTRATION

The administrator carries out the same duties as an executor, but there may be a requirement that the assets of the estate not be distributed within one year of the deceased's death unless the administrator has advertised for creditors. This requirement does not apply if there is an executor, but it is often done for convenience, and for the protection of the executor; an executor can be held personally liable for the debts if a distribution is made to beneficiaries without prior repayment of debts. It is one way to ensure that all creditors are informed of the death and have an opportunity to submit any outstanding bills.

DISTRIBUTING THE INTESTACY

When there is no will (an *intestacy*), the estate is distributed according to the provisions of the appropriate provincial law. An outline of some rules regarding intestacy is shown in Table 3.1 on the previous page. For greater accuracy and completeness you should consult the appropriate provincial statute. You may note a reference to *preferential shares* in this table, which means that the spouse gets a specified share before any other beneficiary. For example, if the spouse's preferential share is $50 000, this must be paid to the spouse before anyone else gets anything. If the estate is less than $50 000, then the spouse gets it all.

GEORGE LEFT NO WILL

George always intended to write a will, but like many people, he never got around to it. After his death, his wife Alma, who was appointed administrator, discovered that his estate totalled about $105 000. According to Ontario law the estate was to be divided as follows:

To Alma, preferential share of $75 000 plus one-third the balance, making a total of $85 000

Two-thirds of the balance to the children:

Son, Simon	$6666
Son, Richard	6666

Deceased son Henry's children:	
Lisa	3333
Sam	3333

CONSANGUINITY   There is a method of classifying relatives according to their nearness to the deceased. To illustrate how the system works, an abbreviated table of consanguinity is shown in Table 3.2. Observe that relatives beyond the nuclear family are grouped in classes. Should the deceased die intestate leaving no spouse or children, the estate may be divided equally among the next-of-kin in the class closest in blood relation. If there are no relatives in Class I, the estate is divided equally among all those in Class II. When there is even one relative in a class, that person gets the whole estate, and the distribution does not continue to the next class. If the deceased leaves grand-children, but no living children, the estate goes to the children through a process called *representation*, because they receive their parents' share.

COMMON-LAW SPOUSES   The status of common-law spouses is changing grad-ually, but at this time there is no generally accepted treatment of such spouses under all conditions. While the Canada Pension Plan, as well as some other pension plans, may provide benefits to a common-law spouse, provincial wills statutes have not considered them to be legal spouses in cases of intestacy. Therefore, care must be taken in generalizing about their rights. At the time of writing, common-law spouses do not automatically receive a share of an intestacy, but may go to the court to argue for a portion because of financial dependency. Of course, if there is a will a common-law spouse can be named a beneficiary.

Table 3.2   ABBREVIATED TABLE OF CONSANGUINITY

All blood relatives, beyond children, are classified into numbered classes as follows:

Class I	father, mother, brother, sister
Class II	grandmother, grandfather
Class III	great grandmother, great grandfather, nephew, niece, uncle, aunt
Class IV	great-great grandfather, great-great grandmother, great nephew, great niece, first cousin, great uncle, great aunt
Class V	great-great uncle, great-great aunt, first cousin once removed, etc.

Transferring Ownership of Assets

In organizing all the details associated with the settling of an estate, it may help to keep in mind that the main purpose is to transfer ownership of assets from the deceased to designated beneficiaries. The various formalities are necessary to ensure that this is correctly done. The diagram in Figure 3.3 summarizes this transfer of the ownership from the deceased to the executor (administrator) in trust, and finally to the beneficiaries.

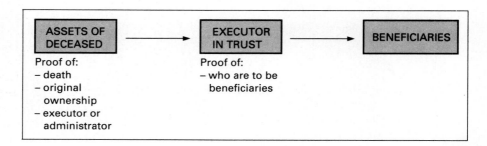

Figure 3.3   TRANSFER OF THE DECEASED'S ASSETS

Estate Assets Not Distributed by the Will

There are two situations in which the deceased's assets go directly to a beneficiary, independently of the will, by contract and at law. Certain financial assets—such as life insurance, annuities, and registered retirement savings plans—may have a designated beneficiary named in the contract by the deceased during his or her lifetime. On proof of death, the financial institution holding these assets automatically transfers ownership to the beneficiary; the will is not involved. If the named beneficiary has predeceased the testator, the assets will probably be paid into the estate unless an alternate beneficiary was named.

Other assets that are not distributed by the will, are those held in *joint tenancy*, a situation that confers the right of survivorship. For instance, if a couple has a joint bank account, the wife, through right of survivorship, becomes the sole owner of the account on her husband's death. Real property held in joint tenancy is handled similarly. Note that joint tenancy is not the same as *tenancy in common*. In this latter instance, each owns an undivided share of the asset. If the family house was held as tenants in common, on the death of one partner, one-half of the value of the house would form a part of the deceased's estate and one-half would continue to belong to the survivor. However, if the house was held in joint tenancy, the ownership of the house would pass to the survivor.

TESTAMENTARY TRUSTS

A will may state that particular assets or property are to be held in trust for some person or persons. This is called a *testamentary trust* because the trust is established by a will, in contrast to a living trust, which becomes operative during the lifetime of the person who established it. In the case of a testamentary trust, someone has to be appointed as trustee to manage this trust. Usually the trustee is named in the will, with perhaps an alternate trustee if the first one should be deceased or unable to act. Trust companies specialize in this service, with trust departments that offer advice in planning the trust. The company acts as trustee when the trust becomes operative. When trust companies are involved in planning an estate, with or without a trust, they usually insist that the company be named executor or co-executor of the will. If there is to be a trust, the company may be named the trustee. Trust companies, obviously, charge a fee for managing assets for others. In fact all trustees, whether corporations or individuals, are entitled to charge a fee, subject to review by the court. In some situations the executor may also be the trustee and decide to appoint someone to carry out the management of the trust property. In such a case, the executor retains ultimate responsibility.

It is wise to select a trustee who does not have a conflict of interest. As an example, Jane has been named the trustee of funds for a her disabled brother, John. The will states that the income from the estate is to be used for John, and after his death the balance of the estate goes to Jane. There can be a conflict of interest in such a situation; if Jane restricts the money available for her brother she may inherit a larger estate. A trustee, however, is obliged to be even-handed between the life interest of one beneficiary and the ultimate interest of another beneficiary.

POWER OF ATTORNEY

Another aspect of financial planning is making provision for the possibility of becoming incapacitated through accident or disease. As has been explained in this chapter, there is a process for handling the affairs of a deceased person, but an incompetent person presents different problems. Sometimes no actions can be taken at all, or in other cases, the individual may make faulty decisions. Without a legally appointed representative for a client, officers of various financial institutions have no choice but to follow the client's instructions, regardless of competency level. Meanwhile, other family members are helpless unless a prior power of attorney has been signed or they initiate the slow and painful court process of having the person ruled mentally incompetent and a legal representative named. In some situations, a joint bank account for depositing income and paying expenses may be a practical and informal alternative, at least for a time.

A *power of attorney* is a legal document that names someone to handle your finances under certain conditions. It is a wise precaution to assign power of attorney to a trusted person who can handle your financial affairs if necessary. Generally, it is advisable to name an alternate in case the first one is unable to act. There are various ways to make a power of attorney restrictive enough that you do not lose control of your affairs prematurely. For instance, the family lawyer can keep the document and release it only when two doctors have stated in writing that the person can no longer handle his or her own affairs.

It is easier, cheaper, and less cumbersome for the family if a power of attorney is signed when the individual is capable. However, additional safeguards are built into the more complex court process of determining incompetency. The person named by the court to manage assets has to submit regular detailed reports to the court for approval.

SUMMARY

Most adults should have a will, and generally should obtain help from a lawyer in drawing it up. A trusted, capable, and willing person should be named executor or executrix, with a second person as alternate. It is wise to review and revise a will periodically to reflect any changes in financial resources or family composition. A will is not operative until death, when it becomes the plan for disposing of the estate. The executor has responsibility for carrying out the provisions of the will. The estates of those who die intestate are disposed of according to provincial law. The status of common-law spouses is changing in Canada, but in most jurisdictions they are not given spouse status in cases of intestacy.

There are sound arguments for giving power of attorney to someone to act as your representative if you should become incompetent to handle your own financial affairs.

PROBLEMS

1.

A CASE OF INTESTACY

At his death, Ed Hogan, who was living with his common-law wife Mrs. Anna Rudd and her children, was operating a successful pig-raising business with the help of Anna's son, Larry Rudd. Because Mr. Hogan left no will, there was much uncertainty about who should look after his affairs, including the growing pigs. Mr. Hogan was divorced, had no children, and his parents were deceased; by the rules of intestacy the collateral relatives would be the heirs, in this case his three brothers. It was agreed that one brother, Tom would apply to be the administrator of the estate.

Initially, Mr. Hogan's affairs appeared quite straightforward. He left two rented barns full of pigs, a truck, some supplies and equipment, personal belongings, and a bank account. A search of his apartment revealed seven burlap bags of personal papers dating from the late 1940s. Among these papers, Tom found that his brother also held two mortgages, several bank accounts, stocks, bonds, and two life insurance policies with named beneficiaries, in one case his deceased mother and in the other his divorced wife.

For a number of years Mr. Hogan had lived with Mrs. Rudd, treating her family as his own. However, Mr. Hogan's brothers and their families, not approving of this situation, kept their distance from both of them. Gradually it was revealed that Mr. Hogan had plans for the disposition of his estate, which he had not put in writing. He had often mentioned taking Larry Rudd into partnership in the business, and he had always meant to change his life insurance policies to name Anna as beneficiary, and also to cancel the mortgage he held for her daughter and son-in-law. His lawyer knew of his intention to make a will naming one brother as executor and recipient of 60 percent of the estate, with the remaining 40 percent to be divided, one half to Anna and one half between the other two brothers. Unfortunately he died before making such a will; therefore his plans could not be implemented.

(a) Would probate be involved in settling Mr. Hogan's estate?

(b) Since Mr. Hogan did not leave a will, what steps would be necessary to have Tom appointed to handle his estate?

(c) Would there be any additional costs, or any delays created because Mr. Hogan did not name an executor?

(d) Who would receive the benefits of the two life insurance policies?

(e) What was the name of the law that specified how Mr. Hogan's estate would be distributed?

(f) Assuming that this situation occurred in your province, estimate the share Anna Rudd would receive under the intestacy law.

(g) Make a list of things that would probably have turned out better if Mr. Hogan had written a will.

(h) Do you think the common-law wife should investigate the possibility of making a claim as a dependent? What law would be involved?

(i) Does Larry Rudd have a basis for contesting the distribution of this estate?

2.

WILLS OF ALL SORTS

When Mrs. Hastings died in 1972 at the age of 94, her family began the search for her will. Someone remembered that there was a letter in her brother's desk, which had been there for years, with instructions to open it after her death. That turned out to be the holograph will reproduced in Figure 3.1. The search did not end there, because someone thought that Mrs. Hastings had once said something about keeping her will at a certain bank. A search of several banks revealed some Canada Savings Bonds, a life insurance policy belonging to her husband, and his will.

After the funeral, a careful search of her room uncovered a second will that had been drawn by a lawyer in 1939 (Figure 3.4). Note that Mrs. Hastings did some revising of this will nine years later when she cut out sections and pasted in a revision. Finally the matron of the nursing home where Mrs. Hastings had been living produced yet another will, which was on a stationery store form (Figure 3.5). This last will was the most recent, and it was submitted for probate.

(a) When Mrs. Hastings died, her holograph will, written in 1933, would have been valid in Quebec if she had not written later wills. Would it be acceptable now in British Columbia or Ontario?

ON THIS twenty first day of the month in February, in the year one thousand nine hundred and thirty nine, at the Village of Rockport, County of Crompton, District of St. Francis, and Province of Quebec:

Before the undersigned Witnesses, Catharine Ross, Advocate, and Mary Goodman, Accountant, both of the Village of Rockport, said County, District and Province,

CAME AND APPEARED

REBECCA M. HASTINGS (nee Cassells), of the Township of Smithton, said District and Province, who being of sound mind, memory and understanding, has declared the following to be her Last Will and Testament:

1. I commend my soul to Almighty God.

2. Hereby revoking any and all former Wills, I hereby will, devise and bequeath any and all property, real and personal, which I now own, or may own or possess at the time of my death, in the following manner:

November 25, 1948.

If my good and faithful husband, Cedric Hastings outlives me, I wish what property is left to be used for his benefit as my dear brother Winston Cassells sees fit. Also that the sun Life Insurance money be used for Cedric's benefit.

I should like a double tombstone erected for both of us, whenever seems most suitable. The cost thereof to come out of our estate. I wish Cedric to have my large trunk and the best black suitcase. Also Dad's gold "Howard" watch. Will Winston and Camille please be my executors?

D. I desire my niece Camille H. Cassells to have the Blue and White bedspread woven by her Grandmother. And my niece Mabel Cassells to have the White bedspread with "Theresa A. Green" woven thereon. And to my niece Beatrice Cassells the silk quilt.

E. I desire my furniture, books, pictures, silverware, and household effects generally, to be divided between my three nieces, Camille, Mabel and Beatrice Cassells abovementioned, as my Executrix may see fit.

After due reading of this Will by the Testatrix, she has signed the same in presence of the Witnesses, who have also signed in her presence and in presence of each other.

WITNESSES   *Rebecca M. Hastings*

Catherine Ross
Mary Goodman

Figure 3.4   MRS. HASTINGS' SECOND WILL

THIS IS THE LAST WILL AND TESTAMENT OF ME, Rebecca Maud Cassells Hastings, at present residing at Eliza Gregson Home, in the Township of Smithton, in the District of St. Frances, retired,

I hereby revoking all former wills and testamentary dispositions heretofore made by me.

I NOMINATE AND APPOINT my brother, Winston Charles Cassells, farmer, residing on Rural Route 4, Crompton, Quebec, and my nieces, Camille Cassells, teacher, residing in Perth, Ontario, and Mabel Cassells, nurse, residing in Toronto, Ontario, and the survivor of them, to be the Executors and Trustees of this, my Will.

I GIVE, DEVISE AND BEQUEATH all the Real and Personal estate of which I shall die possessed or entitled to unto my said Executors and Trustees hereinbefore named, in Trust for the purposes following:

Firstly, to pay my just debts. Secondly, to pay the expenses of my burial which I wish to have undertaken by L.O. Cass and Son. Ltd., funeral directors, of Crompton, Que. Thirdly, to provide for the erection of a modest headstone over the grave of my husband and myself, and to cover all testamentary expenses. Fourthly, to pay to Eliza Gregson Home in the Tonwship of Smithton, Que., whatever may be required for the maintenance of my husband, Mr Cedric Hastings,during his lifetime. Fifthly, to divide between my nieces, Camille Cassells and Mabel Cassells (aforementioned) and Beatrice (Mrs. B.M.Thomas), my pictures, trinkets and personal things. All the rest and residue of my estate both Real and Personal, I GIVE, DEVISE AND BEQUEATH unto Eliza Gregson Home in the Township of Smithton in the Province of Quebec absolutely.

With full power and authority to my Executors and Trustees to sell and dispose of all or any part of my Real or Personal estate, where necessary for the carrying out of the purpose of this my will, and to execute any and all documents that may be necessary for so doing.

IN WITNESS WHEREOF I have subscribed these presents at Eliza Gregson Home in the Township of Smithton, this 14th day of September, Nineteen hundred and sixty-five.

    SIGNED published and declared by the above-named testatrix as and for her last Will and Testament in the presence of us both present at the same time, who at her request and in her presence have hereunto subscribed our names as witnesses.

Rebecca M. Hastings

        (Witnesses)

Name *Terry Petrie*
Address *290 Oba St. Sherbrooke.*

Name *Miss Betty McDonald*
Address *Eliza Gregson Home*

Figure 3.5   MRS. HASTINGS' LAST WILL

(b) What is your opinion of the way Mrs. Hastings revised her second will? Do you think the entire will would be valid or only a part of it? If your will needed revision, how would you do it?

(c) Changes occurred during Mrs. Hastings' long life, and some personal possessions listed in her various wills were disposed of before she died. In your opinion, how might this matter of designating the distribution of personal possessions be handled?

(d) How many executors did Mrs. Hastings name in her third will? Were they to act as co-executors or were some of them alternates in case the others were unable or unwilling to act? How many executors and alternates would you suggest that she needed for a very small estate?

3. Ted Andrachuk died without a will, leaving an estate of approximately $65 000. His nearest relatives are his parents, his wife, and his three children.

(a) How would his estate be divided?

(b) His wife is the beneficiary of a $40 000 life insurance policy. Would this be distributed as part of the estate?

(c) He and his wife had a joint bank account. Would this form part of his estate?

(d) He and his wife owned their house as tenants in common. Would all, a part, or none of the house be considered part of his estate?

4. Marie, who lived common-law for 15 years, tells this story:

INTESTACY AND COMMON-LAW SPOUSES

My common-law husband was a wonderful man, but there was no way I could convince him to marry me. I also tried and tried to get him to make a will, but he said he considered wills meaningless pieces of paper. As the years went by, I worried less about this and concentrated on planning our future together. I never gave up my well-paying job because we could use the money. We pooled all our finances to pay current expenses as we raised his three daughters, bought a house, and established a retirement fund.

Suddenly, my husband died, leaving me not only grief-stricken but also penniless. Here I am living alone in a nearly empty apartment with very few of the lovely things we had over the years. Our house is for sale and the antique furniture that I had collected as a hobby has been distributed among my husband's grasping family who had not approved of me anyway. I never thought my stepchildren would have such lack of loyalty to their father that they would do things he never would have wanted.

(a) What can a common-law wife like Marie do to protect her financial security?

(b) Do you think she has a strong case for contesting the distribution of this estate?

(c) If a person dies without a will in your province, does a common-law spouse automatically get a preferential share? Does the length of time the couple have been living common-law make any difference?

5. Mrs. DeMelo has a dependent daughter who is severely handicapped and who has a limited capacity to handle financial affairs. Mrs. DeMelo's will leaves her estate in equal shares to this daughter and to her son, but she is wondering whether she should revise her will to establish a testamentary trust for the daughter. Because her son is financially independent and her daughter is not, Mrs. DeMelo proposes leaving her total estate in trust for her daughter, with the residue to go to her son after her daughter's death.

(a) List some factors to be considered in deciding whether to leave the estate in trust for the daughter.

(b) Do you think a testamentary trust would be a wise decision in this case?

(c) Do you see a potential conflict of interest for the son if he is made a trustee?

6. Mr. X left a will which stated that his estate was to be divided equally among three of his four children. His youngest son George, now 32, with whom he had been on bad terms for some years, was left out of the will. Does the fact that George was the only child excluded from the will form a good basis for him to contest the will?

7. (a) Why does an executor need a trust account?

(b) The main task of an executor is to assemble the assets of the deceased and distribute them to the designated beneficiaries. Why is there so much formality associated with transferring the assets?

(c) If a beneficiary suspects that an executor may not be acting in the best interests of herself and the other beneficiaries, what can be done to check on this?

8. When Mrs. S. died at an advanced age, it was discovered that her will named her previously deceased husband as executor. How would this estate be settled when there is a will but no executor?

9. After Maisie's death there was a search for a will, since she had often talked about how she would leave her estate, but no will was found. As a result, her estate, which had to be treated as an intestacy, was settled by her cousin

John who acted as administrator. Maisie's estate included the following assets:

Cash and deposits of $26 000
House valued at $185 000 which was owned as a tenant in common with her estranged husband
Canada Savings Bonds, worth $5000
Car valued at $8000
Life insurance policy with face value of $38 000, which named her husband as beneficiary
RRSP of $3600
Pension plan credit of $6849

In addition to her estranged, but never divorced, husband, Maisie left a daughter who is mentally disabled, and an elderly mother.

(a) Make a list of the assets that would form part of Maisie's estate.
(b) Using the rules for intestacy for your province, show how this estate would be divided.
(c) Might there be a reason for an application to the Surrogate Court for a change in this division to favour the daughter who is mentally disabled? What information about the family would you need to know to determine if there is a case to be made?
(d) If the husband wanted the house, would it have to be sold or could it go to him?

10. Arrange for a debate on the resolution:
"Resolved that a young couple without children does not need a will."

References
Books

ANDERSON, BRIAN, and CHRISTOPHER SNYDER. *It's Your Money*. Sixth Edition. Toronto: Methuen, 1989, 264 pp. A reference for the general reader which includes financial planning, budgets, income tax, disability insurance, savings, investments, retirement planning, credit, wills, and estates.

CAROE, LAURENCE C. *Wills for Ontario*. Ninth Edition. Vancouver: International Self-Counsel Press, 1988, 100 pp. A non-technical explanation of wills.

COHEN, DIAN. *Money*. Scarborough, Ontario: Prentice-Hall Canada, 1987, 270 pp. An economist suggests strategies for coping with personal finances in the context of changing economic conditions. Topics include financial plans, buying a home, insurance, income tax, retirement, estate planning, and investments.

DRACHE, ARTHUR B. C., and SUSAN WEIDMAN SCHNEIDER. *Head and Heart, Finan-*

cial Strategies for Smart Women. Toronto: Macmillan, 1987, 348 pp. Recognizing the needs and perspectives of women, a tax lawyer and journalist have collaborated to present basic financial information, taking into account women's concerns at different stages in their lives.

FORMAN, NORM. *Mind Over Money, Curing Your Financial Headaches with Moneysanity*. Toronto: Doubleday Canada, 1987, 248 pp. A psychologist examines the effects money has on behaviour, looking at the origin of money problems and suggesting therapies to help us to better understand ourselves.

GEORGAS, M. STEPHEN. *Power of Attorney Kit*. Second Edition. Vancouver: International Self-Counsel Press, 1988, 30 pp. Instructions and forms for drawing up a power of attorney.

GOTTSELIG, CHERYL. *Wills for Alberta*. Seventh Edition. Vancouver: International Self-Counsel Press, 1987, 128 pp. A lawyer explains the hows and whys of writing a will and some pointers on estate planning.

KRUZENISKI, RONALD, and JANE E. GORDON. *Will/Probate Procedure for Manitoba & Saskatchewan*. Third Edition. Vancouver: International Self-Counsel Press, 1985, 81 pp. A basic explanation of the terminology and procedures involved in drawing or probating a will.

MACINNIS, LYMAN. *Get Smart! Make Your Money Count in the 1990s*. Second Edition. Scarborough, Ontario: Prentice-Hall Canada, 1989, 317 pp. A book for the general reader that includes financial planning and income tax principles, but gives major attention to investing in the stock market.

Money and Family Law. Toronto: Richard De Boo Publishers, monthly. A professional newsletter that concentrates on financial aspects of family law. Includes articles on wills and trusts, pensions and life insurance, support, estate planning, division of family property, and relevant court decisions.

TURNER, MARY, DANIEL LEROSSIGNOL, CLAUDE RINFRET, and RICHARD DAW. *Canadian Guide to Personal Financial Management*. Fourth Edition. Scarborough, Ontario: Prentice-Hall Canada, 1989, 231 pp. Accountants provide guidance on a broad range of topics, including planning finances, estimating insurance needs, managing risk, and determining investment needs. Instructions and the necessary forms for making plans are provided.

WONG, STEVEN G. *Wills for British Columbia*. Thirteenth Edition. Vancouver: International Self-Counsel Press, 1988, 112 pp. Gives the general reader an explanation of basic processes involved with wills.

WYATT, ELAINE. *The Money Companion, How to Manage Your Money and Achieve Financial Freedom*. Markham, Ontario: Penguin Books, 1989, 203 pp. A guide to personal financial management that focuses on planning, investment strategy and retirement needs.

WYLIE, BETTY JANE, and LYNNE MACFARLANE. *Everywoman's Money Book*. Fourth Edition. Toronto: Key Porter, 1989, 223 pp. A journalist and a stockbroker have collaborated on this wide-ranging treatment of a variety of personal finance topics, including women and credit, the budget, insurance, retirement, children and money.

Article

HIRSHORN, SUSAN. "Thy Will be Done," *Canadian Consumer*, 16 No. 11, 1986, 16-20. Suggestions for making a will.

PART 2

FINANCIAL SECURITY

The processes of making financial plans to maximize the use of resources—both during one's lifetime and afterwards—were the focus of Part I. An integral part of financial planning is to ensure financial security for oneself and one's dependents. The objective of Part II is to examine, in some depth, a variety of ways to protect financial security, such as buying insurance or increasing net worth. Before becoming too involved with specific information about insurance, pensions, annuities, bonds, and stocks, it is essential to reflect on the necessity for any of them.

Part II begins with an introductory chapter on economic risks and financial security. This is followed by chapters that explain which risks can be handled by general and life insurance. Funding retirement, a significant aspect of protecting financial security, involves both public programs and private savings. The three final chapters are concerned with saving and investing—indispensable ways of increasing financial security.

ECONOMIC RISKS AND FINANCIAL SECURITY

1. To explain what is meant by financial security.

2. To explain how the need for financial security affects decisions about the use of economic resources, e.g., saving for the future or selecting insurance.

3. To identify events that pose economic risks for individuals or families.

4. To differentiate between assuming risk and sharing risk.

5. To distinguish between steps an individual can take to enhance financial security and the means provided by society.

6. To identify (i) threats to financial security posed by a serious disability and (ii) ways to alleviate the consequences.

7. To analyze the meaning of disability as defined by various insurers.

8. To identify important features in disability insurance coverage.

Introduction

Of prime concern to everyone is maintaining a feeling of financial security, or assurance that we can cope with whatever may happen. This feeling of security can be enhanced if we know what our economic risks are, and can take steps to reduce their consequences. Life is full of economic risk, but sometimes we fail to recognize the particular risks that most threaten our economic well-being. Perhaps that explains why some people buy life insurance regardless of any need for it, and others who really need the protection fail to buy it. This chapter helps to identify those economic risks that pose the greatest threats to welfare, and suggests ways to minimize the risk. Certain risks, such as the untimely death of a person with dependents, or theft or damage of personal property, may be shared through the purchase of insurance. We have social programs (e.g., Old Age Security, Canada/Quebec Pension Plan, Unemployment Insurance, welfare) to ameliorate the effects of some events such as loss of income. The risk of becoming disabled and unable to earn a living is a serious one and too often ignored.

The chapters that follow consider in some detail several important ways to reduce economic risk, such as insuring possessions or your life, planning for retirement income, and saving and investing to build up your net worth.

Financial Security

What do we mean by financial security? You will experience a feeling of *financial security* if you are confident that you will have the economic means to meet your needs in the present and in the future. As there are many conceptions of what is needed for a satisfactory level of living, so there are many notions of what constitutes financial security. Your feelings about risk as well as your economic situation will have much to do with the nature of your concerns about financial security. For instance, a family living on welfare may well consider that having enough money to pay the current bills for food, shelter, and clothing represents financial security for them, while a family living in affluent circumstances may have much more expansive ideas about what is required to maintain their financial security. The latter may feel economically threatened if they have to give up a vacation home, regular holidays, or restaurant meals.

If you feel financially secure, it may be assumed that you feel confident that you will be able to handle the following needs: (i) to maintain your accustomed level of living, (ii) to cope with financial emergencies or unusual expenses, and (iii) to make provision for loss of income resulting from illness, unemployment, retirement, aging, or disability. By knowing that you are protected from financial threats, you can feel reasonably secure about the future. But for how many of us is this true? Who can be certain of future needs or future resources as we move through the various stages in our life cycle?

Both as individuals and as a society, we have taken an increasing interest in ways of providing financial security as we have moved from considerable individual economic self-sufficiency to increasing interdependence. We rely, for the most part, on money income rather than help from others to support our desired lifestyle; anything that interrupts or halts the flow of income is a serious threat. In response to social changes, government-sponsored programs have been instituted to provide partial financial security for the young, the old, the disabled, the unemployed, and the poor. Since most of us want more than partial financial security, we must take steps to protect ourselves against a variety of economic risks.

Economic Risks

Before we can make any plans to enhance our financial security we must first identify those events that pose economic risks for us and could threaten our security. The list of risks will not be identical for everyone, nor the same at all stages of our lives. If you do not own a house, you will not face the risk of it burning down; if you do not have dependent children, you will not have to worry about the risk of being unable to support them; if you do not own a car, damage to it is not one of your risks. It is essential to remember that economic risks and our ideas about financial security are changing constantly as our lives change. Most of our economic risks can be categorized as:

(a) *loss of income*
  – destruction of earning capacity
  – loss of market for your services
(b) *unexpected large expenses*
  – destruction of property
  – illness or death
  – personal liability
(c) *loss in value of capital*
  – drop in market value
  – inflation

Loss of Income

Anything that may cause the income stream to stop poses a very serious threat to economic security. As long as income continues, there are some possibilities of coping with unexpected expenses or loss of capital, but without a regular income it is difficult to obtain enough resources. The reasons for termination of income are usually either the destruction of earning capacity or the disappearance of the market for your services.

DESTRUCTION OF EARNING CAPACITY   Ability to earn income may be lost temporarily through illness, or permanently because of disability, aging, or death. Of these, permanent disability presents a particularly serious risk. Not only would you be unable to work, but you must be supported and may also need expensive care. Our social mechanisms for this financial burden have not been as fully developed as for aging or death, perhaps because we all expect to get older and to die, but not to become disabled.

LOSS OF MARKET FOR YOUR SERVICES   The self-employed must consider the prospect that the market for their goods or services may disappear, leaving them without income. If at all possible, they will need to change what is being produced. Employees may find that their services are no longer needed because the demand for particular skills has fallen, or because economic conditions have reduced economic activity, or for a number of other reasons. Employees, like the self-employed, may have to acquire new skills to fit into the labour market again.

UNEXPECTED LARGE EXPENSES

There can be many kinds of unexpected large expenses that may threaten financial security, but only three will be discussed here:

(a)   destruction or loss of personal property,
(b)   illness or death,
(c)   personal liability.

DESTRUCTION OF PROPERTY   The more we own, the greater the risk of loss or destruction of our possessions. Loss can be the result of many factors, such as theft, fire, or weather. Should a family lose their house and all the contents through fire, they would probably be unable to replace everything from their own resources; for this reason they buy home insurance.

ILLNESS AND DEATH   Many, but not all, of the large expenses associated with illness and death have been shared through our health insurance program. However, the home care of a person who is ill for a long time can be very expensive and some or all of this may have to be borne by the family. Therefore, some personal resources may be needed in addition to health insurance and other social programs.

PERSONAL LIABILITY   Anyone could face a very large unexpected expense if found liable for damage or injury because of negligence. We are probably most aware of this in relation to cars, because of the potential for destruction and death from a moment's inattention while driving. This concept will be more fully developed in the chapter on general insurance.

LOSS IN VALUE OF CAPITAL

Things you own can lose value because of a reduction in the demand for them. If a highway is built close to your house, if interest in a certain painter wanes, or if no one wants your mining stocks, your capital in the form of a house, painting, or shares diminishes through no action of yours.

Inflation has been the cause of substantial loss in the value of money saved. For instance, a dollar earned in 1970 and saved until 1990 would buy only 26 percent of what it had 20 years earlier, a loss of about three-quarters of its purchasing power. That is why it should have been invested to earn a return at least as great as the inflation rate, and preferably greater. Real property, on the other hand, appreciated greatly during this inflationary period.

WHAT ARE YOUR ECONOMIC RISKS?

Make a list of economic risks that could threaten your financial security this year. Which events might cause a loss of income, even for a time? What are some unexpected large expenses that would create hardship? How much of your net worth is at risk from price changes? Next, assign priorities to your list so that you may make plans to handle these risks.

Second, make a list of future economic risks—issues that are not current concerns but may be at another time—such as insufficient retirement income and inability to support children or other relatives.

NEED FOR SAVINGS

Even if you are fortunate enough to go through life managing to escape disability, major illness, or unemployment, you will probably retire sometime. When you do, employment income will stop and you will become dependent on pensions and investment earnings. Unless you spend your work years with the same employer—preferably a government or large and successful company—you may find that your work pension will not support you in the style you would wish. Public pensions will help, but many people find retirement much more comfortable if they have private investment income as well. In order to have investment income you must accumulate some net worth to invest.

HANDLING RISK

Having identified your economic risks, the next step is to decide what to do about them. Essentially there are three possibilities; try to prevent the event from happening, assume the risk yourself, or share the risk with others. The task of thinking of ways to reduce or prevent risks is left to you. A discussion of ways of assuming and sharing risk follows.

ASSUMING RISK

If you have enough financial resources, you can assume your own risks, that is, you are confident you will be able to handle unfortunate events without jeopardizing your level of living. You expect to have the funds to cope with unemployment, an unexpected large expense, illness, or retirement. Accumulating net worth is clearly one way of preparing to handle whatever risks come your way. That is why all advice on financial planning stresses saving for unforeseen needs, emergencies, and retirement.

Another way a family can assume risk is to expect individuals to help each other. When one earner is unable to work, someone else in the family may be able to support the household. Two-income families have spread the risk of something happening to the income stream. Nevertheless, most of us are unable to assume all potential risks, and must depend on some risk-sharing.

SHARING RISK

When a risk is too much for individuals or families to bear alone, it may be shared through private insurance or social income security programs. By collecting small contributions from many people, a fund is created sufficient to compensate those few people who experience the unfortunate event. For example, all car owners contribute to car insurance, but only those who have accidents draw on the fund. Participants in risk-sharing programs enhance their financial security by the knowledge that compensation is available if they should require it.

PUBLIC PROGRAMS   Our public income security programs are based on risk-sharing, one way or another. The Canada and Quebec Pension Plans and Unemployment Insurance are social insurance programs to which most employed people make contributions, and eligibility for benefits depends on having been a contributor. These programs offer protection against the risks of unemployment, disability, aging, and death. There are others, such as Old Age Security and social welfare, which we fund through taxes rather than direct contributions. In this way, those in the labour force provide support for those who are old, or are unable to work.

In addition to these income security programs, society takes other steps to help us plan for our own financial security. The income tax system encourages retirement planning by offering tax deductions if we invest in RRSPs and contribute to employment-related pension plans.

PRIVATE EFFORTS   As mentioned, risk can be handled by trying to reduce it, share it with others, or assume it oneself. In subsequent chapters on general insurance, life insurance, and annuities, various ways of assuming or sharing risks will be examined. Through general insurance, the risks of loss or damage to personal property, as well as personal liability, are shared. Life insurance is designed to protect against the risk of the premature death of a person with dependents. Annuities, by turning capital into an income stream guaranteed for life, protect against the risk of living so long that there are no savings left. Finally, there are personal savings, which although insufficient to cover some risks, can certainly be helpful in any financial crisis.

DISABILITY — A SERIOUS RISK

In this chapter, brief mention will be made of personal disability, a very significant economic risk that we too often ignore. A common hazard is the loss of our ability to earn a living because of temporary or permanent disability due to an accident or an illness. The following case study, based on a real situation, illustrates the disastrous effect that permanent disability can have on a family's financial security.

HIS LIFE WAS CHANGED BY A FALL

Simon, a self-employed mason, fell 15 metres from a scaffold, injuring himself so badly that after months in hospital he now lives in constant pain and walks with difficulty. He can't lift or carry anything. Fortunately he was covered by Workers' Compensation that entitles him to a small pension, but inexplicably he was classified as 25 percent disabled. Two years after the accident Simon was still negotiating with Canada Pension about the extent of his disability. His first application was rejected because of the possibility that he might be able to return to work. He has now applied again.

> At 40, Simon is unable to work to support his wife and three teen-aged children. He gave up his business, sold the house, and they lived on their savings as long as they lasted. The cheque from Workers' Compensation is just large enough to pay the rent on a subsidized apartment. The small amount Simon gets from welfare is insufficient to buy the family's food. Applying for disability benefits from most programs involves considerable red tape and waiting, as Simon has discovered. Simon's fall drastically changed life for himself and his family.

Although, for those under the age of 65, the probability of suffering a disability is greater than dying, most people are more likely to have life insurance than disability insurance. The gender differences in the probability of being disabled for more than six months between the ages of 25 and 55 are illustrated in Figure 4.1. Females face a significantly greater risk of being disabled than dying, but have a lower mortality rate than males of the same age. Experience has shown that anyone who is disabled for more than three months will probably still be disabled five years later. The risk of becoming disabled is one that most of us are financially unable to assume alone. How many young people, or even older ones, have enough savings to support themselves for a year or more?

To protect ourselves against the risk of becoming disabled we can purchase *disability insurance*, sometimes called income replacement insurance. Otherwise we will have to depend on others to support us—our families or the social welfare system.

DISABILITY INSURANCE

Disability insurance may be purchased privately, or more cheaply through a group policy. When an insurance company insures a group of employees in one policy the coverage will be less costly than if each bought it separately. Many employees have some group disability insurance through their place of work. It is critical to find out exactly what coverage you have. Policies vary in the waiting period, the definition of disability, the amount of benefits, the benefit period, and other options. The cost of the coverage will be dependent on the features included; better benefits will cost more.

WAITING PERIOD   It is important to know how long you must be unable to work before disability payments would begin. If you have sick leave coverage at your place of work, you would not need income replacement until that expires. On the other hand, you might not want to wait for months before receiving any payments. Policies may have waiting periods as short as one or

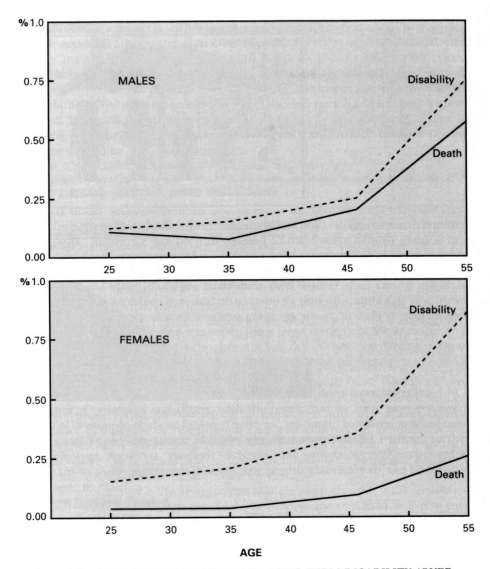

Figure 4.1   PROBABILITY OF DEATH OR LONG-TERM DISABILITY (OVER
SIX MONTHS) OCCURRING WITHIN A YEAR, BY GENDER

Source: Mutual Life's group insurance data reproduced with the permission of Mutual Life of Canada.

two weeks or as long as one to four months. Consider how long you could survive before benefits started, and choose the longest waiting period you could manage, to keep the premium cost down.

DEFINITION OF DISABILITY   How disabled must you be to become eligible for benefits? It is essential that you read this part of the policy very carefully; many disabled people have been surprised to find that, although they had insurance, the definition of disability excluded them. A distinction is usually made between partial and total disability, and whether you could work part-time or at an occupation other than your usual one. By paying more you can get a policy that provides benefits until you are able to return to your usual occupation. For instance, consider a teacher who has suffered some voice impairment. He would perhaps be unable to continue teaching, but might be able to do a clerical job. Since he would not be considered totally disabled, some disability policies would not provide support for him because he appears able to handle different work.

AMOUNT OF BENEFITS   You will want to obtain the most coverage you can afford, but that would probably amount to only 60-70 percent of your usual income. No insurance company will offer a policy that would make it profitable for anyone to become disabled. An additional option to include benefits indexed to inflation will cost more, but will ensure that payments will rise at about the same rate as prices.

BENEFIT PERIOD   Does the policy provide benefits for a limited time such as a few weeks, or one year, or to age 65? Again, you will want the longest benefit period you can afford.

RENEWABILITY   It is possible to have a clause in the policy that guarantees that it is non-cancellable or renewable. You would not want to find, as you get older, that the company will not renew your policy.

SOCIAL SUPPORT FOR THE DISABLED

Should you become disabled, there are some social programs for which you might be eligible. In some instances it will be required that you had previously contributed to the program, or that the disability resulted from an injury on the job or during military service.

Unemployment Insurance—a federal program that provides short-term benefits to contributors.

The Canada and Quebec Pension Plans—a disability pension for contributors with a severe or prolonged disability, and their dependents and survivors.

Workers' Compensation—provincial plans that offer medical, financial, and rehabilitative assistance to workers who become disabled by accidents or illness related to their jobs.

Short-term or Long-term Welfare—municipal and provincial programs for those with few other resources.

SUMMARY

Financial security is something we take for granted when things are going well, actively endeavour to protect if threatened, and vigorously try to regain if lost. It is a feeling of assurance that we have the capacity to maintain our desired level of living. Prudent people take steps to protect their financial security as much as possible from those economic risks that can result in loss of income or unexpected large expenditures. Sharing risks with others by creating a pool of funds to compensate those who are in need is the underlying principle of all forms of insurance. Disability is a much neglected but serious risk to financial security that should be given careful consideration by all working people.

This chapter has perhaps alerted you to some economic risks that could be threatening to your financial security at some time in your life, but has not specified exactly what you can do to protect yourself. Subsequent chapters will address in detail the protection offered by general insurance and life insurance, private and public pensions, and annuities. Net worth, which is helpful in any financial crisis, is achieved by regular saving and wise investing.

PROBLEMS

1. (a) Can you think of anything this family could have done to be better prepared for such an economic disaster as this?

WHEN DISASTER STRUCK

Six years ago, Luke and Vera never imagined that they would be in such dire straits financially as to have to apply for welfare. He was a self-employed, skilled construction worker who was making a good income when suddenly he developed a heart condition that required open-heart surgery. Complications developed. After extended hospitalization he went home, but was not well enough to work. His doctor advised him that any physical activity could cause a coronary.

The stress of Luke's illness, the financial problems, and having to look after the home and children on her own caused a gastric condition that made Vera miserable and not well enough to go out to work. If she did, who would look after the children, who were five years, four years, and ten months old?

When Luke stopped working they had $2000 in the bank, and had built up about $10 000 equity in the semi-detached home they were buying. They did not apply for welfare because they were afraid they would have to sell their house and car, so they lived on their savings as long as they could. Being self-employed, Luke was not covered by unemployment insurance, but he had been paying into the Canada Pension Plan. He had once thought about disability insurance but decided against it because of the high premiums. In addition to regular living expenses, costly drugs were needed for Luke, and a special formula for the baby, who is allergic to milk.

Finally this family became so desperate that they called Social Services. They were immediately put on short-term welfare that included a waiver of premium for health insurance, free prescription drugs and dental care, and an allowance for the special diet. They were advised to see their bank about the mortgage payment, that was one month in arrears, to ask that it be deferred and the mortgage extended a month. They discovered to their surprise that welfare applicants are allowed to have a car and a few assets, and that if they had applied sooner, they could have kept their savings in the bank.

    (b) Should they be applying for disability benefits from the Canada Pension Plan?

    (c) Do you have any other suggestions for ways they could obtain more resources?

2. Think of people you know and outline two instances of families who would have quite different ideas of what financial security means to them.

3. At what stage in the life cycle do you think economic risks may be most threatening?

4. Make a list of four or five economic risks that could threaten your financial security right now. Making a projection to your life five years from now, what changes in economic risks do you foresee?

5. Make a list of several features that it would be desirable to include in a disability insurance policy. Which of these would add to the premium cost?

6. Why do you think people tend to neglect protection for the risk of becoming disabled?

7. In this chapter we have mentioned a variety of economic risks, and suggested various ways to minimize the effects of each. As an aid in summarizing this

information, complete the following chart. In addition to the material in this chapter you should be able to draw on your general knowledge. Distinguish among the various kinds of protection according to whether the initiative comes from yourself or your family, or whether the benefits result from your employment or your citizenship. The first line has been filled in as an example.

Economic risks	Ways to handle economic risks		
	As an individual or family member	As an employee	As a citizen
A. LOSS OF INCOME			
1. Earning capacity destroyed (a) temporarily, e.g., illness	Use savings. Income of another family member.	Sick leave with pay	Health insurance
(b) permanently – disability			
– aging			
– death			
2. Market for earner's services destroyed (a) unemployment			
(b) fall in profits for self-employed			
B. UNEXPECTED LARGE EXPENSES			
1. Destruction or loss of personal property			
2. Illness, death			
3. Personal liability			
C. LOSS OF VALUE OF CAPITAL			
1. Drop in market value e.g., house, stock	Diversify assets	n/a	n/a
2. Price changes e.g., inflation	Diversify assets	n/a	n/a

8. Evaluate this long-term disability plan that covers one group of employees. How effective do you think it will be in meeting the needs of disabled employees? The coverage is as follows:

Benefits: 66 2/3 percent of basic monthly earnings, to a maximum of $3500. This will be reduced by any amount to which you are entitled from Workers' Compensation or Canada Pension (benefits for dependents are excluded). The employer will supplement this at 13 1/3 percent of the basic salary for a period of four months, to a maximum of 80 percent of your basic earnings..

Waiting Period: Benefits begin on the ninety-first consecutive day of total disability.

Benefit Period: until age 65 for total disability; two years for a temporary disability that prevents you from performing the duties of your occupation. It is payable beyond two years if you are disabled to the extent that you cannot engage in any occupation for which you are, or could reasonably become, qualified as determined by your doctor.

9. Decide whether you AGREE or DISAGREE with each of the following statements.

   (a) What you already possess affects your concept of financial security.
   (b) Unemployment Insurance protects against the risk of personal liability.
   (c) You have to contribute to the Canada/Quebec Pension Plan or Unemployment Insurance to become eligible for disability benefits.
   (d) Unemployment Insurance will assist a family when the breadwinner dies suddenly.
   (e) For those aged 30, the probability of becoming disabled (for more than three months) is greater than the probability of dying.
   (f) Social programs tend to provide income support for those unable to work, but leave individuals to arrange their own protection for risks to property or capital.

10. Try to find out the cost of buying disability insurance privately for 25-year-old employed males and females. If possible, compare this to the cost of group protection.

REFERENCES

Books

ANDERSON, BRIAN, and CHRISTOPHER SNYDER. *It's Your Money*. Sixth Edition. Toronto: Methuen, 1989, 264 pp. A reference for the general reader which includes financial planning, budgets, income tax, disability insurance, savings, investments, retirement planning, credit, wills, and estates.

COHEN, DIAN. *Money*. Scarborough, Ontario: Prentice-Hall Canada, 1987, 270 pp. An economist suggests strategies for coping with personal finances in the context of changing economic conditions. Topics include financial plans, buying a home, insurance, income tax, retirement, estate planning, and investments.

THE G. ALLAN ROEHER INSTITUTE. *Income Insecurity, The Disability Income System in Canada*. Downsview, Ontario: The G. Allan Roeher Institute, 1988, 141 pp. Describes and analyzes the various sources of disability income and suggests policy options.

TOWNSON, MONICA, and FREDERICK STAPENHURST. *The Canadian Woman's Guide to Money*. Second Edition. Toronto: McGraw-Hill Ryerson, 1982, 203 pp. A book for the general reader that includes budgets, financial security, life insurance, retirement planning, and credit.

TURNER, MARY, DANIEL LEROSSIGNOL, CLAUDE RINFRET, and RICHARD DAW. *Canadian Guide to Personal Financial Management*. Fourth Edition. Scarborough, Ontario: Prentice-Hall Canada, 1989, 231 pp. Accountants provide guidance on a broad range of topics, including planning finances, estimating insurance needs, managing risk, and determining investment needs. Instructions and the necessary forms for making plans are provided.

WYATT, ELAINE. *The Money Companion, How to Manage Your Money and Achieve Financial Freedom*. Markham, Ontario: Penguin Books, 1989, 203 pp. A guide to personal financial management that focuses on planning, investment strategy, and retirement needs.

GENERAL INSURANCE

1. To identify:
   (a) major financial risks associated with ownership of a house and its contents, personal possessions, or an automobile,
   (b) the appropriate type of insurance coverage for each risk.

2. To understand and demonstrate applications of these basic insurance principles:
   (a) sharing risk,
   (b) indemnification,
   (c) subrogation,
   (d) co-insurance.

3. To distinguish between:
   (a) actual cash value and replacement value,
   (b) insurable interest and insurable risk,
   (c) scheduled items rider and floater clause,
   (d) deductible and policy limits,
   (e) pure cost of insurance and loading charge,
   (f) premium and policy,
   (g) insured and insurer.

4. To explain differences in the functions of:
   (a) actuary,
   (b) insurance agent,
   (c) insurance broker,
   (d) adjuster,
   (e) claims department.

5. To ascertain, from reading an insurance policy, the risks that are: (a) covered, and (b) excluded.

6. To identify some of the factors insurers consider when settling claims.

7. To explain how the concept of negligence may be involved in insurance claims.

8. To explain these terms: depreciation, rider or endorsement, short rate, accident benefits.

INTRODUCTION

The analysis of financial security in Chapter 4 led to the conclusion that some risks could be minimized by purchasing insurance. This chapter identifies economic risks that are of concern to anyone owning real property or personal possessions, explains basic concepts and principles of general insurance, and examines in detail three types of general insurance: property insurance, personal liability insurance, and automobile insurance. Life insurance, which is not considered a type of general insurance, is discussed in the next chapter.

THE ECONOMIC RISKS OF OWNERSHIP

Two types of risk are associated with ownership: (i) the property itself may be damaged, destroyed, or lost, and (ii) you may be held responsible for damage or injury to others or their possessions because of what you own. Fire and theft, examples of the first type of risk, are perhaps more easily understood than the second type, a liability risk. You may have a financial responsibility (or liability) if your car, your dog, or your broken steps should be the cause of damage or injury, although it is usually necessary for those making the claim to prove that you were negligent in some way. All liability risks need not be related to ownership; careless behaviour can also be a cause.

DAMAGE OR LOSS OF PROPERTY

Both tenants and home owners must consider the risk that their furnishings and other possessions may be stolen or damaged by fire, and owners must consider the possibility that their houses may burn. Damage or loss of a car is another risk to consider, but a less serious one than being responsible for injury to people; at the very worst one would be left without a car, but not burdened with a monstrous debt for many years.

LIABILITY FOR DAMAGES

Being found responsible, because of your negligence, for damage to the lives or property of others is one of the risks you may be exposed to. Here we are not speaking about damage to your person or possessions, but claims against you by others for their losses. As a tenant, there is the possibility that you may be held responsible for damage to your rented premises. If, for instance, your careless smoking or forgetfulness in using a heating appliance was the cause of an apartment fire, the landlord's insurer would reimburse the landlord for the damage to the building, but would probably bill you for the cost of the repairs. The extent of your liability would depend on the circumstances.

As a home owner, you face the risk that your walks, yards, trees, and so on may be the cause of an injury. Your tree may fall on the neighbour's car, or someone may fall on your broken steps. As an automobile owner, you face the serious risk of being liable for death or injury, with the enormous financial consequences. Recent Canadian settlements for personal injury in automobile accidents have been as high as several million dollars. Cars can also damage other people's cars or property, but these claims are usually less than for personal injury.

Most of us consider the risks outlined above to be too great to accept entirely on our own, and therefore we buy insurance to share the risks with others. Before examining various types of insurance, it is essential to understand a few basic insurance concepts and principles.

BASIC CONCEPTS AND PRINCIPLES

THE INSURANCE PRINCIPLE

Since a major fire or auto accident can financially cripple an individual or family, methods have been devised to spread the risk. If a large number of people who face a common risk pool their money, there will be sufficient funds to compensate the few who actually experience the disaster. This *pooling or sharing a risk* is the basic principle on which all types of insurance are based. However, it depends on the law of large numbers and will not work for a small group. The insurance companies that collect, manage, and disperse the pooled funds employ specialized mathematicians called *actuaries* to predict the probability of a particular event occurring per 1000 people. They can be fairly accurate for large numbers of people or events, but of course they cannot identify which persons will be affected in a particular year. The amount each person contributes to the insurance pool or fund will depend on:

(a)   the probability of the event occurring,
(b)   the cost of compensation,
(c)   the number sharing the risk.

The simplified example on the next page illustrates this principle.

SHARING THE RISK

I n the town of Bayfield there are 1000 houses, all wooden and of approximately equal value. Past records reveal that, on average, one house burns down each year, and that the cost of rebuilding a house is approximately $100 000. It is not necessary to take into account the value of the land on which the house stands because fire does not destroy the lot.

The loss of a house is such a serious disaster that the community does not expect the affected family to cope alone. In the nineteenth century it was customary for neighbours to come to the rescue, providing temporary shelter for the homeless family while they felled logs and sawed boards to construct a new house. Now the scarcity of trees and the complexity of house construction has caused the house-building bee to be abandoned in favour of property insurance.

How large a fund will be needed in Bayfield to cover the fire losses to houses?

Number of home owners sharing the risk:	1000
Probability of fire:	1 per 1000/year
Cost of compensation:	$100 000

If each owner contributes $100 per year, there will be a fund of $100 000. At the end of a typical year, with one claim for $100 000, the fund will be exhausted.

To summarize, the principle of sharing risk is applied when a large number of people are willing to pay a regular fee that is certain, in exchange for protection against a hazard that is uncertain. This means that those who experience a loss will be compensated and that those fortunate enough not to have had a loss will not need to claim anything from the insurance fund. However, all will have enhanced their financial security with insurance.

FACTORS AFFECTING COST

The cost of property insurance, as we have said, depends on the probability of a particular peril occurring, the cost of compensation, and the number of people sharing the risk. In practice, actuaries take into consideration more complexity than is shown in the above example. The probability of fire and the extent of damage are affected by the availability of fire-fighting facilities, the proximity of hazards such as paint factories or oil storage tanks, and the inflammability of the house. The cost of compensation depends on the value of the property to be repaired or replaced, which can vary considerably in the case of houses.

Once the probability of the event occurring has been established and the cost of compensation estimated, an actuary can determine the cost of covering this risk, which is called the *pure cost of insurance*. To this amount will be added a *loading charge* to cover the costs the insurance company incurs in collecting and managing the insurance funds, settling the claims, and returning profits to the company's shareholders. Not surprisingly, the estimates of all these costs may vary from company to company. The charge to insure a property, called a *premium*, will be paid at regular intervals to keep the insurance in force.

RISK MANAGEMENT

INSURABLE INTEREST   You cannot buy insurance against a risk unless it can be shown that you have an *insurable interest* in the risk in question. In other words, would you suffer a financial loss if the event occurred? If you own property, you have an insurable interest in the possibility of it being stolen or destroyed. A relative or friend who has no legal relation to your property cannot insure your house against fire. This principle applies to all types of insurance, including life insurance.

INSURABLE RISKS   Insurance is concerned with *insurable risks* only; these risks result from chance events and are not caused by deliberate action on the part of the person insured. If a fire starts because of lightning, it is a chance risk, but if the fire was started by the property owner, it is not. Insurance companies have to be sure of the cause of the damage before settling the claim.

HANDLING RISK   Three possible ways of dealing with insurable risks are: (i) take steps to eliminate or reduce the risk, (ii) prepare to handle the loss oneself, or (iii) share the risk with others. An example of reducing risk of injury from fire would be to install smoke detectors in your home. The risk of theft could be reduced by improving the locks on your doors and windows. You may decide to handle some risks yourself if the risk is not too high and your financial resources are adequate. A person who decides not to buy collision coverage on an old car is accepting the risk of destruction of the car instead of sharing it by buying insurance. Sharing risks through insurance is prudent whenever the possible loss would be too heavy to handle alone. In planning for financial security, it may be wise to use a combination of these three options. You will probably need some insurance, but there may be instances where you can reduce the cost of this service if you take steps to minimize the risk and if you assume some portion of the risk yourself.

THE INSURANCE CONTRACT

When you decide to purchase insurance you may contact an *agent* who represents a single insurance company or a *broker* who represents several companies. The broker is able to do comparison shopping for you among the several companies he or she represents to find the most economical and most appropriate coverage for you.

On applying for insurance, the agent may give you an application form to complete but not a copy of the policy, on the assumption that you are not interested in reading it. The agent will obtain a policy for you if asked.

The legal contract or agreement between the person buying insurance, the *insured*, and the insurance company, the *insurer*, is called a *policy*. Although some policies may be in legal language that is difficult to understand, it is encouraging to find insurers now writing their policies in a more simplified form. The policy included in this book represents the latter style of contract-writing. A policy will seem less daunting if you begin by identifying the main components. Examine the sample policy (Figure 5.1 in the Appendix) to identify the following four parts:

(a) preamble or declaration sheet,
(b) insuring agreement,
(c) statutory and policy conditions,
(d) endorsements or riders.

INSURANCE TERMINOLOGY

Policy	the contract between you and the insurance company that specifies the terms of the agreement.
Premium	the regular payment you make for insurance coverage.
Insured	the person whose risks are covered by the insurance, usually the purchaser.
Insurer	the insurance company.
Peril	a risk of some damage or injury.
Endorsement or rider	a statement appended to an insurance policy that may specify additional coverage and a change in ownership or in risk.

DECLARATION SHEET   The *preamble or declaration sheet* is a separate page that is filled in for each insurance buyer, giving the names of insurer and insured, the dates the insurance will be in effect, the amounts paid, and the risks to be covered in the agreement. Without this sheet, it is impossible to know what coverage the insured has bought. The page can be easily identified because the spaces in it have been filled in by writing or typing.

The rest of the policy consists of several printed pages that the company routinely uses for all similar risks. For instance, the company may have a standard fire insurance policy that may be adjusted to fit individual requirements by the selections made on the declaration sheet or preamble. If the space beside a risk on the declaration sheet is not filled in, one may assume that the risk is not covered in this particular agreement. When reading a policy, first determine what coverage is on the declaration sheet, and then locate the sections of the policy's printed portion that are relevant.

AGREEMENT   The printed part of the policy will contain an *insuring agreement*, setting out which kinds of property are covered, which perils are insured against, the exclusions or situations not covered by this policy, and the circumstances under which the insured may receive insurance settlements.

CONDITIONS   *Statutory and policy conditions* include statements about the responsibilities of the insurer and the insured, including misrepresentation, termination of the policy, requirements after a loss, and fraud.

ENDORSEMENTS   Insurance policies may be modified by the use of *endorsements or riders*, which are statements appended to the contract. Some examples include a change in the ownership of the property, a change in the risk situation of the property owner, or an additional coverage.

HOW TO READ A POLICY

Examine a policy such as the one in Figure 5.1 (in the Appendix) to find the answers to these questions.

1. *Who* is covered?
2. *What* property is covered?
3. What *perils* are covered?
4. *Where* does the coverage apply?

5. What are the *exclusions?* (These may apply to who is covered, the perils not covered, or the location where coverage applies.)
6. What are the *extensions* of the coverage?
7. What are the *conditions* of coverage? For example:
   (a) What must the insured do to have coverage continue?
   (b) What must the insured do if there is a loss?
   (c) What must the insured do to recover a loss?

CANCELLATION   You, the insured, may cancel a policy at any time, but the insurer may choose to retain a portion of the premium calculated at the *short rate*. This means that the insurer keeps more than the prorated share of the premium. For instance, if you decided to cancel a one-year policy after six months, you may receive a refund that is less than one half of the premium you paid.

INSURANCE SETTLEMENTS

CLAIMS PROCESS   After a loss has occurred, it is your responsibility to provide proof of the loss. Specialists called *adjusters*, who are either on the regular staff of the insurance company or working independently for a number of companies, immediately go to the scene of the misfortune to begin estimating the extent of the damage. They report their results to the *claims department* of the insurance company, which proceeds with negotiating a settlement. It should be noted that agents and brokers have little, if any, part in the claims procedure.

There are two approaches to determining the amount of an insurance settlement: (i) actual cash value (indemnification), or (ii) replacement value. Traditionally, most claims were settled using the principle of cash value or indemnification but in recent years insurers have offered replacement value coverage. We will consider actual cash value first.

ACTUAL CASH VALUE   Property insurance, but not life insurance, is based on the principle of indemnifying the insured for a loss. *Indemnification* is compensation for you, the insured, at such a level that you will be returned to approximately the same financial position you enjoyed before the loss, because it is not intended that you should profit from an insurance settlement. The concept of indemnification sounds simple, but in practice it may not be easy to determine exactly what the previous financial position of the insured was in regard to the lost or damaged property.

Some property insurance policies promise to indemnify you on the basis of the actual cash value of your property at the date of the loss. It is essential to note that it is the cash value when the loss occurred that is significant, not the value of the property when it was bought, or when it was insured.

There are various methods of arriving at the *actual cash value*, but a common one is to determine the *replacement value* of the loss and then deduct any accumulated depreciation. The replacement value of a house is the cost of rebuilding it, not what it might have sold for. The replacement value of a household possession is the cost of buying a similar new one. *Depreciation* is the monetary value that has been used up since the item was new. Different objects wear out at different rates because of characteristics of the object or the way it was used or cared for. Insurance companies have tables of standard rates of depreciation for many household goods. The adjusters may adapt these rates somewhat to allow for especially good care or very hard usage. The well-established rates of depreciation of cars may be found in tables possessed by most automobile dealers. The way to calculate actual cash value is shown in the example, "Actual Cash Value" below.

ACTUAL CASH VALUE

A small fire in Vickie's living room damaged her sofa and some chairs beyond repair. When she bought the furniture five years ago, she paid $800, but to replace it now would cost about $1200. The insurance adjuster explained to her that the actual cash value of her loss would be calculated as follows:

Actual cash value	= replacement cost — depreciation
	= $1200 − (.30 × $1200)
	= $1200 − $360
	= $840

Vickie was surprised to discover that the insurance settlement would be too small to replace her furniture. When she complained to the adjuster that this furniture had been perfectly good before the fire, she was told that she was not making allowance for the five years of use she had already had from it.

The insurance adjuster had allowed 10 percent depreciation the first year and 5 percent each subsequent year. Vickie's policy promised that she would be indemnified for a loss, which does not mean replacing used furniture with new.

The insurer has the option of offering: (i) a cash settlement, (ii) a similar article to replace the damaged one, or (iii) to repair the damaged article. If the repair results in an improvement of the property, the value of the betterment is charged to you. In addition to the factors mentioned, the condition of the property and the standard of maintenance affects the estimated cash value. In the case of a building that has been destroyed or damaged, the insurer usually settles by paying for the repair or rebuilding, but does not take possession of the property.

In cases of partial loss, you might be reimbursed for a total loss but any *salvage value* of the damaged property belongs to the insurance company. For instance, if your heavily damaged car is replaced by the insurer, you would have no claim on the remnants of the smashed car; it would belong to the insurance company as salvage. If you wish to retain the salvage, you have to pay the insurer for it.

REPLACEMENT VALUE INSURANCE   Although it has been traditional to indemnify the insured on the basis of actual cash value, in recent years insurers have offered *replacement-value insurance*, offering to replace used possessions with similar new ones. This practice increases the cost of compensation and consequently the premium charged. Replacement-value insurance does not follow the classical principle of indemnification of losses because the replacement of used furniture with new may leave the insured in a better position than before the loss. Replacement value insurance is now very popular and some companies report that it predominates over actual cash value coverage. Claimants, pleased to receive settlements that enable them to replace lost articles without considering depreciation, are willing to pay the higher premiums.

INSURER'S LIABILITY   The insured is entitled to compensation for personal loss, but this amount can never be greater than the *policy limits* purchased. A fire insurance policy with limits of $80 000 has limited the insurer's liability on this contract to $80 000. For any claim, the insurer will pay the lesser of the policy limits, the actual cash value, or the replacement value of the loss. A person who had a loss valued at $7000 but with a policy limit of $5000 would receive $5000.

Small claims are expensive for an insurance company to handle, and it is customary to offer the insured the opportunity to pay a lower premium and carry a certain amount of the risk himself. If the insured agrees to assume responsibility for the first $100 of damages, this contract is said to have a *deductible clause* of $100. Obviously, the higher the deductible the lower the premium.

SUBROGATION   When an insurer indemnifies you for a loss, the insurer is entitled to attempt to recover damages from any other persons who may have been responsible for the loss—a procedure called *subrogation*. For instance, if a tenant is responsible for fire damage in an apartment, the insurer of the building may indemnify the landlord and then attempt to collect from the tenant who caused the damage.

PROPERTY INSURANCE

In the interests of clarity, this discussion of property insurance will be limited to coverage on personal possessions, houses, and liability, and will look at each type separately. However, in practice, coverage for several risks is often combined in one policy, as for example homeowners' or tenant's policies.

THE RISKS

The many perils that may befall a house or its contents can be categorized as either: (i) accidental, or (ii) the result of criminal actions. Such perils as fire, smoke, water, windstorm, and falling objects are accidental damage; vandalism and stealing are criminal actions. Examination of a policy will reveal some of the complexity in defining perils and in specifying exclusions not covered in the contract. Two groups of definitions have been singled out for discussion: fires and stealing.

Insurers have given considerable attention to types of fires and their causes. They have classified fires as "friendly" when they are where they are supposed to be, as in a fireplace, and "hostile" when they are where they are not supposed to be. Insurance is concerned with the effects of hostile fires.

It is helpful when reading an insurance policy to know that stealing can be classified as theft, burglary, or robbery. *Theft* means the loss of property by stealing without violence against persons or forced entry. *Burglary* involves theft and forcible entry that leaves visible marks on the premises. *Robbery* is theft accompanied by violence or the threat of violence to a person.

COVERAGE

Most insurance companies sell two types of home owner policies: (i) *named-peril* that provides protection for losses from a list of perils named in the contract, or (ii) *all-risks* that covers all risks except for those specifically excluded in the policy. The more comprehensive coverage may be limited to the house, with the contents covered for named perils only.

It is possible to insure certain possessions against all risks by having an endorsement or rider added to the policy. This coverage would include all risks of direct physical loss or damage, limited only by the exclusions listed. It is usually specified that the damage be accidental and not due to the nature of the property itself, for example, rust or age. When the all-risks coverage is bought for such items as cameras, furs, jewellery, and collections, these items are listed as scheduled property.

The *scheduled property rider* or *valued contract endorsement* lists items with their value, and includes identifying information such as descriptions and serial numbers. To confirm the value, the insurer will require a bill of sale for a recently acquired item, or an official appraisal for a previously purchased article. In the event of loss or damage, the insurer's maximum liability is the value placed on the property when it was insured. Such contracts are generally used to insure items whose true value is difficult to determine after a loss, such as jewellery, works of historic value, antiques, stamp and coin collections. Unfortunately, in periods of rapid inflation the maximum liability established when the insurance was bought can become outdated quickly. Unless insurance companies develop some automatic adjustment for inflation, the owner must have new appraisals done periodically.

SCHEDULED PROPERTY RIDER

Sandra insured her diamond ring and gold necklace for $1000 on a valued contract or special items endorsement (Figure 5.1 in the Appendix). Before insuring them, they were appraised by a qualified jeweller who estimated their worth to be $1000; this information was given to the company. Six years later her jewellery was stolen when thieves broke into her home. Although her ring and necklace now had a replacement value of $1350, the insurance settlement was for $1000—the maximum liability assumed by the company on this contract. If she had wanted to be more fully insured, she should have had this jewellery appraised more frequently. The insurer requires an expert appraisal each time the limits are changed.

PERSONAL PROPERTY FLOATER   Policies often contain a personal property clause or *floater*, that covers personal items taken away from home temporarily. The key word is temporarily; possessions taken on a trip, to a summer cottage for a few weeks, or by a student to a college residence would be considered temporarily away. The amount of coverage for these possessions will vary with the policy. For instance, if the floater clause stated that you are covered for 10 percent of the total coverage you have on all your possessions, and if your household contents were insured for $30 000, you would have floater coverage of $3000. Read the policy to find out what your floater coverage is.

CO-INSURANCE

Actuaries base the premium structure on the assumption that property owners will carry sufficient insurance to cover a total loss of the building. In fact, very few buildings burn completely and most claims are for damage costing a few thousand dollars. Knowing this, the insured may decide to buy a policy with very low limits. If this were to happen, insurance funds would be insufficient to provide compensation for all claims. To prevent such under-insurance, many companies include a co-insurance clause in the policy, which applies to the building, but not to the contents.

The *co-insurance clause* states that the insured must carry policy limits to a level considered adequate by the company. An adequate level may be, for example, 80 percent or 100 percent of the replacement value of the building. If you fail to carry sufficient insurance, any claims made for damage to the building will be prorated. For instance, if your policy limits are one-half what is considered to be adequate, your claim for a small fire will be reduced by one-half. The example, "Under Insured," illustrates how a claim is prorated if the insured does not carry sufficient insurance. The purpose of the co-insurance clause is to encourage you to carry adequate limits. If you do not, you share the risk with the company—hence the term co-insurance.

UNDER INSURED

The Hills bought a policy on their house with limits of $40 000. A few years later they had a bad fire, that resulted in damage valued at $20 000. At that time, their house was estimated to have a replacement value of $70 000. Their policy had a co-insurance clause which required that they have coverage for 80 percent of the replacement value.

Policy limits	= $40 000
Replacement value	= $70 000
Adequate coverage	= 80% of replacement value
	= .80 × $70 000
	= $56 000
Claim	= $20 000

The insurance settlement was calculated as follows:

$$\frac{\text{policy limits they had}}{\text{policy limits they should have had}} \times \text{claim} = \text{settlement}$$

$$\frac{\$40\,000}{\$56\,000} \times \$20\,000 = \$14\,285$$

Although their loss was estimated at $20 000, they received a settlement of $14 285 because they were under insured.

PROPERTY INSURANCE AND MORTGAGES

Property insurance may include a *mortgage clause* which recognizes that there is a mortgage on the property and specifies the rights and obligations of both lender and insurer. The effect of this clause is to express an agreement between the mortgage lender and the insurer that is independent of the agreement between the insurer and the insured, even though this clause is attached to the insured's policy.

The lender has the right to share in any insurance settlement on the property as long as the insured still has an outstanding balance owing. Once the mortgage is completely repaid, the mortgage lender has no claim. The mortgage clause entitles the lender to receive a loss payment regardless of any act or neglect of the home owner or borrower. For example, the insured may breach a condition of the contract with the insurance company, making the claim for damages void; nevertheless, the lender would still be entitled to compensation. An insured who committed arson could not collect insurance, but the lender could.

The mortgage lender has the obligation of informing the insurer of any factors that may change the risk situation. If the risk should increase, and the insured does not pay the additional amount required, the lender is responsible for this amount. The lender's rights in an insurance settlement would take into account the amount still owing on the property at that time. Instead of adding a mortgage clause to the policy, some lending institutions may use forms of their own; or an insurer may issue a separate policy showing the lender as the insured.

THE INVENTORY

When you experience a loss, you are obligated to produce proof of what was lost. In some instances there may be enough evidence remaining for the adjusters to see what sort of possessions you had; at other times little may be left. You should be prepared by keeping an up-to-date inventory of possessions in a secure place away from your house, such as in a safety deposit box. It will not be of much help if the inventory burns up.

If you feel that a written inventory is too tedious, you could use a camera, video camera, tape recorder, or some combination. With video camera or tape recorder, go through the house describing all you see, including the contents of cupboards. These records may be supplemented with sales receipts, lists of serial numbers, and any other relevant information.

Preparing a detailed inventory and attaching current values to each item will assist you in determining how much insurance coverage you require. Consider whether you need any special coverage of such items as jewellery, special collections, or antiques. Doing this inventory is not a one-time event; your list of possessions will change, and some may increase in value.

INFLATION

If your insurance company does not automatically adjust your policy limits in relation to changes in general price levels, you will have to review your coverage regularly. In periods of inflation, replacement costs tend to increase and you could find that your policy limits are too low to cover a total loss. Many homeowners' policies now contain an automatic inflation clause, particularly for the coverage of the building.

PERSONAL LIABILITY INSURANCE

THE RISKS

Your financial security may be jeopardized if you should be found responsible for damage to someone else's property or for an injury to another person. However, it is not quite as bad as it may seem because the person claiming damages must prove that the loss or damage was caused by your negligence. *Negligence* is defined as either failing to do what a reasonable and prudent person would do in such a situation, or doing what a prudent person would not do. Everyone lives under a legal requirement not to cause harm to others or their property and to take reasonable steps to preserve the safety of others. In addition to being held liable for your own negligent acts, you are also responsible for those of an employee that relate to the work he is doing for you. You are responsible for losses caused by your animals and, to some extent, for your children's carelessness. The examples on the next page illustrate some types of claims that have been made.

PERSONAL LIABILITY INSURANCE CLAIMS

1. Ten-year-old Rosa, whose broken leg was in a cast, was sitting in an ice cream parlour with her friends when an elderly woman walking down the aisle tripped and fell over Rosa's cast. The woman broke her leg and claimed $8000 for damages. Rosa's father's insurance company investigated the circumstances, found that the woman's companion, who had preceded her down the aisle, had manoeuvred safely around the cast, and decided that there was not a strong case for finding Rosa negligent. Rather than go through the expense of a suit, the company paid the woman $1800 *ex gratia*, without admitting any liability. The settlement was made under Rosa's father's personal liability insurance.

2. Alan's son broke a neighbour's window while playing baseball. Alan's insurance company paid the neighbour for the window.

3. A child visiting the Duval family fell while playing on their back deck and required root canal work on a tooth. The Duval's insurer paid the dentist.

4. At a campground, a girl broke her neck by diving into water only 1.2 metres deep. She eventually recovered with a 20 percent disability. Because she had various Red Cross swimming certificates, it was established that she was 25 percent at fault for not investigating the water depth, and the campground owner was held to be 75 percent at fault. His insurer paid the girl $50 000.

5. Mr. Nielsen, an independent handyman, was called to a commercial building to check the plumbing. He proceeded to thaw frozen pipes with a blow torch and succeeded in igniting the whole building, resulting in a total claim in excess of $500 000. His liability coverage was $100 000, leaving him responsible for the difference.

COVERAGE

You may buy *liability insurance*, sometimes called public liability, to cover the risk of being found responsible for damage caused by the negligence of yourself, your family members, employees, animals, and so on. This is *third party insurance* because it involves you the insured, the insurer, and some third party who is holding you responsible for a loss. The need to establish who was at fault makes liability insurance claims more involved with legal matters than other kinds of insurance.

Under liability insurance coverage, the insurer agrees not only to pay for damages attributed to you, but also to defend you in court, pay for court costs and interest charged to you, and reimburse you for some immediate costs. Because the insurance company will defend you in a liability suit, it is important that you not admit liability or offer to make payments, because such actions or statements could prejudice your defense. In some situations there must be a court case to prove negligence, in others an out-of-court settlement may be reached. Before the insurance company will settle a liability claim, it must be satisfied that the insured was legally liable in this instance and the policy covers this particular liability.

Liability insurance may be bought separately or, more commonly, as a part of another policy, such as home or auto insurance. A home owner or tenant policy that includes comprehensive personal liability may cover damage to property or injury to people as a result of use or maintenance of property, personal acts of the insured, ownership of animals, ownership of boats, and children's carelessness. It may cover the insured's legal liability for fire, explosion, and smoke in rented premises. In addition, some policies may include a small amount of coverage for damage caused by the insured without reference to negligence. Subject to a list of exclusions, the coverage applies wherever the insured is engaged in normal activities as a private individual; business pursuits are commonly excluded in personal liability policies. Personal liability insurance is a quite inexpensive way to protect yourself against risks that may have a low probability of occurring but that can be extraordinarily costly if they do happen.

AUTOMOBILE INSURANCE

This section is intended to help you gain an understanding of basic principles and concepts associated with auto insurance, not to supply the details of coverage available in each province. The social and financial risks associated with automobiles, considered too significant to be left to personal discretion, are protected to some degree by minimum insurance requirements legislated by each province or territory. Three major categories of risks will be identified and the relevant types of insurance protection explained. With this basic knowledge you will be prepared to investigate the specific arrangements for auto insurance in your province. There is too much variation to go into all the features here.

Two distinguishing points among provincial arrangements for automobile insurance are: (i) who supplies the insurance coverage—whether a public body, private companies, or a public-private combination, and (ii) how fault is handled. It will be more meaningful to leave the discussion of fault until after identifying the risks associated with car ownership and explaining the basic types of insurance protection.

INSURANCE PROVIDERS

In British Columbia, Manitoba and Saskatchewan, basic automobile insurance coverage is government-provided, with extra insurance available from private insurers. Quebec splits auto insurance coverage between government and private companies, and the other provinces and territories leave insurance provision to private companies. Wherever auto insurance is publicly-provided, there is one price and one place to get coverage; where insurance is offered by private enterprise, there may be many competing suppliers.

THE RISKS

As noted, car ownership poses such a significant threat, not only to the financial security of individuals but also to society, that a minimum amount of public liability and accident benefits coverage is mandatory. Three major categories of financial risks that a car owner assumes and the basic types of protection, are as follows:

Risk	*Insurance coverage*
1. Liability to others for injury, death, or property damage	Public liability (third party)
2. Injury or death of self or passengers	Accident benefits
3. Damage to your vehicle	Physical damage (e.g., collision, comprehensive)

LIABILITY TO OTHERS

If you drive or own a car, you face the risk that, because of your negligence, you will be held financially responsible for injuries to others or damage to their property. When assessing your liability risk, reflect on the high probability of being involved in a car accident at some time, simply because of the large number of vehicles on our roads. In spite of the best intentions, a little mistake can cause a serious accident. The consequences of severely injuring one or more persons could be a financial disaster for you; the courts have been awarding increasingly large settlements, sometimes as high as several million dollars. The rising costs of car repair, medical care, and income replacement for killed or injured persons have increased settlements to the point where some insurers are now advising their customers to have at least $1 000 000 in liability coverage. Although all provinces and territories require that anyone who licenses an automobile have a minimum amount of public liability insurance, usually $200 000, it is not enough.

POLICY LIMITS   As with most types of insurance, the liability policy limits determine the maximum that the insurer will pay on your behalf. It may not always be understood that a court can award a settlement to an accident victim that exceeds your policy limits. In such a case, you would be responsible for paying the difference, unless you had specific coverage for such situations.

NEGLIGENCE   Public liability insurance does not apply to damage to your own car or injury to yourself, but is limited to situations where others have suffered loss due to your negligence. Because liability claims depend on proving negligence, it is important to give some thought to the legal concept of negligence. Sometimes distinctions are made between ordinary negligence and gross negligence. Ordinary negligence is the failure to do what a reasonable person would do, or doing what a reasonable person would not do. Gross negligence, on the other hand, is considered to be reckless, wanton, and wilful misconduct in which the person has failed by a wide margin to exercise due care, thereby reflecting an indifference to the probable consequences.

The basic rule in our society is that each of us has the duty to take proper care no matter what we are doing, and must take responsibility for any injury caused by carelessness. Motorists can be held negligent for not keeping a proper look-out or for failing to have their vehicles under complete control at all times. Icy roads or storms are not an excuse; drivers are supposed to adjust their driving to suit conditions. In some jurisdictions, a car owner is responsible for the consequences of any negligence on the part of persons who drive his or her car with consent. If you lend your car to a friend who has an accident with it, liability or collision claims may be handled by your insurance. Find out the terms of your policy. If you are liable, the claim will be submitted to your insurer, who in turn may raise your future premiums if your friend was at fault.

HIGHWAY TRAFFIC ACT   If you are found guilty of an offence under this act it may be evidence for the insurance claims department that you were negligent. However, it is important to note that being found not guilty of a *Highway Traffic Act* charge—such as failure to yield the right of way—does not necessarily absolve you of negligence according to the insurance company.

PROVING FAULT   A serious problem is the difficulty of proving negligence in many auto accidents where events happen very fast and there may be no witnesses. If there is uncertainty about who was at fault, it can be decided in court, or an out-of-court agreement may be reached between the two insurers involved whereby the responsibility for the accident may be divided between the drivers involved. For instance, a 60/40 split would mean that 60 percent of all the damages resulting from the accident would be assessed to one driver and 40 percent to the other, both of whom would in turn refer the claims to their respective insurance companies as third party liability claims. High legal costs, prolonged court processes, and the difficulty of determining fault have created so many problems that some measures have been devised to expedite certain types of claims by not requiring that fault be established. In a later section we will examine so-called "no-fault" auto insurance, but first will consider the two other categories of risks faced by motorists.

QUESTIONS TO ASK ABOUT YOUR LIABILITY COVERAGE

1. *Who is covered by this part of the policy and in which situations?*
   There should be protection for you, the car owner, and persons using the vehicle with your consent, if the driver's negligence caused injury, death, or property damage to others. Find out if you are covered when driving cars that you do not own or use regularly, such as temporary substitute cars or uninsured cars.

   Whose insurance will cover you if you were found negligent in an accident while driving a friend's car?

   Does your liability coverage protect you if family or passengers sue you for negligence?

2. *How much liability coverage do you need?*
   Inquire about the size of recent liability settlements to get an idea of the amount of coverage you need.

3. *What is not covered by your liability insurance?*
   It does not cover injury or death of yourself, damage to your own car, or to property carried in or on it.

4. *What other things does your insurer agree to do?*
   In addition to paying claims resulting from negligence, the insurer may cover the costs of investigating the accident, negotiating a settlement, settling a claim, and defending you in court. Also, the insurer may reimburse you for out-of-pocket costs for immediate expenses associated with the accident, and pay court costs and

interest on the insured portion of settlements charged to you. These costs are in addition to the liability limit of your policy.

PERSONAL INJURY OR DEATH

The second major risk is that you or your passengers will be injured. Medical insurance or accident benefits coverage is designed to provide benefits in case of bodily injury to yourself, the occupants of your vehicle, or to anyone struck by your car. You will note that the term *accident benefits* refers to insurance coverage for personal injury or death. Payment of claims for accident benefits is without reference to fault, and your claims are made to your own insurance company. All provinces, except Newfoundland, require compulsory accident benefits coverage as part of auto insurance. There is some variation by province, but essentially, accident benefits cover, to defined limits, such things as medical payments, disability income, death payments, and funeral expenses. Find out what the accident benefits are where you live.

DAMAGE TO YOUR VEHICLE

The least serious risk is that your car may be stolen or damaged and for this reason insurance coverage is generally not mandatory (with the exception of Saskatchewan and Manitoba). Physical damage coverage does not have a dollar limit, but is based on the actual cash value of your car at the time of the loss. Because of the rapid rate at which cars depreciate, you should review your physical damage insurance from time to time; you may decide to drop this coverage when the premium is too high in relation to the size of the risk being covered. For instance, if your old car has an actual cash value of a few hundred dollars, that would be the maximum settlement in the event of a total loss of your car. How much is it worth to you in annual premiums to protect this small amount of capital in your car?

Coverage for physical damage to your car is often subject to some deductible amount. The deductible is the amount of each claim that you will pay; for instance, collision coverage with $250 deductible means that you are responsible for paying the first $250 in damages. By sharing the risk with the company, you lower your insurance costs.

Most insurance companies will offer you a choice of physical damage coverages, such as: (i) all perils, (ii) specified perils, (iii) collision, and (iv) comprehensive. *All perils* is the broadest, covering everything included in the other three categories and possibly more. Examine your policy to find out what is excluded, because everything else will be covered. By contrast, *specified perils* includes only named risks. The two other coverages, collision and comprehensive, are widely used.

COLLISION Collision covers a collision between your car and another object. Usually a collision involves your car striking or being struck by another car, but it also includes the one-vehicle accident in which the car strikes a tree, guard rail, another object, or the surface of the ground.

If your car is in a collision that was caused by the negligence of another, your insurer will pay your damage claim if it is greater than your deductible and then, by the right of subrogation, will endeavour to collect from the person responsible for the accident. Your insurer has agreed to indemnify you under your collision coverage whether or not it was your fault. If the insurer is successful in collecting from the third party, you will be reimbursed for the deductible amount.

COMPREHENSIVE This covers perils, other than collision, that may happen to your car. The distinction between collision and comprehensive coverage sometimes seems confusing. If a loss is specifically excluded under collision, it may be covered under comprehensive. Some of the perils included in comprehensive coverage are: theft, vandalism, fire, lightning, windstorm, hail, and damage caused by falling or flying objects. This section is usually subject to a deductible amount, but the deductible may not apply in some situations, such as when the entire auto is stolen.

MANDATORY PROVINCIAL COVERAGE

A summary of how auto insurance is provided and what coverage is mandated in various provinces and territories is presented in Table 5.1.

FACTORS AFFECTING INSURANCE RATES

Usually we pay more to insure our cars than our much more valuable houses because cars pose a greater risk to financial security. The increasing number of accidents and the rising cost of settlements have caused car insurance premiums to escalate. Your auto insurance premium will reflect not only the coverage you requested, but also a number of other factors that may be grouped according to: (i) personal characteristics, (ii) type of car, (iii) use you make of the car, and (iv) district where you live.

PERSONAL CHARACTERISTICS Traditionally, statistics linking accident frequency by personal characteristics, such as age, gender, and marital status have been used in determining rates for individuals. More recently, a number of provinces have eliminated these three criteria. Quebec, for instance, has a set premium for a given class of vehicle, regardless of the risk presented by the individual. Young people who have had driver training are often considered better risks than those without such instruction. A driver who for several years

Table 5.1 AUTOMOBILE INSURANCE PROVIDERS AND MANDATED
COVERAGE BY PROVINCE, CANADA, 1989

Province/Territory	Public liability minimum	Mandatory accident benefits	Mandatory collision coverage
Public Insurer			
B.C.	$200 000	X	
Sask.	$200 000	X	X
Man.	$200 000	X	X
Public and Private Insurers			
Que.	*	X	
Private Insurers			
Alta.	$200 000	X	
Ont.	$200 000	X	
N.B.	$200 000	X	
N.S.	$200 000	X	
P.E.I.	$200 000	X	
Nfld.	$200 000		
Yukon	$200 000	X	
NWT.	$200 000	X	

*Quebec residents are compensated for injury without regard to fault. Liability limits are $50 000 for property damage claims within Quebec, and personal injury and property damage claims outside the province.

Source: *Facts*, Insurance Bureau of Canada, Toronto, December 1989, pages 28-29. Reproduced with the permission of the Insurance Bureau of Canada.

has not been responsible for accidents is considered a much better risk than one with accidents or traffic violations on their record. After an accident, insurers reassess the risk classification and usually increase the premium if the insured was at fault.

TYPE OF CAR   The type of car you drive will have an obvious effect on the cost of collision and comprehensive coverage because of repair cost. In addition, insurers may increase liability premiums for powerful cars because of their potential for causing substantial damage.

USE OF CAR   The number of kilometres driven in a year and the number of people who normally drive a particular car affect the risk situation. The more a car is driven, the more the driver is exposed to risk. Whether the car is used for business or pleasure also affects the premium.

TERRITORY   More accidents occur in certain regions of the country, usually because of population density or adverse driving conditions due to weather.

INSURANCE FOR HIGH RISK DRIVERS

There are some drivers whose accident records or other characteristics make them very high risks and thus unacceptable to insurers. However, if they are able to get a driver's license, and car insurance is mandatory, there must be some way to insure them to protect society as well as themselves. The insurance industry solved this problem by creating an arrangement whereby insurers pool the high risks, making it possible to cover all licensed drivers and registered owners. The high-risk driver makes application for auto insurance in the same way as anyone else, but the policy is then transferred to the insurance pool which in turn assigns these high-risk cases to companies in proportion to their share of auto insurance in each province. Thus, no single company will receive more than its share of bad risks, and all those who want insurance will obtain it. Naturally, the premiums paid by high-risk drivers are very high. Claims made on these policies are handled in the usual way by the insurer concerned.

RESPONSIBILITY OF THE INSURED

Your agreement with your insurer requires that you give written notice with details of the accident as soon as possible after it occurs. At the scene of an accident you should collect information about the other driver, such as name, address, name of insurance company, and car license number. Names and addresses of passengers and other witnesses may be useful later. You are not to assume any obligation or accept any responsibility for the accident or make any payment to the victims.

After the accident, you must cooperate with the insurer by providing information as needed, forwarding all summonses, notices of suit, and other correspondence that may come to you, and appearing in court if required. Remember that the victim's claims are being made against you, not the insurer. If there is a court case, it will be the case of Smith vs. you, not Smith vs. your insurer. The insurer's responsibility is to help in resolving the problem, not to take it over entirely.

"NO-FAULT" AUTOMOBILE INSURANCE

THE FAULT SYSTEM

Under the law of torts, which has descended to us from the English common law system, each person has a basic duty to take care not to harm other people or damage their property, either intentionally or unintentionally. When applied to car accidents, this system has created problems because of the difficulty, in many instances, of clearly establishing fault. In addition to driving errors, accidents are caused by adverse road or weather conditions, or by cars or pedestrians not involved in the crash. Naturally, the more extensive the injuries and damage, the greater the need to establish fault in order to receive compensation, but such cases often take years to settle because of long delays in getting court hearings. Some people are never compensated because no one can be shown to have been negligent.

NO-FAULT INSURANCE

Claims under accident benefits and physical damage to one's own car have usually been paid without regard to fault. Much of the discussion surrounding "no-fault" insurance has been in relation to third party liability claims. In a pure "no-fault" system, proof of fault would not be required in order to settle claims for injuries and damages resulting from car accidents. Instead, each person would claim damages from their own insurer thus saving litigation costs and considerable time, and also ensuring that all claims are paid. However, this simple idea raises some important questions. Should your insurance premium be raised because you were paid a large settlement for damages that you did not cause? Should a consistently bad driver continue driving without penalty? Should those seriously injured be deprived of the right to sue for damages?

Many modifications of the basic "no-fault" idea have been tried in a number of provinces and states, with the result that we have now reached a state of terminological confusion. The term "no-fault" has been applied to so many versions of the basic idea that it is not meaningful without further specification. A partial "no-fault" scheme may pay claims without regard to fault up to some maximum amount but permit claimants to sue for further damages in court.

QUEBEC NO-FAULT INSURANCE

BODILY INJURY   In 1978, Quebec completely abolished the fault system of compensating accident victims for bodily injury. Instead of public liability insurance and the right to sue, there are two forms of coverage: (i) a basic compulsory public plan that pays unlimited sums for medical and rehabilitation costs and limited amounts for injuries, and (ii) a supplementary elective private plan to provide no-fault insurance for those who want additional coverage. Under these plans, no legal action may be taken. If the insured disagrees with the decision, application may be made to a tribunal to have the claim reviewed.

PHYSICAL DAMAGE   A compulsory, partial no-fault system for property damage that eliminates third party compensation is administered by private insurers. Car owners are required to purchase property damage insurance to cover the driver's damage to vehicles other than automobiles and to compensate the driver who is not at fault for damage to his own vehicle. When the driver is at fault, based on a simplified fault determination process, he or she must compensate the other driver for damages; collision coverage for this situation is available, but not compulsory.

ONTARIO PARTIAL NO-FAULT INSURANCE

BODILY INJURY   In 1990, Ontario introduced limited "no-fault" insurance that permits lawsuits against those who caused accidents only when the personal injuries are severe or fatal. The mandatory accident benefits coverage, payable without proving fault, provides immediate payments for yourself, your passengers, or injured pedestrians. Claims must be paid within 10-30 days. It is estimated that this new plan will handle 90 percent of claims and the option of suing for damages may be chosen by the remaining claimants.

PHYSICAL DAMAGE   If you are not at fault, you will recover damage to your own car and its contents from your own insurance company. However, if you are at fault or partially at fault, you are responsible for paying all or a portion of the costs, unless covered by optional collision coverage.

SUMMARY

This chapter introduced the insurance principle, and explained its application to risks associated with ownership of property. The importance of identifying your risk exposure before selecting insurance coverage has been emphasized. The concepts of indemnity, depreciation, subrogation, and co-insurance were illustrated in relation to property insurance. Car owners face a number of risks, the most significant being their liability to others. It cannot be too strongly emphasized that adequate liability coverage for car owners is most essential. The age and condition of your car has little to do with the risk of causing damage or injury. Physical damage to your car presents a smaller risk; by accepting some of this risk yourself through a larger deductible amount you can reduce the cost of insurance.

Although there has been much discussion of the merits of a truly no-fault auto insurance system, problems have prevented its implementation. However, modified versions are now in use in several provinces. Modest coverage for personal injuries, where proof of fault is not required for compensation, is mandatory in most provinces.

PROBLEMS

1. Refer to the home insurance policy (Figure 5.1 in the Appendix) to answer this question. Decide whether you AGREE or DISAGREE with each of the following statements.

    (a) The "inflation shield plan" promises that the actual cash value, not the policy limits, will be increased automatically to reflect price changes due to inflation.

    (b) The "inflation shield plan" applies to the house, but not to the contents.

    (c) Sandra Jones' camera was stolen from her locked car while she was on holiday. She has a valid claim under her home insurance policy, but this would not be covered by the comprehensive portion of her auto insurance.

    (d) If the car had been left unlocked when the camera was stolen, the insurance company would not have compensated Sandra.

    (e) Sandra Jones bought her camera and lens six years ago for approximately $500, but she did not have them on a valued contract because of the need for frequent re-evaluations. She might have received a better settlement if she had insured them under a valued contract rider because of the all-risks coverage.

    (f) Sandra's diamond ring is insured against accidental loss, but if prices of diamonds rise, she could be under-insured within a few years.

    (g) The Jones' household insurance policy does not cover their possessions against theft while they are away on holiday.

    (h) The Jones' home insurance policy does not cover them for personal liability.

    (i) If the Jones lost all of their personal possessions in a fire, the maximum settlement would be the actual cash value of their loss, or their policy limits, whichever was less.

2. The Sawchuks came home to find the fire department extinguishing a fire in their living room. It seems that the fire had started from a cigarette carelessly left near some papers. The carpet, walls, and ceiling of the living room of their rented apartment were damaged, as well as some of their furniture. The landlord is claiming damages to his building, the Sawchuks are claiming damages to their possessions, and the landlord's insurer is making claims

against the Sawchuks. The Sawchuks' contents policy was for actual cash value coverage, with $50 000 personal liability.

(a) Who pays for what in this case?

(b) Is there a possibility that the principle of subrogation might be applied in the Sawchuks' situation? If so, who would do what?

(c) Would the Sawchuks receive a settlement large enough to replace the damaged furniture? How would allowances for inflation in furniture prices and depreciation be taken into account?

3. The Arbics have just bought their first home for a price of $170 000. The house alone is estimated to have a replacement cost of $120 000.

(a) Do they need $170 000 insurance coverage on the house? Explain.

(b) Assume that the Arbics decided to save money for a year or two by buying home insurance with policy limits of $50 000, but that during this time they had a fire. The claims manager from the insurance company said that the Arbics are under insured and that the amount they will recover will be determined by the co-insurance clause that requires 80 percent of replacement value. Calculate the amount of the settlement they will receive for damages valued at $9000.

4.
(a) What are the pros and cons of buying a replacement-value insurance policy on your household effects?

(b) How does replacement-value insurance alter the basic principle of indemnification?

5. Obtain an automobile insurance policy and examine it to find answers to the following questions.

(a) If you or your passengers should be injured and unable to work, would there be any income replacement payments? How much? For how long?

(b) If one of your passengers was killed, would there be any compensation for funeral costs?

(c) If your injuries included some that were not covered by the provincial health insurance, would the accident benefits portion of your car insurance policy provide some help? Is there any limit on the amount?

(d) Do you have collision coverage? What is the deductible?

(e) Is there a deductible amount on the comprehensive coverage?

(f) Are there any exclusions to the coverage for damage to the insured's automobile?

6. When Dave Hill's father was buying a new car, he found that his old one was valued at $1900 as a trade-in. He offered it to 19-year-old Dave on condition that Dave handle all the operating costs and insure it. Dave was delighted— he would have his own car at last. The insurance agent was happy to help him

arrange suitable coverage for the car, but Dave was dismayed to find that the premium would be higher than his father had been paying. To economize, he thought that he could cut down on some parts of the insurance. He told the agent that he would take collision coverage but drop the third party liability because the car was getting old; he certainly wanted coverage for theft and fire.

Consider each of the following statements in relation to Hill's case and decide whether you AGREE or DISAGREE.

(a) If Dave doesn't buy public liability coverage, he will not be able to register his car.

(b) If Dave buys an automobile insurance policy, he is required to have at least $100 000 public liability.

(c) In Dave's case, it is probably a good idea for him to skip the public liability coverage because it wouldn't be a great disaster if the old car was wrecked.

(d) If Dave takes out a policy with $250 deductible collision coverage and then runs into a bridge, completely demolishing his car, he would have to pay the first $250 of damages, but his insurance company would pay him $1650 to buy another car.

(e) Dave is wise in insisting on coverage for fire and theft even if he has to do without some other coverage.

(f) Because of the province's mandatory "no-fault" accidents benefits insurance coverage, Dave would not be held accountable if he injured another person in an auto accident.

7. Analyze the following complaints from car owners regarding insurance claims and note how you would explain the situation to each.

(a) Sam writes, "under conditions of icy roads and high winds, our car was blown off the road. When I presented a claim for damage to my car, I was told that my policy did not include collision coverage. On reading the policy I find that we are covered for windstorm damage. The company still insists that they have no responsibility for paying my car repairs."

(b) The summer before last Bob was in a head-on collision with a car that suddenly appeared on his side of the road. Because he had no collision coverage, he was advised to settle on a 50/50 basis since it would cost too much to prove he was in the right. His lawyer will not take the case because she says it will cost more to fight the case than the car is worth. Bob wonders what to do.

(c) Sandra had considered her car insurance quite adequate, as she has collision, comprehensive, and public liability coverage. An unknown driver damaged her car when it was parked legally on the street. She assumed such damage would be covered under the comprehensive clause (with only $50 deductible), since collision must involve her car colliding with another vehicle or some object. The insurer says that since her car was hit by a car, rather than a stone, the accident is classified as a collision. To her, this seems to be an impossibility because she was not even in the car, nor was the car moving. She thinks collision coverage should pay for damage due to her own carelessness, not someone else's. She says comprehensive covers vandalism. The insurer company wants her to pay for the damage because it amounted to less than her deductible amount under collision coverage. Is this right?

8. What is the extent of "no-fault" auto insurance coverage where you live?

9. The following item was from *The Daily Chronicle*.

ONE MAN DEAD, ANOTHER PARALYZED IN TWO-CAR CRASH

Foggy wet weather and poor driving conditions on Saturday evening, March 16, accounted for the head-on collision involving cars driven by Richard Chaney and Russell Talcott. Police reports indicate that Chaney's car went out of control on the northbound lane and crossed the slippery pavement into the southbound lane, where it collided with the vehicle driven by Talcott. On arrival at the General Hospital, Russell Talcott was pronounced dead. He is survived by his wife Mary and their young son Jason. At present Richard Chaney is reported to be in critical condition as a result of a serious spinal injury. No charges were laid in this case.

Assume the following information about the insurance and other security plans of these men:

	Chaney	Talcott
Health insurance	covered	covered
Canada Pension	contributor	contributor
Group life insurance	$70 000	$35 000
Personal life insurance	$75 000	$150 000
Disability insurance	none	pays 1/2 salary

Auto insurance:

Collision insurance	none	$250 deductible
Comprehensive	none	$50 deductible
Accident benefits	yes	yes
Public liability	$200 000	$300 000

(a) Identify by check marks the areas of probable financial need of each family as a result of this accident.

	Chaney	Talcott
Personal injury		
Funeral expenses		
Property damage		
Liability to others		
Loss of income		
Other		

(b) Using the chart below, note the resources these families could call on and what each would cover.

	Chaney	Talcott
Health insurance		
Canada/Quebec Pension		
Group insurance		
Personal life insurance		
Disability insurance		
AUTO INSURANCE: Collision		
Comprehensive		
Public liability		

Note: *Assume that the accident happened in your province when answering the following questions.*

(c) Will Chaney's insurer immediately authorize repairs to his car, and look after the bill? Would you expect Talcott's company to do this? Explain.

(d) Both of these drivers had third-party liability. Explain how claims against this portion of their coverage would proceed. Does the case necessarily have to go to court? What would the claims be for?

(e) If the case did go to court and Chaney was declared to be more than 50 percent responsible for the accident, will Chaney receive any compensation for his disability from Talcott's insurer?

(f) From information provided, which of the two families seems to be in the worse financial position as a result of this accident?

(g) Does the fact that the police did not press charges under the *Highway Traffic Act* mean that the insurer will not make any settlement under the liability coverage?

REFERENCES

Books

FLEMING, JAMES. *Merchants of Fear, An Investigation of Canada's Insurance Industry*. Markham, Ontario: Penguin Books Canada, 1986, 409 pp. An investigative report on the life and general insurance industries.

INSURANCE BUREAU OF CANADA. *Facts*. Toronto: Insurance Bureau of Canada, annual, 58 pp. Annual summary of industry statistics.

MCQUEEN, ROD. *Risky Business, Inside Canada's $86 Billion Insurance Industry*. Toronto: Macmillan, 1985. An investigation into the operation of the insurance industry.

ONTARIO TASK FORCE ON INSURANCE. *Final Report of the Ontario Task Force on Insurance*. Toronto: Ministry of Financial Institutions, 1986, 384 pp. Summarizes findings about property and casualty insurance, particularly in Ontario, and makes recommendations. A summary of the Quebec automobile insurance system is included in an appendix.

QUEBEC CONSUMERS' ASSOCIATION. *The Canadian Insurance Guide*. Montreal: Quebec Consumers' Association, 1988, 126 pp. Explains how to determine home and automobile insurance needs and how to select an insurer; gives most attention to evaluating the solvency of insurers.

TURNER, MARY, DANIEL LEROSSIGNOL, CLAUDE RINFRET, and RICHARD DAW. *Canadian Guide to Personal Financial Management*. Fourth Edition. Scarborough, Ontario: Prentice-Hall Canada, 1989, 231 pp. Accountants provide guidance on a broad range of topics, including planning finances, estimating insurance needs, managing risk, and determining investment needs. Instructions and the necessary forms for making plans are provided.

Article

"Insuring Your Future," *The Financial Post Moneywise*, December 1989, 64-86. Discusses protection for a variety of risks that can be handled by life or general insurance.

6 LIFE INSURANCE

OBJECTIVES

1. To explain the function of life insurance in enhancing financial security.

2. To relate the need for life insurance to changing life cycle requirements.

3. To analyze arguments for and against the use of life insurance as a savings vehicle.

4. To explain the principles of:
   (a) pooling risk,
   (b) pure cost of life insurance,
   (c) level premium.

5. To demonstrate how the basic types of life insurance policies differ with respect to:
   (a) policy reserves,
   (b) duration of insurance protection,
   (c) insurer's liability.

6. To explain how the following policy variations serve specific needs:
   (a) decreasing term,
   (b) limited pay life,
   (c) family policy,
   (d) family income policy,
   (e) universal insurance.

7. To identify the insured's options for using:
   (a) the cash surrender value of a policy,
   (b) dividends.

8. To assess the merits of these options:
   (a) renewability,
   (b) convertibility,
   (c) waiver of premium,
   (d) guaranteed insurability,
   (e) accidental death benefit.

9. To ascertain from an insurance policy the main features of the agreement.

10. To formulate generalizations about:
    (a) trends in per capita insurance coverage,
    (b) insurance coverage per capita and per household,
    (c) reasons for termination of policies,
    (d) share of market held by group insurance,
    (e) the influence of gender, age, and income on the decision to buy individual policies.

11. To explain these terms: face value, premium, beneficiary, policyholder, insurable interest, paid-up policy, dividend, participating policy, group insurance, endorsement or rider, settlement option, loading charges.

INTRODUCTION

The intent of this chapter is to help you to take control of another aspect of your financial affairs. Most Canadians think they ought to have some life insurance, but are bewildered by the process of making a choice. In addition to a natural reluctance to think about their mortality, many people are dubious about insurance agents and unable to evaluate the sales presentation. Their perplexity stems from not understanding life insurance principles and concepts and is compounded by the terminological confusion engendered by the industry. Since there is, unfortunately, no established standard nomenclature for life insurance policies, companies embellish their offerings with a wide variety of names. Much of the confusion felt by buyers can be traced to the naming of policies, varied financing methods, and the multiplicity of renewal provisions. You may be encouraged to learn that there are only a few fundamental types of life insurance, regardless of what they may be called. Therefore, an understanding of basic principles and terms will make it possible for you to assess your need for insurance and make rational choices.

The Economic Risk of Dying Too Soon

If you died tomorrow, would your death create economic hardship for anyone? If the answer is yes, you will want to consider insurance on your life as one way of improving financial security for your dependents. If, as far as you can foresee, the answer is no, you probably do not need life insurance. The primary purpose of life insurance is to provide protection for the economic consequences of the premature death of a person who is providing financial support to others. Young families, who may not have enough net worth to support dependents if a breadwinner should die, may need life insurance as supplementary funds. Another use of insurance, consequential in some instances, is to provide liquidity for an estate when ready cash may be needed by survivors but most of the assets are tied up in property or invested in securities which take time to sell. This chapter does not address other possible functions of life insurance but concentrates on its use to protect a family's income stream.

FINANCIAL RESPONSIBILITIES OF PARENTS

Raising children creates a financial risk that peaks on the day the last one is born; at that time the family has its maximum number of children with the longest period of dependence ahead. As the children grow and the time left to support them decreases, economic risks for the family lessen and, consequently, the size of the estate required to support dependent children becomes less each year. This changing risk is represented in Figure 6.1 by a hypothetical

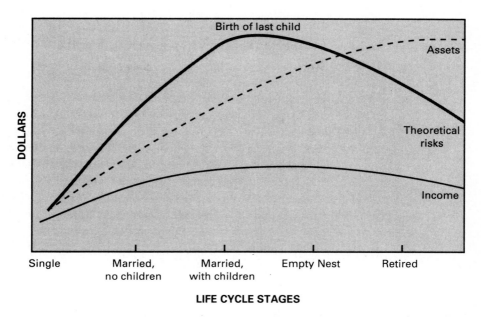

Figure 6.1 RESOURCES AND ECONOMIC RISKS OF PARENTHOOD BY LIFE CYCLE STAGE

curve; for comparison, the average profiles of family income and wealth over the life cycle are superimposed.

For many families, the financial risks associated with dependent children do not correspond to economic resources; financial risks peak before either income or assets reach their highest levels. The average family can expect income to increase until at least middle age, and assets to grow until retirement or after, with the period of greatest wealth occurring after the children have left home. This discrepancy, which poses a significant threat to the financial security of young families, may be minimized by the purchase of life insurance.

Basic Concepts and Principles

Terminology
When you buy life insurance, the company provides an agreement or contract, called a *policy*, that states the risks the company has agreed to assume. This policy specifies in detail all aspects of the agreement, including the maximum liability the company will assume, known as the face amount or *face value*. A

WHEN INSURANCE IS NEEDED

Neither Sue nor Pete had any life insurance when they married, but after baby Daphne's arrival they became aware of their responsibility to support her for at least 18 years. Since both were employed, they decided each should have some life insurance coverage, and they bought two policies. The birth of Adam two years later increased their financial commitments. Now that they were responsible for supporting Daphne for 16 years and Adam for 18, or the equivalent of 34 child-years, an increase in their insurance coverage was needed.

Will Sue and Pete need to carry the same amount of life insurance throughout their lives? Assuming that they have no more children, the economic risks of parenthood will decline each year, going from the peak of 34 child-years to 32 at the end of the next year, then to 30, and so on to zero when they stop supporting the children. By the time Sue and Pete reach retirement, they should have built up some net worth to support their non-earning years. Thus, their need for life insurance should slowly decline to a point where they may need none or very little.

policy with a face value of $100 000 is an agreement that the insurance company will pay your beneficiaries $100 000 on your death. A *beneficiary* is the person named in the policy to receive the proceeds. The regular payments required to keep the policy in force are called *premiums*. Insurance premiums may be paid monthly, semi-annually, or annually, depending on the arrangement with the company, and generally are paid throughout the period the coverage is in force.

As with any type of insurance, a policy cannot be purchased unless there is an *insurable interest*, or a relationship between the insured and the event being insured against. You do not have an insurable interest in the life of another person unless that person's death would have a financial impact on you. Usually, a person is considered to have an insurable interest in his or her own life and in the life of spouse, child, grandchild, employee, or any person on whom he or she may be wholly or partially dependent. For example, a creditor has an insurable interest in the lives of his debtors.

BASIC PRINCIPLES
Three basic principles of life insurance have to do with:

(a) pooling risk,
(b) pure cost of life insurance,
(c) level premium.

POOLING RISK   Life insurance, like general insurance, is a method of pooling small contributions from many people to compensate the few who experience a loss. Actuaries use mortality tables drawn from death records over many years to predict the number of persons of any given age who can be expected to die within the year. Their predictions, quite accurate for large numbers, cannot forecast which persons will die in a given year—only how many. Once the number of expected deaths is known for a specific population, as well as how much money is to be given to the dependents of each, it is possible to determine the size of fund required to make the payments. The over-simplified example, "Pooling the Risk" illustrates this point.

POOLING THE RISK

Population of men aged 30   200 000
Amount to be paid per deceased $50 000
Mortality rate for males aged 30   2.13/1000

Number of deaths expected in the year in this population:

$$200\ 000 \times \frac{2.13}{1000} = 426$$

Fund for dependents: $426 \times \$50\ 000 = \$21\ 300\ 000$
Cost per man:

$$\frac{21\ 300\ 000}{200\ 000} = \$106.50 \text{ for the year}$$

At the end of the year, the fund would be exhausted and more contributions would be needed.

THE PURE COST OF LIFE INSURANCE   As you can see from Figure 6.2, the one-year mortality rate rises with age and is higher at any given age for males than females. The cost of insuring a life for one year is based on the mortality rate for persons of the same age and gender and is called the *pure cost of life insurance*. Consequently, the pure cost of life insurance follows the mortality curve, becoming more expensive each year as one ages, but is less costly for females.

Mortality rate is the primary determinant of the price you will pay for life insurance. To estimate your mortality risk, an actuary would need to know your age and gender, the state of your health, and whether you engage in any

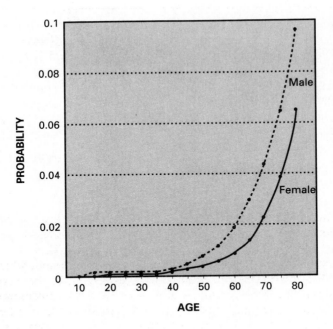

Figure 6.2   PROBABILITY OF DYING BY AGE AND GENDER
Source: *Canada Year Book, 1978-79*. Ottawa: Statistics Canada, 1978 (Catalogue number 11-202), Table 4.45
(page 180). Reproduced with the permission of the Minister of Supply and Services Canada, 1991.

hazardous activities. Your cost will be raised by anything that increases the risk of death. Should the insurance company consider the probability of your dying soon to be too high, it will not insure your life. Fortunately, the proportion of applicants rejected is very small (about two percent) but some people, classified as higher than average risks, have to pay larger premiums.

THE LEVEL PREMIUM   In response to buyer resistance to paying higher premiums each year, insurance companies have devised the level premium. This is the way it works. Rather than charge the pure cost of insurance each year, they establish a constant or *level premium* when a life insurance policy is bought; the policyholder pays this amount regularly for the duration of the policy, whether it be five years or 50. If we superimpose the amount of the level premium on the curve of risk, or the pure cost of insurance, it is obvious that in the early years of the contract the premium is higher than the pure

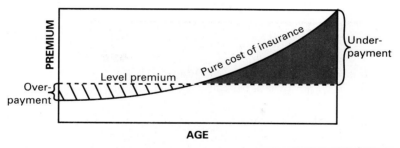

Figure 6.3   OVER-PAYMENT AND UNDER-PAYMENT TO SUSTAIN A LEVEL
PREMIUM

cost, but in later years it is lower (Figure 6.3). The reserve accumulated from
the over-payment at the beginning, together with the interest it generates,
helps to meet the higher cost of coverage in the later period.

A company that writes an insurance policy to cover an individual for his
or her entire life has assumed a liability that is certain. It has promised to pay
a specified sum when the person dies—a situation with 100 percent probability
and an important distinguishing feature between life insurance and other
forms of insurance. Many policies on homes, cars, and personal liability do
not result in claims, and of those that do, few are for the maximum coverage.
When an insurer establishes the premium for a policy to cover a person for
life, it must be set at a level that will accumulate enough reserves in the early
years to pay the certain claim later on.

The level premium and the policy reserves are established to ensure that
there will be enough money to pay the face value to the beneficiary at some
future date. However, if the policyholder decides to cancel the policy, the insurance
company is relieved of the promise to pay this face value and, consequently, the
reserve fund will not be needed and can be refunded to the policyholder.

It is unfortunate that so much of the life insurance literature (and sales
pitch) refers to policy reserves as the savings feature. The policy reserves are
available to the policyholder only if the policy is cancelled or the coverage
reduced; it is impossible to have both full life insurance coverage and access
to the policy reserves at the same time. Life insurance will be easier to understand if you remember that the cash value of a policy is the reserve required
to cover the certain liability that the company has assumed.

FACTORS AFFECTING COST

The cost of a life insurance policy depends not only on your life expectancy
but also on loading charges, the frequency of premium payments, and whether
or not the policy is a participating one.

DAVID CANCELS HIS POLICY

When he was 25, David decided to buy a whole life policy with a face value of $50 000. The premium of $554.50 was payable once a year for the rest of his life.

By the time he was 40 he was divorced, without children or other dependents and saw no need to continue this policy. He informed the insurance company that he wished to cancel his insurance and have a refund of the policy reserves, that had grown to $5950. This cancellation meant that David was no longer insured and the company had no further liability.

LOADING CHARGES   In addition to the pure cost of insuring a life, an amount called the loading charge is included in the premium. The company's *loading charge* includes administrative costs, commissions to sales people, and profit for shareholders. The largest component in loading charges is a commission to life insurance agents, which may be from 25 percent to 85 percent of the first year premium; on renewals the commission may be from two to 15 percent. Individual life insurance policies are sold by sales agents who depend on commissions for income and must search energetically for clients, a very expensive method of selling. Other financial institutions—especially banks and trust companies—are hoping to be allowed to sell insurance at their offices, probably more cheaply. It will be interesting to watch developments.

Offsetting these loading costs to some extent is the interest that may be earned on the pooled funds, which the company can invest until claims are made. Life insurance companies, as managers of the pooled insurance funds, usually collect more than they expect to pay out in claims, not just to establish policy reserves, but also to set up special reserve funds in case their estimates are too low.

FREQUENCY OF PREMIUM PAYMENTS   Your total cost per year will vary slightly depending on the frequency with which the premiums are to be paid. If you pay annually, the total cost will be lower than if you pay semi-annually or monthly. The basis for these differences is the amount of interest the company can obtain by investing the premium funds.

PARTICIPATING AND NON-PARTICIPATING POLICIES   The difference between participating and non-participating policies lies in the way the premiums are calculated. Premiums for *non-participating policies* are estimated as accurately as possible and cannot be increased by the company. If the company under-estimated or over-estimated the cost, the difference is met from the company's funds or a change in premium rates on policies sold in the future. For *participating policies*, the premiums are usually set somewhat higher than for non-participating ones, but the policyholder will receive a refund on any excess. These refunds are called *dividends*, but the term is confusing since they are not a form of income such as stock dividends. Because they are refunds, they are not subject to income tax.

The size of the dividends in any one year will depend on such factors as the efficiency of the company, the return the company obtained on its investments, the amount paid out in claims, and the number of policies cancelled. Dividends may be taken in cash, used to pay the next premium, used to buy more insurance, or left on deposit to earn interest. Although dividends are not considered taxable income, any interest they generate will be taxable.

MAJOR TYPES OF LIFE INSURANCE

DISTINGUISHING FEATURES

A life insurance policy, however it may be labelled to interest prospective buyers, is almost always one of two types—term or whole life—or some combination. Unnecessary confusion has arisen from the inventiveness of companies in naming their many elaborations of the basic kinds. In spite of no uniform terminology, it is usually possible to identify the fundamental policy type if you have a good understanding of the distinguishing features of each. Two important characteristics to consider are: (i) whether the insurance coverage is for *life* or *a specified term*, and (ii) whether the policy *accumulates a cash value* or not. Term insurance is coverage for a specific period, without cash value; whole life provides life-long protection, with cash value; and universal life combines insurance with a cash account.

TERM INSURANCE

Like fire or auto insurance, *term insurance* provides protection against a specified risk for a specific length of time. At the end of that time, or term, the insurance lapses unless renewed. The important characteristic of term insurance is that it is protection for a designated period—not for life. Term life insurance may be purchased for periods of various length: one, five, and ten years are common. It is also possible to buy term to age 65 years, or even to 100. A recent product called "term to 100" is adding to the confusion because it is really a whole life plan, but usually has no cash value until age 65 or later.

Because most buyers of term insurance have a fairly low probability of dying—they are usually under 65 years of age—and because the company does not assume coverage for life, the cost of term insurance is lower than for other types. The premium is made level for the term of the policy. Any policy reserves accumulated are relatively small and will be used up during the term. For these reasons, no cash value will be available to the policyholder. From the company's point of view, the probability of paying claims on term insurance is low; they have not taken on the sure liability they assume in policies with lifelong coverage. To summarize, term insurance is coverage for a specified period, and has no cash value. As with all life insurance, the face value will be paid to the beneficiary if the insured dies while the policy is in force.

Although the premium for term insurance is level for the specified term, at the next renewal the premium must necessarily be raised, since the insured has aged and the probability of dying has increased. Figure 6.4 illustrates the

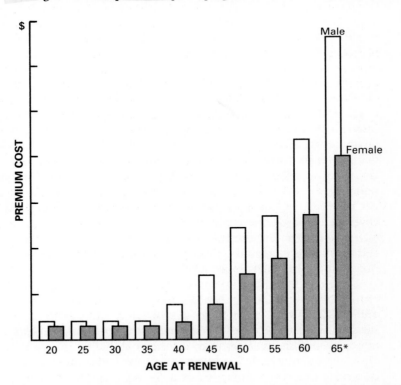

Figure 6.4   PREMIUM LEVELS FOR FIVE-YEAR RENEWABLE TERM INSURANCE BY GENDER AND AGE

changes in premium at each renewal as the pure cost of life insurance rises. By age 65, the pure cost of life insurance has become very high, and few term policies are offered because of the limited market at that age and price.

Term insurance offers the most face value per premium dollar of any type of life insurance because it does not give protection at advanced ages, when the cost of insurance is high. As illustrated in Figure 6.5 (Part A), for every $100 that you can afford to spend each year on life insurance, you will obtain more face value (life insurance coverage) with term insurance than other types of policies. Although this is a useful comparison, two caveats should be made. First, the insurer's liability is not the same with each type of policy, varying from five years to life. Second, the premiums shown in this figure have been made level for different periods, involving varying amounts of reserve funds. Looked at in another way, for a given amount of life insurance the annual cost will be lowest for term coverage (Figure 6.5, Part B).

DECREASING TERM INSURANCE   Thus far we have discussed term insurance with a face value that is constant throughout the term. However, a variant of term insurance that has decreasing face value is useful when the risk being covered is expected to diminish. It is often used as mortgage insurance by persons who wish to leave dependents a debt-free home in the event of their death. At the outset, the face value is equal to the outstanding debt on the house, but decreases at a rate roughly equal to that at which the debt is expected to be reduced. If the insured dies during the term, the face value of the policy should be adequate to pay the outstanding balance on the mortgage. The beneficiary is, of course, under no obligation to use the death benefit for this purpose. It is simply a life insurance policy that will pay a certain sum to the beneficiary when the insured dies. One may argue that special mortgage insurance is unnecessary if overall life insurance coverage is adequate.

Persons supporting a young family may wish to arrange their insurance coverage to match the period of highest financial risk so that coverage is at a maximum when the children are very young. As the children grow, the risk decreases, and so may the need for life insurance. Reducing term insurance may be used for such situations.

The face value of a decreasing term policy falls to zero at the end of the term, with downward adjustments monthly or annually. Premiums, however, are level for the term, probably to discourage policyholders from cancelling the policy when the coverage becomes low. Some companies set a level premium for a period shorter than the entire term; for instance, the premiums on a 20-year decreasing term policy might be paid up in 16 years. The company structures the level premium this way because the incentive to keep the policy in force may be slight when the face value has become quite low. Term and decreasing term insurance are compared in Figure 6.6.

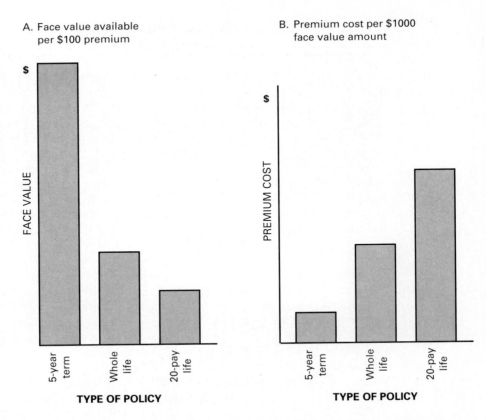

A. Face value available per $100 premium

B. Premium cost per $1000 face value amount

Figure 6.5   EFFECTS ON FACE VALUE AND PREMIUM COST, BY TYPE OF POLICY

GROUP LIFE INSURANCE   Life insurance may be purchased by individuals or groups. In its most common form, group insurance is bought by employers to cover the lives of a large group of employees. Payment for this insurance may be shared by employer and employee, or alternately, one or the other may pay the entire amount. In any event, one policy covers a group of lives. No medical examinations are required as evidence of insurability, but there are some rules intended to avoid a selection of risks that might be adverse to the insurance company. For instance, all employees may be required to join the group plan, or, if there is a choice, employees may be required to join at a specific time, perhaps when they begin employment. In any case, it will be arranged so that most employees cannot avoid being insured. The amount of coverage will also

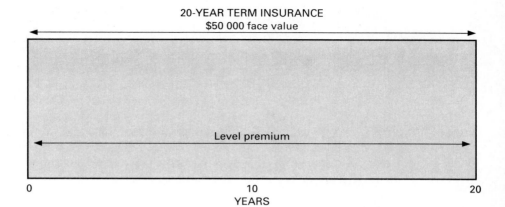

20-YEAR TERM INSURANCE
$50 000 face value

Level premium

0   10   20
YEARS

20-YEAR DECREASING TERM INSURANCE

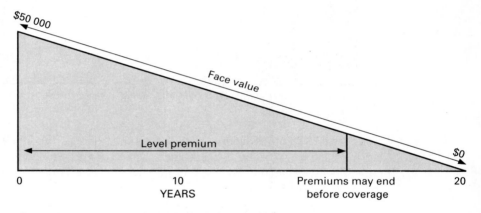

$50 000

Face value

Level premium

$0

0   10   Premiums may end   20
YEARS   before coverage

Figure 6.6   TERM AND DECREASING TERM INSURANCE

depend on a rule: the face value may be some multiple of the employee's annual salary, or all employees may be covered for the same amount.

Group insurance is most often one-year renewable term, but it may also be whole life insurance. Since employees of all ages pay the same premium, group coverage can be a bargain for the older worker. The coverage usually ends whenever an employee terminates employment, but there may be an option of converting, within a month, from the group policy to individual term or whole life. The premiums for group policies are usually lower than for similar insurance bought individually because selling and administration costs are decreased when a single policy covers a large group of lives. The employer collects the premiums and pays the insurer for the group.

CREDIT LIFE INSURANCE   A specialized version of group decreasing term insurance, known as *credit life insurance*, is purchased by lenders to cover the lives of a group of borrowers. If a borrower should die with a debt still outstanding, the insurer will reimburse the creditor for the balance owing. Ultimately, the cost of such insurance is borne by the borrower, who may or may not be given a choice in the matter. This type of insurance is certainly of interest to creditors who are not keen to see debt repayments cease when a borrower dies, and can be useful to anyone who is anxious that there be no outstanding debt to be paid out of his or her estate.

In summary, credit insurance for consumer loans and some mortgages is a type of group coverage arranged by the lender and the benefits must be used to discharge the debt. Alternatively, decreasing term insurance to insure a person who has a mortgage may be arranged privately and need not be used to pay off the mortgage.

WHOLE LIFE INSURANCE

A type of insurance commonly bought by individuals is *whole life* (also called *straight life* or *ordinary life*), that provides insurance protection from the time of purchase until death (Figure 6.7). To maintain this lifelong coverage, premiums must be paid each year as long as the insured lives—unless the premiums are prepaid. Some companies terminate the policies at very advanced ages, such as 95, and pay the policy holder the face value. The premium amount, which is established at the time of purchase, is level for life.

In addition to its long duration, another distinguishing feature of whole life insurance is the accumulation of policy reserves, also known as *cash reserves* or *cash surrender value*. From Figure 6.3, you will recall that in order to have a level premium, the policyholder overpays during the early years and underpays later. These early payments, which exceed the pure cost of insurance, create a reserve that grows over time as more premiums are paid and the reserve funds earn interest.

Any cash reserves created in the first year or two are used for the company's selling and issue expenses, including commissions, and therefore the policy has no cash value at first. A sample whole life policy, reproduced in Figure 6.8, may be found in the Appendix. This policy has a table showing cash values each year the insurance is in force. To read the table, find the column headed by the policyholder's age at time of purchase, which in this case was 25. Assume that you wish to know the cash value five years later. The entries in the table are per $1000 of face value. This policy was for $50 000, therefore the cash value after five years would be $18 \times 50 = \$900$. Each year

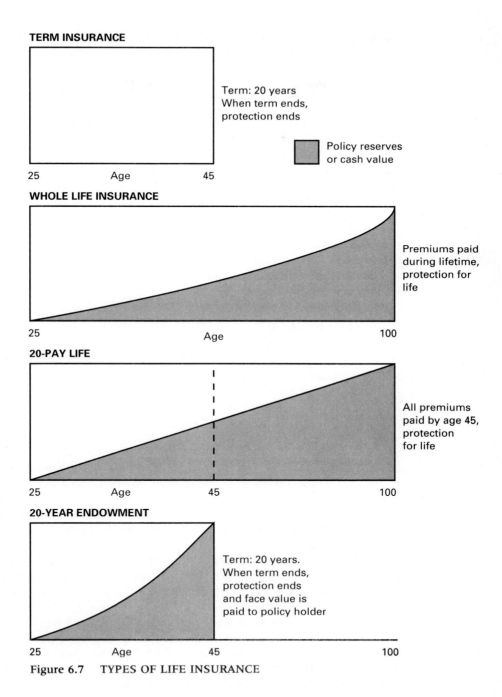

TERM INSURANCE

Term: 20 years
When term ends,
protection ends

Policy reserves
or cash value

25   Age   45

WHOLE LIFE INSURANCE

Premiums paid
during lifetime,
protection for
life

25   Age   100

20-PAY LIFE

All premiums
paid by age 45,
protection
for life

25   Age   45   100

20-YEAR ENDOWMENT

Term: 20 years.
When term ends,
protection ends
and face value is
paid to policy holder

25   Age   45   100

Figure 6.7   TYPES OF LIFE INSURANCE

the reserves continue to grow until around age 100, when the cash value will equal the face value (Figure 6.7). It is impossible to have the use of the cash reserves and also maintain full insurance coverage. The policy states that if the insured person dies, the full face value of the policy will be paid to the beneficiary. Whenever that happens, the policy terminates and so does the cash value. While living, however, the insured can make some use of the cash reserves if he or she is willing to diminish the coverage accordingly. A number of uses for the cash reserves will be outlined.

USES FOR THE CASH RESERVES   The policy reserve, also known as cash value or cash surrender value, has a number of possible uses during the lifetime of the policyholder; five of them will be reviewed here.

(a)   One obvious use of the cash value is to cancel or *surrender the policy* and take the cash value, effectively terminating the insurance coverage.

(b)   It is possible to arrange a *policy loan,* or to borrow from the cash surrender value, at an interest rate that is usually lower than the rate on loans from other sources. There is no pressure to repay a policy loan, but in the meantime the interest continues to accumulate. If the insured should die before the loan is repaid, the unpaid balance and outstanding interest will be deducted from the face value of the policy before the proceeds are paid to the beneficiary.

(c)   The cash surrender value may also be used as *collateral for a loan.* This involves transferring the right to the cash surrender value to the creditor until the loan is repaid. If the insured defaults on the loan, the creditor can cash in the policy and retain whatever is owed. This would effectively terminate the policy. Should the insured die during the term of the loan, the outstanding balance would have to be paid from insurance proceeds or the estate.

(d)   The cash surrender value may be used to pay the premiums if for some reason the policyholder does not do so. This is essentially the same as a policy loan, because the face value will be reduced by the amount used for this purpose. It is called an *automatic premium loan* because the company will use the cash value to pay the premiums rather than let the policy lapse if the policyholder takes no action.

(e)   Instead of cancelling the policy and taking the cash surrender value, another option is to use the cash value to purchase a *paid-up policy* with a smaller face value. This is, in effect, a single premium purchase of life insurance. The amount of the face value will depend on the amount of the cash surrender value at that time. Policies

MIMI TAKES OUT A POLICY LOAN

As she reviewed her finances in preparation for buying a new car, Mimi remembered that she had a whole life insurance policy that she bought 20 years ago. Since her children are now independent and her need for life insurance protection has declined, it occurred to her that a policy loan might be appropriate. On calling her insurance agent, she discovered that the current rate on policy loans was 10.5 percent, with interest calculated annually on the anniversary date of the policy. The maximum cash value available for a loan on this policy was $6850.

Mimi decided to request a policy loan and to let the interest accumulate as a claim against the policy. Five years later when Mimi died, the insurance company paid her beneficiary the face value of the policy less the outstanding debt. The amount was determined as follows:

Face value of policy:	$25 000
Amount of loan:	6 850
Principal + interest due:	
6850 × 1.647 (interest factor)	= $11 281.95
Amount payable to beneficiary:	
25 000 − 11 281.95	= $13 718.05

usually include tables that show the cash value each year the policy is in force and the amount of paid-up insurance the cash value will purchase. Alternatively, the policyholder could use the cash surrender value to purchase term insurance with a larger face value, for a limited time.

LIMITED PAYMENT LIFE INSURANCE   A variation of whole life insurance is the *limited payment policy* that, as the name indicates, is completely paid for during a specified period. Instead of paying premiums for life, the insured pays higher premiums for a shorter time, usually 20 years or to age 65. After it is paid up, the policy remains in force for the rest of the life of the insured. This type of policy is selected when the insured expects to be able to pay for insurance more readily early in life, and thus may be appropriate for people who expect high incomes for a short time—professional athletes, for example. For most families, however, this type of policy cannot provide sufficient coverage when it is most needed.

The more rapid rate of payment causes the cash surrender value to increase faster in limited-pay insurance than in whole life. After the payment period ends, the cash surrender value continues to grow (Figure 6.7). Except for the shorter payment period, limited-pay life is similar in most respects to whole life insurance; the cash surrender value can also be used in the same ways.

ENDOWMENT LIFE INSURANCE

Two combination types of life insurance are: endowment life and universal life. Endowment combines a term with cash values and universal has term insurance with a saving account. We will consider first endowment insurance, a policy type rarely sold nowadays. *Endowment life insurance* provides coverage for a specified period, at the end of which the insurer promises to pay the face value. The insurance company accepts a liability that is 100 percent certain: the face value must be paid if the insured dies during the term or if the insured is alive at maturity. Therefore, the policy reserves must be built up rapidly (Figure 6.7) and consequently the annual premium is necessarily higher than for other types of insurance. While the policy is in force, the cash surrender value may be used by the insured in the ways already described. Endowment insurance shares characteristics with both term and whole life: it is for a term but it has cash values. However, it is not an effective way to build up savings or to obtain life insurance coverage.

Universal Life Insurance

As interest rates soared and inflation continued, insurance companies searched for a way to modify life insurance policies to make them more attractive to buyers. The fixed premiums may become too high in a period of rising interest rates when the insurance companies are receiving more return on invested funds than they predicted. The fixed benefit loses purchasing power after years of inflation. Traditionally, actuaries making forecasts of the estimated return on invested funds far into the future assume conservative rates of interest. To counteract this rigidity, and to make life insurance policies more attractive to buyers, the universal life policy was devised.

The distinctive features of *universal life* are: (i) the flexibility in payments, (ii) the opportunity to withdraw funds, (iii) the freedom to alter the amount of insurance coverage at any time, and (iv) the regular disclosure of fees, interest earned, and other information. These features contrast with traditional policies where the buyer does not know how the premiums are divided among the pure cost of insurance, reserves, and loading charges, or what rate of interest is being credited on the reserves.

Flexible Payments   The payment of money into a universal life policy is voluntary within prescribed limits. The money is used to create a fund from which the company deducts the cost of insurance protection—which is rather like term coverage—and a loading charge. The balance is credited with interest and treated as a sort of investment fund from which the policyholder may make withdrawals. The policyholder can choose how much to put in each year, but if no payment is made for a time, the insurance cost will be deducted from the fund if it has a balance. If the company is deducting the pure cost of insurance each year, you can expect this amount to increase with age.

Withdrawal Privileges   The funds in the cash account are available for you to withdraw or borrow against as you wish. If you leave the money in the account, you will draw interest at current rates. A minimum rate may be guaranteed for a year.

Flexible Coverage   There may be possibilities for changing your coverage, within limits, as your needs change.

Regular Statements   You will receive regular statements showing all the transactions in your account. These statements will keep you informed about your coverage and its cost, loading charges, and the return on the cash account.

EXPENSES   Prospective buyers need to become informed about all the charges that will be assessed, such as one-time administrative fees and surrender charges. Buyers should also be informed as to how the loading charges will be distributed. Some companies deduct loading charges before depositing the premium in the account, while others credit the premium, then deduct charges. Loading charges may be a constant proportion of each premium, front loaded, or back loaded. If in the early years of the policy a larger share of the premium is used for loading charges, the policy is referred to as *front loaded*. When little is deducted from the premiums at the outset for loading charges, but a disproportionate share is added when a policy is surrendered, the policy is *back loaded*. Some companies charge very high surrender charges if the policy is cancelled within a few years. However, if the policy remains in force for some time, the surrender charges diminish.

CAVEATS FOR BUYERS   Prospective buyers should give careful consideration to the benefits of having a term life policy and investment fund combination in one contract, instead of separate arrangements for each. The tax treatment of interest and the payments to beneficiaries should be investigated, along with the nature of the various fees. Some companies charge an initial fee and then a loading charge of 5-10 percent, and a fee for each withdrawal. Companies may use high interest rates to attract buyers, but decrease them later, or project unrealistic future interest rates. It is also possible that some charges may be buried in changed rates for the "pure cost of insurance." The flexibility in premiums may lead the buyer to forget payments, with consequent loss of coverage.

THE INSURANCE POLICY

A life insurance policy is the contract between the insuring company and the policyholder. Some aspects of this complex legal document will be outlined here. A life insurance contract is not a contract of indemnity as is property insurance, where the insured is to be indemnified or returned to the financial position he or she would have been in had the loss not occurred. With a life insurance policy, a predictable sum of money is payable—an important distinction. A sample whole life policy may be found in Figure 6.8 at the end of this chapter.

DESCRIPTION OF POLICY

Near the beginning of the policy there should be such basic information as the period during which the insurance is to be effective, the type of policy, when the face amount is payable, when premiums are to be paid, and how dividends are to be handled if the policy is a participating one.

GRACE PERIOD

The policyholder is usually given a *grace period* of one month after the date the premium is due, during which the premium may be paid without penalty. If the insured should die during the grace period, the beneficiary will receive the face value less the amount of the unpaid premium.

DIVIDENDS

The dividend clause in a participating policy covers the details of the company's payment of dividends and describes the various options available to the policyholder. The insured may take the dividends in cash, use them to reduce the premium, use them to purchase paid-up additions to the life insurance in force or one-year term additions, or leave them on deposit with the company to earn interest. The range of options available will be determined by the company.

INCONTESTABILITY

To protect themselves from future legal actions arising from alleged misrepresentations by the insured, life insurance companies have inserted an *incontestability clause*, stating that after two years in force, the policy will not be invalidated by any non-disclosure or misrepresentation that may be discovered, with the exception of fraud. During these two years, the company can seek to be released from the contract if it discovers that the applicant made false statements.

POLICY LOANS

The conditions under which policy loans are available will be stated somewhere in the policy. Related to these conditions is the automatic policy loan, which provides that if a policyholder fails to pay the premiums or take any other action, the company will use the cash surrender value to pay the premium, repeating the process as required until the cash value has been exhausted. Policyholders who assumed that their policy had lapsed because they had stopped paying premiums might be surprised to learn how much longer their coverage was extended. If the insured should die, of course, the face amount would be diminished by the amount of the policy loan.

OWNERSHIP RIGHTS AND ASSIGNMENT

The rights of the life insurance policy owner include the right to name and change the beneficiary, to use the cash value, to receive any dividends, and to dispose of any of these rights. If one person holds all of these rights, that person is the sole owner of the policy; if ownership is shared with someone, each becomes a part or joint owner. Usually the person insured and the owner are the same. Like other contracts, a life insurance policy is *assignable*—that is, its ownership may be transferred. For example, when a policy is used as collateral for a loan, the policy is assigned to the creditor.

BENEFICIARY

The beneficiary clause identifies who is intended to receive the proceeds of the insurance on the policyholder's death. In most cases, the insured may alter the designation of beneficiary by signing a declaration to be filed with the insurance company. Sometimes people forget to do this when family conditions change, leaving the insurance payable to an estranged, divorced, or deceased spouse. Insurance proceeds payable to a named beneficiary are not distributed through the deceased's will, but go directly to the person designated, free from claims that creditors or others may have on the estate.

If the primary beneficiary dies before the person whose life has been insured, and no alternative (secondary) beneficiary has been named, the company may pay the proceeds to the estate of the deceased. Only rarely will a policyholder name a beneficiary irrevocably, which means that the designation of beneficiary cannot be changed without the consent of the beneficiary himself. In such instances, the policyholder cannot assign the cash surrender value of the policy to a third party without the consent of the named *irrevocable beneficiary*.

SETTLEMENT OPTIONS

The way in which the proceeds of a life insurance policy will be paid to the beneficiary may be settled by the insured, prior to death, or can be left to the beneficiary's discretion. Some of the ways in which life insurance can be paid, other than as a lump sum, will be outlined here. The *interest option* involves leaving the principal sum on deposit with the insurance company and receiving the interest regularly. In the *instalment option*, the proceeds are paid in instalments over a selected period of time by various arrangements, all involving payment of principal and interest. The proceeds can be used to purchase a single payment annuity (life income) with payments to begin either immediately or at a later date; this is sometimes referred to as the *life income option*. (Annuities are explained in the chapter on retirement income.)

POLICY VARIATIONS

Most insurance companies offer quite a range of special policies that are adaptations or combinations of basic policies. Two examples will be considered here as illustrations of possible variations.

FAMILY POLICY

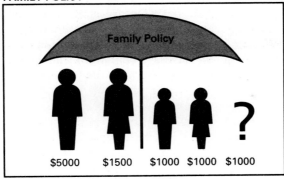

FAMILY INCOME POLICY

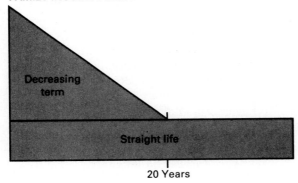

Figure 6.9   FAMILY POLICY AND FAMILY INCOME POLICY

FAMILY INCOME POLICY

Term and whole life insurance are combined in various ways to make a *family income policy* (Figure 6.9). The person insured is usually the family's principal income earner. The whole life portion of the policy covers the insured for life, paying a specified amount on his or her death. The term portion will provide an income for dependents if the insured dies during the term, which might be 20 years. This monthly income will continue for the remainder of the term. For instance, if the insured dies ten years after taking out a policy that has a 20-year term component, the dependents would receive an income for the next ten years, at the end of which they would start receiving a straight life annuity. If the insured lives more than 20 years after buying the policy, the term coverage will have expired, but the whole life insurance will continue.

Family Policy

Some insurers may offer a *family policy* that is a package with separate coverage for the husband, the wife, and each present and future child. This policy may include term insurance only, or a combination of term and whole life. In the latter instance, the whole life coverage would probably be on the husband's life. If any family member should die during the term of his or her coverage, the insurer will pay the coverage for that individual, but the package will continue to cover the lives of the survivors.

Policy Modifications

Endorsements or Riders

An insurance policy may be modified by the addition of *endorsements* or *riders*, that specify various supplementary benefits to be included or omitted without affecting the rest of the policy. Such additions can be worthwhile, but they may change the risk to be covered, thus adding to the cost. Some riders in common use are: guaranteed renewability, waiver of premium, guaranteed insurability, accidental death benefit, and conversion privilege. These features may be available as riders in some instances, or written into policies in other cases, depending on the practices of the company.

Guaranteed Renewability Term insurance buyers may find it desirable to have the option of renewing the policy at the end of the term without providing evidence of insurability by having another medical examination. Guaranteed renewability adds another risk for the life insurance company, but the extra cost may be worthwhile to the insured.

Waiver of Premium A waiver of premium rider usually releases the policyholder from paying premiums when disabled, while keeping the policy in force. A precise definition of what constitutes disability is generally included, and there is often a waiting period of several months. Inspect very closely the definition of what constitutes disability.

Guaranteed Insurability A rider that permits the policyholder to purchase additional life insurance at specified future dates, without evidence of insurability, can be useful. The option may be restricted to persons aged 37 or younger, and the maximum face amount that may be added will probably be specified.

ACCIDENTAL DEATH BENEFIT   Another rider frequently added to basic policies is the accidental death benefit. It provides an additional benefit that may be as much as the face value of the policy if the insured dies as a result of an accident prior to some specified age, such as 65 or 70. The additional premium for this rider is usually small because the majority of deaths are not considered accidental. A buyer of life insurance needs to remember that the amount of insurance bought should be determined by the expected needs of dependents, not by the cause of death. Also, careful note should be taken of the definition of accidental death as far as the life insurance company is concerned. Accidental death coverage, like travel insurance, should not be necessary if the insurance program is carefully planned.

CONVERSION PRIVILEGE   A rider may be added to a term policy, giving the insured the option of converting the policy to another type of insurance without evidence of insurability at any time prior to the end of the term. There may be an age limit on this privilege, such as age 60 or 65.

BUYING LIFE INSURANCE

NATIONAL TRENDS

How much life insurance do Canadians buy, do they prefer individual or group policies, and whose lives do they insure? From national life insurance industry data it is possible to get a general picture of coverage, characteristics of the insured, and their policy preferences. It is well known that some buyers of life insurance change their minds and surrender policies or let them lapse. Data on lapse and surrender rates provide information on the extent to which policies are not maintained in force.

LIFE INSURANCE OWNERSHIP   Canadians are the third most insured people in the world, with an average per capita coverage of $38 000 in 1988. This propensity has continued over time: for instance, the total amount of life insurance in force per capita has increased more than a hundredfold in the last 75 years. However, some of that increase can be explained by inflation. It may be instructive to review recent figures, converted to constant dollars. It is clear that the amounts of life insurance owned between 1977 and 1988 grew significantly, after adjusting for inflation (Table 6.1).

Since not every individual needs or owns life insurance, it is more meaningful to look at the average amounts per policyholder and per household than per capita. Although these figures seem high, very often families are not adequately covered; too often the wrong amounts of the wrong kinds of

Table 6.1   AVERAGE AMOUNTS OF LIFE INSURANCE OWNED BY
            CANADIANS, 1977 AND 1988

Unit	Current $ 1988	Constant 1981 $ 1977	Constant 1981 $ 1988
Per capita	$ 38 100	$18 439	$26 495
Per policyholder	66 400	33 873	46 175
Per household	109 800	61 856	76 356

Source: *Canadian Life and Health Insurance Facts.* Toronto: Canadian Life and Health Insurance Association Inc., various years. Reproduced and edited with permission from the Canadian Life and Health Insurance Association Inc.

insurance are bought on the lives of the wrong persons. The combination of uninformed buyers and high pressure sales techniques can be disastrous.

INDIVIDUAL OR GROUP POLICIES   On examining the total value of life insurance owned in Canada, it is evident that the long-term trend, until recently, has been towards an increasing share for group insurance (Figure 6.10). Group insurance, not available in 1900, represented nearly 60 percent of all insurance owned by 1980 but dropped to 53 percent by 1988 when individual policies gained a slightly increased share.

CHARACTERISTICS OF THE INSURED   The decision to buy life insurance is influenced by a number of variables but most logically by the presence of dependents. However, the available data from the industry association do not mention dependents but do include gender, age, and income of the insured. Each pie graph in Figure 6.11 represents how the total face value of individual life insurance policies purchased in 1988 was distributed by selected characteristics. For instance, there was more coverage on the lives of males (69 percent) than on females (31 percent). Looking at age and income, nearly one-half of the coverage was on those aged 25-44 with about the same proportion on those with incomes between $25 000 and $49 999. One might conclude that insurance coverage is higher for young males with average or slightly higher incomes.

TYPE AND SIZE OF POLICY   Although, historically, whole life policies were the leading type sold to individuals (as opposed to groups), it is interesting to note that by 1988 whole life represented only one-quarter of face value purchased individually (Figure 6.11). There was more term coverage (35 percent) than any other type, with the balance spread among universal life, family life and

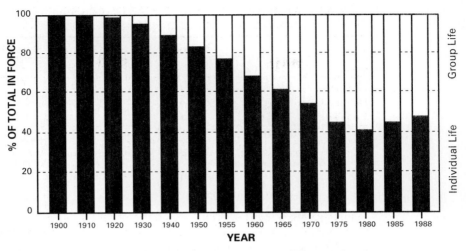

Figure 6.10   PERCENTAGE DISTRIBUTION OF INDIVIDUAL AND GROUP
LIFE INSURANCE OWNED, 1900-1988

Source: *Canadian Life and Health Insurance Facts*. Toronto: Canadian Life and Health Insurance Association Inc.,
1989, page 7. Reproduced and edited with permission from the Canadian Life and Health Insurance Association
Inc.

various combination policies. Considering the size of policies, nearly three-quarters of the coverage had face values of $100 000 or more.

REASONS FOR TERMINATION   From the limited information available it is obvious that many people buy insurance policies that they are unable, or do not want, to keep in force. Some whole life policies are surrendered by policyholders, in exchange for the cash value, because they do not wish to continue the coverage. Other policies are allowed to lapse through non-payment of premiums. The surrender and lapse rate is climbing and far exceeds the rate for termination by death and maturity (Table 6.2). The obvious question is why is this so? It is interesting to consider to what extent this problem is related to the way life insurance is sold.

HOW MUCH TO BUY

The following five steps provide a simplified way of estimating how much life insurance you may need. First, assume that your death could occur tomorrow. Who would need financial support and for how long?

1.   Estimate needs of dependents for as long as they would need support. Call this total A.

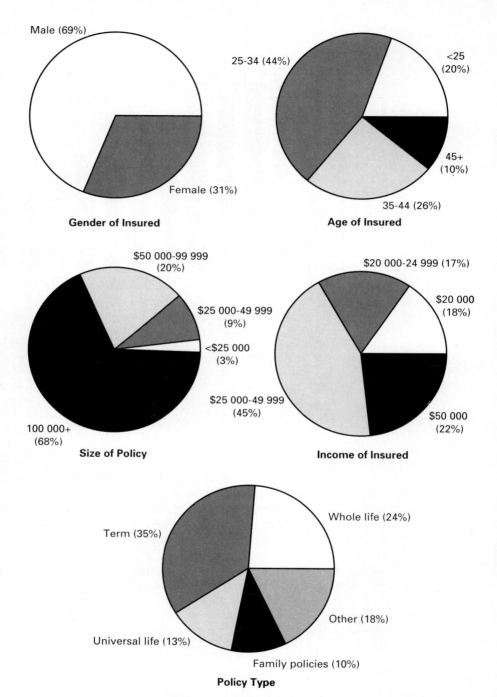

Figure 6.11   PERCENTAGE DISTRIBUTION OF TOTAL FACE VALUE OF INDIVIDUAL LIFE POLICIES PURCHASED, BY SELECTED FACTORS, CANADA, 1988

Source: *Canadian Life and Health Insurance Facts*. Toronto: Canadian Life and Health Insurance Association Inc., 1989, page 12. Reproduced and edited with permission from the Canadian Life and Health Insurance Association Inc.

Table 6.2 PROPORTION* OF LIFE INSURANCE TERMINATED BY REASON, CANADA, SELECTED YEARS

Reason	1955 %	1965 %	1975 %	1987 %
Death, maturity, disability, and expiry	1.1	1.1	1.0	0.9
Surrender and lapse	4.6	6.4	6.4	11.7

*Percentage of face value terminated to total face value in force.

Source: *Report of the Superintendent of Insurance for Canada.* Ottawa: Supply and Services Canada, (Catalogue number 55-1), various years. Reproduced with the permission of the Minister of Supply and Services Canada.

2. Estimate the sources of income your dependents would receive independent of your estate, e.g., Canada or Quebec Pension, family allowances, employment income, investment income. This will be total B.
3. Subtract: A − B = C. This may be either a negative or a positive number. If the result is negative—and your estimates are realistic—it appears that your dependents could manage financially without help from your estate. If the result is positive, continue.
4. List all your assets, estimating their present value. Include life insurance, individual and group policies, pension benefits, Canada Pension death benefit, deposits in savings accounts, term deposits, Canada Savings Bonds, and other bonds. Estimate the value of your stocks and your equity in any real estate that would be sold. From this total, subtract your debts (not mortgages on property, because you counted equity only) to find the net worth of the estate that could be used to support dependents. This will be total D.
5. Finally, compare C and D. Is the net worth of your estate large enough to cover the net needs of your dependents? If so, their financial security seems assured; if not, more life insurance may be in order.

A more sophisticated estimate of insurance requirements would apply a discount factor, because all the funds that you estimated your dependents would need would not have to be available to them immediately. The bulk of the estate could be invested, and this yield should be taken into consideration. Consult some of the references at the end of this chapter for information on forecasting life insurance needs.

SELECTING A POLICY
Buyers of life insurance are advised to first define their needs and then obtain quotations from several companies. Often, it may be difficult to make meaning-

ful comparisons because different companies are offering dissimilar insurance packages which protect against different risks. The more clearly you can specify your requirements before approaching an insurance agent the greater the probability that you will be able to get comparable quotations.

TERM OR WHOLE LIFE?

Tina, who is 30 years old with two dependents, has decided that she requires $100 000 of life insurance coverage but she wonders which type of policy to buy. With the information she collected from agents she plotted the annual premium costs (Figure 6.12). She was surprised to find that five-year term insurance, much cheaper than whole life initially, would increase in cost at each renewal. This graph clarified for her the difference between the level premium for whole life and the increasing premiums for term. It illustrated that, until she was 55, even the increasing premiums for term coverage would be significantly less than those for whole life. She realized that her children should be independent in fifteen years and that she did not need whole life coverage and decided on five-year renewable term insurance.

COST BY GENDER AND TYPE OF POLICY
The cost of insurance, as already explained, is influenced by a number of variables. Factors such as gender and whether or not the insured is a smoker have been found to have a notable effect on cost at any age, as the comparison for several types of policies shown in Table 6.3 attests.

SELLING METHODS
Individual life insurance policies are sold by sales persons who depend on commissions for their livelihood, thus tending to create a conflict of interest when they act as advisors to buyers. When companies pay higher commissions on certain types of policies, sales people attempt to sell these kinds over others. Generally, it has been possible to earn higher commissions from selling cash value policies than term policies. A recent development is that agents are presenting themselves more as general financial planners than as insurance agents. This raises the question of conflict of interest, especially if remuneration comes from commissions rather than fees.

Another difficulty for consumers is the rapid turnover among life insurance sales people; after three years, only 20 percent of agents remain in the

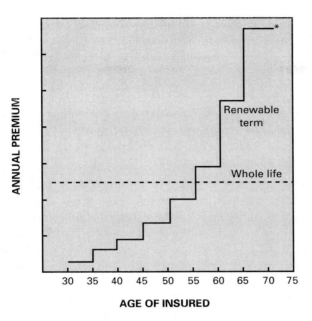

Figure 6.12   ANNUAL PREMIUMS FOR FIVE-YEAR RENEWABLE TERM AND
WHOLE LIFE INSURANCE, BY AGE

*5-year renewable term no longer available after age 65.

Table 6.3   ANNUAL PREMIUM BY TYPE OF POLICY (PER $1000 FACE
AMOUNT OF LIFE INSURANCE)

Type of Policy	Male		Female	
	Smoker	Non-smoker	Smoker	Non-smoker
Term, 25 years	$ 3.21	$ 1.97	$ 2.35	$ 1.75
Term to age 65	4.25	2.77	3.11	2.45
Whole life	9.34	7.87	7.93	7.24
20-pay life	14.58	13.02	13.08	12.35

These data were obtained from one company for participating policies, for a purchaser aged 24.

business. Although some make a career in insurance sales, the large number
of new entrants lowers the overall knowledge and skill. This situation, combined with the pressure on agents to sell, makes it essential that prospective
buyers of life insurance be as well informed as possible.

PROTECTION FOR BUYERS

Although there has rarely been the problem of life insurance companies going out of business and leaving policyholders unprotected, steps have recently been taken by the federal and provincial governments to set up a compensation fund. For holders of RRSPs with life insurance companies, the fund provides protection to a maximum of $60 000, as the Canada Deposit Insurance Corporation does for banks, trust companies, and credit unions. Insurance policyholders are protected to a maximum of $200 000, and annuitants to $2000 per month. This plan is similar to one established a few years previously to protect clients of general insurance companies.

EFFECTS OF INFLATION

The inflation of the 1970s and 1980s created problems for both policyholders and insurance companies. The purchasing power of a fixed amount of face value purchased some years ago is now greatly reduced, effectively reducing the protection planned for the policyholder's dependents; in addition, high interest rates have encouraged families to invest money in other ways to ensure financial security, instead of buying whole life insurance. Consequently, life insurance companies responded by creating new products, such as universal life, new money policies, variable life, and adjustable life.

New-money policies pay higher interest rates on cash reserves, with the rate being adjusted every five years. When rates in the economy rise, the company has a better return and can increase the amount of coverage for the insured without raising the premium. *Variable life*, like universal life, separates premiums and a savings fund, but invests in a wider range of assets. Cash values may increase or decrease daily, depending on investment results. *Adjustable life* allows the insured to change the face value and the premium as desired, although evidence of insurability (medical examination) is required to increase coverage.

Insurance companies have been earning a substantially greater yield on their invested funds because of high interest rates, which are much in excess of the return—3 percent or so—their actuaries had predicted. The higher yield, combined with a drop in mortality rates, has made life insurance cheaper than it used to be, in spite of rising management costs.

SUMMARY

Life insurance, which may have appeared very confusing at first glance, is based on a few fundamental principles, such as pooling risk, the pure cost of insurance and the level premium. Like most other financial sectors, insurance has some specific vocabulary a competent consumer should understand, but the problem is compounded by a lack of common terminology in naming policies. Companies may add numerous special features to the few basic types of insurance policies and call the combinations whatever they wish. It is necessary to reduce this verbiage to fundamental types and principles to make an informed choice.

Before making any market comparisons, identify your need for life insurance, remembering that it is primarily a method of risk management. Very few people need life insurance as a savings vehicle. Uninformed buyers have a tendency to buy the wrong kinds in wrong amounts, and to insure the wrong people. The amounts of money involved are not small, and the need for greater awareness on the part of consumers is great.

PROBLEMS

1. Bert, a 30-year-old chemist, is wondering whether he has enough life insurance, especially since a second child is due to arrive in a few months. His wife Mira, 27, is busy looking after 3-year-old John and does not work outside the home. In reviewing his financial situation, Bert estimated that, if he should die tomorrow he would need to leave a sum of $200 000 in his estate to support his children until they are independent, and his wife for her lifetime. His list of assets and debts is as follows:

Life insurance, five-year renewable term	$55 000
Deposits in bank	1 700
Canada Savings Bonds	400
Equity in home	44 000
Stocks	2 400
Consumer debts	2 400
Funeral expenses	3 000

   (a) If Bert were to die tomorrow, what would be the net worth of his estate? Would it be sufficient to provide the support he desires for his family? Should the equity in the house be included in this analysis? Give your reasons.
   (b) What recommendation would you make to Bert regarding amount and type of life insurance?
   (c) Assuming that he could purchase five-year renewable term insurance for $2.80 per $1000 and whole life for $8.50 per $1000, how much would your recommendation cost him per year?
   (d) Assume that Mira acquires a full-time job. Should she have life insurance also? Would this change Bert's need for life insurance?

2. George, a 49-year-old dentist practising in a small northern town, is active

in sports and flies his own plane. His wife, who is 43, worked as a research assistant before her marriage, but now is at home raising their four children. At this stage in his life, George has put all spare cash into buying property since he has sufficient current income for the needs of the family. George does not believe in life insurance and has not bought any. His reasons are that: (i) his wife has professional training and could support the children, (ii) his property has been appreciating in value, and (iii) he has a registered retirement savings plan.

(a) Do you think George needs any life insurance? Consider the family's need for readily available cash and how they would obtain it. Consider the possibilities for long-term support of his dependents.
(b) What recommendations would you make to George, and what arguments would you advance to support your suggestions?

3. When Dave, 25, got married, he thought about his new responsibilities and decided to buy some life insurance. He consulted agents, read books on life insurance, and selected a whole life policy. The agent presented him with an application form to be completed and a medical report to be filled in by his doctor. When the life insurance company had studied the information provided by Dave and by the agent, checked with the credit bureau, and made other investigations they felt necessary, Dave was accepted. He then received a copy of his policy.

The company examined Dave's finances, his occupation, and his health, among other things. Why did they need to have so much information about him?

4. Decide whether you AGREE or DISAGREE with the following statements.

(a) If George, Bert, and Dave applied to the same company for the same type of life insurance policy and all were accepted, they would pay the same annual premiums.
(b) If they chose whole life, all would pay level premiums for life, or until they reached an age limit such as 85.
(c) If Bert purchases decreasing term insurance, his premiums will decrease each year during the term of the contract.
(d) If Bert changes his job, his present group insurance coverage will continue as long as he pays the premiums.
(e) If Dave chooses a participating policy, he can expect to receive dividends.
(f) Five-year renewable term insurance means that the contract can be renewed after five years at the same premium.
(g) For a given annual expenditure, an endowment policy will provide less insurance protection than other types of insurance.

(h) A dividend may be regarded as interest earned by the money you paid the insurance company.

(i) A group policy is the same as a participating policy.

Senoff

5. Who needs insurance most? When is it most necessary?

6. What difference does it make in the distribution of property after the death of a policyholder whose life insurance is payable to his estate rather than to a named beneficiary, if (a) he dies intestate, or (b) he leaves a will?

7. Analyze each of the following situations and decide whether you AGREE or DISAGREE with the conclusions.

(a) A single woman of 35, without dependents, who has $25 000 of group insurance in association with her employment, has been called on by a life insurance salesman. He encourages her to take out an whole life policy of $50 000. His arguments are: (i) the premium will increase if she postpones buying insurance, and (ii) she should have permanent insurance and not depend on the group policy that covers her only so long as she stays with that employer. She decides that he is right.

(b) A woman widowed at 35 returns to work as a professional librarian to support her four school age children because her husband's estate was small. She asks an insurance agent for a renewable term policy. He recommends that she buy permanent whole life insurance so that she will have something for her old age. She tells him that she doesn't want a small amount of permanent life insurance, but a large amount right now.

(c) A young couple with three small children wonders what kind of life insurance to buy. He earns $38 000 a year, and she stays at home to look after the children. They are thinking of taking out a family policy that would put $10 000 on his life, $4000 on hers and $2000 on each child. That way the couple would cover the major risks.

(d) A retired couple of 75 and 73, who have a whole life policy for $10 000 on the husband's life, wonder whether to keep paying the annual premium of $175 or to cash in the policy and take the cash surrender value of $7200. They are living on Old Age Security, Canada Pension, employer's pension, and the income from their modest investments. They decide not to cash in the policy now but to keep it for the wife's protection in case she should be widowed.

8. Referring to the life insurance policy (Figure 6.8 at the end of the chapter) decide whether you AGREE or DISAGREE with each of the following statements.

(a) Dave bought a limited-pay whole life policy.

(b) Dave should have requested an accidental death rider as better protection for his family.

(c) Dave chose a participating policy.

(d) If Dave decided to cancel the policy one year after purchasing it, he would receive a $130 cash value.

(e) If Dave decided to surrender his policy 10 years after purchase, he could apply for the cash value of $3350 plus accumulated dividends.

(f) He could buy a paid up policy that would have a face value of $15 500 if he surrendered his policy after ten years.

(g) After the children arrived, Dave had difficulty in making ends meet; then his union went on strike for four months. It was impossible for him to pay the premium, due on August 7, 1996. Failure to make this payment meant that his policy was cancelled.

(h) In 1988, the washing machine had to be replaced quickly at a time when cash was short, so Dave applied for a policy loan of $300 for which he was eligible.

(i) Dave should select a lump-sum settlement option for his wife because this will leave her free to elect the settlement option best suited to her situation at the time.

(j) If Dave selects a life income plan as the settlement option for his wife, he is in effect asking that the face value of his policy be used to buy a single-payment life annuity.

(k) If Dave's wife, his named beneficiary, should predecease him and if he neglected to change the beneficiary, on his death the company would pay the face value to his wife's heirs.

(l) When Dave dies, the payment of the face value of this policy is determined by the conditions of his will. His widow will not receive it automatically, even if she is the named beneficiary.

(m) Dave used his life insurance policy as collateral to obtain a loan but died before it was repaid. In this case his wife would not receive any life insurance benefits, but Dave's estate would not have to pay the balance outstanding on the debt.

9. Examine the following statements and identify those that are myths or involve faulty reasoning. Explain the error.

(a) Buying life insurance is a good way to build up savings.

(b) A policyholder's savings in a whole life insurance policy drop to zero on his death.

(c) You should buy life insurance while you are young, when the premiums are less.

(d) The cash surrender value of a whole life policy is your own money and the company should not charge interest when you borrow your own money.

(e) Term insurance is not a good buy because the coverage is temporary but the problem is permanent.

(f) At your death your beneficiary should receive the cash value as well as the face value.

10. Why is it said that "life insurance is sold but not bought?"

11. At retirement a person needs to review his or her insurance coverage in light of future needs. What are some reasons for (a) cashing in or cancelling all life insurance, or (b) retaining some coverage?

REFERENCES

Books

AMLING, FREDERICK, and WILLIAM G. DROMS. *The Dow Jones-Irwin Guide to Personal Financial Planning*. Second Edition. Homewood, Illinois: Dow Jones-Irwin, 1986, 549 pp. Although written for American readers, much of the discussion of financial planning, life insurance, retirement planning, and investments is relevant for Canadians.

BELTH, JOSEPH M. *Life Insurance, A Consumer's Handbook*. Second Edition. Bloomington, Indiana: Indiana University Press, 1985, 216 pp. Examines life insurance from a consumer's point of view.

CANADIAN LIFE AND HEALTH INSURANCE ASSOCIATION. *Canadian Life and Health Insurance Facts*. Toronto: Canadian Life and Health Insurance Association, annual, 68 pp. Provides industry data on purchases and ownership of life and health insurance, and annuities. (Booklet free from the Association at Suite 2500, 20 Queen Street West, Toronto, Ontario, M5H 3S2)

COTE, JEAN-MARC, and DONALD DAY. *Personal Financial Planning in Canada*. Toronto: Allyn and Bacon, 1987, 464 pp. A comprehensive personal finance text that includes financial planning, income tax, annuities, pensions, investments, credit, mortgages, and wills with particular attention to the banking and insurance industries.

FLEMING, JAMES. *Merchants of Fear, An Investigation of Canada's Insurance Industry*. Markham, Ontario: Penguin Books Canada, 1986, 409 pp. An investigative report on the life and general insurance industries.

MATHESON, G. F., and JOHN TODD. *Information, Entry, and Regulation in Markets for Life Insurance*. Toronto: University of Toronto Press, 1982, 117 pp. A detailed analysis of Canadian life insurance.

MCLEOD, WILLIAM E. *The Canadian Buyer's Guide to Life Insurance*. Seventh Edition. Scarborough, Ontario: Prentice-Hall Canada, 1989, 276 pp. A comprehensive guide to various life insurance products, including annuities.

MCQUEEN, ROD. *Risky Business, Inside Canada's $86 billion Insurance Industry*. Toronto: Macmillan, 1985. An investigation into how the insurance industry operates.

SELECT COMMITTEE ON COMPANY LAW. *The Insurance Industry—Fourth Report on Life Insurance*. Toronto: Ontario Legislative Assembly, 1980, 525 pp. A detailed study of life insurance with special attention to selling practices.

TOWNSON, MONICA, and FREDERICK STAPENHURST. *The Canadian Woman's Guide to Money*. Second Edition. Toronto: McGraw-Hill Ryerson, 1982, 203 pp. A book for the general reader that includes budgets, financial security, life insurance, retirement planning, and credit.

TURNER, MARY, DANIEL LEROSSIGNOL, CLAUDE RINFRET, and RICHARD DAW. *Canadian Guide to Personal Financial Management*. Fourth Edition. Scarborough, Ontario: Prentice-Hall Canada, 1989, 231 pp. Accountants provide guidance on a broad range of topics, including planning finances, estimating insurance needs, managing risk, and determining investment needs. Instructions and the necessary forms for making plans are provided.

ZIMMER, HENRY B. *Making Your Money Grow, A Canadian Guide to Successful Personal Finance*. Third Edition. Toronto: Collins, 1989, 260 pp. The focus of this book is on basic calculations needed for personal financial decisions, as applied to compound interest, future and present values, investment returns, RRSPs, annuities, and life insurance.

Articles

"Insuring Your Future," *The Financial Post Moneywise*, December 1989, 64-86. Discusses protection for a variety of risks that can be handled by life or general insurance.

MCLEOD, BILL. "A Life Insurance Check-Up," *Canadian Consumer*, 18, No. 9, 1988, 7-12. Explains recent developmments in life insurance and offers guidance for the buyer.

Policy Data

POLICY NUMBER	*346238*
POLICY DATE	*August 7, 1986*
LIFE INSURED	*David Gerald Hill*
AGE OF LIFE INSURED	*25*
OWNER	*David Gerald Hill, the life insured*
BENEFICIARY	as stated in the application unless subsequently changed
PLAN OF INSURANCE	Whole Life
FACE AMOUNT	$ *50,000.00* **
PREMIUMS	Amount $ *554.50*

The first premium is due on the policy date. Premiums are payable every *twelve* month(s) while the life insured is living.

If this policy includes any Additional Benefits, the premium above includes the premiums for such benefits. When the premium for any Additional Benefit is no longer payable, the premium for the policy will be reduced accordingly.

Additional Benefits included in this policy are:

Policy Data

SPECIMEN

LIR 615-115

Figure 6.8   SAMPLE LIFE INSURANCE POLICY
Source: The Cooperators Life Insurance Company. Reproduced with the permission of the Cooperators Life Insurance Company.

General Provisions

The Contract

The policy and the application are part of the contract. The contract also includes documents attached at issue and any amendments agreed upon in writing after the policy is issued. The policy may not be amended nor any provision waived except by written agreement signed by authorized signing officers of the Company.

Owner

While the life insured is living, all benefits, rights and privileges under the contract belong to the owner.

Beneficiary

The owner may appoint a beneficiary. The owner may change the beneficiary unless the appointment was irrevocable. If there is no beneficiary living when the life insured dies, the owner or the estate of the owner is the beneficiary.

Payment of Premiums

Premiums are due on the dates indicated on the policy data page. If any cheque or other instrument given for payment is not honoured, the premium remains unpaid.

If a premium remains unpaid by the end of the days of grace, dividend accumulations will automatically be applied towards paying the premium. Any portion of the premium still remaining unpaid will be automatically paid by a loan on the policy, subject to the terms of the Automatic Premium Loan clause. If the premium remains only partially paid after the application of dividend accumulations or by payment by an automatic premium loan or both, the policy will stay in force for a pro-rated part of the premium period. This is the only condition under which we will accept a premium payment for less than the amount due.

Currency and Place of Payment

All amounts payable to or by us will be payable in Canadian dollars at any of our offices.

Days of Grace

Thirty-one days of grace are allowed for payment of each premium except the first. During this time, the policy will stay in force. If the life insured dies during this time, any premium due but unpaid will be deducted from the amount payable.

Lapse

This contract will lapse and our liability will cease:

— at the end of the days of grace of an unpaid premium unless:

  i. the premium or part of it is advanced by dividend accumulations or by automatic premium loan, as described in the payment of premiums provision; or
  ii. the policy is changed to Reduced Paid-Up Life Insurance; or

— at the end of a pro-rated part of a premium period, if part of a premium has been advanced by dividend accumulations or by an automatic premium loan, or both; however, the policy will not lapse before the end of the days of grace for an unpaid premium; or

— when the indebtedness equals or exceeds the cash value.

Assignment

We will not recognize an assignment until we receive written notice of it at our Head Office. We are not responsible for the validity of any assignment.

Misstatement of Age

If the date of birth of the life insured or any other person insured under this policy has been misstated, the amount payable shall be increased or decreased to the amount that would have been provided for the same premium at the correct age or ages.

Validity

We may contest the contract if any statement or answer on any application misrepresents or fails to disclose any fact material to the insurance. We shall not contest the contract for these reasons after it has been in force during the lifetime of the life insured for two years from the date it takes effect, either on issue, on reissue for an increased amount or on reinstatement. However, in cases involving fraud, we may contest the contract at any time.

Reinstatement

This contract may be reinstated within three years of lapse. Reinstatement is not allowed on policies where the cash surrender value has been paid or the policy has been changed to Reduced Paid-Up Life Insurance.

Reinstatement requires:

— a written application; and
— evidence which satisfies us that the life insured and any other person insured under this policy is an acceptable risk; and
— all overdue premiums and the indebtedness outstanding at the lapse date must be paid with interest at the yearly rate determined by us.

This policy shall not be deemed to be reinstated until our official notification of reinstatement has been issued.

Self-Destruction

If the life insured dies from suicide or self-inflicted injuries, while either sane or insane:

— within one year of the date of Part 1 of the application for this policy, the amount payable is limited to the premiums paid;
— within one year of the date of the application for any Additional Benefit under this policy, the amount payable in respect of the Additional Benefit is limited to the premiums paid for the Additional Benefit;
— within one year of the date of the application for any reinstatement of this policy, the amount payable is limited to the premiums paid since the date of the last reinstatement.

General Provisions   SPECIMEN   LIR 709 508

Figure 6.8 (continued)

Benefit Provisions

Insuring Clause

We agree that the amount payable under the terms of this policy will be paid on the death of the life insured. Death must occur while this policy is in force.

Benefit Clause

Subject to the terms of this policy, the amount payable will include the face amount, dividends, any Additional Benefit payable on death, less any indebtedness.

Definitions

"Indebtedness" means any policy loans and premium loans and overdue premiums and includes accrued interest.

"Tabular Cash Value" means the value determined in accordance with the "Table of Guaranteed Values".

"Cash Value" means the tabular cash value plus the surrender value of any paid-up additions purchased by dividends. This surrender value will be determined using the same mortality table and rate of interest as used in calculating the "Table of Guaranteed Values".

"Cash Surrender Value" means the cash value plus dividend accumulations less any indebtedness.

"Loan Value" means the cash value less one year's interest, at our current loan interest rate, on the cash value.

"Policy Date" is the date used to determine premium due dates, policy anniversaries and policy years.

"We", "our", and "us" refer to the Co-operators Life Insurance Company.

Payment on Death

The amount payable on the death of the life insured will be paid when sufficient evidence is received as to the death, the age of the life insured, the right of the claimant to be paid and the identity and age of the beneficiary (if any).

Dividends

This policy participates in the surplus distribution of the Company. Our Board of Directors determines the owner's share and we credit it to the policy as a dividend at the end of each policy year. Dividends are applied under the option the owner has elected from those available on this policy. This option remains in effect unless we agree to a change.

Policy Loans

We will grant a loan on the security of the policy. The maximum loan available will be the loan value less any indebtedness. We may require completion of a loan agreement. Interest will accrue from day to day on any loan, whether granted under this clause or under the Automatic Premium Loan clause. The interest rate will be determined by us from time to time. Interest not paid by the end of each policy year will be added to the principal of the loan and will bear interest.

Automatic Premium Loan

We will automatically make a policy loan to pay for any premium not paid by the end of the days of grace. If the loan available is less than the unpaid premium, the loan will be used to keep the policy in force for a pro-rated part of the premium period. Such loans shall bear interest from the end of the days of grace.

Reduced Paid-Up Life Insurance Option

The owner may elect to change this policy to paid-up whole life insurance provided that the new face amount is greater than a minimum value set by us. The new face amount will be the amount provided by the cash value less any indebtedness applied as a single premium and premium payments will cease.

Cash Surrender Option

While this policy has a cash surrender value, it may be surrendered for cash.

On surrender, we will pay the cash surrender value and our liability will cease. Evidence as to the age of the life insured and the right of the claimant to be paid is required on surrender.

Settlement Options

The amount payable on the death of the life insured or on surrender of the policy may be paid in cash, left on deposit at interest, used to provide an annuity or settled on any other agreed basis.

The choice of settlement may be made by the owner. If the owner does not make a choice, the beneficiary shall make the choice of settlement. With our consent, the beneficiary may change a settlement chosen by the owner, unless the owner has specified otherwise.

Details of the options and the conditions under which they are available will be provided on request.

SPECIMEN

Benefit Provisions

LIR 659-308

Figure 6.8 (continued)

Excerpt from a Table of Guaranteed Values

Tabular cash values and paid-up whole life insurance values, per $1000.00 of the face amount, are shown in this table. The values applicable to this policy are those for age shown in the policy data page as Age of Life Insured.

END OF POLICY YEAR	AGE 21 CASH VALUE	AGE 21 PAID-UP VALUE	AGE 22 CASH VALUE	AGE 22 PAID-UP VALUE	AGE 23 CASH VALUE	AGE 23 PAID-UP VALUE	AGE 24 CASH VALUE	AGE 24 PAID-UP VALUE	AGE 25 CASH VALUE	AGE 25 PAID-UP VALUE	AGE 26 CASH VALUE	AGE 26 PAID-UP VALUE	AGE 27 CASH VALUE	AGE 27 PAID-UP VALUE	END OF POLICY YEAR
1	—	—	—	—	—	—	—	—	—	—	—	—	—	—	1
2	—	—	—	—	—	—	—	—	—	—	—	—	—	—	2
3	—	—	—	—	—	—	—	—	1	6	1	6	2	11	3
4	5	33	6	39	7	44	8	48	9	52	10	56	11	59	4
5	12	78	14	87	15	90	17	98	18	100	19	102	21	109	5
6	20	125	22	132	24	139	25	139	27	145	29	150	31	155	6
7	28	168	30	173	32	178	34	183	37	191	39	194	41	197	7
8	36	208	39	217	41	220	44	228	46	229	49	235	51	236	8
9	45	250	48	257	51	264	54	269	56	269	59	273	62	276	9
10	54	290	57	295	60	299	64	307	67	310	70	310	74	318	10
11	62	320	66	329	69	331	73	337	77	343	80	343	84	348	11
12	71	353	75	360	79	365	83	370	87	373	91	376	95	379	12
13	80	383	84	388	88	392	93	399	97	401	102	407	106	407	13
14	89	411	94	418	98	420	103	426	108	430	113	434	118	437	14
15	98	436	104	446	109	450	114	454	119	457	124	459	130	465	15
16	108	463	114	471	119	474	125	480	130	482	136	486	142	490	16
17	118	488	124	494	130	499	136	504	142	507	148	510	155	516	17
18	129	514	135	519	141	522	148	529	154	531	161	536	168	540	18
19	139	534	146	541	153	547	160	552	167	556	174	559	181	562	19
20	151	559	158	565	165	569	172	572	179	575	187	580	194	582	20
Age 60	416	833	413	827	410	821	406	813	402	805	398	797	394	789	Age 60
Age 65	497	874	494	869	491	864	488	858	484	851	481	846	477	839	Age 65

END OF POLICY YEAR	AGE 28 CASH	AGE 28 PAID-UP	AGE 29 CASH	AGE 29 PAID-UP	AGE 30 CASH	AGE 30 PAID-UP	AGE 31 CASH	AGE 31 PAID-UP	AGE 32 CASH	AGE 32 PAID-UP	AGE 33 CASH	AGE 33 PAID-UP	AGE 34 CASH	AGE 34 PAID-UP	END OF POLICY YEAR
1	—	—	—	—	—	—	—	—	—	—	—	—	—	—	1
2	—	—	—	—	—	—	—	—	—	—	—	—	—	—	2
3	2	11	3	16	3	15	4	19	4	19	5	22	5	22	3
4	12	62	13	65	14	67	15	70	16	72	17	73	18	75	4
5	22	110	23	111	25	116	26	116	28	121	29	120	30	120	5
6	32	154	34	158	36	161	38	163	40	166	42	168	44	170	6
7	43	199	45	201	47	202	50	207	52	208	54	208	57	212	7
8	54	241	56	241	59	244	62	248	65	250	68	253	71	254	8
9	65	279	68	282	71	283	75	289	78	290	81	290	85	294	9
10	77	319	80	319	84	323	88	327	91	326	95	328	99	330	10
11	88	351	92	354	96	356	100	358	104	359	109	363	113	364	11
12	99	381	103	382	108	386	113	390	118	393	122	392	127	395	12
13	111	411	116	415	121	418	126	420	131	421	136	422	142	426	13
14	123	440	128	442	134	446	138	447	145	450	151	453	157	455	14
15	135	466	141	469	147	472	153	475	159	477	165	478	172	482	15
16	148	493	154	495	161	500	167	501	174	504	180	505	187	507	16
17	161	517	168	521	174	522	181	525	188	527	196	532	203	533	17
18	174	540	181	543	189	548	196	549	203	551	211	554	219	557	18
19	188	564	195	565	203	569	211	572	219	575	227	577	235	578	19
20	202	586	210	589	218	591	226	593	234	595	243	598	251	599	20
Age 60	389	779	384	769	378	757	373	747	367	735	360	721	354	709	Age 60
Age 65	473	832	468	823	464	816	459	807	454	798	448	788	442	777	Age 65

END OF POLICY YEAR	AGE 35 CASH	AGE 35 PAID-UP	AGE 36 CASH	AGE 36 PAID-UP	AGE 37 CASH	AGE 37 PAID-UP	AGE 38 CASH	AGE 38 PAID-UP	AGE 39 CASH	AGE 39 PAID-UP	AGE 40 CASH	AGE 40 PAID-UP	AGE 41 CASH	AGE 41 PAID-UP	END OF POLICY YEAR
1	—	—	—	—	—	—	—	—	—	—	—	—	—	—	1
2	—	—	—	—	—	—	—	—	—	—	—	—	—	—	2
3	6	25	6	24	7	27	8	30	8	29	9	31	9	30	3
4	19	76	20	77	21	78	22	79	23	80	24	81	26	85	4
5	32	124	34	127	35	126	37	128	39	131	40	130	42	132	5
6	46	171	48	172	50	173	52	174	55	178	57	178	59	178	6
7	60	215	62	215	65	217	68	220	71	222	74	223	77	225	7
8	74	256	77	257	80	258	84	262	87	262	91	265	95	268	8
9	89	297	92	296	96	299	100	301	104	303	108	304	113	308	9
10	104	335	108	336	112	337	117	340	121	340	126	343	131	345	10
11	118	367	123	369	128	372	133	374	138	375	143	376	149	380	11
12	133	399	138	400	143	401	149	405	155	407	161	410	167	412	12
13	148	429	153	429	159	432	166	436	172	438	178	439	185	442	13
14	163	457	169	458	176	462	182	463	189	465	196	468	204	472	14
15	179	485	185	486	192	488	200	492	207	494	214	495	222	499	15
16	194	509	202	513	209	514	217	518	224	518	232	521	240	524	16
17	210	534	218	537	226	539	234	542	242	544	250	545	259	549	17
18	227	559	235	561	243	562	252	566	260	567	269	570	278	573	18
19	243	580	252	583	261	586	269	587	278	589	287	591	297	595	19
20	260	602	269	604	278	606	287	608	296	610	306	613	316	616	20
Age 60	347	695	339	679	332	665	324	649	315	631	306	613	297	595	Age 60
Age 65	436	767	430	756	423	744	416	732	409	719	401	705	393	691	Age 65

Figure 6.8   (continued)

7 RETIREMENT INCOME

1. To identify major sources of retirement income.

2. To explain the sources of funding, eligibility criteria, and tax treatment of the following public income security programs:
   (a) Old Age Security
   (b) Guaranteed Income Supplement
   (c) Spouse's Allowance
   (d) Canada Pension Plan (retirement benefits)

3. To explain the following terms associated with the Canada and Quebec Pension Plans: year's basic exemption, year's maximum pensionable earnings, contributory earnings.

4. To explain the following terms associated with private pensions: portability, vesting, defined contributions, defined benefits.

5. To compare public and private pension plans regarding: coverage of the population, portability, indexing.

6. To explain the annuity principle.

7. To distinguish between the risk covered by life insurance and that covered by a life annuity.

8. To distinguish between the following pairs of terms associated with annuities:
   (a) annuity and annuitant,

(b) accumulation and liquidation periods,

(c) instalment and single-payment purchases,

(d) deferred and immediate annuities,

(e) straight life and certain-period annuities.

9. To distinguish among these types of annuities: refund annuity, escalating annuity, joint and last survivorship annuity, and variable annuity.

10. To identify factors that affect the cost of an annuity.

11. To explain how the use of before-tax or after-tax dollars affects the income tax treatment of annuity income.

12. To examine costs and benefits of buying a life annuity.

13. To explain how the use of an RRSP can enhance financial security in retirement.

14. To outline the rules regarding contribution limits, spousal plans, the number of RRSPs per person, borrowing from an RRSP, withdrawals before maturity, and the death of the RRSP owner.

15. To examine costs and benefits of the four RRSP maturity options.

Introduction

For the student concerned about getting started in a career, retirement certainly seems like an abstraction for later consideration. It is, however, not only the young who defer thinking about retirement. There is a tendency for people of all ages to postpone their retirement planning in the belief that it can best be dealt with when the time comes. Not only do we not want to think about it, we also have an expectation that somehow there will be enough money to live comfortably after retiring, although we may not have any idea how this will come about. The intent of this chapter is to increase your awareness of financial planning for retirement and to convince you to get an early start, rather than leaving your financial future to chance.

The two key questions in financial planning for retirement are: (i) where will the money come from, and (ii) will there be enough? Generally, retirement involves a change in income sources: from employment earnings to pensions and investments. Decisions you make during your working years will have an impact on what you will be able to afford during your retirement years. Although you may become eligible for certain retirement pensions without exerting much initiative, effort will be required to create income-producing assets. If you save and invest while you are in the labour force you can build up assets to support your retirement. Determining how much you will need is more difficult, and the younger you are the more uncertainty there will be about future economic conditions and your probable lifestyle. Some of the references listed at the end of the chapter outline methods of making estimates of future needs. Expect your predictions to increase in accuracy as you get closer to retirement.

How to save and invest to develop the assets that will fund your retirement will be discussed in some detail in later chapters, here the emphasis is on why you will need the savings. This chapter is concerned with identifying sources of retirement income, outlining public and private pension plans, and examining annuities and registered retirement savings plans.

Financial Planning for Retirement

Retirement planning requires a long-term perspective on your personal finances. You will recall from Chapter 1 that you can expect, over your lifetime, to have more variability in your income than in living costs, and that the positive gap between income and expenditures will usually be greatest in the middle years (Figure 1.1, Chapter 1). Then, when earnings cease at retirement, you will have to depend on income from pensions and investments. What you do about pensions and investments during your working years will have a significant bearing on how much retirement income you will have.

The basic rule in planning for retirement income is to begin saving early.

Recognize that you must increase your net worth if you want to achieve financial independence and be able to maintain your preferred lifestyle in retirement. It is truly amazing how, due to the magic of compounding, small regular savings continued over a long period can grow to a substantial sum. Generally, this is to be preferred over attempting to save a great deal during the last few years before retiring. Since it is difficult to predict exactly when you will retire—you may fall ill or decide to retire early—it could be unwise to leave saving for retirement until the last few years.

Sources of Retirement Income

Where will your retirement income come from? If you have been in the labour force, you can expect to receive retirement benefits from the Canada or Quebec Pension Plan and perhaps a pension from your employer. When you reach age 65 you will receive the Old Age Security pension, if the federal government continues the program until that time. The total of these three pensions will surely be less than your pre-retirement income. How can you fill the gap? If you want to maintain your accustomed level of living, you will need income from personal investments.

The major sources of retirement income may be summarized as:

Pensions
Old Age Security (if age 65 or over and meet residence requirement)
Canada or Quebec Pension (if age 60 or over and a contributor)
Employment-related pension (if a contributor or member)

Investment Income
RRSPs converted to annuity or RRIF
Annuities
Interest, dividends
Rent
Business income

You will note that there are certain eligibility requirements for pension benefits, such as age, residence, or having been a contributor to (or member of) the plan during your working life. If you decide to retire early you will have to wait until age 65 for the Old Age Security pension, and until at least age 60 for a Canada/Quebec Pension. If you are a member of an employment-related pension plan, you will probably take a reduced pension should you retire before age 65.

INCOMES OF THE RETIRED

Where do people already retired obtain their incomes? The data presented in Figure 7.1, collected in 1985, illustrate the income pattern by age and gender of those over age 65. Each bar represents the percentage distribution of all the income of one age and gender group. It will be helpful in interpreting these data to know that, regardless of age, males had average incomes about one and a half times larger than females, and that incomes for both men and women declined somewhat with age.

It is evident that the pattern of income sources differed by age and gender. A striking point is the extent to which women depended on Old Age Security (OAS) or the Guaranteed Income Supplement (GIS): these public pensions comprised about 40-50 percent of their incomes. The differential access to Canada or Quebec Pension Plan (CPP/QPP) benefits is apparent. Older men had limited opportunities to participate because the plans did not collect contributions until 1966 and did not pay full benefits until 1976. The restricted labour force participation of many of the women represented in these data excluded them from benefits. Overall, public pension plans (OAS/GIC and CPP/QPP) provided over one-half of all women's income and slightly less of men's.

The combination of private or employment-related pensions and investment income comprised around forty percent of retirement income. Private pensions represented a larger share of income for men as a result of their more sustained labour force participation. Investment income, representing about twenty percent of total income in 1971, has increased in importance over the years. By 1985 those over age 65 received nearly twenty-five percent of their income from investments. A significant income source for men aged 64-69 is part-time employment, as reflected in the category "other."

We will review some highlights of public and private pension plans before looking more closely at two ways to create retirement income from investments: (i) annuities that convert funds into a lifetime income, and (ii) registered retirement savings plans that accumulate funds in a tax shelter.

PUBLIC PENSIONS

The federal, provincial, and municipal governments provide a variety of social security programs, some of which are intended to provide benefits for older or retired persons. The major source of public retirement pensions is from federal programs, but, in addition, some provinces and the territories (Nova Scotia, Ontario, Manitoba, Saskatchewan, Alberta, British Columbia, the Northwest Territories, and the Yukon) supplement the incomes of those in need.

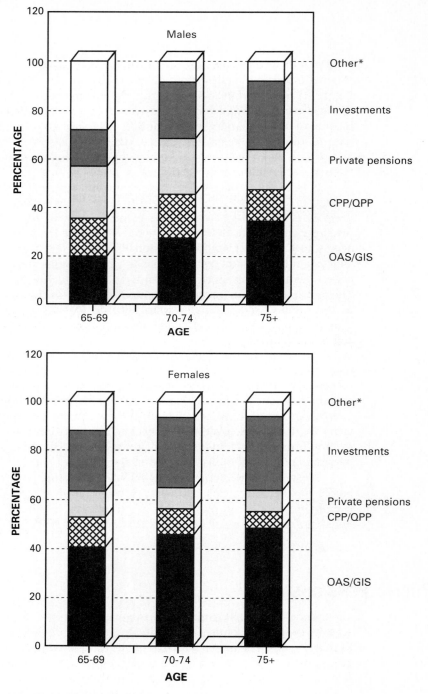

*Includes earnings from employment.

Figure 7.1 INCOME COMPARISON OF PERSONS AGED 65 AND OVER BY GENDER AND AGE, CANADA, 1985

Source: Gail Oja, *Pensions and Incomes of the Elderly in Canada, 1971-1985*, Statistics Canada. Ottawa: Supply and Services Canada, 1988, Table I1 (page 105). (Catalogue number 13-548). Reproduced and edited with the permission of the Minister of Supply and Services Canada, 1991.

Public Retirement Pensions

Federal	*Eligibility Criteria*
Old Age Security	age, residence
Guaranteed Income Supplement	age, residence, need
Spouse's Allowance	age, residence, need
Canada Pension Plan	age, contributor

Provincial	
QPP for Quebec residents	age, contributor
Income support programs	need

OLD AGE SECURITY (OAS)

The two eligibility criteria for Old Age Security pensions are age and residence: the applicant must be aged 65 and have lived in Canada for a substantial period. Details of the residence requirements are rather complex, but essentially require at least ten years residence prior to application. The pension is paid to eligible persons if they apply for it, regardless of any other income they may have, and is taxable.

CLAWBACK OF OAS   The 1989 federal budget introduced measures requiring high-income individuals to repay old age security benefits, at a rate equal to 15 percent of net income in excess of $50 000, up to the total of the pension. For each dollar of net income (income after deductions) over $50 000, 15 cents will be taxed until all is taxed back. Those with net incomes of about $60 000 will be repaying the entire OAS benefit.

INDEXATION   The OAS is fully indexed and adjusted quarterly, which means that every three months the pension amount is increased by the inflation rate of the previous quarter. At the beginning of 1990 the OAS was $340.07 per month or about $4095 a year.

SUPPLEMENTS TO OLD AGE SECURITY

Persons who receive Old Age Security but have little or no other income may apply for the *Guaranteed Income Supplement* (GIS). The amount depends on other income, and whether the pensioner is single or married. There is a sliding scale, with the supplement reduced by $1 a month for each $2 of other income. To simplify matters for the recipient, OAS and GIS benefits are combined in one monthly cheque. Like the OAS, the GIS is adjusted quarterly by the inflation rate, but unlike the OAS, it is not taxed.

The *Spouse's Allowance* pays a pension to the spouse of an Old Age Security pensioner if the spouse is between the ages of 60 and 64, meets residency requirements, and is otherwise eligible for the GIS. This allowance is payable if the combined income of the couple is below a certain amount; it is not taxable.

Canada Pension Plan (CPP)

This federal plan was established in 1966 to provide a measure of economic security for three categories of people: the retired, the disabled, and the dependent survivors of contributors. The province of Quebec, which decided not to participate in the Canada Pension Plan, set up the companion Quebec Pension Plan. There is complete portability between the two plans for those who move into or out of Quebec.

CONTRIBUTIONS   During your working years, you and your employer are required to make contributions to the Canada or Quebec Pension Plan, and at retirement you will receive a lifetime pension. The amount of the pension will be dependent on the length of time you were in the labour force and the amount contributed. The information that follows applies to the Canada Pension Plan; if you live in Quebec you are advised to find out specific details for the Quebec Pension Plan.

The rules for contributions are that each employee must contribute a certain portion of earnings, called *contributory earnings*, which is matched by the employer (the self-employed must contribute both the employee and employer shares of contributory earnings). The contribution rate for employees, which was 2.2 percent of contributory earnings in 1990, is being escalated annually by .1 percent until 1991, and by .075 percent until 2011. Thus the rate became 2.3 percent in 1991, and so on to 3.8 percent in 2011. The terminology used in calculating contributions is shown in Figure 7.2.

The maximum pensionable earnings figure has been changing annually in recent years in response to public demand that we be allowed to make larger contributions in order to qualify for larger pensions. Using 1990 figures, the "Contributions to Canada Pension" example on the next page shows how an employee's contributions are calculated.

BENEFITS   The exact amount of CPP benefits you will receive is determined by your prior contributions and the inflation rate, as each January the benefit levels are adjusted by the inflation rate of the previous year. The benefits are taxable. To suggest the scope of benefits from public pensions, a person retiring in 1990 could receive a maximum of about $6925 from CPP and $4095 from OAS, making a total of $11 020 a year.

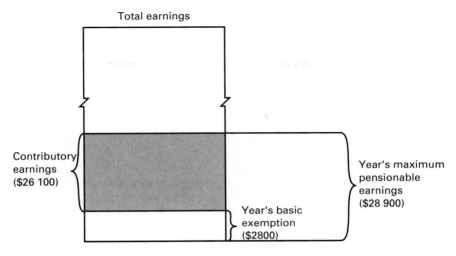

Figure 7.2   TERMINOLOGY ASSOCIATED WITH CPP/QPP CONTRIBUTIONS
(1990 AMOUNTS)

CONTRIBUTIONS TO CANADA PENSION

Alice's earnings in 1990	$41 000
Year's basic exemption	2 800
Year's maximum pensionable earnings	28 900
Contributory earnings ($28 900 − 2 800)	26 100

In 1990 Alice paid 2.2% of $26 100 or $574.20 into the
CPP, and her employer paid the same.

PRIVATE PENSIONS

Private retirement pensions may be arranged from personal savings, but generally when we speak of *private pensions* we mean employment-related ones. Look
upon these terms as synonyms: registered pension plans (RPP), company
pension plans, private pension plans, employer-sponsored pension plans.
Essentially, private pension plans are a way of deferring a portion of your
wages until retirement. There is, however, no uniformity in the benefits from
private pension plans, nor is there universal coverage of paid workers in

Canada. Slightly more than half of all full-time workers are members of private pension plans, the majority of these employed by some level of government or by Crown corporations. This means that many workers are not in private pensions plans and will have to depend on public pensions and their own savings when they retire.

DEFINED CONTRIBUTIONS OR DEFINED BENEFITS

Most private pension plans are *contributory*, that is, employees pay a percentage of their wages to the plan in addition to whatever the employer contributes. Some plans are non-contributory, with all funds coming directly from the employer.

There are two main types of private pension plans: defined contribution and defined benefits. A *defined contribution* or *money purchase* pension plan has rules about the amount to be contributed by the employer and employee, but no promises about the size of the retirement pension. The contributions credited to your pension account, plus interest, will be available at retirement to purchase an annuity for you. A *defined benefits* plan has a formula for calculating your retirement pension that usually depends on years of service and average wages during the last five years. With this plan, the employer promises a certain level of retirement benefits. For the long-service employee, the defined benefits plan is usually preferable to defined contributions. Some employers prefer defined contributions because they have no pension liability to fund as they do with defined benefits.

Although about 90 percent of current private pension plans are defined-benefit the trend is changing. Some employers, finding the new pension regulations onerous, are shifting the risks to employees by setting up defined contribution plans or group RRSPs. Thus, contributions are made to a retirement fund for employees but the employer does not promise any particular level of pension and has less obligation for the effects of future inflation rates or maximizing the yield from the invested pension funds.

PENSION REFORM

During the 1980s, much attention was given to improving the benefits provided by private pension plans. The Federal and Ontario governments, who employ about one-third of pension members, took the leadership in implementing significant reforms. Employment-related pensions fall under provincial jurisdiction and although many provinces are legislating changes, there is at present no uniformity of rules. Important issues in pension reform are: vesting, portability, survivor benefits, and indexation. We will examine each in turn.

VESTING   It is usual for you, as an employee, not to have *vesting rights* until you have worked for the employer for a specified number of years—it used to

be ten, but this is being reduced. For instance, vesting occurs after one year in Saskatchewan, two years in Quebec, Ontario, and for federal employees, and five years in Alberta and Manitoba. If you leave the job before acquiring vesting rights, you will receive a refund of your contributions to the pension fund with interest, but no rights to the amounts contributed by your employer. However, if you leave after you have vesting rights, you will make no more contributions to that pension plan but will still be eligible for retirement benefits. You may have the option of leaving your pension credits with your former employer for a deferred pension at retirement, having your pension credits transferred to a locked-in RRSP, or less likely, transferring the credits to your new employer, or perhaps having your pension funds put into a deferred annuity.

PORTABILITY   Often, when you change jobs, you cannot transfer your pension credits. The lack of *portability* in private pensions has long been a serious problem. A limited degree of portability among certain institutions does exist, but if you did not stay long enough for vesting, all too often a change of job means a loss of pension rights and having to start over in another pension plan. Some of the options for handling the pension credits of those with vesting rights listed above offer a solution to the portability problem. You would have to analyze the costs and benefits of the various options to see which would make a better contribution to your retirement income.

SURVIVOR BENEFITS   Provision of a pension for a surviving spouse has been more common in pension plans for government employees than for those employed in private industries. However, it is now required in Ontario, Alberta, Nova Scotia, and for federal plans, that 60 percent of pension benefits be made to a surviving spouse. Also, if you should die before retirement, your spouse would be eligible for a 60 percent pension.

INDEXATION   Although public pensions are fully indexed, many occupational plans do not have either full or partial indexing. In 1986, about 67 percent of members of public sector (government) plans were provided with full or partial indexation in contrast to about seven percent in the private sector. The limiting factor is the unknown cost. Employers have been reluctant to promise fully indexed pensions for retirees because of uncertainty about their future liabilities and many employees, with more of a present than future orientation, may be averse to reducing take-home pay by making larger contributions to the pension plan to cover future indexing. Among those not yet retired, there may be a lack of awareness of how a fixed pension can be eroded by inflation. For example, with inflation at only four per cent a year, an unindexed pension will lose about a third of its purchasing power in ten years and half in 18 years. If inflation is six percent, purchasing power will be reduced by half in only twelve years. The Province of Ontario has made a commitment to the principle of partially indexing private pensions but has not yet implemented any new rules.

KNOW YOUR PLAN   As one employee you may not have much influence on the pension benefits from your plan, but you can at least become informed about the plan to which you are making contributions. Pension benefits vary so widely that it is wise to ask the following questions:

(a)   Is the plan defined-benefit or defined-contribution?
(b)   If defined-benefit, what formula will be used to calculate pension benefits?
(c)   Are there provisions for early retirement?
(d)   What happens if you should become disabled?
(e)   What are the survivor benefits?
(f)   Will your estate receive any of the employer's contributions?
(g)   Is it possible to split pension credits in the case of marriage breakdown?

LIFE ANNUITIES

At retirement, there may be a need to transform life savings into an income stream and one way to accomplish this is to purchase an annuity. For instance, pension funds or RRSPs may be invested in annuities to produce a monthly income for life. The following discussion of annuities will explain the basic annuity principle and the various ways in which annuities may be bought and paid out.

At retirement, not knowing how long you may live, you face the question of whether to use some of your capital, and at what rate. If you spend too rapidly you may outlive your resources, but if you are too cautious you may scrimp more than necessary. A method of making sure your savings last as long as you do has been devised; it is called a life annuity. The process of liquidating a sum of money through a series of equal payments, made at regular intervals, is called an *annuity*. When you hear someone talking about annuitizing a sum of money, they mean converting it into a monthly income. Originally annuity payments were annual—hence the name annuity—but now they may be monthly, semi-annual, or annual. It is usually safe to assume that the income payment will be monthly, unless stated otherwise.

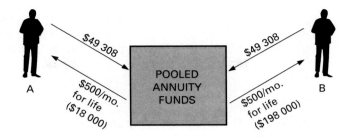

Figure 7.3   EXPERIENCES OF TWO LIFE ANNUITANTS

Accumulation period: At age 65, both A and B purchased immediate, straight life annuities with lump sums of $49 308.

Liquidation period: Immediately A and B began receiving payments of $500 a month, which would continue for life.

A died at age 68 after receiving payments for three years or a total of 36 × $500 = $18 000.
B died at age 98 after receiving payments for 33 years or a total of 33 × 12 × $500 = $198 000.

THE ANNUITY PRINCIPLE

There are two possible ways of protecting yourself against the risk of outliving your savings: either (i) acquire sufficient net worth, or (ii) buy a life annuity. A life annuity, like insurance, is a way of pooling resources with others to ensure that all will be protected against a given risk. Life insurance companies, the only financial institutions that may sell *life annuities*, accept the savings of many people and in return promise each a life income. Those who live a very long time will receive more from the pooled funds than those who die sooner, but all will receive an income as long as they live. It must be emphasized that insurance companies do not promise that you will receive as much as you contributed, as is illustrated in Figure 7.3. A life annuity can be useful for a person with modest means who is more concerned about protecting his or her level of living than creating an estate for heirs.

When you buy a life annuity you make a contract with a life insurance company that, in exchange for a sum of money, the company will pay you, the *annuitant*, a life income of a specified amount from a certain age onward. As an annuity buyer you predict that you will live for a very long time, but the company knows that a certain proportion of annuitants will not. You have covered the risk of outliving your savings and will also receive a larger monthly income than if you had used only the income from your capital, because an annuity includes a gradual liquidation of capital.

Some misconceptions about annuities stem from not understanding the annuity principle. Do not think of an annuity as a way of making money, but rather as *a way of converting a sum of money into a life income*. This principle is illustrated in the following example.

SHOULD HE USE SOME OF HIS CAPITAL?

George, who has just reached age 65, is considering ways of converting his savings of $150 000 into an income stream for his retirement. He is looking at two possibilities. Option A is to deposit the funds and use the interest, which, based on a prediction of eight percent return on average, would generate $1000 per month. At his death the capital would be intact for his heirs,and in the meantime he would have control over the investment.

Another option (B) is to buy a life annuity that would provide George with a guaranteed income of about $1670 a month for life. Why is this annuity income larger than the interest he could earn from depositing the same sum of money? The annuity payments are composed of both interest and capital, since annuities are a way of gradually liquidating capital. Of course, at George's death the annuity payments would cease and none of this capital would be available for heirs.

If a comfortable life in his old age is more important to George than leaving an estate, he should be using some of his capital. But the problem is how fast to use it when he cannot predict his life expectancy. He could use his capital too quickly and perhaps face some lean years in his old age, or he could be too cautious, making do with less. However, if George buys an annuity, his savings are added to those of others, creating a fund that can provide life incomes for all.

The two options George considered are shown diagrammatically in Figure 7.4.

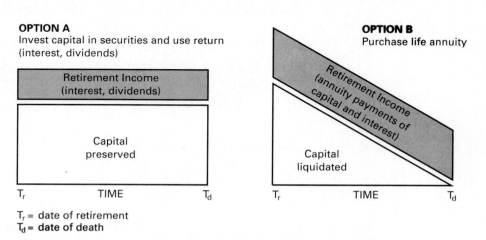

OPTION A
Invest capital in securities and use return (interest, dividends)

Retirement Income (interest, dividends)

Capital preserved

OPTION B
Purchase life annuity

Retirement Income (annuity payments of capital and interest)

Capital liquidated

T_r = date of retirement
T_d = date of death

Figure 7.4   OPTIONS FOR GENERATING RETIREMENT INCOME

Characteristics of Annuities

Your understanding of annuities will be enhanced if you are aware of some important characteristics of annuities such as:

(a) the distinction between the accumulation and liquidation periods,

(b) the method of paying the purchase price,

(c) when the liquidation period is to start,

(d) the number of lives covered,

(e) the refund features.

ACCUMULATION AND LIQUIDATION PERIODS   There are two stages associated with life annuities: (i) the *accumulation period* or the interval during which you pay the insurance company for the annuity, and (ii) the *liquidation period* that begins at the time you receive regular payments from the insurer (Figure 7.5). The accumulation period can last for many years if you choose to buy an annuity by instalments, or be very brief if you make your purchase with a lump sum. Regardless, the accumulation period must be completed before the liquidation period may start.

METHOD OF PAYING   If you have sufficient money to buy an annuity with a lump sum, it will be a *single payment annuity*. The other alternative is to buy

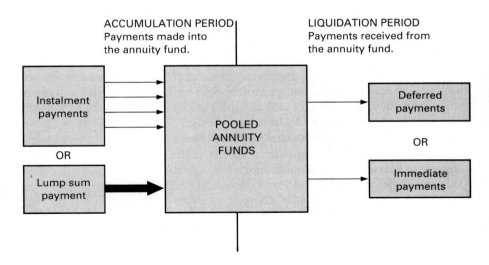

ACCUMULATION PERIOD
Payments made into
the annuity fund.

LIQUIDATION PERIOD
Payments received from
the annuity fund.

Instalment payments

OR

Lump sum payment

POOLED ANNUITY FUNDS

Deferred payments

OR

Immediate payments

Figure 7.5   PAYMENT OPTIONS DURING THE ACCUMULATION AND LIQUIDATION PERIODS OF A LIFE ANNUITY

the annuity gradually, over a number of years, by a series of regular *instalments* or premiums. The instalment method is useful for a person who needs a contractual savings plan, but others may prefer the flexibility of accumulating capital in their own hands and determining later whether to buy an annuity.

STARTING THE LIQUIDATION PERIOD   You may arrange for the proceeds from an annuity to be paid immediately or deferred. An *immediate annuity* will start regular payments to the annuitant at once. By definition, an immediate annuity must be bought in a single payment, since all payments for an annuity must be completed before the liquidation period begins. With a *deferred annuity* the liquidation period is some time after purchase, but the purchase may be made by either single payment or by a series of premiums. For instance, a young person who has inherited a sum of money could decide to use it to buy a single payment, deferred annuity that would begin payments when he or she is older.

NUMBER OF LIVES COVERED   The simplest and cheapest form of life annuity is the *straight life annuity*, that pays an income for the life of the annuitant and ceases at death, with no further payments to beneficiaries. An annuity may be designed to produce a life income for more than one person or, quite commonly, for two. A couple may buy a *joint-life-and-last-survivorship annuity*, guaranteeing income until both are dead. The name of this annuity is derived from joint life, which pays as long as both are alive, and from last survivor, meaning that the annuity will continue during the lifetime of the survivor. These points are illustrated in Figure 7.6.

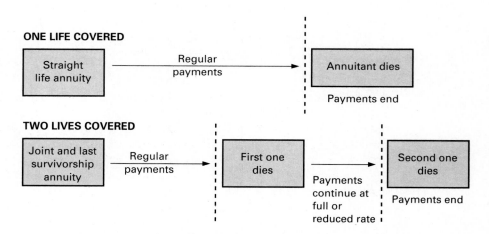

Figure 7.6   LIQUIDATION PAYMENTS BY NUMBER OF LIVES COVERED

Table 7.1   TWO LIFE ANNUITY OPTIONS FOR A COUPLE

Annuitant	Purchase price	Income per month
A. Straight Life Annuity—no certain period (Each has separate life annuity)		
Husband, age 65	$ 67 857	$ 750
Wife, age 62	76 094	750
Total, while both alive	143 951	1500
B. Joint and Last Survivorship Annuity—no certain period (Survivor to receive 50% of monthly income)		
Husband and wife	$143 344	$1500
Survivor		750

Not surprisingly, a joint-and-survivor annuity (to use the abbreviated name) is the most expensive of all annuities. The rates for the couple will be based on the woman's age because of her longer life expectancy and the possibility that she may be younger than her husband. The purchaser must decide whether, after the first one dies, the survivor will continue to receive the full payment or some proportion of it such as two-thirds or one-half. The cost of the joint-and-survivor annuity can be reduced if the payments are planned to decrease after the first death. Another possibility is to buy two separate life annuities, one on each life. Table 7.1 illustrates the costs of both alternatives.

ANNUITY CONTRACT   A sample annuity contract is presented in Figure 7.7 at the end of this chapter. What type of annuity is it?

REFUND FEATURES   As an annuitant, you may be interested in the refund features available during either the accumulation period or the liquidation period. If you should die during the accumulation period, or decide to discontinue payments, it would be desirable to have the amount already paid, plus interest, refunded to your estate or yourself, whichever is appropriate. Or, if you do not wish to continue payments, you may be given the option of converting to a smaller paid-up annuity.

Refund features during the liquidation period are very popular with buyers who worry that they may not live long enough to receive as much as they contributed. In response to this concern, life insurance companies have created annuity plans that include payments for a guaranteed length of time, or to a guaranteed minimum amount, regardless of whether the annuitant lives or dies. Because of these provisions, these plans are called *refund annuities*.

A very popular type of refund annuity is one with a minimum number of instalments guaranteed: for example, for ten years. A *life annuity with ten years certain* promises to make payments as long as the annuitant lives, but for a minimum of ten years regardless. If the annuitant should die within the first ten years of the payout period, a named beneficiary will receive a lump sum equivalent to the balance of payments that the annuitant would have received if he or she had lived until the end of the ten-year period. Note that the certain period refers to the minimum payment period, not the maximum. These ideas are summarized below.

REFUND FEATURES DURING THE ACCUMULATION AND LIQUIDATION PERIODS

ACCUMULATION PERIOD

Situations:

(i) Annuitant decides to stop paying.

 or

(ii) Annuitant dies before completing purchase of annuity.

Refund:

Contributions refunded.

LIQUIDATION PERIOD

Situation:

Annuitant has policy with 10 years certain but dies before 10 years.

Refund:

Sum equivalent to balance of payments remaining in the 10-year period are paid to beneficiary or to estate.

THE COST OF AN ANNUITY

Six factors influence the cost of an annuity:

(a) the size of the monthly payments desired,
(b) life expectancy (as influenced by age, gender, and health),
(c) interest rates,
(d) the length of the accumulation period,
(e) refund, or inflation protection features,
(f) number of lives covered.

SIZE OF PAYMENTS   You can approach the purchase of an annuity in one of two ways: either you are prepared to put a certain amount of money into an annuity and accept the income it will generate, or you want a specific monthly income and will pay the necessary amount to accomplish this. Most buyers of annuities are in the first group; they buy as much monthly income as their limited funds permit, well aware of the relation between cost and expected income.

LIFE EXPECTANCY   Although the price of an annuity is based on a number of factors, life expectancy is a critical one. Three variables used to predict life expectancy are gender, age, and health. Females, younger persons, and healthy persons are expected to live longer than males, older persons, or sickly persons, and therefore the company expects to make annuity payments to them for a longer time. Since this is more costly for the insurance company, the former group will receive a smaller monthly income from a given amount put into an immediate life annuity. The difference gender makes is shown in Figure 7.8.

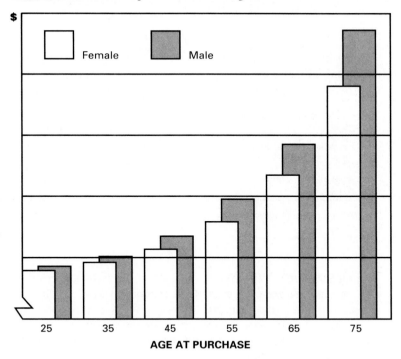

Figure 7.8   MONTHLY ANNUITY INCOME BY AGE AT PURCHASE AND GENDER (SINGLE PAYMENT, IMMEDIATE, STRAIGHT LIFE ANNUITY. ALL PURCHASERS PAY THE SAME PRICE.)

INTEREST RATES   A most important factor determining the cost of an annuity is the probable return that can be earned on your annuity funds while they are held by the insurance company. When interest rates are high, a sum of money can be turned into a higher level of annuity income than when interest rates are low. That is why financial advisors suggest, if possible, that you choose your time carefully when converting capital into an annuity.

LENGTH OF ACCUMULATION PERIOD   If you buy an annuity by instalments over many years, the total cost will be reduced because of the additional interest the company can earn during the longer time your premiums will be on deposit. For instance, if you compare the total cost of a certain level of annuity income (i) bought in instalments over 30 years, with (ii) an immediate annuity, you will find that the first one is less expensive (Table 7.2). Looked at another way, you could have invested the premiums yourself, let the interest compound, and bought an immediate annuity when you needed it.

Table 7.2   PURCHASE PRICE AND MONTHLY INCOME BY METHOD OF PURCHASE

Method of purchase	Purchase price	Monthly income
Single payment, immediate annuity bought at age 60	$204 853	$2 000
Instalment annuity; premiums paid from age 30 to 60. ($1132/yr)	33 960	2 000

Straight life annuity bought by a female with income to start at age 60.

REFUND FEATURES   If you wish to have a guaranteed period, this will add to the cost of an annuity because it changes the probabilities regarding the number of years the insurance company will have to make payments. This is illustrated in Table 7.3. The cost differences reflect the certainty of having to make payments for ten years, regardless of the annuitant's life expectancy.

The same point is made in Figure 7.9, which shows that, in general, a lump sum used to buy an immediate annuity will produce a lower monthly income if there is a refund feature. However, if the annuity is bought before age 45, the difference is small.

Table 7.3   PURCHASE PRICE BY GUARANTEED PERIOD

Type of annuity	Purchase price
Straight life—no certain period	$58 851
Life annuity—ten years certain	$62 242

Immediate annuity to provide a life income of $650 per month for a male, aged 65.

NUMBER OF LIVES COVERED   It will cost more to buy a life annuity to provide an income throughout the lifetimes of two people rather than one. In the case of a couple, the cost is related to gender and the age of the younger one. A younger wife is expected to live longer than her husband.

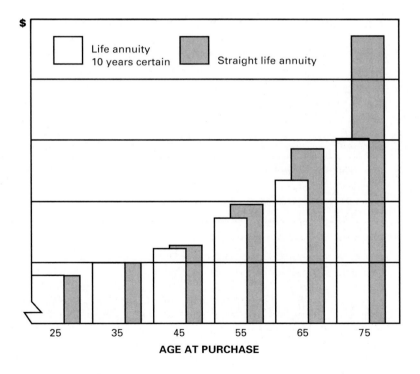

Figure 7.9   ANNUITY INCOME BY AGE AT PURCHASE AND GUARANTEED PERIOD (SINGLE PAYMENT, IMMEDIATE LIFE ANNUITY.)

BUYING AN ANNUITY

In preparation for her forthcoming retirement, Mrs. Alvarez is thinking of converting her three RRSPs to a life annuity to generate a dependable income. With no dependents and a distaste for investment management, she feels that an annuity would be her best choice. Her first thought was to call her life insurance agent and to ask her to make all the arrangements. However, Mrs. Alvarez talked about her plans to several friends, who advised her to consult an annuity broker who could perhaps give her some help. There would probably not be a charge for this service, since brokers get their commissions from the companies issuing annuities. She learned that an annuity broker can obtain quotations from many life insurance companies for a client.

On talking to a broker, she discovered that there was more to buying an annuity than she had supposed. The broker first familiarized himself with Mrs. A's financial situation, considering aspects such as other sources of retirement income, predicted marginal income tax rate, and needs of any dependents; then he presented several options to be considered. He mentioned that if a person's health was poor, she or he might, with the support of medical evidence, qualify for an impaired health annuity, that would pay a higher income for the same premium. Mrs. Alvarez asked the reason and was told that the insurer's liability is reduced if the annuitant is not expected to live long, making it possible for the company to pay a higher rate.

Two possible ways of preserving purchasing power, at least to some degree, were presented to her by the broker. She could investigate escalating annuities offered by some companies, or she could plan to buy a series of annuities in various years. The *escalating annuity* would pay a lower monthly income initially, but would be adjusted annually according to prevailing interest rates. Since an inflationary period would probably cause interest rates to rise she would receive higher annuity payments. If interest rates should fall, the company would not lower payments, but they would increase more slowly. Such escalating annuities are an example of one way that insurers have modified annuities to help preserve purchasing power in inflationary times.

Some brokers suggest that a client buy a series of annuities in different years to take advantage of changing interest rates. The premiums for annuities are very sensitive to the interest rates companies expect to receive on invested funds. Mrs. Alvarez could deregister one of her RRSPs to buy an annuity now, and do likewise with the other two in later years. She realizes that she must have all her RRSPs deregistered by the time she is seventy-one to comply with the income tax laws. In a period of rising interest rates this plan of buying a series of annuities could be advantageous, but if rates are falling, the reverse could be true.

Mrs. Alvarez knew that she wanted an immediate annuity, but she was undecided about the refund feature. She discovered that for a given premium, she could obtain a somewhat larger annual income with a straight life annuity than one with a ten-year guarantee. The broker asked her whether she would rather have the higher income, or the assurance that should she die before ten years, her estate would receive payments for the balance of the decade.

She was advised to make up her mind on the kind of annuity she wanted before the broker obtained quotations for her because annuity prices change rapidly, even daily. For this reason some companies will guarantee their quotations for only one to three days. Since rates vary, not only from time to time, but also among companies, the broker would seek quotations from quite a number of firms for Mrs. Alvarez.

VARIABLE ANNUITIES

Annuities usually provide a fixed income, not a particularly attractive feature to annuitants during periods of inflation. For instance, in 1950, a person may have thought that a deferred life annuity, that would pay $200 per month starting in 1975, would be adequate preparation for retirement. What she could not predict was that by 1975 a 1950 dollar would have lost half of its purchasing power, reducing the $200 per month to the equivalent of $100, and by 1990 it would be worth only $32.

In response to this problem, life insurance companies developed the *variable annuity*, which does not guarantee a specific income. Rather, it promises that the money paid in premiums will be invested in stocks and bonds, with the annuity payments varying according to the investment return. The higher expected return in inflationary times will be reflected in higher annuity payments.

BUYING A VARIABLE ANNUITY

Marg purchased a variable, deferred annuity at a premium of $50 a month. This money was used to buy accumulation units, the price of which varied from time to time. When Marg's first payment was received, the units were $5 each. Therefore, after subtracting $1.50 for expenses, she was credited with 9.7 units.

$$\$50 - \$1.50 = \$48.50$$

$$\frac{\$48.50}{5} = 9.7 \text{ units}$$

If the price of the units had risen to $5.30, her next month's payment would buy

$$\$50 - \$1.50 = \$48.50$$

$$\frac{\$48.50}{5.3} = 9.1 \text{ units}$$

When the accumulation period has been completed and Marg decides to start receiving annuity payments, her accumulation units will be converted to annuity units. This conversion takes place only once, the rate of conversion depending on mortality rates and the return on the company's annuity portfolio.

Suppose that Marg has acquired an entitlement to 100 annuity units per month, and the value of an annuity unit is $2.10 at that time. She would then receive a monthly income of $210 for the first year, after which the company may revise the value of an annuity unit depending on the success of the annuity portfolio. Marg's annuity income will fluctuate as the value of the portfolio supporting it does. Variable annuities are designed so that the annuitant's income varies with investment yields, which (it is hoped) in turn reflect changes in living costs resulting from inflation.

ANNUITIES AND INCOME TAX

The recipient of annuity payments will discover that the income tax treatment of this income is dependent on a number of factors. Since each payment includes both capital and interest, they may be treated separately. If the annuity was purchased with before-tax dollars (they were in a tax shelter, such as an RRSP) both capital and interest components of the income payments are now exposed to income tax. On the other hand, if the annuity was purchased with after-tax dollars (the annuity was not in a tax shelter) the capital portion is not taxable when received. The issuing company will provide the annuitant with annual statements showing the amount of the capital and interest portions. Recent changes to income tax rules require that, during the accumulation period of a deferred annuity, the owner must report the accrued interest at least every three years.

This discussion of annuities is intended to illustrate basic principles, not to describe all variations of annuities that may become available. Financial institutions are quite inventive in constantly creating new services for consumers.

WHETHER TO BUY AN ANNUITY

If you are considering buying an annuity, a number of factors should be reviewed before you make your decision. A major advantage of an annuity is that you will have a guaranteed, usually fixed, income and will not have to be concerned about managing your investments. Nor will you have to worry about how quickly to use your capital to ensure that it lasts as long as you do. On the other hand, you have lost flexibility in handling your money since, once you have bought an annuity, your capital has been committed. If a more beneficial investment opportunity should arise you will not be able to take advantage of it, but conversely, you will be protected against a depressed investment climate. A fixed income loses purchasing power in an inflationary period, but would be an advantage to you should prices fall.

There is no way that you can be sure that you will receive as much or more than you paid into the annuity, but how much does that matter to you? You will have a guaranteed life income, even if your heirs do not receive an estate. Of course, it is possible to put only a portion of your capital into an annuity, leaving a part to bequeath to others.

Annuities are not for everyone, but they are a useful way of making a small estate last for a lifetime. If you are in poor health, concerned about an estate for heirs, or have the time and inclination to manage your investments, you may be wise to put your money elsewhere. However, if you need a contractual savings plan to ensure that you have money for your retirement, a deferred annuity is a reasonable possibility.

REGISTERED RETIREMENT SAVINGS PLANS

WHAT IS AN RRSP?

A *registered retirement savings plan* (RRSP) is a way of sheltering savings from income tax by putting them in specific investments. This is how they work. When you invest your savings outside a tax shelter, you are using after-tax dollars and any income the investment earns, such as interest or dividends, is taxable. If, however, you put money into a RRSP, no tax is payable when you make the investment and the yield is not taxable while in the RRSP. Tax-exempt funds going into an RRSP are referred to as before-tax dollars. You may wish to refer to the diagram in Chapter 2 that illustrates this point.

Since this is only a tax deferment, all funds in RRSPs become taxable whenever they are removed from the tax shelter. The strategy is to put money into an RRSP when your marginal tax rate is high and take it out at a later date when your tax rate drops, usually because you have stopped working or retired. The example below demonstrates how income tax is deferred on RRSP funds.

TAX SHELTER DEFERS TAX

Year 1

Money put into a RRSP = $2000

No income tax on the $2000 to be paid that year.

If marginal tax rate is 40%, you save $800 in tax.

You leave the money in the RRSP for 10 years.

Interest earned was 8% on average, compounded annually, or $2320. No tax has been paid on the interest.

Year 10

You withdraw the funds.

Your marginal tax rate is 26%.

If you take out the $4320 in one year, you will pay about 4320 × .26 = $1123 in income tax.

Two widely-held misconceptions associated with RRSPs are: (i) that everyone needs an RRSP, and (ii) that an RRSP is a specific type of investment. With such energetic promotion of RRSPs, there is a tendency to forget that they are intended for one major purpose—to defer income tax. An RRSP is a way of sheltering savings from tax to allow them to grow at a faster rate than otherwise, and thus accumulate a fund for retirement or something else. If, however, you pay little or no income tax, you do not need an RRSP because you can invest your savings without the restrictions imposed on RRSPs. *An RRSP is not a specific type of investment, but a way of registering a variety of investments to shelter them and defer income tax.* As we will see, many kinds of investments may be put in an RRSP.

To repeat, the chief reason to put money into a registered retirement savings plan is the desire to defer income tax. Your savings will grow faster inside a tax shelter than outside and if you are able to take the money into income in future years, when your marginal tax rate can be expected to be lower, you can reduce your income tax. Refer to Chapter 2 for an explanation of marginal tax rate. The money in an RRSP is taxable eventually, whenever the plan is deregistered and the funds taken into income.

Putting money in an RRSP is investing, and you should take as much care in choosing an RRSP as you would in selecting any other investment. Do not be so caught up in the prospect of deferring income tax that you ignore what you are doing with your money. The principles of investing that are discussed in Chapters 9 to 11 apply to all RRSP decisions.

TYPES OF RRSPs

The *Income Tax Act* permits a broad range of investments to be used as RRSPs. Although some of these types may be unfamiliar to you, that should not matter at this stage. The focus of this chapter is on the tax shelter aspect of RRSPs and not the specifics of the various types of investment, each of which is treated in some detail in other chapters. The various investments acceptable for RRSPs may be categorized as follows:

A. **Guaranteed funds** (promised return of principal and guaranteed rate of return; available from most banks, trust companies, credit unions and life insurance companies)
   1. savings accounts
   2. term deposits or guaranteed investment certificates

B. **Mutual funds** (no promises about rate of return or safety of principal; available from mutual funds companies and agencies, and some trust companies and life insurance companies, and banks)
   1. equity funds
   2. bond funds
   3. balanced funds
   4. money market funds

C. **Self-administered RRSPs** (you make the investment decisions; available from trust companies and investment dealers), that may hold any combination of the following:
   1. cash
   2. treasury bills
   3. bonds, including Canada Savings Bonds
   4. mortgages
   5. mutual funds
   6. stocks

D. **Life insurance** (tied in with a life insurance policy; available from life insurance companies), or *life annuity*.

GUARANTEED FUNDS   These are the safest places to put your RRSP money as long as you are prepared to accept the lower return associated with the low risk. You are promised a return of your principal with interest, and your deposits (up to $60 000 per institution) are insured against loss. It is wise to inquire whether the plan you contemplate investing in is covered by deposit insurance, since there may be some exclusions.

Savings accounts in an RRSP, like any savings account, pay interest regularly at the prevailing rate without locking in the funds for a certain term. Higher interest is usually paid on term deposits or guaranteed investment certificates that promise a given interest rate and lock up the money for a stated term.

When choosing a guaranteed plan, check the following features:

(a) the interest rate,
(b) the frequency of compounding interest,
(c) when interest rates may be adjusted,
(d) the minimum deposit,
(e) the annual fees,
(f) registration, withdrawal, or other fees.

Many banks and trust companies have discontinued all fees on guaranteed funds RRSPs. It is worthwhile to do some comparison shopping before selecting a plan and an institution.

MUTUAL FUNDS   Without going into a detailed explanation of mutual funds (see Chapter 11), suffice it to say that it is a way of pooling the funds of many investors. Instead of actually buying stocks or bonds or mortgages, the investor buys a share in the mutual fund, which in turn invests in such securities. Professional fund managers make the investment decisions for the investors. There are over 250 different mutual funds sold in Canada and they are designed to achieve a range of investment objectives. Some funds are invested in common stock or equities, some in bonds or mortgages, and yet others, called money market funds, in treasury bills and other debt instruments.

Mutual funds are sold directly by some mutual funds companies, by mutual funds sales agents, and also by banks, trust companies, and life insurance companies which have their own funds. There may be costs the buyer has to pay, such as sales commissions (up to nine percent of the initial investment), annual management fees (one to two percent), and sometimes withdrawal fees.

You would use mutual funds for your RRSP if you are prepared to accept more risk than accompanies guaranteed funds, in exchange for the possibility of greater return. There will be no assurance that you will get back your investment or any income from it. Within mutual funds there is a wide spectrum of risk levels, so it is possible to find an appropriate fund for almost any objective.

SELF-ADMINISTERED PLANS   If you have time, expertise, and enough money to make it worthwhile, you might consider a self-administered RRSP that allows you to make your own investment decisions. A wider range of investment types may be held in a self-directed plan, such as Canada Savings Bonds, other bonds, stocks, treasury bills, or mortgages. You can shift your funds from one form of investment to another as you choose, and you can decide how much risk you wish to assume. Institutions that handle self-directed RRSPs, such as most investment dealers and some banks, trust companies, and life insurance companies, charge an annual fee of about $100, as well as commissions on some transactions.

LIFE INSURANCE PLANS   In addition to offering guaranteed funds and mutual funds, life insurance companies provide a combination of life insurance coverage and retirement saving, whereby the cash value is registered as an RRSP. Think carefully before having your RRSP money tied to life insurance coverage. The contract may require fixed annual payments that would limit your flexibility in annual contributions and in moving your RRSP money around. Since the fees and commissions tend to be heaviest in the early years, you would lose if you cancelled the contract after a short time.

Various types of annuities available from life insurance companies are eligible for RRSPs. The schedule of payments may be fixed or flexible. As with life insurance, there will be commissions payable in the early years.

CRITERIA FOR SELECTING AN RRSP

The stiff competition among financial institutions to sell RRSPs has resulted in considerable variety in the criteria and characteristics of the offerings. Before making a selection, as with any investment, you should identify your own objectives. Some questions you could ask yourself are:

1. *Does the RRSP fit in with my investment objectives?*
   How well will it complement my other investments in regard to risk, return, and liquidity?
2. *How much flexibility in contributions do I want?*
   Some RRSPs are contractual with an agreement at the outset to contribute a set amount at regular intervals. Such a plan does not permit a change in the contribution if circumstances change. Other plans require a minimum payment to keep the plan open, but otherwise are flexible; still others may not require an annual payment. When considering flexibility, it is important to remember that there is a maximum limit on annual RRSP contributions. If my income changes, my contribution limit will also change. Having only contractual plans could restrict my flexibility too much.

3. *Will the plan accept transfers of lump sums?*
    If I should change jobs and receive a refund of my pension contribu-
    tions, I may be interested in "rolling over" this lump sum into an
    RRSP in order to postpone paying income tax.
4. *Will there be a penalty if the fund is cashed in before maturity?*
    Suppose I find the performance of a fund unsatisfactory and wish
    to transfer the money to another RRSP. I need to know in advance
    whether this will be possible and, if so, whether the institution will
    exact a penalty or charge a fee.
5. *How much risk and return can be expected?*
    There is usually a trade-off between risk and return, with less risk
    associated with a lower return. What level is appropriate for me?
    Generally, the more distant the retirement date, the more the risk that
    can be handled. As I near retirement I will want to reduce the risk.
6. *How much will the administrative charges be?*
    Is there a sales charge taken off contributions, a management fee
    charged initially, annually or at maturity, redemption fees, or any
    other charge? What is the relation of the charges to the predicted
    yield? Looking for the lowest administrative charges may not always
    be the wisest move.

CONTRIBUTION LIMITS

Anyone with earned income (e.g., salary, wages, royalties, business income,
rental income, alimony) may contribute to a RRSP. The maximum annual
contribution depends on: (i) whether you are a member of a registered pension
plan (employer-sponsored) and, (ii) what type of plan it is. Beginning in 1990,
those not in registered pension plans can contribute 18 percent of the previous
year's earned income up to a specific maximum as follows:

1991	$11 500	1994	$14 500
1992	$12 500	1995	$15 500

For members of registered pension plans, the maximum annual contribution
is 18 percent of the previous year's earned income to the limits shown above,
less a pension adjustment. The pension adjustment will be calculated by
employers and Revenue Canada Taxation and notification sent to employees
late in the year. The calculation is different for defined benefit plans than
defined contribution plans. The intent of these rules is to adjust RRSP limits
to ensure that there is equity for employees who are in different pension plans.
Members of plans with generous benefits will not be able to contribute as
much to their RRSPs as those with more restricted benefits.

RRSP Carry Forward   If you cannot use your RRSP maximum in a particular year, the allowance may be carried forward for up to seven years. Therefore, if you are short of money one year but have more the next, you will not be penalized by your uneven capacity to invest in RRSPs.

Spousal Plans

You may contribute to an RRSP for your spouse, provided that the total you contribute to your own plan and the spousal plan is within your personal limits. The reason for setting up a spousal plan is that you expect, when the funds are taken out, that your spouse will have a marginal tax rate lower than yours. This can be a significant advantage at retirement if one spouse has little pension income. Not only does the family income become split between two people and thus reduce taxes, but the spouse can make use of the pension income deduction.

It is generally not possible to transfer funds from your RRSPs to that of your spouse, retroactively. Therefore, your contributions must be made from current income. The two situations when funds from your RRSPs can be transferred to your spouse without attracting income tax are: (i) at death, if you named your spouse as beneficiary, and (ii) after a marriage breakup, if the court orders a division of RRSPS.

There is a penalty if you set up a spousal RRSP and the spouse deregisters it a short time later. Your spouse must wait three years before taking out funds. Otherwise, you would be taxed on the withdrawals.

Other RRSP Rules

Locked-in RRSPs   To facilitate the portability of pensions, new pension rules make use of locked-in RRSPs. One of the options becoming available to employees leaving an employer is to transfer pension credits to a locked-in RRSP. Also, some employers are sponsoring locked-in RRSPs for employees rather than registered pension plans. At your retirement, the funds in a locked-in RRSP will be used to purchase an annuity for you.

How Many RRSPs?   There is no limit to the number of RRSPs an individual may have. Because of the variation in the types of plans and their yields, you may wish to establish more than one RRSP to diversify your assets.

Can You Borrow From Your RRSP?   You cannot borrow from your RRSP, but you may use the funds as security for a loan. The exact procedure is quite complex because of the way in which it must be reported on the income tax return.

WITHDRAWALS BEFORE MATURITY   You may withdraw money from your RRSP before it matures but you must pay income tax on the funds, including any interest or dividends earned by the plan to date.

DEATH OF THE RRSP OWNER   If you die before your plan matures, there will be a refund of premiums consisting of your contributions plus any yield accumulated in the plan. The income-tax treatment of this refund varies depending on the beneficiary of the refund. A spouse named as beneficiary has the option of rolling the refund over into his or her own RRSP without incurring any income tax, or of accepting the refund as a lump sum and paying the tax. For any beneficiary other than the spouse or certain categories of dependents, refunds from RRSPs will be treated as income of the deceased in the year of death and taxed accordingly.

WHO NEEDS AN RRSP?

If you have earned income and are paying a significant amount of income tax, putting money in RRSPs is a good idea. On the other hand, if you have money to invest but pay very little income tax you are better to forgo the restrictions of the RRSP. The financial press regularly publishes articles on RRSPs that emphasize the amount of tax deferred and the increase in savings possible with RRSPs. Whether this will be true for you depends on your marginal tax rate and the yield from the RRSP you choose. The example below illustrates two cases: one individual who put money into an RRSP, and another who did not.

HOW AN RRSP CAN INCREASE SAVINGS AND REDUCE TAX

Assumptions: 10% average return, compounded annually; started at age 35; marginal tax rate of 40%.

	No RRSP	With RRSP
For One Year		
Pre-tax amount available for investment	$1000	$1000
Taxes on $1000 @40%	400	Nil

Amount left for investment	$600	$1000
Investment yield @10%	60	100
Balance after first year	$660	$1100
For 30-year Period		
Pre-tax amount available over 30 years	$30 000	$30 000
Total amount invested	18 000	30 000
Tax paid on principal and interest @40%	33 520	Nil
Net return on investment	$20 281	$150 943
Value of retirement fund (principal plus interest)	$50 281	$180 943

Note: At the end of 30 years the income tax liability is not the same for the two examples. Income tax has been paid annually on the non-RRSP funds and no more is due. However, the tax-sheltered RRSP funds will become taxable whenever they are converted to income. Presumably the RRSP funds would be taken into income gradually, possibly when the owner's marginal tax rate is lower than 40 percent. Should they be taken out of the shelter in a lump sum after 30 years, the tax could be $180 943 × .40 = $72 377, leaving $108 565 after tax.

MATURITY OPTIONS

Sometime before the end of the year in which you turn 71, you must deregister all of your RRSPs. Deregistering means that you will be changing from accumulating savings to either (a) removing funds from the tax shelter and paying tax, or (b) a liquidation plan to provide income. You can choose one or any combination of these four options:

> *Removal from tax shelter*
> (1) withdraw the funds and pay the income tax
>
> *Income plan*
> (2) purchase a single-payment life annuity
> (3) purchase a fixed-term annuity
> (4) set up a registered retirement income fund (RRIF)

The first of these options differs from the others in that you move funds from the RRSP shelter into your own control. Once you have paid the tax, no more restrictions are imposed by Revenue Canada. The other options provide various ways to convert your RRSP funds into income gradually, over a number of years, and thus spread out your income tax liability. In these cases, the money does not come into your hands, but is transferred directly into the instrument you select. At maturity, you are free to move RRSP funds to other firms if you wish. You should do some comparison shopping before choosing an option and the company to handle it for you.

WITHDRAW THE FUNDS   Funds taken out of an RRSP will be subject to tax in the year they are withdrawn. If you wish to extract your money from the RRSPs and minimize tax, you could make a series of withdrawals over a number of years, or withdraw the funds in a year when your income is less than usual. Otherwise, a complete withdrawal of all RRSP funds at one time could result in a large tax bill.

SINGLE-PAYMENT LIFE ANNUITY   The funds are transferred directly from your RRSP to a life insurance company to buy a life annuity of your choice. You can choose among a variety of annuity products, some of which were mentioned earlier in this chapter. With a life annuity, you convert your RRSP savings into a life income, and pay tax each year on the amount received, effectively spreading the tax burden over your lifetime.

FIXED-TERM ANNUITY   Fixed term annuities are available from life insurance and trust companies, and are a way of gradually converting your RRSP funds into income. A fixed term annuity differs from a life annuity in being unrelated to life expectancy; there is no pooling of funds with others. Your funds are converted into an income stream that will continue until you reach the age of 90. However, if you do not live that long, the balance in your account will be refunded to your beneficiary or estate.

The term of such an annuity will be the number of years from the start until you reach age 90. The monthly payment will be dependent on the length of the term, the sum of money you have to put into the annuity, and interest rates. Later on, if you wish to take your money out of a term annuity, you can deregister it and pay the tax.

With fixed term or life annuities you may have the option of cancelling the contract and being paid the commuted value of the remaining payments. These can be taken out of the shelter and the tax paid, or can be rolled over into a RRIF.

REGISTERED RETIREMENT INCOME FUND   A RRIF is similar to a self-directed RRSP; you can make your own investment decisions if you wish. The same firms that handle RRSPs also look after RRIFs. The choice of possible investments includes savings accounts, term deposits, bonds, stocks, and mutual funds. When you are ready to deregister one or more RRSPs, do some comparison shopping to find terms that suit you.

Once you have set up your RRIF, payments may begin at any time. You are required to take out a minimum amount each year, but there is no maximum. With this flexibility you can manage your funds to provide income when needed, but you must be careful not to deplete your RRIF so quickly that there is not enough for later years.

The minimum annual withdrawal from a RRIF is the amount currently in the plan divided by the number of years until you will be 90. For instance, if there was $95 000 in your plan and you were aged 70, you must withdraw at least $4750 that year.

$$\frac{95\ 000}{90 - 70} = \frac{95\ 000}{20} = \$4750$$

The next year the minimum would be the value of the plan divided by 19, and so on.

Since you can have more than one RRIF, you have the option of diversifying your RRSP funds by using different firms or financial products. You could put some in various kinds of deposits administered by a bank and some in equity mutual funds held elsewhere. You can transfer funds from one RRIF to another if you wish, but it would be wise to find out any restrictions or fees that may be involved.

A RRIF may be set up so that you will be actively involved in the investment decisions, or if you do not wish to supervise it, you can have the funds put into fixed income securities that require little attention.

The advantage of a RRIF over the annuities is the freedom to choose the type of investment and to determine the amount to be withdrawn each year.

SUMMARY

The purpose of this chapter is to increase your awareness about possible sources of retirement income and the need to make preparations early in your working life. At present there are public pension programs, such as Old Age Security and the Guaranteed Income Supplement, that provide benefits to eligible people from the general revenue of the federal government. Those who have been in the labour force contribute to the Canada or Quebec Pension Plans, which pay benefits to the retired, to survivors of contributors, and a lump sum death benefit. About one-half of full-time employees are members of employment-related private retirement pension plans, which vary widely in their benefits.

Life annuities are a way of stretching a sum of money over a lifetime, providing protection against the risk of outliving your savings. By gradually liquidating the principal and interest a life income is created, but there will be no estate for heirs. There are various modifications of the basic life annuity to cover several lives, or to provide a refund if the annuitant dies shortly after starting to receive payments.

At retirement, most people will find public and private pensions inadequate to support their accustomed lifestyle and will need income from their own investments. RRSPs offer a way to invest tax-sheltered funds, permitting the income to compound tax-free until the plan is deregistered. A lower marginal tax rate after retirement makes it beneficial for most people to accumulate funds in RRSPs.

PROBLEMS

1. Use the following annuity quotations for this question. For each $1000 premium, monthly incomes are as follows:

Male, aged 65
    straight life annuity $11.20
    10 years certain $10.58
Female, aged 62
    straight life annuity $9.98
    ten years certain $9.77
Joint and last survivor, male 65, female 62
    no years guaranteed, 100% to survivor $9.45
    no years guaranteed, 50% to survivor $10.25

   (a) When Richard retires next year at age 65, he expects to have $70 000 to invest in immediate life annuities. His objective is to provide supplementary retirement income for himself and his wife, who will be 62, as well as income for her if he should predecease her. List three alternatives he might consider. Compare these options by making a chart with the following headings:
   (i) principal invested
   (ii) annual income
   (iii) advantages
   (iv) disadvantages.
   (b) Would Richard be better advised to invest the $70 000 in guaranteed income certificates at 10 percent for a five-year term? Analyze the consequences of this alternative.

2. Irma is due to retire in one year, and she is giving some thought to her retirement income. Her assets, in addition to her bungalow, are $20 000 in Canada Savings Bonds that pay annual interest, a five-acre piece of land that does not yield any income but may be sold sometime for building lots, a small portfolio of common stocks invested for capital gain that do not pay

much income, and a registered retirement savings plan that has grown to $38 000. She is wondering how to arrange her financial affairs in order to obtain the maximum income during her retirement years.

(a) Do you think she should sell her property and reinvest the money?
(b) She wonders whether to add any more money to the registered retirement savings plan. What information is needed to answer this question?
(c) Why does impending retirement require some review of her finances?

3. (a) Ian earned $43 000 in 1990. Did he have to contribute to the Canada Pension Plan? If so, how much? How much did his employer contribute for him? What is the contribution rate in 1992?
   (b) If Ian should die at age 55, will Ann, his widow and beneficiary, receive anything from CPP, his company pension plan, or his RRSPs?
   (c) If Ian dies during the accumulation period, will Ann receive anything from the deferred annuity he had been buying?
   (d) If Ian used his RRSP funds to purchase an immediate life annuity at age 65, with ten years certain, and lived to age 70, would his wife receive anything from this annuity?
   (e) If Ann buys a variable annuity, when will she learn the amount of her monthly retirement income from it?

4. Ella, aged 67, receives a private pension, the Canada Pension, and Old Age Security, as well as $11 000 a year from part-time employment and return on her investments. Last year she received a lump sum of $15 000 that did not qualify as capital gains. Can you suggest some alternatives for her, as she faces a heavy tax bill? Are there any tax shelters that she could use?

5. Decide whether you AGREE or DISAGREE with each of the following statements.

   (a) More than 80 percent of people now employed are members of occupation-related (private) pension plans.
   (b) If you have been a member of a private pension plan long enough to have obtained vesting rights, your pension automatically becomes portable if you should change jobs.
   (c) Canada Pension Plan benefits are not taxable.
   (d) If you are a contributor to a private pension plan you cannot also put money in an RRSP.
   (e) When an RRSP is deregistered, the funds must be taken out as an annuity.
   (f) You can avoid paying income tax on funds in an RRSP if you take the money out after you are 65; after that age, RRSP funds become tax-exempt.

(g) An annuity with a refund feature is cheaper to buy than a straight life annuity, other things being equal.

(h) The liquidation period of an annuity cannot start until the accumulation period is completed.

(i) The more lives covered by an annuity, the more it will cost, other things being equal.

6. How does the annuity principle differ from the life insurance principle?

7. Analyze the costs and benefits of buying an annuity to provide retirement income.

8. Suggest some pros and cons for contractual RRSPs.

9. These questions refer to the annuity contract in Figure 7.7 (at the end of the chapter).

(a) Is this a deferred annuity or an immediate one?

(b) Was it purchased by instalments?

(c) How much did it cost?

(d) How much will the monthly income be?

(e) How many lives are covered? What type of annuity is it?

(f) When will payments end?

(g) Are payments guaranteed for a certain number of years?

10. Use Figure 7.1 as a reference in deciding whether you AGREE or DISAGREE with each of the following statements.

(a) Regardless of age, females received higher payments from Old Age Security than males.

(b) Public pensions were a more significant source of income for women than for men.

(c) Compared to other elderly persons, women over age 75 had a greater dependence on benefits from the Canada and Quebec Pension Plans.

(d) Males received a larger share of income from private pension plans than females because of their greater labour force involvement and greater probability of being in jobs that had pension plans.

(e) For most elderly persons, investments provided an important source of income—generally over 20 percent.

(f) Regardless of gender, employment income represented a declining share of total income as age increased.

(g) Among persons over age 65, women were less likely than men to have employment income.

REFERENCES
Books

ANDERSON, BRIAN, and CHRISTOPHER SNYDER. *It's Your Money*. Sixth Edition. Toronto: Methuen, 1989, 264 pp. A reference for the general reader that includes financial planning, budgets, income tax, disability insurance, savings, investments, retirement planning, credit, wills, and estates.

BEACH, WAYNE, and LYLE R. HEPBURN. *Are You Paying Too Much Tax?* Toronto: McGraw-Hill Ryerson, annual, 206 pp. A tax planning guide for the general reader that includes a discussion of capital gains, RRSPs, and investment income.

BIRCH, RICHARD. *The Canadian Price Waterhouse Personal Tax Advisor*. Toronto: McClelland-Bantam, 1989, 199 pp. A non-technical guide prepared by tax accountants that outlines how the tax system works and explains the basics of personal income tax, including RRSPs.

BIRCH, RICHARD. *The Family Financial Planning Book, A Step-by-Step Moneyguide for Canadian Families*. Toronto: Key Porter, 1987, 216 pp. An easy-to-read guide to taking control of your personal finances that discusses budgets, income tax, insurance, RRSPs, mortgages, and investments.

COHEN, DIAN. *Money*. Scarborough, Ontario: Prentice-Hall Canada, 1987, 270 pp. An economist suggests strategies for coping with personal finances in the context of changing economic conditions. Topics include financial plans, buying a home, insurance, income tax, retirement, estate planning, and investments.

COTE, JEAN-MARC, and DONALD DAY. *Personal Financial Planning in Canada*. Toronto: Allyn and Bacon, 1987, 464 pp. A comprehensive personal finance text that includes financial planning, income tax, annuities, pensions, investments, credit, mortgages, wills, with particular attention to the banking and insurance industries.

DELANEY, TOM. *The Delaney Report on RRSPs*. Toronto: McGraw-Hill Ryerson, annual, 280 pp. In addition to a comprehensive treatment of RRSPs (types, how to select, and maturity options), private and public pensions plans are explained and suggestions given for planning financial security.

DELOITE, HASKINGS, SELLS. *How to Reduce the Tax You Pay*. Revised Edition. Toronto: Key Porter Books, 1989, 245 pp. A non-technical guide, prepared by tax accountants, that explains the basics of personal income tax.

DRACHE, ARTHUR B. C., and SUSAN WEIDMAN SCHNEIDER. *Head and Heart, Financial Strategies for Smart Women*. Toronto: Macmillan, 1987, 348 pp. Recognizing the needs and perspectives of women, a tax lawyer and journalist have collaborated to present basic finanacial information, taking into account women's concerns at different stages in their lives.

FINLAYSON, ANN. *Whose Money is it Anyway? The Showdown on Pensions*. Markham,

Ontario: Penguin Group, 1989, 278 pp. Examines the issues related to retirement pensions for Canadians.

HEALTH AND WELFARE CANADA. *Basic Facts on Social Security Programs*. Ottawa: Supply and Services Canada, annual, 91 pp. Booklet that summarizes federal income security programs, with recent statistics.

HEALTH AND WELFARE CANADA. *Inventory of Income Security Programs in Canada*. Ottawa: Supply and Services Canada, annual, 247 pp. Compendium of basic information and statistics regarding: federal and provincial programs for the elderly and children; provincial and municipal social assistance programs; provincial taxation and shelter assistance programs; workers' compensation; unemployment insurance; veterans' programs.

HUNNISETT, HENRY S. *Retirement Guide for Canadians: Plan Now for a Comfortable Future*. Tenth Edition. Vancouver: International Self-Counsel Press, 1989, 253 pp. A general guide to retirement planning that includes some chapters on financial aspects.

KELMAN, STEVEN G. *Financial Times Guide to RRSPs: The Authoritative Guide to the Best Retirement Savings Strategies*. Toronto: Financial Times, annual, 193 pp. A detailed guide to selecting a RRSP, with comparisons between financial institutions.

LONGHURST PATRICK and ROSE MARIE EARLE. *Looking After the Future, An Up-to-date Guide to Pension Planning in Canada*. Toronto: Doubleday Canada, 1987, 174 pp. A comprehensive review of both public and private pensions plans—how they work and how to evaluate the benefits.

MACINNIS, LYMAN. *Get Smart! Make Your Money Count in the 1990s*. Second Edition. Scarborough, Ontario: Prentice-Hall Canada, 1989, 317 pp. A book for the general reader that includes financial planning, income tax principles, but gives major attention to investing in the stock market.

MCLEOD, WILLIAM E. *The Canadian Buyer's Guide to Life Insurance*. Seventh Edition. Scarborough, Ontario: Prentice-Hall Canada, 1989, 276 pp. A comprehensive guide to the various life insurance products, including annuities.

OJA, GAIL. *Pensions and Incomes of the Elderly in Canada, 1971-1985*. Statistics Canada, Ottawa: Supply and Services Canada, 1988. Statistical analysis of income data.

PAPE, GORDON. *Gordon Pape's 1990 Guide to RRSPs*. Scarborough, Ontario: Prentice-Hall Canada, 1989, 109 pp. Provides basic rules for contributions, rollovers, transfers, kinds of instruments, and asset mix strategy.

TURNER, MARY, DANIEL LEROSSIGNOL, CLAUDE RINFRET, and RICHARD DAW. *Canadian Guide to Personal Financial Management*. Fourth Edition. Scarborough, Ontario: Prentice-Hall Canada, 1989, 231 pp. Accountants provide guidance on a broad range of topics, including planning finances, estimating insurance needs, managing risk, and determining investment needs. Instructions and the necessary forms for making plans are provided.

WYLIE, BETTY JANE. *The Best is Yet to Come, Planning Ahead for a Financially Secure Retirement*. Toronto: Key Porter, 1989, 206 pp. Emphasis is on financial planning for retirement, but other aspects are also mentioned.

ZIMMER, HENRY B. *Making Your Money Grow, A Canadian Guide to Successful Personal Finance*. Third Edition. Toronto: Collins, 1989, 260 pp. The focus of this book is on basic calculations needed for personal financial decisions, as applied to compound interest, future and present values, investment returns, RRSPs, annuities, and life insurance.

Articles

"Counting Down to Retirement," *Canadian Consumer*, 17, No. 11, 1987, 15-18. Suggestions for financial planning for retirement.

"Enriching Your Retirement," *The Financial Post Moneywise*, December 1989, 100-110. Reviews various forms of retirement income, especially RRSPs.

TOWNSON, MONICA. "A Good Pension Keeps You Sheltered," *The Financial Post 1990 Investor's Guide*, Fall 1989, 76-77. Outlines key points about private pensions and suggests questions employees should ask about their pension plans.

Periodical

The Financial Post Annual Moneyplanner. Annual. The Financial Post Company, 777 Bay Street, Toronto, Ontario, M5G 2E4. Usually contains articles on financial planning, income tax, insurance, investing, and retirement planning.

Policy Data

POLICY NUMBER 350005

POLICY DATE August 7, 1986

ANNUITANT Melvin McDonald
JOINT ANNUITANT Sharon McDonald

AGE OF ANNUITANT 65
AGE OF JOINT
ANNUITANT 65

BENEFICIARY as stated in the application unless subsequently changed

PLAN Joint & Last Survivor Annuity Guaranteed 10 Years, Immediate Annuity

AMOUNT OF ANNUITY $ 334.10 payable on the 23rd day of each month commencing July 23, 1986. These payments will continue monthly until the later of August 23, 1996, or the death of the last Annuitant.

PREMIUM Amount $ 40,000.00

Policy Data

SPECIMEN

Figure 7.7   ANNUITY POLICY

Source: The Cooperators Life Insurance Company. Reproduced with the permission of The Cooperators Life Insurance Company.

PROVISIONS

The Contract

The policy and the application are part of the contract. The contract also includes documents attached at issue and any amendments agreed upon in writing after the policy is issued. The policy may not be amended nor any provision waived except by written agreement signed by authorized signing officers of the Company.

Participation

This policy participates in the surplus distribution of the Company. Any distribution of excess charges or surplus shall remain at the credit of the contract and be used to increase the annuity.

Payment of Premium

The premium is payable either at the Head Office or at any Branch Office or through an authorized representative of the Company.

Currency

All payments to be made in connection with this policy shall be in the lawful money of Canada.

Age

The Company shall be entitled to proof of age of the annuitant before making any payment under this policy. If the age has been misstated, any amount payable hereunder shall be that which the premium would have purchased at the correct age.

Beneficiary

The annuitant may appoint a beneficiary. The annuitant may change the beneficiary unless the appointment was irrevocable. The interest of any legally designated beneficiary who shall die before the Annuitant, or before the surviving Annuitant or Annuitants, if there be more than one Annuitant, shall vest in the Annuitant or the surviving Annuitant or Annuitants, as the case may be, in the absence of any statutory provision as to the disposition thereof and if there be no other legally designated beneficiary.

No Assignment

The policy or annuity payments thereunder cannot be assigned.

SPECIMEN

LIR 705 (01/82) 504

Figure 7.7   continued

8 INTEREST

1. To understand the concept of interest and how it is related to the time value of money.

2. To distinguish between simple and compound interest and to demonstrate the calculation of each.

3. To understand the process of calculating a repayment schedule for a loan to be repaid in equal instalments, with each payment a blend of interest and principal.

4. To explain how frequency of compounding interest affects the effective annual yield.

5. To distinguish between nominal interest rate and effective annual yield.

6. To understand the process of determining the total interest charge on loan contracts for either simple or compound interest.

7. To identify factors that influence the total interest charged on a loan.

8. To understand the concepts of future and present values.

9. To determine future and present values of a single payment, using either formulae or compound interest tables.

10. To calculate the future and present values of a uniform series of deposits made or a uniform series of payments received.

11. To explain the following terms: principal, maturity date, term of a loan, sinking fund, blended payment.

INTRODUCTION

Interest, the subject of this chapter, has important implications for lenders as well as borrowers and is therefore relevant to a variety of transactions. Lest you think that all lenders are people with a great deal of money, keep in mind that when you make deposits in banks or other financial institutions you are a lender. Borrowers pay for the use of other people's money and this goes to lenders (depositors) as interest. This chapter presents some basic principles applicable to interest or the time value of money, and several ways of calculating interest.

The *time value of money* is based on the assumption that money can be lent to others for a rent, called interest, and that funds invested for a time will grow in value. Therefore, a dollar you invest for ten years will be worth more at the end of the decade, but a dollar promised to you in five years' time is worth less than a dollar given to you now. An understanding of interest and how to calculate present and future values should assist you, whether as a borrower or a lender, to make informed choices in various financial transactions.

You will note that this chapter is composed of two major sections: the first is concerned with interest, and the second with future and present values. A thorough understanding of the basic principles of interest and methods of calculation will be helpful for problems found in later chapters on credit, mortgages, and investments. Some acquaintance with the concepts of future and present values, which are applications of compound interest, can be useful in a variety of situations. However, this knowledge is not required for comprehension of later chapters and may be treated as reference material.

This chapter includes an explanation of interest, definitions of basic terms, and illustrations of simple and compound interest calculations. Borrowers are often mystified by repayment schedules used for consumer loans and mortgages, involving blended payments of principal and interest; examples illustrate how this works. Future and present values may be calculated by formulae or with compound interest tables and both methods are demonstrated. Because the tables referred to in the examples and problems are quite detailed, you will find them at the end of the chapter rather than interspersed with the text.

CONCEPT OF INTEREST

Interest, which is payment for the use of someone else's money, is viewed as a cost by borrowers and as income by lenders. For the borrower, interest is the cost of doing something now that otherwise would have to wait. For the lender, interest provides compensation for: (i) the loss of earnings that would have been received if the money had been used for other purposes, (ii) the risk that the loan will not be repaid, and (iii) the administrative costs in making the loan.

The *rate of interest*, which can be defined in a general way as the ratio of the interest payable at the end of a year to the money owed at the beginning of the year, is illustrated in the example, "Annual Interest Rate." This definition will be refined later when the concepts of nominal rate and effective annual yield are explained. It should be remembered that when an interest rate is quoted, it is assumed to be an annual rate unless specified otherwise.

ANNUAL INTEREST RATE

What is the interest rate on a $5000 debt, with interest of $500 payable annually?

$$\frac{500}{5000} = .10 \text{ (or 10\% per annum)}$$

The *total interest charge*, a most important component of any loan transaction, is the amount that must be repaid in addition to the *principal*, or the amount borrowed. It represents the lender's total return or the borrower's total carrying cost. Five factors that determine the magnitude of the total interest charge are: (i) rate of interest, (ii) frequency of compounding, (iii) term or length of time the loan is outstanding, (iv) principal, and (v) method of repayment. The effects of these factors will become apparent as various ways of calculating interest are explained in this chapter or illustrated in mortgage applications in Chapter 15.

SIMPLE INTEREST

Simple interest is used when the total principal and all interest due are to be repaid as a lump sum at a specified time. The date when a loan is due is called the *maturity date*, and the length of time the loan is to be outstanding is the *term of the loan*. The amount of interest due may be calculated with this formula:

Interest = principal × annual rate × time (in years)

SIMPLE INTEREST

Principal: $1500

Annual interest rate: 11%

Term of loan: 2.5 years

Interest = principal × rate × time

    = $1500 × .11 × 2.5

    = $412.50

At maturity, the borrower will pay the lender:

$1500.00	(principal returned)
412.50	(total interest charge)
$1912.50	(total payment)

COMPOUND INTEREST

Compound interest is paid on most savings accounts and charged on many loans, including home mortgages. *Compounding* simply means that, at specified intervals, the accumulated interest is added to the principal; in the next period, interest is earned on the new balance. Thus, interest is reinvested to earn more interest. Compounding may be done as often as daily, monthly, semi-annually, or annually. Naturally, the more frequently interest is compounded, the faster the investment grows. Assuming there is no repayment of principal or interest on a regular basis, the calculation of compound interest is exactly like simple interest, but it is repeated at each compounding interval, using a larger principal each time.

COMPOUND INTEREST

Principal: $1500

Interest rate: 11%, compounded semi-annually

Term of loan: 2.5 years

(a)   *At the end of first 6 months,*

    interest   = principal × rate × time

$$= \$1500 \times .11 \times .5$$
$$= \$82.50$$

new balance	$= $ principal $+$ interest
	$= \$1500 + \$82.50$
	$= \$1582.50$

(b) *At end of second six-month period,*

interest	$= $ principal $\times$ rate $\times$ time
	$= \$1582.50 \times .11 \times .5$
	$= \$87.04$

| new balance | $= \$1582.50 + \$87.04$ |
| | $= \$1669.54$ |

To summarize compound interest calculations over the two and a half year period:

Time period (months)	Balance of principal and interest at beginning of period	Interest at end of period	Outstanding balance at end of period
6	$1500.00	$ 82.50	$1582.50
12	1582.50	87.04	1669.54
18	1669.54	91.82	1761.36
24	1761.36	96.88	1858.24
30	1858.24	102.20	1960.44

At maturity, the borrower pays

$1500.00	(principal returned)
460.44	(total interest charge)
$1960.44	(total payment)

Compound interest is important to the saver because income (interest) is being reinvested regularly and begins earning additional interest. Banks calculate interest on savings accounts at different intervals, depending on the type of account. With a traditional savings account, interest may be calculated monthly on the minimum balance that was in the account during the month, but this interest is not added to the principal until the compounding date, which may be every six months. If you are planning to make a large withdrawal, consider doing so just after the end of the calendar month to avoid losing a month's interest. If you withdraw it too soon, it will not earn any interest for that month.

With a *daily interest acccount*, interest is calculated daily on the minimum balance and compounded perhaps monthly. Although the interest on such accounts is usually slightly lower than on the traditional savings account, a daily interest account can be worthwhile if you have a fluctuating balance in your account. Understandably, the interest rate paid by deposit institutions varies with the type of account: the interest rate may be depressed somewhat by chequing privileges, ready access to the deposit, or more frequent compounding.

RULE OF 72   If you would like to know how fast your money will double, you can use the *Rule of 72*, which gives an approximation of annual compounding. Divide 72 by the compound interest rate to find the number of years it will take to double your money. Alternatively, the compound interest rate can be approximated by dividing 72 by the number of years necessary to double your money.

COMPOUND INTEREST TABLES   To determine how much a sum of money will increase at various rates of interest, compounded annually, and left on deposit for various lengths of time, you may consult a compound interest table such as Table 8.1.

USING COMPOUND INTEREST TABLES

What will be the value of $1000 in 15 years, invested at 6% compounded annually? From Table 8.1, you find the compound value of 1, at 6%, for 15 years to be 2.40.

$$\$1000 \times 2.40 = \$2400.00$$

FREQUENCY OF COMPOUNDING AND YIELD   Whenever you lend or invest money, you expect some return. This return is called *yield* and may be expressed as an annual rate or as the total dollar amount received over some time period. The rate of return or *effective annual yield* is not necessarily the same as the quoted interest rate or nominal rate. *Nominal interest rate* is an annual rate that does not take account of the compounding effect. The more frequently interest is compounded, the faster your savings will grow and the higher the effective annual yield will be. To determine the effective annual yield, use the formula shown below.

$$\text{Effective annual yield (\%)} = \frac{\text{total annual interest}}{\text{principal}} \times 100$$

Working out the annual amount of interest for various compounding periods can become tedious, and therefore it is helpful to know the formula to use or to have convenient tables. If the interest is compounded m times a year at a nominal rate of r, then the effective annual yield can be defined as

$$\text{Effective annual yield} = \left(1 + \frac{r}{m}\right)^m - 1$$

EFFECTIVE ANNUAL YIELD

If the nominal interest rate (r) is 7% and the frequency of compounding (m) is quarterly, then

$$\text{Effective annual yield} = \left(1 + \frac{.07}{4}\right)^4 - 1$$
$$= 0.0719$$
$$= 7.19\%$$

Examine Table 8.2 to observe the effect of compounding frequency on effective annual yield. Would you prefer an investment paying 7.25% compounded monthly, or one at 7.5% compounded semi-annually? Which has the higher effective annual yield?

COMPOUND INTEREST ON INSTALMENT LOANS

BLENDED PAYMENTS Very often loans are repaid in equal monthly instalments, composed of both principal and interest. Each payment will include one month's interest on the amount of principal outstanding, plus a return of some principal. In the succeeding months, as the outstanding principal gradually decreases, payments contain changing proportions of principal and interest. This is illustrated graphically in Figure 8.1. You will observe that the first payment includes a larger share of interest than later payments. As time goes on, the interest component declines and the principal component increases. Such payments, with changing proportions of principal and interest are called

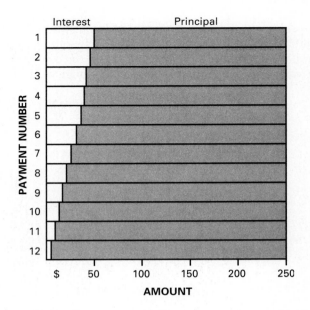

Figure 8.1　PROPORTIONS OF PRINCIPAL AND INTEREST IN EACH
PAYMENT OF A 12-MONTH CONTRACT

blended payments. The example, "Blended Payments" on the next page shows how the changing proportions of principal and interest are calculated and the payments made level.

Finally, there are a couple of points to note regarding compounding and terminology. Although payments on instalment loans are paid monthly interest is probably compounded at some other interval—often semi-annually. You may encounter the term, *amortization* that simply means repayment of a loan over a period of time. For instance, a loans officer might say that the loan will be amortized over three years.

BLENDED PAYMENTS

Principal: $1500
Annual interest rate: 11% compounded semi-annually
Amortization period: 2.5 years
Equal monthly blended payments

(a) *How much will each monthly payment be?*

The monthly payment on a loan of $1500, at 11%, for 2.5 years is $57.25 (Table 8.3).

(b) *How much interest will be paid the first month?*

Refer to a table of interest factors, used to calculate monthly interest on instalment loans (Table 8.4). In this example, the appropriate interest factor is .008 963 3940

interest for	=	outstanding	×	appropriate
1 month		principal		interest factor
	=	$1500	×	.008 963 3940
	=	$13.44		

(c) *What will be the proportions of interest and principal in the first month's payment?*

Interest for 1 month must come out of the payment and then the balance will be repayment of principal.

payment on	=	monthly	−	interest for
principal		payment		1 month
	=	$57.25	−	$13.44
	=	$43.81		

(d) *What will be the principal balance outstanding after the first payment has been made?*

principal	=	principal owing	−	payment on
still owing		before payment		principal
	=	$1500	−	$43.81
	=	$1456.19		

(e) *How much interest will be paid the second month?*

interest for	=	outstanding	×	appropriate
one month		principal		interest factor
	=	$1456.19	×	.008 963 3940
	=	$13.05		

The process of calculating the monthly interest and then determining the size of the repayment on the principal will continue each month until the principal has been reduced to zero, as illustrated in "Excerpts from Payment Schedule for $1500 Loan."

EXCERPTS FROM PAYMENT SCHEDULE FOR A $1500 LOAN (11% FOR 2.5 YEARS)

Payment number	Monthly payment	Principal owing before payment made	Interest paid per month	Principal repaid per month	Principal owing after payment
1	$57.25	$1500.00	$13.44	$43.80	$1456.19
2	57.25	1456.19	13.05	44.20	1411.99
3	57.25	1411.99	12.66	44.59	1367.40
4	57.25	1367.40	12.26	44.99	1322.41
5	57.25	1322.41	11.82	45.40	1277.01
6	57.25	1277.01	11.44	45.80	1231.21
12	57.25	995.96	8.93	48.32	947.64
18	57.25	699.44	6.27	50.98	648.46
24	57.25	386.61	3.46	53.78	332.82
29	57.25	112.81	1.01	56.24	56.57
30	57.08	56.57	0.51	56.57	00.00

To recapitulate, a loan that is amortized using blended payments, as in this last example, will have changing proportions of interest and principal in each payment. As the principal owing is gradually reduced there is less interest to pay, leaving an ever-increasing share for repayment of principal. The relation between the interest and principal portions of each payment will vary with such factors as interest rates, the term of the loan, and the size of the monthly payment. Home mortgages work the same way but the rate of principal repayment can be discouragingly slow if the loan is large, the payments modest, and the term 25 years or longer.

TOTAL INTEREST CHARGES

The same principal, interest rate, and time were used in the three previous examples but they differed in method of repayment and compounding. How do these two differences affect the total amount of interest paid? With an instalment loan that has blended payments, the total interest charge is less apparent than in the examples of simple and compound interest with a single repayment. To find the total interest paid in a blended payment contract, use the following formula:

$$\text{monthly payment} \times \text{number of months} = \text{total amount repaid} - \text{principal borrowed} = \text{total interest charge}$$

$$\$57.25 \times 30 = \$1717.50 - \$1500 = \$217.50$$

Summarizing, the total interest charge on each of the examples is:

(a) simple interest $412.50
(b) compound interest   460.44
(c) compound interest, blended payments   217.50

Can you suggest reasons for the variation?

Five factors that influence the total interest charge, as indicated at the beginning of this chapter, are: (i) rate of interest, (ii) frequency of compounding, (iii) term of the loan, (iv) principal borrowed, and (v) method of repayment. Looking first at interest rate, it is fairly obvious that higher rates will increase the cost of borrowing. On a small, short-term loan, small differences in rate do not change the cost very much; however, when the principal is very large and the term long, as in a home mortgage, a quarter of a percentage point difference in interest rate can make a substantial difference in the total interest charge.

The second factor, the frequency of compounding, is an important one for the borrower to keep in mind. If the interest on a mortgage is to be compounded quarterly instead of semi-annually, the difference in the total interest charge will be significant. The effect of the third factor, the term of the loan or the amortization period, is fairly obvious; the longer your loan is outstanding, the more you will have to pay. Likewise, the larger the principal borrowed, the more the interest charge.

Finally, the method of repayment has an effect on the total interest charge. If you have the use of the total principal for the whole term of the loan, you will have to pay more interest than if you start repaying the principal right away. Most mortgages and consumer loans are instalment loans with blended payments, composed of principal and interest. Since the very first payment includes some return of the principal to the lender this will reduce the total interest charge. Consequently, the method of payment affects the amount of principal outstanding at various times during the term of the loan. Did you notice that the total interest charge was lowest for the instalment loan example with blended payments? The reason is that the borrower did not have the use of the total principal for the entire term.

FUTURE VALUES AND PRESENT VALUES

Two questions investors may ask are: How much will a sum of money increase if left on deposit for a period of time? How much must I invest to have a certain sum at a future date? The answers involve applications of the concept of compound interest in estimating future or present values. Let us suppose that you have $1000 that you can invest today at nine percent for ten years. You want to know the *future value* of $1000 or what the total of principal and interest will be in ten years' time. A different question is, how much will you have to invest now, at nine percent, to have $5000 in five years' time for a down payment on a house? In the latter case, you want to know the *present value* of $5000.

In the two examples above it was assumed that a lump sum would be invested and a single payment received at a later date. These are fairly simple situations but sometimes investments are made in a series of deposits or receipts may be received in a series of payments. For instance, what is the future value of depositing $500 a year for ten years? Or, what is the present value of an annuity of $800 a month that will continue for seven years? For the sake of simplicity, we will examine instances of single payments first, and later explain how to determine future and present values when serial payments are involved.

SINGLE PAYMENTS

FUTURE VALUE OF A LUMP SUM   What will a present sum of money (P) be worth (i.e., its future value F) if the money is to be deposited at interest rate i for a period of n years? A time line will be used to help in visualizing such a problem. On the time line, receipts are shown by the upwards-pointing arrow and payments by the downwards-pointing arrow.

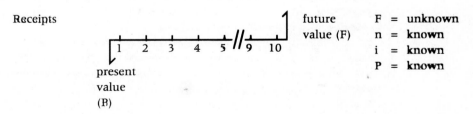

The unknown future value (F) can be found using the following formula which is applicable to a single payment compound amount.

$$F = P(1 + i)^n$$

Another way of expressing $(1 + i)^n$ is F/P at a given rate (i) and number of years (n), where F/P is the *compound amount factor*. Conveniently, there are tables of compound amount factors (F/P) for various combinations of interest rates and number of interest periods. Excerpts may be found in Tables 8.5, 8.6, and 8.7. When tables are used to solve a problem, the equation may be expressed as:

$$F = P(F/P, i\%, n)$$

FUTURE VALUE OF $1000

You have $1000 and wish to know its future value, if invested for 5 years, at 10% compounded annually.

Set up a time line, indicating the knowns and unknowns.

Receipts

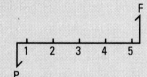

F = unknown
n = 5
i = .10
P = 1000

Payments

Calculate F, using the formula:

F = P(1 + i)^n
F = 1000(1 + .10)^5
 = 1000 × 1.6105
 = 1610.50

Or, use Table 8.6 to find the value for F/P:

F = P(F/P, 10%, 5)
 = 1000 × 1.6105
 = 1610.50

Therefore, the future value of $1000 in 5 years' time will be $1610.50.

PRESENT VALUE OF A LUMP SUM   In this case, we want to know what the present value (P) is of a future sum of money (F) if it can be invested at interest rate i for a period of n years. By cross-multiplying the formula used for future values we get:

$$P = \frac{F}{(1 + i)^n}$$

Or, using tables:

$$P = F\,(P/F, i\%, n)$$
$$= F \times \text{present worth factor (P/F) (Tables 8.5, 8.6, or 8.7)}$$

PRESENT VALUE OF $2000 IN THREE YEARS

Sarah wonders how much she needs to invest now (P), to have a future sum (F) of $2000 saved for a trip in 3 years, if the interest rate is 15% compounded annually? The time line will be:

Receipts

F   F = 2000
      n = 3
      i = .15
1 2 3   P = unknown
P

Payments

Using the formula:

$$P = \frac{F}{(1 + i)^n}$$
$$= \frac{2000}{(1 + .15)^3}$$
$$= \frac{2000}{1.5209}$$
$$= 1315.00$$

Or, using Table 8.7:

$$P = F(P/F, 15\%, 3)$$
$$= 2000 \times 0.6575$$
$$= 1315.00$$

Therefore, if Sarah invests $1315 a year, at 15%, for the next 3 years she will have $2000 for her trip. Or, the present worth of $2000, invested at 15%, is $1315.00.

Uniform Series of Deposits

An interesting question is finding the future value of a series of deposits. For example, if you know how much you can afford to save each year (P) and for how many years (n), you can find out the future value (F) of this savings program.

A practical method to save for a trip or a down payment on a house would be to make regular deposits for several years. If you know how much will be needed (F), and how long you have to save (n), you can calculate the present value (P) in terms of the amount to be deposited each year. The problem is to determine the present value of a series of deposits.

FUTURE VALUE OF A SERIES   What will be the future value (F) of a series of annual deposits (A) for *n* years at interest rate *i*? The time line will be as follows:

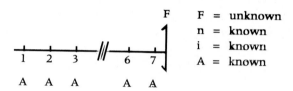

Receipts

F = unknown
n = known
i = known
A = known

Deposits

The appropriate formula is:

$$F = A\left(\frac{(1 + i)^n - 1}{i}\right)$$

Or, using compound interest tables:

F = A × compound amount factor (F/A)
= A(F/A, i%, n)

FUTURE VALUE OF A SERIES OF DEPOSITS

If Frank and Eva can set aside $500 a year for the next 10 years to create a fund for their son's education, how large will the fund be if the interest rate is 6%, compounded annually?

The time line will be:

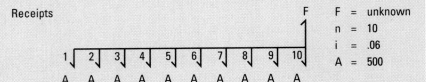

$$F = 500 \frac{(1 + .06)^{10} - 1}{.06}$$

$$= 500 \times 13.181$$

$$= 6590.50$$

Or, using tables:

$$F = A(F/A, 6\%, 10)$$

$$= 500 \times 13.181 \text{ (from Table 8.5)}$$

$$= 6590.50$$

They will accumulate $6590.50 in 10 years. Therefore, the future value of the series of $500 deposits is $6590.50.

PRESENT VALUE OF A SERIES   How much must be deposited in a uniform series to accumulate a future sum of money at a given date? This question is relevant for those planning to retire a debt and is often referred to as a sinking fund problem. A *sinking fund* is a sum being accumulated to retire a debt. The formula is:

$$A = F \frac{i}{(1 + i)^n - 1}$$

Using compound interest tables:

$$A = F \times \text{sinking fund factor (A/F)}$$

$$= F(A/F, i\%, n)$$

PRESENT VALUE OF A SERIES OF DEPOSITS

Since Ed wants to pay off his mortgage as fast as possible, he has decided to make a lump sum payment of $5000 in 4 years' time. At 6% interest, how much should he put aside annually for the next 4 years to reach his objective?

The time line will be:

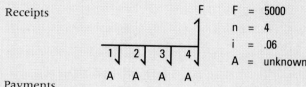

$$A = 5000 \frac{.06}{(1 + .06)^4 - 1}$$

$$= 5000 \times .2286$$

$$= 1142.95$$

Or, using tables:

$$A = F(A/F, 6\%, 4)$$

$$= 5000 \times 0.22859 \text{ (from Table 8.5)}$$

$$= 1142.95$$

If Ed invests $1142.95 a year at 6%, he will be able to reduce his mortgage debt by $5000 in 4 years' time.

UNIFORM SERIES OF PAYMENTS RECEIVED

The previous two examples involved the present and future values of a uniform series of deposits. Now we will consider the present and future values of a uniform series of payments. Often a financial institution faces the question of converting a series of future payments into an equivalent lump sum, known as commuting the values. One instance of this occurs at the death of an annuitant who had an annuity with a guaranteed period. A lump sum may be paid to the beneficiary instead of making payments for the balance of the guaranteed period. This is an example of finding the present value of a series of future payments.

Another problem is deciding how much can be spent each year to exhaust a known sum in a certain length of time. This is called recovery of capital in a uniform series of payments.

PRESENT WORTH OF A SERIES OF FUTURE PAYMENTS   What is the present worth of a property that is now renting at (A) each year, at a given interest rate (i)? The time line will be:

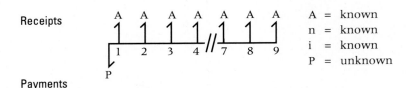

Receipts

Payments

A = known
n = known
i = known
P = unknown

The appropriate formula is:

$$P = A\left(\frac{(1 + i)^n - 1}{i(1 + i)^n}\right)$$

Or, if using compound interest tables:

$$P = A \times \text{present worth factor (P/A)}$$

PRESENT VALUE OF A SERIES OF ANNUITY PAYMENTS

After Ted's death, the insurance company representative called on Marie to tell her that she would receive a lump sum, equivalent to the annuity payments due to her husband. He had been receiving annual payments of $8000 from an annuity that was guaranteed for 6 more years. When commuting the series of payments to a lump sum, the company assumed an interest rate of 10%. The time line would be:

Receipts

A   A   A   A   A   A

1   2   3   4   5   6

P

Payments

A = $8000
n = 6
i = .10
P = unknown

Using the formula:

$$P = A\left(\frac{(1 + i)^n - 1}{i(1 + i)^n}\right)$$

$$= 8000\left(\frac{(1 + .10)^6 - 1}{.10(1 + .10)^6}\right)$$

$$= 34\ 840$$

Using Table 8.5:

$$P = A(P/A, 10\%, 6)$$

$$= 8000 \times 4.355$$

$$= 34\ 840$$

Marie received a lump sum of $34 840 instead of 6 annual payments of $8000. Why did she not receive $48 000?

CAPITAL RECOVERY IN A UNIFORM SERIES OF PAYMENTS   How much can be withdrawn per year (A) from a capital fund with a present value (P) if it is invested at interest rate *i* so that the fund will be exhausted in *n* years? The time line will be:

Receipts

A   A   A   A   A   A   A

1   2   3   4 // 7   8   9

P

Payments

F = unknown
n = known
i = known
A = known

The appropriate formula is:

$$A = P\left(\frac{i(1 + i)^n}{(1 + i)^n - 1}\right)$$

Or, using compound interest tables:

$$A = P \times \text{capital recovery factor (A/P)}$$

$$= P(A/P, i\%, n)$$

MULTIPLE COMPOUNDING PERIODS PER YEAR

Thus far, we have explained how to calculate present and future values when interest is compounded annually, but very often interest is compounded more frequently. There is a simple way to adapt the formulae and procedures given

GRADUAL WITHDRAWAL OF CAPITAL

Jean has $20 000 travel fund that she plans to use up over the the next 10 years. She is wondering how much to spend each year, assuming that she can invest the $20 000 at 10%, compounded annually. The time line will be:

Receipts   A   A   A   A   F = unknown

n = 10

i = .10

A = $20 000

Payments

Using Table 8.6:

$$A = P \times A/P$$
$$= P(A/P, i\%, n)$$
$$= 20\ 000 \times 0.162\ 75$$
$$= 3255$$

If Jean uses $3255 per year for 10 years, her travel fund of $20 000 will be exhausted.

in this chapter to accommodate various frequencies of compounding. Simply change the annual interest rate to the semi-annual or quarterly or whatever rate, and change the number of years to the number of compounding periods. For example, if the interest rate is 10% per year for 6 years, compounded quarterly, it will be expressed as 2.5% per quarter. The number of compounding periods will be 4 × 6 years = 24. When using the formula or tables, $i = .025$ and $n = 24$.

SUMMARY

This chapter has demonstrated the concept of interest as applied to a variety of situations, including compound interest with either a single payment or a series of blended payments. An important consideration in many transactions is the total interest charge, which is dependent on the factors of interest rate, frequency of compounding, term, principal, and method of repayment.

The next time you encounter a problem that involves future or present

SEMI-ANNUAL COMPOUNDING

You wish to know the future value of $1000 in 3 years if the interest rate is 12%, compounded semi-annually.

First put the interest rate into the same time frame as the compounding period. Thus the rate will be 6% per half year. The total number of compounding periods will be 2 per year × 3 years = 6. Therefore n = 6, and i = .06.

$$F = P(F/P, i\%, n)$$
$$= 1000 \times 1.4185 \text{ (Table 8.5)}$$
$$= 1418.50$$

The future value of $1000, compounded semi-annually at 12% for 3 years, will be $1418.50.

values, you should first draw a time line and list your knowns and unknowns. This will permit you to clarify the problem and to classify it as one involving single payments or a series of payments, and to decide whether it is a present or future value that is unknown. By comparing your problem statement and time line with the examples given in this chapter, you can find the appropriate formula to use.

PROBLEMS

1. Calculate the amount of interest due in each of the following cases:

   (a) $500 @ 9% for 6 months, simple interest.
   (b) $850 @ 10% for 1 year, compounded semi-annually.
   (c) The interest component of the first monthly instalment payment on a loan of $1000 @ 12% compounded semi-annually.

2. Assume an instalment loan with the following terms:
   Principal: $3500, monthly blended payments.
   Interest rate: 11%, compounded semi-annually.
   Term: 2 years.

   Would the total interest on this loan be calculated as follows?
   $3500 × .11 × 2 = $770.

   Explain why you agree or disagree with this method. If you disagree, show how it should be done.

3. You have several options for investing $1000 at various interest rates and frequencies of compounding. Which one would you choose from each of the following sets of alternatives, based on the effective annual yield?

   (a) 11.75% compounded daily or 12.50% compounded semi-annually.
   (b) 11.25% compounded annually, 11.0% semi-annually, or 10.75% monthly.

4. Following are pairs of alternative loan arrangements. Calculate the total interest charge for each alternative and identify the preferred choice for the borrower.

   (a) Instalment loan of $3500 at 13% compounded semi-annually. To pay it off completely in 1.5 years or 3 years? (The monthly payments would be $214.52 for 1.5 years and $117.36 for 3 years).
   (b) Single payment loan of $4000 for 2 years. To borrow at 9 3/4% compounded semi-annually or at 9 1/4% compounded monthly?
   (c) Loan of $5000 for 3 years. Instalment loan with monthly blended payments at 11% or single payment loan at 10 1/2%?

5. You have a piece of antique furniture that you are thinking of selling and have received two offers from an interested buyer.

   (a) $1500 now or
   (b) $2000 in 2 years' time.

   Assuming an interest rate of 10% compounded annually, which offer would you accept? Did you make your comparison based on present values or future values?

6. Recently, Fred won $10 000 in a lottery. He would like to spend this sum on holidays, over a five-year period, and is wondering how much he can withdraw annually to make it last 5 years. Assume an interest rate of 15% compounded annually.

7. As an owner of an company that rents office furniture, you have received two offers from one of your clients.

   (a) $3000 per year for the use of the equipment over the next 3 years.
   (b) $9000 at the end of 3 years.

   Which offer will you accept, assuming 6% interest, compounded annually?

8. John wants to know what sum of money he has to save each year in order to have $15 000 available in 5 years' time to buy a new car.

   (a) Assume that the money can be invested at 6% compounded annually.
   (b) Assume that the money can be invested at 12% compounded semi-annually.

9. If you were receiving $3000 a year in rent from 50 acres of farm land, what is the present worth of this land if the interest rates are 10%, compounded annually? (Assume that the rent will be paid at the beginning of the year for the next 3 years.)

10. Lou has determined that his young family should have an educational fund of $10 000 to become available in 8 years' time. If he died tomorrow, how much money would be needed from an insurance settlement to provide this sum if the money could be invested at 8%, compounded annually?

REFERENCES

Books

COTE, JEAN-MARC, and DONALD DAY. *Personal Financial Planning in Canada*. Toronto: Allyn and Bacon, 1987, 464 pp. A comprehensive personal finance text that includes financial planning, income tax, annuities, pensions, interest, investments, credit, mortgages, and wills, with particular attention to the banking and insurance industries.

ESTES, JACK C. *Compound Interest and Annuity Tables*. New York: McGraw-Hill, 1976, 248 pp. Book of tables with wide range of interest rates.

Financial Payment Tables for Canadian Mortgages. Toronto: Stoddart, 1983, 255 pp. Includes mortgage payment tables, loan progress charts, monthly interest factors.

Interest Amortization Tables. New York: McGraw-Hill, 1976, 246 pp. Uses interest rates from 5 to 25 percent.

MUMEY, GLEN A. *Personal Economic Planning*. Toronto: Holt, Rinehart and Winston, 1972, 312 pp. Explains interest calculations.

ZIMMER, HENRY B. *Making Your Money Grow, A Canadian Guide to Successful Personal Finance*. Third Edition. Toronto: Collins, 1989, 260 pp. The focus of this book is on basic calculations needed for personal financial decisions, as applied to compound interest, future and present values, investment returns, RRSPs, annuities, and life insurance.

Table 8.1 COMPOUND VALUE OF 1 AT VARIOUS INTEREST RATES FROM 1 TO 40 YEARS (COMPOUNDED ANNUALLY)

Yrs.	4%	5%	6%	7%	8%	9%	10%	11%	12%	13%	14%	15%	16%
1	1.04	1.05	1.06	1.07	1.08	1.09	1.10	1.11	1.12	1.13	1.14	1.15	1.16
2	1.08	1.10	1.12	1.14	1.17	1.19	1.21	1.23	1.25	1.28	1.30	1.32	1.35
3	1.12	1.16	1.19	1.23	1.26	1.30	1.33	1.37	1.40	1.44	1.48	1.52	1.56
4	1.17	1.22	1.26	1.31	1.36	1.41	1.46	1.52	1.57	1.63	1.69	1.75	1.81
5	1.22	1.28	1.34	1.40	1.47	1.54	1.61	1.69	1.76	1.84	1.93	2.01	2.10
6	1.27	1.34	1.42	1.50	1.59	1.68	1.77	1.87	1.97	2.08	2.19	2.29	2.44
7	1.32	1.41	1.50	1.61	1.71	1.83	1.95	2.08	2.21	2.35	2.50	2.61	2.83
8	1.37	1.48	1.59	1.72	1.85	1.99	2.14	2.30	2.48	2.66	2.85	2.98	3.28
9	1.42	1.55	1.69	1.84	2.00	2.17	2.36	2.56	2.77	3.00	3.25	3.40	3.80
10	1.48	1.63	1.79	1.97	2.16	2.37	2.60	2.84	3.11	3.39	3.71	3.87	4.41
11	1.54	1.71	1.90	2.10	2.33	2.58	2.85	3.15	3.48	3.84	4.23	4.45	5.12
12	1.60	1.80	2.01	2.25	2.52	2.81	3.14	3.50	3.90	4.33	4.82	5.12	5.94
13	1.67	1.89	2.13	2.41	2.72	3.07	3.45	3.88	4.36	4.90	5.50	5.89	6.89
14	1.73	1.98	2.26	2.58	2.94	3.34	3.80	4.31	4.89	5.53	6.26	6.77	7.99
15	1.80	2.08	2.40	2.76	3.17	3.64	4.18	4.78	5.47	6.25	7.14	7.79	9.27
16	1.87	2.18	2.54	2.96	3.43	3.97	4.59	5.31	6.13	7.07	8.14	8.96	10.75
17	1.95	2.30	2.69	3.16	3.70	4.33	5.05	5.90	6.87	7.99	9.28	10.30	12.47
18	2.03	2.41	2.85	3.38	4.00	4.72	5.56	6.54	7.69	9.02	10.58	11.85	14.46
19	2.11	2.53	3.03	3.62	4.32	5.14	6.12	7.26	8.61	10.20	12.06	13.62	16.78
20	2.19	2.66	3.21	3.87	4.66	5.60	6.73	8.06	9.65	11.52	13.74	15.67	19.46
21	2.28	2.79	3.40	4.14	5.03	6.11	7.40	8.95	10.80	13.02	15.67	18.02	22.57
22	2.37	2.93	3.60	4.43	5.44	6.66	8.14	9.93	12.10	14.71	17.86	20.72	26.19
23	2.46	3.07	3.82	4.74	5.87	7.26	8.95	11.03	13.55	16.63	20.36	23.83	30.38
24	2.56	3.23	4.05	5.07	6.34	7.91	9.85	12.24	15.18	18.79	23.21	27.40	35.24
25	2.67	3.39	4.29	5.43	6.85	8.62	10.83	13.59	17.00	21.23	26.46	31.51	40.87
26	2.77	3.56	4.55	5.81	7.40	9.34	11.92	15.08	19.04	23.99	30.17	37.24	47.41
27	2.89	3.73	4.82	6.21	7.99	10.25	13.10	16.74	21.32	27.11	34.39	41.78	55.00
28	3.00	3.92	5.11	6.65	8.63	11.17	14.42	18.58	23.88	30.63	39.20	47.93	63.80
29	3.12	4.12	5.42	7.11	9.32	12.17	15.86	20.62	26.75	34.62	44.69	55.12	74.01
30	3.24	4.32	5.74	7.61	10.06	13.27	17.45	22.89	29.96	39.12	50.95	63.38	85.85
31	3.37	4.54	6.09	8.15	10.87	14.46	19.19	25.41	33.56	44.20	58.08	72.89	99.59
32	3.51	4.76	6.45	8.72	11.74	15.76	21.11	28.21	37.58	49.95	66.21	83.82	115.52
33	3.65	5.00	6.84	9.33	12.68	17.18	23.23	31.31	42.09	56.44	75.48	96.40	134.00
34	3.80	5.25	7.25	9.98	13.69	18.73	25.55	34.75	47.14	63.78	86.95	110.86	155.44
35	3.95	5.52	7.69	10.68	14.79	20.41	28.10	38.57	52.80	72.07	98.10	127.48	180.31
36	4.10	5.80	8.15	11.42	15.97	22.25	30.91	42.82	59.14	81.44	111.83	146.61	209.16
37	4.27	6.08	8.64	12.22	17.25	24.25	34.00	47.53	66.23	92.02	127.49	168.60	242.63
38	4.44	6.39	9.15	13.08	18.63	26.44	37.40	52.76	74.18	103.99	145.34	193.89	281.45
39	4.62	6.70	9.70	13.99	20.12	28.82	41.14	58.56	83.08	117.51	165.69	222.97	326.48
40	4.80	7.04	10.29	14.97	21.72	31.41	45.26	65.00	93.05	132.78	188.88	256.42	378.72

Table 8.2 EFFECTIVE ANNUAL YIELD BY NOMINAL RATE AND FREQUENCY OF COMPOUNDING

Nominal annual interest rate %	Frequency of Compounding				
	Semi-annually %	Quarterly %	Monthly %	Weekly %	Daily %
7	7.12	7.19	7.23	7.25	7.25
7¼	7.38	7.45	7.50	7.51	7.52
7½	7.64	7.71	7.76	7.78	7.79
7¾	7.90	7.98	8.03	8.05	8.06
8	8.16	8.24	8.30	8.32	8.33
8¼	8.42	8.51	8.57	8.59	8.60
8½	8.68	8.77	8.84	8.86	8.87
8¾	8.94	9.04	9.11	9.14	9.14
9	9.20	9.31	9.38	9.41	9.42
9¼	9.46	9.58	9.65	9.68	9.69
9½	9.73	9.84	9.92	9.96	9.96
9¾	9.99	10.11	10.20	10.23	10.24
10	10.25	10.38	10.47	10.51	10.52
10¼	10.51	10.65	10.74	10.78	10.79
10½	10.77	10.92	11.02	11.06	11.07
10¾	11.03	11.19	11.29	11.33	11.34
11	11.30	11.46	11.57	11.61	11.63
11¼	11.57	11.73	11.84	11.89	11.90
11½	11.83	12.00	12.12	12.17	12.19
11¾	12.10	12.28	12.40	12.45	12.47
12	12.36	12.55	12.68	12.73	12.74
12¼	12.62	12.82	12.96	13.01	13.03
12½	12.89	13.10	13.24	13.29	13.31
12¾	13.15	13.37	13.52	13.58	13.60
13	13.42	13.65	13.80	13.86	13.88
13¼	13.69	13.92	14.08	14.15	14.18
13½	13.95	14.20	14.36	14.43	14.45
13¾	14.22	14.47	14.65	14.72	14.74
14	14.49	14.75	14.93	15.01	15.02
14¼	14.75	15.03	15.22	15.30	15.31
14½	15.02	15.30	15.50	15.58	15.60
14¾	15.29	15.58	15.79	15.87	15.89
15	15.56	15.87	16.08	16.16	16.18
15¼	15.83	16.14	16.36	16.44	16.47
15½	16.10	16.42	16.65	16.74	16.76
15¾	16.37	16.70	16.94	17.03	17.00
16	16.64	16.98	17.23	17.32	17.34

Table 8.3   AMORTIZATION TABLE: MONTHLY PAYMENT NECESSARY TO AMORTIZE A LOAN AT 11%

TERM AMOUNT	1 YEAR	1½ YEARS	2 YEARS	2½ YEARS	3 YEARS	3½ YEARS	4 YEARS	4½ YEARS
$ 100	8.83	6.05	4.65	3.82	3.27	2.87	2.58	2.35
200	17.66	12.09	9.30	7.64	6.53	5.74	5.15	4.69
300	26.49	18.13	13.95	11.45	9.79	8.61	7.72	7.04
400	35.31	24.17	18.60	15.27	13.05	11.48	10.30	9.38
500	44.14	30.21	23.25	19.09	16.32	14.34	12.87	11.73
600	52.97	36.25	27.90	22.90	19.58	17.21	15.44	14.07
700	61.79	42.29	32.55	26.72	22.84	20.08	18.01	16.41
800	70.62	48.33	37.20	30.54	26.10	22.95	20.59	18.76
900	79.45	54.37	41.85	34.35	29.37	25.81	23.16	21.10
1000	88.27	60.41	46.50	38.17	32.63	28.68	25.73	23.45
1100	97.10	66.45	51.15	41.99	35.89	31.55	28.30	25.79
1200	105.93	72.49	55.80	45.80	39.15	34.42	30.88	28.13
1300	114.75	78.53	60.45	49.62	42.42	37.29	33.45	30.48
1400	123.58	84.57	65.10	53.43	45.68	40.15	36.02	32.82
1500	132.41	90.61	69.75	57.25	48.94	43.02	38.60	35.17
1600	141.23	96.65	74.40	61.07	52.20	45.89	41.17	37.51
1700	150.06	102.69	79.05	64.88	55.46	48.76	43.74	39.86
1800	158.89	108.74	83.70	68.70	58.73	51.62	46.31	42.20
1900	167.71	114.78	88.34	72.52	61.99	54.49	48.89	44.54
2000	176.54	120.82	92.99	76.33	65.25	57.36	51.46	46.89
2100	185.37	126.86	97.64	80.15	68.51	60.23	54.03	49.23
2200	194.19	132.90	102.29	83.97	71.78	63.09	56.60	51.58
2300	203.02	138.94	106.94	87.78	75.04	65.96	59.18	53.92
2400	211.85	144.98	111.59	91.60	78.30	68.83	61.75	56.26
2500	220.67	151.02	116.24	95.41	81.56	71.70	64.32	58.61
2600	229.50	157.06	120.89	99.23	84.83	74.57	66.90	60.95
2700	238.33	163.10	125.54	103.05	88.09	77.43	69.47	63.30
2800	247.16	169.14	130.19	106.86	91.35	80.30	72.04	65.64
2900	255.98	175.18	134.84	110.68	94.61	83.17	74.61	67.99
3000	264.81	181.22	139.49	114.50	97.87	86.04	77.19	70.33
3100	273.64	187.26	144.14	118.31	101.14	88.90	79.76	72.67
3200	282.46	193.30	148.79	122.13	104.40	91.77	82.33	75.02
3300	291.29	199.34	153.44	125.95	107.66	94.64	84.90	77.36
3400	300.12	205.38	158.09	129.76	110.92	97.51	87.48	79.71
3500	308.94	211.43	162.74	133.58	114.19	100.37	90.05	82.05
3600	317.77	217.47	167.39	137.40	117.45	103.24	92.62	84.39
3700	326.60	223.51	172.04	141.21	120.71	106.11	95.20	86.74
3800	335.42	229.55	176.68	145.03	123.97	108.98	97.77	89.08
3900	344.25	235.59	181.33	148.84	127.24	111.85	100.34	91.43
4000	353.08	241.63	185.98	152.66	130.50	114.71	102.91	93.77
4100	361.90	247.67	190.63	156.48	133.76	117.58	105.49	96.12
4200	370.73	253.71	195.28	160.29	137.02	120.45	108.06	98.46
4300	379.56	259.75	199.93	164.11	140.29	123.32	110.63	100.80
4400	388.38	265.79	204.58	167.93	143.55	126.18	113.20	103.15
4500	397.21	271.83	209.23	171.74	146.81	129.05	115.78	105.49
4600	406.04	277.87	213.88	175.56	150.07	131.92	118.35	107.84
4700	414.86	283.91	218.53	179.38	153.33	134.79	120.92	110.18
4800	423.69	289.95	223.18	183.19	156.60	137.65	123.50	112.52
4900	432.52	295.99	227.83	187.01	159.86	140.52	126.07	114.87
5000	441.34	302.03	232.48	190.82	163.12	143.39	128.64	117.21
5100	450.17	308.07	237.13	194.64	166.38	146.26	131.21	119.56
5200	459.00	314.12	241.78	198.46	169.65	149.13	133.79	121.90
5300	467.82	320.16	246.43	202.27	172.91	151.99	136.36	124.25
5400	476.65	326.20	251.08	206.09	176.17	154.86	138.93	126.59
5500	485.48	332.24	255.73	209.91	179.43	157.73	141.50	128.93

Table 8.3   CONTINUED

TERM AMOUNT	1 YEAR	1½ YEARS	2 YEARS	2½ YEARS	3 YEARS	3½ YEARS	4 YEARS	4½ YEARS
5600	494.31	338.28	260.38	213.72	182.70	160.60	144.08	131.28
5700	503.13	344.32	265.02	217.54	185.96	163.46	146.65	133.62
5800	511.96	350.36	269.67	221.36	189.22	166.33	149.22	135.97
5900	520.79	356.40	274.32	225.17	192.48	169.20	151.80	138.31
6000	529.61	362.44	278.97	228.99	195.74	172.07	154.37	140.65
6100	538.44	368.48	283.62	232.80	199.01	174.94	156.94	143.00
6200	547.27	374.52	288.27	236.62	202.27	177.80	159.51	145.34
6300	556.09	380.56	292.92	240.44	205.53	180.67	162.09	147.69
6400	564.92	386.60	297.57	244.25	208.79	183.54	164.66	150.03
6500	573.75	392.64	302.22	248.07	212.06	186.41	167.23	152.38
6600	582.57	398.68	306.87	251.89	215.32	189.27	169.80	154.72
6700	591.40	404.72	311.52	255.70	218.58	192.14	172.38	157.06
6800	600.23	410.76	316.17	259.52	221.84	195.01	174.95	159.41
6900	609.05	416.80	320.82	263.34	225.11	197.88	177.52	161.75
7000	617.88	422.85	325.47	267.15	228.37	200.74	180.10	164.10
7100	626.71	428.89	330.12	270.97	231.63	203.61	182.67	166.44
7200	635.53	434.93	334.77	274.79	234.89	206.48	185.24	168.78
7300	644.36	440.97	339.42	278.60	238.16	209.35	187.81	171.13
7400	653.19	447.01	344.07	282.42	241.42	212.22	190.39	173.47
7500	662.01	453.05	348.72	286.23	244.68	215.08	192.96	175.82
7600	670.84	459.09	353.36	290.05	247.94	217.95	195.53	178.16
7700	679.67	465.13	358.01	293.87	251.20	220.82	198.10	180.51
7800	688.49	471.17	362.66	297.68	254.47	223.69	200.68	182.85
7900	697.32	477.21	367.31	301.50	257.73	226.55	203.25	185.19
8000	706.15	483.25	371.96	305.32	260.99	229.42	205.82	187.54
8100	714.98	489.29	376.61	309.13	264.25	232.29	208.40	189.88
8200	723.80	495.33	381.26	312.95	267.52	235.16	210.97	192.23
8300	732.63	501.37	385.91	316.77	270.78	238.02	213.54	194.57
8400	741.46	507.41	390.56	320.58	274.04	240.89	216.11	196.91
8500	750.28	513.45	395.21	324.40	277.30	243.76	218.69	199.26
8600	759.11	519.49	399.86	328.21	280.57	246.63	221.26	201.60
8700	767.94	525.54	404.51	332.03	283.83	249.50	223.83	203.95
8800	776.76	531.58	409.16	335.85	287.09	252.36	226.40	206.29
8900	785.59	537.62	413.81	339.66	290.35	255.23	228.98	208.64
9000	794.42	543.66	418.46	343.48	293.61	258.10	231.55	210.98
9100	803.24	549.70	423.11	347.30	296.88	260.97	234.12	213.32
9200	812.07	555.74	427.76	351.11	300.14	263.83	236.70	215.67
9300	820.90	561.78	432.41	354.93	303.40	266.70	239.27	218.01
9400	829.72	567.82	437.05	358.75	306.66	269.57	241.84	220.36
9500	838.55	573.86	441.70	362.56	309.93	272.44	244.41	222.70
9600	847.38	579.90	446.35	366.38	313.19	275.30	246.99	225.04
9700	856.20	585.94	451.00	370.20	316.45	278.17	249.56	227.39
9800	865.03	591.98	455.65	374.01	319.71	281.04	252.13	229.73
9900	873.86	598.02	460.30	377.83	322.98	283.91	254.70	232.08
10000	882.68	604.06	464.95	381.64	326.24	286.78	257.28	234.42
11000	970.95	664.47	511.45	419.81	358.86	315.45	283.00	257.86
12000	1059.22	724.87	557.94	457.97	391.48	344.13	308.73	281.30
13000	1147.49	785.28	604.44	496.14	424.11	372.81	334.46	304.75
14000	1235.76	845.69	650.93	534.30	456.73	401.48	360.19	328.19
15000	1324.02	906.09	697.43	572.46	489.35	430.16	385.91	351.63
16000	1412.29	966.50	743.92	610.63	521.98	458.84	411.64	375.07
17000	1500.56	1026.90	790.41	648.79	554.60	487.52	437.37	398.51
18000	1588.83	1087.31	836.91	686.96	587.22	516.19	463.10	421.95
19000	1677.10	1147.72	883.40	725.12	619.85	544.87	488.82	445.40
20000	1765.36	1208.12	929.90	763.28	652.47	573.55	514.55	468.84

Source: Reproduced from Blended Payments for Loans, Publication #41, p. 10-11, copyright 1964, Financial Publishing Company, Boston, Ma.

Table 8.4 MONTHLY INTEREST FACTORS AT NOMINAL ANNUAL RATES, INTEREST COMPOUNDED SEMI-ANNUALLY

7 % − .005 750 0395	12½% − .010 155 3225
7⅛% − .005 851 2369	12⅝% − .010 254 3331
7¼% − .005 952 3834	12¾% − .010 353 2952
7⅜% − .006 053 4791	12⅞% − .010 452 2088
7½% − .006 154 5240	13 % − .010 551 0740
7⅝% − .006 255 5182	13⅛% − .010 649 8909
7¾% − .006 356 4617	13¼% − .010 748 6596
7⅞% − .006 457 3546	13⅜% − .010 847 3799
8 % − .006 558 1970	13½% − .011 946 0522
8⅛% − .006 658 9889	13⅝% − .011 044 6762
8¼% − .006 759 7303	13¾% − .011 143 2522
8⅜% − .006 860 4214	13⅞% − .011 241 7802
8½% − .006 961 0622	14 % − .010 340 2602
8⅝% − .007 061 6527	14⅛% − .011 438 6923
8¾% − .007 162 1929	14¼% − .011 537 0764
8⅞% − .007 262 6831	14⅜% − .011 635 4128
9 % − .007 363 1231	14½% − .011 733 7014
9⅛% − .007 463 5130	14⅝% − .011 831 9423
9¼% − .007 563 8530	14¾% − .011 930 1355
9⅜% − .007 664 1431	14⅞% − .012 028 2811
9½% − .007 764 3832	15 % − .012 126 3791
9⅝% − .007 864 5735	15⅛% − .012 224 4297
9¾% − .007 964 7141	15¼% − .012 322 4327
9⅞% − .008 064 8049	15⅜% − .012 420 3883
10 % − .008 164 8461	15½% − .012 518 2966
10⅛% − .008 264 8377	15⅝% − .012 616 1575
10¼% − .008 364 7797	15¾% − .012 713 9712
10⅜% − .008 464 6722	15⅞% − .012 811 7377
10½% − .008 564 5152	16 % − .012 909 4570
10⅝% − .008 664 3089	16⅛% − .013 007 1292
10¾% − .008 764 0532	16¼% − .013 104 7543
10⅞% − .008 863 7482	16⅜% − .013 202 3325
11 % − .008 963 3940	16½% − .013 299 8636
11⅛% − .009 062 9906	16⅝% − .013 397 3478
11¼% − .009 162 5381	16¾% − .013 494 7852
11⅜% − .009 262 0365	16⅞% − .013 592 1758
11½% − .009 361 4858	17 % − .013 689 5196
11⅝% − .009 460 8863	17⅛% − .013 786 8166
11¾% − .009 560 2378	17¼% − .013 884 0670
11⅞% − .009 659 5404	17⅜% − .013 981 2708
12 % − .009 758 7942	17½% − .014 078 4280
12⅛% − .009 857 9993	17⅝% − .014 175 5387
12¼% − .009 957 1557	17¾% − .014 272 6030
12⅜% − .010 056 2634	17⅞% − .014 369 6208

Interest for one month on any amount may be obtained by multiplying that amount by this factor.

Table 8.5   6% COMPOUND INTEREST FACTORS

	Single Payment		Uniform Series				
	Compound Amount Factor	Present Worth Factor	Sinking Fund Factor	Capital Recovery Factor	Compound Amount Factor	Present Worth Factor	
n	F/P	P/F	A/F	A/P	F/A	P/A	n
1	1.0600	0.9434	1.000 00	1.060 00	1.000	0.943	1
2	1.1236	0.8900	0.485 44	0.545 44	2.060	1.833	2
3	1.1910	0.8396	0.314 11	0.374 11	3.184	2.673	3
4	1.2625	0.7921	0.228 59	0.288 59	4.375	3.465	4
5	1.3382	0.7473	0.177 40	0.237 40	5.637	4.212	5
6	1.4185	0.7050	0.143 36	0.203 36	6.975	4.917	6
7	1.5036	0.6651	0.119 14	0.179 14	8.394	5.582	7
8	1.5938	0.6274	0.101 04	0.161 04	9.897	6.210	8
9	1.6895	0.5919	0.087 02	0.147 02	11.491	6.802	9
10	1.7908	0.5584	0.075 87	0.135 87	13.181	7.360	10
11	1.8983	0.5268	0.066 79	0.126 79	14.972	7.887	11
12	2.0122	0.4970	0.059 28	0.119 28	16.870	8.384	12
13	2.1329	0.4688	0.052 96	0.112 96	18.882	8.853	13
14	2.2609	0.4423	0.047 58	0.107 58	21.015	9.295	14
15	2.3966	0.4173	0.042 96	0.102 96	23.276	9.712	15
16	2.5404	0.3936	0.038 95	0.098 95	25.673	10.106	16
17	2.6928	0.3714	0.035 44	0.095 44	28.213	10.477	17
18	2.8543	0.3503	0.032 36	0.092 36	30.906	10.828	18
19	3.0256	0.3305	0.029 62	0.089 62	33.760	11.158	19
20	3.2071	0.3118	0.027 18	0.087 18	36.786	11.470	20
21	3.3996	0.2942	0.025 00	0.085 00	39.993	11.764	21
22	3.6035	0.2775	0.023 05	0.083 05	43.392	12.042	22
23	3.8197	0.2618	0.021 28	0.081 28	46.996	12.303	23
24	4.0489	0.2470	0.019 68	0.079 68	50.816	12.550	24
25	4.2919	0.2330	0.018 23	0.078 23	54.865	12.783	25
26	4.5494	0.2198	0.016 90	0.076 90	59.156	13.003	26
27	4.8223	0.2074	0.015 70	0.075 70	63.706	13.211	27
28	5.1117	0.1956	0.014 59	0.074 59	68.528	13.406	28
29	5.4184	0.1846	0.013 58	0.073 58	73.640	13.591	29
30	5.7435	0.1741	0.012 65	0.072 65	79.058	13.765	30
31	6.0881	0.1643	0.011 79	0.071 79	84.802	13.929	31
32	6.4534	0.1550	0.011 00	0.071 00	90.890	14.084	32
33	6.8406	0.1462	0.010 27	0.070 27	97.343	14.230	33
34	7.2510	0.1379	0.009 60	0.069 60	104.184	14.368	34
35	7.6861	0.1301	0.008 97	0.068 97	111.435	14.498	35
40	10.2857	0.0972	0.006 46	0.066 46	154.762	15.046	40
45	13.7646	0.0727	0.004 70	0.064 70	212.744	15.456	45
50	18.4202	0.0543	0.003 44	0.063 44	290.336	15.762	50
55	24.6503	0.0406	0.002 54	0.062 54	394.172	15.991	55
60	32.9877	0.0303	0.001 88	0.061 88	533.128	16.161	60
65	44.1450	0.0227	0.001 39	0.061 39	719.083	16.289	65
70	59.0759	0.0169	0.001 03	0.061 03	967.932	16.385	70
75	79.0569	0.0126	0.000 77	0.060 77	1 300.949	16.456	75
80	105.7960	0.0095	0.000 57	0.060 57	1 746.600	16.509	80
85	141.5789	0.0071	0.000 43	0.060 43	2 342.982	16.549	85
90	189.4645	0.0053	0.000 32	0.060 32	3 141.075	16.579	90
95	253.5463	0.0039	0.000 24	0.060 24	4 209.104	16.601	95
100	339.3021	0.0029	0.000 18	0.060 18	5 638.368	16.618	100

Table 8.6   10% COMPOUND INTEREST FACTORS

	Single Payment		Uniform Series				
n	Compound Amount Factor F/P	Present Worth Factor P/F	Sinking Fund Factor A/F	Capital Recovery Factor A/P	Compound Amount Factor F/A	Present Worth Factor P/A	*n*
1	1.1000	0.9091	1.000 00	0.100 00	1.000	0.909	1
2	1.2100	0.8264	0.476 19	0.576 19	2.100	1.736	2
3	1.3310	0.7513	0.302 11	0.402 11	3.310	2.487	3
4	1.4641	0.6830	0.215 47	0.315 47	4.641	3.170	4
5	1.6105	0.6209	0.163 80	0.263 80	6.105	3.791	5
6	1.7716	0.5645	0.129 61	0.229 61	7.716	4.355	6
7	1.9487	0.5132	0.105 41	0.205 41	9.487	4.868	7
8	2.1436	0.4665	0.087 44	0.187 44	11.436	5.335	8
9	2.3579	0.4241	0.073 64	0.173 64	13.579	5.759	9
10	2.5937	0.3855	0.062 75	0.162 75	15.937	6.144	10
11	2.8531	0.3505	0.053 96	0.153 96	18.531	6.495	11
12	3.1384	0.3186	0.046 76	0.146 76	21.384	6.814	12
13	3.4523	0.2897	0.040 78	0.140 78	24.523	7.103	13
14	3.7975	0.2633	0.035 75	0.135 75	27.975	7.367	14
15	4.1772	0.2394	0.031 47	0.131 47	31.772	7.606	15
16	4.5950	0.2176	0.027 82	0.127 82	35.950	7.824	16
17	5.0545	0.1978	0.024 66	0.124 66	40.545	8.022	17
18	5.5599	0.1799	0.021 93	0.121 93	45.599	8.201	18
19	6.1159	0.1635	0.019 55	0.119 55	51.159	8.365	19
20	6.7275	0.1486	0.017 46	0.117 46	57.275	8.514	20
21	7.4002	0.1351	0.015 62	0.115 62	64.002	8.649	21
22	8.1403	0.1228	0.014 01	0.114 01	71.403	8.772	22
23	8.9543	0.1117	0.012 57	0.112 57	79.543	8.883	23
24	9.8497	0.1015	0.011 30	0.111 30	88.497	8.985	24
25	10.8347	0.0923	0.010 17	0.110 17	98.347	9.077	25
26	11.9182	0.0839	0.009 16	0.109 16	109.182	9.161	26
27	13.1100	0.0763	0.008 26	0.108 26	121.100	9.237	27
28	14.4210	0.0693	0.007 45	0.107 45	134.210	9.307	28
29	15.8631	0.0630	0.006 73	0.106 73	148.631	9.370	29
30	17.4494	0.0573	0.006 08	0.106 08	164.494	9.427	30
31	19.1943	0.0521	0.005 50	0.105 50	181.943	9.479	31
32	21.1138	0.0474	0.004 97	0.104 97	201.138	9.526	32
33	23.2252	0.0431	0.004 50	0.104 50	222.252	9.569	33
34	25.5477	0.0391	0.004 07	0.104 07	245.477	9.609	34
35	28.1024	0.0356	0.003 69	0.103 69	271.024	9.644	35
40	45.2593	0.0221	0.002 26	0.102 26	442.593	9.779	40
45	72.8905	0.0137	0.001 39	0.101 39	718.905	9.863	45
50	117.3909	0.0085	0.000 86	0.100 86	1 163.909	9.915	50
55	189.0591	0.0053	0.000 53	0.100 53	1 880.591	9.947	55
60	304.4816	0.0033	0.000 33	0.100 33	3 034.816	9.967	60
65	490.3707	0.0020	0.000 20	0.100 20	4 893.707	9.980	65
70	789.7470	0.0013	0.000 13	0.100 13	7 887.470	9.987	70
75	1 271.8952	0.0008	0.000 08	0.100 08	12 708.954	9.992	75
80	2 048.4002	0.0005	0.000 05	0.100 05	20 474.002	9.995	80
85	3 298.9690	0.0003	0.000 03	0.100 03	32 979.690	9.997	85
90	5 313.0226	0.0002	0.000 02	0.100 02	53 120.226	9.998	90
95	8 556.6760	0.0001	0.000 01	0.100 01	85 556.760	9.999	95
100	13 780.6123	0.0001	0.000 01	0.100 01	137 796.123	9.999	100

Table 8.7   15% COMPOUND INTEREST FACTORS

	Single Payment		Uniform Series				
	Compound Amount Factor	Present Worth Factor	Sinking Fund Factor	Capital Recovery Factor	Compound Amount Factor	Present Worth Factor	
n	F/P	P/F	A/F	A/P	F/A	P/A	n
1	1.1500	0.8696	1.000 00	1.150 00	1.000	0.870	1
2	1.3225	0.7561	0.465 12	0.615 12	2.150	1.626	2
3	1.5209	0.6575	0.287 98	0.437 98	3.472	2.283	3
4	1.7490	0.5718	0.200 26	0.350 27	4.993	2.855	4
5	2.0114	0.4972	0.148 32	0.298 32	6.742	3.352	5
6	2.3131	0.4323	0.114 24	0.264 24	8.754	3.784	6
7	2.6600	0.3759	0.090 36	0.240 36	11.067	4.160	7
8	3.0590	0.3269	0.072 85	0.222 85	13.727	4.487	8
9	3.5179	0.2843	0.059 57	0.209 57	16.786	4.772	9
10	4.0456	0.2472	0.049 25	0.199 25	20.304	5.019	10
11	4.6524	0.2149	0.041 07	0.191 07	24.349	5.234	11
12	5.3503	0.1869	0.034 48	0.184 48	29.002	5.421	12
13	6.1528	0.1625	0.029 11	0.179 11	34.352	5.583	13
14	7.0757	0.1413	0.024 69	0.174 69	40.505	5.724	14
15	8.1371	0.1229	0.021 02	0.171 02	47.580	5.847	15
16	9.3576	0.1069	0.017 95	0.167 95	55.717	5.954	16
17	10.7613	0.0929	0.015 37	0.165 37	65.075	6.047	17
18	12.3755	0.0808	0.013 19	0.163 19	75.836	6.128	18
19	14.2318	0.0703	0.011 34	0.161 34	88.212	6.198	19
20	16.3665	0.0611	0.009 76	0.159 76	102.444	6.259	20
21	18.8215	0.0531	0.008 42	0.158 42	118.810	6.312	21
22	21.6447	0.0462	0.007 27	0.157 27	137.632	6.359	22
23	24.8915	0.0402	0.006 28	0.156 28	159.276	6.399	23
24	28.6252	0.0349	0.005 43	0.155 43	184.168	6.434	24
25	32.9190	0.0304	0.004 70	0.154 70	212.793	6.464	25
26	37.8568	0.0264	0.004 07	0.154 07	245.712	6.491	26
27	43.5353	0.0230	0.003 53	0.153 53	283.569	6.514	27
28	50.0656	0.0200	0.003 06	0.153 06	327.104	6.534	28
29	57.5755	0.0174	0.002 65	0.152 65	377.170	6.551	29
30	66.2118	0.0151	0.002 30	0.152 30	434.745	6.566	30
31	76.1435	0.0131	0.002 00	0.152 00	500.957	6.579	31
32	87.5651	0.0114	0.001 73	0.151 73	577.100	6.591	32
33	100.6998	0.0099	0.001 50	0.151 50	664.666	6.600	33
34	115.8048	0.0086	0.001 31	0.151 31	765.365	6.609	34
35	133.1755	0.0075	0.001 13	0.151 13	881.170	6.617	35
40	267.8635	0.0037	0.000 56	0.150 56	1 779.090	6.642	40
45	538.7693	0.0019	0.000 28	0.150 28	3 585.128	6.654	45
50	1 083.6574	0.0009	0.000 14	0.150 14	7 217.716	6.661	50
				0.150 00		6.667	

SAVING AND INVESTING

1. To distinguish between the following pairs of terms:
   (a) saving and investing,
   (b) investing and speculating,
   (c) liquidity and marketability,
   (d) debt and equity securities,
   (e) income and capital gain,
   (f) total and liquid assets,
   (g) nominal and real interest rates,
   (h) income and wealth.

2. To categorize reasons for saving and to explain how they affect the choice of investments.

3. To identify reasons why people find saving difficult and investing overwhelming.

4. To examine the trends in the savings rate in Canada.

5. To analyze the effects of age and income on the amount that Canadians save.

6. To explain these terms: portfolio, term, investment pyramid.

7. To distinguish among the different types of risk to which investments are exposed.

8. To identify the type of risk associated with various kinds of investments.

9. To explain the principle of diversification and why it is significant in investment planning.

10. To explain why there are trade-offs between risk and return, return and liquidity, term and return, current income and capital gain.

11. To examine ways of handling risk in an investment portfolio.

12. To identify conflicting investment objectives.

13. To explain how to make an investment plan.

INTRODUCTION

Are you a saver? If not, why not? If you do save, do you invest profitably? While it is quite possible to save without investing, it is rather difficult to be an investor without any savings. Although often linked together, the terms saving and investing are not synonyms: *saving* simply means not spending; *investing* means using your funds with the expectation of yield. For instance, putting money in your sock or under the mattress would be considered saving, but not investing. You would be investing if you deposited the money in a savings account, or bought Canada Savings Bonds, stocks, property, or treasury bills, because there is some prospect of a return. Although savings accounts and term deposits are forms of investments, you may find little discussion of them in the investment literature, probably because it is assumed that their characteristics are well understood.

The range of possible investments is broad. The only characteristic that savings accounts, real estate, stocks, bonds, and precious metals may have in common is the investor's expectation of gain. Even if, in a particular instance, the yield turned out to be nonexistent or less than anticipated, it would still be considered an investment, although an unfortunate one, as long as gain was the intent. Unless you are lucky enough to receive an inheritance or other windfall, you will find it impossible to become an investor without first saving. For that reason, this chapter begins with a consideration of ways to become a better saver, followed by an introduction to investing, including characteristics of investments, identification of investment objectives, and the process of developing an investment plan and portfolio.

In this overview of investments many points are introduced that will be treated in more detail in later chapters, particularly Chapters 10 and 11, that deal with debt securities and stocks. Your understanding will be enhanced if you re-read this chapter after studying the next two.

SAVING

WHY SAVE?

Anyone who receives an income has to make decisions daily about how much of it to spend and how much to save. In our society there is every incentive to spend, but not much pressure to save. Usually we feel that it is more urgent to pay bills or buy some new thing than to save. Saving is for the future, we tell ourselves, and the future is far away. Furthermore, we may feel that our purchases will provide more immediate gratification than a growing balance in a savings account.

To put the need for savings in perspective, it may be helpful to project income and economic needs over the life span (Figure 1.1 in Chapter 1). On average, earnings can be expected to increase until about age 55 or 60, then level off or start to decline. During working years, most people receive increases in wages to reflect growing skill and experience as well as to accommodate price changes, but by late middle age some are forced into early retirement by ill health or loss of jobs. Others may be fortunate enough to maintain income increases for a longer time. At retirement, which may occur between age 60 and 70 but often occurs by age 65, earnings stop and must be replaced by pension and investment income. Investment income is dependent, of course, on first having had some savings to invest.

Long-term consumption needs, as shown in Figure 1.1, generally do not follow the curvilinear pattern of income; most of us want a fairly steady, but perhaps gently rising, level of living throughout our life span. How can this be accomplished? Knowing that expenditure is likely to be more constant than income flow, you can take steps to smooth out the cash flow over your lifetime. This means basing your financial planning on a longer time horizon than just this month or this year. If you are to achieve and maintain financial independence you will have to save some of your income during your working years, and invest it to create retirement income. In addition, you will need savings for short-term needs, for smoothing out any unevenness in cash flow, and for specific goals.

There are at least four important reasons to save. Funds will be needed for (i) emergencies, (ii) liquidity, (iii) short-term goals, and (iv) long-term goals. We will consider each in turn.

EMERGENCY FUND   Since most people start out their working lives with very little net worth, the first need is to create an emergency fund, money that is readily accessible to handle the unexpected expenses that we all have. It is often suggested that several months' take-home pay, perhaps three, should be set aside as the emergency fund. Expect that it will take some time to achieve this goal. These funds could be kept in a savings account, term deposits, Canada Savings Bonds, or any savings instrument that pays interest without locking in funds. Furthermore, high priority should be given, at this stage, to obtaining adequate insurance to cover risks to your property or dependents, as was discussed in previous chapters.

LIQUIDITY NEEDS   You will need to have some funds available to cope with any unevenness in your cash flow and to pay for infrequent large expenses. Ready access to about one month's take-home pay may be adequate. Put these funds where they will earn as much interest as possible but remain readily accessible, possibly in an interest-bearing deposit account that permits chequing.

SHORT-TERM GOALS   How can you distinguish a short-term from a long-term goal? When you review your financial goals, you will find some that can be accomplished within the next five years and some that will take longer. You can decide what time frame best fits your situation, but do make a distinction between short-term and long-term goals. It is best to segregate the funds for short-term goals from those for longer-term goals, either by accounting or keeping the funds in separate accounts. The money being saved for next year's holiday should not get mixed with that being saved for retirement.

Short-term goals might include holidays and trips, and the purchase of vehicles, furniture, appliances, and education for yourself or your children. If your children are very young, planning for their post-secondary education will be a long-term goal. Those interested in becoming homeowners may want to start saving for a down payment or, if they already have a house, to reserve funds for mortgage prepayments.

Home ownership, you may have observed, is the single most important investment for many Canadian families. During periods of rapid inflation, the price of houses has tended to appreciate as much or more than the inflation rate, making property an effective and tax-free storehouse of value. Any capital gain realized on your home has long been excluded from taxation. Another reason for buying a house, from an investment perspective, is as a form of forced saving. The discipline of regular mortgage payments not only results in a place to live but eventually in the ownership of an asset.

Depending on how soon they will be required, funds being saved for short-term goals may be invested in low-risk securities with appropriate maturities. The discussion that follows in this and later chapters should give you some possible ideas.

LONG-TERM GOALS   A key long-term goal will be to increase net worth to enhance financial security, gain financial independence, and ensure support for retirement years. To have a comfortable lifestyle during your retirement, planning must start early in the working years. By the magic of compounding, small amounts will grow to large sums if left invested for long periods. For instance, if you invested $1000 each year at an average annual compound rate of only 5 percent, your savings would more than double to $66 438 in 30 years, or grow even more at 7 percent (Figure 9.1). If saving for retirement is postponed until it can be afforded and left until within a few years of retirement there will be little time for savings to grow. Acquiring capital to fund retirement is a long-term savings goal, and the funds can be invested with a longer time horizon than those intended for short-term goals. That is, they can be invested in securities that are not readily accessible but have prospects for long-term growth.

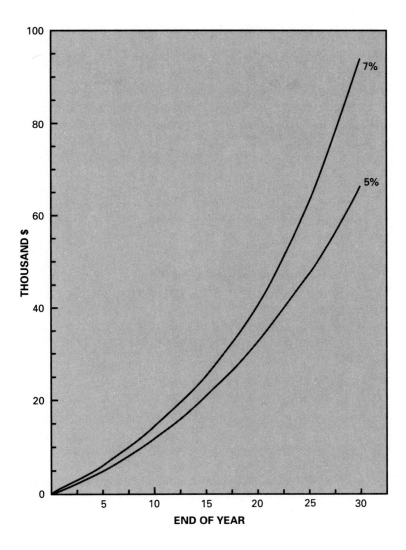

Figure 9.1   COMPOUND VALUE OF ANNUAL INVESTMENTS OF $1000,
              INVESTED AT 5% AND 7%

How to Save

In spite of the widely-held belief that everyone should save some money, these
good intentions tend to be given low priority. Saving can be difficult, easy to
postpone, and not that much fun. To ensure success there must be a firm
commitment and definite plans. There will always be demands on income that

HOW MUCH CAPITAL WILL BE NEEDED?

D eirdre estimates that she will need an income of about $500 a month ($6000 a year) from her investments to supplement her pensions when she retires. She wonders how much capital she will need, based on a conservative return of six percent on average. She makes the following calculations by converting the formula:

$$\text{Interest} = \text{principal} \times \text{rate} \times \text{time}$$

$$\text{Principal} = \frac{\text{interest}}{\text{rate} \times \text{time}}$$

$$= \frac{500 \times 12}{.06 \times 1}$$

$$= \$100\ 000$$

Deirdre has not made any adjustment for inflation because she anticipates that a higher inflation rate will push up interest rates correspondingly. Now that she has a long-term goal of building up a net worth of $100 000, she will make plans for savings and investing.

seem most urgent and require saving to be postponed. You may reason that it will be easier to save later when there will be no unexpected expenses, but eventually you will discover that this pattern is repetitious and that no time ever seems the right time to save. The only solution is to set up an automatic saving plan and follow it determinedly.

There are two basic approaches to saving—taking savings off the top of each pay cheque before spending anything, or waiting to see what will be left at the end of the pay period. Those who follow the first system will accumulate savings and will have funds to invest; the others will never get around to it. Which approach will you take? The best plan is to establish a certain amount or percentage that is to be set aside from each pay, eg., five to ten percent.

When developing a savings strategy, be aware of your strengths and weaknesses. If you are an impulsive spender, you will need a system to make your savings unavailable. Look into payroll savings plans and automatic saving methods at financial institutions and arrange that a certain portion of your income be directed into these plans before it reaches you. For example, each autumn Canada Savings Bonds become available by payroll deduction, some credit unions have automatic savings plans, and a number of mutual funds offer contractual plans.

AN AUTOMATIC SAVINGS PLAN

P eter found saving very difficult. His intention was to bank whatever money was left at the end of the month, but more often than not, nothing was left. A friend who belongs to a credit union told him about an automatic savings plan by which he saves $200 a month. He authorized the credit union to deduct funds on each pay day from the account into which his employer deposited his pay, and to transfer the funds to his savings account.

Peter decided that he would give this plan a try, but when he inquired at his bank, he found that they had no such system in effect. An alternative, they suggested, was for Peter to write a year's supply of post-dated cheques and, at the appropriate time, the bank would transfer funds from his chequing to his savings account. He tried this method, and was very pleased at the end of the year to find that he had saved $2400.

RULES FOR SAVING   The key rules about becoming a successful saver are:

(a)   have a purpose or goal for which you are saving,
(b)   make a plan for accomplishing your goal,
(c)   save regularly.

You have to be committed to a plan for increasing your net worth, or nothing will be accomplished. It would be ridiculous, of course, to go the other extreme and become a miser; letting saving become an end itself is also a mistake. A balance between present and future consumption is the objective. Some financial experts suggest that if you who save 10 percent of your salary throughout your working years and invest it carefully, you can become financially independent by the time of retirement.

How Much Do Canadians Save?

National Savings Rates
To determine how much Canadians save, we examine the macro-economic data from the national accounts, where savings is defined as those sums in the hands of individuals that were not spent for income tax or current consumption. By this definition, Canadians have been saving from 5 percent to 15 percent of their disposable income (after income tax, and CPP and UI

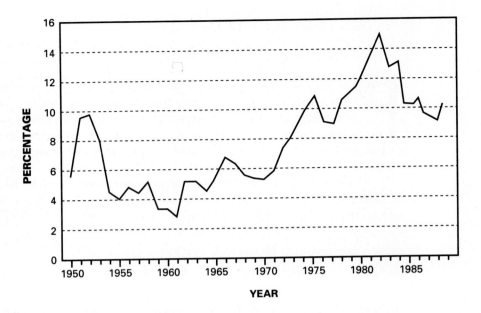

Figure 9.2   SAVINGS RATE*, CANADA, 1950-1989

Source: *Canadian Statistical Review* and *Canadian Economic Observer*, Ottawa: Statistics Canada, various issues.
(Catalogue No. 11-010.) Reproduced and edited with the permission of the Minister of Supply and Services
Canada.

*Personal savings as a percentage of personal disposable income.

premiums) during the past four decades (Figure 9.2). Savings rates are quite
variable and much affected by economic conditions, but in recent years the
rate has risen to the historically high level of 15 percent, then fallen back to
around 10 percent.

Why such high savings rates? The uncertainty created by poor economic
conditions, the high rates paid on deposits, and the encouragement of RRSPs
and other pension plans may be factors. Our present income tax system offers
incentives to put money in RRSPs. In addition, contractual savings in the
Canada Pension Plan and private pension plans have been growing. It has
been estimated that the contractual savings component of the national savings
rate may be about seven percent. That still leaves a significant proportion of
our national savings rate as discretionary. On average, Canadians tend to be
quite good savers.

HOUSEHOLD SURVEYS OF WEALTH

Another important source of information about the savings patterns of Canadians is from household surveys in which people are asked how much they have saved. These surveys provide an estimate of household wealth at a given date (stock) in contrast to the macro data on the rate of saving per year (flow). Do you recall the difference between a stock and a flow, discussed in Chapter 1? Statistics Canada conducts such surveys about every seven or eight years; the last two were in 1977 and 1984. Although the levels of income and wealth are no longer up-to-date, we can still analyze these data for patterns; such behaviour patterns change much more slowly than the averages or medians.

It will be helpful in interpreting these survey results to be aware of some definitions. *Net worth* (total assets less debts) and *wealth* are used as synonyms. *Total assets* refers to all the items of monetary value of the household, including property. In the figures presented in this chapter, a distinction is made between families and households: *families* have two or more members and *households* include families and unattached individuals.

WEALTH OF FAMILIES   It is not unexpected to find that wealth increases with income, but the difference between the mean and the median levels may be a surprise (Figure 9.3). The median (the mid-point in the distribution) is a more useful measure because a few households with very high wealth levels distort the averages. Generally, wealth is distributed more unequally than income. Can you suggest reasons for the large differences between mean and median wealth in the lowest and highest income groups?

NEGATIVE NET WORTH   Although most households have some wealth, there are those with negative net worth, that is, they owe more than they own. The distribution of these households by income shows that as income increases, the probability of having negative net worth declines (Figure 9.4). Are you surprised to find households with negative net worth at all income levels?

DISTRIBUTION OF ASSETS   What pattern do you see between income level and the significance of various kinds of assets? Each bar in Figure 9.5 represents the distribution of total assets within one income group. It should be kept in mind that these data are total assets, not net worth. For instance, the market value of homes is included, without subtracting the outstanding mortgage debt. Owner-

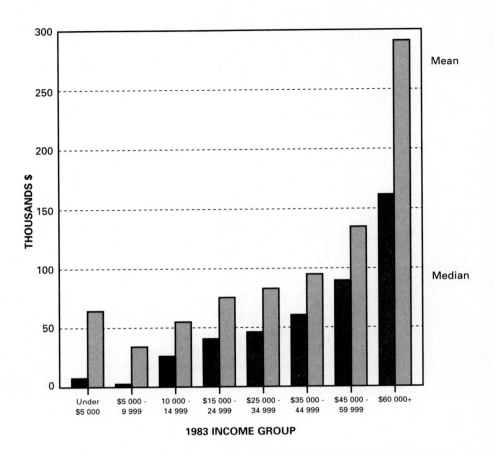

Figure 9.3   MEDIAN AND MEAN WEALTH OF FAMILIES BY 1983 INCOME
GROUP, CANADA, 1984.

Source: *The Distribution of Wealth in Canada, 1984.* Ottawa: Statistics Canada, 1986, Table 1, page 26.
(Catalogue no. 13-580.) Reproduced and edited with the permission of the Minister of Supply and Services
Canada, 1991.

ship of a home is usually the single most important asset, regardless of income
level. Looking at other assets, it is apparent that income influences the forms in
which families hold their wealth. *Liquid assets* are those that can be converted to
cash quite readily with little loss of principal, such as deposits, cash, savings
certificates, Canada Savings Bonds, other bonds. These are the funds we depend
on for emergencies or liquidity. Why do you think liquid assets form a larger
share of wealth at lower income levels, and stocks, RRSPs, and miscellaneous
financial assets form a larger share at higher income levels?

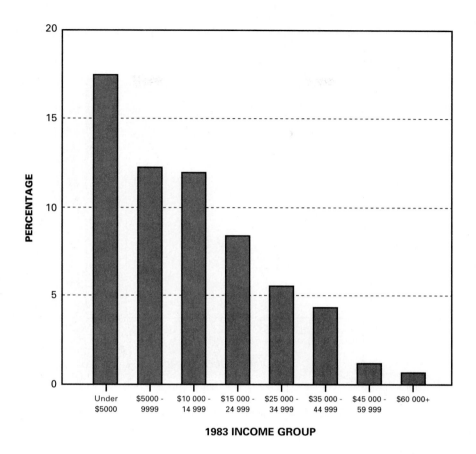

Figure 9.4   PERCENTAGE DISTRIBUTION OF HOUSEHOLDS WITH
              NEGATIVE NET WORTH, CANADA, 1984

Source: *The Distribution of Wealth in Canada, 1984*. Ottawa: Statistics Canada, 1986, Table 1, page 26.
(Catalogue No. 13-580.) Reproduced and edited with the permission of the Minister of Supply and Services
Canada, 1991.

AGE AND WEALTH   To complete this analysis of the wealth of households, we
will consider the relation between age or stage in the life cycle and wealth.
Although the data are not presented here graphically, net worth tends to
increase with age up to about age 64 and then show a slight decline after age
65. However, interpretation of such data is difficult because those households
where the head is aged 65 or more represent a broad age category, some
members of which have been retired for a long time. Older persons accumu-

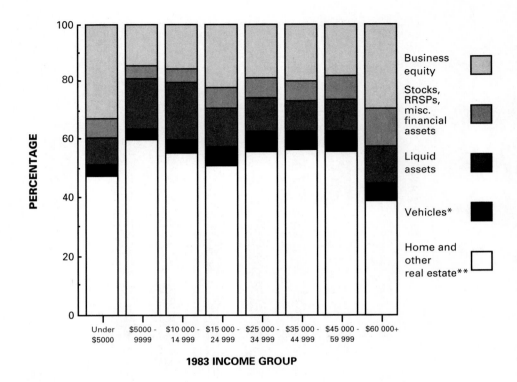

*Includes cars, trucks, and selected recreational vehicles.
**Market value of home, vacation home, and equity in other real estate.

Figure 9.5   PERCENTAGE COMPOSITION OF TOTAL ASSETS OF CANADIAN
HOUSEHOLDS BY INCOME CLASS, SPRING 1984

Source: *The Distribution of Wealth in Canada, 1984.* Ottawa: Statistics Canada, 1986, Table 24, page 64.
(Catalogue No. 13-580.) Reproduced and edited with the permission of the Minister of Supply and Services
Canada, 1991.

lated their wealth many years previously when incomes were much lower, and
may have suffered considerably from the consequences of inflation.

Another way of looking at wealth by age is to observe the pattern of
wealth/income ratios (Figure 9.6). You will note that, on average, households
are in their mid-thirties before they have a net worth equivalent to a year's
income. At peak earning (ages 45-64) the average household has a net worth
about two or two and one-half times income. The higher ratio after age sixty-
five is influenced by the drop in income after retirement and the fact that this
age category is much broader than the others.

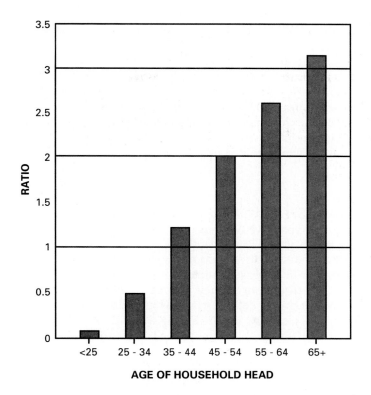

Figure 9.6   WEALTH INCOME RATIOS* BY AGE OF HOUSEHOLD HEAD,
             CANADA, 1984

Source: *The Distribution of Wealth in Canada, 1984.* Ottawa: Statistics Canada, 1986, Table 5, page 32.
(Catalogue No. 13-580.) Reproduced and edited with the permission of the Minister of Supply and Services
Canada, 1991.

*Median wealth divided by mean income. Median income figures were not available.

INVESTING

WHY INVEST?

The primary reason for investing is surely self-evident: your savings must grow
to make your financial goals possible. A secondary reason may be that you
enjoy investing and see the possibilities for an interesting hobby. Some people
who are good savers unfortunately have no idea how to invest their money
profitably. Many Canadians are quite cautious and apprehensive about investing; they deposit their money at the credit union, bank, or trust company, or
buy Canada Savings Bonds because they want safety and ready access to their

funds at all times. The cautious ones probably do not realize how much they may be sacrificing in terms of yield, inflation protection, and tax reduction, or that all investments are exposed to some risk.

In many cases, fear of the unknown and lack of information are the impediments to wise investing, rather than unwillingness to assume some risk. Do not confuse fear of investing with risk. If you do nothing about investing because of anxiety, confusion, and uncertainty, this inaction can be costly. You may pay more income tax than necessary, forego higher yields, and see your savings eroded by inflation.

INVESTING OR SPECULATING

Assuming that you have been successful at saving, what can you do to make your net worth grow? The first thing is to have patience. Investing is not speculating or gambling; you do not want to risk your hard-earned savings, you want them to increase gradually. Although it is commonly believed that investing is putting your money in a safe place and speculating is buying stocks, *investing* can be defined as committing funds in a way that minimizes risk yet protects capital, while earning a return that is satisfactory for the degree of risk. This can be accomplished in a variety of ways, not only with deposits.

Investors are not in a hurry; speculators, on the other hand, look for large profits from a small layout of funds within a short time. *Speculation* tends to be based on a shorter time horizon and involves more risk than investing. Speculators use money with the expectation of capital gain through a change in market value and are primarily motivated by short-term gains rather than long-term yield.

Unless you have several hundred thousand dollars in assets and can afford to hire an investment counsellor, you will have to manage your own investments. The choices are either to become knowledgeable and devote some time to monitoring your portfolio, or to choose investments that require minimum attention. Having a portfolio may sound very grand, but a *portfolio* is simply a list or collection of assets. If money matters are distasteful to you and there seems to be no likelihood of change, find ways to put your savings where they will grow without your efforts. Most of the discussion that follows is based on the assumption that you are interested in learning more about investing.

When you have finished reading this book, you will have been introduced to the basics of investing and should have the vocabulary to understand the articles in the financial press that make it possible for you to keep up-to-date. As mentioned before, lack of knowledge and fear of the unknown deter many people from making wise investment decisions. Since gaining an understanding of basic characteristics of investments is necessary before making a personal investment plan, these will be examined next.

DEBT AND EQUITY INVESTMENTS

DEBT SECURITIES

There are two basic ways to invest: (i) by lending money, or (ii) by acquiring ownership. Lenders become *creditors* and are said to possess *debt securities*. The borrower promises to repay the principal with interest at some specified time. The income from debt instruments is called *interest.* Perhaps you had not thought of yourself as a creditor when you deposited funds at a bank, trust company, or credit union. Were you aware that you were lending money to a government or corporation when you bought a bond or a treasury bill? Deposit accounts, term deposits, guaranteed investment certificates, mortgages (you are the lender), bonds, and treasury bills are types of debt securities. Their characteristics will be reviewed in the next chapter.

EQUITY SECURITIES

Instead of becoming a creditor, you could become an owner or part-owner by purchasing real estate, goods of various sorts— including art, jewellery, antiques—stocks, and all or part of a business. In the ownership role you receive some rights regarding the management of the goods or property, but you obtain no guarantee that the sum you invested will be returned to you, or that it will generate any income. You have acquired an *equity* because you are an owner, with opportunities for gains or losses but no promises. Although more risk is generally associated with equities than with debt securities, it is also possible to find equities that are less risky than some debt instruments. For instance, there is less risk in owning common shares in certain utilities than in lending mortgage money to a person who has a poor record of repayment. Equities are usually chosen because of the expectation of greater gain than is possible from debt securities.

A comparison of average annual yields from three-month treasury bills and common stocks over a 15-year period will illustrate the difference in risk and return from debt and equity securities (Figure 9.7). The salient point is the steady rate of return from the treasury bills and the variability in common stock yield. Between 1975 and 1989, the average annual return was 10.4 percent on treasury bills, and 19 percent on stocks. However, to achieve the higher return the investor had to be prepared to wait out the down swings in the stock market.

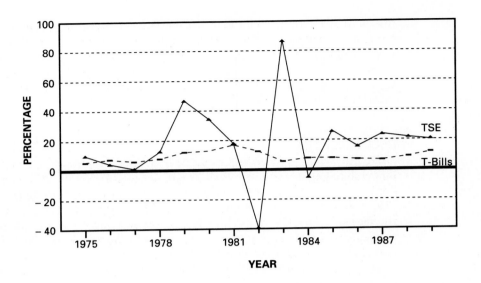

Figure 9.7   AVERAGE ANNUAL RATES OF RETURN ON THREE-MONTH
TREASURY BILLS, AND THE STOCKS IN THE TORONTO STOCK
EXCHANGE INDEX, 1975-1989

INVESTMENT RETURNS

INCOME   The return on an investment may take the form of either income
(interest, dividends, rent, profit) or capital appreciation (capital gain). The
type of return received will vary with the investment. Those who own property
and rent it to others will receive income in the form of rent; owners of shares
in a business hope to receive profit; stock shareholders expect dividends. In
addition to the income generated by ownership, there may be an expectation
that the purchase will increase in value and generate capital gain.

CAPITAL GAIN   The difference between the purchase price of an asset and the
selling price represents capital gain. For example, something purchased at
$2700 and sold for $3500 would result in a capital gain of $800. *Capital gain* is

the windfall accruing to an investor, by virtue of ownership, during a change in prices caused by increased demand or inflation. If an asset, such as a house, was improved and then sold, the value of the improvements would not be counted as capital gain. It should be remembered that the expectation of capital gain always carries with it the possibility of capital loss.

TYPE OF INVESTMENT	FORM OF RETURN
Debt investments	
Deposits, loans	interest
Mortgage loans	interest
Canada Savings Bonds	interest
Treasury bills	interest
Bonds	interest, capital gain (loss)
Equity investments	
Real property	rent, capital gain (loss)
Business	profit, capital gain (loss)
Stocks (shares)	dividends, capital gain (loss)
Gold, silver	capital gain (loss)

CURRENT INCOME OR CAPITAL GAIN?

Generally, it is impossible to maximize both current income and capital gain from the same investment. The creation of capital gain, which comes from ownership of assets as they increase in value, usually takes time if you are an investor, not a speculator. Growth-oriented companies generally re-invest their profits in the business rather than distribute them as dividends (income) to shareholders. Those securities that produce regular income, such as debt investments and preferred shares (less risk than common shares), have limited growth potential. Therefore, we can say that usually the objectives of capital gain and current income are inversely related. To improve the possibility of capital gain, current income would have to be sacrificed, as shown in the example on the next page.

THE CURRENT INCOME/CAPITAL GAIN TRADE-OFF

A fter her husband died, Jean found herself handling investments for the first time, and decided that she needed some help. She consulted a financial planner who asked her what her investment objectives were. She was confused by the question, so the planner asked whether it was more important to her that the $30 000 she planned to invest provide a regular income or that the capital have an opportunity to grow to increase her net worth and provide a hedge against future inflation.

She replied that, since she was 55 and not in the labour force, income was very important, but some provision should be made to cope with any inflation in the future. She was given a card, like the one shown below, with two sets of numbers, zero to ten, and asked to circle the relative importance to her of current income versus future capital gain. The total of the two circled numbers must equal ten. After much thought she gave seven to current income and three to capital gain. Her financial planner now had a better idea about possible investments that might be appropriate for Jean.

CURRENT INCOME

Low										High
0	1	2	3	4	5	6	⑦	8	9	10
10	9	8	7	6	5	4	③	2	1	0
High										Low

CAPITAL GAIN

Jean's son Jeff, who is in his mid-thirties, unmarried, and well-paid, has a small portfolio of growth stocks. He ranks capital gain as ten and return as 0 for his stock portfolio. His emergency funds are in Canada Savings Bonds and guaranteed investment certificates. Taking all of Jeff's assets together, the balance between capital gain and income is about 50-50.

CHARACTERISTICS OF INVESTMENTS

Six characteristics of investments, particularly relevant to investors as they endeavour to decide among all the possible alternatives, are: (i) the risk/return trade-off, (ii) liquidity, (iii) marketability, (iv) term, (v) management effort

Examine your priorities in relation to a specific investment. Circle the numbers that represent your compromise between liquidity and return. The two numbers must add up to ten; as you increase one characteristic, you have to accept less of the other.

Low					RETURN					High
0	1	2	3	4	5	6	7	8	9	10

10	9	8	7	6	5	4	3	2	1	0
High					LIQUIDITY					Low

Figure 9.8   THE LIQUIDITY/RETURN TRADE-OFF

required, and (vi) income tax treatment. Risk, the most important factor in investment decisions, will be examined in more detail than the others and discussed further in Chapter 11. The significance of the other five factors will be considered next.

LIQUIDITY
In the strictest sense, *liquidity* means that an investment can be converted into cash readily and *without loss of principal.* There are degrees of liquidity, ranging from cash which is the most liquid asset, to property or commodities, which are the least liquid. Savings accounts, term deposits, and Canada Savings Bonds can be liquidated during banking hours without loss of principal and thus are considered to be very liquid. Corporate bonds, stocks, and real estate are not very liquid because it may take time to sell them without a loss. Since very high liquidity is associated with an expectation of lower yield, the investor must decide what compromise to make (Figure 9.8). What is the relative importance to you, the investor, of having your investment provide high liquidity versus high return? If you decide to put your money in a savings account, you have chosen high liquidity and low return, but if you invest in a business or property, you may have reversed the situation.

MARKETABILITY
The popular usage of the term liquidity, when marketability is what is really meant, can be confusing. *Marketable assets* are those for which there is an active market. Certain stocks are in greater demand than others, trade more often, and thus are more marketable. Some houses are easier to sell than others and thus are more marketable. An asset may be highly marketable but not very liquid because of price fluctuations. At the time you wish to sell the asset, the prices of all houses, or stocks, for example, may be in a slump, making it impossible to recover your capital totally. Although any asset can be sold if

the price is lowered enough, that is not what is meant by marketability; the aim is to get no less than a fair market price.

Term

Is the investment locked in for a specified period? If not, will the return be adversely affected if the asset is held for a very short time? You can find investments with terms from a few days to many years. Choose investments appropriate to your savings goals. There tends to be a direct relation between term and return because of increasing uncertainty as the maturity date lengthens. Investors demand a higher return in exchange for making a longer-term commitment of their funds. Therefore, short-term investments tend to yield less than long-term ones, although the relationship does become inverted at times.

Personal Management Effort

How much time and attention are you prepared to give to your investments? This is an important consideration in choosing securities. If you are not prepared to put time and effort into supervision, you should select investments that require minimum attention; choose debt securities rather than equities, or buy mutual funds. If you decide not to become involved with investing, you may have to accept a lower return. The relation between effort and return tends to be direct; those who get the highest returns invest their time as well as money. On the other hand, the relation between management effort and liquidity is inverse. Usually the most liquid investments require the least attention and likewise, more attention may be required for less liquid investments.

Tax Considerations

Comparisons of potential yield from investments should be done in after-tax dollars because of the different tax treatment of the various types of investment return: interest is taxed at a higher rate than dividends and some capital gain is exempt from tax. If income tax can be deferred until a time when you expect to have a lower marginal tax rate, two advantages can be achieved. Not only will the total tax be less, but funds in a tax shelter, an RRSP for instance, grow faster because tax on the yield is deferred. Later chapters will have more about income tax in connection with investments.

Investment Risks

Each investor desires maximum return with minimum risk, but unfortunately there are no risk-free investments. Any investment carries some risk—the possibility of losing all or part of the principal or some of its purchasing power, or of receiving a return that is less than anticipated. Unfortunately these are not generally insurable risks. Nevertheless, you can attempt to reduce risk by being as well-informed as possible about investment alternatives and by having some diversity in the choice of assets so that all will not be lost in a single setback. Since investments are not risk-free, it is essential to understand the different types of risks and to know which assets are most subject to which kinds of risks.

TYPES OF RISKS

Four risks associated with investments are: (i) *inflation risk* or the possibility that invested funds will lose purchasing power, (ii) *interest rate risk*, or the likelihood that interest rates will fall, adversely affecting either the return or the price of the asset, (iii) *market risk*, or the chance that the demand for the asset will drop, lowering its value, and (iv) *business risk* or the possibility that the firm invested in will do poorly or fail.

INFLATION RISK   Inflation is measured by the annual percentage change in the Consumer Price Index. To put the high inflation of the early 1980s in perspective, look at the long-term trend in the annual inflation rate from 1948 to 1990 (Figure 9.9). After many years of relative stability, prices began rising rapidly in 1974 and again in 1980. Using an inflation rate of about 3 percent as a satisfactory bench mark, it is easy to see that this ideal has not been achieved in recent years.

Inflation decreases the purchasing power of money. With inflation at 10 percent, $1000 saved one year will buy 10 percent less the next. Although you still have a nominal $1000, it has become less valuable. If you were paid 13 percent interest, however, you would have gained enough to compensate for inflation and would also receive 3 percent real return. *Real rate of return* is the nominal or quoted rate of return less the inflation rate.

INTEREST RATE COMPARISONS

Bob, who remembered receiving 15.5 percent interest when inflation was 11.8 percent, was disturbed to find one year that Canada Savings Bonds were paying only 7 3/4 percent. What he forgot was that the inflation rate had dropped to 4.1 percent. The comparison he should have made was in real rates of return, or 3.7 percent versus 3.65 percent.

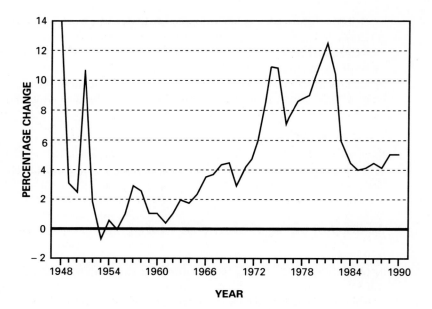

FIGURE 9.9   INFLATION RATE*, CANADA, 1948-1990

Source: *Consumer Prices and Price Indexes*. Ottawa: Statistics Canada, various years. (Catalogue No. 62-010.)
Reproduced and edited with the permission of the Minister of Supply and Services Canada.

*Average annual change in the consumer price index.

In some years, such as in the mid-1970s, the real interest rate was negative, meaning that the inflation rate exceeded interest rates. When investors are receiving a negative real rate of return on investments, they are not getting enough to compensate for inflation, let alone receiving a reward for lending. A comparison of the inflation rate with the average interest rate on three-month treasury bills shows the variation in real interest rates between 1956 and 1990 (Figure 9.10). In 1982 with nominal interest rates at 13.6 percent and inflation at 10.8 percent, the real rate was only 2.8 percent. By contrast, in 1990 the high real rates of eight percent were a result of the nominal rate of 13 percent and inflation of five percent. These examples illustrate how misleading it can be to look at the nominal rates only. Generally, high real rates reflect uncertainty in the investment sector. Over the long term, an investor might look for about 3 percent real return as minimum compensation for lending.

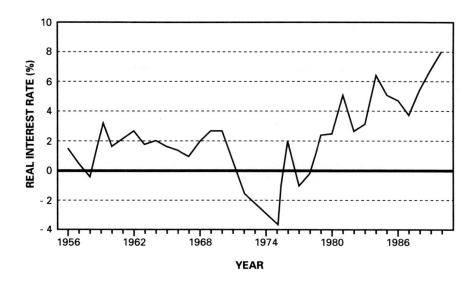

FIGURE 9.10   REAL INTEREST RATES*, CANADA, 1956-1990

*Difference between the three-month treasury bill rate and the inflation rate.

THE INFLATION RISK

When Gerry inherited $100 000 from his grandfather in 1955 he invested it safely in five-year guaranteed investment certificates which, in most years, earned a positive real rate of return. He found it very convenient to use the interest to supplement his salary, and so he did not re-invest it.

At his retirement in 1990 Gerry took a look at this capital and considered ways to generate as much income as possible. At a possible 10 percent rate, he would receive about $10 000 a year, and less if interest rates fell. He had always assumed that this large sum would provide a much better retirement income. What had happened to it?

By adjusting the $100 000 for the effect of inflation at five-year intervals, it is possible to see how inflation eroded the purchasing power of this capital over the past 35 years (Figure 9.11). Would his retirement income have been better if he had not spent the interest but left it to compound?

INTEREST RATE RISK   There is always the risk that a change in interest rates will adversely affect investments. If interest rates rise after a long-term bond has been purchased, the bond will drop in price and create a capital loss if sold. If funds are locked up in a five-year guaranteed investment certificate at six percent and interest rates later rise to 11 percent, an opportunity to benefit from the new higher rates will be lost. If, as is likely, the inflation rate also rises, the return may not cover purchasing power losses. The only protection is to try to diversify holdings, and have debt securities with a range of maturities. Debt securities are not the only assets affected by changes in the general level of interest rates. Common stocks are influenced indirectly because high

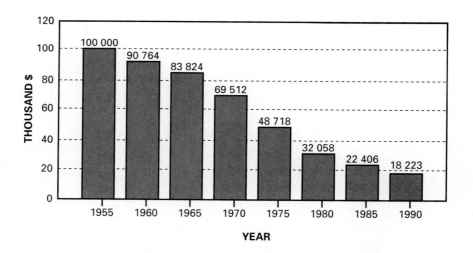

Figure 9.11   PURCHASING POWER OF $100 000 (IN 1955 $), CANADA, 1955-1990

Source: *Consumer Prices and Price Indexes.* Ottawa: Statistics Canada, various years. (Catalogue No. 62-010.) Reproduced and edited with the permission of the Minister of Supply and Services Canada.

HOW COULD SHE LOSE ON A GIC?

Tina invested $5000 in a five-year guaranteed investment certificate in 1973, when interest rates were close to historically high levels at 5.5 percent. She did not want to miss the opportunity to lock her money in at this unusually high interest rate (Figure 9.12). For the next five years she received annual payments at 5.5 percent. But what happened to interest rates during this time? From the graph you can see that nominal interest rates rose to nearly 9 percent then fell to around 12 percent.

Look at the dotted line to see the real rate of return. During most of this time it was close to zero or negative. Tina did not receive enough interest from this GIC to cover the depreciation of her capital by inflation. Not being able to forecast the future, what could Tina have done?

One way to protect assets from such situations is to invest in debt securities with a range of maturities so that some will come due each year, providing the opportunity to re-invest at prevailing rates.

interest rates discourage business expansion, but may push up the dividend rate; low rates do the opposite.

Although they do not follow each other exactly, there is a linkage between interest rates and inflation. Generally, lenders require interest rates high enough to more than compensate for inflation.

A lack of stability in interest rates complicates matters for investors. In times when interest rates are volatile, it is difficult to make wise investment decisions because there is so much uncertainty about future rates. When investors feel uncertain, as in the early 1980s, they demand higher real interest rates as compensation.

MARKET RISK   There is the possibility that general economic conditions may change the demand for one of your assets, resulting in lower prices just when you wish to sell. For instance, if you bought a house in Calgary at the height of economic activity, when work was plentiful and houses were in short supply, the price would have been high. Suppose that you had to sell your house and move to another city at a time when economic activity had slowed down and house prices were in a slump. You now face the effects of a market risk, not

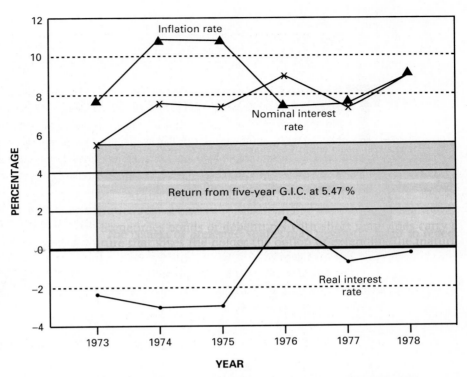

Figure 9.12   RETURN FROM A FIVE-YEAR GIC, NOMINAL AND REAL
INTEREST RATES, CANADA, 1973-1978, (GIC INVESTED
AT 5.5% IN 1973)

because your house has any less quality but because a lower demand for houses caused prices to fall. Similarly, your shares in a gold mining company could drop in price because of a reduction in demand for gold.

BUSINESS RISK   There is a risk that the business you invested in might fail totally, but more often the risk is that earnings from the business will decline, thus reducing not only your equity but also your return. Investors are attracted to companies with growing or stable earnings and usually pay a higher price for investing in them. As an investor, your risk is that you may pay too high a price for the security.

How to Reduce Risk

Since uncertainty about the future creates investment risk, the further into the future you try to predict the quality of an investment, the greater the

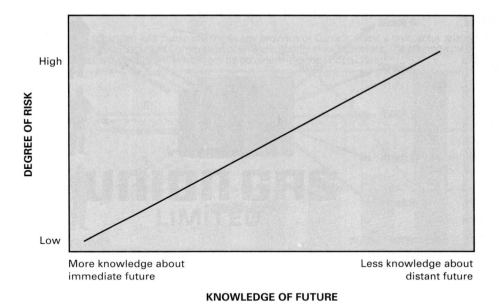

Figure 9.13   DEGREE OF RISK AND KNOWLEDGE ABOUT THE FUTURE

uncertainty—hence, the greater the risk. Risk is thus related to both time and knowledge. This relationship is summarized in Figure 9.13, which shows that risk exposure increases as knowledge about the future decreases. The best defence against risk in your investment portfolio is an understanding of current economic conditions, knowledge of particular investments, and diversification within your portfolio to spread risk.

KNOWLEDGE   There is a wide range of investment alternatives to consider, some of which will be discussed in later chapters. A successful investor should be well informed about the securities held. Anyone who plans to invest in real estate must learn a great deal about the real estate market; to make money in the stock market it is necessary to take an interest in the market in general and some specific stocks in more detail. Leaving money in deposits requires less of the investor. A compromise might be to buy mutual funds and leave investment decisions to the fund manager.

THE RISK/RETURN TRADE-OFF   Everyone wants the highest return and the lowest risk, but most will accept somewhat more risk if the expected return is greater. This brings up the risk/return trade-off. How much safety will you give up in

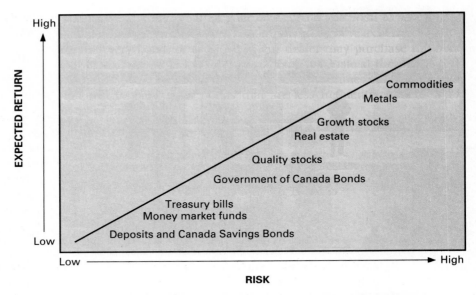

Figure 9.14   EXPECTED RETURN AND ESTIMATED RISK OF SELECTED
INVESTMENTS

the expectation of an additional unit of return? This inverse relationship is
illustrated in Figure 9.14.

Once you know what your priorities are with respect to risk and return,
look for investments that provide the desired qualities. It is difficult to generalize about classes of investments and risk because there are always exceptions
and qualifications. Figure 9.14 is intended as a general illustration of the
relation between risk and return.

RISK MANAGEMENT

WHAT ARE YOUR RISKS?

Analyze the various kinds of assets you have or might acquire, in order to
identify which risks may apply to them. Plan to avoid concentration in any
one risk category. When most assets are fixed-income debt securities there is
exposure to interest rate and inflation risks but much less to market and
business risks. Try to diversify by choosing investments with different risks.

A portfolio with a balance between debt and equities should offer protection against a broad range of risks.

BALANCE INVESTMENT AND OTHER RISKS

LIFE CYCLE AND RISK   The amount of risk that will be acceptable will vary with the stage in the life cycle. A young single person who has an adequate income and no dependents may be in a position to handle more risk than will be possible a few years later when starting a family. The middle years, when income is more than enough to handle expenses, permit a higher proportion of risk in the portfolio than will be desirable during retirement. If there is a loss, a young person has time to recoup, but retired persons should not put their retirement income at risk unless their net worth is very large.

INCOME AND RISK   Some people have more risk associated with income than others. A civil service employee can usually count on more security than a person who is self-employed, or who is in a cyclical industry that often lays off workers. Farmers and other self-employed people often invest in their businesses instead of the stock market. To balance the high risk associated with their equity-based income, they may put some savings in very low-risk debt securities.

At this first level of diversification, look at total net worth as well as the income source. If, for instance, your income is dependent on the real estate market, you would not want to put your savings into the same sector. In addition to planning for a balance among a broad range of risks, attention should also be given to spreading risk within an investment portfolio by diversifying the types of assets.

DIVERSIFY INVESTMENTS

A basic principle in portfolio management is *diversification*, which means reducing total risk by choosing securities that are not subject to the same types of risk. If there is enough money to work with, the risk to your whole portfolio can be reduced by spreading the risk over a variety of investments. Small investors can achieve diversification by using mutual funds, a topic to be discussed in Chapter 11. Since it is impossible to maximize safety, yield, and growth in any one portfolio, decide which is the highest priority but do not neglect the other two. Expect to adjust a portfolio from time to time as needs and economic conditions change.

DIVERSITY IN PORTFOLIOS

Three investors, Ann, Bob, and Carl, are at different stages in life and have different attitudes toward investments, as you can see from this summary of their portfolios.

Investment	Ann	Bob	Carl
	%	%	%
Canada Savings Bonds	0	50	15
Guaranteed investment certificates	0	25	10
Mutual fund (balanced)	0	25	30
Corporate bonds	0	0	15
Common stocks	60	0	25
Gold	40	0	5
TOTAL	100	100	100

Which one is probably young, single and not averse to risk? Who likely spends the least time looking after his or her portfolio? Who seems to have spread the risk most widely?

Bob, who appears to be the most conservative in this group, as he has three-quarters of his portfolio in debt securities, is exposed to interest rate and inflation risks. This is offset by the balanced mutual fund (invested in stocks and bonds) which offers some opportunity for growth and inflation-protection without very high risk. Perhaps he is retired, has a lower marginal tax rate, and needs income-producing securities.

Ann, with no debt securities, has the most risk in her portfolio. She is very heavily exposed to market and business risks but should be protected against inflation. But what will she use for emergency funds or short-term goals? If she should need funds when the market is low, she might be forced to take a capital loss.

Carl, the seasoned investor, may have the largest net worth. At any rate, he has diversified his holdings more than the others, and thus has protection against a range of risks.

INVESTMENTS AND THEIR CHARACTERISTICS

In spite of the difficulties in classifying investments by various characteristics, the following summary chart is presented as a general guide (Table 9.1).

Table 9.1   INVESTMENT CHARACTERISTICS BY ASSET CATEGORY

Asset category	Investment characteristics				
	Safety	Liquidity	Income/ capital gain	Mgt. effort	Inflation protection
Deposits: (savings accounts, CSBs, term deposits)	Exc.	Exc.	Fixed income	Very little	None
GICs	Exc.	Poor	Fixed income	Very little	None
Treasury bills, money market funds	Exc.	Very good	Fixed income	Little	None
High quality bonds	Exc. to good	Varies	Fixed income, gain possible	Not much	Not much
High quality preferred shares	Good to fair	Varies	Both possible	Some	Some
Common stock	Good to poor	Poor	Both possible	Some to much	Good in long run
Real estate (income property)	Good to poor	Poor	Both possible	Necessary	Usually good
Mutual funds	Good to poor	Poor	Both possible	Not much	Varies

PERSONAL INVESTMENT PLANS

INVESTMENT OBJECTIVES

Within the general framework of an overall aim of maximizing investment return with minimum risk and effort, you must establish personal priorities with respect to your total portfolio before considering specific investments. What is your personal preference for risk, and for spending time and effort managing investments? At your stage in the life cycle, what are your needs for current income? Use Table 9.2 to record your preferences, on a scale of zero to ten. With paired characteristics, the combined values must equal ten to reflect the trade-off involved.

ANALYZE PRESENT PORTFOLIO

Make a list of the assets you now own, their values, their share of the total, and annual rate of return. Use Table 9.3 to classify each according to its prime investment objective.

Compare your investment priorities with this asset analysis, but do not be surprised if you find that your expressed preferences do not exactly corre-

Table 9.2   PRIORITIES FOR YOUR TOTAL PORTFOLIO

Objectives	Priorities										
1. Return	0	1	2	3	4	5	6	7	8	9	10
Safety	10	9	8	7	6	5	4	3	2	1	0
				(combined value = 10)							
2. Current income	0	1	2	3	4	5	6	7	8	9	10
Capital gain (growth)	10	9	8	7	6	5	4	3	2	1	0
				(combined value = 10)							
3. Liquidity	0	1	2	3	4	5	6	7	8	9	10
Return	10	9	8	7	6	5	4	3	2	1	0
				(combined value = 10)							
4. Inflation protection	0	1	2	3	4	5	6	7	8	9	10
Safety	10	9	8	7	6	5	4	3	2	1	0
				(combined value = 10)							
5. Management effort	0	1	2	3	4	5	6	7	8	9	10
6. Tax reduction	0	1	2	3	4	5	6	7	8	9	10

Table 9.3   ANALYSIS OF PRESENT PORTFOLIO

Asset	Present value	% of total	Annual rate of return	Investment objective
Savings account				
GIC				
Term deposits				
Canada Savings Bonds				
RRSPs				
Mutual funds				
Bonds				
Stocks				
Real estate				

spond to your current holdings. You might have indicated that you gave a high priority to inflation protection but discover that you have mostly fixed-income assets. This analysis of your objectives will be a guide in planning changes to your portfolio and in choosing additional investments.

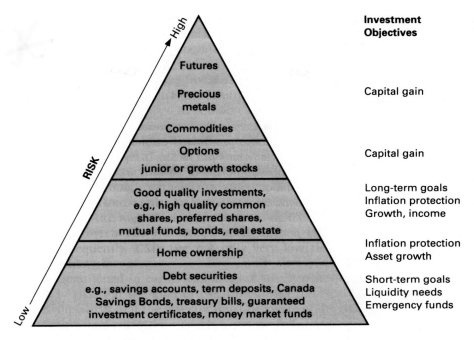

Investment Objectives

Capital gain

Capital gain

Long-term goals
Inflation protection
Growth, income

Inflation protection
Asset growth

Short-term goals
Liquidity needs
Emergency funds

Figure 9.15   THE INVESTMENT PYRAMID

INVESTMENT PYRAMID

A widely-used guide to investment planning is the investment pyramid, which depicts a summary of an individual's portfolio (Figure 9.15). As the height of the pyramid increases, so does the risk; those investments at the base of the pyramid carry the least risk. If drawn to scale, each slice of the pyramid would represent the distribution of the portfolio among the various risk categories. The order of priority is from bottom to top. First, ensure that you have invested money for emergencies, liquidity needs, and short-term goals in secure but accessible securities. For those who choose home ownership, investment in a home property will be the next priority. After taking care of these needs, investments can be made in good quality securities to fund long-term goals. The top slices of the pyramid are high-risk securities that should not represent a significant share of most portfolios and should be considered only if other investment goals have been adequately funded.

Make a drawing of your own portfolio pyramid to see how well you have implemented your priorities. There is no one right way to divide the pyramid; it will depend on your stage in the life cycle, your personal objectives, and your financial situation. Those who are very young or very wealthy may be more aggressive than older or retired investors. Nevertheless, everyone needs a safety cushion of funds for short-term needs before moving into other types of investments. The purpose of this pyramid exercise is to become more aware of portfolio planning and to avoid haphazard investing, which may not be the best way to achieve your financial goals.

What Will Your Next Investment Be?

Once you have a clear picture of your overall objectives, you will be in a position to determine the specific objectives of an additional investment. If your portfolio is largely low-risk, low-return, fixed-income securities, you would probably want your next investment to offer more inflation protection, more return, and somewhat less safety.

An Investment Plan

A well-designed plan for saving and investing is the road to financial independence. As was mentioned in Chapter 4, Economic Risks and Financial Security, financial security is the assurance that you can maintain your desired level of living now and in the future. In spite of public income security programs and personal insurance, a significant component of financial security is dependent on individual net worth. Should you wish to retire early from the labour force to pursue other interests, or to have a comfortable life after the conventional retirement age, the size of your net worth will be a determining factor. Furthermore, a saving and investment plan is a good defence against impulse spending or social pressure to buy things.

Earlier in this chapter there was discussion of the need to save for emergency funds, liquidity needs, and short-term and long-term goals. This money should be invested in securities with appropriate maturities and with characteristics that match your priorities. Your investment plan will include a forecast of the total amount required, the amounts to be saved each pay period, and indications as to how these savings will be invested.

Summary

This general discussion of investment provides an introduction to chapters on the specifics of debt securities and stocks. This chapter emphasized that you must save money if you wish to invest. You should devise ways to give saving a high priority, examine reasons for investing and, finally learn how to make an investment plan. All investors want to maximize return and yet minimize risk, the effects of inflation, and income tax. To accomplish these objectives it is necessary to have clear investment goals, and some knowledge about securities, and to be prepared to invest time as well as money in the process. Although there are no risk-free investments, the wise investor understands the risk inherent in various types of securities and uses diversification to reduce overall risk.

PROBLEMS

1. Decide whether you AGREE or DISAGREE with each of the following statements. State reasons for your decision.

   (a) Do not invest your emergency funds in common stocks because the liquidity is too high.
   (b) Investing means putting money in high-risk assets.
   (c) A savings account is not really a type of investment.
   (d) If you lend money to someone to buy a house and take back a mortgage, you have acquired an equity security.
   (e) If you own rental property, the rent you receive is not considered capital gain.
   (f) Interest is one form of income received from equity securities.
   (g) Accumulating enough money to pay the annual taxes on the house is an example of a need for a liquidity fund.

2. (a) When do you think a person should start saving for retirement?
   (b) What kind of retirement saving would you suggest, if any, for a person who is 25 and in a first job?
   (c) What are some of the costs and benefits of leaving retirement saving until about age 50?
   (d) Look at Figure 1.1 (Chapter 1) and identify the life cycle stage(s) when you think the financial pressures will be the greatest.

3. Suppose that a young couple consulted you about their financial affairs. They claimed that it was impossible for them to save anything at all because they had credit card bills to pay each month for a wide range of necessities. In fact, the amount outstanding on the two credit cards was gradually increasing. What suggestions might you make?

4. Decide whether you AGREE or DISAGREE with each of the following statements, based on the information provided in this chapter.

   (a) Most Canadian families have some wealth.
   (b) For most families, their home is the single largest asset.
   (c) The lower the income level, the more the diversity in the average family's portfolio.
   (d) Stocks and miscellaneous financial investments are more significant forms of assets for higher-income families than for low-income or middle-income households.

(e) All low-income or middle-income families have a positive net worth.
(f) The ratio of wealth to income increases with age.
(g) With age, a household's wealth becomes greater than its average annual income because of increasing propensity to save.
(h) On average, families under age 45 have enough wealth to replace their income for a couple of years if they faced unemployment or illness.
(i) Those who own stocks are more likely to have high incomes.
(j) The savings rate in Canada has been rising steadily for a decade or more.
(k) The aggregate savings rate in Canada has varied but has rarely exceeded 10 percent.

5. (a) It is apparent from Figure 9.2 that, on average, Canadians are successful savers. However, the results of a household survey indicate that only around 10 percent of Canadians invest in the stock market. Suggest reasons for this.
(b) Do you think many people equate buying stocks with speculating?

6. (a) List four factors that are inversely related to return on investments.
(b) Why is there usually an inverse relation between income and capital gain?
(c) Why is more risk generally associated with equity than with debt investments?

7. Which of the following pairs of investments is more liquid?

(a) Canada Savings Bond or five-year guaranteed investment certificate.
(b) common stock or a term deposit.

8. In the example about Gerry and his $100 000 inheritance (Figure 9.11), it seems that safety of principal was given the highest priority.

(a) Identify some risks he failed to protect against.
(b) How would you have invested such a sum to be a source of retirement income?

9. Refer to Figure 9.12. This investor locked in funds in 1973 when interest rates were close to a historical high, a decision that seemed very rational at the time.

(a) Did the investor receive enough return during this period to compensate for inflation and also to gain from having lent the money?
(b) If you planned to invest several thousand dollars in debt securities, is there any way to hedge against a sudden change in interest rates?

10. Why do we say that stocks are not liquid investments?

11. Assume that a friend, who has just inherited $40 000, asked your advice on investing it. Before offering any ideas you need to know something about

your friend's situation. Write out five essential questions you would ask your friend.

12.

WHAT ARE HIS INVESTMENT OBJECTIVES?

Jim is an affable person who admits he is a spendthrift and generally unable to save money. At 28 he has plans to marry within the year and possibly to build his own house. As a welder-fitter, he finds his income more than sufficient for his needs. He owes $7000 on a car loan, which is life-insured. When asked how he would invest a windfall of $11 000 he said he was not averse to taking some risk. He recognizes that inflation can erode capital and thinks that perhaps he should try for capital gain. He wants this investment to be highly liquid and invested for a short term in a safe place. He does not want to risk the capital.

table-9. 2

(a) From this limited information, make a list of Jim's investment priorities.
(b) How do you suggest he should invest this money to achieve all of his goals?
(c) If you were Jim's investment advisor, what advice would you have for him?

13.

INVESTMENT PRIORITIES

Sid, 45, has grown, independent children; his house is paid for and he is the owner of a well-established business. He has reached the stage of having a large margin between his current income and his expenses. He owns bonds and common stock, and is saving for his retirement. When asked how he would invest his next $6000 of savings, he listed his highest priorities as safety of principal, current income, capital appreciation; liquidity and inflation protection were less essential. He thinks he might invest in mining stock and a second mortgage as soon as his savings build up enough.

(a) Examine Sid's investment objectives in light of what you know about his financial situation.

(b) Identify any inconsistencies between his stated objectives and his plans.

(c) It is not uncommon to find such inconsistencies. Why is that?

14.

HOW MUCH RISK?

Claude and Janet are consulting you about their investments. They are in their mid-forties, with two teen-age daughters. Claude is employed as a computer programmer with a large company, and Janet is a teacher. They have a mortgage on their house, but no other debts. Their assets include Canada Savings Bonds and term deposits, but they are now thinking of buying some common stocks. In conversation you discover that they want their investment to be a hedge against inflation. They would prefer an investment that does not require much attention from them, and that offers the prospect of capital gain. They are nervous about assuming risk and want their funds readily available in case of an emergency.

(a) What would you say to this couple?

(b) What kind of investment would you suggest for them?

REFERENCES

Books

AMLING, FREDERICK, and WILLIAM G. DROMS. *The Dow Jones-Irwin Guide to Personal Financial Planning.* Second Edition. Homewood, Illinois: Dow Jones-Irwin, 1986, 549 pp. Although written for American readers, much of the discussion of financial planning, life insurance, retirement planning, and investments is relevant for Canadians.

ANDERSON, BRIAN, and CHRISTOPHER SNYDER. *It's Your Money.* Sixth Edition. Toronto: Methuen, 1989, 264 pp. A reference for the general reader which includes financial planning, budgets, income tax, disability insurance, savings, investments, retirement planning, credit, wills, and estates.

BIRCH, RICHARD. *The Family Financial Planning Book, A Step-by-Step Moneyguide for Canadian Families.* Toronto: Key Porter, 1987, 216 pp. An easy-to-read guide to taking control of your personal finances that discusses budgets, income tax, insurance, RRSPs, mortgages, and investments.

CHAKRAPINI, C. *Financial Freedom on $5 a Day*. Fourth Edition. Vancouver: International Self-Counsel Press, 1989, 200 pp. Presents a method of increasing net worth by consistently saving and investing small sums.

COHEN, DIAN. *Money*. Scarborough, Ontario: Prentice-Hall Canada, 1987, 270 pp. An economist suggests strategies for coping with personal finances in the context of changing economic conditions. Topics include financial plans, buying a home, insurance, income tax, retirement, estate planning, and investments.

COSTELLO, BRIAN. *Your Money and How to Keep It*. Fifth Edition. Toronto: Stoddart, 1990, 248 pp. Particular emphasis on investments and income tax.

COTE, JEAN-MARC, and DONALD DAY. *Personal Financial Planning in Canada*. Toronto: Allyn and Bacon, 1987, 464 pp. A comprehensive personal finance text that includes financial planning, income tax, annuities, pensions, investments, credit, mortgages, and wills with particular attention to the banking and insurance industries.

DRACHE, ARTHUR B. C., and SUSAN WEIDMAN SCHNEIDER. *Head and Heart, Financial Strategies for Smart Women*. Toronto: Macmillan, 1987, 348 pp. Recognizing the needs and perspectives of women, a tax lawyer and journalist have collaborated to present basic financial information, taking into account women's concerns at different stages in their lives.

DRACHE, ARTHUR B. C., and PEGGY WATERTON. *Dollars and Sense, The Complete Canadian Financial Planner*. Toronto: Grosvenor House, 1987, 207 pp. An overview of a range of financial topics, including budgets, credit, investing, taxes, insurance, retirement planning, estates, and effects of changes in family status.

FORMAN, NORM. *Mind Over Money, Curing Your Financial Headaches with Moneysanity*. Toronto: Doubleday Canada, 1987, 248 pp. A psychologist examines the effects money has on behaviour, looking at the origin of money problems and suggesting therapies to help us to better understand ourselves.

FRIEDLAND, SEYMOUR, and STEVEN G. KELMAN. *Investment Strategies, How to Create Your Own and Make it Work for You*. Markham, Ontario: Penguin Canada, 1988, 125 pp. Offers guidance for the general reader in defining objectives and establishing an investment program.

GOHEEN, DUNCAN. *Planning for Financial Independence, Choose Your Lifestyle, Secure Your Future*. Vancouver: International Self-Counsel Press, 1988, 111 pp. Detailed guidance for making a financial plan, including the necessary charts and tables.

HATCH, JAMES E. and MICHAEL J. ROBINSON. *Investment Management in Canada*. Toronto: Prentice-Hall Canada, 1989, 836 pp. A technical university text with in-depth coverage of many aspects of investing.

MACINNIS, LYMAN. *Get Smart! Make Your Money Count in the 1990s*. Second Edition. Scarborough, Ontario: Prentice-Hall Canada, 1989, 317 pp. A book for the general reader that includes financial planning, income tax principles, but gives major attention to investing in the stock market.

MOTHERWELL, CATHRYN. *Smart Money, Investment Strategies for Canadian Women*. Toronto: Key Porter, 1989, 192 pp. A financial journalist explains how to get started investing, how to evaluate the products and how to build a portfolio.

PAPE, GORDON. *Building Wealth, Achieving Your Financial Goals*. Scarborough, Ontario: Prentice-Hall Canada, 1988, 246 pp. An easy-to-read guide for the novice financial manager and investor that considers interest rates, credit cards, mortgages, RRSPs, mutual funds, and the stock market.

PAPE, GORDON. *Low-Risk Investing*. Scarborough, Ontario: Prentice-Hall Canada, 1989, 244 pp. A book written to encourage the novice investor to get started on saving and investing. Outlines the basics of investing in debt and equity investments.

TURNER, MARY, DANIEL LEROSSIGNOL, CLAUDE RINFRET, and RICHARD DAW. *Canadian Guide to Personal Financial Management*. Fourth Edition. Scarborough, Ontario: Prentice-Hall Canada, 1989, 231 pp. Accountants provide guidance on a broad range of topics, including planning finances, estimating insurance needs, managing risk, and determining investment needs. Instructions and the necessary forms for making plans are provided.

WYATT, ELAINE. *The Money Companion, How to Manage Your Money and Achieve Financial Freedom*. Markham, Ontario: Penguin Books, 1989, 203 pp. A guide to personal financial management that focuses on planning, investment strategy, and retirement needs.

WYLIE, BETTY JANE, and LYNNE MACFARLANE. *Everywoman's Money Book*. Fourth Edition. Toronto: Key Porter, 1989, 223 pp. A journalist and a stock broker have collaborated on this wide-ranging treatment of a variety of personal finance topics, including women and credit; the budget; insurance; retirement; children and money.

Article

"Investing Your Wealth," *The Financial Post Moneywise*, 1990 Annual Moneyplanner, December 1989, 36-62. Discussion of investment objectives and various ways to meet them through mutual funds, stocks, and debt securities.

Periodicals

Canadian Consumer. Monthly. Box 9300, Ottawa, Ontario, K1G 3T9. In recent years, the personal finance articles have been concentrated in the November issue, "Personal Money Guide."

Canadian Money Saver. Monthly. Box 370, Bath, Ontario, K0H 1G0. Includes short articles on a range of personal finance topics, with special emphasis on investments.

Financial Times. Weekly. Suite 500, 920 Yonge Street, Toronto, Ontario, M2W 3L5. Provides current information on a range of business and economic topics.

Report on Business. Daily. A section of *The Globe and Mail.* Important source of information on the financial markets.

The Financial Post. Daily and weekly. 777 Bay Street, Toronto, Ontario, M5G 2E4. Up-to-date information on business, economics, income tax, and investments.

The Financial Post Annual Moneyplanner. Annual. 777 Bay Street, Toronto, Ontario, M5G 2E4. Usually contains articles on financial planning, income tax, insurance, investing, and retirement planning.

The Financial Post Magazine. Monthly. 777 Bay Street, Toronto, Ontario, M5G 2E4. Includes a section on personal finance.

10 DEBT SECURITIES

1. To distinguish among the following types of debt securities: guaranteed investment certificates, term deposits, treasury bills, commercial paper, money market funds.

2. To understand the significance of the following features when comparing deposits offered by financial institutions:
   (a) maturities or term,
   (b) accessibility of invested funds,
   (c) minimum deposit,
   (d) interest rate and frequency of compounding.

3. To explain the purpose and coverage of deposit insurance.

4. To distinguish between the following pairs:
   (a) bearer and registered bonds,
   (b) mortgage and collateral trust bonds,
   (c) nominal rate and yield to maturity,
   (d) an investment dealer acting as a principal and as an agent in the distribution of bonds,
   (e) the money market and the bond market,
   (f) bonds and debentures,
   (g) extendible and retractable bonds,
   (h) interest on a cash basis and on a receivable basis.

5. To outline the process of underwriting and selling a bond issue and to identify factors that affect the interest rates of new bond issues.

6. To calculate the approximate yield to maturity on a marketable bond.

7. To explain how changing bond prices affect yield to maturity.

8. To explain why accrued interest is added to the price of a bond.

9. To explain the differences in the tax treatment of two types of bond yield: interest and capital gain.

10. To explain these terms: maturity date, term, call feature, denomination, par, discount, premium, redemption, coupon, underwriter, bank rate, bond certificate, convertible bond, floating rate, sinking fund, stripped bonds.

11. To explain why Canada Savings Bonds are more like savings certificates than bonds.

INTRODUCTION

This chapter is about debt securities, those for which the investor becomes a lender rather than an owner, and as a result generally assumes less risk and less management responsibility. Four groups of debt securities, those of most interest to individual investors, will be discussed: (i) deposits, (ii) money market securities, (iii) bonds and debentures, and (iv) Canada Savings Bonds. Most of these are low-risk, very liquid investments, appropriate as a base for any portfolio. Deposits and Canada Savings Bonds are not transferrable to other investors, but money market securities and bonds may be traded in the financial markets. It is important to distinguish between Canada Savings Bonds, which are more like savings certificates, and the other types of bonds.

This chapter provides an introduction to basic principles and terminology associated with debt securities, but does not address portfolio management strategies. You are referred to other books to continue your study of investing in debt securities.

DEPOSITS

The easiest and simplest way to invest is to lend capital to financial institutions by placing it in deposit securities in the form of savings accounts, term deposits, and guaranteed investment certificates. Although these savings vehicles may differ in interest rates, term, minimum deposit, and accessibility, all are very low risk, pay interest regularly, and require minimum attention from the investor.

SAVINGS ACCOUNTS

Banks, trust companies, and credit unions offer a bewildering array of accounts, which may or may not permit chequing, but generally pay higher interest rates on accounts that require the least service. Should you plan to leave funds relatively untouched in a savings account, look for an account that combines the best interest rate with the most frequent compounding. If, however, your account balance tends to fluctuate, a daily interest account might be advantageous, in spite of a lower interest rate. Interest will be paid on the daily balance, compounded monthly rather than on the minimum monthly balance, compounded semi-annually as in many savings accounts. The highly competitive markets of today force financial institutions to make frequent changes in the types of accounts offered; do some comparison shopping to find the best account for your purposes. Some criteria to be considered when comparing accounts are shown in Table 10.1 that compares fees among several banks and trust companies.

Table 10.1   FEES FOR SELECTED BANK SERVICES, 1990

| | General service charges | | | | Cheque related charges | | | Chequing/Savings Account | | | Savings Account only | | |
	Stop payment	Bill payment at branch	Transfer between accounts	Monthly statements	Certification	Chargeback (wrong date, etc.)	NSF (insufficient funds)	Minimum balance	Cost per cheque	Cost per withdrawal at ATM	Minimum monthly balance	Cost per withdrawal at counter	Penalty for account closed within 90 days of opening	Packaged services*
Bank A	$6.50	$1.05	$4.00	na.	$3.50	$3.50	$16.00	$200	$0.46	$0.75	$600	no charge	$10.00	$7.50 mo.
Bank B	$6.00	$1.00	$4.25	$4.25	$3.50	$3.00	$15.00	$200	$0.70	$0.70	$600	no charge	$6.00	$8.50 mo.
Bank C	$7.00	$1.15	no charge	$3.50	$3.75	na.	$16.00	$200	$0.44	no charge	$1000	no charge	$10.00	$8.50 mo.
Trust A	$6.50	$1.00	$5.00	$2.00	$3.50	na.	$15.00	na.	$0.40	$0.45	na.	no charge	$10.00	na.
Trust B	$9.00	$1.00	$5.00	$2.25	$4.00	no charge	$19.00	$1200	no charge	no charge	$1200	no charge	$15.00	na.

na: information not available, or service not offered.
*: a package of services for day-to-day banking needs.

TERM DEPOSITS

As the name implies, *term deposits* are for a specified term at a guaranteed interest rate, and in some cases require a minimum investment. Savings accounts, by contrast, have no guaranteed interest rate, no minimum deposit, and no set term that the funds are required to be on deposit. The rate of return on term deposits is usually higher than on savings accounts, and although the money is invested for a specified term, funds can usually be withdrawn before maturity by sacrificing some interest. Since the frequency of interest payments affects the interest rate, expect a lower rate if interest is to be paid monthly.

GUARANTEED INVESTMENT CERTIFICATES

These savings certificates have terms ranging from one to five years, during which time the interest rate is guaranteed and the money usually locked in until maturity, except in the case of settling an estate after death. If you have funds in a guaranteed investment certificate and need the money before maturity, the issuing trust company will not redeem the certificate but you may be able to sell it through some brokerage houses. The price will depend on interest rates prevailing at the time; it could be discounted or sold at a premium, terms to be discussed later in this chapter in relation to bonds.

For certain rates and maturities, a minimum deposit may be required. Some certificates provide regular interest payments and others offer automatic compounding. Generally, the interest rate will be slightly less if interest payments are to be made more often than once a year.

DEPOSIT INSURANCE

Funds deposited in a bank, trust company, or credit union are insured against loss if the institution should become insolvent. In 1967, the federal government established the Canada Deposit Insurance Corporation (CDIC) as a Crown corporation to insure deposits in member institutions. You may notice signs on the windows of banks and trust companies indicating membership.

The CDIC insures savings and chequing accounts, money orders, deposit receipts, guaranteed investment certificates, debentures, and other obligations issued by the member institutions. The maximum coverage is changed from time to time, but is currently $60 000 per depositor for each institution, which applies to a combined total of deposits at all branches of the same institution. One restriction is that term deposits, to be insurable, must be redeemable no later than five years after deposit. Joint accounts are insured separately from individual accounts, meaning that if you had both a personal and a joint account in the same bank, you would have the maximum coverage of $60 000 on each account. Credit unions, through their provincial leagues, offer similar deposit insurance.

MONEY MARKET SECURITIES

From time to time, corporations and governments need to borrow money to support their various activities. Corporations borrow from banks, or borrow by selling bonds, debentures, or short-term commercial paper. The federal government borrows by selling Canada Savings Bonds, treasury bills, or

Canada bonds; provincial and municipal governments borrow by selling debentures. These various types of loans are usually classified as either short-term (money market instruments) or long-term (bonds or debentures). We will look first at money market securities, which include treasury bills, commercial paper, and money market funds.

THE MONEY MARKET

A large pool of cash moves from lenders to borrowers for short periods through a mechanism known as the *money market*. The major actors in this market are the banks, other financial institutions (trust companies, small loan and sales finance companies), corporations, governments, and our central bank, the Bank of Canada. The lenders are usually corporations or institutions with spare cash that can be invested for a short period, and the borrowers are those who temporarily need extra funds. There is no physical site where money market transactions take place, only a communication system. Because of the large minimum investment required, few individual investors are aware of all this activity.

The money market, as has been mentioned, deals with short-term loans, mostly for 30, 60, 90, or 365 days, but occasionally for as long as three to five years. Commercial paper and treasury bills are two widely used instruments in the money market. *Commercial paper* (discounted paper) is the name used for short-term loans or promissory notes; instead of borrowing a principal sum and repaying it with interest at maturity, the lender may invest a discounted sum and at maturity receive an amount equivalent to the loan plus interest. For instance, a 30-day note for $50 000 might be purchased for $49 600 by the lender, who would receive $50 000 at maturity. The difference between the amount invested and the amount received is the interest on the loan, which in this instance is 9.6 percent.

TREASURY BILLS

Short-term promissory notes issued principally by the federal government but also by other levels of government are called *treasury bills*. The usual denominations are $1000, $5000, $25 000, $100 000, and $1 000 000, with terms of 91, 182, or 365 days. Treasury bills, like commercial paper, do not carry specific interest rates but sell at a discount with the purchaser's yield determined by the difference between the price paid and the value at maturity. Since investors can sell treasury bills before maturity at a price dependent on current interest rates, they are marketable securities.

T-BILLS

When Jim inherited $25 000, he needed a short-term investment until he made other plans. He chose a 91-day treasury bill, discounted at 12.5 percent. The price he paid was determined as follows:

$$\text{Principal} + \text{interest paid at maturity} = \text{discounted amount (X)} + \text{interest for 91 days}$$

$$
\begin{aligned}
25\,000 &= X + (X \times .125 \times 91/365) \\
&= X\,[1 + (1 \times .125 \times .249)] \\
&= X\,[1 + (.0311)] \\
&= X \times 1.0311 \\
X &= \frac{25\,000}{1.0311} \\
&= \$24\,246
\end{aligned}
$$

Jim invested $24 246 for 91 days; at maturity he received $25 000 which included a gain of $794, equivalent to an interest rate of 12.5 percent. Revenue Canada Taxation treats this gain as interest, not capital gain.

If Jim had needed to sell the treasury bill before it matured, the return would be re-calculated to reflect the current T-bill rate at the time of the sale.

Each Thursday, Government of Canada treasury bills are auctioned in Ottawa by the Bank of Canada. The previous week, the Bank of Canada announces the amounts and maturities of the bills to be auctioned, and interested investors, i.e., banks and investment dealers, submit bids. At the auction the bills are sold to the highest bidders, with the Bank of Canada possibly tendering reserve bids. This treasury bill auction is a mechanism whereby the federal government exerts influence on all interest rates. The *bank rate*, the rate at which the Bank of Canada lends funds to the chartered banks, is tied to the weekly auction; for instance the bank rate may be 1/4 percent higher than the auction rate on 91-day treasury bills. Usually, the evening news on Thursdays includes an item on the change in the bank rate as a result of this weekly auction.

Most of the treasury bills are bought by banks, to be kept as part of their reserves, or by investment dealers who sell them on the secondary market. In

Table 10.2   COSTS AND BENEFITS OF SEVERAL DEBT SECURITIES

Debt security	Interest rate %	Costs and benefits
Savings Accounts		
daily interest	8.5	Liquid, less interest
T-bill account*	10.1	Liquid, minimum balance required
Term deposit*†	11.5	Locked in, higher interest
Treasury bill†	12.76	Liquid, need broker's account‡, highest rate

* Minimum of $5000.
† Invested for three months.
‡ Some banks will sell treasury bills with a minimum deposit of $25 000 to $50 000; otherwise it is necessary to have an account with a broker who may sell them in units of $5000.

recent years, some investment dealers have made treasury bills available to small investors with a minimum purchase of $1000, in increments of $1000. Anyone who wishes to invest for a short term in a top quality, low-risk, very liquid investment, should consider treasury bills. To buy treasury bills it may be necessary to open an account with a stock broker. Usually treasury bills pay somewhat higher interest than savings accounts or term deposits as noted in Table 10.2.

MONEY MARKET FUNDS

Savings accounts are not the only places to put small sums in low-risk, highly liquid, interest-earning securities. If you do not have enough money to buy treasury bills directly from a broker, you can put your savings in the money market through a *money market fund*, which is a way of pooling contributions from many small investors. A money market mutual fund accepts small amounts from many people, and under the supervision of a paid manager these are invested in a portfolio of treasury bills and commercial paper. The individual investor thus acquires shares in the money market fund that can be sold at any time. The return from money market funds, in the form of interest, may be received regularly by the investor or reinvested in additional shares of the fund.

Sponsors of money market funds vary in their selling practices and commission fees. Some are sold directly to customers, others are available through brokers. Some funds do not charge a fee, but require a large initial deposit, while others may charge an acquisition fee of two to nine percent depending on the size of the investment; the larger the deposit, the smaller the rate. Most money market funds charge annual management fees, which are deducted before return is paid to the investor. (Mutual funds and their fee systems will be elaborated on in Chapter 11.)

INVESTING IN A MONEY MARKET FUND

Janice has $5000 that she wants to invest in a money market fund because she likes the liquidity and high interest rates. But she has discovered, on making inquiries, that for her modest investment the acquisition fee may amount to nine percent or up to $450.

Last year the average return paid by the more conservative companies was 11.2 percent. At that rate, the first year interest could be almost equivalent to the initial fee, although in future years this fee would not recur.

In the mail, Janice received a prospectus from ABC Money Market Fund, which states that no commission will be charged on investments over $2500. Recently, this company has been paying 12.5 percent and its past record is comparable with similar money market funds. Janice thinks that she will invest her money in this fund.

BONDS

BONDS AND DEBENTURES

Debt securities with longer-term maturities include bonds and debentures, which may have terms up to 25 years or more. There is a distinction between bonds and debentures, although occasionally the terms appear to be used interchangeably. Technically, *bonds* are secured with property, while *debentures* are unsecured loans. To further confuse matters, Government of Canada bonds are really debentures, but they are customarily called bonds. In this chapter, bonds will be used as the generic term to include both bonds and debentures.

Bonds are issued by the federal, provincial, and municipal governments, by public utilities, and by private corporations when they need to borrow money. If you buy their bonds, you become their creditor and receive a promise that interest will be paid on specific dates, and the principal repaid at maturity.

HOW BONDS ARE ISSUED

When a government or corporation wishes to float a new bond issue, one or more investment dealers will be consulted for advice on terms. After an agreement is reached, the bonds will be printed and transferred by the issuer (borrower) to the investment dealers who are underwriting this particular issue. *Underwriters* are involved not only in designing the terms of the issue but also in its sale and distribution. They may *act as principals* by buying the entire issue for resale to the public, or *act as agents*, in which case they agree to find buyers. Their profit comes from being able to purchase the issue below par or from a commission paid by the issuer.

The *par value*, the face value of the bond or other security, is printed on the bond—for example, $1000. Investment dealers advertise each new issue of bonds and sell them to buyers at a price that may be at par or slightly below, depending on the market at the time.

BOND ISSUE ANNOUNCEMENT   Examine the announcement of a new bond issue reproduced in Figure 10.1. It gives the name of the bond issuer (Newfoundland and Labrador Hydro) and the total value of the bond issue ($40 million). The terms of the issue are: interest at 10 percent of the face value will be paid for 25 years from June 27, 1978 to June 27, 2003; Hydro will not recall these bonds before June 27, 1998; and the principal and interest are guaranteed by the Province of Newfoundland. Note that when first issued, the bonds could be purchased for 99, which means that a $1000 bond cost $990. It is a convention to list bond prices in hundreds of dollars, although a $1000 bond is frequently the lowest denomination available. Although the bonds described in such an announcement (known as tombstones in the industry) may have already been sold to investors by the time it appears in the papers, they will be trading on the bond market at the going price.

The investment dealers, listed at the bottom of the advertisement, underwrote this issue and initially may have bought all the bonds from Hydro. However, once sold by the investment dealers, the bonds would trade on the bond market. Bondholders who no longer wish to keep their bonds cannot redeem them from Hydro until 1998, but may sell them to another investor. It might be interesting to find out from a broker the price at which these bonds are currently selling. Later in this chapter you will find out why they may be priced at less or more than 100.

FACTORS AFFECTING INTEREST RATES   Three significant factors that affect the rate of interest on a new bond issue are general level of interest rates in the country at the time, the length of time to maturity, and the credit rating of the issuer. At a time when general interest rates are quite high, bond issuers will have to offer equivalent rates to attract investors. Since money has a time value, the longer the term, the more uncertainty about the future; consequently, a higher rate is needed to interest investors in very long-term bonds.

The credit rating of a bond issuer is dependent on its financial status and

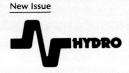

$40,000,000

NEWFOUNDLAND AND LABRADOR HYDRO

10% Sinking Fund Debentures, Series L
to be dated June 27, 1978 and mature June 27, 2003
(Non redeemable before June 27, 1998)

Guaranteed unconditionally as to principal and interest by
Province of Newfoundland

We, as principals, offer these Debentures, subject to prior sale and change in price, if, as and when issued by Newfoundland and Labrador Hydro and accepted by us and subject to the approval of Counsel. Subscriptions will be received subject to rejection or allotment in whole or in part and the right is reserved to close the subscription books at any time without notice. It is expected that definitive Debentures will be ready for delivery on or about June 27, 1978.

A copy of the circular will be furnished upon request.

PRICE: 99 to yield approximately 10.11%

_____

A. E. Ames & Co. Limited	**Burns Fry Limited**

Wood Gundy Limited	**Greenshields Incorporated**	**Dominion Securities Limited**
McLeod Young Weir Limited	**Morgan Stanley Canada Limited**	**Merrill Lynch, Royal Securities Limited**
Richardson Securities of Canada	**Nesbitt Thomson Securities Limited**	**Pitfield Mackay Ross Limited**
Midland Doherty Limited	**Walwyn Stodgell Cochran Murray Limited**	**Bell, Gouinlock & Company, Limited**
Lévesque, Beaubien Inc.	**Scotia Bond Company Limited**	**Pemberton Securities Limited**
Tassé & Associés, Limitée	**René T. Leclerc Incorporée**	**Mead & Co. Limited**
	Molson, Rousseau & Cie Limitée	

_____

The Bank of Nova Scotia	**Bank of Montreal**

Canadian Imperial Bank of Commerce	**The Toronto-Dominion Bank**	**The Royal Bank of Canada**

May, 1978

Figure 10.1   ANNOUNCEMENT OF A BOND ISSUE

its revenue base. The federal government, considered to have the highest credit rating, can borrow more cheaply than the provinces. Municipalities are considered to be in the third level of safety and must pay somewhat more interest than the two senior governments. Generally, corporations rank below all governments and must pay somewhat higher interest rates on their bonds. However, among corporations there is great diversity, and credit ratings differ widely. This ranking of credit status from the federal government at the top to corporations at the bottom is a useful generalization but does not cover all cases.

BOND RATINGS   If you wish to find the credit rating of a government or corporation you may consult the bond ratings published in Canada by the Canadian Bond Rating Service or Dominion Bond Rating Service. Two U.S. agencies—Moody's, and Standard and Poor's—rate those Canadian issuers who borrow in American markets. The ratings go from AAA at the top to AA, A, BBB, and so on.

BOND CERTIFICATES

If you buy a bond you will receive a *bond certificate*, stating the *denomination* of the bond, which may be $500, $1000, $10 000 or more (usually $1000 is the smallest denomination), and the terms of the issue. It will also give the *maturity date*, the date when the issuer promises to repay the principal—a process known as *redemption*. The certificate also states the interest rate and the way in which interest will be paid. Interest payments are usually made twice a year on the dates indicated on the bond. A typical bond certificate is shown in Figure 10.2.

Interest on bonds may be paid either by cheque or coupon. A *coupon bond* has a series of coupons attached to the bond certificate. Each coupon has a value printed on it, as well as the date when it may be cashed (Figure 10.2). For example, a bond with a ten-year term will have 20 coupons, dated at six-month intervals, each worth a half year's interest. The coupons or the certificate will indicate at which financial institutions they may be cashed. When the specified date arrives, cut off the coupon and exchange it for cash at the bank or investment dealer's office. You should cash in the coupons promptly so that the funds may be reinvested. Bond coupons are the equivalent of cash and care should be taken not to lose them.

There are bearer bonds, bonds registered as to principal, and fully registered bonds. *Bearer bonds* have no proof of ownership; as with currency, whoever possesses them can sell them or cash in the coupons. These bonds should never be left in an unsecured place, since there would be no way to trace them. Bearer bonds always have coupons because the bond issuer has no way of knowing to whom the interest cheques should be sent. Bonds *registered as to*

THE TELEPHONE COMMISSION OF QUEBEC
9¼% Bond Due February 1, 1995
(Subject to Prior Redemption)

$1000   **$1000**

Guaranteed as to Principal and Interest by the Province of Quebec

The TELEPHONE COMMISSION OF QUEBEC (hereinafter called the "Commission") for value received hereby promises to pay to the bearer or if registered to the registered holder hereof on the 1st day of February 1995, or on such earlier date as this bond may be redeemed in accordance with the provisions for redemption hereinafter set forth, on presentation and surrender of this bond, the sum of

ONE THOUSAND DOLLARS

in lawful money of Canada at any branch of any chartered bank in Quebec, or in any of the cities of Saint John, Quebec, Montreal, Winnipeg, Regina, Calgary, Edmonton, Vancouver, or Victoria, Canada, at holder's option, with interest thereon from the 1st day of February 1995 at the rate of nine and one-quarter per centum (9¼) per annum payable half-yearly in like money at any of the said places at holder's option on the 1st days of February and August in each year of the currency of this bond on presentation and surrender of the interest coupons hereto annexed as they severally become due.

The Commission shall have the right at its option to redeem the bonds of this issue, either in whole or in part, in advance of maturity, on any interest payment date on or after the 1st day of February 1991, at the places where and in the money in which the said bonds are expressed to be payable, upon payment of the principal amount thereof together with interest accrued thereon to the date of redemption, and upon giving previous notice of such redemption. In the event that less than all of the said bonds shall be redeemed, the bonds to be redeemed shall be chosen by lot in such manner as the Commission may deem equitable, and for the purpose of redemption and selection for redemption, each bond of a denomination greater than $1,000 each and any part of the principal amount of such bond comprising one or more of such units may accordingly be selected and called for redemption. In the event of the selection for redemption of a portion only of the principal amount of any coupon bond, payment of the redemption price of such portion will be made only upon surrender of such bond with all unmatured unredeemed balance of such principal amount, with all unmatured interest coupons attached. In the event of the selection for redemption of a portion only of the principal amount of any fully registered bond, payment of the redemption price of such portion will be made only upon surrender of such bond in exchange for a fully registered bond or bonds of this issue for the unredeemed balance of such principal amount.

This bond is subject to the conditions endorsed hereon which form part hereof.

This bond is issued under the authority of the Telephone Commission Act and of an order of the Lieutenant Governor in Council.

In witness whereof the Commission has caused its corporate seal and the engraved facsimile signature of its chairman or a vice-chairman to be affixed hereto and this bond to be duly signed by an authorized signing office of the Commission and to be dated the 1st day of February 1975.

GUARANTEE by QUEBEC

By virtue of the powers conferred by the legislature of Quebec and of an order of the Lieutenant-Governor in Council, Quebec hereby guarantees to the holder for the time being of this bond and to the holder for the time being of any of the coupons attached thereto, due payment of the principal of this bond and of the interest thereon according to the tenor of the said bond and of the coupons attached thereto.

Thomas Carlyle
Chairman

Authorized Signing Officer

John Ruskin
Officer of the Treasury Department

Specimen

Figure 10.2   FACSIMILE OF A BEARER BOND AND COUPON

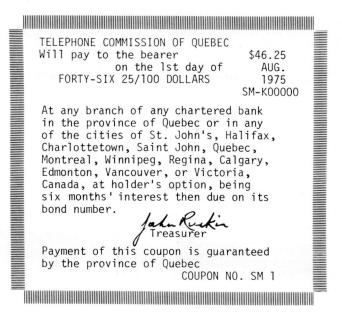

Figure 10.2 (continued)

principal have the name of the owner typed on them, but they carry coupons which, if detached, may be cashed by anyone. However, it will be difficult for any but the registered owner to redeem a bond registered as to principal. Other bonds are *fully registered*, which means that not only is the owner's name on the bond certificate but the interest is paid directly to the owner by cheque, thus no coupons are required. When bonds are sold from one owner to another, the coupon bonds can be simply handed over, but the two registered types require a transfer-of-ownership form to be signed and witnessed.

TYPES OF BONDS

GOVERNMENT OF CANADA BONDS   Debt securities issued by the federal government are considered to be of the highest quality and safer than those of any other Canadian borrower. With its broad taxing powers the government is most unlikely to fail to pay interest or redeem the "Canadas" or Government of Canada bonds. In the Canadian market, the federal government is the largest issuer of bonds, and the frequent trading of "Canadas" makes them very marketable. In addition to its own bonds, the Government of Canada guarantees bonds issued by various Crown corporations. Although the federal government also issues Canada Savings Bonds, these are more like savings certificates than bonds and will be considered separately.

PROVINCIAL GOVERNMENT BONDS   The provinces also issue bonds in their own right and guarantee bond issues of those commissions, hydro-electric corporations, and school boards, which fall under their jurisdiction. As previously mentioned, provincial bonds are usually considered to be a notch or two below the 'Canadas' in security.

MUNICIPAL BONDS   Local governments issue debentures to pay for their public projects, such as streets, waterworks, schools, and hospitals, which cost a great deal but are expected to last for some time; by issuing bonds, the cost is spread over a number of years. The fact that the provinces usually exert some regulatory control over the borrowing of municipalities may be a comfort to investors. Municipal debentures do not trade as frequently as the more senior provincial and federal debentures, and therefore are generally less marketable. The quality of municipal securities is dependent on the tax base: municipalities with a broader range of industries are preferable to single-industry towns or regions. Generally, municipal debentures are ranked below provincial and federal issues, but it is difficult to generalize because some Canadian cities have larger budgets than the smallest provinces.

CORPORATION BONDS   When long-term funding is needed, corporations issue a variety of bonds and debentures, a few of which will be mentioned here. If the corporation's credit rating is high enough, unsecured debentures may be issued, otherwise, their bonds are backed by some type of security. As a loan secured by property, a *mortgage bond* is similar to any mortgage. However, because the sums corporations borrow are so large, the loan is divided into smaller units enabling a number of investors to be involved. Property put up as security will be used to compensate bond holders if the corporation should default. Among mortgage bonds, as in home mortgages, there are *first mortgage bonds* and *second mortgage bonds*, which are an indication of the order in which creditors would rank in compensation claims.

If a corporation does not have a high enough credit rating to borrow with unsecured debentures, and has no property to offer as security, it may issue *collateral trust bonds*, which are secured with financial assets such as bonds and stocks that the company holds.

SPECIAL FEATURES

Bonds and debentures are often issued with special characteristics, such as being callable, convertible, extendible, or retractable. These characteristics are intended to make an issue more attractive to investors.

CALLABLE   Some bond certificates state that the issuer can recall the bond before the maturity date. If borrowers wish to reserve the right to pay off a bond debt before maturity, they issue *callable bonds*. The call or redemption feature usually includes an agreement to give the bondholder a month's notice of the intention to redeem. The issuer may agree to pay the owner somewhat more than the face value of the bond as compensation for the early recall, although the Government of Canada usually does not do so. Bonds are assumed to be *non-callable* unless indicated otherwise. With a call feature the initiative remains with the issuer; bondholders do not have the option of redeeming a callable bond whenever they wish. Unless the bond is called by the issuer, they must find a buyer or wait until the maturity date.

A BOND REDEMPTION

The paper of June 25, 1990 contained the announcement that, on July 25th, the Consolidated Group would be redeeming certain 10.5 percent sinking fund debentures due to mature on June 1, 1997. The company would pay a redemption price of 102.05 plus accrued interest. The announcement listed the serial numbers of all the debentures to be called. Bondholders were asked to redeem the bonds being called in at any branch of the Canadian Imperial Bank of Canada. After the redemption date no more interest would be paid on these bonds.

CONVERTIBLE   Bonds may include a clause that gives the holder the option of exchanging the security for a specified number of common shares of the company. The terms of the conversion are established when the bonds are issued, and do not change. This feature gives the holder of a debt security the possibility of capital gain. The investor would profit if, in the future, the price of the common stock should rise above the set conversion price. The option of converting to common stock may be a factor in supporting the price of a bond which would otherwise drop. The terms of one series of convertible debentures are shown in the following example.

CONVERSION TERMS

A corporation issued convertible debentures with the following conversion terms:

> The conversion price of Class B non-voting shares would be $11.75 and the conversion rate approximately 85.11 shares per $1000 debenture. The right of conversion may be exercised at any time prior to the close of business on July 15.

EXTENDIBLE   Sometimes bonds or debentures with short maturities carry an extendible feature that gives the holder the option of extending the maturity date, perhaps for ten years, at the same or a slightly higher interest rate.

RETRACTABLE   Long-term bonds may carry an option permitting the holder to shorten the maturity. Investors may be attracted by this retractable feature and be willing to accept a slightly lower interest rate. An example of a debenture series with a retraction privilege is shown in Figure 10.3.

FLOATING RATE   In recent years when interest rates were changing very rapidly, some bonds with a floating rate were issued. The interest rate is set at certain intervals in relation to the treasury bill rate. This feature means that neither the lender nor the borrower is locked into a set interest rate. Whether the lender or the borrower will benefit in the long run will depend on which way interest rates move, but the price of the bond will not fluctuate very much.

SINKING FUND PROVISION   Many debt securities carry a sinking fund provision, which means that the issuer will be setting aside sums of money each year to provide for their redemption. These funds are held in trust by a trustee, usually a trust company, until needed. A sinking fund provision is useful to the corporation as a way of reducing debt, but not particularly helpful to the investor who may not want to have the bonds redeemed before maturity. Note that the bond announcement in Figure 10.1 carries a sinking fund provision.

BUYING AND SELLING BONDS

If you have a bond that will not mature for many years, but need the cash now, you must find a buyer. Bonds are bought and sold on the *bond market*, which is not a physical place but a communication system linking investment

New Issue

UNION GAS
LIMITED

$75,000,000
10⅝% Debentures, 1986 Series
(unsecured)

To be dated February 26, 1986   To mature December 15, 2005

Multiple Retraction Privilege and Interest Rate Adjustment

The Debentures will be retractable at the option of the holder on December 15, 1995 and on December 15 each year thereafter at par plus accrued interest thereon to the date of retraction. Prior to each retraction date, Union Gas Limited may, at its option, increase the interest rate. Any increase in interest rate will be effective for a period of one year from such retraction date.

Price: 100

Nesbitt Thomson Bongard Inc.	Gordon Capital Corporation	Merrill Lynch Canada Inc.
Midland Doherty Limited	Dominion Securities Pitfield Limited	McLeod Young Weir Limited

February 1986

Figure 10.3   ANNOUNCEMENT OF A RETRACTABLE DEBENTURE

dealers and brokers. When you tell your broker that you wish to sell a bond, this information may be sent to other brokers who may have a client interested in buying that very bond, or the investment dealer may purchase the bond from you. Commission is not charged on bonds, but instead the dealers add their profit to the price at which they buy or sell, sometimes called the *spread*. The spread will be greater for bonds that are less frequently traded, or for small orders of bonds.

SPREAD IN BOND PRICES

Bond Quotation:

Bell Canada 10 percent, due 1996, bid 69.1, ask 70.1

This $1000 bond may be sold to a broker for $691.00 or purchased for $701.00. The $10 difference between these two prices, called the spread, represents the broker's commission. The amount of the spread depends on the trading activity in a particular bond and the size of the transaction. If a certain issue of bonds trades thinly, the broker may have more difficulty in finding a buyer or seller and thus may take a larger spread. Investors who place large bond orders may be able to negotiate a smaller spread per bond than a very small investor. Usually the minimum spread is about $10.

FLUCTUATION OF BOND PRICES When a bond is issued, the interest rate is fixed for the entire term, which may be 10, 20, or more years. But economic conditions generally cause interest rates to change during that period. This creates a problem if you wish to sell a bond paying 5 percent when rates on other, more recently issued debt securities are closer to 10 percent. To interest a purchaser, you will have to lower the price of your bond, or sell it *at a discount*. Likewise, if interest rates have fallen since your bond was issued, you will be able to sell it at a higher price, or *at a premium*. If a bond sells at its face value, it sells *at par*.

YIELD TO MATURITY In the financial world, *yield* usually means the annual return from an investment expressed as a percentage of its market price. In the case of bonds, the time value of future interest and principal payments must be taken into account. Payments received in the near future are worth more to the investor than those to be received in the uncertain, distant future. A precise calculation of bond yield to maturity takes into account the present

YIELD TO MATURITY

M arie bought a 10.9 percent Royal Bank bond due January 15, 1999. After a few years she needed the money and decided to sell the bond; by then interest rates were around 12 percent. When she asked a broker for the price she might get for this bond, she was quoted 97.65. This meant a selling price of $976.50 for the bond, which had originally cost her $1000, or a capital loss of $23.50. Why would anyone buy a bond that pays lower interest than term deposits? The answer is that the yield to maturity is approximately 11.35 percent and part of this yield is capital gain that attracts much less or no income tax.

Jim bought an Alberta Energy bond at a purchase price of 95.80. The spread between the selling price of 94.80 and the purchase price of 95.80 is $10 per $1000. The yield he would receive if held to maturity can be approximated by the following calculation.

Face value	$1000
Nominal interest rate	10.5%
Price quotation	95.80
Amount paid	$958.00
Maturity date	30 June 1996
Date of purchase	31 Dec. 1990

The average annual return from this bond, if held to maturity, consists of interest and capital gain.

Annual interest	$105.00
Capital gain over 5.5 years	$42.00
Average annual capital gain	$42.00/5.5 = $7.64
Total average annual return	$105.00 + $7.64 = $112.64
(Add capital gain, deduct capital loss)	

$$\text{Annual yield to maturity} = \frac{\text{ave. annual return} \times 100}{\text{purchase price}}$$

$$= \frac{112.64 \times 100}{958}$$

$$= 11.76\%$$

Why is Jim's yield to maturity lower than Marie's?

value of coupon payments and the present value of the principal repayment at maturity. Bond traders use a complex formula to work out this involved calculation. The simple method used in the above example serves to show how the nominal interest rate and the potential capital gain or loss influence the yield. The results using this method will be somewhat different from those found in bond yield quotations. For one thing, we have made no adjustment for the time value effect.

The buyer of a bond takes into account the possibility of capital gain or loss, in addition to considering the amount of interest the bond will pay. If the bond is held until maturity, the owner will receive the face value regardless of the price paid for it.

ACCRUED INTEREST   Bond interest is paid on fixed dates, usually every six months from the date of issue. This presents problems for buyers and sellers of bonds who may transfer ownership at any time. Whoever owns the bond on the interest payment date will receive six months' interest, but perhaps this person has held the bond for two months only. The seller should not lose four months's interest because the bond was sold to someone else. The solution is to charge the buyer accrued interest. Bonds are sold at a certain price plus *accrued interest*, that is, the buyer pays the seller for the interest due to the seller but which will come to the buyer in the next interest payment. The example below will clarify this process.

ACCRUED INTEREST

Bond denomination	$1000
Interest rate	10.5
Interest payment dates	March 15, September 15
Sale date	June 15

George sold a bond at par to Elizabeth on June 15. The previous interest payment had been on March 15 and there would not be another until September 15. At the time of the sale, three months' interest was due to George, so Elizabeth paid him 1000 × .105 × 3/12 = $26.25. In September when the next interest payments will be sent to bondholders, Elizabeth will receive six months' interest or $52.50. Thus, the system of paying the seller for accrued interest adjusts for the inflexibility of bond interest payments.

BOND QUOTATIONS   Financial papers do not provide as much information about bond quotations as they do about stock prices, probably because it is more difficult to get the information together when bond trades are not concentrated on a few exchanges as are stock transactions. When you do find some bond quotations, as in *The Financial Post* or the *Globe and Mail*'s *Report on Business* (on Mondays), you will notice that bond prices are given in hundreds and that bonds of the same issuer are distinguished by the interest rate and the maturity date. Thus we speak of the 11.75 percent "Canadas" of 15 Dec 92, meaning that this issue of Government of Canada bonds carried an interest rate of 11.75 percent and will mature on December 15, 1992. The quotation will also give a recent price at which these bonds traded, and the yield to maturity (Table 10.3).

STRIPPED BONDS

You may have heard about stripped bonds, which are another way of investing in debt securities. Investment dealers buy large denomination bonds, issued by federal or provincial governments or Crown corporations, and strip off the coupons. Long-term bonds with maturities of at least 20 years are usually selected for coupon stripping. In a *stripped bond* the interest has been separated from the principal (bond residue) and both sold separately. Each coupon, with a fixed payment date, becomes a little bond that may be sold at a discount dependent on the prevailing interest rates.

For instance, in 1990 $4079 would buy stripped bonds maturing at $10 000 in 1998. At the end of eight years the investor would have earned $5 921 in interest but would receive no yield in the interim. The purchase price reflects the time value of money, or the time the investor has to wait to receive the yield and current interest rates. Investors have a choice of discounted coupons maturing every six months.

Dealers usually pool the funds and give a deposit receipt or certificate. These go by a variety of names depending on who issues them, such as TIGRS

Table 10.3   BOND QUOTATIONS, JUNE 1990

Issuer	Maturity	Coupon	Quote	Yield
Canada	15 Dec 92	11.75	99.65	11.92
Canada	1 Oct 06	14.00	122.25	11.02
Nova Scotia	1 Dec 96	7.63	81.00	11.92
Montreal Ur	7 Apr 03	13.25	108.00	12.00
SimpsonSearsAc	1 Apr 96	14.75	106.38	13.13
3-mo. T-Bills				13.55

(term investment growth receipt), Cougars, and Sentinels. In the latter case, the investor has a share in a pool of coupons or residuals held in trust. These certificates are registered in the name of the investor who may sell them at any time on the secondary market. The sale price, which changes with general interest rates, will generally fluctuate more than bond prices.

A STRIPPED BOND HELD TO MATURITY

In the newspaper, George saw an offering of stripped bonds maturing in five years. The asking price was $560 per $1000 face value. Because the bonds had been stripped of their coupons, there would be no semi-annual interest payments. Instead he would receive $1000 in five years' time.

George's return will be $440 on an investment of $560, which works out to about 10.25 percent per annum. This was slightly higher than current rates for some other five-year debt securities.

TAXATION OF BOND YIELD

The return from bonds is composed of interest income and the possibility of capital gain or loss, if traded before maturity. Interest is added to taxable income and taxed accordingly. Net capital gain (capital gain less any capital loss) is exempt from tax to a maximum of $100 000 over your lifetime. The tax treatment of capital gains has become most complex and will not be explained here. Consult books on income tax for details.

The differential treatment of interest and capital gain provides an incentive for some investors to prefer their bond return in the form of capital gain rather than interest. The yield from stripped bonds is considered by the Revenue Canada Taxation to be interest, not capital gain, and for this reason they are often selected for self-administered RRSP accounts where the return is tax-sheltered. If these bonds are not in a tax shelter, accrued interest must be reported annually, even though not received.

CANADA SAVINGS BONDS

Although they are called bonds, Canada Savings Bonds (CSBs) are more like savings certificates and do not have many of the attributes of bonds or debentures. Since they cannot be traded but only redeemed, their value does not fluctuate. Canada Savings Bonds, developed from the Victory bonds which were so successful in raising funds for the war effort between 1940 and 1944, have become a significant part of federal government borrowing for the past 50 years.

TERMS OF THE ISSUES

Once each year, in November (and often for a limited time) a new issue goes on sale and is available to Canadian residents only. In addition, the amount an individual may purchase in any one year is usually restricted. Issues may be bought at the face value in denominations of $100, $300, $500, $1000, $5000, and $10 000 from banks, trust companies, credit unions, and investment dealers. No commission is paid by the buyer at the time of purchase or redemption. Although the bonds are not transferrable, except in the case of death, the government will redeem them at their face value on any business day. Consequently, CSBs are not only very low risk, but also very liquid investments.

TYPES OF CSBs

Bonds issued since 1977 carry no coupons, are fully registered, and are available in two forms: *regular interest bonds* and *compound interest bonds*. Interest is mailed each November to holders of regular interest bonds, and left to compound until maturity or redemption if the bond is a compound one.

INTEREST

Before 1977, CSBs had coupons and set interest rates, but a period of very high and rapidly changing interest rates created difficulties for both investors and the government. Now, CSB issues have no coupons or any guaranteed rate for the whole term. Instead, each autumn the federal government announces the interest rate to be paid for the coming year on both the new issue and all outstanding issues. The rate on CSBs, previously slightly higher than on savings accounts, has been lowered in recent years to encourage Canadians to invest in other securities. Nevertheless, CSBs are popular because of their safety and high liquidity.

INCOME TAX

Before 1991, holders of compound interest bonds were allowed to choose whether to report interest: (i) as received, on a *cash basis* or, (ii) as earned, on a *receivable basis*. Revisions to the *Income Tax Act* require that interest on bonds purchased since 1990 be reported annually.

SAVINGS BONDS VERSUS OTHER BONDS

In spite of their name, Canada Savings Bonds lack many of the attributes of bonds. Instead, think of them as a type of savings certificate. To summarize the unique features of CSBs, six of their attributes are listed below.

1. *Sale* They are sold directly to investors, are not traded on the bond market, are not transferrable, and carry no commission charges.
2. *Eligibility* Distribution is limited to Canadian residents.
3. *Redemption* Face value available on any business day.
4. *Denominations* Available in smaller denominations than other bonds.
5. *Types* There are two types: regular interest bonds (interest mailed annually), and compound interest bonds (interest paid at redemption or maturity).
6. *Annual interest* Interest is paid each November.

CSBs OR PREFERRED SHARES?

I t is November and you have $5000 to invest. Should you buy some of the current issue of Canada Savings Bonds which carry a 10 percent rate for the first year or put your money into preferred shares of B.C. Telephone which have a return of 9.9 percent? To answer the question, the following assumptions are made: your combined federal and provincial marginal tax rate is 40 percent; the income tax on share dividends is reduced by the tax dividend credit (explained in Chapter 11).

Annual return on the CSBs:

$5000 × .10 = $500 before tax
$500 × .40 = $200 income tax
$500 − 200 = $300, or an after-tax yield of 6%

Annual return on the preferred shares:

$5000 × .099 = $495 before tax
Income tax = $115.96 (see Chapter 11 for method)
$495 − 115.96 = $379.04, or an after-tax yield of 7.6%

The preferential tax treatment of dividends from Canadian corporations results in a higher after-tax return from the preferred shares than the CSBs. Investment decisions require other considerations but this example illustrates the importance of comparing yields on an after-tax basis.

Summary

Debt securities represent not only a very large share of the financial transactions in the country but also a significant portion of the portfolios of individual investors. As a lender of funds, the investor does not acquire either the opportunity to influence management decisions or the potential for gain that is possible with equities. On the other hand, there is generally less risk with debt securities, which are considered senior to equity in the case of company failure. Deposits, money market instruments, Canada Savings Bonds, and bonds and debentures promise regular interest payments and the return of the principal at some specified time. Capital gain or loss is a possibility with bonds and debentures if traded prior to maturity, but that is not so with the other debt securities discussed in this chapter.

Canada Savings Bonds are very secure liquid investments. They have more attributes of savings certificates than bonds because they do not trade on the bond market, are redeemable at par at any time, do not carry an interest rate fixed for the term, are available in small denominations, and are sold only to Canadian residents.

Problems

1. On July 11, 1990, the *Report on Business* of *The Globe and Mail* reported the following information about interest rates:

    CANADIAN ADMINISTERED RATES
Bank of Canada	13.73%
Prime	14.75%

    MONEY MARKET RATES
    (for transactions of $1-million or more)
Three–month treasury bills	13.46%
30–day commercial paper	13.82%
60–day commercial paper	13.78%
90–day commercial paper	13.62%

   (a) Look in the financial section of a recent paper to find current interest rates, and update the above table.

   (b) Why is the bank rate lower than the prime rate?

   (c) Why is the rate higher on commercial paper than on treasury bills?

   (d) Do the interest rates on commercial paper increase as the term increases? If not, why so?

   (e) What is commercial paper and who would buy and sell it?

(f) If you had $5000 to invest in the money market, would the interest rate quoted be the same as those above? Explain.

(g) How would you go about investing the $5000 in the money market?

2. Try to find a newspaper advertisement announcing a new bond issue. (These are usually found in the financial section, but occur irregularly.) Otherwise, analyze the announcement in Figure 10.1.

Look for the following information in the advertisement:

(a) Name of the bond issuer,
(b) Names of the underwriters,
(c) Offering price,
(d) Maturity date,
(e) Interest rate,
(f) Special features, e.g., callable, retractable, extendible, convertible.
(g) Denominations available,
(h) Size of the issue (amount to be borrowed).

3. Examine these two bond quotations:

Issuer	Maturity	Coupon	Quote	Yield
Stelco	1 Oct 00	13.50	104.63	12.67
Canada	15 Dec 00	9.75	93.85	10.74

(a) Are these bonds selling at par, at a discount or at a premium? Suggest reasons why.

(b) What is the probable minimum denomination available in these bonds?

(c) Calculate the yield to maturity if purchased in 1990 at the quoted price on June 15 and July 11, respectively. How does your result compare with the published yield?

(d) Suggest reasons why the Canada bond has a lower yield to maturity than the Stelco bond.

4. Assume that you bought a 13 percent B.C. Hydro and Power $1000 debenture, maturing 15 June 1996, on March 15, 1990.

(a) How much accrued interest would you pay?
(b) Will you get this interest back? If so, when?
(c) Why did you have to pay accrued interest?
(d) If you could buy this debenture at a price $117.88, how much capital loss would you suffer at maturity?

5. The following questions refer to Figure 10.4.

(a) How do dealers distinguish among the various issues of Canada bonds — only a few of which are listed here?

(b) Why is there one B.C. Hydro & Power bond quoted at 81.75 and another at 118.12?

(c) Suggest two reasons for such a wide range of coupon interest rates on the bonds (In June 1990 the bank prime rate was about 14 percent).

(d) Are some of these bonds really debentures? If so, which?

(e) In this list of bonds there seem to be more selling at a discount than at a premium. Can you suggest any reasons?

6. Decide whether you AGREE or DISAGREE with each of the following statements:

(a) Bonds are a form of equity security.

(b) Bond prices vary inversely with changes in general interest rates.

(c) All coupon bonds are bearer bonds.

(d) Fully registered bonds have no coupons.

(e) Both Canada Savings Bonds and Government of Canada bonds trade on the bond market.

(f) The price of a bond quoted at 93.5/8 is always $1000, but the face value can vary.

(g) All bond interest is exempt from income tax.

(h) Most bonds pay interest annually.

(i) As a bondholder, you have no promise from the issuer of the bond regarding payment of interest or repayment of the principal.

7. Explain why you have to pay more than the face value if you buy a Canada Savings Bond by payroll deduction. Is this extra sum called interest? Can it be used as an income tax deduction?

8. Assume that you decide to redeem three $1000 Canada Savings Bonds on March 1. You will receive the face value and accrued interest. These bonds are paying 10.5 percent interest at the moment. Calculate the amount of accrued interest you will receive.

9. Look at bond quotations in a recent newspaper.

(a) How do bond yields compare with the current rate on treasury bills?

(b) Are most bonds selling at a discount or a premium? Why?

10. In 1991, Kase invested $5000 in a compound series of Canada Savings Bonds. For income tax purposes, should he report interest on the receivable basis?

11. How might a high marginal tax rate affect a decision to buy a discounted bond?

12. Why would anyone buy a bond selling at a premium when there would be a capital loss if held to maturity?

13. Why would anyone want to buy stripped bonds instead of regular bonds?

Issuer	Maturity	Coupon	Quote	Yield
Canadas				
Canada	1 Jul 90	8.00	99.70	12.33
Canada	1 Aug 90	7.50	99.00	13.98
Canada	1 Aug 90	9.00	99.25	13.70
Canada	1 Sep 90	10.75	99.30	13.48
Canada	5 Sep 90	10.25	99.15	13.52
Canada	1 Oct 90	10.50	99.05	13.39
Canada	1 Oct 90	12.50	99.60	13.51
Canada	5 Dec 90	10.25	98.65	13.16
Canada	15 Dec 90	10.25	98.55	13.22
Canada	1 Feb 91	12.50	99.50	13.26
Canada	1 Mar 91	9.25	97.45	12.96
Canada	5 Mar 91	11.00	98.60	12.98
Canada	1 May 91	9.75	97.45	12.82
Canada	1 May 91	14.50	101.10	13.11
Canada	6 Jun 91	10.50	97.65	13.09
Canada	1 Jun 91	11.00	98.45	12.72
Canada	1 Jul 91	8.50	95.65	13.00
Canada	1 Sep 91	9.00	96.05	12.53
Canada	6 Sep 91	10.25	97.35	12.58
Municipals				
M.F.A. of BC	15 Jun 03	12.38	106.00	11.48
M.F.A. of BC	12 Jun 05	12.00	104.25	11.40
Metr Toronto	1 Oct 90	8.75	98.75	12.68
Metr Toronto	15 Feb 92	8.00	94.00	12.01
Metr Toronto	15 Sep 92	8.38	93.50	11.70
Metr Toronto	19 Apr 93	11.75	99.38	12.00
Metr Toronto	30 Oct 93	8.38	91.50	11.46
Metr Toronto	15 Nov 93	12.00	100.50	11.81
Metr Toronto	15 Apr 94	9.13	92.63	11.54
Metr Toronto	30 Jun 98	9.75	93.25	11.03
Metr Toronto	15 Nov 99	11.25	100.00	11.25
Montreal	22 Jul 97	10.25	93.75	11.56
Montreal Urb	7 Apr 93	12.25	99.63	12.39
Montreal Urb	15 Jun 93	16.50	111.00	12.04
Montreal Urb	15 Sep 96	10.75	95.75	11.72
Montreal Urb	4 Jan 97	10.75	95.63	11.72
Montreal Urb	25 May 98	10.50	94.25	11.62
Montreal Urb	7 Apr 03	13.25	108.88	11.88
Otwa-Cltn	30 Nov 93	8.50	91.50	11.53
Otwa-Cltn	15 Dec 93	12.00	100.25	11.91
Otwa-Cltn	15 Apr 97	9.50	91.75	11.25
Provincials				
Alberta	15 Jun 91	8.13	95.50	12.97
Alta Gov Tel	15 Dec 91	7.50	92.88	12.81
Alta Gov Tel	31 May 03	11.50	101.75	11.24
Alta Mun Fc	15 Mar 93	7.25	90.13	11.50
Alta Mun Fc	15 Dec 02	12.25	106.13	11.32
BC Hyd & Pwr	15 Dec 93	5.25	81.75	11.73
BC Hyd & Pwr	15 Oct 00	10.00	91.50	11.42
BC Hyd & Pwr	14 Apr 06	14.50	118.12	11.92
BC Hyd & Pwr	15 Jan 11	13.50	112.25	11.89
Br Columbia	20 Oct 93	12.00	99.88	12.03
Man Hydro	15 Sep 91	8.50	94.88	12.98
Man Hydro	31 Aug 92	8.25	92.63	12.11
Man Hydro	10 Jun 94	10.00	94.50	11.76
Man Hydro	1 Aug 98	8.38	83.50	11.55
Man Tel	15 Nov 91	7.88	93.50	12.97
Man Tel	1 Mar 99	8.75	86.25	11.26
Manitoba	15 Mar 93	11.75	99.13	12.11
Manitoba	1 Oct 93	8.75	91.25	12.02
Manitoba	15 May 95	11.50	98.25	11.97
Manitoba	5 Dec 99	10.00	92.25	11.35
N Bruns Elec	8 Feb 93	11.75	98.88	12.24
N Bruns Elec	15 May 95	10.38	94.63	11.84

Issuer	Maturity	Coupon	Quote	Yield
Utilities				
AEC Power	30 Jun 96	10.75	94.38	12.08
Alta Gas Tr	15 Jun 90	9.75	100.00	9.75
Alta Gas Tr	1 Dec 92	8.13	90.50	12.71
Alta Gas Tr	1 Aug 95	11.38	96.38	12.34
BC Tel	1 Apr 91	14.25	100.63	13.34
BC Tel	1 Apr 92	16.38	105.38	12.92
BC Tel	15 Nov 92	9.63	94.25	12.43
BC Tel	15 Oct 93	8.63	90.13	12.30
BC Tel	1 Apr 95	10.25	93.38	12.10
BC Tel	15 Jan 96	11.00	95.50	12.12
BC Tel	15 Jun 99	9.70	89.38	11.63
BC Tel	15 Oct 01	10.25	91.88	11.55
BC Tel	1 Nov 03	9.88	89.13	11.48
Bell Canada	14 Aug 90	9.38	99.13	13.82
Bell Canada	1 Dec 93	9.38	92.63	12.03
Bell Canada	1 May 94	8.13	88.13	12.02
Bell Canada	3 Jun 96	10.00	92.50	11.78
Bell Canada	1 Apr 99	9.88	90.63	11.60
Bell Canada	1 May 00	13.88	108.00	12.44
Bell Canada	15 Feb 02	9.40	87.63	11.33
Bell Canada	15 Oct 04	11.00	96.88	11.44
Bell Canada	15 Oct 05	9.85	89.38	11.32
Calgary Pwr	1 Nov 90	9.38	98.38	13.56
Calgary Pwr	15 Jun 93	8.50	90.63	12.31
Calgary Pwr	1 Apr 94	9.13	90.25	12.40
Calgary Pwr	1 Feb 00	10.50	93.50	11.63
Cdn Util	15 Dec 91	9.63	94.88	13.46
Cdn Util	2 Jul 93	8.75	91.75	12.04
Cdn Util	15 Mar 94	9.13	90.63	12.30
Corporations				
B F Goodrich	15 Apr 96	11.00	95.00	12.21
B F Goodrich	1 Nov 98	10.25	90.63	12.05
Bank of NS	15 Sep 97	9.50	88.88	11.82
Bramalea	27 Feb 98	10.50	90.88	12.36
C.I.L.	15 Dec 93	12.38	99.88	12.42
C.I.L.	15 Apr 96	14.50	105.50	13.11
C.I.L.	15 Jul 96	10.63	93.13	12.25
C.P. Ltd	15 Nov 95	11.25	95.75	12.34
Cad Fairview	28 Feb 95	11.25	100.75	11.03
Cad Fairview	1 May 07	11.00	94.75	11.72
Campeau Corp	20 Dec 91	11.25	96.50	14.20
Campeau Corp	1 Dec 93	11.25	94.25	13.70
Can Cement	15 Feb 95	11.25	96.25	12.32
Can Cement	15 Dec 97	9.75	89.25	11.96
Cdn Tire	15 Aug 95	10.75	95.88	11.83
Cominco	15 Feb 95	10.88	93.88	12.63
Dofasco	15 May 95	10.88	95.63	12.07
Dofasco	15 Mar 96	10.38	92.88	12.12
Dofasco	1 Nov 00	13.50	104.90	12.63
Dom Textile	15 Jan 93	14.00	101.63	13.22
Domtar	1 Aug 95	11.00	95.88	12.09
Dupont	1 May 95	10.50	92.88	12.48
Eaton Acc	15 Jul 94	10.50	94.00	12.40
Eaton Acc	15 Sep 99	11.00	94.75	11.94
Edmonton Ctr	15 Oct 09	10.38	91.25	11.79
Fed Inds cv	15 Jun 06	8.00	82.00	10.32
Genstar	1 Jun 95	11.75	97.88	12.33
Genstar	15 Mar 96	11.25	95.50	12.35
Genstar	15 Jun 99	10.75	93.50	11.95
Gt West Life	15 Nov 93	12.75	100.00	12.75
Hud Bay Acc	15 Nov 96	10.50	89.88	12.86
Hud Bay Acc	1 Feb 01	13.75	105.50	12.78
Hud Bay Prop	15 Jan 95	11.50	94.63	13.08
Hud Bay Prop	15 Mar 98	10.00	87.50	12.56
I.A.C.	15 Nov 99	11.75	98.50	12.02
Imperial Oil	31 Mar 93	12.00	99.50	12.20
Imperial Oil	15 Aug 94	10.63	96.13	11.81

Figure 10.4   EXCERPTS FROM BOND QUOTATIONS, JUNE 1990

REFERENCES

Books

BEACH, WAYNE, and LYLE R. HEPBURN. *Are You Paying Too Much Tax?* Toronto: McGraw-Hill Ryerson, annual, 206 pp. A tax planning guide for the general reader that includes a discussion of capital gains, RRSPs, and investment income.

BIRCH, RICHARD. *The Family Financial Planning Book, A Step-by-Step Moneyguide for Canadian Families*. Toronto: Key Porter, 1987, 216 pp. An easy-to-read guide to taking control of your personal finances that discusses budgets, income tax, insurance, RRSPs, mortgages, and investments.

CANADIAN SECURITIES INSTITUTE. *How to Invest in Canadian Securities*. Third Edition. Toronto: Canadian Securities Institute, 1984, 251. Provides detailed explanations about various types of bonds, and stocks.

COSTELLO, BRIAN. *Your Money and How to Keep It*. Fifth Edition. Toronto: Stoddart, 1990, 248 pp. Particular emphasis on investments and income tax.

COTE, JEAN-MARC, and DONALD DAY. *Personal Financial Planning in Canada*. Toronto: Allyn and Bacon, 1987, 464 pp. A comprehensive personal finance text that includes financial planning, income tax, annuities, pensions, investments, credit, mortgages, and wills, with particular attention to the banking and insurance industries.

DRACHE, ARTHUR B. C., and SUSAN WEIDMAN SCHNEIDER. *Head and Heart, Financial Strategies for Smart Women*. Toronto: Macmillan, 1987, 348 pp. Recognizing the needs and perspectives of women, a tax lawyer and journalist have collaborated to present basic financial information, taking into account women's concerns at different stages in their lives.

FRIEDLAND, SEYMOUR, and STEVEN G. KELMAN. *Investment Strategies, How to Create Your Own and Make it Work for You*. Markham, Ontario: Penguin Canada, 1988, 125 pp. Offers guidance for the general reader in defining objectives and establishing an investment program.

HOGG, R. D. *Preparing Your Income Tax Returns*. Toronto: CCH Canadian, annual, 589 pp. A complete and technical guide to income tax preparation.

HUNTER, W. T. *Canadian Financial Markets*. Peterborough, Ontario, Broadview Press, 1986, 193 pp. An economist gives an overview of the workings of the bond market, the mortgage market and the stock market.

HATCH, JAMES E. and MICHAEL J. ROBINSON. *Investment Management in Canada*. Toronto: Prentice-Hall Canada, 1989, 836 pp. A technical university text with in-depth coverage of many aspects of investing.

MACINNIS, LYMAN. *Get Smart! Make Your Money Count in the 1990s*. Second Edition. Scarborough, Ontario: Prentice-Hall Canada, 1989, 317 pp. A book for the general reader that includes financial planning, income tax principles, but gives major attention to investing in the stock market.

MOTHERWELL, CATHRYN. *Smart Money, Investment Strategies for Canadian Women*. Toronto: Key Porter, 1989, 192 pp. A financial journalist explains how to get started investing, how to evaluate the products and how to build a portfolio.

PAPE, GORDON. *Building Wealth, Achieving Your Financial Goals*. Scarborough, Ontario: Prentice-Hall Canada, 1988, 246 pp. An easy-to-read guide for the novice financial manager and investor that considers interest rates, credit cards, mortgages, RRSPs, mutual funds, and the stock market.

PAPE, GORDON. *Low-Risk Investing*. Scarborough, Ontario: Prentice-Hall Canada, 1989, 244 pp. A book written to encourage the novice investor to get started on saving and investing. Outlines the basics of investing in debt and equity investments.

TURNER, MARY, DANIEL LEROSSIGNOL, CLAUDE RINFRET, and RICHARD DAW. *Canadian Guide to Personal Financial Management*. Fourth Edition. Scarborough, Ontario: Prentice-Hall Canada, 1989, 231 pp. Accountants provide guidance on a broad range of topics, including planning finances, estimating insurance needs, managing risk, and determining investment needs. Instructions and the necessary forms for making plans are provided.

WYATT, ELAINE. *The Money Companion, How to Manage Your Money and Achieve Financial Freedom*. Markham, Ontario: Penguin Books, 1989, 203 pp. A guide to personal financial management that focuses on planning, investment strategy, and retirement needs.

ZIMMER, HENRY B., and JEANNE V. KAUFMAN. *Your Investment Strategies for the 1990s*. Toronto: Collins, 1988, 249 pp. The authors, with backgrounds in accounting and taxation, discuss financial planning and a wide range of investment possibilities, including RRSPs, insurance, real estate, stocks, mutual funds, and metals.

Articles

DE THOMASIS, TONY. "Making the Most of Stripped Bonds," *Canadian Consumer*, 15, No. 11, 1985, 12-13. Explains what stripped bonds are and identifies pros and cons of this investment.

HIRSHORN, SUSAN. "Taking Accounts," *Canadian Consumer*, 18, No. 9, 1988, 34-43. A detailed examination of service charges, interest rates and other aspects of saving, chequing and investment accounts.

JACKSON, TED. "Bonds Come Up Roses," *The Financial Post 1990 Investor's Guide*, Fall 1989, 39-40. An analysis of the risk and return from bonds.

JACKSON, TED. "When Choosing is Just Too Difficult," *The Financial Post 1990 Investor's Guide*, Fall 1989, 41. Explanation of convertible bonds.

Periodicals

Canadian Consumer. Monthly. Box 9300, Ottawa, Ontario, K1G 3T9. In recent years, the personal finance articles have been concentrated in the November issue, "Personal Money Guide."

Canadian Money Saver. Monthly. Box 370, Bath, Ontario, K0H 1G0. Includes short articles on a range of personal finance topics, with special emphasis on investments.

Financial Times. Weekly. Suite 500, 920 Yonge Street, Toronto, Ontario, M2W 3L5. Provides current information on a range of business and economic topics.

Report on Business. Daily. A section of *The Globe and Mail*. Important source of information on the financial markets.

The Financial Post. Daily and weekly. 777 Bay Street, Toronto, Ontario, M5G 2E4. Up-to-date information on business, economics, income tax, and investments.

The Financial Post Annual Moneyplanner. Annual. 777 Bay Street, Toronto, Ontario, M5G 2E4. Usually contains articles on financial planning, income tax, insurance, investing, and retirement planning.

The Financial Post Magazine. Monthly. 777 Bay Street, Toronto, Ontario, M5G 2E4. Includes a section on personal finance.

11 STOCKS AND MUTUAL FUNDS

OBJECTIVES

1. To evaluate advantages and disadvantages of investing in the stock market.

2. To distinguish between common and preferred shares.

3. To outline the process of stock trading.

4. To interpret a stock quotation.

5. To explain the meaning and usefulness of a stock market index.

6. To examine long-term and short-term trends in stock prices.

7. To distinguish between
   (a) cash and stock dividends,
   (b) board and odd lots,
   (c) stock split and warrant,
   (d) redeemable and retractable preferred shares,
   (e) convertible and cumulative preferred shares,
   (f) open-end and closed-end investment funds,
   (g) acquisition and redemption fees,
   (h) bid and ask prices,
   (i) full-service and discount brokers,
   (j) sales and management fees.

8. To explain the limited liability of a stockholder.

9. To differentiate between equity, debt, and balanced mutual funds.

10. To explain how to use information on mutual fund performance in choosing or monitoring an investment.

11. To evaluate advantages and disadvantages of investing in mutual funds.

12. To identify the kinds of risks associated with different types of investments.

13. To explain how the risk in a portfolio may be reduced by diversification.

14. To explain how the three forms of investment yield are taxed.

INTRODUCTION

View this chapter as an introduction to the workings of the stock market—an important, complex, and vast subject—rather than a complete explanation of all aspects. It is intended to give a basic understanding of how the stock market works, to explain some of the vocabulary, and to provide a sketch of fundamental characteristics of common and preferred stocks and mutual funds. Armed with this knowledge, you should be able to increase your understanding of the subject by reading some of the many books and articles on investing, and especially the financial papers. Learning how to evaluate the quality of various stocks, although not addressed here, is a useful topic for future study.

Initially, this introductory treatment of a complex subject may seem confusing, but after careful study some of the mystery and apprehension you may feel about the stock market should dissipate.

INVESTING IN THE MARKET

When requirements for emergency funds, liquidity, and short-term savings have been met, it may be possible for you to broaden your asset holdings by investing in the stock market. Stocks, in contrast to debt securities, are a form of ownership that carry no promise of any return, but offer possibilities for greater gain. Before investing in the stock market you should recognize the trade-off between safety and the opportunity of greater return. Aware of this trade-off, you may then consider the broad spectrum of stocks encompassed by the stock market, from quite low-risk, blue chip, preferred stocks to very high-risk, speculative ones. Even very conservative investors can find appropriate stock market choices.

Over the long term, the stock market has proven a better hedge against inflation than debt securities. For instance, between 1975 and 1989, when consumer prices increased an average of about 7.5 percent a year, treasury bills paid about 10.4 percent interest on average. Unless taxable income was quite low, much of that 2.9 percent real return was paid in income tax. During the same period, stocks (those included in the Toronto Stock Exchange composite index) produced an average annual return of 19 percent. The variability of return from common stocks is illustrated in Figure 9.7 in Chapter 9. This annual *real* return of about 11.5 percent was taxed at a lower rate than interest income, as will be explained later, making the after-tax return on stocks attractive.

LOW LIQUIDITY OF STOCKS

Even though stocks have been more profitable over the long term than debt securities, their lower liquidity presents drawbacks. Stock prices fluctuate all the time, and also follow the business cycle of approximately four years, during which stock prices move from lows to highs and start around again. If it is necessary to sell stocks at one of the lows, there is a strong possibility of losing. The ideal is to buy stocks when prices are low and sell when they are high. Unfortunately, many small investors stay away from the stock market when it is down and only get in when it nears a high; as stock prices start to fall they panic and sell, vowing never to invest in the market again. Their mistake is in thinking of stocks as short-term rather than long-term investments. Some people seem to consider their investment alternatives limited to either various kinds of deposits or to trying to make money quickly in the stock market, not realizing that there are many intermediate possibilities.

COMMON SHARES

Corporations, especially large ones, often have many owners who provide the capital for the business. These owners, called shareholders, may hold two types of shares—common or preferred. Common shareholders take the greater risk and may gain or lose more than preferred shareholders, who usually accept a smaller voice in the management of the enterprise in exchange for greater safety of principal and income. The characteristics of common shares will be examined first.

CHARACTERISTICS

An investment in common stock has two attributes that differentiate it from a debt security: (i) equity (ownership) with its attendant rights, and (ii) the uncertainty of return. *Common shareholders* become part owners in a corporation, with certain rights that include: (i) having a vote at annual meetings, (ii) sharing in the company's success or lack of it by making or losing money, (iii) receiving dividends (income) when declared, (iv) receiving regular financial statements from the company, (v) sharing in the company's assets should it be dissolved.

Buying common stock represents a deliberate decision to give up some measure of safety in favour of the prospect of greater return. This equity investment carries neither a promise that the capital will be returned nor any guarantee of income. If the company does well the shareholders will benefit, but if it does poorly, some or all of the investment could be lost. Fortunately, a shareholder has *limited liability* for the losses of the corporation: if the firm should become bankrupt the maximum loss would be the funds invested.

It is normal for stock prices to fluctuate, but the result is low liquidity for the investor who cannot be sure of selling without a loss on a given day. Those who are investors, rather than speculators, look upon stocks as relatively long-term investments for which timing is essential. It is important to choose carefully when to buy and when to sell.

Stock Trading

Businesses require working capital, obtained by selling shares in the corporation, and if the shares are sold to the public, it becomes a publicly-owned corporation. Shares in such a corporation are sold at the start of a new business, or whenever the company requires additional capital. Once sold, the shares usually trade in the market where they may change hands quite often. Anyone who buys shares of Canadian Pacific and no longer wishes to hold them, must find a buyer; generally Canadian Pacific would not buy them from the investor. The function of stockbrokers and stock exchanges is to facilitate contact between buyers and sellers.

Traditionally, stocks have been bought and sold at *stock exchanges*, places where members of the exchange can execute orders for their clients. Each exchange has a limited number of *seats* or member trading permits, which entitle members to trade listed securities on the floor of the exchange. A firm of investment dealers, wishing to trade on a certain stock exchange, must either purchase one of these seats or work through a dealer who has one.

With the advent of computer technologies, there is a move towards electronic selling through a communication system, called CATS (computer assisted trading system) rather than by the physical presence of representatives of buyers and sellers at an exchange.

How a Stock Trade is Made

If an investor decided to buy 100 shares of Bank of Montreal, she would telephone her stockbroker to place the order. Assuming that she already has an account with this broker, who works for XYZ Investment Dealers, the order would be sent directly to the trading department at XYZ head office, which in turn would transmit the order to the XYZ booth at the Stock Exchange. There, the order would be transmitted to an XYZ floor trader, who would move to the post where Bank of Montreal stock is traded to look at posted recent prices. The floor trader would call out that he wants to buy 100 shares of Bank of Montreal and thus attract the attention of traders who have sell orders. If the two traders can agree on a price, the sale will be made and recorded on slips of paper. The progress of this order is illustrated in Figure 11.1.

Information about this sale is immediately relayed to the stock exchange's computer and becomes widely available across the nation or the world. Details of the trade are quickly sent to the broker, who in turn can inform the client of the results. All this activity may be accomplished within a very few minutes. After an order has been executed, the client has five business days to pay for the shares.

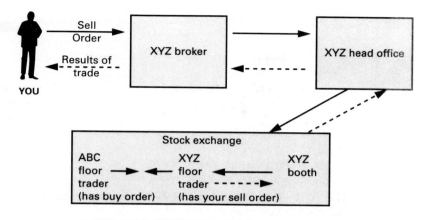

Figure 11.1   **TRANSACTING A STOCK TRADE**

Transactions involving large sums of money are carried out through verbal agreement, dependent solely on trust. Consequently, a broker will not conduct business for a client until an account has been opened, usually involving a meeting with the broker in which the investor will outline his or her investment objectives and financial status. This may be followed up by a check with the credit bureau to ensure creditworthiness.

BROKER'S COMMISSION   Stockbrokers, or registered representatives as they are often called, charge a commission for arranging either a sale or purchase of securities. There is no longer a standard commission rate; each firm determines its fee schedule. Generally, commission is charged on a sliding scale, with lower rates for larger orders. Anyone planning to place a small order should inquire about the minimum commission charge, which may be $50.

Investment dealers may be classified as full service brokers or discount brokers. *Full service brokers* charge higher commission rates but also offer advice, research reports on companies, and other information, in contrast to *discount brokers* who charge less but may offer no information at all.

STOCK QUOTATIONS   Considerable information about the previous day's stock trades is carried in the financial press. There one can find the price range within which the stock traded yesterday, the price at the closing of the exchange, and how many shares traded. In addition, the high and low prices of the past year and the amount of the most recent dividend are usually given. Weekly summaries in some papers give additional information.

JANE SELLS SHARES

Jane telephoned her full service broker and asked her to sell 300 shares of Power Corporation at the market price, which that day was 26 3/8. The confirmation of the sale she received in the mail a few days later showed this information:

Sold 300 shares Power Corp.	@ 26.375
Gross amount	$7912.50
Commission	147.41
Net amount	$7765.09

Jane received a cheque for $7765.09 as a result of this transaction.

Newspapers differ somewhat in the way that the stock quotations are expressed; the example below shows a quotation from one paper. Sometimes there is a reference to bid and ask prices; the *bid price* is what a buyer is willing to pay and the *ask price* is what the seller is willing to accept. Unless they reach an agreement there will be no transaction, of course.

READING STOCK QUOTATIONS

On July 13, 1990 Bell Canada Enterprises common stock was quoted as follows:

52-week								
High	Low	Stock	Div	High	Low	Close	Ch'ge	Vol
46 1/2	37 7/8	BCE	2.52	38 3/8	37 7/8	38 3/8	+ 1/8	239 681

This quotation means that over the previous 52 weeks the common stock of Bell Canada Enterprises traded as high as $46.50 and as low as $37.875, and the most recent dividend rate was $2.52 per share, per annum. During the previous day's trading, 239 681 shares changed hands at prices as high as $38.375 and as low as $37.875, ending the day at $38.375. This closing price was $0.125 higher than the previous day.

When you hear on the evening news that Bell Canada Enterprises was up a quarter, it means that the closing price was 25 cents higher than the previous day.

STOCK MARKET INDEX   Accompanying the newspaper stock quotations is a graph showing recent changes in the Toronto Stock Exchange Composite Index (Figure 11.2). Its outstanding feature is the variation in the index. On any one day some stocks rise in price while others fall, but the index gives an indication of the overall trend. The *Toronto Stock Exchange Composite Index* (TSE Index) is a statistical measurement of the percentage change in the prices of a group of 300 representative common stocks. Within this index there are 14 sub-groups representative of major sectors, such as metals and minerals, oil and gas, paper and forest products, transportation, utilities, and financial services. Each day the change in the overall index and in each sub-index is reported. These indexes are useful to the investor, who can measure the progress of a personal portfolio against that of the stocks represented in the index. If your stocks consistently under perform the market you may want to make some changes.

In the United States there are several stock indexes, including the well-known Dow Jones Industrial Index, which is based on 30 stocks.

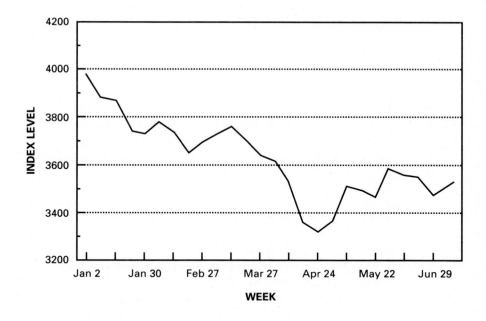

**Figure 11.2   TORONTO STOCK EXCHANGE COMPOSITE INDEX
WEEKLY CLOSE, JANUARY–JUNE 1990**

Source: Index Section, Toronto Stock Exchange. © 1990 Reprinted with the permission of the Toronto Stock Exchange.

Although the TSE Index fluctuates all the time, the long-term trend has been upward (Figure 11.3). It is apparent that if one happens to buy stocks at one of the highs and must sell when prices are down, there will be a loss. That is why stocks are considered to be low in liquidity, although many are highly marketable. To find out the marketability of a particular stock look at the figures on the volumes of shares traded; those that trade actively are more marketable.

TRADING QUANTITIES   Just as a dozen is used as the basic unit for buying eggs or oranges, there are trading units for shares. Stock exchanges have selected convenient numbers of shares, called *board lots*, to facilitate trading because it is more difficult to match buy and sell orders for odd numbers of shares. The number in a board lot is related to the share price, as shown below, but most shares are priced to sell in board lots of 100.

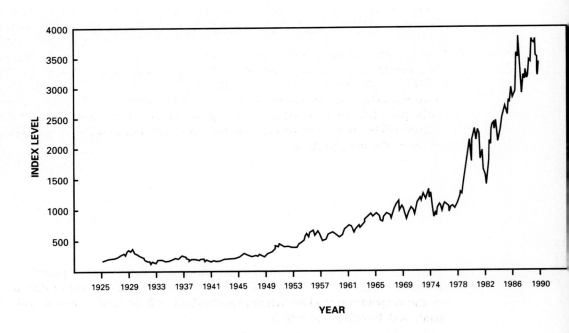

Figure 11.3   TORONTO STOCK EXCHANGE COMPOSITE INDEX,
MONTHLY CLOSE, JANUARY 1925–JUNE 1990

Source: Index Section, Toronto Stock Exchange. © 1990 Reprinted with the permission of the Toronto Stock Exchange.

Price of shares	Number in board lot
Under .10	1000
From .10 to under $1	500
From $1 to under $100 (includes most stocks)	100
$100 and over	10

When less than a board lot is traded it is referred to as an *odd lot*. Since it is more difficult to find buyers or sellers for odd lots, the price may be somewhat higher or the trade less quickly executed. When reading stock quotations, you should note that the prices of stocks trading for less than $5 are quoted in cents; the prices of other stocks are shown in dollar amounts. Those priced at $5 or less are often referred to as *penny stocks*.

KINDS OF ORDERS   A number of different orders may be placed with a broker. A *market order* is to be executed immediately at the best available price; any order on which no specific price has been placed will be handled as a market order. It is left up to the trader to get the best possible price. An *open order* names a price and remains open until either executed or cancelled. Should an investor decide to buy a certain stock if the price falls to a certain level, the broker may be given an open order that will be executed if and when that price is reached. A *stop loss* order gives the broker authority to sell the shares if the price falls to a named level. A stop loss order is used to ensure that the shares will be sold at the set price should prices fall, but makes it unnecessary to sell if the price keeps rising.

INVESTMENT RETURN

Investors buy common stock in expectation of return on their capital. The yield from investments in the stock market may take the form of one or more of these: cash dividends, stock dividends, or capital gain.

DIVIDENDS   Income from common stocks, called *dividends*, is not promised in advance or paid automatically as with debt securities. The board of directors of the corporation decides whether a dividend will be paid, when it will be paid, and how large it will be. As to be expected, the amount paid out in dividends will vary with the profitability of the company. At times the directors may decide not to declare any dividend, because of low profits in the past quarter, the need to invest most of the profit back into the business, or to conserve cash flow. Dividends, when declared, are usually paid quarterly.

Since common shares are continually being bought and sold, there must be some way to determine to whom the dividend cheque should be sent. Each time a dividend is declared, a date is established for determining ownership. For instance, notices are published in the financial press stating that a dividend will be paid to *shareholders of record*, or those who owned shares at the close of business on a certain date. This date may be two weeks before the payment date, giving the company time to prepare dividend cheques. During this two-week interval the stock will continue to trade, but the corporation will send dividends to those who were owners on the dividend record date.

DIVIDEND NOTICE

The Board of Directors of ABC Corporation has declared the following dividends of the company payable on December 2 to the shareholders of record at the close of business on October 31:

Class A common shares	10 cents per share
Class B common shares	12.5 cents per share

By Order of the Board
John A.Doe, Secretary
Dated this 17th day of October.

The stock exchange sets a date, known as the ex-dividend date, on or after which the stock sells *ex-dividend*, or without a dividend for that quarter. During this time the sellers, not the buyers, will receive the dividend. If you purchased 100 shares of Stelco, which was trading ex-dividend, the person selling the shares, not you, would receive the next dividend.

STOCK DIVIDENDS   Sometimes companies offer new shares in the company instead of cash dividends. Known as *stock dividends*, they are allotted in proportion to the number of shares held by each stockholder. Those who receive stock dividends have the option of adding them to the shares already owned or of selling them on the market. The tax treatment of stock dividends is the same as cash dividends. The investor will receive statements from the investment dealer and must report the amounts when making an income tax return.

Some major companies have *automatic dividend reinvestment plans*, whereby dividends are used to buy more stock in the firm. This can be arranged directly with the company, without the assistance of a broker. The advantage for the investor is that there is no commission charge on the new shares and it may be possible to purchase them below the current market price. These plans are not only a useful way to increase net worth with little effort, but can be a disciplined way of reinvesting, instead of spending cash dividends as they arrive.

CAPITAL GAINS   Most investors in common stock are looking for capital gains in addition to dividends, or, in the case of growth stocks, in lieu of dividends. They hope to sell the shares at a higher price than they paid, but face the possibility of a capital loss. Capital gain (loss) is calculated as follows:

$$\text{Total receipts from sale} - \text{selling commission} - \text{purchase price} = \text{capital gain (loss)}$$

By *growth stocks*, we usually mean companies that are thought to have very good prospects for increasing their business and thus their profits. Such companies tend to invest profits back in the business to make it grow, rather than pay large dividends to shareholders. You would buy a growth stock in the hopes that the price of the shares would rise so that you could sell them and reap a capital gain. If you wanted current income, you would eschew growth stocks.

RIGHTS AND WARRANTS

Sometimes shareholders are offered *rights*, which are privileges to buy additional shares directly from the company. It can be a useful way for a firm to raise more capital and an advantage for the shareholder who can obtain more shares, often at lower than market price and without paying commission. There is usually a short period during which these rights may be exercised before they become valueless. The recipient of rights has the option of exercising them or selling them on the market to someone who is interested in the opportunity to buy shares at the special price.

A RIGHTS OFFER

XYZ Corporation has been cleared for a rights offering to shareholders of record July 28 on the basis of one right for each share held. Five rights and $2.25 will be needed to purchase three additional shares. The offer expires August 25.

There is more than one usage of the term *warrant*, but the common one refers to a certificate attached to bonds and new issues of shares to make them more saleable. A warrant allows the owner to buy shares of the issuing company at a certain price within a specified time period. Warrants do not usually expire as quickly as rights, but like rights, may be detached and sold separately.

BELL CANADA ENTERPRISES WARRANTS

On July 6, 1990 BCE announced a new issue of preferred shares with attached warrants. Each common share carries one common share purchase warrant. These warrants may be exercised until the close of business on April 28, 1995 and each warrant may be used to buy one common share at a price of $45.75.

These examples illustrate that rights and warrants are similar in many ways; both offer the holder the opportunity to buy shares from the company under certain conditions. Rights may be offered to existing shareholders with a limited time to exercise them. Warrants tend to be attached to new issues of bonds or stocks and do not expire as quickly. Since warrants do not cost as much as shares, an investor might buy warrants as a cheaper way to get capital gain; if the underlying stock rises in price, so will the warrants. Then the warrants can be sold at a profit.

STOCK SPLITS

Sometimes corporations split their stock by exchanging each share for several shares. For example, early in 1986 when Canadian Imperial Bank of Commerce common shares were trading around $40-44, the directors decided to split the stock, two-for-one. That meant that a shareholder who previously had 200 shares became the owner of 400, now trading around $20 each. The lower price made the stock more attractive to investors; instead of paying $4000 to buy a board lot of 100 shares the price became a more manageable $2000. In addition, by doubling the number of outstanding shares the bank increased the possibility of its shares being held by more people.

PREFERRED SHARES

In addition to common stock, companies often issue another class of shares, called *preferred shares*, which represent limited ownership in a corporation. One would choose preferred shares because of a preference for less risk than the common stockholder, accepting the probability that there will be less opportunity to benefit from the growth of the company. If the company prospers, the common shareholders will probably see the price of their shares rise more than the preferreds. While there is no set dividend rate associated with common shares, most preferred shares promise a certain rate of return.

A company has an obligation first to pay interest on bonds, and then to pay dividends to preferred shareholders, before paying anything to the common shareholders. This puts preferred shareholders in a position midway between bondholders and common shareholders. Any company that does not pay dividends on its preferred shares will not be looked upon with favour by investors. If a company closes down, bondholders (who are creditors not owners) have claims on assets that take precedence over those of preferred and common shareholders.

DIVIDENDS

Preferred shareholders are usually entitled to a fixed rate of return on the investment, but the dividends may be deferred or omitted if the company has had a poor year. Most Canadian preferred shares have a stated par value and carry a fixed dividend rate that may be expressed either as a percentage of par value or as an amount per share. The issue of preferred shares described in Figure 11.4 has a par value of $20 per share and promises annual dividends of $2.70 per share, which is a return of 13.5 percent a year. As shown in the example below, another company, Nova, has a preferred share issue with par value of $25 and dividends @ 9 1/8 percent.

When shares are first issued, each has a stated value, known as the *par value* or face value. Investors can buy the new issue at the par value, but afterwards the shares will trade at various prices depending on demand, not necessarily at the par value. The promised dividend rate, however, is based on the par value and remains fixed. New issues of preferred shares frequently have a par value of $20 or $25.

It is interesting to note in Figure 11.4 that this particular Bell preferred stock, issued in 1982 at $20 per share was trading at $41.75 by February 27, 1987. Interest rates, which were very high in 1982, had fallen five years later,

---

$225,000,000

Bell Canada

11,250,000 shares

$2.70 Cumulative Redeemable Convertible Voting Preferred Shares. Class E. Series I. of the par value of $20 each

This offering may be increased, at the option of the underwriters by up to $11.250.000 (562,500 shares).

Conversion Privilege

Each $2.70 Preferred Share will be convertible into one common share of Bell Canada on or before March 15, 1992.

Price: $20 per share to yield 13.50%

Figure 11.4   A NEW ISSUE OF PREFERRED SHARES

making the dividend yield on this stock most attractive. In addition, since each preferred share may be converted to one common share at a later date, the rising prices of Bell common shares enhanced the demand for the preferred stock. Both of these factors contributed to the price increase of the Bell $2.70 preferred stock. These shares are no longer on the market.

To find preferred shares in newspaper stock quotations, look for such designations as *p, pfd.,* or simply the dividend rate after the name of the corporation. The various issues of Bell Canada Enterprises preferred stock may be shown as BCE 1.05, BCE 1.95, and so on.

NOVA 9 1/8 PERCENT PREFERRED SHARES

Issued at the end of 1984, these shares had the following features:

Cumulative with a *par value* of $25.

Dividends, to be paid in equal amounts on the fifteenth of February, May, August, and November at an annual rate of 9.125 percent, until Feb. 15, 1990. Thereafter, at a floating rate, equal to one-quarter of 70 percent of the average prime rate of a specified Canadian chartered bank.

Redeemable at the option of the company on Feb. 15, 1995, or at any time afterwards, on 30 days prior notice, at $25 per share plus accrued and unpaid dividends. Not redeemable before 1995.

Retractable at the option of the holder by advance notice given on or before Feb. 6, 1995, for payment on Feb. 15, 1995 at $25 per share plus accrued and unpaid dividends.

Convertible into another class of preferred shares of the company on Feb. 15, 1995, if notice given 30 days prior.

SPECIAL FEATURES

Issues of preferred shares often carry features intended to make them more attractive to investors. They may be cumulative, redeemable, retractable, or convertible.

CUMULATIVE   Dividends on preferred shares may be cumulative or non-cumulative, although most Canadian preferred shares are cumulative. Dividend payments on *cumulative shares* are expected to be paid quarterly, and if they are not, the unpaid amounts accumulate or become *in arrears*. All arrears of cumulative preferred shares must be paid before common dividends are paid; the existence of unpaid dividends will cause the market price of the shares to drop. Whenever the company's financial condition improves, dividends in arrears will be paid to the current shareholders but no interest will be paid for the period they were in arrears. In stock quotations, companies with dividends in arrears are shown with an *r* or other designation.

Dividend payment on *non-cumulative* preferred shares is not obligatory, but must be declared by the firm's board of directors. If a decision is made not to declare a dividend in some particular quarter, the shareholder has no future claim.

REDEEMABLE   The issuers of preferred shares may retain the right to redeem the issue at some future date. *Redeemable preferred shares*, like callable bonds, may be called in by the company at its option, usually at a price slightly higher than the par value.

RETRACTABLE   If there is a retractable feature, the investor may sell the preferred shares back to the company at a specific date. The decision to exercise this privilege belongs to the stockholder, in contrast to redeemability, in which the option belongs to the issuer of the stock.

CONVERTIBLE   Some preferred shares give the investor the option of converting these shares into other stock of the company, often common stock, at a specified price and within a certain time period. This gives the shareholder the opportunity of deciding at a later date whether it will be more beneficial to hold common or preferred stock.

INVESTMENT FUNDS

Two features of investing in the stock market, seen as obstacles by some small investors, are the management effort required and the need to have a sizeable portfolio in order to achieve diversity. One solution is to invest in pooled funds, known collectively as *investment funds*. The moneys of many investors are collected by investment funds companies, which in turn hire professional managers to invest the pooled funds in a diversified portfolio of many stocks and bonds. Each investor acquires shares in the fund, not in the individual securities that make up the portfolio of the fund (Figure 11.5). The investor

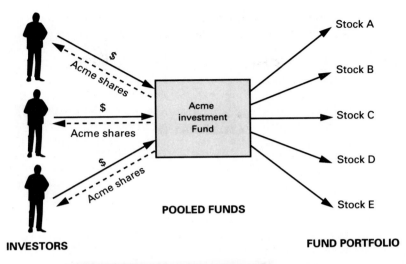

POOLED FUNDS

INVESTORS   **FUND PORTFOLIO**

Figure 11.5 BUYING AN INVESTMENT FUND

pays fees for the service of having the investment decisions looked after, and receives return from the fund in the form of dividends or capital gain.

CLOSED-END AND OPEN-END FUNDS

Investment funds may be organized as either (i) closed-end, or (ii) open-end (Figure 11.6). *Closed-end investment funds* issue a fixed number of shares. After the initial offering of shares, anyone who wishes to invest in a closed-end fund must find someone with shares to sell. BGR Precious Metals and Germany Fund of Canada are examples of closed-end funds; their shares trade on the stock exchanges and recent trades are listed in the daily stock quotations. After the initial offering one cannot invest directly with the corporation, but must buy or sell shares on the market through a broker.

MUTUAL FUNDS

Open-end investment funds, commonly known as *mutual funds*, are more numerous than closed-end funds. These funds do not have a fixed number of shares. Investors buy shares directly from the funds company, which promises to redeem them at any time. Mutual fund shares are not sold from investor to investor like common or preferred stock or closed-end funds. A mutual fund

1. Closed-end fund

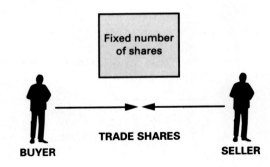

TRADE SHARES

BUYER   **SELLER**

2. Open-end fund—Mutual fund

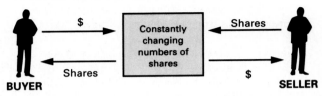

BUYER   **SELLER**

Figure 11.6   **CLOSED-END AND OPEN-END INVESTMENT FUNDS**

will accept as much money as the investor wishes to put into it; therefore, the total assets in the portfolio are constantly changing.

Think of a mutual fund as an ever-changing common pool of funds, which belongs to many investors who have arranged for professional managers to invest in a portfolio on their behalf. The value of each share is related to the net asset value of the fund's portfolio on any given date. At the end of a business day the total value of the portfolio may be estimated, liabilities and management costs deducted, and the net value divided by the number of outstanding shares. The result is the *net asset value per share*, which is published regularly in the financial papers.

A buyer of mutual fund shares will pay the current net asset value per share plus any sales fee. To withdraw money from a mutual fund, all that is needed is to inform the agent or the company, and the current net asset value less any redemption fees will be paid.

TYPES OF FUNDS

The 250 or more mutual funds being sold in Canada, intended to meet a wide variety of objectives, can be divided into three major groups acccording to how

NET ASSET VALUE PER SHARE

Total value − (liabilities + management) = Net asset
of fund   charges   value of
portfolio   portfolio

$$\frac{\text{Net asset value of portfolio}}{\text{Total no. shares outstanding}} = \text{Net asset value per share}$$

they are invested: (i) equity funds, (ii) debt security funds, (iii) balanced funds invested in both debt and equities, and (iv) others. A summary of the categories of investment funds is shown in Table 11.1.

EQUITY FUNDS   Although all of these funds invest in common stocks, they vary in risk level. The financial press usually classifies them as low, intermediate, and high variability (risk) funds, reflecting the price volatility of the stocks

Table 11.1   CLASSIFICATION OF MUTUAL FUNDS

Category	Description
I. Equity Funds (Risk levels: high, intermediate, or low.)	
A. Broad portfolio of stocks	
1. Growth funds—invested in growth companies for capital gain; higher risk	
2. Income funds—invested in lower risk, dividend-paying stocks for current income, e.g., dividend funds	
B. Specialty funds	
1. Invested in specific sector of market, e.g., oils, energy, high technology	
2. Invested in specific countries, e.g., Japan or USA.	
II. Debt Funds	
A. Money market funds—invested in treasury bills, acceptances, short-term bonds	
B. Fixed income funds—invested in bonds, mortgages	
C. Guaranteed income funds—invested in various deposits	
III. Balanced Funds	
Invested in both debt and equity securities	
IV. Other Funds	
A. Gold funds—invested in gold bullion or gold certificates	
B. Real estate funds—invested in property	

in each fund portfolio. High variability funds make great gains when the stock market is rising, but conversely lose rapidly in a falling market. The low risk funds will neither make nor lose as much money.

Within the various risk groups are equity funds that invest in a broad range of stocks, and those that specialize in one sector of the market, such as Gas and Energy Fund, Hi-Tech Fund, or Computer Trend Fund. Others invest in a certain country, such as the Japan Fund, or in a number of countries such as the Worldwide or Global Funds. Another group of funds, which invest in preferred shares, are known as dividend income funds because they emphasize low risk and a regular income.

DEBT FUNDS   Among the funds specializing in debt securities there are: (i) money market funds that are low risk and highly liquid, (ii) fixed income funds that invest in mortgages or bonds, and (iii) guaranteed income funds invested in deposits, often sponsored by banks or trust companies. Although the portfolios of these funds earn interest, the payments to shareholders are called dividends. However, reflecting their origin as interest, these dividends are not eligible for the tax dividend credit (to be explained later in this chapter). The income from debt funds, while perhaps referred to as dividends, is treated as interest income for tax purposes. In addition, there may be capital gain from some debt funds, such as bond funds. Receipts provided for tax purposes will separate these different kinds of return.

BALANCED FUNDS   These funds spread the risk by investing in both stocks and bonds, adjusting the proportions of each according to economic conditions. Again, a lower return is associated with less risk.

OTHER FUNDS   Real estate funds and gold funds invest in these commodities exclusively and thus limit their diversity. Nevertheless, they make it possible for the small investor to have exposure to this portion of the market.

BUYING MUTUAL FUNDS

Anyone interested in buying mutual funds should take the following steps: (i) determine personal objectives for this investment, (ii) find a fund that matches these personal objectives, (iii) investigate the fees that will be charged, and (iv) analyze the past performance of several possible funds.

OBJECTIVES   A cursory glance at the names of mutual funds listed in the papers shows that they have different objectives, e.g., growth, income, dividend, and money market fund. More information about the objectives of a fund may be obtained by requesting a prospectus listing the securities currently held in the portfolio. Since many mutual fund companies operate a number of funds with different objectives, you should contact a few companies, state desired objectives, and request the prospectus of any appropriate funds. The financial papers carry many advertisements for mutual fund companies with coupons for obtaining further information; take advantage of these. Otherwise, find an agent for a number of mutual funds and ask for prospectuses.

FEES   The costs associated with investment funds include sales commissions and fees for managing the funds. If a fee is imposed at the time of purchase, it is called an *acquisition fee*, a *sales fee*, or a *front-loading charge*. Some funds have no sales fees, others charge as much as nine percent of all amounts invested. Another way of covering these costs is to charge a *redemption fee* or *rear-end load*, paid at the time money is withdrawn from the fund. Redemption fees may be a set amount per transaction (e.g., $15 to $25) or a percentage (e.g., two percent).

Funds that do not charge sales fees are called *no-load funds*. However, the fee may be disguised. One group of supposedly no-load funds imposes a distribution fee of one percent a year which is added to the management fee for the first few years as a way of compensating sales people.

The no-load funds, most of which have no sales force, use other methods of finding investors, such as advertising, direct mail, and arrangements with stockbrokers. Also, there is a system of reciprocal commissions whereby managers of mutual funds, who need the services of stockbrokers, agree to send business to a broker who, in return, will promote sales of that particular mutual fund. In these instances, the investor does not pay an acquisition fee, but may receive advice somewhat biased in favour of certain funds because of the reciprocal arrangements.

The costs of managing the funds (the management fees) are deducted from the assets of the fund before the total return on the fund is calculated. These charges range from one to two percent a year.

PERFORMANCE   The prospective buyer of a mutual fund must find out how well the fund has performed in the past. How does the return on it compare to that of similar funds? *The Globe and Mail*, *The Financial Post*, and *Financial Times* publish monthly surveys of mutual fund performance over one, three, five, and ten years. These figures usually exclude any direct charges such as sales or redemption fees. When making comparisons it would be wise to take into account the effect of any sales fee on investment return. Note that the yield figures are based on annual compound rates of return, assuming dividends and capital gain are re-invested in the fund.

INVESTING IN A MUTUAL FUND

With $1000 to invest and no time to look after it, Sarah decided to buy shares in a mutual fund. The fund she chose had a sales fee of 8.5 percent and a net asset value per share of $14.72.

Sales commission (1000 × .085)	$85.00
Sum to invest (1000 − 85)	915.00
Number of shares bought (915/ 14.72)	62.160

Some months later a dividend of .30 per share was declared.

Dividends received (62.160 × .30)	18.648

If Sarah had arranged to have dividends reinvested in more shares of the mutual fund, which now had a net asset value per share of $13.50, she would gain 1.381 more shares.

Dividends to reinvest	18.648
Number of shares received (18.648 / 13.50)	1.381
Total shares owned (62.160 + 1.381)	63.541

As mentioned, the mutual funds are classified according to the volatility of their net asset value per share, and also whether or not they qualify for tax shelter eligibility (can be used in RRSPs). The rules for eligibility of funds for tax shelters are quite complex and will not be treated here.

In some papers, at the end of each category of mutual funds, information is given on the yield for the top and bottom performers and the average in that class. These data are useful bench marks for evaluating the performance of a specific fund. One should shun a fund that has consistently been the lowest performer in its class, and look with interest on those that have shown better than average return over long and short terms. Historical rates of return, while important information, should not be the sole basis for a choice. A key factor is the person who manages the funds, but managers often change companies. Watch the financial papers for information about the managers of funds and where they are presently working.

ADVANTAGES AND DISADVANTAGES

Some of the advantages of mutual funds are: (i) professional management by someone who monitors the portfolio continually, (ii) diversification, either broadly over the market or within a specific sector, that could not be attained by a small investment, (iii) marketability or the opportunity to withdraw funds at any time, (iv) the variety of purchase plans that include lump sum purchases as well as automatic saving plans, and (v) the many types of mutual funds available to meet almost any investment objective.

Among the disadvantages of mutual funds is the low liquidity of equity funds. Since those invested in equities fluctuate in net asset value per share as the whole market rises and falls, the optimum time for selling may not coincide with the need for funds. In addition, a high sales fee will reduce the net yield on the investment in the short term. With the exception of money market funds, most mutual funds are poor short-term investments, best planned for the long-term. The success of a particular fund is dependent on the skill of the managers, and some are better than others.

INVESTMENT RISK

As was mentioned in earlier chapters, all investments are exposed to some degree of risk, but the kind of risk varies with the type of investment. The essential point is that the investor must be aware of the risks associated with various kinds of securities and plan investments to achieve the best results without undue risk. After discussing several types of investments, it is advisable to review the kinds of risks to which the investor may be exposed, and ways to reduce risk.

TYPES OF RISK

As explained in Chapter 9, investors must consider the risks posed by (i) inflation, which causes the value of cash and debt securities to fall, (ii) interest rates, which have differential effects on various investments, (iii) market risk or the possibility that demand for the security falls, and (iv) business risk or the chance that the business in which you invested may do poorly. Market and business risks, which are of particular concern to investors in the stock market, will be reviewed here.

MARKET RISK   This is the possibility that, without any adverse happenings in the business operation or in interest rates, an asset may lose favour. The price of equity assets is dependent on demand in a market that is variable (Figure 11.3). It is normal for stock prices to fluctuate for reasons unrelated to earnings or dividend changes. As a great deal of emotion may be associated with stock ownership, irrational factors may influence prices. It is difficult to predict the direction or magnitude of the change in stock prices in the short run, but over the long run stock prices have produced real gains (in excess of inflation). The problem for the investor is timing. The ideal is to buy low and sell high and those who do the reverse will certainly lose. Since timing is so important with equity investments, the investor should be in a position to wait until an opportune time to sell. That is why funds for emergencies or short-term goals should not be invested in equities.

BUSINESS RISK   There is a risk that the business one invested in fails totally, but more often it is the risk that the earnings will decline, thus reducing not only one's equity but also the return. Investors are attracted to companies with growing or stable earnings and usually pay a higher price for this. The risk is that the investor paid too high a price for the security.

For instance, anyone who invested in the giant nickel mining company Inco at $24 a share, when the demand for metals was high, received dividends regularly. Later, an oversupply of nickel resulted in low profits for the company and a fall in dividends, which in turn caused the share price to drop to $14. These investors suffered from a business risk and were not able to recover all the capital invested or receive as much dividend income as anticipated unless they waited until the market for nickel improved. However, by 1990 patient investors saw Inco shares selling at $35.

DEBT SECURITIES AND RISK

Inflation and interest-rate risks are particularly important for fixed dollar investments, such as most debt securities. Therefore, attention should be given to real interest rates to ensure that, if possible, the return after inflation, is positive. Rising interest rates present problems whenever funds are locked in for some time at a fixed return. This creates not only a concern about inflation, but also the loss of opportunity to benefit from the new higher interest rates. It will, of course, be beneficial if, during falling interest rates, investments are locked in at higher rates.

Bonds might seem free of business risks, but corporations that are doing very poorly may be unable to keep the promise to pay bond interest. Interest from government bonds, however, usually arrives on schedule because governments can use taxing power to raise money when needed. In summary, if funds are invested with senior governments or stable financial institutions there is not much need to worry about business or market risks, or that interest will not be paid, but the risks of inflation or changing interest rates are of concern, as discussed in Chapter 9.

EQUITIES AND RISK

Ownership of stocks is subject to market, business, and interest rate risks. An investor may have chosen a company that did not do as well as expected or that has lost favour with other investors. Declines in profit mean dividends are reduced or omitted. In the more drastic case of complete failure, all or part of initial investment could be lost. Equity investments are especially vulnerable to market risks. Anyone who follows the stock market for some months will observe that prices may go up, down, or sideways, and the changes may be large or small. Some of the price variation is due to business risk and some to market risk. Not only stocks, but precious metals and property are subject to market risk.

The interest rate risk, which is especially important for debt securities, also has effects on other investments. Generally, falling interest rates are more beneficial to the stock market and real estate than to the bond market. When interest rates are low, businesses can afford to borrow and to expand and people decide to buy houses, all of which may be reflected in rising stock prices.

Over the long term, equity investments have been better than debt securities as a method of protecting net worth from inflation. Real estate prices have risen during periods of inflation, resulting in significant capital gain if the asset were sold. Over time, stocks have substantially outpaced inflation, but in the short run it may be difficult to find stocks that will out-perform inflation because of fluctuating market prices. In the rare periods of deflation or falling prices, debt securities generally do better than stocks or real estate.

RISK REDUCTION

Since there is no way to pick investments that will do well under all circumstances or to avoid some possible bad results, the rational approach is to take steps to reduce risk, recognizing that some risk will always remain. The future may not turn out as expected, but optimistically, investment risk carries with it the possibility of investment gain.

The distribution of risk in each portfolio must be carefully planned, taking into account individual personality, stage in the life cycle, and risk associated with the income stream. Some people are more *risk averse* than others, that is, they are less comfortable with uncertainty about future return. The most risk-averse people will be uneasy with any but the most secure fixed-income investments, and might as well recognize that they prefer certainty to the possibility of greater yield. Although they may never get rich, they will at least be free of worry.

DIVERSITY OF STOCKS
In addition to overall diversity, a stock portfolio should have diversity within. A well-constructed portfolio will not concentrate on any one sector. For example,

instead of buying only shares in oil companies, you could diversify your holdings by buying some in transportation, utilities, and industrial products. The odds are that, in a diversified portfolio, some securities will do better than expected, which will balance those that did not do as well as hoped. If a portfolio is well balanced, the overall risk will be less than that associated with any particular stock. Diversity reduces risk because the poor performance in one sector will be offset by successes in another, as individual companies react differently to economic and other conditions.

Although spreading risk is the primary reason for diversifying assets, convenience can be another. It is wise to have debt securities maturing at different times, to make it easier to re-invest the funds. Instead of being forced to find suitable investments for a large proportion of a portfolio at a time when opportunities may be limited, it would be better to re-invest on a number of occasions. Those who have invested for income should plan to have interest and dividend payment dates spread over the year to ensure an even flow.

Finally, do not overdo diversification. No one investor can effectively monitor a portfolio of many kinds of assets. For a small portfolio, six to ten stocks may be appropriate. A rule of thumb is that with less than $50 000 (excluding your house), each asset should be limited to about 10 percent of the total. Those with a larger net worth may be able to handle 20 securities.

INCOME TAX

Investment return may take the form of interest, dividends, or capital gain. Generally, these three types of return are taxed differently.

INTEREST

All interest must be added to taxable income and taxed accordingly. This has made debt securities less attractive to investors than equities.

INCOME TAX ON INTEREST

Assume that you have $2000 of interest income. Your federal marginal rate is 26 percent, and the provincial rate is 52 percent of the federal tax. What will your after-tax return be on $2000 of interest?

Total interest	$2000.00
Federal income tax (2000 × .26)	520.00

Provincial income tax (520 × .52)	270.00
Total income tax	790.00
After-tax return (2000 − 790)	1210.00

DIVIDENDS

Dividends from Canadian corporations are eligible for the tax dividend credit explained below. This preferential treatment of dividends has been designed to encourage Canadians to invest in our corporations.

At these income tax rates, a handy comparison can be made between the after-tax return from interest and dividends. To be equivalent, the interest rate must be 1.27 times the dividend rate. For instance, if deciding between preferred shares paying 8 percent in dividends and a debt security paying 10 percent, multiply 8 percent by 1.27. In other words, an interest rate of 10.16 percent would be needed to produce the equivalent after-tax income of an 8 percent dividend.

DIVIDEND TAX CREDIT

The rules for calculating the dividend tax credit require that the actual amount of dividends received be *grossed-up* or increased by a specific percentage, which in 1990 was 25 percent. Assume that you had received $2000 in dividends and had a federal marginal tax rate of 26 percent and a provincial marginal tax rate that is 52 percent of the federal tax.

Total dividends actually received	$2000.00
Grossed-up by 25 percent (2000 × 1.25)	2500.00
Federal income tax (26 percent)	650.00
Dividend tax credit is 16 2/3 percent × grossed-up amount (2500 x .167)	417.50
Federal tax payable (federal tax − dividend credit) (650.00 − 417.50)	232.50
Provincial tax (52 percent of federal tax) (232.50 × .52)	120.90

Total tax	
(federal + provincial)	$353.40
After-tax return	
($2000 − $530.67)	$1646.60

Capital Gain

Each person has a lifetime exemption of $100 000 in net capital gains. *Net capital gain* is the gross capital gain less any capital loss. After that exemption has been used, three-quarters of net capital gains must be added to taxable income and taxed along with other income. Recent tax reform has added considerably to the details of handling the taxation of capital gains and therefore you are advised to consult income tax publications for more specific information.

Summary

This brief treatment of equity investments introduced the vocabulary and characteristics of common and preferred shares as well as mutual funds. The mysteries of stock trading and the interpretation of stock quotations were revealed in preparation for reading the often-ignored financial section of the newspaper. There is much useful information in the financial section for the investor who understands the language. If you intend to invest, you should do further research for the information needed to evaluate various stocks.

It has been pointed out that while investing in the stock market usually entails more risk than many debt securities, not all stocks are highly speculative. Conservative investors who buy preferred shares of strong companies can expect a predictable dividend income as well as some prospect that the shares will increase over the years. Those who are interested in growth or capital gain can find stocks of growing companies for which the risk is higher but the possible rewards greater.

Mutual funds, which experience a boom when the stock market is rising, offer great diversity to suit a range of investment objectives. It is important to choose a fund to match personal objectives, and to be aware of the various fees attached.

As a conclusion to this section on investments, some associated risks were identified and the necessity of diversifying a portfolio to minimize risk was emphasized. When comparing the yield on investments, it is important to use after-tax return because different types of investment are taxed at different rates. Capital gains are exempt from tax up to $100 000 and dividends are taxed less heavily than interest income.

PROBLEMS

1. Use stock quotations from a recent newspaper to answer the following questions. It will be helpful to look at the legend, which should be located somewhere on the newspaper page, for explanation of the footnotes.

   (a) How much was the most recent dividend per share, in annual terms, on Stelco common stock? On Bell Canada Enterprises (BCE)?
   (b) Try to find an example of a preferred share for which the dividend is in arrears.
   (c) Look at the volume figures and find a stock that traded very actively.
   (d) Find a quotation for stock warrants. It may be indicated by a *w* after the name of the corporation.
   (e) Examine the quotations for B.C. Tel preferred shares to find out how many issues there seem to be.
   (f) Look for a stock that has issued stock dividends recently.

2. Decide whether you AGREE or DISAGREE with each of the following statements:

   (a) If an investor's primary objective is safety of principal, common stock should be considered.
   (b) Preferred stocks have some attributes of both bonds and common shares.
   (c) An investment firm must have a seat on the stock exchange if it is to have traders on the floor.
   (d) All mutual funds are highly speculative.
   (e) If you wish to buy shares in a mutual fund, you or your broker must find someone with shares to sell.
   (f) All mutual funds have sales fees.
   (g) A no-load mutual fund will not have any management fees.
   (h) A mutual fund is a type of investment fund.
   (i) The main reason for investing in mutual funds, rather than directly in the stock market, is to obtain the highest possible return on your money.
   (j) If you sell shares and use the money to buy more shares of another company immediately, your broker will charge you commission on one transaction only.
   (k) An open-end investment fund offers new shares without limit to the investing public, but does not offer to redeem the shares.
   (l) An investor who buys shares in a mutual fund with a front-end load and decides to sell them within a few months would probably lose money.

RIGHTS OFFERING

A news report states that Montreal Trustco plans to raise approximately $80 million in new capital through an issue of rights to shareholders, who will receive one right for every four common shares held. With one right and $12, the holder can buy another share of Montreal Trustco. The offer will be mailed to shareholders in late October and will expire 21 days later. With this new issue, rights will be offered to shareholders of record on October 15.

At the time of this announcement Montreal Trustco shares were trading at $12. By Nov. 1, they were up to $13. Over the previous year the shares had traded between 7 1/4 and 14.

3. (a) Why is the company making this offer?
    (b) As a shareholder, would you be interested in this offering? Comment.
    (c) If you were a shareholder, what choices would you have in regard to this rights offering?
    (d) If you bought Montreal Trustco stock on October 30, would you be eligible for rights? Explain whether you would be considered a shareholder of record as far as this offering is concerned.

4. An investor with a high marginal tax rate is interested in planning her investments to minimize her income tax. What would be the relative merits for her of interest, dividends, and capital gain?

5. Bell Enterprises Inc. announced that, on Nov. 4, the $1.80 preferred shares would be redeemed at $21.365 each unless the shareholder wished to convert them to common shares at the rate of .67 common share for each preferred. At the time this notice appeared, the preferred shares were trading at $24.50 and the common at $37.50.

    (a) Assume that you held 100 of the preferred shares. Calculate the amount you would receive if you accepted the redemption offer, and the value of your holdings if you converted to common shares. Which is higher?
    (b) What are some reasons for accepting the redemption offer?

6. Identify the type of investment risk that seems to predominate in each of these cases.

    (a) Shares of a lumber company dropped in price after news of a duty on wood products to be imposed by the United States.

(b) Stock market prices, which had been rising for several years, continued to fall for months.

(c) An investor who inherited $100 000 invested it all in five-year GICs at 8 percent, then interest rates moved to 11 percent.

7. A survey of mutual funds, published in the financial press reported the following information about Cundill Security and Dynamic Income Funds. Also, data about the average of all the equity funds of intermediate risk are shown.

EQUITY MUTUAL FUNDS

	Cundill Security	Dynamic Income	Ave. of group
Net asset value ($)	14.09	5.33	
Total assets ($ millions)	19.9	96.0	
Maximum sales fee (percent)	8.7	5.0	
Variability over 5 years	ave. —	ave.	
Average annual compound rate of return, including dividends			
Over past 3 years	+2.8	+8.6	−0.07
Over past 5 years	+8.3	+9.4	+6.0
Over past 10 years	+10.0	+12.9	+9.1

Annual compound rates of return on other investments, and the inflation rate:

	TSE*	T-bill (3-mo.)	Inflation rate
Three years	2.5	10.8	5.6
Five years	9.0	10.0	5.0
Ten years	11.2	11.1	6.0

*TSE—the return on the stocks in the Toronto Stock Exchange Index.

(a) Which fund has the larger sum of money to invest?

(b) Compare the past performance of each fund to the group average. What is your conclusion? Was one more successful over the short term as well as the long term?

(c) Based on this information, would you consider the higher fee of the Cundill Security Fund a deterrent to investing in it?

(d) Compare the return on these two mutual funds to the average return on the 300 stocks in the TSE, and to three-month treasury bills. Use the inflation rate to estimate real rates of return. Did the funds do as well as the TSE? Would you have had a better return if you had bought treasury bills? How well did these investments protect the investor against inflation?

REFERENCES

Books

ANDERSON, HUGH. *Bulls and Bears*. Markham, Ontario: Penguin, 1990, 172 pp. A guide for the investor that explains the language of the stock market, the functions of analysts and brokers, the difference between fundamental and technical analysis, and a variety of investment possibilities.

BEACH, WAYNE, and LYLE R. HEPBURN. *Are You Paying Too Much Tax*? Toronto: McGraw-Hill Ryerson, annual, 206 pp. A tax planning guide for the general reader that includes a discussion of capital gains, RRSPs, and investment income.

CANADIAN SECURITIES INSTITUTE. *How to Invest in Canadian Securities*. Third Edition. Toronto: Canadian Securities Institute, 1984, 251. Provides detailed explanations about various types of bonds and stocks.

COHEN, DIAN. *Money*. Scarborough, Ontario: Prentice-Hall Canada, 1987, 270 pp. An economist suggests strategies for coping with personal finances in the context of changing economic conditions. Topics include financial plans, buying a home, insurance, income tax, retirement, estate planning, and investments.

COSTELLO, BRIAN. *Your Money and How to Keep It*. Fifth Edition. Toronto: Stoddart, 1990, 248 pp. Particular emphasis on investments and income tax.

COTE, JEAN-MARC, and DONALD DAY. *Personal Financial Planning in Canada*. Toronto: Allyn and Bacon, 1987, 464 pp. A comprehensive personal finance text that includes financial planning, income tax, annuities, pensions, investments, credit, mortgages, and wills, with particular attention to the banking and insurance industries.

DEMONT, JOHN and TRACY LEMAY. *Financial Post Guide to Mutual Funds*. Toronto: Random House, 1988, 176 pp. An explanation of mutual funds, written for the general reader.

DRACHE, ARTHUR B. C., and PEGGY WATERTON. *Dollars and Sense, The Complete Canadian Financial Planner*. Toronto: Grosvenor House, 1987, 207 pp. An overview of a range of financial topics, including budgets, credit, investing, taxes, insurance, retirement planning, estates, and effects of changes in family status.

THE FINANCIAL POST. *Preferred Shares and Warrants*. Toronto: The Financial Post, annual. Provides details about all outstanding issues of preferred shares and warrants.

FRIEDLAND, SEYMOUR, and STEVEN G. KELMAN. *Investment Strategies, How to Create Your Own and Make it Work for You*. Markham, Ontario: Penguin, 1988, 125 pp. Offers guidance for the general reader in defining objectives and establishing an investment program.

GRAHAM, BENJAMIN. *The Intelligent Investor, A Book of Practical Counsel*. Fourth Edition. New York: Harper & Row, 1973, 318 pp. A classic guide to investing in the stock market.

HATCH, JAMES E. and MICHAEL J. ROBINSON. *Investment Management in Canada*. Scarborough, Ontario: Prentice-Hall Canada, 1989, 836 pp. A technical university text with in-depth coverage of many aspects of investing.

HOGG, R. D. *Preparing Your Income Tax Returns*. Toronto: CCH Canadian, annual, 589 pp. A complete and technical guide to income tax preparation.

HUNTER, W. T. *Canadian Financial Markets*. Peterborough, Ontario: Broadview Press, 1986, 193 pp. An economist gives an overview of the workings of the bond market, the mortgage market, and the stock market.

KELMAN, STEVEN G. *Understanding Mutual Funds*. Markham, Ontario: Penguin, 1989, 207 pp. Explains different types of mutual funds, how to select a fund, and how to analyze performance. Provides a detailed directory of funds with dates of establishment, historical rates of return, fees, and addresses.

MACINNIS, LYMAN. *Get Smart! Make Your Money Count in the 1990s*. Second Edition. Scarborough, Ontario: Prentice-Hall Canada, 1989, 317 pp. A book for the general reader that includes financial planning, income tax principles, but gives major attention to investing in the stock market.

MOTHERWELL, CATHRYN. *Smart Money, Investment Strategies for Canadian Women*. Toronto: Key Porter, 1989, 192 pp. A financial journalist explains how to get started investing, how to evaluate the products and how to build a portfolio.

PAPE, GORDON. *Building Wealth, Achieving Your Financial Goals*. Scarborough, Ontario: Prentice-Hall Canada, 1988, 246 pp. An easy-to-read guide for the novice financial manager and investor that considers interest rates, credit cards, mortgages, RRSPs, mutual funds, and the stock market.

SIEVERS, MARC. *Investing Successfully in Canadian Mutual Funds*. Toronto: Stoddart, 1988, 230 pp. A guide for the general reader.

Through the Mutual Funds Maze. Toronto: Grosvenor House Press, 1988, 185 pp. A detailed guide on what mutual funds are, how they work, how to evaluate performance, how to select a fund and how to evaluate costs.

WOODS, SHIRLEY E. *The Money Labyrinth: A Stock Market Guide by a Canadian Broker*. Toronto: Doubleday Canada, 1984, 221 pp. Explains how the stock market works, how to choose a broker and the difference among bonds, stocks, options, mutual funds, and commodities.

WYATT, ELAINE. *The Money Companion, How to Manage Your Money and Achieve Financial Freedom*. Markham, Ontario: Penguin Books, 1989, 203 pp. A guide to personal financial management that focuses on planning, investment strategy, and retirement needs.

ZIMMER, HENRY B. *Making Your Money Grow, A Canadian Guide to Successful Personal Finance*. Third Edition. Toronto: Collins, 1989, 260 pp. The focus of this book is on basic calculations needed for personal financial decisions, as applied to compound interest, future and present values, investment returns, RRSPs, annuities, and life insurance.

ZIMMER, HENRY B. and JEANNE V. KAUFMAN. *Your Investment Strategies for the 1990s*. Toronto: Collins, 1988, 249 pp. The authors, with backgrounds in accounting and taxation, discuss financial planning and a wide range of investment possibilities, including RRSPs, insurance, real estate, stocks, mutual funds, and metals.

Periodicals

Canadian Consumer. Monthly. Box 9300, Ottawa, Ontario, K1G 3T9. In recent years, the personal finance articles have been concentrated in the November issue, "Personal Money Guide."

Canadian Money Saver. Monthly. Box 370, Bath, Ontario, K0H 1G0. Includes short articles on a range of personal finance topics, with special emphasis on investments.

Canadian Shareowner. Bimonthly. Suite 204, 1090 University Avenue West, Windsor, Ontario, N9A 5S4. Intended for investors who wish to become knowledgeable about managing their own stock portfolio. Special attention to growth stocks.

Financial Times. Weekly. Suite 500, 920 Yonge Street, Toronto, Ontario, M2W 3L5. Provides current information on a range of business and economic topics.

Report on Business. Daily. A section of *The Globe and Mail*. Important source of information on the financial markets.

The Financial Post. Daily and weekly. 777 Bay Street, Toronto, Ontario, M5G 2E4. Up-to-date information on business, economics, income tax, and investments.

The Financial Post Annual Moneyplanner. Annual. 777 Bay Street, Toronto, Ontario, M5G 2E4. Usually contains articles on financial planning, income tax, insurance, investing, and retirement planning.

The Financial Post Magazine. Monthly. 777 Bay Street, Toronto, Ontario, M5G 2E4. Includes a section on personal finance.

PART

CREDIT

3

This section presents a comprehensive treatment of consumer and mortgage credit, beginning with a review of trends in the use of consumer credit in Canada. This is followed by two chapters on consumer loans and vendor credit that examine the various institutions that provide credit, types available, terminology used, and contracts that borrowers sign. Although the language in consumer credit contracts is becoming more comprehensible, it is important for borrowers to understand what they are signing. Therefore, samples of credit contracts are included to familiarize the reader with them.

It is a convention to make a distinction between consumer credit and mortgage credit and following this practice, there is a separate chapter on home mortgages, an ever-increasingly complex subject. The chapter on credit reporting and debt collection explains processes that are mysterious and challenging to many. Finally, strategies are outlined for handling problems with debt.

12

THE USE OF CONSUMER CREDIT

8. To examine, from the borrower's perspective, some advantages and disadvantages of using credit.

9. To understand the following terms: debtor, creditor, principal, interest, total consumer credit outstanding, current dollars, constant dollars, flexibility cost of credit, debt burden, personal disposable income, discretionary income.

Introduction

To set the stage for this study of consumer credit, we will examine empirical information on the amounts of credit used in Canada over several decades. The data on consumer credit comes from two sources: macro or national data obtained from creditors, and micro data from household surveys. These micro surveys are not conducted very often but they do provide information about variables associated with the use of consumer debt. Finally, some reasons for using credit will be considered.

What is Credit?

Credit and Debt

Every borrowing transaction has two aspects. There is the lender (creditor) who supplies money for a loan in exchange for a credit, and who looks upon the transaction in terms of the amount of credit that has been extended. The other actor is the borrower (debtor) who receives the money and views the transaction as an accumulation of debt. Therefore, that which is consumer debt to you, the borrower, is *consumer credit* to the lender or creditor. Information about this transaction may be reported as debt or credit, depending on the perspective of the reporter. Although it is really the same phenomenon, data obtained from households about their borrowing are usually reported as consumer debt, while the statistics gathered from lenders are referred to as consumer credit. In this chapter both kinds of data will be examined.

The *debtor* in a credit/debt transaction accepts a commitment to repay the debt sometime in the future, and thus must be prepared to give up future purchasing power in order to have extra resources available at present. The debtor, making the decision that it is more important to have extra funds now than to wait until the money can be saved, should realize that a cost of using credit is the commitment of future income to interest payments; these funds will not be available for other uses. The debtor makes a promise to repay, not only the *principal,* or the sum borrowed, but also the *interest*, which is the charge for borrowing. Thus the lender or the *creditor* holds a claim that the borrower will repay interest and principal as promised.

It is a convention to make a distinction between consumer debt and mortgage debt; *total debt* is the sum of these two. *Consumer debt* is defined as all the personal debt incurred by households, exclusive of mortgage debt or business debt. *Mortgage debt* is debt secured by real property, such as buildings and land. To summarize:

$$\begin{array}{c}
\text{consumer} \\
\text{debt}
\end{array} + \begin{array}{c}
\text{mortgage} \\
\text{debt}
\end{array} = \begin{array}{c}
\text{total debt of} \\
\text{households}
\end{array}$$

For analytical purposes, it is useful to make a distinction between mortgage debt and consumer debt. Mortgage debt generally involves much larger amounts and for a much longer term than consumer debt; therefore combining these statistics would obscure trends in consumer debt. From the household's perspective, mortgage debt can be viewed as the ongoing cost of housing—a regular expense in contrast to short-term debt. Also, borrowing to invest in property can be an effective way to accumulate assets but borrowing for current consumption is not. For a discussion of mortgages see Chapter 15.

CONSUMER CREDIT—NATIONAL DATA

SOURCE OF INFORMATION

Lenders are required to make regular reports to Statistics Canada about the amount of credit they have extended; this is called the *total consumer credit outstanding*. From this national information it is possible to identify the amounts of credit held by various lenders, but it is impossible to know anything about the borrowers. Such data are, however, quite useful in giving a picture of national trends. These data were not available before 1951, which is probably an indication of the increasing significance of consumer credit in our society.

HOW MUCH CREDIT DO WE USE?

You may have heard people say that Canadians now use more consumer credit than ever before. To verify this statement, we will examine the trends in the total consumer credit outstanding since 1951 (Figure 12.1). It is clear from this graph that there has been a dramatic increase in total credit outstanding. By looking at one decade at a time, it is evident that the rate of increase changed significantly after 1970. What are some possible explanations for this? It may be that: (i) the population grew rapidly and thus more credit was needed in Canada, or (ii) prices of goods rose substantially necessitating larger loans, or (iii) each person used more credit. Each of these possibilities will be examined in turn.

POPULATION CHANGES   The data shown in Figure 12.1 make no allowance for any changes in the population of Canada. This can be corrected by dividing the total credit figures by the population of Canada for each year. Examine the line in Figure 12.2 labelled "current dollars", showing the amounts of consumer credit outstanding per capita. Generally the slope of this line

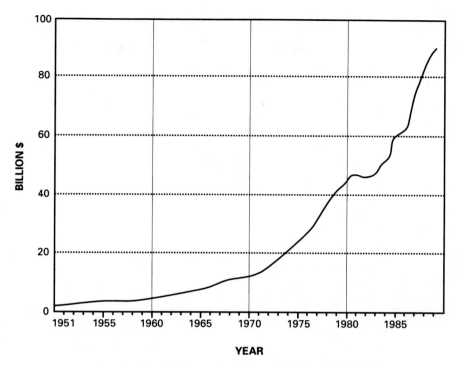

BILLION $

100								
80								
60								
40								
20								
0								

1951   1955   1960   1965   1970   1975   1980   1985

YEAR

Figure 12.1   TOTAL CONSUMER CREDIT OUTSTANDING, CANADA,
1951-1989

Source of data: *Bank of Canada Review*, Ottawa: Bank of Canada, various issues. *Canada Year Book, Canadian Statistical Review, Canadian Economic Observer,* and *Historical Statistical Supplement*, Ottawa: Statistics Canada, various issues. Reproduced with the permission of the Bank of Canada and the Minister of Supply and Services Canada.

matches that in Figure 12.1, indicating about the same rate of increase. Apparently, it is not possible to explain the rapid increase in total consumer credit outstanding by a change in the population of Canada. Other causes must be sought.

INFLATION   Perhaps rising prices caused people to use increasing amounts of consumer credit. For example, as the prices of cars rose, the size of each car loan necessarily increased. In this case, it would not mean a broadening of the use of credit, but rather that inflated prices of goods increased loan amounts. To check whether the rapidly rising amounts of consumer credit were caused by inflation, the credit outstanding per capita will be adjusted for changes in consumer prices. The statistical procedure is to convert the values that were

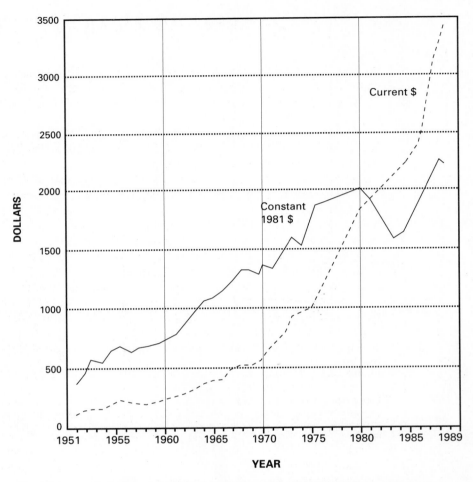

Figure 12.2   CONSUMER CREDIT OUTSTANDING PER CAPITA, CANADA,
1951-1989 (IN CURRENT AND CONSTANT 1981 DOLLARS)

Source of data: *Bank of Canada Review*, Ottawa: Bank of Canada, various issues. *Canada Year Book, Canadian Statistical Review, Canadian Economic Observer*, and *Historical Statistical Supplement*, Ottawa: Statistics Canada, various issues. Reproduced with the permission of the Bank of Canada and the Minister of Supply and Services Canada.

in *current dollars* that is, the dollar amounts recorded in each year, into *constant dollars* which estimate the values if prices had remained constant. The numbers plotted in Figure 12.1 were in current dollars, but may be converted to constant dollars by using the following formula:

$$\frac{\text{Value in current dollars in Year X}}{\text{Consumer Price Index in Year X}} \quad \text{x } 100 = \quad \begin{array}{l} \text{Constant \$} \\ \text{in Year X} \end{array}$$

This is a way of eliminating, statistically, the effect of changes in prices. In other words, if consumer prices had remained unchanged since 1951, the amount of consumer credit extended would be approximately that shown in constant dollars in Figure 12.2.

If the increase in consumer credit outstanding had been entirely due to population changes and rising prices, the constant dollar line in Figure 12.2, which has been corrected for both, should be perfectly horizontal. On the contrary, it shows a rising trend and therefore we can conclude from these data that, regardless of any changes in population or consumer prices, Canadians did use more consumer credit. Much of the difference between the two lines in Figure 12.2 can be attributed to the effects of inflation; as prices of goods and services rose, so did the amounts borrowed.

It is clear from these data that the recession of 1982-3 created a turning point in the use of consumer credit. Economic events such as the slowdown in the economy, escalating interest rates, and high unemployment combined to create uncertainty and a natural reluctance to incur more debt. Many of those with debts found it very difficult to maintain their payment schedules, and bankruptcies were not uncommon. For a while, attitudes toward using consumer debt became more cautious. How long did these effects last? What has been the trend since 1983?

DEBT BURDEN

Another way of analyzing the use of consumer credit is to relate it to income levels. If about the same proportion of income is committed to the repayment of debt year after year, one may conclude that the burden of debt would be unchanged. *Debt burden* is often measured as a ratio of debt or credit to income. Continuing to use macro data, a comparison will be made between the ratio of total consumer credit outstanding to total personal disposable income in each of the years since 1951. *Personal disposable income* is all the income received by Canadians after income tax was paid.

Debt burden increased until about 1981, when it began to decline for a few years before rising again (Figure 12.3). It appears that Canadians carried an average debt burden of about 10 percent in 1951, which grew to over 20 percent before dropping after 1980. Between 1951 and 1980, the real incomes of Canadians increased substantially, leaving most families with more *discretionary income,* which is income left after paying for such necessaries as food, clothing, and shelter. This new prosperity made it possible to buy more consumer durables and recreational goods, which are the items most frequently bought on credit. In this period of

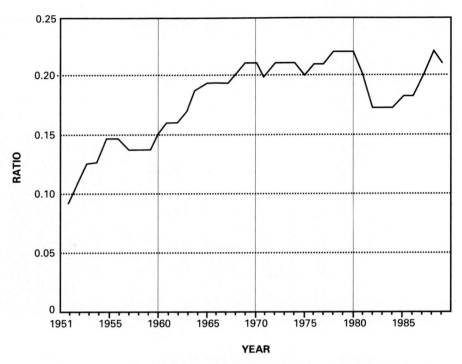

Figure 12.3   RATIO OF TOTAL CONSUMER CREDIT OUTSTANDING TO
PERSONAL DISPOSABLE INCOME, CANADA, 1951-1989

Source of data: *Bank of Canada Review*, Ottawa: Bank of Canada, various issues. *Canada Year Book, Canadian Statistical Review, Canadian Economic Observer*, and *Historical Statistical Supplement*, Ottawa: Statistics Canada, various issues. Reproduced with the permission of the Bank of Canada and the Minister of Supply and Services Canada.

steadily rising incomes, it became easier to repay debt because incomes tended to increase annually while most debt contracts remain fixed for several years. Thus, the combination of fixed debt commitments and rising income was beneficial for borrowers. However, when we are in a time of slower economic growth a reduction in our debt burden is wise.

A look at what has been happening to family incomes may be helpful in interpreting trends in the use of consumer credit. Between 1965 and 1988, median incomes of Canadian families increased six-fold, or on average nearly 4% a year (Figure 12.4). However, this does not mean that economic welfare grew at the same rate. By converting these data to constant 1981 dollars it is possible to estimate the purchasing power of each year's income. Assuming that the prices of goods and services had remained unchanged for these 23 years, the constant dollar figures give an estimate of changes in purchasing

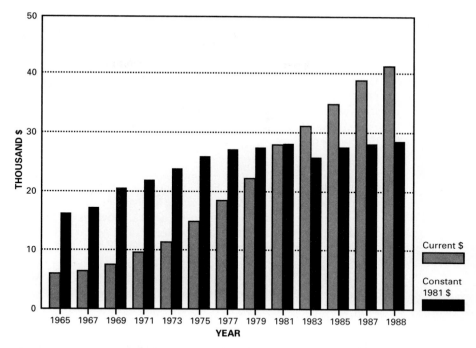

Figure 12.4 MEDIAN INCOMES OF CANADIAN FAMILIES, 1965-1988
(IN CURRENT AND CONSTANT 1981 DOLLARS)

Source: *Income Distributions by Size in Canada* (1975, 1977, 1988), Catalogue number 13-207, Table 1; and the *Canadian Economic Observer, Historical Statistical Supplement, 1989/90*, Catalogue number 11-210, Table 3.2, Ottawa: Statistics Canada. Reproduced and edited with the permission of the Minister of Supply and Services Canada, 1991.

power of family incomes, also known as *real incomes*. Note the steady increase in real incomes from 1965 to 1981, until the down turn in 1983. How do you think this affected the use of credit?

CONSUMER DEBT USE AT THE HOUSEHOLD LEVEL

The information examined thus far has been macro data from national statistics that give a general picture of credit use in Canada over a number of years. Another source of information about credit or debt is micro data obtained by interviewing householders. Statistics Canada has conducted infrequent surveys of consumer debt; the last three were in 1969, 1977, and 1984. By asking people about their debts, incomes, and other variables, it is possible to explore relationships between debt levels and variables such as income, age, education, and occupation. Here we will examine the relation between the use of consumer debt and both income and age.

It will be less confusing if you realize that different definitions of consumer credit may be in use. Although debt can generally be classified as consumer debt or mortgage debt, a somewhat different terminology is used in Statistics Canada household surveys where "personal debt" refers to all non-mortgage debt. For our purposes, consider personal debt and consumer debt as synonyms.

INCOME AND CONSUMER DEBT

Are people with higher incomes more likely to incur consumer debt than those with lower incomes? Each bar in Figure 12.5 divides all households according to whether or not they have any personal debt. What pattern do you see here? Low income families may wish to use credit, but usually are denied it because of their lack of ability to repay. From these data one may generalize that the probability of having consumer debt increases with income. Were you surprised to find a significant proportion of Canadian households with no consumer debt at all?

We have seen that households with the greatest probability of incurring consumer debt had middle or high incomes. Another way of looking at the relation between income and debt is illustrated in Figure 12.6, which shows how average debt load varies by income group. Compare Figures 12.5 and 12.6. Why is the difference between the bottom and top income groups more marked in Figure 12.6? Keep in mind that these data are for all Canadian households, not only those with debts. If information were available for debtors only, the average debts would of course be much higher.

STAGE IN THE LIFE CYCLE AND CONSUMER DEBT

Is the stage in the life cycle (or age) associated with the probability of having certain kinds of debt? A curvilinear relation between age and the incidence of personal and mortgage debt is clearly shown in Figure 12.7. It appears that those who are 35 to 44 years old are most likely to have both kinds of debt, and those over 65 to have neither. This is consistent with the needs at different stages in the life cycle. Younger families start buying houses and collecting household durables, and by retirement they have usually discharged these debts.

The relation between average debt and the age of the household head follows a pattern similar to the incidence data. Those aged 35 to 44 have the highest levels of consumer debt (Figure 12.8 on page 384). Again these data are for all households, not only debtors.

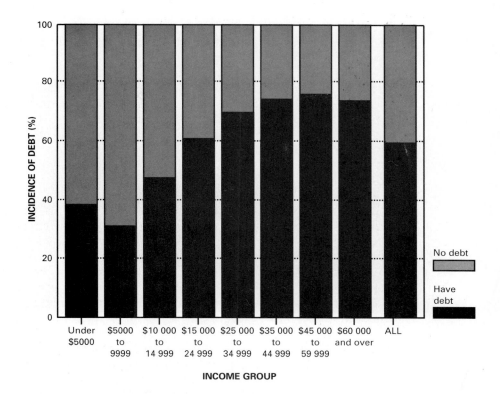

Figure 12.5   PERCENTAGE DISTRIBUTION OF CANADIAN HOUSEHOLDS BY STATUS OF CONSUMER DEBT AND BY INCOME GROUPS, SPRING 1984

Source: *The Distribution of Wealth in Canada, 1984*, Ottawa: Statistics Canada, 1986, Table 25, page 67 (Catalogue No. 13-580). Reproduced and edited with the permission of the Minister of Supply and Services Canada.

DEBT/INCOME RATIO

The data examined thus far show how income and stage in the life cycle (age) affect (i) the probability that households will use consumer debt, and (ii) how much debt is used. Another way to analyze the use of consumer debt is to look at the ratio of consumer debt to income, or debt burden. No recent data are available, but in the past it has been found that middle-income households had a higher propensity to incur a heavy debt burden. This is quite understandable, considering that very low-income families are often very young or very old, and not good candidates for consumer credit. Those with high incomes, while heavy users of credit, have large enough incomes to make the burden manageable.

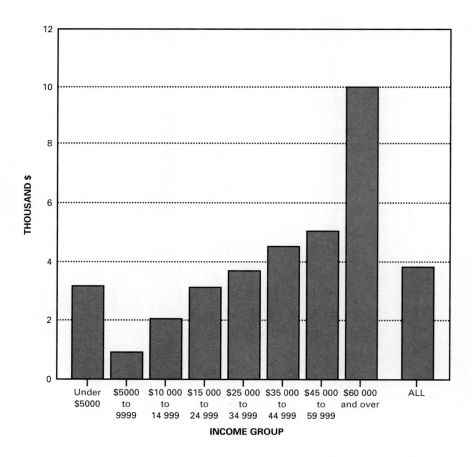

Figure 12.6   AVERAGE TOTAL PERSONAL DEBT OF CANADIAN
HOUSEHOLDS BY INCOME GROUPS, SPRING 1984

Source: *The Distribution of Wealth in Canada, 1984*, Ottawa: Statistics Canada, 1986, Tables 1 and 24, pages 26, 64 (Catalogue No. 13-580). Reproduced and edited with the permission of the Minister of Supply and Services Canada, 1991.

MEASURING USE OF CONSUMER CREDIT

To determine which population segments use more credit, it is necessary first to decide how to measure consumer credit activity. Three possible ways are: (i) the probability that any consumer credit will be used (Figures 12.5 and 12.7), (ii) the average amount of consumer debt carried by the household (Figures 12.4 and 12.6), or (iii) the debt burden.

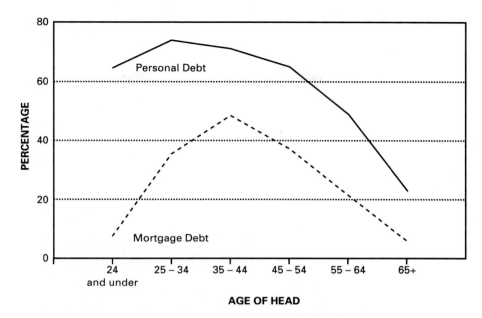

Figure 12.7   INCIDENCE OF CONSUMER AND MORTGAGE DEBT OF
CANADIAN HOUSEHOLDS, BY AGE OF HEAD, SPRING 1984

Source: *The Distribution of Wealth in Canada, 1984*, Ottawa: Statistics Canada, 1986, Table 27, page 73
(Catalogue No. 13-580). Reproduced and edited with the permission of the Minister of Supply and Services
Canada.

WHY DO WE USE CREDIT?

Undoubtedly, there are many reasons why we use credit, but most can be classified into four main categories. Credit is used: (i) for convenience, (ii) to obtain something before saving enough to pay for it, (iii) to bridge the gap if income is insufficient, infrequent, or irregular, and occasionally (iv) to consolidate debts. Each of these reasons may have costs as well as benefits.

CONVENIENCE
It is very handy to use a credit card instead of carrying cash, and to be able to use one cheque to pay for a number of bills. As long as the amount outstanding is paid monthly, it is an interest-free convenience. Some charge accounts require that the total bill be paid monthly, but there are others, such as bank credit cards and retail revolving accounts, that offer a choice of paying all or a portion of the debt. Although this option makes it quite easy to let bills

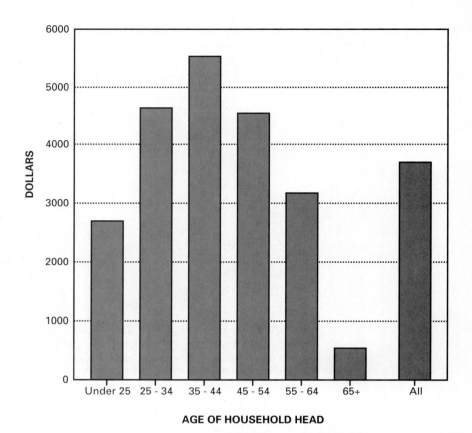

Figure 12.8   AVERAGE TOTAL PERSONAL DEBT OF CANADIAN
HOUSEHOLDS BY AGE OF HEAD, SPRING 1984

Source: *The Distribution of Wealth in Canada, 1984*, Ottawa: Statistics Canada, 1986, Tables 5 and 26, pages 32, 70 (Catalogue No. 13-580), Ottawa, 1986. Reproduced and edited with the permission of the Minister of Supply and Services Canada, 1991.

accumulate, the interest rates charged on unpaid balances are usually rather high. Another disadvantage is that a credit card tends to encourage impulsive shopping tendencies; having to pay in cash is a more effective restraint.

IMMEDIACY

As advertisers eagerly point out, credit allows us to have things immediately and pay later. This is a very successful means of selling high-priced goods and services because buyers do not have to consider whether they can afford the selling price, but merely whether they can manage the monthly payments.

Each individual must decide whether or not the benefits outweigh the costs. Sometimes, the opportunity to have a good or service immediately can be worth the cost. When you take into account the costs of being without a car or certain equipment, you may discover monetary benefits in using credit.

Most of the benefits of using credit for this reason, however, are not monetary. It is very appealing to have something we want as soon as we see it, but whether the resulting satisfaction offsets the cost is a personal decision. There are people who find it almost impossible to save enough to accumulate the purchase price of expensive items; using credit is the only way they can acquire such things. In such instances, credit becomes a form of forced saving, although an expensive one.

Two costs of using credit to obtain immediate satisfaction are the interest to be paid and the loss of financial flexibility. Interest is a direct monetary cost that varies directly according to the time taken to repay the debt. Another cost that can be very significant, but is perhaps less visible, is the *flexibility cost* of having committed some future income to debt repayment. Using credit means accepting an obligation to make future payments that may curtail freedom to spend in other ways. If something happens to the income stream because of illness or loss of a job, debt payments can become a substantial burden. Or, if unexpected emergencies occur, there will be less money available for large expenses. When consumer durables or vehicles are bought on credit, one must consider not only the flexibility cost but also whether it is possible to handle the recurring expenses of operation and maintenance.

To Bridge the Gap

Individuals with an irregular income, such as many self-employed persons, may require loans to pay regular costs until the next income cheque. Until a sufficient reserve fund is built up, loans to bridge this gap may be necessary. Even with a regular income, on occasion there may not be enough money to cover reasonable needs. When income prospects appear good, it may be worthwhile to incur debt to furnish a first home, to support a growing family, or to provide education for oneself or children.

Consolidation Loans

When all the bills and debts exceed income, some people borrow enough to repay all outstanding debts and then owe a larger amount to one lender for a longer time, through a consolidation loan. Such a loan is one way to reduce the financial pressure, but it tends to lock a person into continual debt. This will be discussed in more detail in the chapter on debt strategies.

INFLATION

In inflationary periods, borrowers tend to benefit at the expense of lenders. As prices rise and incomes tend to increase, borrowers pay back loans that have fixed payments. This makes it comparatively easy to handle debt. The lender, on the other hand, is paid back in dollars that will buy less than when they were lent. Another aspect of very rapid inflation is the advantage of making a purchase before the price goes up any more. Under these conditions it may be quite rational to use credit rather than accumulate savings. However, if economic conditions change as they did in the early 1980s and the early 1990s, the loss of a job creates hardship for debtors.

SUMMARY

Consumer debt and consumer credit are synonyms, with the choice of term dependent on one's perspective. By convention, data on mortgage debt are kept separate from consumer debt. Canadians have significantly increased their use of consumer credit during the past several decades but only a small portion of the increase may be attributed to population growth. Inflation had a significant effect on the total amount of credit extended, but when the data are corrected for price change, it is apparent that we have been making greater use of consumer credit. Information about consumer credit use may be obtained from lenders or from borrowers themselves. In this chapter, we examined data from both macro and micro sources.

Three measures of the "use of consumer credit" by households are:(i) the proportion of families that make some use of credit or incidence, (ii) the average debt level of the household, and (iii) the ratio of consumer debt to income. Income level tends to be positively related to the probability of using consumer credit and there is a curvilinear relation between credit use and age. Middle-income families that use consumer credit tend to carry the heaviest debt burdens.

PROBLEMS

1. Refer to Figures 12.1 and 12.2 when answering these questions:

   (a) What numbers were plotted to make Figure 12.1? Who supplied these credit figures to Statistics Canada?
   (b) Do these data refer to all Canadians, those with debts, or to whom?
   (c) Is it possible to tell from these data how many people had large debts and how many had no debts?
   (d) Do these figures include mortgage credit?

(e) Why is the slope of the line in Figure 12.1 steeper each decade? Suggest several possibilities.

(f) Why is the constant dollar line in Figure 12.2 the more meaningful one?

(g) Suggest two or three reasons why Canadians increased their levels of debt since 1951.

(h) Why did we convert the data from current dollars into constant dollars?

(i) Why did the constant dollar line in Figure 12.2 curve downward in the early 1980s? What has been happening more recently?

2. These questions relate to Figure 12.3.

(a) What adjustment was made to the total consumer credit outstanding figures to create the ratios plotted in this graph?

(b) How are the data presented in Figure 12.3 different from those shown in the two previous graphs?

(c) Explain how debt burden was measured.

(d) What would it have meant if the line in the graph had been perfectly horizontal?

(e) Write a sentence that summarizes Figure 12.3.

(f) Is it true that the debt burden of Canadians in 1988 was about the same as 20 years before?

3. What is the difference between

(a) total debt and consumer debt?

(b) consumer debt and personal debt?

(c) current and constant dollars?

(d) consumer debt and consumer credit?

(e) personal disposable income and personal discretionary income?

(f) debt burden and average debt?

(g) principal and interest?

4. (a) Why is it important to use constant dollars when comparing the trend in family incomes?

(b) What is the significance of the information presented in Figure 12.4 in explaining use of consumer credit?

5. Is it true that in 1984,

(a) slightly over one-half of Canadian households had some personal debt?

(b) about one-fifth of households in the lowest income class had consumer debt?

(c) the probability of having consumer debt exceeded that of having mortgage debt at all stages in the life cycle?

(d) those households headed by a person aged 24 or under were very much more likely to have consumer debt than mortgage debt?

(e) the probability of having mortgage debt is highest when the head of the household is between the ages of 25 and 44?

6. (a) What is the difference between the kinds of information plotted in Figures 12.7 and 12.8?

   (b) How can the information in Figure 12.7 be used in interpreting that in Figure 12.8?

7. Suggest some examples or situations in which the flexibility cost of credit could be so high that borrowing might be unwise.

8. In this chapter, four reasons for using consumer credit were advanced. Can you suggest others? In your opinion, which reason is the most common?

9. Do you think Canadians should use less credit? Comment.

10. Have you observed any difference between people of your parents' generation and your own in attitudes toward using credit? Comment.

REFERENCES

Statistical Reports

STATISTICS CANADA. *Canadian Economic Observer*. Ottawa: Supply and Services Canada, monthly. (Catalogue No. 11-010)

STATISTICS CANADA. *The Distribution of Wealth in Canada, 1984*. Ottawa: Supply and Services Canada, 1986. (Catalogue No. 13-580)

STATISTICS CANADA. *Income Distribution by Size in Canada*. Ottawa: Supply and Services Canada, annual. (Catalogue No. 13-207)

13 CONSUMER LOANS

9. To ascertain, by examining a chattel mortgage:
   (a) security pledged,
   (b) repayment conditions,
   (c) penalties for late payments,
   (d) conditions under which a creditor may enforce security and the means to be used.

10. To explain these terms: spread, common bond, debit card, fiduciary, living trust, testamentary trust, term of a loan, loan terms, fully secured loan, collateral, maturity date, skip, seize or sue law.

11. To compare the cost of a cash advance on a credit card with a personal bank loan.

INTRODUCTION

This chapter and the next are about various forms of consumer credit, who the chief lenders are, and the lending process. One way to organize this subject is to classify credit transactions as either: (i) obtaining a loan from a financial institution or (ii) making a purchase and arranging with the vendor for credit financing. This chapter will focus on *consumer loans* where credit is obtained separately from a purchase. Although a person may borrow from the bank and use the funds to buy a car, these are separate transactions with two different firms. *Vendor credit*, the subject of the next chapter, occurs when the purchase and the extension of credit occur in the same transaction.

READING CREDIT CONTRACTS   Generally you cannot obtain credit without, at some point, signing a contract. Do you understand what you are signing? Many people, intimidated by the legal terminology and small print, sign their acceptance of terms they do not understand. To help you to develop skill in reading credit contracts, several samples are presented in this and the next chapter. You are advised to read them carefully and to do the related problems. Although the contracts may seem forbidding at first glance, with practice you will find your ability to understand them grows and that in future you will never again sign an agreement that you have not read and do not fully understand.

THE CONSUMER LENDERS

Funds can be borrowed from a number of places, but four financial institutions particularly active in providing consumer loans are banks, credit unions, trust companies, and small loan companies. In addition, the owner of a whole life insurance policy may borrow against it. Other possibilities that do not fit this discussion are family and friends, the pawnbroker, and the loan shark.

MARKET SHARES

In the previous chapter, we saw that the long-term trend in Canada was towards an increase in the use of consumer credit. Here we will examine how the consumer credit market is shared by various creditors. In Figure 13.1 each bar represents all the consumer credit outstanding in Canada in a given year, and the divisions show how the business was divided among lenders. These data include both consumer loans and vendor credit, and since some creditors offer both, the data are difficult to separate. Bank credit cards, for instance, represent a mixture of loan and vendor credit.

It is clear from Figure 13.1 that significant changes in market shares have occurred over past decades. The most striking point is the shift to banks

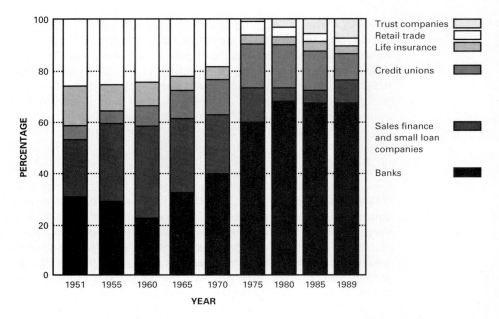

Figure 13.1   SHARE OF TOTAL CONSUMER CREDIT OUTSTANDING BY
SOURCE, CANADA, 1951-1989

Sources of data: *Bank of Canada Review*, Ottawa: Bank of Canada, various issues. *Canada Year Book*, Ottawa:
Statistics Canada, various issues. Reproduced with the permission of the Bank of Canada and the Minister of
Supply and Services Canada.

from sales finance and small loan companies and retail trade. Credit unions
have increased their share of the consumer credit business somewhat and life
insurance policy loans have declined slightly. Trust companies entered the
consumer credit business more recently, but have been gaining an increasing
market share. Keep these trends in mind as we review the major consumer
lenders and think about possible reasons for the changes.

FINANCIAL INSTITUTIONS

At one time banks, credit unions, trust companies, and small loan companies
were distinctly different in structure and the services they provided but now
the trend is towards greater similarity. Each wants to provide the same broad
range of services and they wait impatiently for expected federal legislation
that will change what they are permitted to do. Banks want to sell insurance,
stocks, and bonds; trust companies and life insurance companies want to be
bankers and investment dealers. If this happens, distinctions among the so-

called four pillars of our financial market—banks, trust companies, investment dealers, and insurance companies—will diminish or vanish.

The following overview of major consumer lending institutions includes a brief discussion of some institutions that are probably already familiar to you, such as banks and trust companies, with a more detailed review of credit unions for the benefit of those who have never been members.

Banks

The chartered banks, many of which have large systems of branch offices, are in the business of borrowing from depositors to lend to those who need money. They charge sufficient interest on the money they lend to pay interest to their creditors, the depositors. The difference between the rate charged on loans and the rate paid on deposits is called the *spread*, and covers the cost of operation and profit for bank shareholders. Chartered banks are regulated by the federal *Bank Act* which is revised about once a decade. Until the 1967 revision, banks were restricted in their consumer loan activity by the *Act*. Afterwards banks became very active in consumer loans as can be seen in Figure 13.1.

Trust Companies

Trust companies, active in Canada since the latter part of the nineteenth century, provide financial and trustee services to individuals and corporations. A *trustee*, which may be a person or a trust company, manages financial affairs for others—either during their lifetime or after death. Sometimes people stipulate in their wills that a trust fund be set up on their death, naming a person or trust company as trustee to handle the funds. In Canada, trust companies are the only corporations that may act as trustees. At the present time banks and other financial institutions are not permitted to conduct *fiduciary* business, that is, to act as trustees, but this may change.

Trust companies have certain advantages over individuals acting in a trustee role because they can provide continuous service over a long period of time. In addition, the expertise of trust companies may be invaluable if the trust is a complex one and involves large sums of money. In exchange for their services, trust companies charge an annual fee, which is usually a percentage of the capital being managed. For individuals, trust companies handle both *living trusts*, which have been established by persons still alive, and *testamentary trusts*, which are created by a will, on a persons's death. A large part of the business of trust companies is acting as trustees for other corporations in handling pension funds, bond issues, and the like.

Because the charters of trust companies do not limit them to fiduciary business, they are active financial intermediaries, taking in deposits and making loans of various kinds. Generally, only the larger trust companies are in the consumer loan business, but mortgage lending is a different matter. In recent years the trust and mortgage loan companies have provided about one-third of all mortgage funds in Canada.

SMALL LOAN COMPANIES

Many small loan companies and money lenders are affiliated with other financial institutions, especially sales finance companies. It is not uncommon for a firm to operate both a small loan and a sales finance business from the same premises; because of this close affiliation their statistics are often combined. The principal distinction is that *small loan companies* and *money lenders* make cash loans, while sales finance companies buy credit contracts arranged by retailers (as will be explained in Chapter 14). The cost of credit at these small loan companies tends to be high because of such factors as their acceptance of higher risk borrowers, the cost of processing small loans, and the fact that they are not deposit-taking institutions but must borrow from other sources. Note that before 1975 they had a significant share of the consumer credit business which has since diminished (Figure 13.1).

LIFE INSURANCE POLICY LOANS

Loans may be made against life insurance policies that have a cash surrender value, such as whole life, but not against term or most group policies that have no cash value. It takes two or three years for cash surrender value to build up to make the policyholder eligible for a loan. The cash value of the policy grows each year that the policy is in force and the amounts are shown in the policy. Generally, policies permit about 90 percent to 100 percent of the cash value to be borrowed.

The interest rate on life insurance policy loans is usually lower than from other commercial sources. Before 1968 the maximum loan rate was 6 percent, but policies written since are not so restricted and now the usual practice is not to state a lending rate in the policy. There is no difficulty in obtaining the loan because the policyholder borrows from the cash value of his or her own policy. Also, there is no time limit for repaying the loan; interest due will automatically be added to the loan. A loan on a policy does not invalidate life insurance coverage. When the policyholder dies, the policy remains intact, but any outstanding debt is subtracted from the payment to the beneficiary. The terms of the loan are stated in the life insurance policy. Look at the sample life insurance policy at the end of chapter six to find out what the terms are for a policy loan.

As a share of all consumer credit outstanding in Canada, life insurance policy loans are not very significant and, in fact, are decreasing. In 1955, policy loans represented less than nine percent of all consumer credit, but by 1989 this share was down to three percent. Some possible reasons are that the demand for consumer credit has increased at a much faster rate than the purchase of life insurance, that more life insurance without cash value is being sold now than previously, or that loans are more readily available elsewhere. Life insurance companies do not especially promote policy loans.

CREDIT UNIONS

The financial cooperatives in the consumer lending and saving business are the *credit unions*, originally created to offer services to low-income families whose only alternative was a loan shark. By pooling the funds of savers, money could be lent at reasonable rates to those who needed to borrow, resulting in an arrangement advantageous to both savers and borrowers. Early credit unions were small, members knew one another, and personal needs received careful attention. When a debt to one's credit union was seen as a personal obligation to friends or associates, social pressure to repay loans was strong and losses minimized, but this has now changed considerably.

HISTORY

The credit union movement began in 1847 when mayor and lay preacher, Friedrich Raiffeisen, became concerned about the peasants of southern Germany, who were hopelessly in debt following a series of crop failures. The only sources of loans available to them were banks, which required gilt-edged security, or loan sharks who exacted punitive interest rates. He was instrumental in establishing credit societies, using the small savings of members to create funds to be borrowed by others. By the time of his death in 1888, there were 423 credit unions flourishing in Germany.

At the turn of the century a legislative reporter, Alphonse Desjardins of Lévis, Quebec, noted the high rates being charged by money lenders to the poor people of the region. Using some of Raiffeisen's ideas, Desjardins started La Caisse Populaire de Lévis with an initial membership of 80 people and assets of $26. This venture was so successful in meeting a widespread need that credit unions were organized in many Quebec parishes. As the credit union idea spread, first from Lévis to Boston, then to Nova Scotia, Saskatchewan, and across the continent, it was adapted to meet local requirements. Few credit unions were established in Ontario before 1945, when the move towards industrial credit unions began.

ORGANIZATION

COMMON BOND   To do business with a credit union one must be a member and, furthermore, it is a legal requirement that members share a *common bond*, which may be the same place of employment; membership in the same church, labour union, or fraternal organization; or residence in a community or on a military base. Potential members must meet the common bond requirement and buy a share in the credit union, which may cost as little as five dollars. Recently, as a result of mergers, larger credit unions with residential common bonds have replaced small credit unions with their very specific common bonds (such as place of employment or church membership).

MEMBER INVOLVEMENT   As part of a non-profit cooperative, members have a say in the credit union's operation through the elected Board of Directors, which determines general policy and either handles operating decisions or delegates them to a paid manager. The net earnings of credit unions are returned to members, both borrowers and depositors, in a variety of ways, such as dividends on the share accounts, higher interest rates on deposits, lower charges for loans, or additional services.

PROVINCIAL DIFFERENCES   The credit union movement is strongest in Quebec (over 60 percent of the population are members) and in Saskatchewan (more than half of the population are members). In most other provinces, credit union members represent less than a third of the population. In terms of credit union assets, the Quebec credit unions, or caisses populaires, exceed any other province with nearly one-half of all the Canadian assets. Saskatchewan and Quebec far outrank the other provinces in credit union assets per capita (Figure 13.2).

NETWORK   All credit unions are linked into regional, provincial and national networks. Starting at the top, there is the World Council of Credit Unions made up of national associations such as the Canadian Cooperative Credit Society. In Canada, the three-tiered structure is composed of provincial chapters or centrals, regional groupings, and local credit unions. This leaves credit unions with much local autonomy but with connections to the larger organization. Local credit unions, with their separate Boards of Directors, are more independent than the branches of large banks. Nevertheless, there is a move to coordinate services so that a member of one credit union can conduct business at another credit union.

The provincial centrals offer important assistance to credit unions, including: investing their surplus funds or lending them additional money; supplying legal assistance, lobbying power, and educational services; and providing central purchasing of supplies. Deposit insurance, which is very important to savers, is arranged through the provincial centrals.

SECURITY   Borrowers at credit unions may be asked to provide several forms of security. For example, they may be required to maintain the equivalent of

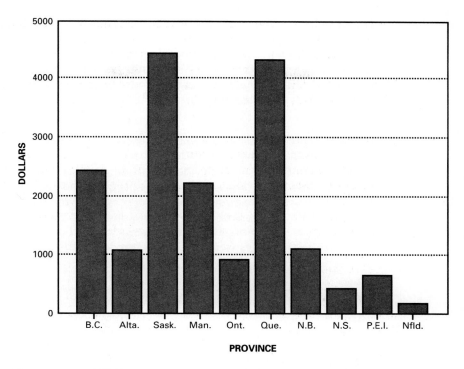

**Figure 13.2   CREDIT UNION ASSETS PER CAPITA BY PROVINCE,
CANADA, 1987**

Sources: *Canada Year Book 1990*, Ottawa: Statistics Canada, 1990. (Catalogue number 11-402), Table 18-15.
Canadian Economic Observer, Historical Statistical Supplement, 1987. Ottawa: Statistics Canada, 1988, (Catalogue number 11-210), Table 11.1. Reproduced and edited with the permission of the Minister of Supply and Services Canada, 1991.

ten percent of the outstanding balance on their loans in a deposit account, and in addition to sign a promissory note, a wage assignment and, if appropriate, a chattel mortgage. In some instances a co-signer may be required. These terms will be explained later in this chapter.

RECENT TRENDS

NUMBERS OF CREDIT UNIONS   Historically, most credit unions were operated by volunteers in premises that were often rent-free. These small, amateur operations were low cost and intimate, but in recent years they have been unable to compete with the larger-scale and more professional activities of banks and trust companies. As a consequence, many small credit unions merged to form fewer, larger unions, and hired staff to run them, making them into more efficient and impersonal institutions. The pattern of change in numbers of credit union locals is illustrated in Figure 13.3 that shows the gradual growth in the early years, rapid expansion between 1950 and 1960, and the effects of the mergers after 1970.

SERVICES   Credit unions vary considerably in size and in the range of services offered. All receive deposits and make loans, but some offer a variety of deposit accounts and savings vehicles, chequing services, mortgage loans, and automatic tellers. The larger credit unions have become quite competitive with banks and trust companies in interest rates and services offered.

   With the creation of larger credit unions, volunteer staff are being replaced with paid professional managers, loan officers, and independent auditors. These changes were necessary if credit unions were to become com-

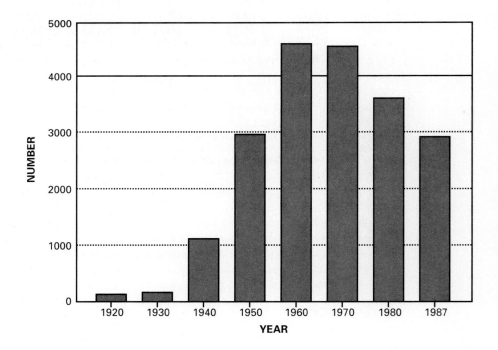

Figure 13.3   NUMBER OF CREDIT UNIONS IN CANADA, 1920-1987
Sources: *Canada Year Book* (1948-49, page 1051; 1961, Table 18, page 1130; 1962, Table 18, page 1108; 1972, Table 17, page 1245; 1990, Table 18.14), Catalogue number 11-402, Ottawa: Statistics Canada. Reproduced and edited with the permission of the Minister of Supply and Services Canada, 1991.

petitive with other financial institutions. Interestingly, credit unions were the leaders among financial institutions in offering weekly payment mortgages, daily interest savings accounts, and exploring the use of debit cards. To expedite the blurring of distinctions among financial institutions, British Columbia recently revised its *Financial Institutions Act* making credit unions subject to the same rules as other institutions and giving them the right to sell equity shares to members.

Obtaining a Loan

Loan Application

The procedure for obtaining a loan is about the same at any lender. The credit manager will request the completion of a *loan application form* (Figure 13.4), which requires considerable detail about the applicant's past financial activities. On the basis of this and other information that may be obtained in a credit report (as will be explained in Chapter 16), the loan officer will decide whether or not to grant the loan. If the decision is favourable, the next step is to settle the *terms of the loan*, i.e., the principal to be lent, the interest rate, the length of time to repay, and the security required. The date when the loan must be completely repaid is known as the *maturity date*, and the length of time the loan is to be outstanding is called the *term*. Notice the distinction between the "terms" of the loan and the "term" of the loan.

Types of Loans

The kinds of loans available to individuals at financial institutions differ in their terms and conditions. Interest rates are dependent on the risk level presented by the borrower and the services provided. Some arrangements provide funds on an on-going basis and others are contracts drawn up for a specific instalment loan. Examples of the on-going types of loans are: (i) line of credit, (ii) overdraft protection, and (iii) cash advances on a bank credit card. All of these give the borrower advance permission to borrow within set limits if the need arises. The advantage of these arrangements is that the funds are available if needed, but there are no interest charges if not used. At other times, a sum may be borrowed for a specific purpose with a set repayment schedule, such as: (i) a demand loan or (ii) an instalment loan.

Personal Line of Credit   Banks, trust companies, and credit unions may offer their creditworthy customers a personal line of credit as a convenient substitute for personal loans. A *personal line of credit* is a flexible way to use credit because the financial institution makes funds, up to a set limit, available to a customer

Loan Officer's I.D. No.   Application No.

What are your loan requirements? (Please Print in Ink)

How much do you wish to borrow? $ 13 000.00   For what purpose do you require this loan? PURCHASE OF FORD TEMPO

Do you wish to apply for insurance on this loan? ☐ Yes ☒ No

What monthly payment can you make? $ 320.00

Are you a present borrower or former borrower? ☒   ☐ Branch EDMONTON MAIN   Loan Number _____   Balance $ 80 000

☐ Do you wish to add to this Loan? OR ☒ Do you wish a separate Loan?

Is this a joint application? ☒ Yes ☐ No

If "yes", who is the co-applicant? ☒ My spouse ☐ Other   Name ALISON PORTER

NOTE: if your co-applicant is not your spouse, he/she must complete a separate application

Please tell us about yourself.

☒ Mr.   ☐ Miss   First Name TIMOTHY   R.   Last Name PORTER
☐ Mrs   ☐ Ms.   & Initial

Date of Birth   Day 02 Month 02 Year 54   Social Insurance No. 1 2 3 4 5 6 7 8 9

☐ Single   ☒ Married   ☐ Separated   ☐ Divorced   ☐ Widow(er)   ☐ Unknown

Spouse's First Name & Initial ALISON M.   Spouse's Last Name PORTER   Date of Birth   Day 09 Month 08 Year 57

Street Address 26 BAYVIEW CRESC   City EDMONTON

Province ALBERTA   Postal Code T 6 J 5 G 1   Residence Telephone (4 0 3) 2 1 3 4 5 4 5   How long? 3½ Years

Do you   ☒ Own   ☐ Room and Board   ☐ Live with Parents or Relatives   No. of Dependents (Excluding Spouse) 1
    ☐ Rent   ☐ Other (Please Specify) _____

Previous address (if less than 3 years at present address) _____   How long? ___ Years

Name and Address of Relatives or Close Friends
1) WILLIAM PORTER, 35 HOPEWELL CRESC. EDMONTON
2) JIM FRIEND 24 BAYVIEW CRESC. EDMONTON

Tell us about your household income.

Name of Employer EDMONTON PAPER PRODUCTS   What is your occupation? SALESMAN

Employer's Address 200 INDUSTRIAL RD. EDMONTON   Business Telephone (4 0 3) 2 1 3 6 9 0 1 1   Gross Monthly income $ 2923

How long? 5 Years   Where did you work before? (if less than 3 years with present employer) _____   How long? ___ Years

Are you? ☒ Full-Time   ☐ Part-Time   ☐ Self-Employed   ☐ Unemployed   ☐ Retired   ☐ Other   ☐ Seasonal

Spouse's Employer Dr. DAVID COOK   Occupation DENTAL HYGIENIST   How long? 7 Years

Address 14 BELLVIEW Dr. EDMONTON   Telephone (4 0 3) 2 1 3 1 4 2 1   Gross Monthly income $ 2281

Other Income Source(s) and Amount(s) ANNUAL BONUS - APPROX. $1000

Some information on your assets.

						Estimated Value
Your Residence	Do you ☐ Own your home ☒ Have joint ownership	Year Purchased 19 87	Purchase Price $ 110 000			$ 149 000
Your Vehicles	1985 Year	HONDA Make	ACCORD Model			$ 5000
	Year	Make	Model			$ _____
Other Assets (RRSP'S, Bonds, Real Estate, etc.)	RRSP BANK OF MONTREAL EDMONTON					$ 7500
	CANADA SAVINGS BONDS					$ 1500

Where do you bank? BANK of MONTREAL   Branch Address ANY STREET, EDMONTON

		Balance
Savings Account No. 0041 - 5000 - 000		$ 1000
Chequing Account No. 0041 - 8000 - 000		$ 500

TOTAL ASSETS $ 164 500

PLEASE COMPLETE REVERSE

Figure 13.4   PERSONAL LOAN APPLICATION FORM
Source: Reproduced with the permission of Bank of Montreal.

Tell us about your financial dealings.

USE A SEPARATE PAGE FOR DETAILS IF SPACE IS INSUFFICIENT IN ANY AREA

	NAME	ADDRESS	Maturity Date	AMOUNT OWING	MONTHLY PAYMENT (including taxes)
1st Mortgage Holder	BANK OF MONTREAL	EDMONTON	Jan 1991	$ 80 000	$ 910.43
2nd Mortgage Holder			Maturity Date	$	$
Landlord					Monthly Rent $

LOANS	WITH WHOM?	ADDRESS	AMOUNT OWING	MONTHLY PAYMENT
Auto			$	$
Other			$	$
Other			$	$
Other			$	$

CREDIT CARDS	CARD NUMBER	WITH WHOM?	CREDIT LIMIT	AMOUNT OWING	MONTHLY PAYMENT
MasterCard	5191 0000 0000 000	BANK of MONTREAL	$ 2000	$ 1500	$ 75
VISA			$	$	$
American Express			$	$	$
Other	804 132 160	THE BAY	$ 1200	$ 1100	$ 55
		TOTALS		$ 2600	$ 130

When and where may we conveniently contact you during business hours?

Best Day ___MONDAY___   Best Time ___11:00___   ☑ A.M. ☐ P.M.   ☑ At Home   ☐ At Work

Please read and sign below with your full signature. You can drop off your application at your Bank of Montreal branch during normal hours, mail it or drop it in your Bank of Montreal branch Night Depository.

If a Co-Applicant signs below, the words "I" and "me" refer to each of the Applicant and Co-Applicant. I authorize the Bank to obtain personal and credit information about me from any source.

This information, as well as that provided by me on this application, will be referred to in connection with this loan/credit and other banking relationships we may establish from time to time. **I also authorize the Bank to disclose from time to time to other lenders, credit bureaux or other credit reporting agencies personal and credit information about me.** I certify that the information in this application is true and correct.

If this application is for a MasterCard card, please indicate your preferred choice of card:

APPLICANTS INITIALS   SPOUSES INITIALS (IF CARD REQUESTED)

☐ Regular MasterCard card for which there is no annual fee.

☐ Gold MasterCard card. Annual fee applies. Current fee available on request. Annual fee as of January, 1990 is $40.00. If this application for a gold MasterCard card is not approved, please treat this application as a request for your regular MasterCard card and applicable plan service for which there is no annual fee.

I request a Bank of Montreal MasterCard card and renewals or replacements thereof from time to time at the Bank's discretion. I also request a Personal Identification Number (PIN) in order to allow use of the card in Bank of Montreal Instabank units, and, if available, other automated banking machine systems. If a MasterCard card is issued, I agree to abide by the terms and conditions of the applicable Bank of Montreal MasterCard Cardholder Agreement accompanying the Master Card. If there is an annual fee, I agree that the fee is for the card and for other available plan services and will be billed directly to the card account. If an additional card is requested in Co-Applicant's name, each of the undersigned agrees to be jointly and severally liable for indebtedness and obligations incurred through use of the cards issued pursuant to such request and authorizes through use of such cards, deposits to and withdrawals from bank accounts designated by either of the undersigned.

I authorize the Bank to credit the proceeds of the loan to the account designated below and to debit the account designated below

Transit	Account No.		Transit	Account No.
Deposit Proceeds to 0 0 4 1	8 0 0 0 0 0 0	Debit Payments to ☑ Same Account No. OR		

APPLICABLE IN PROVINCE OF QUEBEC ONLY. It is the express wish of the Parties that this agreement and any related documents be drawn up and executed in English. Les parties conviennent que la présente convention et tous les documents s'y rattachant soient redigés et signés en anglais.

___May 16, 1990___   _Timothy R. Porter_   _Alison Porter_

Date   Signature of Applicant   Signature of Co-Applicant (if joint application)

Figure 13.4   (continued)

whenever they are needed. There is no interest charge until some or all of the funds are used.

Once the application has been approved, a customer is granted a line of credit up to a specified maximum amount. There is usually a minimum monthly payment required in addition to interest on the outstanding monthly balance. A line of credit could be as low as $2500 or $5000, with payments of at least three to five percent of the outstanding balance. The interest rate on a line of credit is related to the prime rate and is adjusted monthly. For those eligible, a line of credit may be a cheaper alternative to a personal loan.

OVERDRAFT PROTECTION   The difference between a personal line of credit and overdraft protection may be blurred by some financial institutions. *Overdraft protection*, available at banks, trust companies, and credit unions allows deposit accounts to become overdrawn to a set limit, for instance, $1000. The overdraft becomes a loan and is subject to interest rates about the same as those charged on credit card loans. The rates on a personal line of credit may be six to seven percent lower than on overdraft protection so, clearly, it is worthwhile to check this.

CREDIT CARD CASH ADVANCES   Anyone with a credit card issued by a financial institution (bank, credit union, trust company) has the option of obtaining a loan, called a *cash advance*, without making a special application each time funds are needed. The maximum amount of the loan was established previously. Interest, calculated daily, begins at once at rates usually higher than a line of credit or a personal loan.

DEMAND LOAN   Rather than flexible credit, customers with a good credit rating may arrange for a *demand loan* by signing an agreement to repay the loan in full at a certain date, with interest due monthly. The lender has the right to recall a demand loan at any time, hence the name. Holders of demand loans often renegotiate them at maturity. Interest charges will be set slightly above the prime rate and will fluctuate according to the prevailing rate. The *prime rate* is the lowest interest rate that financial institutions charge their best corporate customers and is the guide for setting other interest rates.

INSTALMENT LOANS   Instalment loans usually have a set interest rate, a maturity date, and certain security requirements, as will be explained shortly. The contract signed varies with the kind of security pledged.

W hen Sarah and Matt applied at the bank for a personal instalment loan of $10 000 to buy a sailboat they had outstanding balances on several credit and charge cards but their credit rating had been well established. After the loans officer heard about their debts of $1100 to Mastercard, $500 to American Express, and $950 to Sears she strongly recommended that they consolidate these debts into one loan with the bank, and have only one payment to make. The bank would be happy to lend them the $10 000 they asked for and, in addition, enough to pay off all their debts.

Sarah and Matt were not keen to consolidate their credit card debt with the bank loan, but they got the impression that their loan application would be looked at more favourably if they did.

What factors should they consider before deciding to consolidate their debts?

SECURITY FOR LOANS

Lenders must consider the risk of not being repaid, and wisely take steps to minimize the consequences. They can choose to accept as borrowers only those who appear to be good risks, or can lend to a wider range of people but ask them for certain assurances. It is common practice to require a borrower to sign documents that give the lender permission *in advance* to take over specified possessions or assets of the borrower, should the latter fail to make the payments as agreed. These various claims on the borrower, which are arranged at the time the loan is taken out, are referred to as the *security for the loan*.

SECURITY AND COLLATERAL   It is sometimes difficult to make a clear distinction between security and collateral. It may help to consider security as a claim or right that the borrower has voluntarily assigned to the lender in order to reduce the lender's risk. The term collateral is applied to certain tangible assets used as security, such as financial assets or durable goods. Therefore, the signature of a guarantor or co-signer is a form of security for the lender, but is not a tangible object and therefore not collateral. Promises may have some security value but are not collateral.

Fully and Partially Secured Loans

Loans may be fully or partially secured. If the borrower signs over to the lender assets equal in value to the total loan, that loan is said to be *fully secured*. Naturally, very few consumer loans are fully secured, because those with enough assets would buy the goods for cash. There are occasions, however, when requesting a fully secured loan is a reasonable decision. For instance, if funds are needed for a few months only, it may be preferable to use assets as security rather than sell the assets to pay in cash. If these assets were invested at a higher yield than available in the current market, it might be better to retain the assets and take a loan for a short time. By using bonds or similar assets as security for the loan, the borrower can expect to be charged a very favourable interest rate because the lender is taking no risk at all.

More often, loans are *partially secured* because buyers do not have sufficient assets to obtain fully secured loans. A car buyer may use the car as security for the loan, but this debt will not be fully secured because cars and other durables may depreciate faster than loans are repaid.

Signature Loans

A borrower considered to present little risk to the lender may be asked for nothing more than a signature on a *promissory note*, which is an unconditional promise to repay the loan. Such a loan, also called a *signature loan*, is considered to be unsecured by the lender. In other words, if the borrower does not repay the loan as promised, the lender has nothing of value belonging to the borrower that can be liquidated to pay the debt. The legal contract used for signature loans is the promissory note, which is simply a promise to repay the loan. A sample promissory note used for a personal loan is shown in Figure 13.5.

Many people are not eligible for signature loans and those who are may choose a personal line of credit because of its greater flexibility. Long-time customers of financial institutions, whose character and credit record are judged to be exemplary, are permitted signature loans with no other security, but most borrowers are required to provide something tangible in the way of security, in addition to their promise. Thus, promissory notes are often incorporated into more complex credit contracts of the sort to be discussed below. Four frequently used forms of security for loans are: (i) co-signers, (ii) future wages, (iii) financial assets, and (iv) durable goods.

Co-signer

The lender may require that the borrower find another person to sign the loan agreement. By signing, the *co-signer* or guarantor agrees to repay any outstanding balance on the loan if the borrower fails to do so. Sometimes, people agree to co-sign loans as a gesture of friendship, without fully realizing the commitment they have made. The extent of their responsibility becomes

Bank of Montreal   **Personal Loan Plan - Promissory Note**

Branch Domicile Stamp

PLEASE PRINT

Full Name of Borrower(s)		
TIMOTHY R. PORTER & ALISON PORTER		
PLP Account No.	Date	
2 0 0 0 - 0 0 0	MARCH 10 19 87	

In this promissory note the words "I" and "me" mean the borrower, or if more than one, all borrowers jointly and severally.
In return for lending me money I promise to pay to the order of Bank of Montreal at the branch named above the principal sum of

$ _____ 800 oo/xt _____ . I promise to pay interest on that sum at the rate of __ 14.5 __ % per year calculated on the dates payments are due as set out below.

I will pay the principal sum and interest by paying $ __ 38.45 __ on __ APRIL 10 __ , 19 __ 87 __ and then by paying

$ __ 38.45 __ every __ MONTH __ starting on __ MAY 10 __ , 19 __ 87 __ through and including
                                       (specify frequency)

__ MARCH 10 __ , 19 __ 89 __ when I will pay any balance owing.
  (specify date of maturity**)

If I fail to pay any amount when it is due I will pay interest at the rate shown above on the amount until it is paid. This interest will be calculated and

payable on the dates payments are due until the maturity date and every __ MONTHLY __ after that date.
                                                         (specify frequency)

If I fail to make any payment when it is due, Bank of Montreal may require me to pay immediately the entire balance of what I owe.

_____
Signature of Borrower

_____
Signature of Borrower

Figure 13.5   PERSONAL LOAN PROMISSORY NOTE
Source: Reproduced with the permission of Bank of Montreal.

GUARANTEE OF PROMISSORY NOTE

In this Guarantee the words "I", "me" and "my" mean the Guarantor or if more than one, all Guarantors jointly and severally. The words "the Note" mean the promissory note on the reverse side of this Guarantee. The words "the Borrower" mean each borrower named in the note.

In return for Bank of Montreal lending money to the Borrower I guarantee payment on demand of the total amount secured by the Note, and all costs, expenses and legal fees incurred in the collection and enforcement of the Note.

I agree that:

(a) my obligations under this Guarantee are unconditional.

(b) Bank of Montreal may extend the time for payment of the Note, take, release and not register any interest in collateral securing the Note and deal with the Borrower as it wants without notice to me or my consent.

(c) Bank of Montreal does not have to use any of its remedies against the Borrower or other Parties or in respect of collateral securing the Note before being entitled to payment from me.

(d) I waive presentment for payment, notice of dishonour, protest and demand of the Note.

(e) demand for payment under this Guarantee may be made by letter sent by ordinary mail to me at my last known address contained in the records of Bank of Montreal.

(f) my obligations under this Guarantee are continuing and extend to any renewals or substitutions of the Note.

(g) Bank of Montreal has made no representations concerning my liability under this Guarantee.

This clause applies to the Province of Quebec only

It is the express wish of the Parties that this agreement and any related documents be drawn up and executed in English. Les parties conviennent que la présente convention et tous les documents s'y rattachant soient rédigés et signés en anglais.

SIGNED AND SEALED AT ___ANY BRANCH___ on ___march 10___ , 19 87

In the presence of:

Stephen Williamson   _Andrew Steel_ (Seal)

Signature of Witness   Signature of Guarantor

STEPHEN WILLIAMSON   ANDREW STEEL

Witness's Name   Guarantor's Name & Address

_____   _____ (Seal)

Signature of Witness   Signature of Guarantor

Witness's Name   Guarantor's Name & Address

Figure 13.5   (continued)
Source: Reproduced with the permission of Bank of Montreal.

evident when the lender requires them to make restitution for the friend or relative who has disappeared without repaying the loan. Such people are referred to in the credit business as *skips*.

FUTURE WAGES

Sometimes borrowers sign an agreement that if they do not maintain the repayment schedule, the lender has permission to collect a portion of their wages directly from their employers. This contract is called a *wage assignment*. To protect borrowers from abuses of this system which have occurred in the past, the use of wage assignments has been curtailed. For instance, credit unions are the only creditors in Ontario that are permitted to use wage assignments. Note in Figure 13.6 the borrower voluntarily agrees that, if the debt is not repaid, the credit union may collect 20 percent of her wages directly from her employer. Whether the 20 percent is based on gross or net wages varies according to jurisdiction.

In practice, the credit union would not enforce a wage assignment until less drastic measures had failed. The debtor would, of course, be informed that this was about to happen, giving her time to repay the debt or to petition for a reduction in the amount of wages to be taken. The decision to enforce the wage assignment is made by the loan officer or the Board of Directors, who may grant an exemption or reduction if the borrower's situation seems to warrant it.

FINANCIAL ASSETS

To secure a loan, a lender may require a borrower to lodge in the lender's possession some form of *collateral*, such as bonds, stock certificates, life insurance policies, or deposits. These types of collateral are financial assets that can be readily converted to cash, which is what the lender will do if the borrower fails to maintain the terms of the loan agreement. With each form of collateral offered, the borrower will be asked to sign an appropriate agreement giving the lender the power to realize these assets in case of default on the loan. Different contracts are used, depending on the nature of the asset pledged.

Credit unions sometimes use deposits as one form of security, requiring the borrower to keep on deposit a sum of money equal to a specified percentage of the loan, e.g., ten percent. This deposit is frozen for the duration of the loan and unavailable to the owner.

A borrower who has a life insurance policy with sufficient cash surrender value may assign it to a lender as security for a loan. This process is discussed in more detail in the chapter on life insurance. Essentially it means that the policy is held by the lender until the debt is cleared, but the policyholder must continue to pay the premiums. If the borrower defaults on the loan, the lender can cash in the policy.

ASSIGNMENT OF WAGES

TO: .... G̲U̲E̲L̲P̲H̲ ̲&̲ ̲W̲E̲L̲L̲I̲N̲G̲T̲O̲N̲ .... CREDIT UNION LIMITED
(hereinafter called the "Credit Union")

I. .... S̲A̲R̲A̲H̲ ̲W̲A̲K̲E̲F̲I̲E̲L̲D̲ ....
(Name of Assignor)

for Valuable Consideration hereby assign, transfer and set over unto the Credit Union, 20 per cent of all the wages, salary, commission and other monies owing to me, or hereafter to become owing to me in the employ of: W̲E̲L̲L̲I̲N̲G̲T̲O̲N̲. .... C̲O̲U̲N̲T̲Y̲ ̲B̲O̲A̲R̲D̲ ̲O̲F̲ ̲E̲D̲U̲C̲A̲T̲I̲O̲N̲ .... or any other person, firm, corporation or entity by whom I may be hereafter employed.

AND I HEREBY AUTHORIZE AND DIRECT my said employer or any future employer to pay the said 20 per cent of all wages, salary, commissions and other monies to the Credit Union, and I hereby irrevocably authorize the Credit Union to take all proceedings which may be proper and necessary for the recovery of any amount or amounts above assigned and to give receipts for same, or any part thereof, in my name, and I hereby release and discharge my said employers and each of them from all liability to me for or on account of any or all monies paid in accordance with the terms hereof. Nothing herein shall prevent the Credit Union from exercising any other right of recovery available in law or any amount lawfully owing to the Credit Union in excess of the amounts assigned above.

Signed, Sealed and Delivered this .... 3̲1̲ˢᵗ .... day of .... M̲A̲Y̲ .... 19 9̲0̲..

at .... G̲U̲E̲L̲P̲H̲ .... Ontario in the presence of:

WITNESS:

Jennifer M. Bucholz
(Signature of Assignor)

(FORM O.L.-D 1923/12-88)

Figure 13.6   ASSIGNMENT OF WAGES
Reproduced with the permission of Credit Union Central of Ontario Limited.

Durable Goods

When consumer durables such as vehicles, appliances, and furniture are bought with credit, these articles are usually offered as security. If the consumer obtains a loan from a bank, credit union, small loan, or trust company, a *chattel mortgage* will be signed that transfers the ownership of the goods to the lender (Figure 13.7). Note that the term *chattel* applies to moveable goods, but not to land or buildings (called real property), which are used as security in home mortgages. The borrower has possession of the goods and full use of them, but agrees to maintain them in good condition and, in most cases, to insure them.

During the term of the chattel mortgage, which is the time until the debt is repaid, the borrower does not have the right to sell the pledged goods without the permission of the lender. If the borrower defaults on the loan, the lender has prior permission to repossess the goods and sell them. In some provinces, Ontario for instance, the creditor may have the right to repossess and also to sue for any balance outstanding if the proceeds from the sale are insufficient to extinguish the debt. However, there has been a trend toward "seize or sue" laws (as in British Columbia, Alberta, and Newfoundland) that give the creditor the option of repossessing the goods or suing the debtor, but not both.

It is important to take careful note that chattel mortgages are the contracts used by lenders when taking the title to goods as security. Vendors of goods, who already have title to the goods they are selling, are in a position to retain the title until the total cost is paid; for these transactions a different contract, called a conditional sales contract, is used. In the case of default, the vendor enforces his security by repossession. Credit sales are discussed in the next chapter.

Lien

In popular usage, the term lien is often encountered as a synonym for a chattel mortgage, but there is a distinction in law. A *lien* is a claim registered against certain property, generally in the case where the goods or service provided cannot be seized. For example, if a contractor paved a driveway, but payment is overdue, the creditor may register a lien against the house. This would represent a claim against the property that must be settled before the owner can obtain a clear title. Another instance could occur when a service station has not been paid for repairing a car. An automobile lien could be registered, which gives the garage the right to retain the car until the debt is satisfied, or if the default continues, to sell the car.

 **Bank of Montreal**　　　　　　　　　　　　　　**Chattel Mortgage - Personal Loans**

(For use in all provinces except Quebec, British Columbia and Yukon)

A

THIS INDENTURE made (in duplicate)

BETWEEN

TIMOTHY RAY PORTER
(First Name - Middle Name - Last Name - No Abbreviations)

_02 - 02 - 54_
Date of Birth - DD - MM - YY

Show full name and address

of _26 BAYVIEW CRESC._ in the _____ CITY _____ of _____ EDMONTON_
(Street Address)　　　　　　　　　(City, etc.)　　　　　　　　(Name of City)

in the Province of _____ ·ALBERTA _____ , _T6J 5G1_
Postal Code

(hereinafter called the "Mortgagor")

— and —

BANK OF MONTREAL

of _____ ANY STREET _____ in the _____ CITY _____ of _____ EDMONTON_
(Street Address)　　　　　　　　(City, etc.)　　　　　　　(Name of City)

in the Province of _____ ALBERTA_

(hereinafter called the "Mortgagee").

Insert net amount of note

WITNESSETH that in consideration of the sum of _THIRTEEN THOUSAND_
_____ Dollars (\$ _13 000 ⁰⁰_),
lent and paid to the Mortgagor by the Mortgagee, (the receipt of which the Mortgagor hereby acknowledges)

Insert gross amount of note

and to secure payment of _NINETEEN THOUSAND ONE HUNDRED_
AND SEVENTY-SIX _____ Dollars (\$ _19 176 ⁰⁰_) (hereinafter called the

Insert amount of interest

"said amount owing") being the said sum so lent and paid together with _SIX THOUSAND ONE_
HUNDRED AND SEVENTY-SIX Dollars (\$ _6 176 ⁰⁰_), being the cost of the said

sum so lent and paid, the Mortgagor by these presents grants, bargains, sells and assigns to the Mortgagee the following chattels and all proceeds thereof and accessions thereto, namely :

1990 FORD TEMPO
SERIAL # 1FBAP 306 J 20010714
LICENCE # TRJ 111

Insert detailed description of chattels

(hereinafter sometimes called the "property") all of which are now owned by the Mortgagor and are located at
26 BAYVIEW CRESC. EDMONTON　　　　　_ALBERTA_
(Address)　　　　　　(City or Town)　　　　　(County or District)　　　　(Province)

TO HAVE AND TO HOLD the same unto the Mortgagee forever :

Insert gross amount of note

PROVIDED that if the Mortgagor shall pay to the Mortgagee the said amount owing of _NINETEEN_
THOUSAND ONE HUNDRED SEVENTY-SIX Dollars (\$ _19 176 ⁰⁰_) and interest according to the terms of and as evidenced by a promissory note of even date herewith and any and all renewals thereof, and upon the due and timely performance by the Mortgagor of all the terms and covenants on the Mortgagor's part to be performed hereunder, then this mortgage shall be void.

The Mortgagor covenants with the Mortgagee as follows :

1. THAT the Mortgagor will pay to the Mortgagee the said sum of money and interest thereon as in the above proviso mentioned.

2. THAT the Mortgagor is the sole owner of the property and there are no liens, mortgages, charges or other encumbrances thereon.

Figure 13.7　CHATTEL MORTGAGE

Source: Reproduced with the permission of Bank of Montreal.

3. THAT if the property is at the time of the making of the loan, or thereafter becomes, subject to any charge in favour of any person other than the Mortgagee, the Mortgagee may pay such charge and the amount so paid shall, together with interest thereon at the rate specified in the said promissory note, become a charge on the property in favour of the Mortgagee and be added to the sum secured hereby and the sum secured hereby, including the amount so added, shall, at the option of the Mortgagee, forthwith become due and payable.

4. THAT the Mortgagor will insure and keep insured the property for its full insurable value against loss or damage by fire or theft and if the property includes a motor vehicle, collision, and hereby assigns to the Mortgagee all such policies of insurance and all amounts payable thereunder. If the Mortgagor fails to effect or maintain such insurance, the Mortgagee may effect and maintain the same and all moneys expended by it for such purpose, together with interest thereon at the rate specified in the said promissory note, from the time the same has been expended, shall become a charge on the property and be added to the sum secured hereby.

5. THAT the Mortgagor will not sell or dispose of or part with the possession of the property or any part thereof and will not permanently remove it from the premises where it now is without first obtaining the written consent of the Mortgagee.

6. THAT if the Mortgagor fails to pay any of the moneys mentioned in the proviso in accordance with the terms there set out, or fails to observe or perform any of the covenants contained herein, or institutes or does anything which permits to be instituted any proceedings leading to the Mortgagor becoming a bankrupt, or if the Mortgagor dies, then all the moneys secured hereby shall, at the option of the Mortgagee, forthwith become due and payable and the Mortgagee, its servants or agents, may, with or without legal process, take possession of the property (and may for that purpose enter upon the premises where the property is located) and sell the same at public auction or private sale or otherwise realize on the property by any method not prohibited by law, including by lease or by sale for deferred payment, with or without notice to the Mortgagor, and after payment out of the net proceeds of such sale of all amounts due to the Mortgagee hereunder the Mortgagee shall pay over to the Mortgagor or such other person who may be entitled thereto any surplus but if such proceeds are not sufficient to pay all amounts due to the Mortgagee hereunder the Mortgagor will pay the deficiency to the Mortgagee.

7. That the Mortgagor will pay on demand to the Mortgagee all costs (including legal costs as between a solicitor and his own client) incurred by the Mortgagee in realizing on the property and enforcing the covenants in this Mortgage and the promissory note, all of which sums shall be secured hereunder and bear interest at the rate specified in the note.

8. THAT the Mortgagee may, in order to recover any amount owing to it, hereunder, pursue either singly or concurrently the remedy of action and the remedy of taking possession and selling given to it hereby and shall not be precluded by the exercise of either remedy from proceeding to exercise the other remedy. The Mortgagee shall not be responsible for any loss or damage to the property, whether caused by the negligence or fault of the Mortgagee, its servants or agents, or a sheriff or receiver, and the Mortgagee shall not be obliged to preserve rights against other persons or prepare the property for disposition, and shall only be liable to account for funds (net of costs of collection, realization and sale, including solicitor and his own client legal costs), actually received by the Mortgagee.

Applicable in
Alberta only

9. The Mortgagor waives receipt of any financing statement registered by the Bank and any confirmation of registration.

10. The Mortgagor acknowledges receipt of a copy of this Chattel Mortgage.

ALL grants, warrants, covenants, agreements, rights, powers, privileges and liabilities contained in this indenture shall enure to the benefit of and be binding upon the heirs, executors, administrators, successors and assigns of the parties hereto respectively ; all covenants and agreements on the part of the Mortgagor shall be construed as both joint and several and when the context so requires the singular number shall be read as if the plural were expressed.

This mortgage was executed on the _16th_ day of _May_ 19_90_

IN WITNESS whereof the Mortgagor has hereunto set his hand and seal.

SIGNED, SEALED AND DELIVERED

In the presence of

SEAL

Figure 13.7   (continued)

 **Bank of Montreal**   **Statement of Disclosure**

<u>Any Branch, Edmonton, Alberta</u>   <u>May   16</u>   19 <u>90</u>
Branch/Domicile Stamp   Date Disclosure Made

<u>TIMOTHY PORTER   &   ALISON PORTER</u>
Name of Borrower(s)

(1) Your loan takes effect on   <u>MAY 16</u>   , 19 <u>90</u>

(2) The principal sum of your loan is secured by <u>1990 FORD   TEMPO</u>   and is made up of :

    (a) the amount of money paid to you or as you direct .... $ <u>13 000 $\frac{00}{\times}$</u>

    (b) the amount of money used to repay previous loan(s) .... $ _____

    (c) the cost of Life Insurance (if applicable) .... $ _____

    (d) the cost of Disability Insurance (if applicable) .... $ _____

    for a total principal sum of (a) + (b) + (c) + (d) .... $ <u>13 000 $\frac{00}{\times}$</u>

(3) You will pay interest on the principal sum at the rate of <u>$16\frac{1}{2}$</u> % per year*

(4) Your Cost of Borrowing* for the whole term of the loan is .... $ <u>6 176 $\frac{00}{\times}$</u>

(5) Your Total Obligation* is ((2) + (4)) .... $ <u>19 176 $\frac{00}{\times}$</u>

(6) The term of your loan is <u>60</u> months. Your payments are amortized over <u>60</u> months.

(7) Your Total Obligation is repayable in one payment of $ <u>319.60</u>   on   <u>JUNE 16</u>   , 19 <u>90</u> , and then in equal

    payments of $ <u>319.60</u>   every   <u>MONTH</u>   starting on   <u>JULY 16</u>   , 19 <u>90</u> through and including
                       (specify frequency)

    <u>MAY 16</u>   , 19 <u>95</u> on which date a Final Payment* of approximately $ <u>NIL</u>   is due.
       (specify date of maturity**)

(8) If you fail to pay any amount when it is due, you will pay interest at the rate shown above on the amount until it is all paid. This interest will be calculated and

    payable on the dates payments are due until the maturity date and every   <u>MONTH</u>   after that date.
                                      (specify frequency)

(9) If you fail to make any payment when it is due, the Bank may require you to pay immediately the entire balance of what you owe.
(10) You will pay all reasonable expenses including legal expenses which the Bank incurs in protecting or collecting your loan.
(11) You may prepay your loan or any part of your loan before the date for final payment without penalty. Interest on any amount of the loan prepaid before the final payment date is only payable up to the date of prepayment.
(12) If the term of this loan, original or as extended, is not equal to the amortization period and if there have been no default of payments on their due dates nor any default under any security given to secure this loan, you shall have the right to extend this loan for the balance owing on the Maturity Date to a new Maturity Date and at the interest rate required by the Bank at the time of such extension. Varying terms of extension at varying interest rates may be available. If you do not exercise this right of extension on or before the Maturity Date or any subsequent new Maturity Date by advising the Bank of your intention to extend, the Bank may extend or further extend the loan to a new Maturity Date and at an interest rate as required by the Bank and advise you accordingly. If the Bank does not receive from you before the 15th day after such advice has been mailed to your last known address (as shown by the Bank's records) your written advice that you do not accept such extension you shall be deemed to have accepted the same.

   *   Interest on the principal sum of your outstanding loan is determined on a daily basis and is calculated and payable on the dates payments are due. You make the same equal payment for each payment period but the number of days in each payment period may vary, for example there are 28 days in February and 31 days in March. As a result, your Cost of Borrowing, your Total Obligation and your Final Payment are estimated amounts which reflect interest calculated on the basis of monthly intervals of an equal number of days. The interest rate per year remains the same whether a daily or monthly interval is used.
** The maturity date may not coincide with the exact date on which the last payment would be scheduled depending on the payment frequency specified on the agreement.

                                                                  Timothy R Porter
                                                     Signature of Borrower

                                                                  Alison Porter

John Smith
Signature of Bank Officer   Signature of Borrower

Figure 13.7   (continued)

Cost of Borrowing

Insurance

On signing a credit contract, the borrower assumes not only the responsibility of repaying the debt, but also the risk that something will happen to make it impossible or difficult to carry out this intent. Unexpected illness, unemployment, disability, or death may disrupt a payment schedule. It is possible to obtain insurance to give protection against two of these risks—death or disability.

Credit Life Insurance

Lenders often require that their consumer loans be life-insured. They do this by having a group life insurance policy that covers the lives of their borrowers against the risk of someone dying before their debts have been repaid. This insurance on the life of the borrower is often called *credit life insurance*. When an insured borrower dies, the insurance company will pay the lender the outstanding balance due on the debt. The borrower's estate does not receive anything, but the survivors may be relieved that the debt has been paid.

Some lenders automatically include credit life insurance without an additional charge; others offer it as an option with a specific cost. Either way, the borrower ultimately pays for this service. If it is optional, a borrower might give some thought to the need for it. When a borrower with an outstanding debt dies without credit life insurance, the balance of the debt is a charge on the estate, which must be paid before any funds are distributed to the heirs. If the estate is adequate there may be no difficulty; however, if the family has many needs and few assets, a large debt could create hardship for the survivors.

Credit Disability Insurance

Not all lenders offer disability insurance, but credit unions often do. For an additional fee, *disability insurance* covers the borrower for the risk of being unable to make payments because of a personal disability. It is important to find out what the conditions of such insurance are as well as what it will cost. How does the insurance company define disabled? How long must one be disabled before the insurance will take effect? If the borrower meets the criteria for disability, the insurance company will assume responsibility for the debt payments as long as the disability lasts.

Interest Charges

The cost of borrowing depends on the lender's cost of money, the assessment of the risk of the loan not being repaid, and the services offered. Deposit-taking institutions, with a ready supply of funds to lend, can charge lower rates than small loan companies which have to borrow funds to lend. To cover their costs, banks, trust companies, and credit unions allow a one to three percent spread between the rate paid to depositors and the rate they charge borrowers.

On receipt of a loan application, a creditor assesses the degree of risk involved. Some lenders, notably small loan companies who will lend to higher risk borrowers, charge higher rates to cover losses on bad debts. Other lenders establish the level of risk they will accept and refuse loans to those who do not qualify.

INTEREST RATES   At the present time there is little variation in rates between financial institutions for the same type of loan but there are significant differences by the type of loan. This disparity is illustrated in Figure 13.8.

ENFORCEMENT OF SECURITY

IN ARREARS

When a debtor does not adhere to the repayment schedule originally agreed on, the account is first considered to be *in arrears* or *delinquent* because the payments are somewhat behind. However, if the borrower contacts the lender and explains the problem, it is usually possible to make some adjustments. If the borrower is ill or unemployed, the lender may agree to freeze loan payments, or ask for interest only. An account in arrears, provided that it does not last too long, is not as serious a blot on the debtor's record as an account that is in default.

IN DEFAULT

The difference between an account in arrears and one in default is largely a matter of degree. In both cases the regular payment schedule has not been maintained. An account *in default* is one that is hopelessly behind, and the lender is not having any success in collecting the debt. Such an account may be turned over for collection to a special department within the firm or to an outside collection agency. Default has a negative effect on one's credit record.

ENFORCING SECURITY

When a debtor defaults, the lender is in a position to *enforce* the security, that is, to realize funds from whatever was put up for security by the borrower before the loan was granted. If there was a co-signer, the lender will attempt to collect from this person, using various amounts of pressure. If the creditor

Figure 13.8

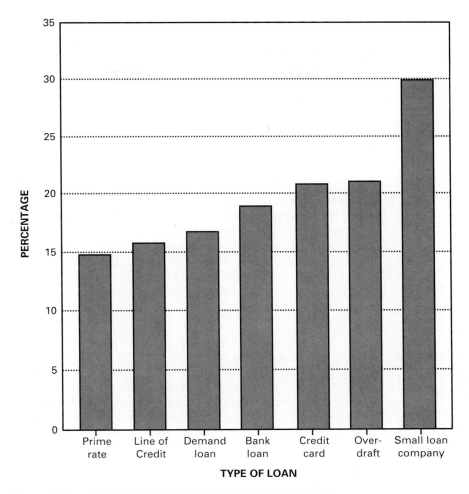

Figure 13.8   INTEREST RATES BY TYPE OF LOAN, 1990

is a credit union, a decision may be made to exercise the wage assignment, which means directing the debtor's employer to deduct up to 20 percent of wages due on each pay day and send it to the creditor. If financial assets, such as bonds, stocks, deposits, and life insurance, were used as security, the lender can now convert these into cash to cover as much of the debt as possible. Finally, if consumer durables were the security, the lender can take possession and offer them for sale.

Enforcement of security is limited to whatever the particular credit contract specifies; it means taking steps to obtain funds from the goods, assets, or co-signers according to the pledges made when the loan was initially arranged. At this stage, the creditor cannot seize goods unless they were listed as security in the credit contract. A creditor may choose not to enforce his or her security, especially in the case of chattel mortgages or conditional sales contracts, if the pledged goods have been in use for some time. Whether exercised or not, the possibility of repossession serves as a powerful threat to debtors.

ENFORCEMENT OF SECURITY VERSUS COURT ACTION   There is a distinction between enforcing security and using the courts to collect debts. In the first instance, the lender exercises a right given by the borrower at the time the loan was arranged, and as explained above, the creditor can take any of the steps specified in the contract without resorting to the courts. If the creditor does not realize enough from the sale of the pledged assets, or if a decision is made not to enforce the security, the debtor can be sued in the appropriate court. The court will determine the validity of the creditor's claim on the debtor and make a decision about the amount owed. If the creditor wins the case, there are ways to coerce the debtor to make payment. Court collection of debts is discussed in Chapter 16.

REGULATIONS AND POLICIES

Consumer credit practices are governed by federal laws and provincial statutes, as well as by the policies of lenders. It may be difficult at first to distinguish among these. Laws can be changed only by legislatures, regulations by order-in-council, but lender policies can be altered more readily and often are modified in response to the pressures of competition.

FEDERAL REGULATION

The power to regulate consumer credit is shared between the federal and provincial governments. The federal government has jurisdiction over banks, promissory notes, bills of exchange, interest, and bankruptcy. In general, there is no legislated ceiling on interest rates on consumer loans. The *Small Loans Act* does state that it is an indictable offense to charge more than the *criminal rate of interest*, which is 60 percent.

PROVINCIAL REGULATION

All provinces have consumer credit laws requiring that borrowers be informed about the cost of credit, expressed both as an annual rate and as a total dollar cost. Also, all provinces have an *Unconscionable Transactions Relief Act*, which permits a debtor to apply to court for a review of a loan contract. If the court finds, considering the circumstances, that the cost of the loan is excessive and the contract harsh and unconscionable, the transaction may be reopened and all or part of the contract set aside.

SUMMARY

This chapter focused on consumer loans obtained from financial institutions such as banks, credit unions, trust companies, and life insurance companies. The market shares of these creditors have changed over the years, with the banks now the major suppliers of consumer credit. Differences among these institutional lenders have become blurred as all have attempted to broaden their range of services. Credit unions, the financial cooperatives, have changed considerably as they became competitive members of the financial community.

Financial institutions, anxious to make loans, offer a bewildering range of possibilities including, personal lines of credit, overdraft protection, credit card cash advances, demand loans, and instalment loans. The security required for a loan differs with the borrower's financial status and the type of loan requested, but may include promissory notes, co-signers, wage assignments, pledging of financial assets or durable goods. There is not much regulation of consumer loans, other than to require full disclosure of the cost, leaving it to competition to maintain economic rates.

PROBLEMS

1. Suggest some reasons for the shift in consumer credit market shares from small loan companies, sales finance companies, and retail vendors to the banks.

2. What are the responsibilities of a person who co-signs a loan?

3. Do you AGREE or DISAGREE with the following statements?

   (a) If you borrowed $1500 from a small loan company, the lender could charge any rate the market will bear (excepting the criminal rate) since there is no maximum set by law.
   (b) The provincial government sets a maximum interest rate on loans from banks.
   (c) Being a good credit risk is important in obtaining a policy loan from your life insurance company.
   (d) Using a life insurance policy as collateral for a loan is essentially the same thing as getting a policy loan.

(e) Life insurance policies issued in recent years state the rate to be charged on policy loans.

(f) There has been a trend among Canadians to prefer to obtain credit from vendors of goods and services rather than cash lenders.

(g) Banks now supply more than two-thirds of all consumer credit, which is double their share in 1965.

4. Which of the following forms of security would be considered collateral? How can you distinguish them?

(a) wage assignment,
(b) bonds,
(c) life insurance with cash value,
(d) promissory note,
(e) durable goods, such as cars,
(f) deposits in a savings account.

5. (a) Try to find out from local lenders whether disability insurance is available with most loans.

(b) When do you think it is worth the extra cost to have a consumer loan insured for disability?

6.

BORROWING TO BUY A CAR

The Porters have had two experiences with consumer loans. First, they borrowed money from the bank to buy a washing machine. By using Alison's Canada Savings Bonds as collateral, they were able to obtain a fully secured loan at a low interest rate.

A year later, Tim and Alison realized that they needed a new car but they could not pay cash for it. They thought about approaching the credit union at the factory where Tim worked, but since he had never joined it, he wasn't sure how their request would be received. Remembering how easy it had been to borrow at the bank, they went back for a larger loan. The loan officer asked them to sign a chattel mortgage on the car and gave them the loan. (The forms and contracts signed by the Porters may be found earlier in this chapter.)

(a) Why did the Porters pay a lower rate of interest on the fully secured loan?

(b) Was the loan for the car fully or partially secured? How can you tell?

(c) The loan officer at the bank told the Porters that credit life insurance would be included at no additional cost. Does that mean if Tim should die, Alison will receive some money from the insurance? Explain.

(d) There are real estate mortgages and chattel mortgages. What characteristics of the security pledged differentiate these mortgages?

(e) Must the Porters carry insurance on this car? Does it matter to the bank?

(f) If they wish to trade in the car and get another before the debt is repaid, do they need to consult the bank, as long as they maintain their payments?

(g) Does the chattel mortgage contract make mention of any penalties for late payments? What do you think might happen if the Porters made a payment a month late?

(h) According to the contract they signed, does the bank have the right to seize anything but the car if the Porters should default on the loan?

(i) If the Porters defaulted, and the bank repossessed and sold the car, but failed to realize enough to cover the outstanding debt, could the bank sue the Porters for the balance owing? If the bank incurs costs in the repossession and sale of the car, who pays this?

(j) If the loan officer at the bank had reservations about the ability of the Porters to repay the loan on schedule, would she:
  (i) offer them a signature loan?
  (ii) offer them a loan without credit life insurance?
  (iii) require more security before making the loan?

7.

SARAH JOINS THE CREDIT UNION

When Sarah began her new teaching job in the city, a friend told her to consider joining a credit union where she could obtain similar, but more personal, services than at a bank. The credit union officer, Mrs. Stein, explained that as a result of several mergers with small credit unions, this was now a community credit union with a common bond requirement that members live or work in the city or surrounding county. Sarah was thus eligible to become a member if she opened a share account with a small deposit.

Mrs. Stein told her about the services available to members of this credit union, which included the option of having her pay cheque deposited in the credit union account by her employer and the opportunity to authorize the credit union to deposit a portion of each cheque into a true savings account and a portion into a chequing account.

Later, when Sarah applied for a loan to buy a car, she found that she had to sign not only a promissory note, but also a wage assignment (Figure 13.5) and a chattel mortgage. Feeling very healthy she declined the disability insurance. However, as luck would have it, she fractured her leg very badly in a skiing accident the next winter. Her income was reduced while she was unable to work, but her living costs and debt payments continued as before. In these circumstances, Sarah was unable to make her loan payments to the credit union. Fortunately, she called to tell them of her problem, and the credit union arranged for her to make interest payments only until she returned to work.

(a) What are some common bond requirements used by credit unions?
(b) What will be the consequences for Sarah of paying interest only for a couple of months?
(c) If Sarah disappeared without repaying her loan, what security would the credit union be able to enforce? If she defaulted, but failed to disappear, what further security could be enforced?
(d) If Sarah had decided to get her car loan from a bank, would she have signed a wage assignment? Why or why not?
(e) Does the credit union offer Sarah any benefit she could not get from other financial institutions?

8. If a person arranged to have loan payments deducted monthly from a chequing account at a credit union or bank, would this be considered a wage assignment? Explain.

9. Distinguish between the following pairs:

(a) enforcement of security and taking a debtor to court to collect a debt,
(b) a demand loan and a credit card cash advance,
(c) a living trust and a testamentary trust,
(d) term of a loan and terms of a loan,
(e) collateral and security,
(f) a personal line of credit and overdraft protection.

10. Who makes the decision to use a wage assignment? Can the amount of money taken from a pay cheque be reduced? If so, how?

11. Why are some loans cheaper than others?

REFERENCES

Books

Canadian Commercial Law Reports. Don Mills, Ontario: CCH Canadian, subscription service. Two-volume reporting service with up-to-date federal and provincial laws regarding sales contracts, conditional sales, instalment sales, chattel mortgages, and consumer protection.

COTE, JEAN-MARC, and DONALD DAY. *Personal Financial Planning in Canada*. Toronto: Allyn and Bacon, 1987, 464 pp. A comprehensive personal finance text that includes financial planning, income tax, annuities, pensions, investments, credit, mortgages, and wills, with particular attention to the banking and insurance industries.

DYMOND, MARY JOY. *The Canadian Woman's Legal Guide*. Toronto: Doubleday, 1987, 449 pp. Includes a section on women and credit.

FORMAN, NORM. *Mind Over Money, Curing Your Financial Headaches with Moneysanity*. Toronto: Doubleday Canada, 1987, 248 pp. A psychologist examines the effects money has on behaviour, looking at the origin of money problems and suggesting therapies to help us to better understand ourselves.

PARKER, ALLAN A. *Credit, Debt, and Bankruptcy*. Seventh Edition. Vancouver: International Self-Counsel Press, 1988, 109 pp. A handbook on Canadian credit law for credit users.

TOWNSON, MONICA, and FREDERICK STAPENHURST. *The Canadian Woman's Guide to Money*. Second Edition. Toronto: McGraw-Hill Ryerson, 1982, 203 pp. A book for the general reader that includes budgets, financial security, life insurance, retirement planning.

Articles

STEVENSON, DEREK. "Playing Your Cards Right." *Canadian Consumer*, 19 (No. 10), 1989, pp. 8-15. This article about credit cards includes a discussion of personal line of credit, overdraft protection, instalment and other loans.

TOWNSON, MONICA. "A Straight Line to Credit." *Canadian Consumer*, 16 (No. 11) 1986, pp. 31-33. Explains how a line of credit works.

Periodical

Canadian Consumer. Monthly. Box 9300, Ottawa, Ontario, K1G 3T9. In recent years, the personal finance articles have been concentrated in the November issue, "Personal Money Guide."

14 VENDOR CREDIT

OBJECTIVES

1. To identify various forms of vendor credit.

2. To outline trends in the use of credit cards.

3. To suggest situations in which each of the following credit arrangements might be used:
   (a) charge card,
   (b) revolving charge account,
   (c) conditional sales agreement.

4. To distinguish between
   (a) vendor credit and consumer loans,
   (b) charge card and credit card,
   (c) charge card and revolving credit,
   (d) credit card and debit card,
   (e) variable credit and conditional sales,
   (f) transaction fee and annual fee (credit cards).

5. To explain why comparing the nominal rates is an inadequate basis for evaluating credit card costs.

6. To suggest some reasons for the discrepancy between credit card interest rates and the bank rate.

7. To explain the differences in the calculation of interest charges on a bank card and a retail credit card according to
   (a) frequency of calculation,
   (b) when charges apply,
   (c) whether a partial payment is over 50 percent of the balance.

8. To explain why a conditional sales contract would be used in a credit transaction rather than a chattel mortgage.

9. To ascertain by reading a conditional sales contract:
   (a) the security offered,
   (b) who holds title to the goods,
   (c) who has possession of the goods,
   (d) the penalties for late payment or default,
   (e) whether there is a promissory note included in the contract,
   (f) the name of the financial institution that may buy the contract from the vendor,
   (g) whether the provincial disclosure rules were followed.

10. To evaluate the extent to which conditional sales contracts serve the consumers' interest by:
    (a) protecting their rights in the transaction.
    (b) explaining the terms of the contract in understandable language.

11. To explain the following terms: revolving charge account, variable credit, grace period, conditional sales contract, acceleration clause, itinerant (direct) seller, "cooling-off" period (or recision rights).

12. To assess the value to consumers of a "cooling-off" period.

13. To explain the main provisions of the protection provided to consumers by the provincial consumer protection statutes in the following areas:
    (a) disclosure of information about credit transactions,

(b) supervision of itinerant sellers,
(c) repossession of goods when the borrower defaults,
(d) advertising of credit,
(e) unsolicited credit cards and unsolicited goods.

14. To calculate the amount of rebate to which a borrower is entitled if the balance of an instalment contract (with precomputed interest) is paid sometime before maturity.

15. To explain the significance of the words "consumer purchase" on the promissory notes included in conditional sales agreements.

16. To outline some current issues of concern to credit card users.

INTRODUCTION

The subject here is credit arranged at the point of sale in contrast to the cash loans discussed in the previous chapter. The difference is that instead of approaching a financial institution for a loan, you are primarily involved in a purchase transaction with a retailer, but choose to use credit rather than cash. Various ways of extending vendor credit, such as charge cards, credit cards, and conditional sales will be examined. In addition, samples of some associated contracts are presented to give you an opportunity to continue your practice in reading and understanding such documents. Provincial legislation that regulates certain aspects of vendor credit varies somewhat by province but the general outline given here will serve as an introduction; check your provincial legislation for details. Finally, attention is given to certain issues and problems of concern to credit users.

ECONOMIC SIGNIFICANCE

As everyone knows, our society depends on credit for much economic activity and from the data presented in the two previous chapters it is evident that our use of consumer credit has been accelerating quite rapidly. The most recent change is our dependence on credit cards: approximately two-thirds of Canadians have at least one credit card. This trend is reflected in the increasing value of sales charged to credit cards issued by Visa and Mastercard between 1977 and 1988 (Figure 14.1.) In eleven years, sales increased nearly seven and one-half times, or if converted to constant dollars, about three-fold. During this same period, the number of Mastercard and Visa cards in circulation more than doubled to about 19.4 million cards. It is estimated that these two cards are used for nine percent of all consumer purchases with retail credit cards accounting for another three percent.

VENDOR CREDIT ARRANGEMENTS

If credit is obtained from a vendor at the point of sale, it is called *vendor credit*, in contrast to loan credit, which is available from institutions that do not sell goods or services. Three of the most common kinds of vendor credit arrangements—charge cards, credit cards, and conditional sales—will be the focus of our attention. A distinction is being made between a *charge card*, used for accounts that require payment in full each month and a *credit card,* used for accounts that permit instalment payments. To dispel any possible confusion with credit cards, debit cards will be mentioned briefly here, although they are not a form of credit.

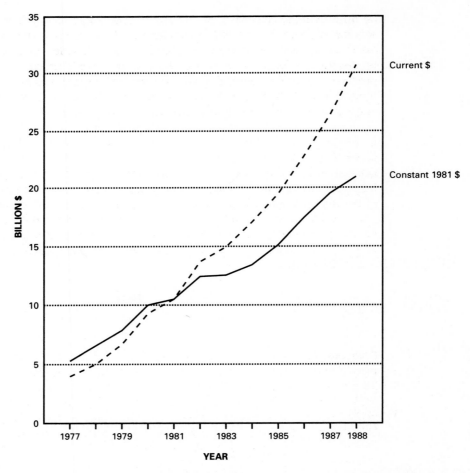

Figure 14.1   DOLLAR SALES USING MASTERCARD AND VISA, CANADA,
                1977-1988 (IN CURRENT AND CONSTANT 1981 DOLLARS)
Source: *Charge It, Credit Cards and the Canadian Consumer.* Report of the Standing Committee on Consumer and
Corporate Affairs and Government Operations, House of Commons, Ottawa, 1989, Appendix 2.

DEBIT CARDS

A *debit card*, also called a *payment card*, differs from a credit card in that
purchases are immediately deducted from the purchaser's regular chequing
account, possibly with a line of credit to handle overdrafts. Debit cards may
also be used as a means of access to automatic teller machines.

Credit unions initiated the use of debit cards, usually at the local level.
More recently other financial institutions, especially banks, have been working

on a nationwide electronic system that would allow payment for goods and services without the use of cash or cheques. It is proposed that once such an *electronic payments system* is put in place, you will be able to use a plastic card to instantly debit your bank account for the week's groceries, right at the check-out counter. Several financial institutions are working together to launch a joint venture debit card system in the near future. To gain wide support, debit cards must be acceptable almost everywhere.

CHARGE CARDS

Charge cards are provided for short-term credit (about a month) primarily by oil companies, and travel and entertainment clubs such as American Express or Diner's. They offer charge accounts requiring full payment within a specified *grace period*, or the number of days after the statement date before a late payment penalty becomes effective. The grace period varies but may be from 25 to 45 days. After that, late payments will attract a penalty at a fairly high rate of interest.

CREDIT CARDS

REVOLVING ACCOUNTS   Credit cards are used for *revolving charge accounts*, so named because it is possible to continue charging purchases to the account as long as a portion of the bill is paid each month. There are two major types of credit cards: (i) those issued by banks, trust companies, credit unions, and other financial institutions (often called "bank cards") and (ii) those issued by retailers. The credit card accounts at financial institutions and retailers differ in two respects: (i) in one case the lender is a retailer and the other a provider of consumer loans, and (ii) the way credit charges are calculated.

To open a revolving charge account, referred to in legislative documents as *variable credit*, an application form similar to the one in Figure 14.2 must be completed. The credit department evaluates the information provided in the application and also may obtain a credit report from the credit bureau (to be explained in the chapter on credit reporting). On the basis of the applicant's current financial situation and previous credit record, the credit manager assesses the individual's credit-worthiness and establishes a ceiling on the amount of credit that may be outstanding at any one time.

Once the account has been opened, credit purchases may be made within the set limit and monthly statements will report the status of the account, including the minimum payment, the outstanding balance, and the credit limit. Whenever the balance reaches the established limit on the account, the use of the card must cease until the debt has been reduced.

ST. GEORGE'S SQUARE
GUELPH, ONT.

Canadian Imperial Bank of Commerce

CIBC *Convenience Card* WITH VISA APPLICATION

PLEASE PRINT IN INK

Use a separate page for details if space is insufficient in any area.

Branch domicile for Chargex credit card application.

A Please tell us about yourself

1. Mr 3. Miss 5.
2. ☑Ms 4. Mrs.

First Name **KIMBERLY** Initial **M** Last Name **TRAVINSKI**

Street Address **1611 PRINCESS ST.** Apt. No. City and Province **PETERBOROUGH ONTARIO** Postal Code **P1P 1O1**

How long have you lived there? **3 YEARS** Home Telephone **705 111-2345** Business Telephone **705 234-1790**
☐ Own your home ☐ Board ☐ Live with parents Monthly payments $ **720**
☑ Rent

If less than 2 years, previous address

Social Insurance Number (optional) Date of Birth — Day **01** Month **03** Year **59** Telephone

☑Single ☐Divorced ☐Widow(er) ☐Married ☐Separated
Spouse's Name
Number of Dependents
Please tell us the name and address of nearest personal reference
Address
Relationship
City, Province, Postal Code
Telephone

B Please tell us about your household income

Employer Name, Department and Address **ACME CLINIC 12 SENECA BLVD., PETERBOROUGH** Telephone **705 234-1790** Occupation **SOCIAL WORKER** How long? **4 YRS** Gross Monthly Income **2887.76**

Previous Employer (if less than 2 years) Telephone Occupation How long? Gross Monthly Income

Other Income Source(s) and Amount(s) Spouse now employed by Telephone Occupation How long? Gross Monthly Income

C Please tell us about your financial obligations and credit references

	Amount Owing	Monthly Payments	Name and Location of Creditor	Account No. (if applicable)	Other (please specify)	Amount Owing	Monthly Payments	Name and Location of Creditor
Bank Loans	$	$				$	$	
Car Loans	$ **3 400**	$ **308.43**	**CIBC PETERBOROUGH**		Mortgages	$	$	
Credit Cards	$	$			Mortgages	$	$	
Credit Cards	$	$			Estimated value of home			

Where do you bank? **CIBC** Branch and Location **MAIN STREET PETERBOROUGH** Savings Account No. **34-476** Chequing Account No. Previous Bank (if less than 2 yrs) Branch

D Secret Code

You will automatically receive a Secret Code to access your VISA account through Instant Teller. I understand that Instant Teller access to my CIBC VISA Account is granted automatically on acceptance of this application, and I request a Secret Code be issued to me. I agree to comply with the Bank's Instant Teller Agreement, which you will send me. Use of the Secret Code at any automated banking machine which is part of the Instant Teller Service shall evidence that I have received such Agreement.

E Additional Card

Do you want another card and renewals and replacements of it? If so, what name do you want on it? Your name ... or in the name of the following authorized user.

First Name Initial Last Name

F CIBC CONVENIENCE CARD WITH VISA Transaction Fee/Annual Fee

TRANSACTION FEE ☐
ANNUAL FEE ☐

TRANSACTION FEE/ANNUAL FEE: A Transaction fee or an annual fee is payable in respect of the VISA account. The amount of the fees and how they are charged are available from any branch of CIBC or your CIBC VISA Centre. Please indicate the fee which is to apply – if no choice is indicated, the transaction fee will apply. I (the applicant) certify the above information to be true, I request a CIBC Convenience Card with VISA, renewals and replacements (and the additional card(s) indicated above) and request CIBC open a VISA account in my name. The authorized user and I will be bound by the CIBC Cardholder Agreement (as amended or replaced from time to time) which CIBC will send me. I will be responsible for all charges to the account and the authorized user and I will both be responsible for charges resulting from use of Cards issued in the authorized user's name and by any other use of the account by the authorized user (except in the case of loss or theft of a Card, as described in the Cardholder Agreement). Use of any Card applied for will show that I received the Cardholder Agreement. CIBC is advised that the authorized user will have the same mailing address as the applicant.

THE BANK MAY OBTAIN CREDIT INFORMATION ABOUT ME (THE APPLICANT) IN CONNECTION WITH THIS APPLICATION AND MY OBLIGATIONS AND MAY DISCLOSE (AUTOMATICALLY OR UPON REQUEST) CREDIT INFORMATION ABOUT ME TO CREDIT BUREAUX AND PERSONS WITH WHOM I HAVE OR PROPOSE TO HAVE FINANCIAL DEALINGS OR IF THE BANK BELIEVES DISCLOSURE IS REQUIRED BY LAW.

DATE **03/11/90** APPLICANT'S SIGNATURE **Kimberly Travinski** AUTHORIZED USER'S SIGNATURE

FOR OFFICE USE ONLY

ACCOUNT NO. LIMIT PLASTICS TYPE LOC CODE STMT CODE PCC (ATM) HOME TELEPHONE BUSINESS TELEPHONE TF ☐ **0** HH AF ☐ BRANCH NO.

COMM POSTAL CODE LANGUAGE PREFERENCE ADD SERV DC MO DY YR INSTANT TELLER LIMIT CODE **2** **5** $ TRANSIT NO.

Figure 14.2   CREDIT CARD APPLICATION
Source: Reproduced with the permission of the Canadian Imperial Bank of Commerce.

GRACE PERIOD   All credit card issuers offer the cardholder a certain number of days, the *grace period*, in which to make full payment without interest charges. Generally, bank, trust company and credit union accounts have a grace period of 21 days and retailer accounts from 21 to 30 days. There is no grace period on amounts carried over from previous months nor on cash advances.

CASH ADVANCES   Credit cards issued by financial institutions permit cash advances, within limits, as well as retail purchases. These loans are treated as small daily loans, with interest charged at a daily rate from the date the funds were advanced.

COMPARATIVE INTEREST RATES   It is instructive to compare the relation between the bank rate and the rates charged on retail and bank cards over the past decade (Figure 14.3). Most of the time there has been a substantial spread

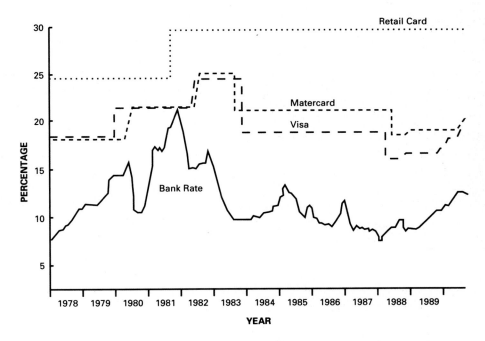

Figure 14.3   REPRESENTATIVE CREDIT CARD RATES VERSUS THE BANK RATE, CANADA, 1977-1989

Source: *Charge It, Credit Cards and the Canadian Consumer.* Report of the Standing Committee on Consumer and Corporate Affairs and Government Operations, House of Commons, Ottawa, 1989, Appendix 2.

between the bank rate and credit card rates. During this period, retail card rates were the highest of all and the most infrequently adjusted. You will note, also, that credit card rates change slowly in response to changes in the bank rate. Two contributing factors that make credit card rates "sticky" are the requirement to give cardholders a month's notice of a change and the large fixed costs of running a credit card operation. Before concluding that it will cost more to make partial payments on a retail card than on a bank card, you must know about the different methods of calculating interest charges, as will be explained shortly.

LOST OR STOLEN CREDIT CARDS   If a credit card is lost or stolen, the owner's responsibility tends to vary with the policy of the company issuing the card. However, in Alberta, Manitoba, or Quebec, cardholders have no legal obligation for any debts incurred after they have notified the company of the loss. If there should be any bills charged after the loss and before notification, the cardholder's responsibility in Alberta and Manitoba is limited to about $50.

CONDITIONAL SALES AGREEMENT

For the sale of high-priced items—such as vehicles, appliances, and furniture—that are to be paid for in instalments, the retailer may use a conditional sales contract rather than a revolving charge account in order to increase the vendor's security in case of default. With charge accounts, the vendor has no claim on the merchandise purchased but only the borrower's signature with a promise to repay. A *conditional sales agreement*, however, permits the creditor to retain title of the goods until they are paid for, with the option of repossessing them if the buyer defaults.

RATES FOR VENDOR CREDIT

There is no regulation of the rates charged on revolving charge accounts or conditional sales. It is expected that competition among creditors will keep rates in line with other forms of consumer credit. At present, there is less rate variation among lenders with similar forms of credit than between types. Some examples of rates charged for various types of vendor credit are shown in Figure 14.4.

CREDIT CARD COSTS

Credit card holders may be charged for two types of costs: (i) transaction or annual fees, and (ii) interest. Each will be examined in turn.

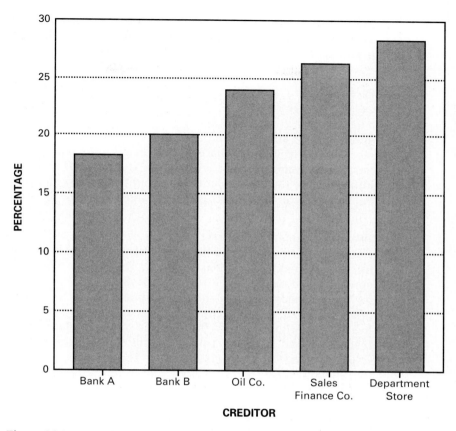

Figure 14.4   INTEREST RATES FOR VENDOR CREDIT, CANADA, APRIL 1990
Source: *Credit Card Costs*, Consumer and Corporate Affairs Canada, Ottawa, April 1990.

TRANSACTION OR ANNUAL FEES

Some financial institutions impose either an annual fee ($6-$12) or a transaction fee (15 cents) but retailers usually do not charge fees for their credit cards. Annual fees for travel and entertainment cards are much higher ($30-$55). With this much variation in costs, it is worthwhile to check out these fees before applying for a credit card.

INTEREST CHARGES

Interest charges are not a concern for the fifty percent of credit cardholders who pay their total outstanding balances each month, but are of great importance to the rest of us. Two significant factors affecting interest costs on partial or instalment payments are: (i) frequency of interest calculation, and (ii) timing in the application of interest charges.

FREQUENCY OF INTEREST CALCULATION   Banks, trust companies and credit unions calculate interest on the daily outstanding balance. For example, assume that a bank card was used to charge three purchases made on March 2, March 12, and March 23 and a partial payment was made after the first statement was received. Daily interest charges on Purchase A would begin March 2, on Purchase B March 12, and on Purchase C March 23. This makes it virtually impossible for the cardholder to figure out the interest charges on bank cards. Retailers, on the other hand, usually charge interest on the monthly balances.

TIMING OF APPLICATION OF INTEREST CHARGES   When a credit cardholder receives a statement, he or she has the option of paying the balance in full without interest, or making a partial payment. The person who chooses the latter option may be surprised to find that some financial institutions charge interest for three periods: (i) from the date of purchase (or the date the credit card office posted the transaction) to the next statement date, (ii) from one statement date to the next, and (iii) from the statement date to the payment date (called residual interest). This is illustrated in Figure 14.5. The amount of residual interest due appears on a later statement.

Retailers, on the other hand, generally charge interest on a monthly basis, starting from the statement date, not the purchase date (except in Quebec, where all interest must be calculated daily) and do not charge residual interest. For the same purchases in the example above, interest charges would be on the balance outstanding after the partial payment was made, accruing from the previous statement date, as illustrated in Figure 14.5.

EFFECT OF SUBSTANTIAL PAYMENT   If the partial payment is 50 percent or more of the balance owing, credit card issuers differ in when they apply interest charges. Retailers usually subtract the partial payment from the outstanding balance before calculating the new interest charges. Financial institutions, however, calculate interest on the previous balance and then subtract the partial payment. When the partial payment is less than 50 percent of the balance, retailers do not subtract the payment before the interest is calculated.

NOMINAL AND EFFECTIVE INTEREST RATES   Nominal interest rates on revolving credit accounts can vary significantly; recently the range was from 17.9 to 28.8 percent. From Chapter 8 you will recall that the nominal interest rate is the quoted rate but it may not be the same as the more significant effective rate.

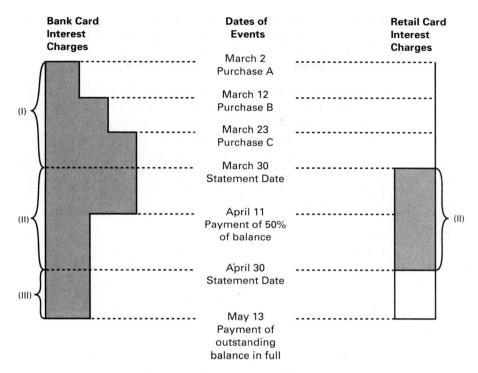

Bank Card Interest Charges	Dates of Events	Retail Card Interest Charges
(I)	March 2 Purchase A	
	March 12 Purchase B	
	March 23 Purchase C	
	March 30 Statement Date	
(II)	April 11 Payment of 50% of balance	(II)
(III)	April 30 Statement Date	
	May 13 Payment of outstanding balance in full	

Figure 14.5   BANK AND RETAIL CREDIT CARD INTEREST CHARGES ON ACCOUNTS WITH PARTIAL PAYMENTS

GINA'S CHARGE ACCOUNTS

Soon after she started her first job, Gina got two credit cards—a bank card and a department store card. She made purchases using each card on March 2, 12 and 23. At the end of the month statements arrived from the bank and the retailer and it so happened that both were dated March 30.

When she settled down to pay bills on April 11 she knew that if she paid these credit card bills in full, there would be no interest charges. However, she was a bit short of funds and decided to pay half of each bill. Each statement indicated the minimum payment but did not show any interest charges.

On April 30, new statements arrived from both credit cards, showing how much she had paid and how much interest had accrued. She knew that there was a difference in interest rates (21% on the bank card and 28.8% on the store card) but she did not understand how the interest was calculated. After some investigation she learned that the retailer had charged interest on the unpaid portion of her bill for the month between statement dates. The bank card interest charges had begun from the date of her purchases and were divided into three periods: (i) from the purchase date to the statement date, (ii) from one statement date to the next, and (iii) residual interest as shown in Figure 14.5. After her partial payment on April 11, the bank charged her interest on the new balance.

On May 13 she paid the total outstanding balance shown on the April 30th statement. Although she did not charge anything more to her bank card in the meantime, she was surprised to find a charge for interest on the May 30th statement. That, she found out, was a residual interest charge for the period between April 30 and May 13.

Unfortunately, it is quite difficult to compare effective annual interest rates on credit cards because of the complex calculation methods. For example, a comparison between a retail card carrying 28.8 percent interest and a bank card at 19 percent (identical transactions and timing of partial payments) resulted in the retail card having a lower effective rate. The difference was in the application of interest charges.

CONDITIONAL SALES CONTRACTS

When you examine the sample contract in Figure 14.6 you will notice that a conditional sales agreement is quite similar to a chattel mortgage in providing a statement of the terms of the credit agreement, a description of the security pledged, and the penalties for failing to keep the terms of the contract. The main difference is that it is a sales rather than a loan agreement. The vendor retains title to the goods until complete payment has been received, reserving the right to repossess the pledged goods if the buyer does not make payments as scheduled.

ACCELERATION CLAUSE

A statement indicating that the lender can demand immediate payment of the total outstanding debt if the borrower is late with one or more payments, or does anything to make the lender feel "insecure," is called an *acceleration clause*. Such a clause is often included in credit agreements for the benefit of the lender. By making the total balance due at once, the lender is in a position to initiate court proceedings to collect the debt without waiting for each monthly instalment to become in arrears.

CONDITIONAL SALE CONTRACT

SELLER: _Bargain Joe's Appliance_
Name

23 Lindsay St.
Address

Peterborough, Ont _P5T 2K8_
City   Province   P.C.

BUYER(S): _Kimberley Travinski_
Name(s)

1611 Princess St.
Address

Peterborough, Ont. _P6T 1O1_
City   Province   P.C.

Dear Customer:
We are writing this Contract in easy-to-read language because we want you to understand its terms. Please read your Contract carefully and feel free to ask us any questions you may have about it. We are using the words, *you, your* and *yours* to mean all persons signing the Contract as the Buyer. The words *we, us* and *our* refer to the Seller.

Contract Coverage: We sell and you buy the following Property and/or Services:

Description of Goods	Make	Model	Serial No.	Price
Dishwasher	Kenmore	V5	PR 2342	$749

Disclosure of your credit costs:

Cash Price	$ _749.00_
Less Trade-In	$ _—_
Net Cash Price	$ _749.00_
Provincial Sales Tax	$ _59.92_
Fees for Registration	$ _5.00_
Total Cash Price	$ _813.92_
Cash Down Payment	$ _13.92_
Amount Financed	$ _800.00_
Scheduled Finance Charge	$ _120.01_
Total Amount of Contract	$ _920.01_
Annual Percentage Rate _26.62_ %	

Payment Schedule: Your payment schedule is _12_ payments of $ _76.70_, except the last which shall be the balance owing. Each payment shall be due on the _first_ day of each month beginning _June 1_, 19 _90_, or one month from the date of this Contract if not otherwise specified.

Date of Contract _May 18th_, 19 _90_

SEE REVERSE SIDE FOR TERMS OF THIS CONTRACT

Notice to Buyer: Do not sign this Contract before you read it, or if it contains any blank spaces.

1. Please note that in connection with this credit application a consumer report containing credit information or personal information may be obtained by the prospective creditor. If you so request the creditor will inform you of the name and address of the consumer reporting agency supplying the report. Any information obtained in connection with this credit application may be divulged to other credit grantors or to a consumer reporting agency. 2. When you sign this Contract, you acknowledge that you have read and agreed to all its terms. 3. Be sure and read the terms and conditions contained on the reverse side of this Contract as they are binding on you as well. 4. All copies must be individually signed in ink.

J. Britehouse
Seller's Signature

I hereby guaranty payment of the total of payments of this Contract:

_____
Guarantor's Signature

You confirm receiving a completed copy of this Contract with disclosures of your credit costs.

Kimberley Travinski
Buyer 1's Signature

Paul Wong
Buyer 2's Signature

AP 24 ONT. Ed. 9/89

Figure 14.6   CONDITIONAL SALES CONTRACT
Source: Reproduced with the permission of Beneficial Canada.

TERMS AND CONDITIONS

1. Promise to Pay: You promise to pay the total amount of contract according to your payment schedule.

2. Interest Rate: The rate shown on the front page as Annual Percentage Rate shall be the rate agreed upon for the computation of pre-judgment and post-judgment interest and shall be used in the computation of any such interest by a Court of Justice when making an order or granting a judgment to enforce this contract.

3. Credit Statement: You certify that all statements in your credit statement are true and complete and were made for the purpose of obtaining credit.

4. Warranties: Unless you have been given a written warranty, there is no warranty on the goods purchased and no statements or promise made by any party shall be valid or binding.

5. Title: Title, and therefore legal ownership, to the goods which you have purchased by this Contract does not pass to you until payment in full of this Contract. You understand and acknowledge that the Seller, and any assignee of the Seller, retains a continuing security interest in the goods which you have purchased until payment in full of this Contract. Furthermore, you agree not to transfer possession or control of the property to any other person without first notifying us by registered mail of your intention to do so.

6. Location: You agree that the goods are to remain at the address indicated on the front of this Contract. If you wish to move the goods, you must notify us by registered mail before you do so. The registered letter can be sent to the same address where you send us your payments. If you move from the address shown on the reverse side, you must notify us of your new address without delay.

7. Insurance: It is your obligation to keep the property insured against fire and theft. You acknowledge that any loss, injury or destruction of the property covered by this Contract does not relieve you of your obligation to pay the full amount owed on the Contract.

8. Default: You will be considered in default under the terms of this Contract if:

a) you fail to make any payment on time;
b) you fail to meet any promise you have made in this Contract;
c) you become insolvent or bankrupt;

d) the property is lost or destroyed;
e) the property is seized in any legal proceeding.

9. Remember: If you are in default under this Contract, we have certain legal remedies available to us. We may, at our election,

a) demand that the full balance owing be paid immediately;
b) take possession of the goods according to law;
c) commence legal proceedings for recovery of the balance owing.

Where we have taken possesion of the goods, you will be sent the required notice which will explain how you may regain possession of the goods. If you do not do so, we will be entitled to dispose of the goods at a public or private sale, or at an auction. We may exercise our rights at any time. Where a deficiency has resulted from such a sale, we may commence legal proceedings for recovery of the deficiency, if permitted by law.

10. Additional Charges on Default: You agree to pay a delinquency charge of 5¢ per each $1.00 of any instalment which is not paid within 5 days after the instalment due date. You agree to pay interest at the same annual percentage rate as stated in this contract after maturity on any unpaid balance which remains.

11. Insufficient Funds Charge: In the event a cheque tendered for payment is returned for insufficient funds, we may collect a $10.00 charge as a reasonable charge for expenses incurred, over and above any other charges.

12. Refund: If you repay in full one month or more before the maturity date of this Contract, a portion of the Total Amount of Contract shall be refunded to you, calculated according to the Consumer Protection Act of Ontario and the regulations. We are entitled to retain an additional amount of $20 or one half of the refund, whichever is less. You are not entitled to the rebate if after deducting the amount we can retain, the rebate is less than two ($2.00) dollars.

13. Assignment: You understand that this Contract may be assigned by the Seller. The assignee will then be entitled to all the rights which the Seller may have had.

14. Applicable Law: Any part of this Contract which is contrary to the laws of any province shall not invalidate the other parts of this Contract.

THIS CONTRACT CONTAINS THE ENTIRE AGREEMENT BETWEEN THE PARTIES

ASSIGNMENT WITHOUT RECOURSE

TO BENCHARGE CREDIT SERVICE (A Division of Beneficial Canada Inc.)

FOR VALUE RECEIVED, we hereby sell, assign, and transfer to you, without recourse, all our rights, title and interest in and to the preceding Contract together with the chattels therein described with full power to take legal proceedings in our name or your own.

_____ (Seal)
(Corporate, Firm or Trade Name of Dealer)

Date _____ , 19 _____   _____ (Seal)
(Authorized Signature)

ASSIGNMENT WITHOUT RECOURSE

TO BENCHARGE CREDIT SERVICE (A Division of Beneficial Canada Inc.)

FOR VALUE RECEIVED, we hereby sell, assign, and transfer to you, without recourse, all our rights, title and interest in and to the preceding Contract together with the chattels therein described with full power to take legal proceedings in our name or your own.

Bargain Joe's Appliance (Seal)
(Corporate, Firm or Trade Name of Dealer)

Date ___ May 18th ___ , 19 90   J. Britehouse (Seal)
(Authorized Signature)

Figure 14.6   (continued)

Assignment of a Conditional Sales Contract to a Third Party

The signing of a conditional sales agreement gives a purchaser the opportunity to buy and enjoy the use of a high-priced durable good by distributing the cost over a number of months or years. Retailers find this encourages sales, but presents a problem by tying up working capital that they need to buy new stock. This difficulty is solved by sales finance companies and some banks, which make a business of buying conditional sales contracts from retailers—a transaction sometimes referred to as *selling credit paper.*

Careful examination of most conditional sales contracts will reveal a statement specifying that the contract may be assigned to a third party, a named financial institution. The blank contract forms, often supplied to the retailer by the sales finance company, may bear the name of that company. The arrangements made between retailers and sales finance companies vary, but usually the sales finance company will buy the contract from the retailer for a sum equal to the purchase price of the item; this makes it equivalent to a cash sale from the retailer's perspective. The purchaser now makes payments directly to the sales finance company that holds the contract.

The sales finance company gains its money from the interest part of the contract. Depending on competition and economic conditions, the sales finance company may offer the retailer an additional premium or charge a discount.

Regulation of Vendor Credit

Historical Background

The proliferation of consumer protection legislation, which began in the mid-1960s, continued until all provinces had one or more acts confirming the rights of consumers in credit transactions. The reason for this legislative activity is not difficult to find. You will recall that the rate of increase in the use of consumer credit was fairly gradual in the 1950s but accelerated in the 1960s (Figure 12.1). A situation had developed where many consumers with little expertise in the credit market were at a disadvantage in their dealings with large corporate creditors. Consequently, the provincial governments attempted to come to the aid of consumers with consumer protection legislation.

Historically, most credit transactions had been conducted between businessmen experienced in the credit market. Except for informal charge accounts at the local store, most consumers did not enter the credit market. This changed after 1950 with the advent of mass production of high-priced consumer durables, which were merchandised on a "buy now, pay later" arrangement. Unsophisticated buyers, unversed in credit or contracts, entered the market and enlarged the demand for both the durables and the credit, but unfortunately many signed contracts they did not understand, waiving rights they did not know they enjoyed.

Not surprisingly, some borrowers got into difficult situations for which they had no legal defense. This prompted provincial legislatures to entrench certain rights of consumers in law and to set up ministries of consumer affairs. The aims were laudable, but the budgets were rarely sufficient to provide help on the scale that was needed. Although consumers acquired rights that lawyers and creditors knew about, most consumers were unaware of them. Insufficient resources were allocated for public information or law enforcement. Nevertheless, consumers benefited from the legislation because lenders knew the rules and endeavoured to follow them.

Provincial statutes regulating vendor credit have many similar provisions, with minor variations. The very general discussion that follows is limited to some of the highlights; for greater detail or precision the relevant statutes should be consulted. These statutes are called the *Consumer Protection Act* in most provinces; the equivalents are the *Cost of Disclosure Act* in New Brunswick and Saskatchewan, and the *Credit and Loan Agreement Act* in Alberta.

DISCLOSURE OF CREDIT CHARGES

One of the main achievements of the consumer protection legislation was to require creditors to disclose all the costs of credit, both as total dollar amounts and as annual percentage rates. Because of divided federal-provincial jurisdiction regarding the regulation of consumer credit—interest is a federal matter and trade is provincial—there was uncertainty about exactly which costs of borrowing could be called interest. Consequently the provincial acts usually avoid the use of the word interest, and substitute the broader term, *credit charges*. This disclosure of the cost of credit, both as a rate and as an amount (referred to as "truth in lending" in the United States) is now mandatory in all provinces and states.

After the disclosure laws had been in effect for a number of years, some research was done to determine whether consumers make use of this information to comparison shop for credit. Many borrowers were found to be generally insensitive to interest rates and more concerned with the size of the monthly payments. Apparently, many users of consumer credit are more interested in shopping for the purchase than for financing.

The disclosure requirements for variable credit or revolving charge accounts are that the borrower be told in advance what the interest rate will be and that, after extending the credit, the lender will provide a statement showing the outstanding balances at the beginning and end of the period, amounts and dates of each transaction, and the cost of borrowing expressed in dollar amounts.

The rules for disclosure of credit costs apply to conditional sales contracts whether signed at the vendor's premises or in the customer's home. The method of calculating credit charges on conditional sales is set forth in the regulations that accompany the various provincial acts. Included in the disclosure legislation is a list of information that must be included in *executory contracts* (e.g., a conditional sales contract) if the total cost of the purchase, exclusive of credit charges is above a specified amount, which may be around $50. Essentially, the contract must contain names and addresses of the buyer and seller, a description of the goods being purchased, and details about the financial transaction.

SUPERVISION OF ITINERANT SELLERS

Do door-to-door sellers exert undue pressure on people to buy their products? Perhaps. At any rate, each province has legislation that allows consumers time to change their minds about contracts signed in their own homes. In fact, the consumer's right to cancel the agreement can apply to any contract signed at a location other than the company's place of business. The length of this "cooling-off" period varies from province to province, but within the specified time, a consumer may cancel the contract simply by informing the company of that intention. This is best done by registered mail, but verbal notice is acceptable in some provinces. Usually the postmarked date on the letter is considered to be the time the notice was received by the company. The "cooling-off" period does not include Sundays or statutory holidays. When a contract is cancelled, the consumer is expected to return any goods received and possibly to pay compensation for the use of them; the seller is expected to return any down payment. A summary of this legislation by province is shown in Table 14.1.

PREPAYMENT OF PRECOMPUTED CREDIT CONTRACTS

Some creditors arrange the repayment of accounts by calculating the credit charges on the outstanding balance at the end of each month, as discussed in the chapter on interest. Others use a precomputed schedule of credit charges. In both instances, the monthly payments will be of equal size, composed of varying amounts of principal and interest. The difference is that the proportions of interest and principal are established in advance in the precomputed schedule, instead of being computed monthly. The first method offers more flexibility to a borrower who may wish to repay the debt faster than scheduled. In such a case, the lender simply charges interest on whatever principal sum is outstanding at the end of the month, subtracts this amount from the payment, and uses the remainder to reduce the principal. (You may wish to review the calculation of compound interest on instalment loans in Chapter 8.) Precomputed charges create more complexity if the borrower wishes to repay early. The following discussion applies to precomputed contracts.

Table 14.1   COOLING-OFF PERIODS BY PROVINCE

Province	Legislation	Length of cooling-off period	Notification of cancellation	Minimum amount of sale
Newfoundland	*The Direct Sellers Act*	Within 10 days of date on which contract was signed.	Written, personally delivered, or sent by registered mail; in which case it is deemed effective on the day after it is mailed.	no min.
Prince Edward Island	*The Direct Sellers Act*	Within 7 days of date on which contract was signed.	In writing or by personal delivery, telegram, or registered mail to vendor's last known address. When sent registered mail, it is deemed effective on the day after it is mailed.	$40
Nova Scotia*	*Direct Sellers Licensing and Regulation Act*	Within 10 days of date on which contract was signed.	Written or by personal delivery to direct seller or one of his salesmen or by registered mail to address shown on contract, in which case it is deemed effective at time of mailing.	$25
New Brunswick	*Direct Sellers Act*	Within 5 days of date on which contract was signed.	Written, to direct vendor or one of his salesmen or by personal delivery or registered mail to address in contract in which case it is deemed effective at time of mailing.	$25
Quebec*	*The Consumer Protection Act*	Not later than 10 days after buyer receives copy of contract.	By returning goods to vendor's address or by written notice.	$25
Ontario*	*The Consumer Protection Act*	Within 2 days after duplicate original copy of contract is received by buyer.	Written, by personal delivery or by registered mail to address stated in the contract, in which case it is effective at time of mailing.	$50
Manitoba*	*The Consumer Protection Act*	Within 4 days of date on which contract was signed.	Written, by personal delivery, or by registered mail to address of vendor stated in contract.	no min.
Saskatchewan	*The Direct Sellers Act*	Within 10 days of date on which contract was signed.	Written, or by personal delivery, telegram or registered mail to vendor's last known address. In case of registered mail, it is deemed effective on date of postmaster's receipt.	no min.

Table 14.1   CONTINUED

Province	Legislation	Length of cooling-off period	Notification of cancellation	Minimum amount of sale
Alberta	*The Direct Sales Cancellation Act*	Not later than 4 days after date on which purchaser received his copy of contract by personal delivery or mail.	Written, by personal delivery or mailed to vendor named in contract. If no contract, notice sent to any address of salesman known to buyer. It is deemed effective at time of mailing.	$25
British Columbia*	*Consumer Protection act*	Not later than 7 days after date when buyer receives copy of contract.	Written, by personal delivery or mailed to seller's address stated in contract or any address of seller known to buyer.	$20

 * In some provinces, legislation is only effective when the purchase exceeds a minimum dollar price.
1. In Manitoba and Nova Scotia, if the contract does not include rescission rights the cooling-off period is 30 days after the goods or services were delivered.
2. All provinces, except Ontario and Quebec, provide for cancellation after longer periods if certain conditions are not met.

RULE OF 78   If the holder of a credit contract with a precomputed schedule wishes to repay the debt early, the *Rule of 78* may be used to determine the amount of interest that will be rebated. The Rule of 78 is so-named because the credit charges for a contract requiring 12 payments are divided into 78 units. For the first month, when the interest charges are at the maximum, the number of units of credit charges will be 12, the next month 11, then ten, nine, and so on until only one unit of credit charges is owed by the last month (Table 14.2). For an 18-month contract, the credit charges would begin with 18 and go down to one. The numbers in Table 14.2 are shown diagrammatically in Figure 8.1.

Although called the Rule of 78, that in fact is something of a misnomer if the contract is for more or less than 12 payments. For example, with a three-year contract, the total number of units of credit charges would be 666, not 78. While most provinces follow the Rule of 78, the Sum of the Balances Method is used in Alberta; the results are generally about the same if all payments are equal and paid as scheduled.

RETENTION BY LENDER   The amount the lender is allowed to retain when such contracts are prepaid is $20 in most provinces ($15 in British Columbia, $10 in Newfoundland and Prince Edward Island) or half of the rebate, whichever is less. In Newfoundland and Prince Edward Island, the prepayment is to be made within the first half of the term of the agreement. In all provinces except British Columbia, the borrower is not entitled to anything if the rebate works out to less than $2. The rationale for retaining a portion of the rebate is that

Table 14.2   COMPONENTS OF CREDIT PAYMENTS AMORTIZED OVER
12 MONTHS (PRINCIPAL $3500)

Payment number	Total monthly payment $	Amount of principal owing $	Amount of credit charge $	Units of credit charge	Amount of principal repaid each month $
1	317.50	3500.00	47.69	12	269.81
2	317.50	3230.19	43.71	11	273.79
3	317.50	2956.40	39.75	10	277.76
4	317.50	2678.64	35.77	9	281.73
5	317.50	2396.91	31.79	8	285.71
6	317.50	2111.20	27.82	7	289.68
7	317.50	1821.52	23.84	6	293.66
8	317.50	1527.86	19.87	5	297.63
9	317.50	1230.23	15.90	4	301.60
10	317.50	928.63	11.92	3	305.58
11	317.50	623.05	7.95	2	309.55
12	317.50	313.50	3.97	1	313.53
Totals	3810		309.97	78	3500.03

a creditor should be compensated for having to reinvest the capital. The example "Prepayment of a Credit Contract" illustrates an application of the Rule of 78.

PREPAYMENT OF A CREDIT CONTRACT

Carlos borrowed $3500 to be paid back in 12 monthly payments of $317.50, with total credit charges of $310. After making the sixth payment, Carlos chose to repay the balance of the contract. He thought that since he was exactly halfway through the schedule, he would receive an allowance for half of the credit charges or $310 × 1/2 = $155. However, he learned that it was not that simple.

Carlos was shown the schedule (Table 14.2) which set forth the components of each payment. It was pointed out to him that the credit charges were highest during the early stages of the contract and by the end of six months he had already paid more than half of the total credit charge. He was interested to find out how units of credit charges are calculated.

There are two ways to find the total number of credit units in a contract. You can add: $12 + 11 + 10 \ldots + 1 = 78$ units. Or, you can use this formula, where N = the number of payments in the contract:

$$\text{Total credit units} = \frac{N}{2} \times (N + 1)$$

For a 12-month contract:

$$\text{Total credit units} = \frac{12}{2} \times (12 + 1)$$
$$= 78$$

Since Carlos has six more payments to make, the number of credit units outstanding is:

$$\begin{array}{l}\text{Credit units for}\\\text{last 6 months}\end{array} = \frac{6}{2} \times (6 + 1)$$
$$= 21$$

The value of one credit unit is 1/78 of the total credit charge of $310:

$$1/78 \times \$310 = \$3.97$$

His rebate will be:

$$21 \text{ units} \times \$3.97 = \$83.37 \text{ less } \$20 \text{ to compensate the lender.}$$

Therefore, to close out this contract Carlos will pay a lump sum of:

$$(6 \text{ months} \times \text{his monthly payment}) - (\$83.37 - \$20)$$
$$(6 \times 317.50) - (\$83.37 - 20)$$
$$\$1905 - \$63.37$$
$$= \$1841.63$$

UNSOLICITED CREDIT CARDS AND GOODS

Provincial legislation sets limits on your responsibility for unsolicited goods or credit cards you may receive.

UNSOLICITED CREDIT CARDS   Five provinces prohibit the issuing of unsolicited credit cards (Table 14.3). Other provinces do not make it illegal to send out such cards, but they make it quite clear that if a credit card was not requested, the intended recipient has no legal responsibility for transactions made with it unless some indication of acceptance was made, such as signing the card and presenting it to a vendor.

Table 14.3   PROVINCIAL LAWS CONCERNING UNSOLICITED CREDIT
             CARDS

The law states that . . .	Provinces where this law applies
issuing of unsolicited credit cards is forbidden.	Alberta, Manitoba, New Brunswick, Prince Edward Island, Quebec.
if an unsolicited credit card is received, the recipient has no legal obligation for transactions made with it, unless he writes to the issuer of the card stating his intention of accepting it.	Alberta, British Columbia, Newfoundland, Nova Scotia, Ontario, Saskatchewan.
signing and using an unsolicited credit card is considered to be acceptance of responsibility for the card.	Alberta, Newfoundland, Nova Scotia, Ontario.
if the unsolicited credit card has not been accepted, the intended recipient has no responsibility if the card is lost or misused.	Alberta, Ontario, British Columbia, Newfoundland, Nova Scotia, Saskatchewan.

UNSOLICITED GOODS   Prince Edward Island is the only province that prohibits sending unsolicited goods. In British Columbia, Newfoundland, Nova Scotia, Ontario, and Saskatchewan, the recipient of unsolicited goods has no responsibility to return, pay for, or take any special care of such goods. However, if residents of British Columbia or Saskatchewan acknowledge the receipt of such goods, they lose their immunity from responsibility.

ADVERTISING THE COST OF CREDIT

All provinces regulate the advertising of the cost of credit. This became necessary when retailers and lenders deceived potential customers by advertising their credit arrangements in such a way as to be misleading. For instance, an advertisement might have stated that there would be no down payment, but did not tell the rest of the story. Lenders who advertise the cost of credit must now indicate the cost of borrowing expressed as an annual percentage rate. If other information about the credit terms is to be advertised, lenders are required to present all relevant information, which includes the number of instalments, the amount of the down payment, and the size of each instalment.

REPOSSESSION OF SECURED GOODS

If a debtor is in default, the creditor can usually seize the secured goods without a court judgment. However, provincial laws place some restrictions on this process. In practice, most creditors prefer to press for payment of the debt rather than become involved in the complications of repossession. Although threat of repossession is a powerful weapon for encouraging borrowers to make payments, it is not worthwhile for creditors unless the pledged goods are of significant value. The creditor usually has the right to repossess the goods, sell them, and claim against the debtor for any balance not covered by the sale. However, because of unscrupulous practices such as selling the goods at a lower price to friends, some provinces have "seize or sue" laws that allow the creditor to repossess secured goods or to sue, but not both (British Columbia, Alberta, and Newfoundland).

Promissory Notes on Conditional Sales Agreements

A promissory note is not only an unconditional promise to repay a debt, but is also a negotiable instrument. Like a cheque, it can be endorsed and made payable to a third party. There is usually a promissory note included in a conditional sales agreement but in such cases there are some restrictions to protect borrowers. The words "consumer purchase" must be written on them to distinguish them from other promissory notes. The reason is that a person who holds the usual type of promissory note can demand payment regardless of any responsibilities for delivery, quality of goods, and so on. However, if the note is marked "consumer purchase," anyone who buys this contract from a retailer shares responsibility with the retailer in ensuring that obligations associated with the goods are met. This is of some significance when conditional sales agreements are assigned to a third party, as already explained. The vendor and the third party, usually a sales finance company or bank, share in the responsibility that the goods or service are satisfactory for their intended purpose.

Issues and Problems

Credit Cards

Need for Standardized Disclosure   In spite of the widespread use of credit cards, their costs are not well understood. The available cards differ significantly in two kinds of costs: (i) non-interest costs such as annual or transaction fees, and (ii) terms and conditions associated with interest charges. To make rational choices consumers must understand the terms and conditions of each credit card. However, that is not possible with the present state of information disclosure. Although the nominal interest rates are readily available, as you have seen they are not an accurate basis for comparing costs.

Some of the information card issuers do provide is not presented in an easily understandable form. For instance, it is commonly believed that a partial payment will proportionately reduce the interest charges but this is not the case with any credit card. There is a need for a standardized set of terms and conditions for calculating interest charges, as is now the case for consumer loans.

In 1987, in response to a demand for better information about credit card costs, Consumer and Corporate Affairs Canada began to issue a brief release called "Credit Card Costs" three times a year. Contact the department if you wish to be on the mailing list. It includes a chart comparing credit cards by fees, grace period, interest rates, and the period when interest charges apply.

DISPUTES WITH RETAILERS   A complicating aspect of purchases made with bank cards is that if there is a dispute about goods or services purchased with them, one has to deal with a retailer who has already been reimbursed by the financial institution. The bank or other institution, which specifically stated in the cardholder agreement that it does not take responsibility for merchandise or services, will not be interested in hearing about the dispute (Figure 14.7). Payments to the issuer of the credit card must be kept up-to-date; withholding payment will not succeed, more credit charges will be added to the unpaid amount. The problem will have to be handled as an unsatisfactory cash purchase would have been.

Some consumers have faced a quite different problem. They have had the unfortunate experience of having their credit cards rejected at the point of sale, in spite of a good payment record. The cause could be an employee error or it could be that the card issuer's computer has detected unusual purchasing patterns. When this occurs, it is difficult to get the problem resolved in a store or hotel lobby. One alternative is to have an another method of payment available, such as cash or another credit card.

CONTRACTS

The conditional sales agreement, when used for a consumer purchase, is subject to provincial consumer protection legislation regarding disclosure of credit charges and the content of the contract. The statutes concerned with conditional sales agreements may refer to them as a type of *executory contract*, that is, one in which both parties have made promises regarding future action, but have yet to act.

Two significant problems consumers have to face when they sign credit contracts are their weak bargaining position and the difficulty of understanding the legal terminology used in the contracts. Chattel mortgages and conditional sales agreements have been drawn up by lawyers hired to protect the interests of creditors, not those of consumers. A borrower has the choice of accepting the contract as it stands or rejecting it and going elsewhere for

VISA CARDHOLDER AGREEMENT

In this Agreement, the words "you" and "your" mean "Canadian Imperial Bank of Commerce" and the words "I", "me" and "my" mean the person in whose name you have opened a VISA* account (the Account) and whose name is embossed on one or more of your charge cards which carry the Chargex* and/or VISA* name ("Cards"). "Authorized User" means each person whose name is embossed on a Card or Convenience Cheque at my request.

I and each Authorized User agree with you as follows:

1. Use of Cards and Convenience Cheques

I will ensure that each Card is signed immediately upon receipt. I will not use a Card or Convenience Cheque prior to any validation date embossed on a Card or after the expiry date embossed on a Card. Cards and Convenience Cheques are your property. They may be used to purchase goods and services and to obtain cash advances, and the Account may be used in any other way you may permit (a "Transaction"). I can not stop payment on any Transaction (except a Convenience Cheque).

2. Liability for Indebtedness

The purchase price of goods and services, the amount of cash advances and Convenience Cheques and all other amounts payable under this Agreement, except interest, are called Indebtedness. I am liable for all Indebtedness and interest on it (including Indebtedness incurred by each Authorized User, any family member or any other person, to whom I have given either express or implied authority to use the Account (an "Authorized Person")). If I or any Authorized Person sign a sales or cash advance draft or give the Account number to make a purchase or obtain a cash advance without presenting the Card (such as for a mail order or telephone purchase), the legal effect shall be the same as if the Card was used by me and a sales or cash advance draft was signed by me. Each Authorized User is jointly and individually liable with me for all Indebtedness and interest on it incurred by such Authorized User or with such Authorized User's Card.

3. Credit Limit

I will not permit the Indebtedness to exceed the credit limit established by you from time to time. However you may (but are

not required to, even if you have done so before) permit the Indebtedness to exceed the credit limit established from time to time. The credit limit appears on the document which accompanies a Card when it is issued and also appears on the monthly statement. I am liable for all Indebtedness, whether or not it exceeds the credit limit.

4. Payment

I will pay the Indebtedness and interest on it by the Payment Due Date on the monthly statement as follows:

(a) in full, or

(b) by a part payment equal to the greater of $10.00 or 5% of the unpaid balance shown on the statement, or

(c) by any payment greater than (b).

In addition, I will immediately pay any Indebtedness exceeding the credit limit, and if the balance shown on a statement is less than $10.00, I will pay it in full by the statement's Payment Due Date. Payments received at your VISA Center, or by 3:00 p.m. on a banking day at any of your Canadian branches, will be applied to the Account as of the day of receipt. I will not use the Account to pay the Indebtedness.

5. Interest

(a) **Payment in Full.** There is a benefit to me if I pay my Account in full by the Payment Due Date. If I pay the entire balance in full by the Payment Due Date shown on the statement, interest is charged only:

(i) on cash advances from and including the date they are obtained

(ii) on Convenience Cheques from the date they are charged to the Account, and

(iii) on Indebtedness shown on the statement which also appeared on the previous statement.

(b) **Partial Payment.** If I do not pay the entire balance in full by the Payment Due Date then interest is charged;

(i) on cash advances from and including the date they are obtained, and

(ii) on all other Indebtedness from the date they are charged to the Account.

(c) **Interest Rate.** Interest is charged at the rate specified in the Disclosure Statement which accompanies this Agreement. The

interest rate is subject to change in accordance with paragraph 14, and the current rate at any time appears on the monthly statement. Interest is calculated by totalling the interest bearing Indebtedness owing at the end of each day in the period in question and multiplying the result by the daily interest rate.

6. Application of Payments

Payments are applied, in accordance with paragraph 4, in the following order: previously billed interest; previously billed cash advances and Convenience Cheques; previously billed purchases, fees and charges which are interest-bearing, previously billed purchases, fees and charges which are not yet interest-bearing; unbilled cash advances and Convenience Cheques; and, at the end of a billing period, any unapplied payments are applied to unbilled purchases.

7. Special Services

You may make available to me and/or to any Authorized User special services or benefits (a "Service"). The Services shall be subject to the terms and conditions applicable to them (which may vary from time to time) and may be cancelled with or without notice. You are not liable for any Service not directly supplied by you.

8. Fees and Charges

I will pay the fees and charges described in the Disclosure Statement and those described in any notice or monthly statement sent to me from time to time.

9. Monthly Statements

The number of days covered by each monthly statement will vary as a result of several factors, including holidays, weekends and the different number of days in each month, and will normally be between 28 and 33 days.

10. Loss or Theft of Card

If a Card is lost or stolen, I will immediately notify you and you may take whatever steps you consider necessary in order to recover the Card including reporting the lost or stolen Card to the appropriate authorities to facilitate its recovery. Until notification, I am liable for up to $50 for unauthorized use.

Figure 14.7 CREDIT CARDHOLDER AGREEMENT
Source: Reproduced with the permission of the Canadian Imperial Bank of Commerce.

Cardholder Agreement

For CIBC VISA Cards

11. Failure to Honour Cards or Accept Convenience Cheques; Claims Against Merchants

You will not be liable if a Card is not honoured, a Convenience Cheque is not accepted, or the Account cannot otherwise be used. I will settle all claims and disputes regarding any Transaction or any credit voucher issued by a merchant directly with the merchant. You will credit the Account upon receipt of a merchant's credit voucher for a purchase made with a Card. If you have not received a credit voucher when a monthly statement is prepared, I will pay the balance shown on the statement as required by this Agreement, and any credit will appear on a subsequent statement following your receipt of the voucher.

12. Foreign Currency

I will pay Indebtedness incurred in a foreign currency in Canadian dollars. If you convert the Indebtedness to Canadian currency, you will use a conversion rate no higher than your selling rate in effect at the time that the Transaction is processed by you or by your agents. If you are charged in Canadian currency, you will use the conversion rate billed to you plus a service charge based on the converted amount.

13. Errors in Statement; Copies of Documents

If I or an Authorized User do not notify you in writing within 30 days after the date of a monthly statement of any error or omission, the statement will be conclusively settled to be complete and correct except for any amount improperly credited to the Account. A microfilm or other copy of a sales draft, cash advance draft, Convenience Cheque or other document relating to a Transaction will be sufficient to establish liability.

14. Changes

You may change this Agreement and/or any Disclosure Statement from time to time, by mailing a notice (or sending it in any other way) to me at the most recent address appearing in the records of your VISA Center. The notice will bind the Authorized User if it is also mailed or sent to the Authorized User at my address. The Authorized User directs you to use that address for such purposes. A change may apply both to existing Indebtedness and to Indebtedness arising after the change is made. I will give your VISA Center prompt written notice of any change in my address.

15. Termination of Agreement

I may terminate this Agreement at any time without notice. You may terminate this Agreement at any time without notice if I am in breach of this Agreement, if I am in default in respect of any other loan arrangement I may have with you, or if you receive information about me which leads you to believe that I may be unable to repay the Indebtedness.

If this Agreement is terminated, you may do any or all of the following without notice:

(a) refuse to honour any Convenience Cheques (whether made before or after such termination),

(b) require that all Indebtedness and interest be paid immediately,

(c) debit any bank account I have with you and apply the funds against the Indebtedness and interest owing under this Agreement,

(d) request that all Cards and unused Convenience Cheques be returned to you,

(e) take possession of all Cards and unused Convenience Cheques.

If this Agreement is terminated, I will continue to be liable for Indebtedness and interest and I am responsible for returning the Cards and unused Convenience Cheques to you. If a Card or a Convenience Cheque is used after this Agreement is terminated I will be liable for the Indebtedness and interest incurred even though the Agreement was terminated.

I will pay to you all legal fees and expenses (on a solicitor and client basis) incurred by you to recover any Indebtedness or interest and all expenses incurred by you to take possession of a Card.

CIBC VISA Cards are owned and issued by Canadian Imperial Bank of Commerce.

*CIBC Registered User of Marks

CX 921E - 4/89

Figure 14.7   (continued)

credit. The sales person or credit manager usually lacks the authority to renegotiate the terms to suit the borrower and rarely understands the contract any better than the customer does. It is encouraging, however, to find that some creditors have started to rewrite these contracts in language much easier to understand.

SUMMARY

Vendor credit, which may take the form of charge cards, credit cards, or conditional sales, plays a significant part in consumer transactions. The use of credit cards has grown at an accelerating rate in recent years but consumer understanding of the associated terms and conditions has lagged. Charge cards are for short-term credit and do not attract interest unless payment is overdue. Credit cardholders have the option of paying monthly balances in full without interest or making partial payments with interest. The methods used to determine interest charges on partial payments are very complex, making it virtually impossible to use nominal interest as a basis of comparing costs. There is a need for a standardized method of calculating interest charges and a improved means of communicating this to consumers.

In view of the weak bargaining position of most consumer borrowers in relation to corporate creditors, provincial consumer legislation has been enacted to redress the balance, but some problems still remain. Generally, consumers are unaware of their rights. The legislation requires full disclosure of credit costs and terms, but borrowers tend to be insensitive to interest rates. "Cooling-off" laws are intended to assist those who sign credit contracts at home and who may have been subject to undue sales pressure, but in most cases they do not know of this right.

PROBLEMS

Note: You must consult the appropriate consumer protection legislation for your province to find the information needed to answer these questions.

1. Kim is frustrated because the lawn mower she purchased from Handy Appliances, using her Visa card, has been defective from the time she brought it home. She took it back to the store but was not able to get satisfaction. At first they said, "Bring it in, we'll look it over," but it turned out that the store was a sales business only, without any service personnel. The sales clerks commented that the lawn mower looked to be in order and suggested that Kim try it again. In the meantime the Visa bill arrived. Since she was contesting this sale, she wrote Visa to say that she wasn't paying the bill until the lawn mower was fixed or replaced. Time passed and along came another

Visa statement. The bill for the lawn mower was on it as well as a credit charge for the delay in paying.

(a) Where can Kim find out what her rights are in her dispute with Visa?
(b) What are these rights?
(c) What is your opinion of the situation? What would you do?
(d) What rights does Kim have in her dispute with the retailer?
(e) What interest rate would Kim pay if she obtained a cash loan with her Visa card? How does this compare with the rates that banks charge for personal loans? (Refer to Chapter 13 or call a bank.)

2. Kim also bought a dishwasher using a conditional sales agreement. Her partner, Paul Wong, co-signed the contract (Figure 14.4).

(a) At the time she signed the contract was it possible for her to predict that it might be sold to a third party?
(b) Explain who will have possession and who will have the title to the dishwasher during the payment period.
(c) Will there be additional costs if Kim misses a few payments and has her contract extended?
(d) If the couple's house is damaged by fire and the dishwasher destroyed, can Kim cancel the contract since she no longer has a dishwasher?
(e) Is there an acceleration clause in Kim's contract? What does an acceleration clause usually say?
(f) If, after she has paid two-thirds of the purchase price of the dishwasher, Kim is unable to make further payments, can the holder of the contract repossess the dishwasher? Explain.
(g) If the dishwasher has been repossessed, but not sold, and Kim has found some money to make up the payment, will she have to pay any extra charges? If so, for what?
(h) If the holder of the conditional sales contract uses the services of a lawyer to enforce some aspect of the contract, who pays the lawyer's fee?
(i) Could Kim have saved money by obtaining credit from another source?
(j) From Kim's perspective, what difference is there between a chattel mortgage and a conditional sales contract? What is the legal distinction?
(k) Does the contract specify that it is for a consumer purchase? What is the significance of these words on a contract?

3. Susan and David are about to book a vacation to Puerto Vallarta through the travel section of a major department store. They want this, their first real holiday, to be special so they have been looking at packages costing about $1500 each. Knowing that they will be rather short on cash with the trip coming right after Christmas, they are planning to use either a bank card or the store's credit card to pay for the trip. The store accepts either, leaving

them in a quandary as to which card to use. The nominal interest rate is 28.8 percent on the store card and 18.6 percent on the bank card.

(a) Their first thought is that the decision is easy; it seems obvious that the bank card would be the best choice. What other factors beside the nominal interest rate might they consider before making a choice?

(b) Susan and David realize that there will be other things that they will need before the trip. If they spend an additional $750 on gifts and clothes at various times during the second month, could this influence their decision about which account to choose?

(c) David might get a bonus of about $1600 in three months' time. Should they use all of it to reduce their credit card balance or put it in a high-interest bank account?

(d) Are there other possibilities you think this couple should explore before making their final decision?

4. (a) What minimum monthly payment is required on a Visa account?
   (b) If you obtain a cash advance and repay it all when the bill arrives, will you pay any credit charges?

5. How is an itinerant seller defined in the consumer protection legislation of your province? Can you think of examples of door-to-door selling that are not regulated by this legislation?

6. The "cooling-off" legislation is intended to provide consumers with some protection from itinerant sellers.

(a) What are the conditions regarding a door-to-door sale that make the "cooling-off" legislation applicable?

(b) How much and what kinds of protection from itinerant sellers do you think consumers need?

(c) How effective do you think the present legislation in your province is in meeting these needs?

(d) Do you think the right to cancel the contract should be written on the contract? Why or why not?

7. Make a list of arguments for and against this statement: "In the area of vendor credit, consumers have enough protection in law; what they need is more education about their rights and responsibilities."

8. What is your responsibility regarding:

(a) debts charged against you by someone who found or stole your credit card?

(b) paying for unsolicited goods you received in the mail?

(c) an unsolicited credit card received in the mail?

9. Decide whether you AGREE or DISAGREE with each of the following statements:

  (a) There is a provincial law that regulates the maximum rates that retailers can charge on revolving accounts.

  (b) There is no legal limit to the credit rate that sales finance companies may charge on conditional sales agreements.

  (c) The contract will be void if a conditional sales agreement omits any of the following:
    (i) the total cost of credit in dollar amounts,
    (ii) a guarantee of the quality of the merchandise,
    (iii) the credit rate expressed as an annual rate,
    (iv) the name and address of the manufacturer of the goods.

10. Peter financed his car by borrowing $7000 for three years at an effective annual rate of 12 percent. There was a credit life insurance premium of $35.86 to be added to the cost of the loan. This meant that he borrowed $7035.86 with monthly payments of $232.75. Immediately after he made the eighteenth payment, Peter was surprised to receive an inheritance of $5500. His first thought was that now he could prepay the balance of his loan.

  (a) How much would the interest rebate be?
  (b) What is the total amount he would pay to discharge this loan?

11. Make inquiries to find out if bank cardholders are charged a fee. If there is one, is it by the month or by the transaction?

12. Assume that you have a choice between buying a television set with a credit card or with a conditional sales agreement. In either case you plan to pay for it over 12 months. Identify some of the costs and benefits for you of each alternative.

13. Suppose that you made a purchase using a debit card, and a friend made a similar purchase with a credit card. From your perspective, what differences would there be between the two transactions?

14. If you had saved $11 000 to buy a new car, would it be better to buy the car for cash or, as some salesmen have suggested, put $1500 down, use credit for the balance, and invest the $9500? The credit terms were 13.5 percent with payments of $255.50 for 48 months. Money could be invested at 9 percent compounded annually in a guaranteed investment certificate.

  (a) Calculate the total cost of credit if the car were to be purchased this way.
  (b) Find the total interest that could be earned from the guaranteed investment certificate. (Remember to use a compound interest table or formula.)

(c) How much tax would be paid on the interest income? Assume a combined federal and provincial marginal income tax rate of 40 percent.

(d) Subtract the income tax from the GIC income to find the after-tax return. Compare this with the cost of borrowing.

(e) Look at this situation in another way. Suppose that you had bought the car for cash, and then had invested $255 a month for 48 months. How much would this amount to in four years? To find the answer use the formula for the future value of a uniform series of deposits, but adapt it for semi-annual compounding by using an interest rate of 4.5 percent and change $n = 4$ to $n = 8$ to reflect the eight compounding periods.

REFERENCES

Books

Canadian Commercial Law Guide. Don Mills, Ontario: CCH Canadian, Topic Law Reports. Subscription service in two volumes on federal and provincial law regarding the sale of personal property and consumer protection.

DYMOND, MARY JOY. *The Canadian Woman's Legal Guide.* Toronto: Doubleday, 1987, 449 pp. Includes a section on women and credit.

FORMAN, NORM. *Mind Over Money, Curing Your Financial Headaches with Moneysanity.* Toronto: Doubleday Canada, 1987, 248 pp. A psychologist examines the effects money has on behaviour, looking at the origin of money problems and suggesting therapies to help us to better understand ourselves.

PARKER, ALLAN A. *Credit, Debt, and Bankruptcy.* Seventh Edition. Vancouver: International Self-Counsel Press, 1988, 109 pp. A handbook on Canadian credit law for credit users.

Articles and Reports

Charge It, Credit Cards and the Canadian Consumer. Ottawa: Consumer and Corporate Affairs Canada, 1989, 53 pp. Minutes and proceedings of a House of Commons Committee that reviewed the background to the problems with credit card costs, the extent of market competition, current disclosure practices, and made proposals for legislation. Data in appendix.

Credit Card Costs. Ottawa: Consumer and Corporate Affairs Canada, three times a year, 5 pp. Lists fees, interest rates, grace periods, and date from which interest is calculated by name of creditor. Free copy on request.

Credit Cards in Canada. Ottawa: Queen's Printer, 1987, 58 pp. Minutes and proceedings of a House of Commons Committee that examined credit card operations in Canada (including pricing, calculation of interest charges, disclosure requirements, and competition) and made recommendations.

Discussion Paper on Credit Card Interest Charges. Ottawa: Consumer and Corporate Affairs Canada, 1988, 24 pp. An analysis of the pricing of credit cards that examined how interest is calculated and recommended more standardization.

STEVENSON, DEREK. "Playing Your Cards Right." *Canadian Consumer*, 19 (No. 10) 1989, pp.8-16. Explains the complexities of selecting credit cards and how the various charges are calculated.

Periodical

Canadian Consumer. Monthly. Box 9300, Ottawa, Ontario, K1G 3T9. In recent years, the personal finance articles have been concentrated in the November issue, "Personal Money Guide."

15 HOME MORTGAGES

1. To explain why opportunity cost and non-money income are considerations when deciding to buy a house.

2. To distinguish between:
   (a) mortgagor and mortgagee,
   (b) chattel mortgage and real estate mortgage,
   (c) term and amortization period,
   (d) first and second mortgages (consider risk, interest rate, and term from both the lender's and the borrower's perspectives),
   (e) mortgage insurance and mortgage life insurance,
   (f) lending value and purchasing price,
   (g) repayment and prepayment,
   (h) open and closed mortgages.

3. To explain the processes used by lenders in determining whether a potential borrower qualifies for a loan.

4. To calculate the size of loan for which an applicant is eligible, given income, debts, and the taxes on the prospective property.

5. To distinguish between these methods of repayment:
   (a) equal instalments of principal,
   (b) blended payments.

6. To calculate the interest and principal components in a mortgage payment.

7. To explain the effect of each of the following variables on the total cost of a house:
   (a) interest rate,
   (b) amortization period,
   (c) frequency of compounding interest,
   (d) size of down payment.

8. To explain the differences between a conventional mortgage and an insured mortgage regarding:
   (a) down payment,
   (b) special costs,
   (c) constraints on the borrower.

9. To explain how private lenders relate to the National Housing Act and the Canada Mortgage and Housing Corporation in the provision of home mortgages.

10. To compare the costs and benefits of alternative ways of obtaining mortgage funds, including private sources, a vendor-take-back, assuming an existing mortgage, and using a mortgage broker.

11. To identify costs associated with a house purchase (other than the down payment and the monthly mortgage payments).

12. To identify the following components in a mortgage contract:
   (a) description of the property,
   (b) identification of the parties,
   (c) the covenants,
   (d) repayment terms, including prepayment restrictions.

13. To explain how a reverse income mortgage may be used to turn a non-liquid asset into an income stream.

14. To explain these terms: gross debt service, total debt service, closing costs, closing date, appraisal, foreclosure, discharge of mortgage, interest bonus or penalty, prepayment privilege, capital gain, commitment period, equity, maturity date, amortize, mortgage broker, equity of redemption, high ratio mortgage, non-money income, pre-approved mortgage, interest adjustment date, variable rate mortgage.

Introduction

This chapter explains the basic process of using credit to buy personal real estate; it is not about how to choose a house, but rather about how to understand mortgages. There is, of course, much more to buying a house than the financing and many books have been written on whether to buy or rent, and how to select a house. Such issues are important but are beyond the scope of this book, which focuses on financial issues, rather than all aspects of consumer decision making.

Sometimes prospective buyers are so enthusiastic about the new house that they leave all the financial arrangements to the real estate agent. Perhaps they feel overwhelmed by the terminology and mathematics that seem to be associated with mortgages. After studying this chapter, it should be possible to talk intelligently with mortgage officers, ask knowledgeable questions, and do some comparison shopping.

The Economics of Home Ownership

To Buy or Rent

For most families, the decision whether to buy or rent is not strictly an economic one, but a choice between two different lifestyles. However, the economics of this question involve consideration of the *opportunity costs* of ownership as well as any differences in regular monthly expenditures. A decision to buy a house means tying up funds that otherwise could have been invested in an income-producing asset. To find the opportunity cost of buying a house, estimate how much interest has been given up by not investing the money at current interest rates and leaving it to compound over future years.

The house you live in does not usually yield money income but provides services or *non-money income* in the form of shelter. In addition to a stream of non-money income, home ownership has the potential for capital gain. When a house is sold for more than it cost, the difference is called *capital gain*. In times of rising prices, houses may be appreciating in value faster than they are wearing out, thus creating a potential capital gain.

Finally, consider the income-tax implications of buying a house. If savings are invested in a house, there will be no income tax to pay on any capital gain that may occur, because capital gain on a principal residence is not subject to income tax. If, instead, funds are invested in deposits, bonds, or stocks, the income will be taxable.

How Much to Spend

Assuming that the decision had been made to buy a house, how much should be spent on it? Sometimes financial advisers suggest that a house should not cost more than two or three times one's annual salary, but these guidelines are much too imprecise to be helpful. The rules do not specify gross income or take-home pay, and the difference can be quite significant. Families live so differently and have such varied financial goals that general rules are often not applicable. It is preferable to work out the details based on consideration of each unique situation.

To start, determine how much of your savings can be spared for a down payment. Add to this the amount that can be borrowed to get an approximation of the purchase price that can be afforded. The next step is to find out what all the costs would be on a monthly basis.

HOW MUCH CAN THEY AFFORD?

The Martens decided that they could afford a down payment of $12 000 on a house. Their banker agreed to lend them $88 000 at 10 percent, amortized over 25 years. They found their expenses for a $100 000 house might be as follows:

	Per month
Mortgage payment	$787.00
Taxes	92.00
Insurance	20.00
Utilities	125.00
Maintenance and repairs (annually 2% value of house)	167.00
Total	$1191.00
Interest foregone on $12 000 @ 9.5% annually	95.00
Grand Total	$1286.00

The Martens must now examine their income and expenditures to determine if they can afford $1286 a month for housing. If they are paying $900 a month for rent at present, the opportunity cost of buying a home is about $389 a month or $4668 a year.

FINANCING A HOME

Most buyers of homes or other real estate will probably need credit to finance the purchase, but because the loan is likely to be large and the term long, they will find the borrowing process somewhat more complex than the usual personal loan. To obtain such a large loan they must pledge security of some significance, usually the property being purchased.

When real estate (immovable property) is used to secure a loan, the borrower signs a contract called a *mortgage*, distinguished from a chattel mortgage, which is used for movable goods. The mortgage contract refers to the borrower as the *mortgagor* because this person is giving the mortgage to the lender, who in turn becomes the *mortgagee*, or the one who receives the mortgage as security for the loan. The alternative terms, chargor and chargee, are used sometimes.

MORTGAGE DEBT   Most of the total debt of households is mortgage debt, although the pattern varies somewhat with income level (Figure 15.1). Single

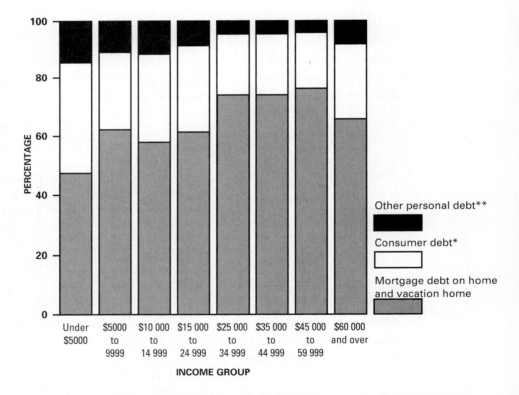

Figure 15.1   PERCENTAGE COMPOSITION OF TOTAL DEBT OF CANADIAN FAMILIES BY INCOME GROUPS, SPRING 1984

Source: *The Distribution of Wealth in Canada, 1984*, Ottawa: Statistics Canada, 1986, Table 24, page 65. (Catalogue No. 13-580). Reproduced and edited with the permission of the Minister of Supply and Services Canada.

individuals, who are less likely to be homeowners, are not included in this graph. Each bar, which represents the average total debt of households in one income class, shows how the total is divided between consumer and mortgage debt. It is perhaps not surprising to find that, regardless of income level, mortgage debt represents the largest component of total family debt. There appears to be a tendency for mortgage debt to represent a larger proportion of total debt among higher income households, which can afford more expensive houses and may also have vacation homes.

EQUITY IN REAL ESTATE

Equity refers to the value that the owner has in a property, and can be estimated by subtracting the outstanding debt on the property from a fair market price. If house prices fall, equity falls too, as people living in areas that have experienced severe economic down-turns have discovered.

HOW MUCH EQUITY?

Jim and Marie bought a $105 000 house with a down payment of $20 000 and a mortgage of $85 000. Initially they had an equity of $20 000, but a year later similar houses were selling for $115 000.

If they were to sell they would have about $30 000 left after discharging the mortgage, assuming that the small amount they had repaid on the principal during the first year would probably not cover the costs of the sale. Because of price increases their equity increased by $10 000 in one year. As they reduce this mortgage, their equity will also increase.

TYPES OF MORTGAGES

SECURITY FOR THE LENDER

Mortgage money may be obtained privately or from financial institutions such as banks, trust companies, and credit unions. As a mortgage is a large loan, the lender must have assurance that it is a sound investment. To protect the lender, the mortgagor must make a sizeable down payment or have the mortgage insured. When the down payment is less than 25 percent of the value of the property, the buyer's equity might not be enough to cover costs if, in the case of default, the lender had to take back the property and sell it. When the buyer cannot provide a downpayment of at least 25 percent of the property's value, the mortgagee will not offer a loan without mortgage insurance.

Mortgage insurance covers the risk to the lender that the borrower will default on the loan. The two institutions that insure mortgages are: Canada Mortgage and Housing Corporation (a Crown corporation) and Mortgage Insurance Company of Canada. These insurers reimburse the lender for loss in cases of default but, correspondingly, they impose a number of restrictions on the granting of the mortgage, as will be explained later. First, the differences between conventional mortgages and insured mortgages will be examined.

CONVENTIONAL MORTGAGES

A *conventional mortgage* is not usually insured, but the down payment is at least 25 percent of the value of the property. A number of financial institutions, notably trust and mortgage companies, offer conventional mortgages. Privately arranged mortgages are always conventional mortgages, in that they are not insured. However, the down payment can be whatever the parties involved agree on.

INSURED MORTGAGES

At one time, all mortgages were conventional mortgages, but in 1954 the federal government established a system to guarantee mortgage loans made by approved financial lenders as a means of increasing the mortgage money available to home buyers and builders. The legislation is the *National Housing Act*, and the Crown corporation that administers it is the Canada Mortgage and Housing Corporation, usually known as CMHC. A lender making a mortgage loan approved by CMHC or the Mortgage Insurance Company of Canada (MICC) can extend a mortgage that is more than 75 percent of the value of the property. These *insured mortgages* permit the buyer to obtain a mortgage with less than 25 percent of the value of the property as a down payment.

The buyer pays an insurance fee, from 1 percent to 3 percent of the total loan, which is added to the principal at the outset. The lender collects the mortgage insurance premium and forwards it to the insurer—CMHC or MICC. This insurance, which protects the lender in case of default, may not seem to offer much benefit to the borrower. However, without it, mortgages with low down payments would not be available at all. These mortgages, which represent a high proportion of the value cost of the house, are sometimes referred to as *high ratio loans*.

FINDING A MORTGAGE

When a mortgage is needed, there are a number of ways to obtain one. It may be possible to arrange a private mortgage with a relative or other individual who has money to lend. In this case, a lawyer would draw up a contract stating the terms agreeable to both borrower and lender. Most mortgages, however, are obtained from financial institutions: banks, trust companies, and credit unions.

In some cases, it is possible to arrange a *vendor take-back* mortgage for all or part of the required financing, which means that the seller lends part of the selling price to the buyer. Perhaps the buyer has found a desirable house and the vendor offers to sell it for $90 000, with the arrangement that the buyer pay $25 000 on closing and the rest in monthly instalments. Since the vendor is providing the loan of $65 000, it is called a vendor take-back mortgage. Often, this takes the form of a second mortgage.

ASSUMPTION OF EXISTING MORTGAGE

At times it may be advantageous to take over a mortgage already existing on the property. If the vendor has a mortgage with four more years remaining in the term and with an interest rate lower than could be obtained for a new mortgage, the buyer may wish to take over the vendor's mortgage. Investigate whether the mortgagee's approval would be required for such a transfer and if it may be obtained. Mortgage contracts vary in this regard. If an existing mortgage is assumed, the buyer would take the place of the original mortgagor regarding the agreements in the mortgage contract, but, in case of default, the original borrower may still be bound by the personal covenant, which is the promise to repay the debt. In practice, when the purchaser has been approved to assume the existing mortgage, the vendor often obtains a written release of this covenant from the lender as protection from this contingency.

MORTGAGE BROKERS

Mortgage brokers specialize in making contact between those who have funds to invest in mortgages and those who need a mortgage. The rates charged for arranging a mortgage vary, depending on the amount of work involved, but are payable by the borrower at the time of closing. As with any mortgage, the property in question has to be satisfactory to the lender. A borrower might need the services of a broker because of his or her poor credit rating, previous bankruptcy, very short employment history, or seasonally fluctuating income. Sometimes, home buyers will ask a broker to find them a mortgage, because they do not qualify at the local bank or trust company.

Qualifying for a Mortgage

The rules and procedures that govern the mortgage-granting process originate from three sources: (i) legislation, both federal and provincial, (ii) insurers' requirements for high ratio mortgages, and (iii) the policies of each financial institution. Essentially, the criteria for determining whether or not to grant a mortgage relate to: (i) the quality of the property as security, and (ii) the creditworthiness of the borrower.

The Property

Before agreeing to arrange a mortgage on a property, a lender will have it appraised to determine its *lending value*, that is, the value the lender's appraiser assigns the property, which is not necessarily the same as the selling price. It is conceivable that a buyer may be prepared to pay $150 000 for a much-desired property that the lender considers to be worth $143 000. In such a case, the mortgage loan is based on the lending value, not the selling price.

CMHC has rules, that vary from time to time and from place to place, relating to the proportion of the lending value that may be lent for an insured mortgage. For example, CMHC insured loans could be as large as 90 percent of the first $80 000 of the lending value, plus 80 percent of the remainder.

The Borrower

A potential lender will want a full report on the buyer's credit history as well as complete details about income, assets, and debts. The applicant will be asked to provide statements from an employer verifying current income, from a banker about funds available for a down payment, and from employers about employment history of the applicant and spouse.

From these facts the lender will calculate two ratios to determine capacity to handle the proposed mortgage: the gross debt service and total debt service. The first, *gross debt service*, is the percentage of annual gross income needed to cover the mortgage payments plus municipal taxes. If a condominium is to be purchased, 50 percent of the condominium fee is usually included in the calculation. Lenders have guidelines, changed from time to time, about the maximum gross debt service that is acceptable to them; it may range from 25-32 percent.

A quick way to determine the maximum that can be afforded is to find 30 percent (or whatever the ratio is) of gross annual income, subtract the estimated annual property taxes, and divide by 12. The resulting amount is the monthly payment one can presumably afford for principal and interest. The size of the loan can be found from an amortization table if you know the current mortgage interest rate and the desired amortization period.

GROSS DEBT SERVICE

The Rinaldis have a family income of $56 900 from the husband's salary; the wife is not employed. The property taxes on the house they want to buy are about $1200 a year. If they obtain a mortgage of $92 000, 11.5 percent amortized for 25 years, the monthly payment will be $918.16. How much is their gross debt service?

$$\text{Gross debt service} = \frac{(\text{payment/mo.} \times 12) + \text{taxes/yr.}}{\text{gross annual income}} \times 100$$

$$= \frac{(918.16 \times 12) + 1200}{56\ 900} \times 100$$

$$= \frac{11\ 017.92 + 1200}{56\ 900} \times 100$$

$$= \frac{12\ 217.92}{56\ 900} \times 100$$

$$= 21.47\%$$

Another measure of capacity to handle a mortgage is *total debt service*, the percentage of annual income needed to cover mortgage payments, taxes, and consumer debt payments. This should not exceed 37-38 percent, or 40 percent if heating costs are included. Lenders may use this rule for any type of mortgage, conventional or insured.

A third requirement is that the buyer have enough personal funds to make a down payment that is some minimum proportion of the selling price. For a conventional mortgage this would be 25 percent, for a high ratio mortgage it might be as low as 10 percent. If the total available for a down payment combined with the maximum mortgage is less than the price of the house, a second mortgage might be a consideration. The cost of servicing the second mortgage would have to be included in the gross and total debt service ratios. In qualifying purchasers for a mortgage, some conservative lenders may wish to satisfy themselves that the down payment is actually from the borrower's own resources and not a gift or undisclosed loan. To this end, the lender may require evidence of the source of the funds, such as the history of a savings account.

TOTAL DEBT SERVICE

The Rinaldis owe $9200 in consumer debts, which they are repaying at the rate of $3600 a year. What is their total debt service? (All the figures below are *annual.*)

$$\text{Total debt service} = \frac{\text{payments} + \text{taxes} + \text{consumer debt}}{\text{gross annual income}} \times 100$$

$$= \frac{11\ 017.92 + 1200 + 3600}{56\ 900} \times 100$$

$$= \frac{15\ 817.92}{56\ 900} \times 100$$

$$= 27.8\%$$

Since their total debt service is well below the 38% guideline of the lending institution, the Rinaldis are interested in knowing the largest mortgage they would be eligible for with a 25-year amortization.

$$\frac{\text{Payments} + \text{taxes} + \text{consumer debt}}{\text{gross annual income}} \times 100 = \frac{\text{total debt service}}{\text{(TDS)}}$$

Transposing the equation:

$$\text{Payments} + (\text{taxes} + \text{consumer debt}) = \frac{\text{TDS} \times \text{gross income}}{100}$$

$$\text{Payments} = \left(\frac{\text{TDS} \times \text{gross income}}{100}\right) - (\text{taxes} + \text{consumer debt})$$

$$= \left(\frac{38 \times 56\ 900}{100}\right) - (1200 + 3600)$$

$$= 21\ 622 - 4800$$

$$= \$16\ 822.00 \text{ per year} (\$1401.83 \text{ a month})$$

Looking at Table 15.3, the monthly payment per $1000 for a mortgage at 11.5% for 25 years is $9.98.

$$\text{Maximum mortgage} = \frac{1401.83}{9.98} \times 1000$$

$$= \$140\ 463.93$$

Based on their total debt service, the Rinaldis would be eligible for a maximum mortgage of $140 463.93, providing the property qualifies.

The Mortgage Contract

Equity of Redemption

In the mortgage document, the mortgagor agrees to transfer the ownership of the property to the mortgagee (a financial institution or an individual lender) as security for the loan until such time as it is repaid. The mortgagor will receive a copy of the signed mortgage and the mortgagee will retain the original. The mortgage leaves the mortgagor with an interest in the property, called the *equity of redemption*, which is the right to redeem the property and have the ownership transferred back when the mortgage is discharged. It states that the mortgagor will retain possession of the property and may enjoy the use of it, but must take good care of it and keep it insured, with the mortgagee as joint beneficiary of the insurance policy. If there is a fire while the mortgage is outstanding, the insurance money would be paid to the mortgagee, who can decide what to do about the repairs.

The Contract

The essential features of a mortgage are: (i) a description of the property; (ii) identification of the mortgagor and mortgagee; (iii) the amount of the mortgage with terms of repayment; (iv) an agreement that the mortgagor will give a charge on the property to the mortgagee, but will keep the right of possession and the right to redeem the property when the mortgage is discharged; and (v) certain promises or covenants.

Sample Mortgage Contract

A sample mortgage contract is reproduced in the Appendix (Figure 15.2). This lender gives the borrower a legal mortgage contract as well as a version written in plain English. The legal version is not reproduced in this book. This contract uses the alternative terms, chargee and chargor, instead of mortgagee and mortgagor.

Mortgage Covenants

Apart from the main contract, every mortgage contains a number of *covenants*, or promises made by the borrower or mortgagor, which are binding. Particularly important is the personal covenant, which is the mortgagor's promise to pay principal and interest. It is called a personal covenant because the mortgagee can sue the mortgagor personally to obtain repayment in full or those payments that are in arrears. The mortgagee can take a number of other actions to recover the loan, as will be mentioned later.

TAXES   Other covenants bind the mortgagor to pay the taxes, to insure the property, and to maintain it in good repair. It is important that taxes be paid on time, because taxes are a prior claim on property, taking precedence over a first mortgage. If taxes are allowed to fall into arrears the mortgagee's security may be impaired, as in the case of a property being sold for taxes. Some lenders require that the mortgagor pay one-twelfth of the annual taxes with each monthly mortgage payment, in order to build up a fund to pay the taxes when they become due. This saves the mortgagee the annual bother of finding out if the taxes have been paid. Interest on this tax fund may be credited to the mortgagor or it may not, depending on the agreement. Penalties for inadvertent late payment of taxes by the lender are usually debited to the borrower's account.

PROPERTY INSURANCE   Before mortgage money is advanced, the mortgagor may be required to insure the property against fire and other possible risks, and to have the policy made in favour of the mortgagee. The insurance policy will be endorsed to ensure that the mortgagee's interest in the property is known to the insurer.

FIRST AND SECOND MORTGAGES

A particular property may have more than one mortgage on it, which will be ranked as first, second, etc., according to the order in which they were recorded at the local Registry Office. The distinguishing characteristic between *first* and *second mortgages* is simply the order in which they were registered against the property. If the first mortgage on a property is discharged, the second mortgage would then automatically become the first mortgage. This does not happen often, because first mortgages are usually for larger sums and longer terms than second mortgages.

In the event that the buyer defaults on the mortgage payments and the property must be taken back and sold, the holder of the first mortgage would have first claim on the proceeds from the sale. After this has been paid, the second mortgagee's claims would be settled. If there were insufficient funds to pay all claims, the second mortgagee might have to accept a loss. This is the reason that second mortgages are considered to be higher risks than first mortgages, and consequently carry higher interest rates.

The exchanges involved when using real property as security for loans are summarized in Figure 15.3. The purchaser briefly acquires title to and possession of the property, but on giving the first mortgage, legal title is surrendered to the first mortgagee; the mortgagor retains the equity of redemption. Should the mortgagor give a second mortgage on this property, the equity of redemption would be transferred to the second mortgagee as security.

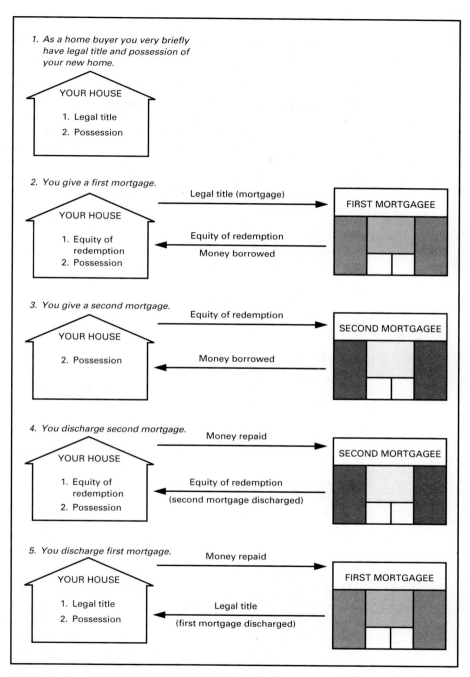

1. As a home buyer you very briefly have legal title and possession of your new home.

YOUR HOUSE
1. Legal title
2. Possession

2. You give a first mortgage.

YOUR HOUSE
1. Equity of redemption
2. Possession

Legal title (mortgage) →
← Equity of redemption
Money borrowed

FIRST MORTGAGEE

3. You give a second mortgage.

YOUR HOUSE
2. Possession

Equity of redemption →
← Money borrowed

SECOND MORTGAGEE

4. You discharge second mortgage.

YOUR HOUSE
1. Equity of redemption
2. Possession

Money repaid →
← Equity of redemption
(second mortgage discharged)

SECOND MORTGAGEE

5. You discharge first mortgage.

YOUR HOUSE
1. Legal title
2. Possession

Money repaid →
← Legal title
(first mortgage discharged)

FIRST MORTGAGEE

Figure 15.3   EXCHANGES WHEN REAL PROPERTY IS SECURITY FOR LOAN

Sale of Mortgages

A person or institution who holds a mortgage (mortgagee) may decide that they would prefer to have the cash at once instead of receiving a monthly income stream for the term of the mortgage. They can sell the mortgage without asking the mortgagor's permission, although they would be informed. Mortgages may be sold at their face value, or for more or less (at a premium or at a discount) depending on interest rates at the time. Refer to Chapter 10, Debt Securities, to review how changing interest rates affect the price of a security. For the mortgagor, one of the risks of assuming a vendor-take-back mortgage is that the vendor may sell the mortgage and the mortgagor has to deal with another person or institution. This is the principal reason why all of the terms of the loan should be written into the mortgage document, especially any terms favourable to the mortgagor.

Breach of Mortgage Contract

If the mortgagor fails to carry out any of the promises agreed to in the mortgage contract, this failure will be considered a default and he or she may be subject to a variety of penalties. The mortgage contract stipulates that the mortgagor must: (i) make payments on time, (ii) pay the taxes, (iii) keep the property insured, (iv) keep the property in good condition, and (v) not sell the property without the mortgagee's written approval.

Anyone who finds it impossible to make a payment on time should immediately contact the mortgagee to search for a solution to the problem before it gets worse. The mortgagor is usually liable for late interest charges which would be added to the outstanding principal and thus cause interest to be paid on interest. A mortgagee has a number of options to force a defaulting mortgagor to pay, which may include taking possession of the property, suing the borrower under the personal covenant, exercising the acceleration clause, selling the property, and foreclosure. Before any of these actions begin, the mortgagor would receive notice of the mortgagee's intentions and have an opportunity to take some preventative steps if desired. The details of procedures that follow default are explained in several of the references listed at the end of this chapter, but will not be discussed here.

Discharge of Mortgages

When a mortgage has been repaid in full, steps are taken to obtain a legal *discharge of the mortgage* and transfer of the property ownership back to the mortgagor. Either the mortgagor or the lawyer will take a signed statement, which indicates that the debt has been paid, from the mortgagee to the local land registry office. For a small fee the claim against the property will be removed and the title cleared.

METHODS OF REPAYMENT

TERM AND AMORTIZATION PERIOD

Repayment of a mortgage is a long-term process that may take up to 25 or 30 years. The time it takes to completely repay a mortgage, established when the mortgage is arranged, is called the *amortization period*. Although it has not always been so, nowadays the term is usually much shorter than the amortization period. The length of time before the lender can demand repayment of all the outstanding principal is the *mortgage term*. In most cases, the interest rate and monthly payments are fixed for the term. Recently mortgage terms have been as short as six months or as long as seven years. At the end of the term, or at the *maturity date*, the lender can demand full payment for all the outstanding balance, but usually will offer to renew the mortgage at the prevailing rate. There have been times in the past when the term and amortization period were the same, but in recent years the high variability in interest rates made it impossible for lenders to offer mortgages with interest rates fixed for 20 to 25 years.

SHORT TERM, LONG AMORTIZATION

When Tom and Sandra were buying a house, they were told that the mortgage would be amortized over 25 years, but that the term would be five years. That meant that the monthly payments were worked out so that, at current interest rates, the mortgage would be completely repaid in 25 years.

Since the lender did not want to be committed to a fixed interest rate for the next 25 years, when rates might move in any direction, the mortgage contract had a term of five years. During the term, the interest rate and monthly payments would be fixed; at the end of the term, or maturity, the contract would terminate, and all of the outstanding balance would become due. This is an opportunity for Tom and Sandra to reduce their principal as much as desired, without penalty.

Unless they could discharge the entire mortgage, they would have to renegotiate their mortgage at the prevailing interest rates. Their monthly payments could be adjusted at this time.

Table 15.1 MORTGAGE REPAYMENT SCHEDULE, EQUAL INSTALMENTS OF PRINCIPAL

Principal	$80 000
Term	20 years
Interest	10% annually on outstanding balance
Annual payment	$4000 plus interest

Payment number	Payment to consist of		Total payment	Balance outstanding
	principal	interest		
1	$4 000	$8 000	$12 000	$76 000
2	4 000	7 600	11 600	72 000
3	4 000	7 200	11 200	68 000
4	4 000	6 800	10 800	64 000
5	4 000	6 400	10 400	60 000
6	4 000	6 000	10 000	56 000
7	4 000	5 600	9 600	52 000
8	4 000	5 200	9 200	48 000
19	4 000	800	4 800	4 000
20	4 000	400	4 400	nil

Total interest paid in 20 years = $84 000

Table 15.2 PORTION OF MORTGAGE REPAYMENT SCHEDULE, EQUAL BLENDED PAYMENTS

Principal	$50 000
Interest	11% compounded semi-annually
Amortization	25 years
Payments	monthly

Payment number	Monthly payment	Payment to consist of		Balance outstanding
		Principal	Interest	
First year				
1	481.26	33.09	448.17	49 966.91
6	481.26	34.60	446.66	49 796.96
12	481.26	36.50	444.76	49 582.74
Final year				
230	481.26	255.37	225.89	24 946.04
240	481.26	279.21	202.05	22 263.00
300	481.26	476.92	4.34	6.93

Mortgage loans may be repaid in a number of ways as long as an agreement can be reached between the mortgagor and the mortgagee. Since it is not practicable for most people to repay an entire mortgage with interest in a lump sum, most mortgages are *amortized*, that is, the debt is extinguished by regular payments of interest and principal.

Two methods of repayment will be explained in this chapter: (i) equal instalments of principal, and (ii) blended payments. The difference between them, which is in the proportions of interest and principal in each payment, is illustrated in Figure 15.4. Each horizontal bar represents one payment and the way it is divided between principal and interest. These diagrams show the proportions in a general way; an exact plot of blended payments would result in a curved line rather than a straight one dividing interest and principal. As will be explained below, if a mortgage is repaid with equal instalments of principal, the amount of interest owing declines, making succeeding payments smaller. By contrast, if all payments are to be level, as in blended payments, the proportions of interest and principal must vary over the repayment period.

EQUAL INSTALMENTS OF PRINCIPAL

In this repayment schedule, the principal is repaid at a constant rate but each consecutive payment becomes smaller because, as the principal owing is reduced, the interest due also decreases (Table 15.1 and Figure 15.4). This arrangement is used for various payment intervals—for instance, annually, semi-annually, or quarterly—but seldom monthly.

EQUAL BLENDED PAYMENTS

Repayment of a loan in equal instalments of principal, as described above, is quite easy to understand but is not a widely used method because of the very large, unequal payments. Most people prefer to repay loans with smaller and more frequent level payments that fit more easily into their budgets. To accomplish this, the arithmetic becomes somewhat complicated. Essentially, each payment will include one month's interest on the total outstanding balance, with the remainder of the payment used to reduce the principal. As the principal owing slowly drops each month, the interest component declines. This allows more of each payment to be used to reduce the principal, as is illustrated in Figure 15.4 and Table 15.2.

CALCULATING THE REPAYMENT SCHEDULE FOR EQUAL BLENDED PAYMENTS   The procedure for calculating the repayment schedule for mortgages is identical to that used for instalment loans as described in Chapter 8. (Refer to Table 15.4 in the Appendix for a complete mortgage schedule.) The steps in calculating interest and principal components in each payment are reviewed in the example "Calculations for Blended Payments."

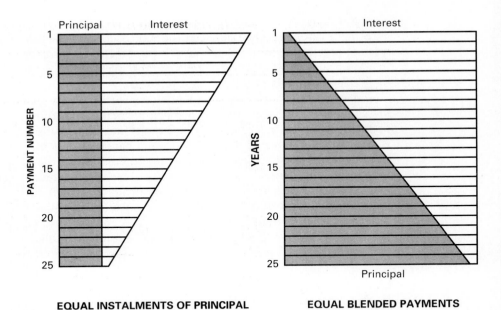

Principal Interest

Interest

PAYMENT NUMBER

YEARS

Principal

EQUAL INSTALMENTS OF PRINCIPAL   **EQUAL BLENDED PAYMENTS**

Figure 15.4   PROPORTIONS OF PRINCIPAL AND INTEREST PER PAYMENT,
EQUAL INSTALMENTS OF PRINCIPAL, AND EQUAL BLENDED
PAYMENTS

CALCULATIONS FOR BLENDED PAYMENTS

Mortgage terms:

Principal	$100 000
Interest rate	10.5%
Compounding	semi-annual
Amortization period	25 years
Term	5 years
Monthly payment	$929 (Table 15.3)
Interest factor	.008 564 5152 (Table 8.4)

Table 15.3   MONTHLY PAYMENTS REQUIRED TO AMORTIZE A $1000 LOAN, INTEREST COMPOUNDED SEMI-ANNUALLY

Nominal interest rate	Amortization period (years)						
%	5	10	15	20	25	30	35
	(dollars per thousand)						
9	20.68	12.58	10.05	8.90	8.25	7.93	7.72
9$^1/_4$	20.08	12.71	10.19	9.05	8.45	8.11	7.90
9$^1/_2$	20.92	12.84	10.34	9.21	8.62	8.28	8.08
9$^3/_4$	21.04	12.98	10.48	9.36	8.78	8.46	8.26
10	21.15	13.11	10.63	9.52	8.95	8.63	8.45
10$^1/_4$	21.27	13.24	10.77	9.68	9.12	8.81	8.63
10$^1/_2$	21.39	13.37	10.92	9.84	9.29	8.99	8.81
10$^3/_4$	21.51	13.51	11.07	10.00	9.46	9.17	9.00
11	21.63	13.64	11.22	10.16	9.63	9.34	9.18
11$^1/_4$	21.74	13.78	11.37	10.32	9.80	9.52	9.37
11$^1/_2$	21.86	13.91	11.52	10.49	9.98	9.71	9.56
11$^3/_4$	21.98	14.05	11.67	10.65	10.15	9.89	9.74
12	22.10	14.19	11.82	10.81	10.32	10.07	9.93
12$^1/_4$	22.22	14.32	11.97	10.98	10.50	10.25	10.12
12$^1/_2$	22.34	14.46	12.13	11.15	10.68	10.43	10.31
12$^3/_4$	22.46	14.60	12.28	11.31	10.85	10.62	10.50
13	22.59	14.74	12.44	11.48	11.03	10.80	10.69
13$^1/_4$	22.71	14.22	12.59	11.65	11.21	10.99	10.88
13$^1/_2$	22.83	15.02	12.75	11.82	11.39	11.17	11.07
13$^3/_4$	22.95	15.16	12.90	11.99	11.56	11.36	11.26

(a)   Amount of monthly payment:

Consult an amortization table (Table 15.3) to find the monthly payment for a loan of $1000, at 10.5%, for 25 years.

Monthly payment = 100 × 9.29
              = $929

(b)   Interest at end of first month:

Interest for   = outstanding × appropriate interest
one month   principal   factor (Table 8.4)

            = 100 000 × 0.008 564 5152
            = $856.45

(c)   Principal component of the first month's payment:

Repayment = monthly − interest for
of principal   payment   one month

$$= 929 - 856.45$$
$$= \$72.55$$

(d)   Principal outstanding after first payment:

Principal   = principal owing   − payment on
outstanding   before payment   principal

$$= 100\ 000 - 72.55$$
$$= \$99\ 927.45$$

(e)   Second month's interest:

Interest for = outstanding x appropriate interest
one month   principal   factor (Table 8.4)

$$= 99\ 927.45 \times 0.008\ 564\ 5152$$
$$= \$855.83$$

(f)   Mortgage schedule for the first six months:

Payment number	Date of payment	Total payment	Interest portion	Principal portion	Outstanding balance
1	June 1	$929	$856.45	$72.55	$99 927.45
2	July 1	929	855.83	73.17	99 854.28
3	August 1	929	855.20	73.80	99 780.48
4	September 1	929	854.57	74.43	99 706.05
5	October 1	929	853.93	75.07	99 630.98
6	November 1	929	853.29	75.71	99 555.27

RENEWING A MORTGAGE

If a mortgage has a term of five years and an amortization period of 25 years, every five years the contract will have to be renewed. At the maturity date, all the outstanding balance on the principal is due and must be repaid or renegotiated for a further term. At this time one can either: (i) renew with the same lender at the prevailing interest rate, or (ii) change lenders. If the second option is selected, there will be additional costs of a new appraisal and any other fees a new lender may levy. By changing lenders it may be possible to obtain a lower interest rate, but this should be weighed against the additional costs. A new mortgagee will often want an independent appraisal of the property, a check against the title for any other claims on it, and probably a credit check on the borrower. Currently, many lenders are offering low or no cost mortgage transfer promotions. Find out all of this information before making a decision to change lenders.

At the end of a term when the total outstanding balance becomes due, there is an opportunity to reduce the principal before renegotiating the mortgage. As illustrated in the examples included in this chapter, any reduction in principal will result in considerable interest savings over the long run.

PREPAYMENT OF PRINCIPAL

The difference between repayment and prepayment is that *repayment* means following the mortgage schedule in extinguishing the loan, while *prepayment* is a way to accelerate the reduction of the principal during the term. A mortgagor may wish to repay a mortgage faster than the original schedule, make lump sum payments to reduce the principal, or discharge the mortgage on selling the property, but the possibilities of doing so will be dependent on the terms established when the original mortgage contract was drawn up.

OPEN AND CLOSED MORTGAGES

There tends to be some confusion about open and closed mortgages because of the degrees of openness and the fact that few are completely closed. A *fully open mortgage* permits prepayments without restriction or penalty and the loan may be paid off completely at any time. A *totally closed mortgage*, on the other hand, permits no prepayments. In practice, most so-called closed mortgages permit some prepayments without penalty under certain conditions, and mortgages referred to as open may actually be only partially open. Some mortgage contracts permit limited amounts to be prepaid at specified times, while others are more liberal. In summary, prepayment may be totally unrestricted, or restricted in amount allowed, or in timing of the payment.

PREPAYMENT PENALTIES

When you make a prepayment, the lender may charge a fee that, depending on your perspective, is called a *prepayment penalty* or a bonus. Having to pay a penalty to make a prepayment of principal is not unusual and is based on the rationale that the mortgagee has invested money in this mortgage for a regular income and is inconvenienced by having to reinvest unexpected repayments. The penalty may be three months' interest. When interest rates are such that the lender must reinvest the prepaid money at a rate of interest less than the contract rate of the mortgage, the lender may charge an amount, additional to the prepayment penalty, representing the interest differential for the remainder of the term.

Since mortgage lenders change their policies about prepayment from time to time it is important that a borrower find out the prepayment opportunities being offered by competing lenders. Regardless of verbal representations made by the lending officer, a mortgage contract should be read carefully to find out exactly what the prepayment conditions are. There may be a requirement that the lender be given notice of the intention to repay and also paid a penalty.

When prepayments are made, it is common practice for the lender to make no change in the size of the monthly payments, thus shortening the time that the loan will be outstanding. The reduced amortization period will result in less total interest.

To calculate the savings in making a prepayment, it is necessary to use an amortization schedule, showing the principal and interest components of each payment (Table 15.4 in the Appendix). A prepayment eliminates a number of payments from the schedule, thus reducing both principal and interest for the mortgagor. Consequently, the mortgage will be repaid in less time than originally expected.

COSTS AND BENEFITS OF A PREPAYMENT

The Changs, who had a CMHC insured-mortgage for $50 000 at 11%, were in a position to repay an additional $7000 two years later. The mortgage stated that they could make a prepayment of 10% of the original loan at the end of the second year with three months' interest penalty. In their case, the maximum prepayment would be:

$$\text{Prepayment} = 50\ 000 \times .10$$
$$= \$5000$$

How much interest penalty (bonus) would they have to pay?

$$\text{Penalty} = 5000 \times \text{interest rate} \times 3/12$$
$$= 5000 \times .11 \times 3/12$$
$$= \$137.50$$

What are some of the costs and benefits of making this prepayment?

Costs: (a) penalty of $137.50.
      (b) interest foregone because the money they used for the down payment cannot be invested in an income-paying security.

Foregone interest:

Assuming that they could have invested the $5000 for 23 years (the time remaining in their amortization period) at an average rate of 7%, what is the opportunity cost of this prepayment?

$5000 invested at 7%, compounded annually for 23 years would grow to:

$$\text{Compound value} = 5000 \times 4.74 \text{ (Table 8.1)}$$
$$= \$23\ 700$$
$$\text{Interest} = 23\ 700 - 5000$$
$$= \$18\ 700$$

Assuming 30% average income tax rate:

$$\text{Income tax} = 18\ 700 \times .30$$
$$= \$5610$$

$$\text{After-tax income} = 18\ 700 - 5610$$
$$= \$13\ 090$$

$$\textbf{Total costs} = 137.50 + 13\ 090$$
$$= \$13\ 227.50$$

Benefits: (a) reduction in total interest
(b) reduction in time the loan will be outstanding

Reduction in interest:

Use the Chang's amortization schedule (Table 15.4 in the Appendix).
Balance outstanding after payment #24 = $49 118.33.
After prepayment:

$$\text{Outstanding balance} = 49\ 118.33 - 5000$$
$$= \$44\ 118.33$$

In the mortgage schedule, the outstanding balance after payment 106 is $44 185.90.

$$\begin{matrix} \text{Interest} \\ \text{saved} \end{matrix} = \begin{matrix} \text{accumulated interest} \\ \text{at payment \#106} \end{matrix} - \begin{matrix} \text{accumulated interest} \\ \text{at payment \#24} \end{matrix}$$

$$= \$45\ 198.75 \qquad - 10\ 668.57$$
$$= \$34\ 530.18$$

Reduction in time:

$$\text{Number of payments eliminated} = 106 - 24$$
$$= 82$$

Mortgage discharge is nearer by 82 divided by 12 months.
$$= 6 \text{ years, 10 months.}$$

TOTAL INTEREST

Not infrequently the total interest paid during the life of a mortgage greatly exceeds the purchase price of the house. For example, a mortgage of $80 000 at 10 percent for 25 years would result in total interest charges of $134 677. Consult the mortgage schedule in the Appendix to find out the total interest on that $50 000 loan. The three influential and interrelated factors affecting total interest are: (i) the principal, (ii) the interest rate, and (iii) the amortization period. If it is possible to reduce any of them, the total interest will be decreased. (You may wish to refer to Chapter 8 to review the method of calculating total interest.)

The first opportunity to reduce total interest is when the mortgage is being arranged. If you can lower the principal of the loan by making a larger down payment, you will pay less total interest (Figure 15.5). A second factor is the interest rate. If you can find a loan at a lower rate, that will be to your advantage. What appear to be quite small differences in interest rates can have a significant effect on the total interest. Using the example above, a 1/4 percent reduction in interest rate on the $80 000 loan would mean $4026 less in total interest. Finally, the shorter the amortization period, the less total interest, as illustrated in Figure 15.5; it is, of course, necessary to make larger monthly payments to accomplish this.

CLOSING COSTS

When a property is purchased, the agreement to purchase may be signed some time before the date for closing the deal. At the time of closing, the buyer must pay: (i) the seller for the property, (ii) the lawyer for services and disbursements, such as registration of the transaction at the registry office,

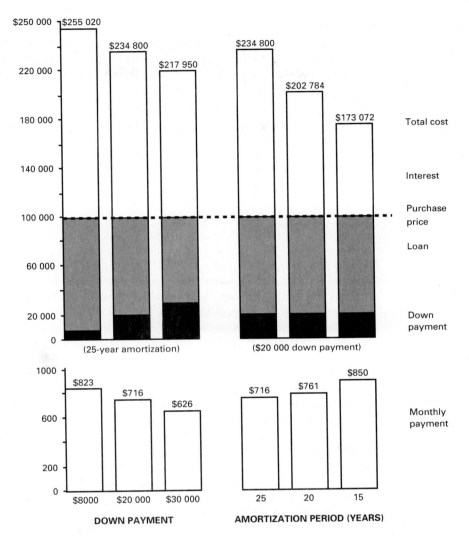

Figure 15.5   TOTAL COST OF A HOUSE, VARIOUS DOWN PAYMENTS AND
AMORTIZATION PERIODS (PURCHASE PRICE AND INTEREST
RATE HELD CONSTANT)

(iii) land transfer or property purchase tax, if applicable, and (iv) adjustment costs. With or without a mortgage, there will be closing costs when property is purchased.

STATEMENT OF ADJUSTMENTS

Before the closing date for the house purchase, the lawyer will send a *statement of adjustments*, which sets forth the accounts between buyer and seller relating to this sale. It may include such items as purchase price, deposit, property taxes, insurance, and fuel. Since the vendor has been paying property taxes and insurance, the buyer will have to reimburse the vendor for any prepaid taxes and insurance when ownership changes. For example, if a house was bought in June, the insurance may have been paid until September and the taxes until November. The buyer would pay three months' insurance and five months' taxes to the vendor. Sometimes there is fuel oil in the tank to be paid for. The new property must be insured against fire, as noted in the mortgage contract. At this stage, the buyer can decide whether to take over the vendor's property insurance policy, convert a previous policy to fit this new property, or take out a new one.

LEGAL FEES AND TAXES

The lawyer's bill usually includes fees for services and any expenditures made on the buyer's behalf, such as fees for title searches, registration of various documents, and any provincial taxes. The lawyer's fee is dependent on the complexity of the transaction and the local guidelines for fees.

Some provinces impose a land transfer or property-purchase tax on real property at the time of registration of the deed. In 1990, the Ontario land transfer tax rates were: $5 per $1000 of purchase price up to $55 000; $10 per $1000 up to $250 000; then $15 per $1000 from $250 001 to $400 000. In British Columbia, the property-purchase tax is one percent of the first $200 000 and two percent of the balance.

A copy of an up-to-date land survey is usually required by all lenders. It may be possible to obtain a copy of the survey from the vendor or the vendor's mortgagee at the time of the offer to purchase the property. Otherwise, the purchaser may be liable for significant surveyor fees in conjunction with placing a new mortgage on the property.

The goods and services tax is being applied to some purchases of property. This will be another closing cost to be considered.

LIFE INSURANCE AND MORTGAGES

If they so wish, home buyers may arrange a decreasing term life insurance policy with their own insurance company or with the lender to make provision for enough funds to discharge the mortgage in the event of their death. Initially, the life insurance policy will be for approximately the same amount as the mortgage loan, with periodic reductions in value to roughly correspond to the declining debt on the property. If the person whose life is insured should die before the mortgage is fully repaid, the beneficiary of the life insurance will have some funds to discharge the mortgage debt, but is not obligated to do so.

Some lenders, who have group policies covering the lives of a number of borrowers, offer mortgage life insurance as part of the mortgage package. If this coverage is selected, the survivors will not have any choice in the use of the insurance money since the policy is not a personal one. In such cases, the outstanding balance on the mortgage would be repaid by the insurer directly to the lender. If the income of the two persons purchasing a residence is required for debt servicing, it is important to determine whether the lives of both wage earners are covered. If not, additional private life insurance may be prudent. In any event, it is always wise to compare the cost of optional group life insurance offered by the mortgagee with similar coverages available in the market place.

This reducing term insurance is sometimes called *mortgage life insurance*, but it should not be confused with the mortgage insurance that lenders use to cover the risk of losing money if the borrower defaults. This latter type of insurance is mandatory for mortgages insured by CMHC or MICC.

MORTGAGE FEATURES AND OPTIONS

From the previous discussion of basic mortgage principles, one might think that choosing a mortgage would not be too difficult. However, keen competition among financial institutions has created a rapidly changing mortgage market in which we find little variation in interest rates among lenders but intense competition in a fascinating and often confusing array of mortgage features and options. Such policies of individual firms are readily changed, making it impossible to predict which special features or options will be available at any given time or place. However, a few will be outlined according to this classification: (i) pre-approval, (ii) interest rate adjustments, (iii) accelerated payment opportunities, and (iv) monthly payment adjustments.

PRE-APPROVED MORTGAGES

It is not unusual for home buyers to select a property, sign an offer to purchase conditional on obtaining financing, and then start looking for a mortgage. In the excitement of choosing a new house they have neglected to give as much attention to the financing as they did to finding the property. This method has two significant disadvantages: the buyers have to do their mortgage shopping under time pressure and they have made a commitment to a property before determining how large a loan they may qualify for.

Lenders are now offering *pre-approved* or *pre-arranged mortgages* which is tentative approval for a mortgage amount based on an assessment of the borrower, with final approval dependent on an appraisal of the property. By applying for a pre-arranged mortgage buyers can shop around for the best financing terms before making a commitment to a property, and at the same time find out how much lenders are willing to lend them. Armed with this knowledge, they will be in a position to make a more attractive offer on a property, one not conditional on obtaining financing, but rather only on a satisfactory appraisal.

With pre-approved mortgages, there is an opportunity to apply to several lenders, usually no fee for the assessment, and no obligation to deal with any particular institution. However, the guaranteed interest rate period may be quite short, perhaps from none to three months. The tendency of borrowers to accept the first institution's terms rather than comparison shop for a mortgage works very well for lenders trying to increase their market share, but not so well for borrowers. Applicants may feel so pleased to receive approval that they do not look any further.

MORTGAGE SHOPPING STRATEGY   A better strategy is to first make one's own estimate of how much debt can be handled, given current interest rates, then go to lenders to find out what terms and options are currently being offered. With this information, it is possible to decide which features are most important and to make a list of the most essential ones before making an application for a pre-approved mortgage from a lender who offers the best combination of the desired options.

INTEREST RATE ADJUSTMENTS

COMMITMENT PERIOD   After a mortgage is approved, there is usually a period of weeks or months before the closing date. The day when the purchase transaction is completed—the buyer pays the vendor and receives possession of the property—is known as the *closing date*. If interest rates are changing frequently, will the borrower be charged the rate prevailing at the time of approval or that at the closing date? A lender may make a commitment to an agreed-upon rate at the time of approval with the option that if rates drop in the interim, the mortgage rate will be reduced accordingly. Find out the lender's policy and how long their commitment period is.

INTEREST ADJUSTMENT DATE   Mortgage payments are usually made at the end of each month, "not in advance." That means if mortgage money was advanced on February 21 the first payment would be due a month later on March 21.

This would seem to be quite straightforward but some institutional lenders prefer to collect all mortgage payments on the first of each month. Since closing dates can be any business day, the lender solves this problem by collecting interest for the period from closing to the beginning of the next month. When lenders refer to the *interest adjustment date* they mean the day the mortgage starts.

AN UNEXPECTED COST

When Tony and Maria bought their first house they closed the deal on March 12, getting their mortgage from a firm that collected mortgage payments on the first of every month. Their mortgage adjustment date became April first, nineteen days later. They were surprised to find that their lender collected 19 days' interest on the whole mortgage ($80 000 × .13 × 19/365 = $541) at the time of closing. This amount was subtracted from the mortgage funds being advanced to them, forcing them to find the extra money to complete the house purchase. Later they discovered that some lenders calculate this interest with daily compounding, making an even higher interest payment. Their first regular mortgage payment will be made on May first, a month after the interest adjustment date.

VARIABLE RATE MORTGAGES   Variable or floating rate mortgages were devised in the early 1980s to reduce uncertainty for lenders in a period of rapidly changing interest rates. Financial institutions had difficulty matching the interest rates and maturities of the deposits they accepted with those of the mortgage funds they lent. With variable rate mortgages, lenders pass the risk of fluctuating rates on to the borrower who has the advantage of a fully open mortgage that can be discharged at any time. On this type of mortgage, the interest rate is adjusted frequently, usually monthly. A payment schedule, based on 20-year or 25-year amortization, is drawn up for a specified period, usually one year, during which the borrower is committed to regular payments of a predictable amount. The rate quoted on variable rate mortgages, which may be half a percent lower than for other types, may look especially attractive, but you should remember that the interest is compounded monthly rather than semi-annually.

While reducing uncertainty for lenders, variable rate mortgages can create problems for borrowers by making it difficult for them to accurately predict their future liabilities. If interest rates rise, a mortgagor could find that the fixed monthly payment is composed entirely of interest with no reduction in principal. It is conceivable that some payments would be insufficient to cover all the interest due, and that the balance of the interest owing could be added to the unpaid principal. In such a case, the home buyer would be increasing liabilities rather than assets.

In times of more stable interest rates, borrowers are less interested in variable rate mortgages. More recently lenders have offered a short term, fully open mortgage with the interest rate guaranteed for the period, for example six months.

ACCELERATED PAYMENT OPPORTUNITIES

Repayment of the principal may be accelerated by: (i) lump sum prepayments (as was discussed earlier), (ii) increases in monthly payments, or (iii) more frequent payments.

INCREASING MONTHLY PAYMENTS   Lenders may permit mortgagors to increase their monthly payments, once a year or on any payment date, by as little as 10 percent or as much as 100 percent.

WEEKLY PAYMENTS   Weekly or bi-weekly payment mortgages are a way of shortening the amortization period by making payments more frequently. If the usual monthly payment is divided by four and paid each week, the borrower will make 52 weekly payments in a year, instead of 12 monthly ones that are equivalent to 48 weekly ones. The effect of making four extra weekly payments each year will be a reduction in total interest and the time needed to repay the mortgage. The bi-weekly mortgage scheme is similar, except that payments are made fortnightly or 26 times a year, instead of the equivalent of 24.

The mortgagor should be aware of the method being used to calculate the payments. If the monthly payment is divided by 4 or 2 and paid weekly or bi-weekly, the mortgage will be reduced faster than by 12 monthly payments. However, if the annual amount of interest and principal is divided by 52 or 26 this will not happen.

MONTHLY OR WEEKLY PAYMENTS?

Mike plans to take out a $70 000 mortgage, but cannot decide what frequency of payment best suits him. He is aware that a monthly payment schedule is the most common one but would like to know what difference weekly payments would make. The mortgage officer gave Mike the following figures.

	Conventional amount paid monthly	Monthly amount paid in 52 weekly payments
Mortgage	$ 70 000	$ 70 000
Interest rate	10.5%	10.5%
Amortization	25 years	19.5 years
Payment	$ 649.84/mo.	$ 162.46/wk.
Payment/yr.	$7798.08	$8447.92
Total repaid	$194 952	$164 734
Total interest	$124 952	$ 94 734

When comparing these options, two points stood out. First, with weekly payments, the total interest charge would be less by over $36 000. Second, the rate of repayment would not be exactly the same. The weekly payment was arrived at by dividing the monthly payment by four, but since there are 52 weeks in a year, he would be making payments equivalent to 13 months. If he can handle the weekly payments he will extinguish his mortgage 5 1/2 years sooner. Mike decided he preferred a weekly payment plan.

COMPARISON SHOPPING FOR A MORTGAGE

When shopping for a mortgage, the following chart can be used to record the information gained from a number of lenders.

Item	Lender		
	1	2	3
Interest rates			
First mortgage			
Second mortgage			
Fixed for term or variable			
Frequency of payment			
(monthly, bi-weekly, weekly)			
Flexibility			
Charges			
Appraisal fee			
Application fee			
Qualification guidelines			
GDS			
TDS			
Prepayment privileges			
Amount			
Time			
Penalty			
Flexibility			
Renewal conditions			
Fee			
Time before maturity			

After a mortgage has been selected, it is important that the borrower insist that any special features be written in the mortgage contract.

REVERSE INCOME MORTGAGES

Most people spend years paying off their mortgage debt and are very relieved when it has been discharged, looking forward to living in a debt-free house in their retirement years. However, some find that in their old age they are short of income, but have a significant asset tied up in the house. There is a way to live in the house but also get some income from it—the *reverse income mortgage*. Essentially, a financial institution takes a claim on the property in return for monthly payments to the owners. Eventually, the debt must be paid, perhaps by selling the house after the death of the owners.

Several strategies have been used to implement reverse income mortgages in various countries. These are described in some of the references listed at the end of this chapter. In Canada there has not been much demand for such mortgages. For people who have saved for years to buy a house, the idea of re-mortgaging it, although rational, may not be appealing. Such an action would possibly be seen as a threat to financial security, since no one knows what his or her life span will be.

Summary

Although a mortgage is simply a large loan, secured by real property, the magnitude of the sum borrowed, the long repayment period and the nature of the security create considerable complexity. The most common way of repaying a mortgage is with a series of equal blended payments that have changing proportions of principal and interest. Mortgage financing involves four interrelated factors: principal, interest rate, amortization period, and monthly payment. Often the total interest paid over the life of the mortgage may be much greater than the price of the house, but it may be reduced by decreasing the principal, the interest rate, or the amortization period. The opportunity to do this, once the mortgage has been signed, depends on the rules of the lending institution. It is worthwhile to investigate the mortgage conditions offered by various institutions to find those best suited to your needs. Special attention should be given to prepayment privileges, payment frequency and renewal policies.

To safeguard their investment, mortgage lenders have regulations regarding down payments, insurance of the property, insurance against default, and prepayments. Conventional mortgages require larger down payments than high ratio loans. The mortgage document sets forth all the conditions and obligations of the borrower. First and second mortgages are distinguished by the order in which they were registered and the consequent risk. A new home buyer should be aware that the down payment and monthly payments do not represent all the costs to be covered; some funds must be reserved for a variety of closing and moving costs.

Problems

1. (a) Assume that you bought a house for $100 000 with a $20 000 down payment and $80 000 mortgage. Sometime later when you are considering selling the house, you have an unpaid balance on the mortgage of $23 500. How much would your equity be if you could sell it for $120 000?

(b) If you are making mortgage payments of $444 per month, do your payments add to your equity in the property? Explain.

(c) Does the down payment represent part of your equity in the property?

(d) Explain what has happened to Rick and Jean's equity in this situation. They paid $150 000 for a house in Vancouver when prices were very high, financed with a down payment of $30 000 and a mortgage for $120 000. Now that Rick has been moved to a job in Toronto, they must sell the house at a time when the outstanding balance on the mortgage is $110 000 and the best offer on the house is $98 000.

2. Refer to the mortgage contract signed by Jim and Petra Schwartz (Figure 15.2 in the Appendix).

(a) Who is the mortgagee (chargee) in this contract?

(b) How long is the term of this mortgage? What will happen at the maturity date?

(c) What are some property rights that the Schwartz family has given up for the duration of the mortgage?

(d) What is required of Jim and Petra by the insurance covenant?

(e) Six months after they gave this mortgage, they won $5000 in a lottery, which they would like to use to reduce their mortgage. When can they make a repayment? How much can it be? What will the penalty be?

(f) If Jim dies before the mortgage is discharged, and Petra does not have enough income to maintain the payments, will she lose her equity in the house?

3. (a) How much did Jim and Petra pay for mortgage insurance? If you can't find this figure in the contract, assume 2.5%.

(b) When is this mortgage insurance paid?

(c) What protection does this insurance offer the mortgagors?

(d) Did Jim and Petra have a choice about taking this insurance?

4. (a) Why would a person obtain a mortgage loan instead of a personal bank loan to buy a house?

(b) Would you expect a bank to charge a higher rate on a loan secured by a chattel mortgage than on one secured by a real estate mortgage? Why?

5. A mortgage officer suggested to Duncan, a prospective client, that he could save on legal fees by engaging the same lawyer to look after his interests in the transaction as the lending institution is employing to look after their interests. Would there be a possible conflict of interest involved here? What would you do?

6.

THEIR FIRST HOUSE

Beth and David finally located a house they really liked, with an asking price of $125 000, which seemed reasonable. They realized that the house would require redecorating as soon as possible in two downstairs rooms, and that they would have to buy major appliances. The taxes on the property had been $1150 the previous year. Their offer to purchase the house for $118 900 was conditional upon the arrangement of financing.

At the bank the mortgage officer inquired about the family income and how much money they could use as a down payment. David explained that his annual income was $56 900 and Beth's part-time earnings came to $12 500; their only debt was for their car, which cost $280 a month. They had accumulated $14 000 for a down payment. The mortgage officer calculated their gross debt service and their total debt service for a mortgage of $104 000 at 11%, amortized over 25 years, and suggested they apply for a CMHC-insured mortgage. They were told that the application would cost $100 and that an appraiser would be looking at the house they wanted to buy and would determine its lending value. The appraisal fee would be $150.

In a few days' time they learned that the house had a lending value of $116 000 and that they were eligible for a mortgage for $104 000.

(a) List the criteria that the lender would use to determine the eligibility of (i) Beth and David, and (ii) the property.
(b) Would this couple be eligible for a conventional mortgage?
(c) How much would the monthly payments be on this mortgage?
(d) Calculate the gross debt service and the total debt service.
(e) Work out the interest and principal components of the first payment.
(f) How much total interest will this couple pay over 25 years, assuming no change in interest rates and no prepayments?
(g) How much would the total interest be reduced if they could get a mortgage for 1/2% less?
(h) How much interest could they save if they amortized this mortgage over 20 years instead of 25?
(i) Use the chart below to estimate some of the costs (in addition to the down payment and mortgage) that David and Beth will probably encounter as they complete the purchase and move from their apartment. How much is the total?

SOME COSTS ASSOCIATED WITH HOME BUYING

The numbers used here are estimates; find out current costs.

		Totals
Mortgage Fees		
Appraisal fee	$ _____	
Mortgage insurance fee (added to mortgage; assume 2.5%)	$ _____	$ _____
Statement of Adjustments		
Tax adjustments (allow six months)	$ _____	
Fire insurance	$ __200.00__	
Fuel oil (part of a tank)	$ __100.00__	$ _____
Goods and Services Tax (if applicable)		$ _____
Lawyer's Account		
Disbursements by lawyer for land transfer tax (if applicable)	$ _____	
Deed registration	$ __16.00__	
Legal fees	$ __750.00__	$ _____
Moving and Related Costs		
Moving two men and a truck, five hrs. @ $55/hr.)	$ _____	
Connection of utilities		
Telephone	$ __28.50__	
Cable TV	$ __43.20__	
Electricity	$ __7.50__	
Others	$ __22.00__	$ _____
Appliances, Repairs		
Purchase of major appliances	$ __2500.00__	
Decorating supplies	$ __500.00__	
Repairs	$ __500.00__	$ _____
Grand total		$ _____

What are some other costs that might be anticipated but are not included here?

7. The Baileys' offer to purchase a house has been accepted. Now they are considering ways of financing it. The purchase price is $187 000 and they have $18 000 for a down payment. The alternatives they are considering are:

	Down payment	First mortgage	Second mortgage
(i)	$18 000	$169 000 @ 12%, 25 yrs.	none
(ii)	$18 000	$169 000 @ 12%, 20 yrs.	none
(iii)	$10 000	$169 000 @ 12%, 25 yrs.	$8000 @13% for 5 years ($245.33/mo.)

(a) Which of these alternatives would result in the lowest
   – monthly cost?
   – total interest?
(b) What are some factors the Baileys should consider when making their choice?

8. When the Karlovs bought their house, they took over the vendor's mortgage because it was at 9% and had 4 more years to maturity. The purchase price was $91 900, the down payment $16 000 and the vendor's mortgage was $65 640. How will they raise the balance of the purchase price? What interest rate will they probably have to pay?

9. Barbara and George have decided to buy a house, but before looking they would like some information on the size of mortgage they might be able to obtain. They have monthly credit payments of $250 on the car and $150 for furniture. Their joint income is $48 000 a year. They found out that the annual taxes on houses of the type they would like are about $900.

(a) How much might they expect to borrow at 10 3/4%, amortized over 25 years?
(b) If they would prefer a 20-year mortgage, what will the maximum loan be?
(c) With a down payment of $12 000, and the mortgage amortized over 20 years, what price of home could they purchase if the mortgage was:
   (i) conventional?
   (ii) insured?

10. Use the Chang's amortization schedule (Table 15.4 in the Appendix) to answer this question.

(a) How much principal and interest will they pay in the
   – first five years?
   – the last five years?
(b) Compare the difference in total interest saved, and the effect on the time to repay the mortgage, if a prepayment of $5000 is made after:
   – five years.
   – ten years.

(c) If they made two prepayments—after five years and after ten—when would the mortgage be extinguished?

11. Find out if there is a property tax credit for taxpayers in your province. If so, what are the eligibility criteria? This information will be included in the federal income tax materials.

12. Sometimes mortgage lenders include property taxes, as well as principal and interest (P.I.T.) in the monthly payments. What is the reason for this?

REFERENCES

Books

BIRCH, RICHARD. *The Family Financial Planning Book, A Step-by-Step Moneyguide for Canadian Families*. Toronto: Key Porter, 1987, 216 pp. An easy-to-read guide to taking control of your personal finances that discusses budgets, income tax, insurance, RRSPs, mortgages, and investments.

COHEN, DIAN. *Money*. Scarborough, Ontario: Prentice-Hall Canada, 1987, 270 pp. An economist suggests strategies for coping with personal finances in the context of changing economic conditions. Topics include financial plans, buying a home, insurance, income tax, retirement, estate planning, and investments.

GOLDENBERG, DAVID M. *Mortgages and Foreclosure, Know Your Rights*. Fifth Edition. Vancouver: International Self-Counsel Press, 1989, 128 pp. Explains the legal terms found in a mortgage contract, the different types of mortgages, and how foreclosure law works.

PAPE, GORDON. *Building Wealth, Achieving Your Financial Goals*. Scarborough, Ontario: Prentice-Hall Canada, 1988, 246 pp. An easy-to-read guide for the novice financial manager and investor that considers interest rates, credit cards, mortgages, RRSPs, mutual funds, and the stock market.

ROSE, STANLEY M. *Real Estate Buying/Selling Guide for Ontario*. Seventh Edition. Vancouver: International Self-Counsel Press, 1987, 224 pp. A non-technical discussion of housing transactions with special emphasis on legal aspects.

SILVERSTEIN, ALAN. *Hidden Profits in Your Mortgage, The Smart-Money Guide to Canadian Home Ownership*. Toronto: Stoddart, 1985, 221 pp. A real estate lawyer offers suggestions for minimizing costs of mortgages and explains the details of some payment plans.

SILVERSTEIN, ALAN. *The Perfect Mortgage, Your Key to Cutting the Cost of Home Ownership*. Toronto: Stoddart, 1989, 136 pp. Explains, in non-technical language, basic mortgage terms, the most common options and how to make an informed choice.

STEACY, RICHARD. *Canadian Real Estate*. Seventh Edition. Toronto: Stoddart,1987, 456 pp. Includes a section on mortgages.

STEWART, GEORGE C. *Real Estate Buying/Selling Guide for Alberta*. Fourth Edition. Vancouver: International Self-Counsel Press, 1985, 159 pp. Explains the processes involved in real estate transactions; for the general reader.

SYBERG-OLSEN, E. *Real Estate Buying/Selling Guide for British Columbia*. Eighth Edition. Vancouver: International Self-Counsel Press, 1988, 208 pp. An introduction to the general area of mortgages and buying real estate.

WYATT, ELAINE. *The Money Companion, How to Manage Your Money and Achieve Financial Freedom*. Markham, Ontario: Penguin Books, 1989, 203 pp. A guide to personal financial management that focuses on planning, investment strategy and retirement needs.

ZIMMER, HENRY B. *Making Your Money Grow, A Canadian Guide to Successful Personal Finance*. Third Edition. Toronto: Collins, 1989, 260 pp. The focus of this book is on basic calculations needed for personal financial decisions, as applied to compound interest, future and present values, investment returns, RRSPs, annuities and life insurance.

ZIMMER, HENRY B. *The Revised and Expanded Canadian Tax and Investment Guide*. Edmonton: Hurtig, annual, 315 pp. Very comprehensive treatment of income tax and investments.

16 CREDIT REPORTING AND DEBT COLLECTION

1. To explain the operation of a credit bureau, including:
   (a) how it is financed,
   (b) how information is obtained,
   (c) who has access to the information,
   (d) how it serves the interests of both debtors and creditors.

2. To identify:
   (a) factors considered in the assessment of an individual's credit rating,
   (b) the roles of the credit bureau and the creditor in making this assessment.

3. To explain the rights given consumers in the provincial legislation on credit reporting regarding:
   (a) prohibited information in credit files,
   (b) disclosure of information,
   (c) notice that a credit report may be obtained,
   (d) consumer access to own file.

4. To outline:
   (a) the operation, and
   (b) the functions of collection agencies.

5. To evaluate the protection provided debtors by the provincial regulation of collection agencies.

6. To explain these terms: credit file (history), credit report, consumer information, personal information, third-party collecting.

7. To explain ways in which debts may be collected without resorting to the courts.

8. To explain the process of suing a debtor to obtain a court judgment.

9. To explain how garnishees and execution orders are used to collect judgment debts.

10. To identify forms of garnishment other than wage garnishment.

INTRODUCTION

Credit reporting and debt collection are combined in this chapter, not because their functions are more closely related than other aspects of credit, but because credit bureaus often own collection agencies and operate both under the same roof. *Credit reporting*, an information service provided to lenders to help them assess the potential risk associated with a loan application, occurs in the initial stage of a credit transaction. Debt collection, on the other hand, is the final process for a small proportion of loans or accounts.

CREDIT REPORTING

If you apply for credit, the lender must assess the probability that you will be able to repay the debt as scheduled. What does a lender need to know to predict your reliability and capacity to repay this debt? When you filled out the application for credit, you gave information about your residence, occupation, bank, salary, mortgage, and consumer debts (Figure 14.2). In addition, it may be useful for the lender to know how you handled previous credit transactions. The lender can obtain information about your credit history by contacting the local credit bureau. A *credit bureau* is a business that sells information about credit transactions to its subscribers.

THE CREDIT BUREAU

Credit bureaus are usually privately owned by individual businesses that belong to provincial organizations and thus are linked with the Associated Credit Bureaus of Canada. Each bureau covers a specific geographic region, usually a county or city. Cooperation among credit bureaus is important because it is frequently necessary to forward files from one location to another as consumers move about the country or continent, or sometimes the world.

Credit bureaus depend on selling memberships to firms that extend credit—such as financial institutions and retailers—as well as to a variety of other businesses that need information on the credit histories of customers. Employers and landlords have an interest in subscribing to the credit bureau, as do life insurance companies. However, in order to become a member, each must have a legitimate business interest in such credit information.

Credit bureau subscribers pay an annual membership fee in addition to a charge for each credit report that they obtain. Most credit reports are transferred electronically from the credit bureau to the member (computer to computer) instead of by telephone as in the past. The service contract signed by members binds them to inquire for *bona fide* business purposes only, and also requires that they give the credit bureau any relevant credit information they have about their customers.

THE CREDIT FILE

Anyone who has credit cards or charge accounts, has ever obtained a mortgage or other loan, has rented accommodation, or is connected to utilities such as telephone or hydro, probably has a file at a credit bureau. Most of the information in the file comes from three major sources: the individual, the individual's creditors, and public records. Each time an application is made for credit, the facts supplied on the application form will be transferred to the credit bureau file by the credit grantor whenever a credit report is drawn.

In addition, it is common practice for all the major credit grantors, such as the bank credit card companies, large retailers, and financial institutions, to send their entire credit files to the credit bureau every month or two. These computer files, reporting the status of all their credit accounts, are electronically merged with those already in the credit bureau files, or new files are set up if the person in question does not already have one. The information includes the account number, the outstanding balance, and whether payment has been made on time.

Items of public record, such as chattel mortgages and conditional sales agreements registered with provincial authorities, and reports on court judgments or bankruptcies, are obtained by the credit bureau and added to the files.

Nowadays, most credit bureaus store their files in computers where they are immediately accessible to other bureaus. The sample credit report (Figure 16.1) illustrates the types of information that may be kept in a credit bureau file. The record, that is entered in code or an abbreviated form for conciseness, includes the individual's usual manner of payment classified on a nine-point scale, as well as information from a number of sources.

INTERPRETING THE CREDIT FILE   The first line under Credit History in the sample credit report can be interpreted as follows. An October 1982 report showed that there had been a claim (lien) registered against property by a bank (BB) to secure a loan with terms of 27 payments of $1248 each. The original instalment loan was for $33 735, but it was repaid by October 1981 and the balance is now zero. During the repayment period some instalments fell into arrears, from 90-130 days, as indicated by the code (I4). In an actual report, there would be code numbers after BB to show which branch of which bank extended the loan. Later credit transactions indicate that Mr. Love was making his payments on time (I1).

THE CREDIT CHECK

Whenever an application is made for a loan, to purchase an appliance with a conditional sales contract, or to open a charge account, the borrower is asked to complete an application form and then await the credit grantor's decision.

DATE RECEIVED
MO DAY YEAR
10/27/86
DATE MAILED

10/27/86

40

2625258

08/79

FACTUAL CONFIDENTIAL REPORT FOR
TRAINING,ATTN-

This information is furnished in response to an inquiry for the purpose of evaluating credit risks. It has been obtained from sources deemed reliable, the accuracy of which this organization does not guarantee. The inquirer has agreed to indemnify the reporting bureau for any damage arising from misuse of this information and this report is furnished in reliance upon that indemnity. It must be held in strict confidence and must not be revealed to the subject reported on except by a reporting agency in accordance with Provincial Regulations.

REPORT ON (SURNAME)

LOVE,RALPH,,
SOCIAL INSURANCE NUMBER   AGE OR DATE OF BIRTH

BORN 09/20/54

SPOUSE'S NAME

NANCY
MARITAL STATUS

MARRIED

PRESENT ADDRESS   FROM   INDICATOR

31,ORCHARD,PK,ST JACOBS,ON,   *   03/86F

COMPLETE TO HERE FOR FILE SUMMARY OR REVISED TRADE REPORT AND SKIP TO CREDIT HISTORY

PRESENT EMPLOYER AND OCCUPATION   FROM   SALARY & BASIS   INDICATOR

RALPH LOVE LTD,PRESIDENT   01/82   *   03/83R

COMPLETE TO HERE FOR SHORT REPORT AND SKIP TO CREDIT HISTORY

OWNS   RENTS   BOARDS

NUMBER OF DEPENDENTS INCLUDING SPOUSE   *   UNABLE TO SECURE
FORMER ADDRESS   FROM   TO   INDICATOR

21,BIRDLAND,DR,ELMIRA,ON,   *   *   08/79R
FORMER EMPLOYER AND OCCUPATION   FROM   TO   SALARY & BASIS   INDICATOR

CENTRAL SYSTEMS,   *   *   *   09/79R
SPOUSE'S EMPLOYER AND OCCUPATION   FROM   TO   SALARY & BASIS   INDICATOR

RALPH LOVE LTD,SECRTY-TREASURER   *   *   *   03/83R

CREDIT HISTORY

DATE REPORTED	SOURCE	ACCOUNT TYPE	DATE OPEN	HIGH CREDIT	LAST PAID	BALANCE	PAST DUE	HOW PAY	TRADE KEY	DATE CLOSED
10/82R	BB/	REGISTERED LIEN	11/78	33735		00		I4		10/81
	TERMS-27X1248									
01/85C	BT	REAL ESTATE LOAN	05/84	56000	12/84	55446		I1	JT	
	TERMS-669/PIT,CREDITOR-1ST MTG 31 ORCHARD PKWY ST JACOBS									
01/85C	BB/	REGISTERED LIEN	03/81	12637	01/85	526		I1	JT	
	TERMS-48X263,CREDITOR-1980 GMC PICK-UP									
09/86R	DC		11/78	594	08/86	493		R1		
	TERMS-10/M									
09/86R	DC		04/79	1000	07/86	893	25	R2	LT	
	TERMS-25/M									

-BANK-
12/84C BB/   PERSONAL CHEQUING 01/83,BAL-L3,OVERDRAFT/UNSATIS

-LEGALS-
08/82R COURT-1ST CC WTL,TYPE-JU999/82,DATED-08/82,AMOUNT-$455,DEFENDANT-RALPH
LOVE,PLAINTIFF-COLBYCO MGT
07/85R COURT-3RD WTL,TYPE-JU 2424-79,DATED-06/85,AMOUNT-$150,PAID-07/85
DEFENDANT-RALPH LOVE,PLAINTIFF-ROYAL BANK CHARGEX

-BANKRUPTCY-
10/80R TYPE-BD,DATED-10/81,LIABILITIES-$99878,TRUSTEE-KILLDEER & ASSOC/ELMIRA
RALPH LOVE/FILED 10/80

-OTHER-

* UNABLE TO SECURE

NUMBER OF ADDRESSES
SINCE ON FILE DATE   0

NUMBER OF EMPLOYMENTS
SINCE ON FILE DATE   0

NUMBER OF INQUIRIES
SINCE ON FILE DATE   99

FORM 100
000904

MEMBER
ASSOCIATED CREDIT BUREAUS OF CANADA   1----CONTINUED

Figure 16.1   SAMPLE CREDIT REPORT
Source: Reproduced with the permission of Golden Triangle Credit Bureau Inc.

The credit officer at the bank, trust company, or store may contact the credit bureau through a computer terminal or, less frequently nowadays, by telephone. Two conditions must be met before the credit officer can receive information about the individual's credit history: (i) the inquiring firm must be a member of the credit bureau, and (ii) the file that the credit bureau retrieves must apply to this person and not to someone else.

Safeguards are built into the credit reporting system to ensure that access to credit information is restricted to members of the credit bureau only. This is done electronically when the data are transferred from one computer system to another, with a code number if making a telephone request. To be sure that the retrieved file is the right one, a comparison is made between the information on the application form and that in the file at the credit bureau. In addition to name and address, other identifying information used are birth date, social insurance number, credit card account numbers, and place of employment.

Assuming that the credit application matches the file at the credit bureau, there will be an exchange of information between the lender and the credit bureau. The file at the credit bureau will be updated with any new facts from the application, and the creditor will find out how the individual has handled credit in the past.

CREDIT RATING

The decision whether or not to extend credit is made by the credit grantor, not the credit bureau. Credit bureaus collect and sell information, but do not make assessments of anyone's capacity to handle credit. In the interests of efficiency and cost, large firms are coming to depend heavily on an automatic assessment system, called *credit scoring*, whereby points are given for certain characteristics. Although the weight given different factors may vary somewhat among companies and vary from time to time as credit is made easier or harder to obtain, there is general agreement that the traditional three Cs of capacity, character, and collateral play an important part. Higher scores are assigned to those who are owners of property, show stability in residence and in their jobs, possess several credit cards, have paid past obligations on time, do not write bad cheques, and have low debt/income ratios.

Lenders have programmed their computers to quickly score the information on the application form and indicate whether the applicant is a good risk, a bad risk, or an uncertain one. In the first two instances, the decision to grant or not grant credit is fairly obvious and may be made without contacting the credit bureau. It may be that the top 10-15 percent are automatically accepted and the bottom 30 percent rejected. That leaves about half of the applicants in the uncertain category, where more information is needed to reach a decision; credit bureau reports will be drawn for these people.

Since the lender makes the assessment of creditworthiness, an applicant may find that at any one time, some lenders will grant credit while others will not. Obviously, this is more apt to be true if the individual falls in the uncertain category, because creditors vary in the levels of risk they are willing to accept. Nevertheless, whether or not credit will be granted may be influenced by factors other than personal history. Lender policies are affected by conditions in the economy and the situation in the lender's own business. Sometimes a lender has surplus funds and is very anxious to lend, but at other times scarce funds or poor economic conditions, such as high unemployment, may discourage lending.

THE CONSUMER AND THE CREDIT BUREAU

Many users of consumer credit are unaware that there is a record of some of their financial transactions on file at the credit bureau; in fact, they may never have heard of the credit bureau. Some people discover the credit bureau when there is a mix-up over their files or when they are refused credit. It is the policy of the Associated Credit Bureaus of Canada, and also a legal requirement in most provinces, that consumers be permitted to know what is in their files, if they ask.

LEGISLATION

All provinces except Alberta and New Brunswick have passed laws to regulate consumer reporting agencies, which include credit bureaus. The two basic concerns reflected in these laws are the consumer's privacy in regard to credit information and the right not to suffer from inaccurate credit or personal information.

CREDIT REPORTING LEGISLATION

Province	Title
British Columbia	*Credit Reporting Act*
Saskatchewan	*Credit Reporting Agencies Act*
Manitoba	*Personal Investigations Act*
Ontario	*Consumer Reporting Act*
Quebec	*Consumer Protection Act*
Nova Scotia	*Consumer Reporting Act*
Prince Edward Island	*Consumer Reporting Act*
Newfoundland	*Consumer Reporting Agencies Act*

INFORMATION IN FILES   These acts distinguish *consumer information*, which includes such details as name, address, age, occupation, residence, marital status, education, employment, estimated income, paying habits, debts, assets, and obligations, from *personal information*, which has little to do with financial transactions, e.g., character, reputation, and personal characteristics. The details differ, but all of these acts set limits on the type of information that can be included in a consumer report; generally they must be restricted to consumer information. In addition, there are limits on the inclusion of detrimental information in a credit report. For example, information about previous bankruptcies may not be reported after 14 years (six years in British Columbia and Nova Scotia; and seven years in Ontario, Prince Edward Island and Newfoundland). Disclosure of other detrimental information, more than seven years old, is also prohibited. Restrictions are set on the situations in which consumer reporting agencies may make reports. Acceptable circumstances are court orders and requests from those who are concerned with extending credit, renting, employment, or insurance.

PERMISSION FOR CREDIT REPORT   Consumer reports, also known as credit reports, may not be requested unless a consumer has either given written consent or is sent written notice that the report was obtained. Ontario and Newfoundland require that notice be given before the report is obtained; in Manitoba, notice must follow within ten days of granting or refusing credit. The permission to obtain a report may be included in a credit application, as in the form in Figure 14.2.

In 1988 the Ontario government revised the *Consumer Reporting Act* in response to misuse of credit bureau files. Businesses were obtaining credit reports to identify consumers as possible targets in promotional campaigns, such as offers of new credit cards. If an individual has not made an application for credit, the credit bureau cannot give a credit report to a third party without informing the person of the request and the name and address of the third party.

ACCESS TO OWN FILE   The consumer has the right to know what is in his or her file at a credit bureau, and if arrangements are made with the local bureau an individual will be told the contents of the record. Should the accuracy of information found there be questioned, the agency must make every effort to verify the record and to correct any errors.

OTHER CREDIT REPORTING AGENCIES

Although this chapter is about credit bureaus, brief mention should be made of two other types of reporting agencies. *Information exchanges* are formed by groups of creditors, such as the small loan and sales finance companies, to share information about their debtors as a way of preventing the occurrence of bad debts. Information exchanges are interested in the same kinds of information as credit bureaus, but differ in their organizational structure. *Investigative agencies*, on the other hand, collect a wider range of information, including very personal data about family relations, addictions, and so on, and may visit neighbours for opinions on character.

DEBT COLLECTION

When debts are in arrears or in default, the creditor is concerned with retrieving the money owed as quickly and as cheaply as possible, and with as little destruction as possible of the debtor's goodwill towards the firm. The collection of a difficult debt may go through three phases. First, the creditor tries notices and reminders, but if these fail the debt may be referred to a special collection division of the creditor's firm or to an independent collection agency. Finally, the creditor may sue the debtor in court. All three stages will be considered here. Ways in which the debtor may respond to debt problems are reviewed in the next chapter.

WHO DOES THE COLLECTING?

There is no simple answer to this question because creditors will choose a procedure that is suitable for them and seems feasible for the particular debt. In general, one finds that firms in the finance business, such as banks, small loan companies, or credit unions, tend to have their own collection facilities to collect their own overdue accounts. Large retailers also may conduct much of their own collecting. Smaller companies and independent professionals, particularly, prefer to devote their energies to their specialities and tend to turn over delinquent accounts to a collection agency. Sometimes, a firm will pursue overdue accounts for a time, turning over only the very difficult ones.

COLLECTION AGENCIES

A *collection agency* is a provincially licensed business that specializes in collecting overdue accounts for others. Its income depends on its success in collecting, because from 30 percent to 50 percent of the amounts collected is retained, with no fees if unsuccessful. It is not surprising, then, that collection agencies are quite energetic in their efforts to collect. A collection agency is often found under the same roof as a credit bureau, although the two are licensed as separate business operations. Access to each other's information is a convenience for both.

COLLECTION PRACTICES   Collection practices vary, but it is usual to begin with polite reminder notices or telephone calls. At this stage, the bulk of the overdue accounts are collected without harassment or much personal contact. Debtors who are still resistant will find the techniques becoming progressively more aggressive because, at this stage, maintaining goodwill is no longer a concern of the creditor. Although the debt has been written off in the accounts of the business, there may still be some hope of collecting a portion of the debt by referring the matter to a lawyer or an independent collection agency.

Before the point when a debt comes into the courts, collection procedures often depend heavily on psychological tactics. Some steps are hoped to be intimidating to some degree: for example, using legal-looking forms and letterheads, referring the debt to a lawyer or collection agency, or making threats that may not be enforceable but go unchallenged by uninformed debtors. The debtor can slow down or stop the collection process at any stage by making some payments.

The persuasive, intimidating, or dunning techniques will be ineffective if the debtor cannot be found. Nowadays, computer linkages of credit bureaus make it much more difficult for defaulters to disappear. An alert is placed in the files of missing debtors and whenever or wherever they next apply for credit and their credit history is examined, the creditor will become aware of their default status and the credit bureau will automatically acquire their most recent address. Not all defaulters skip deliberately; some have moved, and never informed their creditors.

ENFORCEMENT OF SECURITY   In this discussion of debt collection, it has been assumed that a creditor will have enforced any security, if considered worthwhile, before beginning aggressive collection processes. When the creditor holds security in the form of assets, durables, or promise of future income, the security also includes the debtor's prior permission to realize on any of these in the case of default. But sometimes the security is not sufficient to cover the balance owing, and alternate procedures are needed.

REGULATION OF COLLECTION AGENCIES   The legislation regulating collections does not apply to all those who collect debts, but in the main is directed at third party collections, where the collector is not the creditor. Therefore, it is chiefly concerned with regulating collection agencies. The professions and institutions exempt from the requirements of this legislation vary among provinces. In British Columbia and Ontario, for instance, credit unions, banks, trust companies, barristers, real estate agents, and insurance agents, among others, are exempt. Refer to the appropriate provincial legislation to determine which collectors are regulated.

LEGISLATION REGULATING COLLECTION AGENCIES

Province	Title
British Columbia	*Debt Collection Act*
Alberta	*Collection Practices Act*
Saskatchewan	*Collection Agents Act*
Manitoba	*Consumer Protection Act*
Ontario	*Collection Agencies Act*, and *Debt Collectors Act*
Quebec	*Act Respecting the Collection of Certain Debts*
New Brunswick	*Collection Agencies Act*
Nova Scotia	*Collection Agencies Act*
Prince Edward Island	*Collecting Agencies Act*
Newfoundland	*The Collections Act*

The Criminal Code of Canada prohibits indecent, threatening or harassing telephone calls. This applies to all collection endeavours and, thus, provides some recourse for the consumer who is being pursued for payment by someone whose activities are not regulated under legislation.

USING THE COURTS TO COLLECT DEBTS

As mentioned earlier, the creditor who has an account in default has the right to enforce security and use reasonable collection procedures. If these are not sufficient, the next alternative is to sue the debtor. The details of the procedure vary from province to province, but a summary of the Ontario process will indicate the general procedure for collecting debts through the courts.

The creditor files a claim at the appropriate court giving names, addresses, and reasons for suing. The court clerk mails the claim and a summons to the debtor who has three alternatives:

(a) try to settle the dispute out of court,
(b) file a defense,
(c) do nothing.

If the first alternative is selected, the debtor and creditor reopen negotiations about payment of the debt, and if an agreement is reached, the creditor will drop the claim. If the second alternative is chosen, the debtor must file a defense in this same court within the number of days specified by the summons, stating reasons for disputing the creditor's claim. Failure to file a defense may result in a judgment against the debtor by default.

When a defense has been filed, there may be a trial to hear both sides of the matter. On the date of the trial, all witnesses, the creditor, the debtor, and any lawyers for either party, will appear before the judge. Small Claims Courts are meant to be informal courts where legal counsel is not required. After both sides of the story have been heard, the judge will announce the decision. On very small claims no appeal may be permitted. The judge's decision or judgment may have two possible outcomes. Either the debtor does not owe the money and the case is dismissed, or the debtor does owe some or all of the money claimed by the creditor. In the latter instance the debtor is responsible for paying what is owed. If the debtor voluntarily makes the necessary payment, the matter is ended.

ENFORCEMENT OF JUDGMENT   If the debtor either cannot or will not repay the debt, there are several courses of action to enforce the judgment. The creditor may choose to garnishee the debtor's wages, if employed, or to seize some of the debtor's goods under an execution order. *Execution* is a creditor's right, acquired as a result of a judgment in his favour, to seize and sell goods and land possessed by a debtor to discharge a judgment debt. The goods seized must be completely owned by the debtor without liens or mortgages attached to them. The provincial *Execution Acts* exempt the seizure of certain possessions such as essential household furnishings.

Wages or bank accounts may be garnisheed to satisfy a judgment debt. *Wage garnishment* is a court order to an employer to pay into court some percentage of the debtor's wages. If a debtor has more than one garnishee order outstanding, the court will send them out one at a time. The debtor will not be taken by surprise but will receive a statement from the court that the creditor has requested a garnishee, and there is time to respond to the court. The debtor can plead for a reduction in the amount taken off his or her wages and can stop the garnishee, if it can be shown that steps to handle the debt problems are being taken.

Garnishment is governed by a number of regulations, including those regarding exemption of certain persons, exemption of a portion of wages, and protection of employees from dismissal when their wages have been garnisheed. The social security income of those receiving welfare, Unemployment Insurance, or Old Age Security is exempt from garnishment. The proportion of wages that may be garnisheed is specified in provincial legislation (70-80 per cent of gross wages may be exempt) but can be reduced if the debtor can persuade the court of need. When an employer receives a garnishee order, there may be an inclination to dismiss the employee on the assumption that he or she is not very reliable. Provincial laws attempt to prevent this, but sometimes it is difficult to find out the real reason for dismissal.

A *bank account garnishment* can be taken to obtain money from a debtor's account to satisfy a judgment debt. Like a wage garnishee, the process is initiated through the court.

DEMAND ON A THIRD PARTY   A demand on a third party may be issued by the federal government for debts incurred against the federal government, for instance, income tax arrears and Unemployment Insurance benefit overpayments. It is like a garnishee in many ways, but it does not require a court judgment and does allow attachment of a larger share of income. In the case of a self-employed individual, a demand on a third party may be issued against the person's bank account.

FAMILY COURT ACTION   Whenever payments on a maintenance order are not kept up-to-date, the family court can also issue an attachment on wages that has a continuing effect, similar to a demand on a third party. Again, the percentage of the wages that can be attached may exceed limits set under provincial wages legislation. In Ontario, the Director of Support Custody Enforcement can issue a garnishee for 50 percent of gross wages. To apply for relief, the person would have to file a dispute with the courts and await a hearing. At the hearing, the judge decides whether or not to reduce the percentage garnisheed.

SUMMARY

Our consumer credit system depends on reliable means for a lender to quickly assess the risk potential of each borrower. To meet this need, a network of credit bureaus, that sell credit information about borrowers to the member lenders, has been established. As a control on the zeal of credit bureaus in collecting and preserving information about consumers, provincial legislation has specified what types of information may be included in a credit report. Credit bureaus provide information to creditors but do not determine credit ratings; each lender makes this decision in light of company policies.

Overdue debts may be collected by the creditor or turned over to a third party such as a collection agency for collection. Various forms of pressure may be exerted on delinquent debtors to encourage payment, including legal action. Provincial legislation tends to regulate the licensing of collection agencies without defining what undue harassment is, or exerting control over creditors who do their own collecting. However, there are provisions under the Criminal

Code of Canada which prohibit certain threatening or harassing actions on the part of anyone trying to collect a debt.

PROBLEMS

Note: You are advised to consult the appropriate legislation for the province where you live, in order to obtain more detail than is provided in this chapter. The following problems are based on the assumption that you will have this additional information.

1. With reference to provincial legislation regarding credit reporting, decide whether you AGREE or DISAGREE with the following statements:

   (a) Information about judgments that occurred more than seven years ago may be included in a credit report.
   (b) A credit report may indicate the race, creed, colour, or ethnic origin of the subject of a credit report.
   (c) A credit bureau is required to reveal the contents of a consumer's file, if requested by that consumer.
   (d) Prospective employers cannot obtain credit reports from a credit bureau.
   (e) A creditor must advise the consumer involved before obtaining a credit report.
   (f) If a consumer makes a written request for the information on file and the sources of this information, the credit bureau can decide whether or not to respond.

2. What are the roles of the lender and the credit bureau in evaluating a consumer's credit-worthiness? What criteria are used?

3. What is your opinion of the close association between some credit bureaus and collection agencies?

4. Evaluate the consumer-protection aspects of the legislation regarding collection agencies.

   (a) What abuses will it control?
   (b) Do you see any problems in enforcing it?
   (c) Has the law specified what constitutes undue harassment?
   (d) Does the credit reporting legislation apply to the majority of debt collection activity?

5. Why might an individual be granted credit at one institution and refused it at another, on the same day and in the same town?

6. Find the section of the act regulating credit bureaus that relates to "notice of intention to procure consumer report," and then examine the credit application form in Figure 14.2 to discover if the form complies with the act.

7. What is the difference between:

(a) a credit file (history) and a credit report?

(b) a collection agency and a collection department?

(c) consumer information and personal information?

(d) a credit bureau and a collection agency?

8. Regarding the collection of debts, decide whether you AGREE or DISAGREE with the following statements:

(a) Most debts can be collected without aggressive action.

(b) Collection agencies and collection departments are essentially the same.

(c) Most creditor collection activities are regulated through provincial legislation.

(d) The amount a creditor can obtain through garnishment is limited by provincial legislation or a court decision.

9. Explain the similarities and differences of the following:

(a) wage assignments,

(b) wage garnishees,

(c) demand on a third party,

(d) family court garnishees.

10. If debtors learn that they are about to have their wages garnisheed, is there anything they can do to stop or alter the process?

11. Can a creditor garnishee the wages of a debtor before successfully suing the debtor? Can the creditor do this after the suit is started but before judgment is decided in the creditor's favour?

12. What is the difference between a garnishee and an execution order?

REFERENCES

Books

Canadian Commercial Law Reports. Don Mills, Ontario: CCH Canadian, Subscription service. Two-volume reporting service with up-to-date federal and provincial laws regarding sales contracts, conditional sales, instalment sales, chattel mortgages, consumer protection.

DYMOND, MARY JOY. *The Canadian Woman's Legal Guide*. Toronto: Doubleday, 1987, 449 pp. Includes a section on women and credit.

PARKER, ALLAN A. *Credit, Debt, and Bankruptcy*. Seventh Edition. Vancouver: International Self-Counsel Press, 1988, 109 pp. A handbook on Canadian credit law for credit users.

TOWNSON, MONICA, and FREDERICK STAPENHURST. *The Canadian Woman's Guide to Money*. Second Edition. Toronto: McGraw-Hill Ryerson, 1982, 203 pp. A book for the general reader that includes budgets, financial security, life insurance, retirement planning, and credit.

17 STRATEGIES FOR OVERCOMMITTED DEBTORS

1. To identify major causes of overindebtedness.

2. To describe alternatives available to overcommitted debtors.

3. To explain the process of a debt repayment program.

4. To identify the responsibilities of the applicant, the creditors and the trustee in a personal bankruptcy.

5. To outline consequences of bankruptcy for:
   (a) creditors,
   (b) the discharged bankrupt.

6. To distinguish between a court consolidation and a consolidation loan.

INTRODUCTION

Within one generation, our society has made a major shift from paying cash for nearly everything to dependence on credit, a change that may have contributed to economic growth by increasing demand but has not been without attendant social costs. The combination of rising real incomes and readily available credit made it seem unnecessary to postpone purchases until sufficient money had been saved. For many people this worked quite satisfactorily, but for an increasing number the result was overindebtedness, followed by despair and crisis. This chapter is concerned with ways to handle situations faced by people who run into difficulties with consumer debt. What can they do to resolve their problems?

OVERINDEBTEDNESS

Overindebtedness is a result of having more debts than one can or is willing to repay. The consequences of reneging on a promise to a lender may begin with gentle reminders, leading to more urgent requests, possible enforcement of security, and referral of the debt to a collection agency or department. When these measures fail to obtain results, the lender may sue the debtor in court. You will recall the court procedures for debt collection outlined in the previous chapter. A lender who wins the case has some additional means to try, such as garnisheeing wages or seizing property and possessions.

At any stage of overindebtedness, the debtor can contact the creditor and attempt to negotiate a new arrangement, or go to a credit counsellor for assistance to improve personal financial management or identify possible solutions to debt problems.

WHY DEBTORS DEFAULT

Reasons why people become overindebted are myriad, but the following classification, adapted from Caplovitz, captures the major reasons, although it does not cover all cases.[1] Caplovitz made distinctions between the inability to pay and an unwillingness to do so, and also between voluntary and involuntary causes of overindebtedness.

I.   Inability to pay
   A.   Unanticipated loss of income, e.g., illness, unemployment
   B.   Rival demands on income
      1.   Demands assumed voluntarily, e.g., over-use of credit, poor financial management.

1. David Caplovitz, *Consumers in Trouble: A Study of Debtors in Default*, New York: Free Press, 1974, Chapter 4.

2. Unexpected or involuntary demands, e.g., personal difficulties such as marital problems, addiction to drugs or alcohol, or other family crisis.
3. Chronic low income and inability to meet living costs.

II. Unwillingness to pay
    A. Debtor feels that the treatment received from the creditor has been unfair, or has some other problem with a credit transaction.
    B. Irresponsibility of the debtor who lacks commitment to debt repayment.

INABILITY TO PAY   Some people become over-indebted because of events beyond their control, such as illness, strikes, or loss of work, which reduce expected income. Unanticipated large expenses due to an illness or accident may force a family to borrow. Most creditors, if they know the reasons for the default, may take a more tolerant attitude towards debtors who have suffered from some unexpected crisis if the debtor seems anxious to resume payments as soon as possible.

IMPULSIVE SPENDING   Anyone who takes a carefree attitude toward the use of credit cards is voluntarily assuming debt that may or may not be too much to handle. Our consumer market encourages impulse spending, which some find irresistible. In the excitement of the purchase one may not think of the reality of the future payments. If a creditor discovers that the debtor is able to pay but is unwilling, energetic steps will probably be taken to force compliance. However, if the debtor has little or no capacity to repay the debt, the creditor may decide to drop the matter for the present and review the debtor's situation at a later date.

COMBINATION OF FACTORS   It is not unusual for an individual's overindebtedness to have been caused by a combination of reasons. Marital difficulties may create a situation in which there is both inability and unwillingness to pay debts, or the debtor refuses to pay because of a misunderstanding with the creditor. On occasion, debtors may claim that they were not being credited with the payment they had made, did not know where to pay, or had returned the merchandise and considered the matter closed. Some had co-signed for a friend or relative and felt betrayed when the creditor tried to collect from them, because they had not fully understood the implications of co-signing.

FLEXIBILITY COST   As mentioned in the chapter on the use of credit, one of the costs of credit is the flexibility cost—with future income committed to debts, there are fewer resources for emergencies or the unexpected. Families with high debt commitments are vulnerable when changes in their employment situation reduce or stop the flow of income. Debtors may be insured against the possibility that death or disability may impair their ability to repay the debt, but perhaps there is an equally compelling need to insure debtors against loss of income.

ALTERNATIVES FOR THE OVERCOMMITTED DEBTOR

The creditor has a number of options to try to force a debtor to repay a debt, some of which may be quite unpleasant. What rights does the debtor have and what steps can he or she take? Assuming that the present debt commitments exceed the current capacity to pay them, the options include: (i) negotiating new terms with creditors, (ii) obtaining a consolidation loan, (iii) requesting help from a credit counselling service, (iv) declaring bankruptcy, and (v) arranging a court consolidation order. Unfortunately, from fear and ignorance some over-extended debtors do nothing at all, letting the situation worsen rapidly.

NEGOTIATION WITH CREDITORS

Anyone who becomes overindebted should, first of all, talk to creditors as soon as it is apparent that things are out of hand. Tell them what has happened and ask what adjustments can be arranged. Above all, creditors prefer to see their money returning, even if delayed slightly, rather than to be forced to take strong measures. The policies of the particular institution will determine which alternatives may be available to the debtor. The creditor may offer to freeze the loan—that is, to accept no payments at all for a time. Additional interest payments may or may not be charged for this time, but of course, the date for the completion of the credit contract will be moved forward.

CONSOLIDATION LOAN

Some lenders offer consolidation loans to overcommitted debtors. A *consolidation loan* is a new loan used to discharge a number of existing debts and is usually requested when the debtor is unable to maintain previous repayment commitments. Advertisements often exhort credit users to borrow enough money to pay off all their debts and thus owe just one company. Unfortunately, this is not a perfect solution. To borrow sufficient funds to cover all outstanding obligations and yet make smaller monthly payments than before will have two predictable consequences—the loan will be for a longer term and the total interest charges will be increased. A consolidation loan may be a reasonable solution in some cases, but for many people it is the beginning of a vicious cycle from which it is difficult to escape. Unfortunately, the smaller monthly payments may tempt a debtor to take on even more debt, and so the problem worsens.

Before deciding on a consolidation loan, examine the interest rate that will be charged and make a comparison with the rates on existing obligations. It is unwise to transfer to a consolidation loan those debts that now carry a lower interest rate or none at all. Since consolidation loans are made to people who are not very good credit risks, the interest rate tends to be high. If a loan contract is close to completion, the final payments are composed mostly of principal and very little interest. If such a contract were prepaid and transferred to a new consolidation loan, the debtor would significantly increase the amount of interest to be paid.

CREDIT COUNSELLING

Another solution for the overcommitted debtor is to approach one of the government or community-sponsored credit or debt counselling services usually found in larger centres. Although the organizational structure may vary from province to province, all of these agencies have the same objective and offer services without charge. They help clients to find an appropriate solution to their financial problems, which in some instances involves acting as a mediator between the overindebted family and their creditors to alleviate the crisis and to facilitate the eventual repayment of the debt.

ASSESSMENT INTERVIEW   The first step the credit counsellor takes is to interview the debtor with his or her partner to obtain detailed information about the family's financial situation in order to assess the type of solution that might be appropriate. The financial analysis includes a complete listing of: (i) income, (ii) living expenses, and (iii) debts. If the family's monthly income is sufficient to cover living expenses and debt obligations, the counsellor may spend some time discussing ways of improving their financial management so that they can make their income stretch from one pay day to the next. If there is a prospect of allocating a reasonable amount toward debt repayment, although less than the family's present commitment, a debt repayment plan may be developed. If, however, there is insufficient income to cover living expenses and partial debt payments, another solution may be needed.

DEBT REPAYMENT PROGRAM   The counsellor may work out with the family the amount that can be used to repay debts, and allocate this among their creditors in proportion to each creditor's share of the total outstanding debt. This process is a *debt repayment program*, also known as orderly payment of debts, debt adjustment, or prorating. For instance, the creditor who is owed the largest part of the family's total debt will receive the largest share of any repayment. Once a debt repayment plan acceptable to both the debtor and creditors is set up, a contract is signed by the debtor specifying the amount to be forwarded to the counselling agency on a regular basis. The agency, acting as a trustee, handles the distribution of the funds to the creditors.

The success of a debt repayment program depends on the willingness of the family to cooperate by living within the budget drawn up in consultation with the counsellor, the stability of the family's circumstances, and also on the willingness of the creditors to participate in the plan. Often creditors prefer to accept reduced but regular payments instead of trying more collection procedures or writing the account off as a bad debt. If the family fails to maintain the agreed payments, the agency will cancel the plan. The case study, "Credit Counselling and Debt Adjustment," illustrates how a debt repayment program may be set up.

CREDIT COUNSELLING AND DEBT ADJUSTMENT

Constant strife about bills made life so unpleasant that Michael and Susan decided to seek the help of a credit counselling service. With the counsellor's assistance, they began to get a picture of their financial situation. When the counsellor asked them to list all their expenses and all their income, they were surprised at the result. Their monthly living costs were exceeding their income before any consumer debt payments were made. The figures below show that they were short nearly $850 per month.

MONTHLY CASH FLOW

Total family take-home pay		$2750
Living expenses	2465	
Debt commitment	1135	
Total monthly expenses		$3600

Michael and Susan were also surprised to discover how much they owed in total, since their loan balance at the credit union was low. They hadn't realized how quickly their credit card debts had mounted up. When the counsellor went over the monthly statements from their various credit cards with them, there was another surprise: the balances were increasing in spite of sporadic payments and recent purchasing restraints.

After a careful review of their financial affairs, several possible solutions were discussed and carefully analyzed. Michael and Susan decided that they would go on an agency-administered debt repayment program. The counsellor explained that this would require reductions in living expenses or an increase in income. The potential for augmenting the family income was low but they felt that they could cut back on some of their expenses.

For a start, they decided to reduce their gift giving and forego vacations until their situation improved. The effect of these changes on their deficit would be approximately $100 per month. They proposed a further cut in their expenses by dropping "Super Channel" on their TV cable package and also agreed to reduce the number of restaurant meals and "take-outs." The anticipated gain there was another $90 a month. Before making any more sacrifices, the counsellor suggested that they take more time to consider the implication of these suggestions and to decide what other appropriate action to take.

When Susan and Michael returned a week later they offered these ideas: to reduce the telephone bill by making fewer long distance calls and to lower child-care costs by having their eldest child take more responsibility. They estimated that this would save about $125 per month. However, they realized that they had been a little over-zealous the week before and decided even if they didn't go away for vacations, they would spend extra money while they were off work, probably $200 a year. The counsellor, also recognizing that such changes are easier to plan than to implement, suggested that they allocate $650 per month toward repayment of their consumer debt.

The counsellor confirmed the outstanding balances with each creditor and was not surprised to find that the couple's debt was about $747 more than they had estimated—a total of $19 186. The counsellor's debt profile for this family shows the following list of creditors and amounts of debt, and the proportions of the total to be paid each month to each creditor.

Creditor	Reason for debt	Payment per mo.	Confirmed balance	Prorate %	Prorate Amt
Credit union	cars	295	4917	25.6	166.40
The Bay	stove, refrigerator, dishwasher, stereo	249	4023	21.0	136.50
Eatons	clothing, household goods, Christmas gifts	227	3813	19.9	129.35
Sears	washer, dryer, clothes, gifts, VCR	228	3967	20.7	134.55

Visa	car repairs, vacuum, cash advances, misc.	136	2304	12.0	78.00
Esso	gas		162	0.8	5.20
Total		$1135	$19 186	100.0	$650.00

Susan and Michael will require approximately three and a half to four years to repay these debts, and during this time they must refrain from assuming any new ones. If the family is successful in making the necessary adjustments in their lifestyle, they will probably succeed in eliminating their debt and becoming more effective financial managers. Unfortunately, some families cannot accept such a regimen, or their circumstances change and they do not complete the debt adjustment program.

BANKRUPTCY

Bankruptcy, the last resort of the overindebted, is much dreaded because of the attached social stigma and detrimental effect on a credit rating. However, it may be the only alternative for families who do not have enough income to cover their regular living expenses and also make some debt repayment. Not uncommonly, a substantial drop in income caused by illness or unemployment is the reason the debt load becomes impossible. The case study, "Bankruptcy or Asset Liquidation," illustrates a situation in which a heavily overindebted family faces a choice between bankruptcy or a negotiated settlement with creditors.

BANKRUPTCY OR ASSET LIQUIDATION?

When a credit counsellor encounters a family whose debts are far in excess of its ability to repay, an agency-administered debt repayment program may not be an option. Sheila was such a case. Until separation from her alcoholic husband, Sheila had managed to keep all the bills paid and the family lived well on a combined income of over $100 000. After the separation, she had hoped that with her salary as an executive secretary and substantial support payments for the two young children she would still be able to keep on top of her expenses. However, her ex-husband lost his middle management job a few months after the separation and the sporadic support payments ceased.

Now, Sheila was behind on the mortgage, owed the gas company for fuel, the bank was threatening to take her car and her credit cards and charge accounts were at their limit. She still owed money to the lawyer for handling her separation. The pressures from her present financial situation made Sheila sometimes wonder if she and the children were really better off living apart from her abusive husband. It seemed to her that things were always going wrong.

The situation that Sheila found herself in is not uncommon today with the frequency of marriage and relationship breakdown and employment instability at all levels. What was manageable on two incomes is not manageable on one. Sheila was so angry at what she felt to be the injustice of her circumstances that it was hard for her to take any kind of an objective look at her financial situation.

It soon became evident to both Sheila and the counsellor that keeping the house was not going to be possible nor, on her income alone, would she be able to meet her other monthly debt commitments. The counsellor suggested two possible alternatives for relief from her financial burdens. Bankruptcy is one possibility because Sheila is insolvent. Another option is to make use of the equity in her home and some valuable antiques by selling them and using the proceeds to offer her creditors a cash settlement. Neither solution was ideal. Before making any financial decisions, Sheila was advised to try to resolve some of her other problems by seeing a separation counsellor. The credit counsellor also recommended that Sheila seek legal advice, particularly concerning her right to sell the house and antiques.

BANKRUPTCY PROCEDURE   In all provinces, both corporate and personal bankruptcies are regulated by the federal *Bankruptcy Act*, but this discussion will be limited to personal bankruptcy. Bankruptcy proceedings may be initiated by an individual voluntarily assigning his or her property to a trustee, or it may be involuntary if a creditor submits a petition. In either case, the result is the same; the debtor's assets are liquidated and distributed on a *pro rata* basis to the creditors and, in time, the debtor is released from all the debt obligations included in the bankruptcy.

There are four main actors in the bankruptcy drama: (i) The *bankrupt*, who must be insolvent, i.e., have debts of at least $1000 and be unable to meet debt obligations; (ii) the *official receiver*, a civil servant who oversees the process of a bankruptcy and accepts the initial assignment of property, chairs the first meeting of creditors, and oversees the activities of the trustee; (iii) the *trustee in bankruptcy*, usually a chartered accountant licensed by the Superintendent of Bankruptcy, who collects and liquidates the estate of the debtor and distributes the proceeds to the creditors; and (iv) the *creditors*, who are all those who can prove a claim against the bankrupt. They control the bankruptcy proceedings through their agents, the inspectors. The creditors affirm the appointment of the trustee, and the trustee must consult with and follow the instructions of the inspectors.

The first step in bankruptcy is the assignment of all the debtor's assets to a licensed trustee. This is done through the official receiver, and may be regarded as an application for bankruptcy. From this time, until released from debts by the court, the debtor is an *undischarged bankrupt*. Next, a meeting of creditors will be called, at which the appointment of the trustee will be affirmed and instructions given concerning the administration of the estate. The trustee will then proceed to liquidate the estate. All the property of the debtor is available for payment of debts, except that which is exempt from execution or seizure under the laws of the province. All creditors must prove their claims against the estate. Secured creditors will be paid first because they have a claim on specific assets. By law, any remaining assets are then distributed in the following order:

1. payment for the costs of administration of the bankruptcy,
2. payment for wages and salaries owed,
3. municipal taxes,
4. rent arrears,
5. all other creditors.

Once the existing assets have been distributed, the court may grant the bankrupt a discharge. This releases the debtor from all claims of creditors except those for court fines, bail bond, alimony or support payments, certain debts incurred by fraud, and debts or liability for goods supplied as necessaries of life.

When the administration of the bankruptcy is complete (i.e., the assets have been distributed and the bankrupt discharged), the trustee applies for his or her own discharge. This releases the trustee from all liability for the administration of the bankruptcy and for conduct as a trustee.

In 1949, the existing *Bankruptcy Act* of 1918 was revised. Since 1966 there has been much discussion of revisions to the *Act*, a great deal has been written about problems with it, and many recommendations have been made. There is hope that new legislation will eventually be forthcoming.

Personal bankruptcy may cost the debtor $900 or more in fees, which is more than some overcommitted debtors can afford. Such people may contact the regional office of the Bankruptcy Branch, Consumer and Corporate Affairs for information on how to proceed under these circumstances.

The federal *Bankruptcy Act* provides for an Orderly Payment of Debts program (i.e., debt repayment plan) to be administered by the provinces if they choose. Six provinces—British Columbia, Alberta, Saskatchewan, Manitoba, Nova Scotia, and Prince Edward Island—have implemented the O.P.D. program, but there is no particular uniformity in procedures among these provinces. Essentially, this section of the *Bankruptcy Act* permits a debt administration program to be established under government sponsorship.

THE CASE OF PENNY AND TONY

Sometimes bankruptcy is not the panacea that people hope for. The case of Penny and Tony illustrates some of the problems that can be involved in a bankruptcy. Penny and Tony had been managing well on a government-sponsored debt repayment program for a year and a half. However, the birth of a seriously handicapped child left them both financially and emotionally drained. Weeks of commuting to a hospital in a larger centre, followed by the baby's death, seemed more than they could bear. When they contacted the agency handling their debt repayments they had made up their minds that they were filing for bankruptcy and nothing the counsellor said would dissuade them.

Several days after they signed the bankruptcy papers, the finance company, which had a chattel mortgage on their household goods, arrived with a truck and picked up most of their furniture leaving them without a stove and barely a chair to sit on. Ironically, they had to borrow money right away to get some furniture. The credit union placed a wage assignment on Tony's wages, to be in effect until his release from bankruptcy, and there was also the bankruptcy trustee's fee. To their surprise, they discovered that their debt was reduced by only $1100 through the bankruptcy.

COURT CONSOLIDATION OF DEBTS

It may be advantageous for a person who has several small claims court judgment debts outstanding (it must be three or more in Ontario) to apply to the court for a *consolidation order*. The judge will arrange a hearing with the debtor and the creditors to establish the capacity to repay these debts and, if feasible, will determine a repayment schedule. The debtor must make regular payments to the court which distributes the funds on a *pro rata* basis to the creditors. The court charges a fee of about ten percent of the debt, which is shared equally by the debtor and creditor. As long as the debtor maintains the repayment schedule, he or she is protected from other collection or court procedures in relation to those debts.

COMPLEXITIES OF OVERINDEBTEDNESS

The case study, "Debt Problems of a Blended Family," illustrates how interconnected family relations and financial matters can become. None of the alternatives that were identified appears to be a perfect solution, forcing the family to look for the least cost possibility.

DEBT PROBLEMS OF A BLENDED FAMILY

When the mail brought a summons to appear in family court regarding arrears in his support payments, it was the last straw. Robert persuaded Denise that they had better get some help.

Robert and Denise were obviously feeling very overburdened and stressed by their financial situation when they approached the social agency offering credit counselling. They were considering separating. In addition to their debt problems, Denise's recurring medical problem had flared up again and the school principal had called about some serious problems Denise's son, Tim, was having at school. Denise has been missing a fair amount of work recently and Robert's boss has told him to do something about his personal problems. It was apparent to the counsellor that the family needed relief from their financial problems soon.

The counsellor asked the couple to outline their family situation as necessary background for any new plans. Denise and Robert explained that they have been living common-law for several years, and are caring for Denise's twelve-year-old son Tim, from a previous marriage. Robert, who had also been married before, was ordered by the court to make support payments of $600 per month to his ex-wife for the support of their three teenage children. These children spend every other weekend with Denise and Robert, as well as much of the summer. Both Robert and Denise resent having to make such large support payments; Denise feels that she works for Robert's ex-wife. To aggravate matters, Denise's ex-husband is $2400 behind in support payments to her as he rarely sends his $100 a month payments.

When Robert and his wife separated two and a half years ago, he had to assume their debts of approximately $12 000 ($7000 for the car and $5000 on charge accounts) because she went on long-term social assistance.

Anxious to establish her own credit rating after her separation, Denise borrowed $5000 to buy a car with her elderly parents as co-signers. Denise still owes about $3500 on that loan and has another $2500 in credit card debt. Cash advances on Robert's credit cards and loans from her family to keep up their commitments have added another $6500 to their debts.

Their resources for financial aid were exhausted months ago and now creditors are calling both Robert and Denise at work about their delinquent payments. Robert has received a summons to appear in family court regarding the $1050 owing in support payments. The arrears occurred when Denise was laid off earlier in the year. The only payment that is up-to-date is Denise's bank loan that her parents co-signed. She says that she would starve before she would let her parents use their old age pension to pay that debt.

Before the counsellor could help the couple look at possible solutions to their problems, everyone needed to have a clearer picture of their financial position. The counsellor's assessment revealed the following.

BALANCE SHEET

Assets

Small bank account, two cars, household furnishings	$9 500	
Support arrears owed to Denise	2 400	
Total Assets		$11 900

Liabilities

Robert's old debts	$12 000	
Robert's support payments in arrears	1 050	
Denise's loan	3 500	
Robert's current debts	6 500	
Total Liabilities		$23 050
Net Worth		**− $11 150**

MONTHLY CASH FLOW

Income	$3 022	$3 022

Expenses

Net living expenses	2 286	
Robert's support payments	600	
Consumer debt payments		
Charge accounts, credit cards	675	
Bank loans	502	
Total Expenses		$4063
Deficit		**− $1041**

The counsellor helped the couple to look objectively at their situation, and together they drew up the following possible solutions.

1. *Both seek legal recourse regarding support payments in arrears.* Denise might be successful in obtaining a form of garnishee for support payments and those in arrears. This could increase the family's income by at least $100 a month. Robert could apply to the family court for a reduction in support payments, but it is unlikely, however, that a judge would be sympathetic to his situation.

2. *Find cheaper living accommodation.* Robert and Denise are renting a four-bedroom townhouse so there will be space for Robert's children when they come to visit. They could reduce their housing expenses by at least $300 a month if they moved into a two-bedroom apartment. However, they would be very cramped when Robert's children came to stay.

3. *Consolidate their debts.* Charge account and credit card interest rates are usually higher than consumer loans. A consolidation loan might reduce their monthly debt load and the total amount owed. Since the couple have a negative net worth, it is doubtful that they can find a lender willing to give them a loan for the total owed.

4. *Arrange an orderly payment of debt program, either through a governmental agency or a social agency.* This would allow the couple to repay their debts with more manageable monthly payments, over a longer period of time. There are potential risks involved in this choice. If the *pro rata* share on Denise's bank loan was less than the contractual amount, Denise's parents might be asked by the bank to make up the deficit. Unless interest concessions were negotiated, the total debt could increase substantially through accrued interest charges. It is possible that a creditor might decide to exercise rights to security, and thus take possession of household chattels or a car. And last, but not necessarily least, the family would have to make changes in their lifestyle to reduce living expenses, and exercise considerable self-discipline for the program to be a success, and maintain this over approximately four years.

5. *Declare bankruptcy.* This would relieve the family of their monthly debt burden with the exception of support arrears. They, however, would undoubtedly lose some of their possessions. There is also the stigma attached to bankruptcy and the limit it may place on the ability of an individual or family to get credit

in the future. Denise's elderly parents would, no doubt, be forced to take over her bank loan if she were to file for bankruptcy.

What do you think they should do?

Summary

People may become overindebted through circumstances beyond their control that reduce the stream of income, or through careless and impulsive use of credit. Anyone in this position will find that they begin to have much more frequent contact with creditors who will use every possible tactic to collect the debts. A debtor in this situation has several options to consider, including negotiation with the creditors, obtaining a consolidation loan, going to a credit counsellor, or filing for bankruptcy.

Problems

1. Refer to the case studies: "Credit Counselling and Debt Adjustment" and "Bankruptcy or Asset Liquidation."

   (a) In both instances, the families were referred to a credit counselling service. Which aspects of these cases were similar and which were different?
   (b) Do you think the Sheila should file for bankruptcy, or try for a negotiated settlement? What are the pros and cons of each alternative?
   (c) How does a credit counsellor arrive at an expenditure plan for an overcommitted debtor?
   (d) Do you think the Michael and Susan should continue to make their debt payments to the agency for four years, or do you think they should assume responsibility for their financial affairs before that time?
   (e) What would be the consequences for Susan and Michael if they failed to maintain the repayment schedule established by the agency?

2. Some books suggest that a debtor arrange a prorate or debt pooling plan directly with his or her creditors, without the use of a counselling agency. For whom would this work? What problems do you see arising?

3.

THE NOVICE COUNSELLOR

My first assignment in a student counselling practicum involved Glen and Mary. An administrator for the local housing authority wanted me to visit them because they had fallen behind in their rent payments. I made my first call at their house, confident that with a bit of help from me, this family would soon find itself able to cope with its financial problems.

When I arrived at their home at the appointed time, Mary was out shopping but returned within the hour. This friendly woman, in her mid-30s, was most cooperative, telling me that her husband was employed at a local factory and that she did part-time work at a nursing home, and that they have four children between the ages of five and 13. During this interview, I tried to determine the actual amount of their debts, but Mary was very vague about the amounts.

My second visit was very pleasant and Mary made every attempt to answer my questions. However, it appeared that she really did not know much about their financial situation. She wasn't sure what her husband's usual take-home pay was, but we made an estimate of their main debts, which were about $4000 in total.

I was astonished to find two large television sets in the midst of a rather poorly furnished living room. Mary said they were both quite new and in working condition, and that they had bought the first one about a year ago and the second one last month. She said "The man that sold them to us is a very good friend of ours and whenever he gets a really good deal he calls us and we go down and look at it. He is awfully nice about letting us pay for the televisions when we can."

When I looked at the contracts for their television sets, I realized that they were paying a substantial amount of credit charges. I mentioned this to Mary and she was most surprised because she didn't realize that her friend was charging them anything extra. She said they are paying them off fairly quickly because every so often they use Glen's whole pay cheque for some of the television debt. When I asked what they did about their other debts on these occasions, Mary said that frequently they let hydro, rent, and telephone bills accumulate for a few months. As we talked about their debts it became obvious that Mary really had no understanding of credit contracts or credit costs.

During the period of my visits to this household, Glen absolutely refused to meet me, although I was willing to go when he would be at home. I discovered that they have two cars although Mary doesn't drive. The whole family enjoys going out to eat once or twice a week, and Glen usually meets a friend to have a few drinks at their club every week.

My visits to this family ended without meeting the husband, and with the wife repeatedly stating that unless Glen agrees to make some changes there is very little that she can do. I learned later that they will probably be evicted from their low-rental townhouse. From this experience, I realize that solving financial problems is more complicated than I had thought, and that simply providing this family with information would not change much. This particular couple did not seem anxious to make a change, and until they are motivated to review their goals and values in light of their resources, a counsellor cannot be of help. This experience was obviously more beneficial for me than for the family.

(a) Why was the counsellor so unsuccessful?
(b) Could a more experienced counsellor have assisted this family? What would you have done?
(c) What changes would be necessary to improve this family's success in managing their finances?

4. Explain the difference between a court consolidation order and a consolidation loan, indicating differences in eligibility, procedures and consequences.

5. Refer to "The Debt Problems of a Blended Family."

(a) Do you think this family should declare bankruptcy? What would be some advantages for them?
(b) Can they afford the cost of bankruptcy?
(c) Will the creditors get anything at all?
(d) Will they lose their household furnishings?
(e) How will the bankruptcy affect their credit rating if they want another loan?
(f) What could they have done to avoid their present predicament?
(g) Are there other solutions to the family's financial problems that might have been discussed in a later interview? If so, what?

REFERENCES

Books

ANTEN, JUHLI. *Small Claims Court for British Columbia*. Eighth Edition. Vancouver: International Self-Counsel Press, 1986, 138 pp. Complete manual for proceeding with or defending an action in small claims court.

LIPTRAP, PATRICIA R., and AMY E. G. COUSINEAU. *Manual for Credit Counsellors*.

Second Edition. Grimsby, Ontario: Ontario Association of Credit Counselling Services, 1983. Provides guidance for credit counsellors. Available from the Association at Box 189, Grimsby, Ontario, L3M 4E3.

PARKER, ALLAN A. *Credit, Debt, and Bankruptcy*. Seventh Edition. Vancouver: International Self-Counsel Press, 1988, 109 pp. A handbook on Canadian credit law for credit users.

TOPHAM, MARK, and PATRICIA LIPTRAP. *Guidelines and Standards for Credit Counsellors*. Second Edition. Grimsby, Ontario: Ontario Association for Credit Counselling Services, 1988, 64 pp. A listing of professional standards for credit counselling in Ontario. Available from the Association at Box 189, Grimsby, Ontario, L3M 4E3.

VAN ARSDALE, MARY G. *A Guide to Family Financial Counseling, Credit, Debt and Money Management*. Homewood, Illinois: Dow Jones Irwin, 1982, 381 pp. Provides guidance for financial counsellors on such topics as, building the relationship, obtaining client information, diagnosis, generating alternatives, and evaluation of results.

YOUNG, JENNIFER. *Small Claims Court Guide for Ontario*. Sixth Edition. Vancouver: International Self-Counsel Press, 1986, 176 pp. A complete manual to proceeding with or defending an action in small claims court.

ZINKHOFER, FRED. *Small Claims Court Guide for Alberta*. Fourth Edition. Vancouver: International Self-Counsel Press, 1985, 122 pp. A complete manual for proceeding with or defending an action in small claims court

APPENDIX

Homeshield Policy

Form _____ Coverage Summary

Name of Policyholder	Ron J. Jones and Sandra Jones

Policy Period

	DAY	MONTH	YEAR		DAY	MONTH	YEAR	Your Policy begins and ends at 12:01 a.m. on these dates	This Policy Replaces Cancelled/Expired
from	15	6	xx	to	15	6	xx		Policy No. 68130

Your Agent John Dickie
Street Address 80 Great King Street
City, Province, Postal Code Guelph, Ontario N1S 2R4

Agency Number	Sub. Number	Company Code

Address of Home Insured
City, Province, Postal Code
Home is occupied as [X] Dwg. [ ] Apt. [ ] _____
Within 1000' of a fire hydrant [X] Yes   Within 5 miles of

Year Built 68 Construction brick veneer firehall.

Mortgageholder Royal Trust
Street Address 88 St. George's Square
City, Province, Postal Code Guelph, Ontario

Mortgageholder Bank of Montreal
Street Address St. George's Square
City, Province, Postal Code Guelph, Ontario

If we are to pay a mortgageholder for loss to your home, this is a certified copy only

Limits of Your Coverage— you're insured up to the limits shown below. These limits may be altered by special provisions described in this Policy or by any attached riders or endorsements.

Principal Home	Additional Buildings	Personal Belongings	Additional Living Expense		Personal Liability Protection	Voluntary Medical Payments	Voluntary Property Damage
$ 50,000	$ 5,000	$25,000	[X] 20% of Home Insurance	[ ] 20% of Personal Belongings Insurance	$ 100,000 for each occurrence	$ 500.00 for each person	$ 250. for each occurrence

This Policy contains a clause which may limit the amount payable

Your Deductible on this Policy is $ 50.00

Your Basic Premium $123.00

Additional Coverage

Rider No.		Deductible Applicable	Additional Coverage Premium
	[X] INFLATION SHIELD PLAN		NO CHARGE
	[ ] EXTENDED AUTO THEFT COVERAGE		
	[ ] OPTIONAL EXTENDED EARTHQUAKE PROTECTION		
	Special Items Endorsement (jewellery valued at $1,000.)		$11.00

Your Total Premium $ 134.00

Additional Liability Coverage

Personal Liability — unless indicated differently in the Additional Liability Coverage above, we won't cover claims others make against you relating to: homes owned by you or your spouse other than the one described on this page; elevators, escalators or inclinators; business use of your home; your permanent household employees; any watercraft you own that's over 26 feet, or has an outboard motor over 24 h.p. or an inboard with more than 50 h.p.

F 2 13 46 91
Policy Number

6 ROYAL INSURANCE COMPANY OF CANADA   4 THE WESTERN ASSURANCE COMPANY
3 QUEBEC ASSURANCE COMPANY
You are insured by the company indicated in the company code number box.

This Policy is not valid until countersigned by an authorized representative of the company.

Ralph Chapman
Authorized Representative

R. A. Hansford

Figure 5.1   SAMPLE HOME INSURANCE POLICY
Source: Reproduced with the permission of Royal Insurance Canada.

(Where mortgage is on building(s) only, the standard mortgage clause printed below is applicable unless special mortgage clause attached)

STANDARD MORTGAGE CLAUSE
(APPROVED BY THE INSURANCE BUREAU OF CANADA)

It is hereby provided and agreed that:

BREACH OF CONDITIONS BY MORTGAGOR OWNER OR OCCUPANT

1. This insurance and every documented renewal thereof - AS TO THE INTEREST OF THE MORTGAGEE ONLY THEREIN - is and shall be in force notwithstanding any act, neglect, omission or misrepresentation attributable to the mortgagor, owner or occupant of the property insured, including transfer of interest, any vacancy or non - occupancy, or the occupation of the property for purposes more hazardous than specified in the description of the risk;

PROVIDED ALWAYS that the Mortgagee shall notify forthwith the Insurer (if known) of any vacancy or non - occupancy extending beyond thirty (30) consecutive days, or of any transfer of interest or increased hazard THAT SHALL COME TO HIS KNOWLEDGE; and that every increase of hazard (not permitted by the policy) shall be paid for by the Mortgagee - on reasonable demand - from the date such hazard existed, according to the established scale of rates for the acceptance of such increased hazard, during the continuance of this insurance.

RIGHT OF SUBROGATION

2. Whenever the Insurer pays the Mortgagee any loss award under this policy and claims that - as to the Mortgagor or Owner - no liability therefor existed, it shall be legally subrogated to all rights of the Mortgagee against the Insured; but any subrogation shall be limited to the amount of such loss payment and shall be subordinate and subject to the basic right of the Mortgagee to recover the full amount of its mortgage equity in priority to the Insurer; or the Insurer may at its option pay the Mortgagee all amounts due or to become due under the mortgage or on the security thereof, and shall thereupon receive a full assignment and transfer of the mortgage together with all securities held as collateral to the mortgage debt.

OTHER INSURANCE

3. If there be other valid and collectible insurance upon the property with loss payable to the Mortgagee - at law or in equity - then any amount payable thereunder shall be taken into account in determining the amount payable to the Mortgagee.

WHO MAY GIVE PROOF OF LOSS

4. In the absence of the Insured, or the inability, refusal or neglect of the Insured to give notice of loss or deliver the required Proof of Loss under the policy, then the Mortgagee may give the notice upon becoming aware of the loss and deliver as soon as practicable the Proof of Loss.

TERMINATION

5. The term of this mortgage clause coincides with the term of the policy; PROVIDED ALWAYS that the Insurer reserves the right to cancel the policy as provided by Statutory provision but agrees that the Insurer will neither terminate nor alter the policy to the prejudice of the Mortgagee without the notice stipulated in such Statutory provision.

FORECLOSURE

6. Should title or ownership to said property become vested in the Mortgagee and/or assigns as owner or purchaser under foreclosure or otherwise, this insurance shall continue until expiry or cancellation for the benefit of the said Mortgagee and/or assigns.

SUBJECT TO THE TERMS OF THIS MORTGAGE CLAUSE (and these shall supersede any policy provisions in conflict therewith BUT ONLY AS TO THE INTEREST OF THE MORTGAGEE), loss under this policy is made payable to the Mortgagee.

RELEASE OF INTEREST

This is to certify that the undersigned has no further interest in this policy for insurance

Date _____ 19 _____   _____
                                                                    Signature

Figure 5.1   (continued)

Contents

Your Homeshield Policy

Protection for Your Home

Personal Liability Protection

Please remember that throughout this policy the words **you** and **your** refer to the person named on the Coverage Summary page and his or her spouse or any relatives living in the same household. **You** and **your** also mean anyone under 21 living in the same house under the care of the person named on the Coverage Summary page, his or her spouse, or one of the relatives. **We** and **our** mean the company providing the insurance.

Effective Date. Your coverage begins at 12:01 a.m. on the date shown on the attached Coverage Summary page. If we decide to broaden this Homeshield coverage within 45 days before your policy begins *or* while it's in effect, you'll automatically receive this increased coverage at no additional premium.

Optional Extended Coverages. This policy is designed to meet your individual insurance requirements. So, for an additional premium, we provide extra protection in those areas where you need it. These extended coverages are clearly marked in each section of the policy where they apply.

You can order an extended coverage at any time during the life of this policy. Any extended coverage you've already ordered is indicated on the Coverage Summary page.

Conflicts. If any terms of this policy conflict with provincial or local law, we'll enforce these terms as if they were changed to conform with the law.

Paying Claims. Basically all claims are paid directly to the person named on the Coverage Summary page. In some instances these payments may be made to others as specifically noted in the policy.

Policy Limits. Please note the *Limits of Your Coverage* shown on the attached Coverage Summary page. These limits, along with any applicable allowance for inflation, represent the maximum amount we'll pay for any *one* accident or incident, no matter how many people insured under this policy are involved. However, the limits of your coverage will not be reduced by any claims paid during the policy period.

Inflation Allowance. Your Homeshield Policy automatically protects you against inflation at no extra cost to you. We'll increase the limits of your coverage on your home, personal belongings and additional living expenses by 2% after your policy has been in effect for 3 months. And by another 2% when your policy has been in effect for 5, 7 and 9 months. This means that at the end of 9 months these limits will have been increased by a total of 8%. Moreover, on the renewal date of the policy, we'll automatically increase these limits to reflect the latest residential building price index published by Statistics Canada.

This inflation allowance will be terminated immediately if the limits of your coverage are reduced. And, in no case will we pay more than the cost of replacing or repairing your home or the actual cash value for personal belongings or additional living expenses.

Deductibles. Your Home coverage carries a deductible unless we specifically tell you differently. This means you'll pay the first part of your loss and we'll pay the rest up to the limits of your coverage shown on the Coverage Summary page. No deductible applies to your Liability coverage. See page 4 for further details.

Figure 5.1   (continued)

Your Home

Your home described on the Coverage Summary page is protected under this policy. So is the property surrounding your home, and any private driveways and roads leading to it.

We protect the glass windows and doors in your home, and fittings and fixtures such as light fixtures, storms or screens and furnaces. Fittings and fixtures are also insured against accidents while being transported for repair or seasonal storage. And they're protected while being repaired or stored away from home for up to 10% of the limit of your Home Insurance shown on the Coverage Summary page.

You leave your chandelier with a decorator to be repaired. It's covered for up to 10% of your Home Insurance shown on the Coverage Summary page.

A garage **connected** to your home and any other **attached** extensions are protected. Permanently installed outdoor equipment located anywhere on the property, including swimming pools, is also covered.

We cover any construction materials or supplies located on the property — or adjacent to it — that will be used to build, repair or alter your home.

Detached Buildings. If a detached garage or other **separate** building is damaged or destroyed, you can apply up to 10% of your Home Insurance shown on the Coverage Summary page to cover the loss. This insurance can also be used to cover the loss of any construction materials and supplies intended for use on these detached buildings. This coverage is in addition to the amount of the Home Insurance shown on the Coverage Summary page.

Your home, insured under this policy for $50,000, and a detached garage are destroyed by fire (a hazard you're protected against). You could recover as much as $55,000 for your loss ($50,000 + 10% for the detached garage).

If you have **more than one detached building on your property,** we'll pay for losses in proportion to the value of **all** the detached buildings damaged or destroyed at any one time.

Your garage valued at $4,000 is damaged by fire. You're covered for the damage up to 10% of your Home Insurance, which is $5,000. But you also have a $2,000 detached tool shed on your property. Here's how we'll compute the limit of your coverage:

Value of damage detached building Value of all detached buildings on property		Coverage limit for detached buildings (up to 10% of Home Insurance limit)		Amount of coverage for damaged detached building
	X		=	

$$\frac{\$4,000}{\$6,000} \quad X \quad \frac{\$5,000}{\text{(Extent of 10\% limit)}} = \$3,334$$

With the 10% limit you'll only be able to recover up to $3,334. If this will not fully protect you, additional insurance on detached buildings should be purchased from your agent.

Use of Property. You're free to use the property for normal dwelling purposes and make any alterations, repairs or improvements without contacting us. You may also complete any construction already begun when this policy became effective.

Protecting Your Property. If your property is damaged we expect you to take all reasonable steps to protect it from further damage. You should make all reasonable repairs and keep accurate and complete records of your expenses. We'll reimburse you for these costs and they'll be included in figuring the total amount we'll pay for the loss.

Personal Belongings

This policy covers contents of your home: Your furniture. Clothing you normally keep at your home. And any other personal belongings kept on the property. Your personal belongings are also covered when you temporarily take them from your home, up to the full limit of your Personal Belongings coverage shown on the Coverage Summary page. We won't, however, cover personal belongings you store in a warehouse. If you need such coverage, your agent will be glad to assist you.

We'll cover books, tools and instruments used in connection with your business while they're in your home. However, we won't cover anything held for sale or as samples. Please be sure that the total coverage on your personal belongings is sufficient to include the value of these business items.

There are also special rules and coverage limits for some types of personal belongings. And, a few kinds of personal belongings — automobiles, for example — that we won't cover at all. These rules, limits and exclusions are clearly spelled out throughout this policy.

Other People's Personal Belongings. We also cover personal belongings you borrow, both on your property and while temporarily removed from it.

You borrow a neighbor's camera and take it on a holiday to England. While there, the camera is stolen. The loss of the camera is covered under this policy up to the limits of your Personal Belongings Insurance shown on the Coverage Summary page.

And, if you want, you can have us cover other people's personal belongings, including those of a guest or a housekeeper, while they're at your home. Coverage will extend up to the limit of **your** Personal Belongings Insurance for all claims (both yours and theirs). For example, you can have us cover the clothes of an overnight guest that were ruined when your home burned down. We won't, however, cover personal belongings of unrelated fulltime boarders.

You can also choose to cover the personal belongings of your household employees while they're traveling with you. This coverage will extend up to the limits of your Personal Belongings Insurance shown on the Coverage Summary page.

Personal Belongings in Your Second Home or Seasonal Residence. Personal belongings you **bring** to your second residence are covered while you're there just as they are in your principal home. Personal belongings that **normally remain** at your second residence are not covered and should be specifically insured. Your agent will be glad to assist you.

If a member of your family is a student, we'll cover their personal belongings in a residence they occupy while attending school as

Figure 5.1   (continued)

long as the student has been there within 45 days before any loss.

Additional Living Expenses

If you're forced to leave your home by one of the hazards you're protected against under this policy, we'll cover the cost of moving your furniture and personal belongings. We'll also pay any increased living expenses required to maintain your normal standard of living. These payments will continue until you rebuild or settle in a new permanent home, even if this extends beyond the term of the policy. But, we'll only pay for a reasonable period of time. These payments are not subject to a deductible, can be up to 20% of your Home Insurance, and are in addition to it. What do we consider increased living expenses? Expenses over and above the amount you normally live on.

Your home is left uninhabitable by a fire. You're forced to move your family into a hotel and to eat in restaurants. Normally, your expenses — including groceries — come to $200 a week. Now, your expenses average $300 a week. We'll pay the difference.

We'll also pay any increase in living expenses for up to two weeks if you are ordered from your home by a civil authority because of a hazard you're insured against under this policy that occurs on a neighbor's property.

Your neighbor's house is destroyed by fire. The police are worried that gas pipes in the area might explode. They order you to leave your home until the pipes can be checked. We'll pick up your hotel bill and any other increased living expenses you have.

Reimbursed Rental Payments. If you rented a portion of your home or other structure covered by your policy and your tenant can no longer live there, we'll reimburse you for the lost rent minus any savings in electric bills or other expenses.

And if you were trying to rent a portion of your home at the time when the hazard struck, we'll pay you the fair rental value you could normally have expected to receive.

Hazards You're Protected Against

Your home and other property insured under this policy are protected against direct losses and damage caused by any of the hazards described below.

Fire. We protect against **fire. Lightning.** And any **explosions,** such as your kitchen stove blowing up. We also protect against sudden and accidental **smoke damage,** such as damage to your curtains and rugs caused by smoke when you accidentally forget to open the draft in your fireplace before starting a fire. But we won't pay for any smoke damage caused by pollution, agricultural smudging or industrial operations.

Theft. We protect against **theft and attempted theft** including loss from a known place when it's likely that the item has been stolen.

While you are away, vandals maliciously ransack your home. When you return, you discover that your television set is missing and your living room rug has been destroyed. We'll cover the loss of both items up to the limit of your Personal Belongings Insurance shown on the Coverage Summary page as well as the cost of replacing the window that the vandals broke to get into your home.

However, we won't cover items stolen while your home is under construction. Coverage will begin when your home is completed and ready for occupancy.

We cover personal belongings stolen from *your locked* car, truck, trailer or other motor vehicle. But, the vehicle must have been locked when the theft occurred and you must be able to show us signs of forcible entry.

If your car or other motor vehicle is stolen and not recovered within 30 days, we'll assume your personal belongings inside are permanently gone. We'll cover your loss. We'll also cover personal belongings in or attached to your car while it's in an attended parking lot provided you've given the keys to the parking attendant.

Optional Extended Auto Theft Coverage

If you've paid an additional premium and the box marked "Extended Auto Theft Coverage" on the Coverage Summary page is checked, we'll protect personal belongings stolen from an *unlocked* car, truck, trailer or other motorized vehicle.

But, under no circumstances will we cover the theft from a motor vehicle of Citizen's Band radios, tape decks, tape recorders or any other instruments used for recording or reproducing sound that may be powered by the electrical system of a motor vehicle. Nor will we cover theft of any tapes, records or other similar materials.

Civil Disturbances. We cover damage done during a **riot.** You're also protected against damage from **vandalism** and **malicious acts,** as long as you're not responsible for it.

Aircraft. We cover damage to your property caused by **aircraft.** This includes windows broken by **sonic boom.**

Motorized Vehicles. We cover damage *caused by* **motorized vehicles.** We won't cover injuries to animals or damage to driveways and walks done by a motorized vehicle owned or driven by you.

Transportation. We cover personal belongings while they are being **transported** in a truck, car or trailer attached to a car against damage caused by collision, upset or sinking. We also cover your personal belongings against the same hazards if they are being transported by a common carrier. Fittings and fixtures removed from your home for repair or seasonal storage are similarly covered. But under no circumstances will we cover damage to watercraft or equipment attached to it or outboard motors while they're being transported.

Water-Steam Damage. We cover the accidental discharge or overflow of **water** or **steam** from your plumbing, heating or air conditioning system, and from your household appliances, swimming pool or a public watermain.

We'll pay for repair of the defect itself, unless caused by rust or corrosion. We'll also pay to replace any walls, ceilings or other parts of your home that must be torn apart before the defective system or appliance can be repaired. However, we won't pay for damage to your home caused by continuous or repeated seepage or leakage. Or if the water or steam damage is the result of freezing.

And if your steam or hot water heating system, air conditioning or appliance for heating water suddenly and accidentally cracks,

Figure 5.1   (continued)

burns, bulges or is torn apart — we'll cover the resulting damage, and pay for repair of the system or appliance.

But we won't cover the damage if it was caused by freezing, nor damage to the system or appliance caused by rust or corrosion. We won't cover any damage caused by the rupture, backing up or escape of water from a sewer.

Freezing. We automatically cover damage caused by the **freezing** of your pipes, heating and air conditioning systems and household appliances while you're living in the house, or while you are away on a holiday. But if you're away, you must have taken reasonable care to make sure the heat is continued or the water turned off and all pipes and appliances drained.

Fuel Tanks. We cover damage caused by the bursting or overflowing of your domestic fixed **fuel tank,** apparatus or pipes in your home.

Wind or Hail. We cover damage to buildings insured under this policy that is caused by **wind** or **hail.** For example, if wind rips shingles off your home we'll cover the damage to the exterior of the building. But damage to the contents is only covered if the wind or hail first rips a hole in the building.

We also cover boats and other watercraft kept in a fully enclosed building from damage caused by wind. But we won't cover any damage to outdoor radio or TV antennas caused by wind or hail.

Falling Objects. We cover buildings and their contents insured under this policy against damage caused when tree branches, utility poles or other objects **fall** against the outside of the building.

But we won't pay for damage caused by objects that fall on the building because of a landslide, snowslide or other earth movement.

Glass Breakage. We cover the **glass** in any building insured under this policy against breakage. This includes the glass in storm windows and doors.

Weight of Ice, Snow, Sleet. We cover any structural damage to an insured building or its contents caused by the **weight of ice, snow, or sleet.** However, we won't cover damage to outdoor equipment such as awnings, fences, swimming pools, patios, or radio and TV antennas. Moreover, we won't cover any damage caused by snow itself, or ice, waves, high water, floods or objects in the water, even if they're driven or caused by wind.

A bad snow storm hits your area. Your attached garage collapses from the weight of the snow on the roof. We'll cover the loss of your garage up to the limit of your Home Insurance shown on the Coverage Summary page. But we won't cover damage to your greenhouse done by windblown snow.

Collapse. We cover damage that results when any building or part of a building insured under this policy **collapses.** This coverage is limited to the loss of the actual building and any damage directly stemming from the collapse. This section does not cover the settling, cracking, shrinking, bulging or expansion of any building.

Electricity. We cover sudden and accidental damage caused by artificially generated electricity. But we won't cover any damage to tubes, transistors or similar electronic components.

Additional Homeshield Coverage
Besides the standard coverage we've just described, your Homeshield Policy also provides you with the following additional coverage at no extra premium. This additional coverage does not increase the amount of your insurance shown on the Coverage Summary page.

We pay for the **removal of debris** left by a hazard against which you're insured under this policy.

We cover any loss to personal belongings caused by **temperature change** after your home or other structure insured under this policy has been damaged by an insured hazard. For example, if lightning damages your electrical panel, we'll pay for any food in your freezer that spoils, up to the limits of your Personal Belongings coverage.

You may protect your **trees, plants, shrubs and lawn** against certain hazards for up to 5% of the limit of your Home Insurance. These hazards are: Fire. Lightning. Explosion. Aircraft. Vehicles. Theft. Riot. Vandalism and Malicious Acts. We'll pay up to $250 for any one item including the cost of carting away any debris. But we won't cover anything grown for commercial purposes.

If you have an agreement with a **fire department** outside the municipality where your home is located, we'll reimburse you for up to $250 (without deductible) if that fire department charges for attending your home because of an insured hazard.

If your **personal credit card** is forged, altered or stolen, we'll pay the first $1,000 you become liable for under Canadian law. We'll even pay for losses that occur while this policy is in effect but that aren't discovered for up to one year after its cancellation or termination.

To obtain this protection, however, you must have complied with all the conditions under which the credit card was issued. And you must co-operate fully with us. You promise to notify the credit card company and us as soon as you discover the loss, and to file a detailed "Proof of Loss" Statement within four months of the discovery. We'll pay all attorney's fees and court costs.

You're covered if you **accept counterfeit Canadian or United States paper money** up to $50 for any one transaction and to a total of $100 in any one year.

How We Compute Your Loss
Deductible Clause. Losses to your home or personal belongings from one accident or incident that we determine total less than $1,000 are subject to a deductible. You first pay the amount shown on the Coverage Summary page. We pay the rest of your loss, up to the limits of your coverage. If the loss comes to more than $1,000, we'll pay the full amount.

Some losses to your home or personal belongings are not subject to a deductible. These are clearly marked wherever they appear in the policy.

Buildings. If your home or other insured building is damaged or destroyed by a hazard you're protected against under this policy, you may elect to:

Figure 5.1 (continued)

- Rebuild, repair or replace the building on the same location with materials of similar quality. We'll pay the cost, up to the limits of your Home coverage.

- Elect not to rebuild. We'll pay you the actual cash value of the damaged or destroyed building up to the limits of your Home coverage.

Actual cash value is *the cost of replacing the property minus any depreciation.* Among the items we'll consider in determining depreciation are the condition of the property immediately before it was damaged or destroyed. Resale value. The normal life expectancy of the article. And, if relevant, the location of the property.

Your home on Green Street in Vancouver is destroyed by fire. You decide not to rebuild. We determine that it will cost $35,000 to rebuild on that lot, but since the house hasn't been maintained in the last 15 years, its actual cash value (replacement cost minus depreciation) is $25,000.

Contents. We'll pay you actual cash value for contents of your home that are damaged or destroyed. Your coverage extends up to the limits shown on the Coverage Summary page. You can, however, purchase a replacement cost endorsement to cover the contents.

Special Items. We also have limits on the amount we'll pay for certain "high risk" items. The extent of your coverage depends on the category listed below.

We'll pay up to the following amounts when the loss is caused by **any insured hazard.**

- $100 in total for: Money or bullion

- $1,000 in total for: Securities. Manuscripts. Passports. Stamps. Accounts. Tickets. Deeds. Letters of credit and notes other than bank notes. Watercraft, their trailers, furnishings, equipment and accessories. Trailers not used with watercraft.

We'll also pay up to the following amounts for property that's **stolen.**

- $1,000 in total for: Jewellery. Precious and semi-precious stones. Watches. Furs and garments trimmed with fur.

- $100 in total for numismatic property (coin collections).

- $500 in total for philatelic property (stamp collections).

If you need more insurance on any of these items, your agent will be glad to assist you.

Claims We Won't Cover
Although your Homeshield Policy provides you with truly broad protection for your home, there are a few things it can't cover.

- We won't cover any damage to a building that you use for business or farming.

- We won't cover damage to your home after it's vacant for more than 30 days. But we will cover your property while your home is under construction against all hazards except theft. We'll also cover you if you are temporarily away — for example, on an extended holiday. If you are going to be away for more than 30 days, you should *let your agent know.*

- We won't cover damage to motorized vehicles or their equipment. But we will cover damage to lawnmowers, snowblowers and garden tractors.

- We won't cover damage to articles you insure separately under any other insurance. For example, if you insure a wedding ring under our Special Items Endorsement you cannot also claim for this item under your personal belongings coverage.

- We won't cover damage to goods caused by the application of heat by an iron, blowtorch or any other process. But we will cover fire that results from this heat. For example, you're not covered if you scorch a shirt while you're ironing. But, if the iron sets fire to your home, we'll cover this damage.

- We won't cover damage to anything that is illegally acquired or kept. Nor will we pay for any damage you or anyone else whose property is insured under this policy intentionally or criminally caused by your action or failure to act.

- We won't cover any injuries or damage caused by war, invasion, act of a foreign enemy, declared or undeclared hostilities, civil war, civil commotion, rebellion, revolution, insurrection or military power.

- We won't cover losses or damage caused by radioactive material, including radioactive fallout.

- We won't cover losses that result from laws or ordinances regulating zoning or the demolition, repair or construction of buildings.

- We won't cover damage caused by earthquake unless you have the Optional Extended Earthquake Protection. Nor will we cover any other earth movement such as land slippage or erosion, however caused.

Optional Extended Earthquake Protection
If the box on the Coverage Summary page marked "Optional Extended Earthquake Protection" is checked, your Homeshield Policy has been extended to cover your property against earthquakes. We'll cover any losses or damage caused by an earthquake that occurs after this optional provision becomes effective and before the policy expires. You will pay the first 5% of the value of any property damaged or destroyed within 72 hours of the first shock, and we'll pay the rest. You promise to do all you can to reduce losses. For example, to move your belongings to a safer area. We'll pay additional living expenses.

And if an earthquake damages the walls or roof of a building insured under this policy, we'll cover any resulting damage inside the building done by snow, rain, wind, or hail.

But we won't cover any damage or loss caused by the following hazards even though they're directly caused by an earthquake: Floods. Waves. High water. Ice. Or objects in the water.

Figure 5.1 (continued)

Your Homeshield Policy covers you for claims made against you for accidental physical injury to others or damage to their property. You're covered whether the incident takes place on or off your property — but the injury or damage must have been unintentional.

Why is this coverage important? Say, for example, someone trips over a garden hose you left on the sidewalk in front of your home. You're legally responsible. The person's medical bills come to $300. We'll pay the full amount — no deductible applies. We'll even pay for accidents that aren't your fault, but specific limits apply.

We'll defend any suit brought against you, even if it is groundless, and pay all costs of your defense, including investigation and court costs. We may investigate, negotiate and settle any claim or suit if we decide this is appropriate.

We'll pay up to the limits of your Personal Liability Coverage shown on the Coverage Summary page for all claims stemming from any one accident or occurrence. There's no limit on the number of accidents or occurrences we'll pay for during your policy period.

Here are the details of your Personal Liability Coverage:

Who's Covered
You're covered. So are your spouse and any relatives living in your household as well as anyone under 21 in their care or yours living with you. And some people employed by you under certain circumstances.

They are:

• Residence employees while they're using farm tractors, trailers, and other motorized, animal-drawn or self-propelled farm equipment on your behalf.

• Any person or organization that's legally responsible for animals or watercraft you own. For example, the owner of the stable where you board your horse. Or the owner of the boatyard where your watercraft is kept.

• The legal representative of the person named on the Coverage Summary page after his or her death, but only while that representative is actually attending to the property covered under this policy.

Where You're Protected
Your Personal Liability protection covers you when you're responsible for unintentional physical injury or damage. You're covered whether the injury or damage occurs in your home or your spouse's or at anyplace you are temporarily renting or staying.

Damage to property you are renting or leasing is not covered. For example, if you rent a snowmobile, we won't cover damage to the snowmobile itself. However, we will cover damage to premises you are temporarily leasing or renting caused by fire, explosion, sudden accidental smoke damage, and the accidental discharge or overflow of water or steam from your plumbing, heating or air conditioning system. But if the damage is caused by freezing while you're away, you must have taken reasonable

care to insure that the heat was left on or that the water was turned off and all pipes and appliances drained.

You're covered with respect to individual or family burial plots or burial vaults, and on vacant land including land where an independent contractor has begun to build a one- or two-family residence. But this coverage does not extend to farm land. You're also covered with respect to any land you acquire during the term of this policy as long as you don't farm or conduct any business there. But you must notify us of the acquisition within 30 days. (Apartment houses with fewer than 5 apartments are not considered to be a business). Of course, the person named in the Coverage Summary page must pay any additional premiums required as a result of the new acquisitions.

You're also covered for claims made against you when you're away from home. Anywhere in the world.

Responsibilities You've Assumed. You're covered if you assume by written agreement the liability of other people while they're on your property.

You hire a roofing company to repair your roof and sign a waiver releasing them from liability. We'll cover claims made against you because of an injury they caused while on the job.

Special Coverage for Watercraft. We won't cover damage to watercraft you have rented, but we will cover you for Personal Injury or damage claims made against you while you're using it. You're also covered while using watercraft you own, provided it's an outboard under 24 horsepower, an inboard with less than 50 horsepower, or is under 27 feet in length. Any larger watercraft you own must be specifically insured under this policy for you to be protected. However, we'll protect you with regard to any watercraft you acquire after this policy is in effect. Coverage extends for up to 30 days from the time of acquisition.

Special Coverage for Autos. Generally, claims for personal injury or property damage caused by automobiles are not covered under this policy. By autos we mean any self-propelled land vehicle, amphibious vehicle or air-cushioned vehicle. However, your Homeshield Policy does give you specific protection against such claims in certain special circumstances. We will cover claims for injury or damage made against you while you're using an automobile you don't own provided the auto is not licensed, is primarily designed for use off public roads, and isn't used for business or organized racing. For example, you'll remember that we won't cover damage to a snowmobile you have rented, but we will cover you for personal injury or damage claims made against you while you're using it.

Your Homeshield Policy also protects you against claims for injury or damage caused by a golf cart you own, while you're using it on the golf course. And from a self-propelled lawnmower, snowblower, garden-type tractor, or farm or gardening implement used or operated mainly on your property. But you're not covered if this equipment is being used for compensation.

What You Must Do
You must tell us as soon as you learn of a situation that may give rise to a claim. You'll also notify us as soon as someone files a claim or brings a suit against you and send us any legal papers received by you or your representative.

Figure 5.1 (continued)

You must do all you can to help us while we're defending a suit against you. We'll reimburse you for expenses and loss of salary up to $25 a day while you're testifying in court or performing other duties at our request.

You may also be able to recover all or part of your loss from someone other than us. Because of this you must do all you can to preserve any rights of recovery you have. For example, you must not release any of the parties to the suit from their potential obligation to pay. Or agree to pay any expenses without our permission, except for emergency medical or surgical treatment following an accident or occurrence.

However, under no circumstances will we be required to pay any amount unless you have complied with all the terms of this policy and until a final settlement or decision has been reached.

We'll also pay premiums for appeal bonds and bonds to release any property and personal belongings that are being held as security, in addition to the limit of our liability shown on the Coverage Summary page. And if all appeals have been denied, we'll also pay any interest on any part of the judgement that we're paying, in addition to the limits of your coverage.

Voluntary Medical Payments

Even if you're not legally responsible, your Homeshield Policy will pay reasonable medical expenses if you, or anyone else protected for liability under this policy, accidentally injure another person. And this coverage applies anywhere in the world. But we won't pay for injuries to you or to anyone else covered by this policy.

Reasonable medical expenses include bills for: Surgery. Dental work. Hospitalization. Professional nursing. Ambulance service. And funeral expenses.

A neighbor's daughter comes to play in the backyard. She falls off a swing, spraining her wrist. You're not legally responsible, but you can choose to have us pay the cost of her x-rays and other reasonable medical treatment, up to the limits of your coverage.

Payments Limits. We'll pay up to the limits shown on the Coverage Summary page for each person injured in any one accident. These expenses can be incurred up to one year after the accident. But these payments won't begin until the injured person has received all other payments available under any medical, surgical or hospitalization plan or law. Or under any other insurance policy.

Verifying the Injury. You must help us to confirm the injury should it be necessary.

Voluntary Payments for Property Damage

We'll pay up to the limits shown on the Coverage Summary page for any property damage you or anyone else covered for liability cause anywhere in the world, even though you're not legally obligated to pay. We'll even cover damage *intentionally done* by an insured child under the age of 12. In all these cases, you don't have to choose or decide whether to use your coverage under this policy until after the damage or destruction actually takes place.

Your son is playing baseball in a neighbor's backyard and he breaks a window with a wild throw. If you want, the cost of replacing the window can be covered under this policy.

Limits on Coverage. We won't cover any loss to property owned or rented by you or anyone else insured under this policy. Nor will we cover any loss in connection with property you own or rent to others. We also won't cover damage to or destruction of personal belongings of anyone else living in the same home as the person named on the Coverage Summary page.

In addition, we won't cover any loss resulting from the use or operation of automobiles, farm machinery or equipment or watercraft. And, of course, we won't cover any losses that result in the course of your business.

Verifying the Loss. Should it be necessary, you must help us verify the damage.

Claims We Won't Cover

Although your Personal Liability Protection is broad in scope, there are some claims that it can't cover.

• Generally we won't cover claims for injuries or damage connected with your business, profession or occupation. For instance, we won't cover malpractice claims.

But we will cover business-related claims if you work for *someone else* as a salesman, collector, messenger, or clerk — as long as the claim doesn't involve injury to a fellow employee. We'll also cover claims made against you as a teacher, provided the claim doesn't involve physical disciplinary action. And if you're 18 or under, you're covered while working at a part-time job such as baby-sitting, stocking shelves or delivering papers.

There are also certain business uses of your premises that are covered if you have specifically reported them to us and they are included on the Coverage Summary page. For example, you're covered if you, as a salesman, use your home as an office and a client visiting you is injured.

• We won't cover injuries or damage to anyone who's eligible to collect under Workmen's Compensation.

• We won't cover any injuries or damage caused by war, invasion, act of a foreign enemy, declared or undeclared hostilities, civil war, civil commotion, rebellion, revolution, insurrection or military power.

• We won't cover any damage or injury that results from the use, operation or ownership of an airplane. Nor will we cover any activities resulting from the use of any property as an airport or landing strip.

SPECIMEN

Figure 5.1   (continued)

Conditions Applicable to the Various Coverages Provided Herein

In respect of your Personal Liability Protection (including Residence Voluntary Compensation when added) — Statutory Conditions 1, 3, 4, 5 and 15 only, apply. Otherwise, all of the Conditions set forth under the titles Statutory Conditions and Additional Conditions apply with respect to all of the perils insured by this policy except as these Conditions may be modified or supplemented by the Forms or Endorsements attached.

Statutory Conditions

Misrepresentation

1. If a person applying for Insurance falsely describes the property to the prejudice of the Insurer, or misrepresents or fraudulently omits to communicate any circumstance that is material to be made known to the Insurer in order to enable it to judge of the risk to be undertaken, the contract is void as to any property in relation to which the misrepresentation or omission is material.

Property of Others

2. Unless otherwise specifically stated in the contract, the Insurer is not liable for loss or damage to property owned by any person other than the Insured, unless the interest of the Insured therein is stated in the contract.

Change of Interest

3. The Insurer is liable for loss or damage occurring after an authorized assignment under the Bankruptcy Act or change of title by succession, by operation of law, or by death.

Material Change

4. Any change material to the risk and within the control and knowledge of the Insured avoids the contract as to the part affected thereby, unless the change is promptly notified in writing to the Insurer or its local agent, and the Insurer when so notified may return the unearned portion, if any, of the premium paid and cancel the contract, or may notify the Insured in writing that, if he desires the contract to continue in force, he must, within fifteen days of the receipt of the notice, pay to the Insurer an additional premium, and in default of such payment the contract is no longer in force and the Insurer shall return the unearned portion, if any, of the premium paid.

Termination

5. (1) This contract may be terminated,
(a) by the Insurer giving to the Insured fifteen days' notice of termination by registered mail or five days' written notice of termination personally delivered;
(b) by the Insured at any time on request.
(2) Where this contract is terminated by the Insurer,
(a) the Insurer shall refund the excess of premium actually paid by the Insured over the pro rata premium for the expired time, but, in no event, shall the pro rata premium for the expired time be deemed to be less than any minimum retained premium specified; and
(b) the refund shall accompany the notice unless the premium is subject to adjustment or determination as to amount, in which case the refund shall be made as soon as practicable.
(3) Where this contract is terminated by the Insured, the Insurer shall refund as soon as practicable the excess of the premium actually paid by the Insured over the short rate premium for the expired time, but in no event shall the short rate premium for the expired time be deemed to be less than any minimum retained premium specified.
(4) The refund may be made by money, postal or express company money order or cheque payable at par.
(5) The fifteen days mentioned in clause (a) of subcondition (1) of this condition commences to run on the day following the receipt of the registered letter at the post office to which it is addressed.

Requirements After Loss

6. (1) Upon the occurrence of any loss of or damage to the insured property, the Insured shall, if the loss or damage is covered by the contract, in addition to observing the requirements of conditions 9, 10 and 11,
(a) forthwith give notice thereof in writing to the Insurer;
(b) delivery as soon as practicable to the Insurer a proof of loss verified by a statutory declaration,
(i) giving a complete inventory of the destroyed and damaged property and showing in detail quantities, costs, actual cash value and particulars of amount of loss claimed;
(ii) stating when and how the loss occurred, and if caused by fire or explosion due to ignition, how the fire or explosion originated, so far as the Insured knows or believes;
(iii) stating that the loss did not occur through any wilful act or neglect or the procurement, means or connivance of the Insured;
(iv) showing the amount of other insurances and the names of other insurers;
(v) showing the interest of the Insured and of all others in the property with particulars of all liens, encumbrances and other charges upon the property;
(vi) showing any changes in title, use, occupation, location, possession or exposures of the property since the issue of the contract;
(vii) showing the place where the property insured was at the time of loss;
(c) if required, give a complete inventory of undamaged property and showing in detail quantities, cost, actual cash value;
(d) if required and if practicable, produce books of account, warehouse receipts and stock lists, and furnish invoices and other vouchers verified by statutory declaration, and furnish a copy of the written portion of any other contract.
(2) The evidence furnished under clauses (c) and (d) of sub-paragraph (1) of this condition shall not be considered proofs of loss within the meaning of conditions 12 and 13.

Fraud

7. Any fraud or wilfully false statement in a statutory declaration in relation to any of the above particulars, vitiates the claim of the person making the declaration.

Who May Give Notice and Proof

8. Notice of loss may be given and proof of loss may be made by the agent of the Insured named in the contract in case of absence or inability of the Insured to give the notice or make the proof, and absence or inability being satisfactorily accounted for, or in the like case, or if the Insured refuses to do so, by a person to whom any part of the insurance money is payable.

Salvage

9. (1) The Insured, in the event of any loss or damage to any property insured under the contract, shall take all reasonable steps to prevent further damage to such property so damaged and to prevent damage to other property insured hereunder including, if necessary, its removal to prevent damage or further damage thereto.
(2) The Insurer shall contribute pro rata towards any reasonable and proper expenses in connection with steps taken by the Insured and required under sub-paragraph (1) of this condition according to the respective interests of the parties.

Entry, Control, Abandonment

10. After loss or damage to insured property, the Insurer has an immediate right of access and entry by accredited agents sufficient to enable them to survey and examine the property, and to make an estimate of the loss or damage, and, after the Insured has secured the property, a further right of access and entry sufficient to enable them to make appraisement or particular estimate of the loss or damage, but the Insurer is not entitled to the control or possession of the insured property, and without the consent of the Insurer there can be no abandonment to it of insured property.

Appraisal

11. In the event of disagreement as to the value of the property insured, the property saved or the amount of the loss, those questions shall be determined by appraisal as provided under The Insurance Act before there can be any recovery under this contract whether the right to recover on the contract is disputed or not, and independently of all other questions. There shall be no right to an appraisal until a specific demand therefor is made in writing and until after proof of loss has been delivered.

When Loss Payable

12. The loss is payable within sixty days after completion of the proof of loss, unless the contract provides for a shorter period.

Replacement

13. (1) The Insurer, instead of making payment, may repair, rebuild, or replace the property damaged or lost, giving written notice of its intention so to do within thirty days after receipt of the proofs of loss.
(2) In that event the Insurer shall commence to so repair, rebuild, or replace the property within forty-five days after receipt of the proofs of loss, and shall thereafter proceed with all due diligence to the completion thereof.

Action

14. Every action or proceeding against the Insurer for the recovery of any claim under or by virtue of this contract is absolutely barred unless commenced within one year next after the loss or damage occurs.

Notice

15. Any written notice to the Insurer may be delivered at, or sent by registered mail to, the chief agency or head office of the Insurer in the Province. Written notice may be given to the Insured named in the contract by letter personally delivered to him or by registered mail addressed to him at his latest post office address as notified to the Insurer. In this condition, the expression "registered" means registered in or outside Canada.

Additional Conditions

Notice to Authorities

I. Where the loss is due to malicious acts, burglary, robbery, theft, or attempt thereat, or is suspected to be so due, the Insured shall give immediate notice thereof to the police or other authorities having jurisdiction.

No Benefit to Bailee

II. It is warranted by the Insured that this insurance shall in no wise enure directly or indirectly to the benefit of any carrier or other bailee.

Pair and Set

III. In the case of loss of or damage to any article or articles, whether scheduled or unscheduled, which are a part of a set, the measure of loss of or damage to such article or articles shall be a reasonable and fair proportion of the total value of the set, but in no event shall such loss or damage be construed to mean total loss of set.

Parts

IV. In the case of loss of or damage to any part of the insured property whether scheduled or unscheduled, consisting, when complete for use, of several parts, the Insurer is not liable for more than the insured value of the part lost or damaged, including the cost of installation.

Figure 5.1 (continued)

**Royal Insurance**
Canada

Special Items Endorsement

This endorsement provides you with extra protection against physical loss, damage or destruction of special "high risk" items caused by an external risk. These include such items as photographic equipment, firearms, furs, jewellery and watches, musical instruments, radios and typewriters, silver and goldware, and stamp and coin collections.

The following are totals, by type of property, for the individual items you have listed.

Property Class

Description	Category Limit	Premium
Cameras projection equipment, film and photographic equipment	$	$
Firearms	$	$
Furs and garments trimmed with fur	$	$
Jewellery, precious stones and watches	$1,000	$11.00
Musical instruments and accessories	$	$
Portable radios and portable typewriters	$	$
Silverware, silver plated ware, goldware, gold plated ware and pewterware. (Not including pens, pencils, flasks, smoking implements or accessories and articles of personal adornment.)	$	$
Stamp and coin collections, including philatelic and numismatic equipment	$	$
Total	$1,000	$11.00

Property Schedule

Each item below is insured separately for its replacement value, but not more than the amount listed in this property schedule

Item Number	Description	Limits of Your Coverage
1	Diamond ring	$1,000

Special Conditions

Limits on stamp and coin collections. Unless specifically listed in your property schedule above, we won't pay more than $250 for any one item in a coin or stamp collection. For example, one stamp, coin or other individual article or pair, strip, block, series, sheet, cover frame, card, etc.

Musical instruments. You agree not to use any musical instrument insured under this endorsement professionally without written permission from us.

Newly acquired property. You're covered for losses or damage to any items you acquire during the term of this policy as long as you don't exceed the category limit for that item. But you must notify us of the acquisition in writing within 30 days. And in no case will we pay more than $5,000 for losses to these items.

Claims We Won't Cover

This endorsement provides you with truly broad protection for these "high risk" items. However, there are a few losses or damage we won't cover.

- We won't cover damage from normal wear and tear.

- We won't cover losses due to mechanical breakdown.

- We won't cover losses to property that's illegally acquired, kept, stored or transported. Or property seized or confiscated by order of a public authority or as the result of a violation of the law.

- We won't cover losses or damage caused by deterioration, insects or vermin.

- We won't cover losses or damage caused by war, invasion, act of foreign enemy, declared or undeclared hostilities, civil war, rebellion, revolution, insurrection or military power.

- We won't cover losses or damages caused by radioactive material, including radioactive fallout.

Figure 5.1   (continued)

Charge/Mortgage of Land

Form 2 — Land Registration Reform Act, 1984

Province of Ontario

Canada Trust **B**

(1) ☑ Registry ☐ Land Titles	**(2)** Page 1 of ___ pages

(3) Property Identifier(s)   Block   Property

Additional: See Schedule ☐

(4) Principal Amount

--ONE HUNDRED THOUSAND--   Dollars $ 100,000.00

(5) Description

Part of Lot Number One, Concession 15, Township of Middleton, County of Wellington.

New Property Identifiers

Additional: See Schedule ☐

Executions

Additional: See Schedule ☐

FOR OFFICE USE ONLY

(6) This Document Contains   (a) Redescription New Easement Plan/Sketch ☐   (b) Schedule for: Description ☒   Additional Parties ☐   Other ☒

(7) Interest/Estate Charged
Fee Simple

(8) Standard Charge Terms — The parties agree to be bound by the provisions in Standard Charge Terms filed as number 8544 and the Chargor(s) hereby acknowledge(s) receipt of a copy of these terms.

(9) Payment Provisions

(a) Principal Amount $ 100,000,.00	(b) Interest Rate 13.25 % per annum	(c) Calculation Period semi-annual not in advance

	Y	M	D			
(d) Interest Adjustment Date	91	06	15	(e) Payment Date and Period	15 th of each month	(f) First Payment Date Y 91 M 06 15
(g) Last Payment Date	96	06	15	(h) Amount of Each Payment	One thousand, one hundred nineteen and 82/100	Dollars $ 1119.82
(i) Balance Due Date	96	06	15	(j) Insurance	Full replacement cost	Dollars $

(10) Additional Provisions

Continued on Schedule ☐

Figure 15.2   SAMPLE MORTGAGE CONTRACT
Source: Reproduced with the permission of Canada Trustco Mortgage Company.

(11) Chargor(s) The chargor hereby charges the land to the chargee and certifies that the chargor is at least eighteen years old and that

..I. am .a. spouse.... The. person. consenting. below. is .my .spouse..............................

The chargor(s) acknowledge(s) receipt of a true copy of this charge.

Name(s)	Signature(s)	Date of Signature Y M D
James P. Schwartz	*James P. Schwartz*	
Petra O. Schwartz	*Petra O. Schwartz*	

(12) Spouse(s) of Chargor(s) I hereby consent to this transaction.

Name(s)	Signature(s)	Date of Signature Y M D
Petra O. Schwartz	*Petra O. Schwartz*	

(13) Chargor(s) Address for Service 12 Maple Drive, Fergus, Ontario, N1F 4H0

(14) Chargee(s)

................Canada .Trusto .Mortgage. Company...........................

............Wyndham .Street,. Guelph,. Ontario.......................

(15) Chargee(s) Address for Service

(16) Assessment Roll Number of Property	Cty.	Mun.	Map	Sub.	Par.		Fees	
	32	08	020	011	20300		Registration Fee	22.00

(17) Municipal Address of Property	**(18) Document Prepared by:**		
	Smith and Smith 100 Douglas Street Guelph, Ontario		
		Total	22.00

05-359 (1285)

Figure 15.2 (continued)

SCHEDULE 1 A

1 TO 5 YEAR

All terms that are defined in the Standard Charge Terms referred to in box 8 of the attached Charge/Mortgage of Land have the same meaning when used in this Schedule.

PAYMENT PROVISIONS

Interest

Interest is payable on the balance of the principal amount outstanding from time to time as follows:

(a) from the date that any part of the principal amount is advanced until ___June 15___ , 19 96 , interest is payable at the rate of _13.25_ percent (_____ %) per annum, calculated half-yearly, not in advance, before and after default, demand, maturity and judgment; and

(b) after ___June 15___ , 19 96 , interest is payable at the rate which, on any day, is the greater of the rate specified in (a) and Canada Trust's Prime Demand Rate on such day, calculated half-yearly, not in advance, before and after default, demand, maturity and judgment. Canada Trust's Prime Demand Rate is subject to change from time to time without notice to you.

Interest is also payable at the rate payable on the principal amount on any amount not paid when due (including interest) and on any judgment. If interest on an overdue amount is not paid within six months of the date the amount was due, such interest will become due and payable at the end of such six months and, therefore, will itself bear interest at the same rate thereafter.

Payments

Canada Trust may, at its option, deduct from any advance of the principal amount the interest that has accrued on previous advances or any other amount payable to it. The principal amount and accrued interest will be payable by monthly instalments of $ 1119.82 on the _15th_ day of each month beginning June _____ , 19 91 , and ending ___June 15___ , 19 96 , on which date the balance of the principal amount and accrued interest become payable on demand. Any demand for payment made by Canada Trust may be delivered personally to you or may be mailed, postage prepaid, to your most recent address appearing in Canada Trust's records relating to the mortgage. ANY SUCH DEMAND SHALL BE CONCLUSIVELY DEEMED TO BE GIVEN AND RECEIVED ON THE DATE OF DELIVERY OR THE FIFTH DAY AFTER MAILING. All amounts paid to Canada Trust will be applied first to accrued interest and then to the principal amount, except that, if you fail to comply with any of your obligations under the mortgage, Canada Trust may apply any amount it receives to any amount secured by mortgage.

Weekly, Bi-Weekly or Semi-Monthly Payments

Canada Trust has agreed that instead of paying the regular monthly instalments stated above, you may, on written notice to Canada Trust, select one of the following payment options:

A. WEEKLY PAYMENTS equal to 1/4 of the regular monthly instalment stated above, payable on the 7th day after the final advance of the principal amount and on every 7th day thereafter,

or

B. BI-WEEKLY PAYMENTS equal to 1/2 of the regular monthly instalment stated above, payable on the 14th day after the final advance of the principal amount and on every 14th day thereafter,

or

C. SEMI-MONTHLY PAYMENTS equal to 1/2 of the regular monthly instalment stated above, payable on the 15th day and the last day of each month beginning with the first such day after the final advance of the principal amount,

until the balance of the principal amount and accrued interest become payable on demand.

However, if at any time your payments are in arrears in an amount which equals or exceeds the regular monthly instalment stated above, this privilege of making payments weekly, bi-weekly or semi-monthly will, at Canada Trust's option, cease to apply and you must pay the regular monthly instalment stated above on the regular monthly instalment date stated above until the balance of the principal amount and accrued interest become payable on demand.

Figure 15.2 (continued)

ADDITIONAL PROVISIONS

Prepayments

During each year of the mortgage (that is, each twelve-month period starting on the day the final advance of the principal amount is made or on an anniverary of that date), you may (provided you have complied with all of your obligations under the mortgage):

(a) make one or more prepayments, which in aggregate total not more than fifteen percent (15%) of the principal amount; and/or

(b) once in each year, increase the amount of your regular weekly, bi-weekly, semi-monthly or monthly payment by up to fifteen percent (15%) of the amount of such payment established above.

You may not, in any such year, prepay more than 15% of the principal amount or increase your regular payment by more than 15%, whether or not you prepaid less than 15% or increased a regular payment by less than 15% in previous years.

Early Renewal

If you have complied with all of your obligations under the mortgage, and Canada Trust receives a written notice (the "notice") that you wish to extend the period during which the balance of the principal amount is payable in regular instalments for an additional term commencing on a date (the "effective date") specified in the notice (which date may not be more than 12 months before the day your last regular payment under the mortgage is due), then such period will be so extended on the effective date. In such event, the rate at which interest is then payable under the mortgage (the "then existing mortgage rate") will be changed, commencing the effective date, to Canada Trust's rate on such date for mortgages having a term equal to the additional term specified in the notice (the "new rate"). The provisions of this paragraph will apply to a notice only if Canada Trust is, on the effective date, offering mortgages having a term equal to the additional term specified in the notice and only if you pay, prior to the effective date, an interest differential adjustment in an amount which is calculated in accordance with Canada Trust's usual procedures and is based on the difference between the new rate and the then existing mortgage rate. You may, on the effective date, prepay any portion of the principal amount of the mortgage and you may also reduce the mortgage's remaining amortization period by specifying the reduced period in the notice. The amount of your regular weekly, bi-weekly, semi-monthly or monthly payment will be changed, commencing on the effective date, to the amount specified by Canada Trust as approximately reflecting the new rate, the balance of the principal amount and accrued interest outstanding on the effective date and the mortgage's remaining amortization period (as reduced, if applicable, in accordance with the notice).

Sale of Property

If you enter into a genuine agreement to sell the property to a person with whom you deal at arm's length, then you may pay off the mortgage from the proceeds of the sale provided you pay us, in addition, the greater of:

(a) three months interest on the balance of the principal amount then outstanding, calculated at the rate that interest is then payable under the mortgage; and

(b) an interest differential adjustment in an amount which is calculated in accordance with Canada Trust's then usual procedures and is based on the difference between (i) Canada Trust's then current rate for mortgages having a term equal to the remaining period during which the balance of the principal amount is payable in regular monthly instalments and (ii) the rate at which interest is then payable under the mortgage.

No Other Right of Prepayment

You shall have no right of premature repayment except as provided above. You agree that any right of prepayment given to you by the provisions of any present or future law (including the rights under Section 10 of the Interest Act and any similar provincial law) will not apply to the mortgage and you waive any such right.

Figure 15.2 (continued)

Mortgage Portability

If you pay off the mortgage in full in connection with a genuine sale of the property to a person with whom you deal at arm's length and complete the purchase of a new residence within sixty days of paying off the mortgage, Canada Trust will, on application by you but subject to (c) below, provide financing for the purchase of your new residence on the security of a mortgage (the "new mortgage") on such residence, on the following basis:

(a) if the amount to be advanced under the new mortgage (the "new principal") does not exceed the balance of the principal amount outstanding under the mortgage immediately before the mortgage was paid off (the "portable amount"), then, for the period during which the portable amount would have been payable in regular instalments if the mortgage had not been paid off, (rounded to the nearest full year) interest will be payable under the new mortgage at the last rate at which interest was payable under the mortgage and, at the end of such period, the balance of the portable amount then outstanding will become payable on demand and will bear interest at the rate determined in accordance with paragraph (b) above under the heading "Interest";

(b) If the new principal exceeds the portable amount, then at the time you apply for the new mortgage, a blended rate and term will be determined using Canada Trust's then current procedure for blended rate and term financing.

(c) Canada Trust's then current policies, procedures and documentation will apply to the new mortgage (including its terms) and your application for it and, in particular, Canada Trust's obligation to provide mortgage financing will be subject to your application meeting its approval criteria in effect at the time you make the application and you must pay Canada Trust's then standard processing fees, all legal and appraisal fees and all other expenses incurred in connection with the new mortgage.

Figure 15.2   (continued)

LAND REGISTRATION REFORM ACT, 1984

SET OF STANDARD CHARGE TERMS

FILED BY

FILING NO. 8544

THE CANADA TRUST COMPANY

— and —

CANADA TRUSTCO MORTGAGE COMPANY

The following set of standard charge terms shall be deemed to be included in every charge in which the set is referred to by its filing number, as provided in section 9 of the Act.

1.   In this set of standard charge terms, "Mortgage form" means a Charge/Mortgage of Land which refers to the filing number of this set of standard charge terms and all schedules to it. "Mortgage" means the Mortgage Form and this set of standard charge terms, and includes the mortgage as amended from time to time. "You" and "your" refer to each person who signs the Mortgage Form as chargor and their heirs, executors, administrators, successors and assigns and "Canada Trust" refers to the chargee named in the Mortgage Form and its successors and assigns. "Principal amount" means the principal amount set out in the Mortgage Form and "property" means the land described in the Mortgage Form and all buildings, improvements and other structures now or later on it.

2.   You own the property and have the right to charge it in favour of Canada Trust in accordance with the terms of the mortgage. Except as you have advised Canada Trust in writing, there are no mortgages, charges, liens or other encumbrances or claims on the property.

3.   By signing the Mortgage Form, you agree to make the payments as and when required by it and to perform and observe all of your other obligations under the mortgage, and you charge all of your present and future interest in the property as security for the payment of all amounts you are required to pay under the mortgage and the performance of all of your other obligations under it. However, Canada Trust is under no obligation to advance money to you even if the Mortgage Form is signed and registered and whether or not any money has previously been advanced. If more than one person signs the Mortgage Form, each is liable and all are jointly liable under the mortgage.

4.   You agree not to demolish or make any major alterations, improvements or additions to any part of the property without Canada Trust's written consent. You agree to keep the property in good condition and repair and not to do, fail to do or permit anything to be done that might diminish its value. Canada Trust may enter and inspect the property and may (but does not have to) make and pay for any repairs it considers necessary.

5.   You will pay all taxes assessed against the property and provide Canada Trust with evidence of such payment and with all tax bills, receipts, notices of assessment and other notices relating to property taxes. Canada Trust may (but does not have to) pay such taxes either before or after they are due. If you are required to make monthly payments under the mortgage, Canada Trust may, at its option, estimate the amount of taxes for the year in which case you will pay one-twelfth of the estimated taxes, and one-twelfth of any overdue taxes, to Canada Trust along with each monthly payment. If property taxes have or will become payable in the calendar year in which you are to receive the balance of the money advanced on the security of the mortgage, Canada Trust may pay such taxes and deduct the amount paid from the final advance.

Figure 15.2 (continued)

6. You will keep the property insured with an insurance company and for an amount acceptable to Canada Trust against loss or damage caused by fire, against other risks usually covered by fire insurance policies and against those risks requested by Canada Trust. You will provide Canada Trust with evidence that you have obtained the necessary insurance and, at least ten days before any insurance policy expires, evidence that the insurance coverage has been continued. If you do not, Canada Trust may (but does not have to) insure the property and pay the premiums. By signing the Mortgage Form, you transfer to Canada Trust your right to receive the proceeds of any insurance on the property, and Canada Trust may apply them to the amount you owe whether or not that amount is then due. Every policy of insurance on the property must include a mortgage clause acceptable to Canada Trust stating that the proceeds are payable to it.

7. If you sell, transfer, dispose of, lease or otherwise deal with all or part of the property (or agree to do so), then Canada Trust may, at its option, require you to immediately pay all amounts payable under the mortgage.

8. Canada Trust may pay or satisfy any existing or future mortgage, charge, lien or other encumbrance or claim against the property and may pay the fees and expenses of any receiver or of any real estate broker, realtor or agency (including Canada Trust Realtor) appointed or retained by Canada Trust in connection with the mortgage.

9. You will immediately pay Canada Trust all amounts it is permitted to pay under the mortgage and all expenses (including legal costs as between a solicitor and his or her own client, allowances and expenses for the time and expense of Canada Trust employees, and management, real estate or leasing fees for services performed by Canada Trust charged at Canada Trust's normal rates for such services) that Canada Trust incurs in investigating title, evaluating the property, registering the Mortgage Form and any related documents, collecting the amounts secured by the mortgage, taking and keeping possession of and managing the property and taking any other proceedings or exercising any of its other rights under the mortgage. You will also pay interest at the rate set out on page 2 of the Mortgage Form on all such amounts and expenses from the date Canada Trust paid the amount or incurred the expense.

10. If you fail to (i) make any payment required by the mortgage, (ii) comply with any of your other obligations under the mortgage, (iii) comply with any of your obligations under any charge which is entitled to priority over the mortgage or (iv) immediately discharge any construction lien registered against the property, or if any statement contained in paragraph 2 above or any other part of the mortgage is untrue, then all amounts secured by the mortgage will, at Canada Trust's option and without notice to you, become payable immediately. In the event of any such failure, Canada Trust may do any one or more of the following, in any order and at any time:

    A. Canada Trust may enter on and take possession of all or any part of the property, repair or complete the construction of any buildings or improvements on the property, collect any rents and otherwise protect or manage the property.

    B. Canada Trust may sell and/or lease all or any part of the property after giving any notice required by law. For this purpose, Canada Trust may list the property with and sell or lease the property through a licensed real estate broker, realtor or agent (including Canada Trust Realtor). Any sale or lease may be for cash or credit (or partly for cash and partly for credit) and Canada Trust will only be accountable for proceeds received by it in cash. Canada Trust may cancel or change the terms of any sale or lease and will not be responsible for any resulting loss.

    C. Canada Trust may commence court proceedings to foreclose your right, title and equity of redemption to and in the property or to take possession of, sell, lease or otherwise deal with the property.

    D. Canada Trust may sue you for any amount secured by the mortgage. Any judgment Canada Trust obtains will provide that interest is payable at the rate payable under the mortgage and will not affect your obligations under the mortgage.

    E. Canada Trust may apply any amount paid to it for property taxes in satisfaction of any amount secured by the mortgage.

    F. Canada Trust may also exercise any other rights it may have.

    You will not interfere with Canada Trust's possession of the property nor with the possession of anyone to whom it is sold or leased.

Figure 15.2 (continued)

11. Should you breach your obligations under the mortgage, Canada Trust does not have to exercise any rights it may have under the mortgage and may decide not to do so, but no such decision will be considered to have been made unless it is communicated to you in writing. Any decision by Canada Trust not to exercise its rights as a result of any particular breach of your obligations shall not be considered a waiver of compliance with any of your obligations in the future nor excuse any other breach.

12. Canada Trust's rights against you or any other person will not be affected by (i) any extension of the time for making payments under the mortgage or any consent to a change in the amount or frequency of payments or in the rate of interest payable under the mortgage or in any other provision of the mortgage given by Canada Trust to you or to anyone to whom the property is transferred or (ii) the release of any part of the property from the mortgage.

13. Canada Trust's charge on the property will terminate when all amounts secured by the mortgage have been paid in full and all other obligations secured by the mortgage have been performed. Within a reasonable time thereafter, Canada Trust will prepare or execute a discharge or, if you request, an assignment of the mortgage. You will pay Canada Trust's usual administrative fee for preparing, reviewing or signing either document and all of its related legal and other expenses.

14. The mortgage is in addition to and does not replace any other security Canada Trust may hold. Canada Trust may exercise its remedies under the mortgage or any other security in any order it chooses. Any judgment or recovery under the mortgage or under any other security shall not affect Canada Trust's right to realize upon the mortgage or any other security.

15. The mortgage may be amended from time to time pursuant to a written agreement between you and Canada Trust, and such amendments may extend the time for payment and change the frequency of payments or the rate of interest payable under the mortgage. Whether or not there are any subsequent encumbrances at the time of any such amendment, it will not be necessary to register the amendment on title in order to retain priority for the mortgage as amended over any instrument registered after the mortgage.

16. You will sign any document and do any other act or thing reasonably requested by Canada Trust to carry out the intent of the mortgage. You will tell Canada Trust if there is a change in your marital status or if you sell the property so that Canada Trust will be kept fully informed at all times of the name(s) and adddress(es) of the owner(s) of the property and of the spouse of each such owner.

17. The covenants deemed to be included in the mortgage by the Land Registration Reform Act, 1984 are excluded from the mortgage.

18. Clause 2 of this paragraph 18 only applies if you now or subsequently rent all or part of the property to a third party.

    (1) You agree that the following, whether now or later on the property, will be considered to be affixed to and to form part of the property: all fences, aerials, heating, lighting, ventilating and air conditioning apparatus, elevators and plant and machinery, whether movable or stationary, together with all gear, connections, appliances, gas pipes, wiring, gas, plumbing and electrical fixtures and fittings, cooling and refrigeration equipment, radiators and covers, fixed mirrors, window blinds, fitted blinds, storm doors, storm windows, window screens and screen doors, shutters and awnings, wall-to-wall floor covering and growing things.

    (2) If, pursuant to paragraph 10 above or any other provision of the mortgage, all amounts secured by the mortgage may become, or become, payable immediately at Canada Trust's option, then Canada Trust may do any one or more of the following, in any order and at any time, in addition to all other things it is permitted to do under the mortgage:

        A. Canada Trust may appoint in writing a receiver (which term wherever used in the mortgage includes a receiver and manager) or a new receiver to replace a receiver previously appointed to do any or all of the things Canada Trust is permitted to do under the mortgage. Any receiver appointed will be considered your agent and all actions taken by the receiver will be considered to be your actions. Nothing done by the receiver puts Canada Trust in possession of the property nor makes it accountable for any money not received by it. The receiver may apply any income received from the property to pay any amount Canada Trust is permitted to pay under the mortgage (including the receiver's fees and expenses) and the balance will be paid to Canada Trust to reduce the amount secured by the mortgage, whether or not such amount is then due.

        B. Canada Trust may distrain or attorn rents for overdue interest, principal or other payments and for overdue taxes (including interest and penalties payable because the taxes are overdue).

Figure 15.2 (continued)

Table 15.4   MORTGAGE AMORTIZATION SCHEDULE

Loan	$50000.00		Rate %11.0000		Compounded Semi-Annually	Term 300
Payment	$ 481.26		Paid Monthly		Factor 0.0089633939	

No.	Due Date		Interest	Principal	Payment	Accumulated Interest	Balance
1	0	0	448.17	33.09	481.26	448.17	49966.91
2	0	0	447.87	33.39	481.26	896.04	49933.52
3	0	0	447.57	33.69	481.26	1343.62	49899.84
4	0	0	447.27	33.99	481.26	1790.89	49865.85
5	0	0	446.97	34.29	481.26	2237.86	49831.56
6	0	0	446.66	34.60	481.26	2684.52	49796.96
7	0	0	446.35	34.91	481.26	3130.87	49762.05
8	0	0	446.04	35.22	481.26	3576.90	49726.82
9	0	0	445.72	35.54	481.26	4022.62	49691.28
10	0	0	445.40	35.86	481.26	4468.03	49655.43
11	0	0	445.08	36.18	481.26	4913.11	49619.25
12	0	0	444.76	36.50	481.26	5357.86	49582.74
13	0	0	444.43	36.83	481.26	5802.29	49545.91
14	0	0	444.10	37.16	481.26	6246.39	49508.75
15	0	0	443.77	37.49	481.26	6690.16	49471.26
16	0	0	443.43	37.83	481.26	7133.59	49433.43
17	0	0	443.09	38.17	481.26	7576.68	49395.26
18	0	0	442.75	38.51	481.26	8019.43	49356.75
19	0	0	442.40	38.86	481.26	8461.83	49317.89
20	0	0	442.06	39.20	481.26	8903.89	49278.69
21	0	0	441.70	39.56	481.26	9345.59	49239.13
22	0	0	441.35	39.91	481.26	9786.94	49199.22
23	0	0	440.99	40.27	481.26	10227.94	49158.96
24	0	0	440.63	40.63	481.26	10668.57	49118.33
25	0	0	440.27	40.99	481.26	11108.83	49077.33
26	0	0	439.90	41.36	481.26	11548.73	49035.97
27	0	0	439.53	41.73	481.26	11988.26	48994.24
28	0	0	439.15	42.11	481.26	12427.42	48952.14
29	0	0	438.78	42.48	481.26	12866.19	48909.65
30	0	0	438.40	42.86	481.26	13304.59	48866.79
31	0	0	438.01	43.25	481.26	13742.60	48823.54
32	0	0	437.62	43.64	481.26	14180.23	48779.91
33	0	0	437.23	44.03	481.26	14617.46	48735.88
34	0	0	436.84	44.42	481.26	15054.30	48691.46
35	0	0	436.44	44.82	481.26	15490.74	48646.64
36	0	0	436.04	45.22	481.26	15926.78	48601.42

This schedule has been processed with interest calculated not in advance.

Table 15.4 (continued)

Loan	$48601.42		Rate %11.0000		Compounded Semi-Annually	Term 300
Payment	$ 481.26		Paid Monthly		Factor 0.0089633939	

No.	Due Date	Interest	Principal	Payment	Accumulated Interest	Balance
37	0 0	435.63	45.63	481.26	16362.41	48555.79
38	0 0	435.22	46.04	481.26	16797.64	48509.76
39	0 0	434.81	46.45	481.26	17232.45	48463.31
40	0 0	434.40	46.86	481.26	17666.85	48416.45
41	0 0	433.98	47.28	481.26	18100.82	48369.16
42	0 0	433.55	47.71	481.26	18534.37	48321.45
43	0 0	433.12	48.14	481.26	18967.50	48273.32
44	0 0	432.69	48.57	481.26	19400.19	48224.75
45	0 0	432.26	49.00	481.26	19832.45	48175.75
46	0 0	431.82	49.44	481.26	20264.27	48126.31
47	0 0	431.38	49.88	481.26	20695.64	48076.42
48	0 0	430.93	50.33	481.26	21126.57	48026.09
49	0 0	430.48	50.78	481.26	21557.05	47975.31
50	0 0	430.02	51.24	481.26	21987.07	47924.07
51	0 0	429.56	51.70	481.26	22416.63	47872.37
52	0 0	429.10	52.16	481.26	22845.73	47820.21
53	0 0	428.63	52.63	481.26	23274.36	47767.58
54	0 0	428.16	53.10	481.26	23702.52	47714.48
55	0 0	427.68	53.58	481.26	24130.20	47660.90
56	0 0	427.20	54.06	481.26	24557.41	47606.85
57	0 0	426.72	54.54	481.26	24984.13	47552.31
58	0 0	426.23	55.03	481.26	25410.36	47497.28
59	0 0	425.74	55.52	481.26	25836.09	47441.75
60	0 0	425.24	56.02	481.26	26261.33	47385.73
61	0 0	424.74	56.52	481.26	26686.07	47329.21
62	0 0	424.23	57.03	481.26	27110.30	47272.18
63	0 0	423.72	57.54	481.26	27534.02	47214.64
64	0 0	423.20	58.06	481.26	27957.22	47156.58
65	0 0	422.68	58.58	481.26	28379.90	47098.00
66	0 0	422.16	59.10	481.26	28802.06	47038.90
67	0 0	421.63	59.63	481.26	29223.69	46979.27
68	0 0	421.09	60.17	481.26	29644.78	46919.10
69	0 0	420.55	60.71	481.26	30065.34	46858.40
70	0 0	420.01	61.25	481.26	30485.35	46797.15
71	0 0	419.46	61.80	481.26	30904.81	46735.35
72	0 0	418.91	62.35	481.26	31323.72	46673.00

This schedule has been processed with interest calculated not in advance.

Table 15.4   (continued)

| Loan | $46673.00 | Rate %11.0000 | Compounded Semi-Annually | Term 300 |
| Payment | $ 481.26 | Paid Monthly | Factor 0.0089633939 | |

No.	Due Date		Interest	Principal	Payment	Accumulated Interest	Balance
73	0	0	418.35	62.91	481.26	31742.07	46610.09
74	0	0	417.78	63.48	481.26	32159.85	46546.61
75	0	0	417.22	64.04	481.26	32577.07	46482.57
76	0	0	416.64	64.62	481.26	32993.71	46417.95
77	0	0	416.06	65.20	481.26	33409.77	46352.75
78	0	0	415.48	65.78	481.26	33825.25	46286.97
79	0	0	414.89	66.37	481.26	34240.14	46220.60
80	0	0	414.29	66.97	481.26	34654.43	46153.63
81	0	0	413.69	67.57	481.26	35068.12	46086.06
82	0	0	413.09	68.17	481.26	35481.21	46017.89
83	0	0	412.48	68.78	481.26	35893.69	45949.11
84	0	0	411.86	69.40	481.26	36305.55	45879.71
85	0	0	411.24	70.02	481.26	36716.79	45809.69
86	0	0	410.61	70.65	481.26	37127.40	45739.04
87	0	0	409.98	71.28	481.26	37537.37	45667.75
88	0	0	409.34	71.92	481.26	37946.71	45595.83
89	0	0	408.69	72.57	481.26	38355.40	45523.26
90	0	0	408.04	73.22	481.26	38763.45	45450.05
91	0	0	407.39	73.87	481.26	39170.83	45376.17
92	0	0	406.72	74.54	481.26	39577.56	45301.64
93	0	0	406.06	75.20	481.26	39983.61	45226.43
94	0	0	405.38	75.88	481.26	40389.00	45150.56
95	0	0	404.70	76.56	481.26	40793.70	45074.00
96	0	0	404.02	77.24	481.26	41197.72	44996.76
97	0	0	403.32	77.94	481.26	41601.04	44918.82
98	0	0	402.63	78.63	481.26	42003.66	44840.18
99	0	0	401.92	79.34	481.26	42405.58	44760.84
100	0	0	401.21	80.05	481.26	42806.79	44680.79
101	0	0	400.49	80.77	481.26	43207.28	44600.02
102	0	0	399.77	81.49	481.26	43607.05	44518.53
103	0	0	399.04	82.22	481.26	44006.09	44436.31
104	0	0	398.30	82.96	481.26	44404.39	44353.35
105	0	0	397.56	83.70	481.26	44801.95	44269.65
106	0	0	396.81	84.45	481.26	45198.75	44185.19
107	0	0	396.05	85.21	481.26	45594.80	44099.98
108	0	0	395.29	85.97	481.26	45990.09	44014.01

This schedule has been processed with interest calculated not in advance.

Table 15.4   (continued)

| Loan | $44014.01 | Rate %11.0000 | | Compounded Semi-Annually | | Term 300 |
| Payment | $ 481.26 | Paid Monthly | | Factor 0.0089633939 | | |

No.	Due Date		Interest	Principal	Payment	Accumulated Interest	Balance
109	0	0	394.51	86.75	481.26	46384.60	43927.26
110	0	0	393.74	87.52	481.26	46778.34	43839.74
111	0	0	392.95	88.31	481.26	47171.29	43751.43
112	0	0	392.16	89.10	481.26	47563.45	43662.33
113	0	0	391.36	89.90	481.26	47954.82	43572.44
114	0	0	390.56	90.70	481.26	48345.37	43481.73
115	0	0	389.74	91.52	481.26	48735.12	43390.22
116	0	0	388.92	92.34	481.26	49124.04	43297.88
117	0	0	388.10	93.16	481.26	49512.14	43204.72
118	0	0	387.26	94.00	481.26	49899.40	43110.72
119	0	0	386.42	94.84	481.26	50285.82	43015.88
120	0	0	385.57	95.69	481.26	50671.38	42920.18
121	0	0	384.71	96.55	481.26	51056.09	42823.63
122	0	0	383.85	97.41	481.26	51439.94	42726.22
123	0	0	382.97	98.29	481.26	51822.91	42627.93
124	0	0	382.09	99.17	481.26	52205.00	42528.76
125	0	0	381.20	100.06	481.26	52586.20	42428.70
126	0	0	380.31	100.95	481.26	52966.51	42327.75
127	0	0	379.40	101.86	481.26	53345.91	42225.89
128	0	0	378.49	102.77	481.26	53724.40	42123.12
129	0	0	377.57	103.69	481.26	54101.96	42019.42
130	0	0	376.64	104.62	481.26	54478.60	41914.80
131	0	0	375.70	105.56	481.26	54854.30	41809.24
132	0	0	374.75	106.51	481.26	55229.05	41702.73
133	0	0	373.80	107.46	481.26	55602.85	41595.27
134	0	0	372.83	108.43	481.26	55975.68	41486.84
135	0	0	371.86	109.40	481.26	56347.55	41377.45
136	0	0	370.88	110.38	481.26	56718.43	41267.07
137	0	0	369.89	111.37	481.26	57088.32	41155.70
138	0	0	368.89	112.37	481.26	57457.22	41043.34
139	0	0	367.89	113.37	481.26	57825.11	40929.97
140	0	0	366.87	114.39	481.26	58191.98	40815.58
141	0	0	365.85	115.41	481.26	58557.82	40700.16
142	0	0	364.81	116.45	481.26	58922.63	40583.71
143	0	0	363.77	117.49	481.26	59286.40	40466.22
144	0	0	362.71	118.55	481.26	59649.12	40347.68

This schedule has been processed with interest calculated not in advance.

Table 15.4　(continued)

Loan	$40347.68		Rate %11.0000		Compounded Semi-Annually		Term 300
Payment	$　481.26		Paid Monthly		Factor 0.0089633939		

No.	Due Date		Interest	Principal	Payment	Accumulated Interest	Balance
145	0	0	361.65	119.61	481.26	60010.77	40228.07
146	0	0	360.58	120.68	481.26	60371.35	40107.39
147	0	0	359.50	121.76	481.26	60730.85	39985.63
148	0	0	358.41	122.85	481.26	61089.25	39862.77
149	0	0	357.31	123.95	481.26	61446.56	39738.82
150	0	0	356.19	125.07	481.26	61802.75	39613.75
151	0	0	355.07	126.19	481.26	62157.83	39487.57
152	0	0	353.94	127.32	481.26	62511.77	39360.25
153	0	0	352.80	128.46	481.26	62864.57	39231.79
154	0	0	351.65	129.61	481.26	63216.22	39102.18
155	0	0	350.49	130.77	481.26	63566.71	38971.41
156	0	0	349.32	131.94	481.26	63916.03	38839.47
157	0	0	348.13	133.13	481.26	64264.16	38706.34
158	0	0	346.94	134.32	481.26	64611.10	38572.02
159	0	0	345.74	135.52	481.26	64956.84	38436.50
160	0	0	344.52	136.74	481.26	65301.36	38299.76
161	0	0	343.30	137.96	481.26	65644.65	38161.79
162	0	0	342.06	139.20	481.26	65986.71	38022.59
163	0	0	340.81	140.45	481.26	66327.52	37882.14
164	0	0	339.55	141.71	481.26	66667.08	37740.44
165	0	0	338.28	142.98	481.26	67005.36	37597.46
166	0	0	337.00	144.26	481.26	67342.36	37453.20
167	0	0	335.71	145.55	481.26	67678.07	37307.65
168	0	0	334.40	146.86	481.26	68012.47	37160.79
169	0	0	333.09	148.17	481.26	68345.56	37012.62
170	0	0	331.76	149.50	481.26	68677.32	36863.12
171	0	0	330.42	150.84	481.26	69007.74	36712.28
172	0	0	329.07	152.19	481.26	69336.80	36560.08
173	0	0	327.70	153.56	481.26	69664.50	36406.52
174	0	0	326.33	154.93	481.26	69990.83	36251.59
175	0	0	324.94	156.32	481.26	70315.77	36095.27
176	0	0	323.54	157.72	481.26	70639.30	35937.54
177	0	0	322.12	159.14	481.26	70961.43	35778.41
178	0	0	320.70	160.56	481.26	71282.12	35617.84
179	0	0	319.26	162.00	481.26	71601.38	35455.84
180	0	0	317.80	163.46	481.26	71919.18	35292.38

This schedule has been processed with interest calculated not in advance.

Table 15.4 (continued)

Loan	$35292.38	Rate %11.0000	Compounded Semi-Annually	Term 300
Payment	$ 481.26	Paid Monthly	Factor 0.0089633939	

No.	Due Date	Interest	Principal	Payment	Accumulated Interest	Balance
181	0 0	316.34	164.92	481.26	72235.52	35127.46
182	0 0	314.86	166.40	481.26	72550.38	34961.06
183	0 0	313.37	167.89	481.26	72863.75	34793.17
184	0 0	311.86	169.40	481.26	73175.62	34623.78
185	0 0	310.35	170.91	481.26	73485.97	34452.87
186	0 0	308.81	172.45	481.26	73794.78	34280.42
187	0 0	307.27	173.99	481.26	74102.05	34106.43
188	0 0	305.71	175.55	481.26	74407.76	33930.88
189	0 0	304.14	177.12	481.26	74711.89	33753.75
190	0 0	302.55	178.71	481.26	75014.44	33575.04
191	0 0	300.95	180.31	481.26	75315.39	33394.73
192	0 0	299.33	181.93	481.26	75614.72	33212.80
193	0 0	297.70	183.56	481.26	75912.42	33029.24
194	0 0	296.05	185.21	481.26	76208.47	32844.03
195	0 0	294.39	186.87	481.26	76502.87	32657.17
196	0 0	292.72	188.54	481.26	76795.59	32468.63
197	0 0	291.03	190.23	481.26	77086.61	32278.39
198	0 0	289.32	191.94	481.26	77375.94	32086.46
199	0 0	287.60	193.66	481.26	77663.54	31892.80
200	0 0	285.87	195.39	481.26	77949.41	31697.41
201	0 0	284.12	197.14	481.26	78233.53	31500.27
202	0 0	282.35	198.91	481.26	78515.88	31301.36
203	0 0	280.57	200.69	481.26	78796.44	31100.66
204	0 0	278.77	202.49	481.26	79075.21	30898.17
205	0 0	276.95	204.31	481.26	79352.16	30693.86
206	0 0	275.12	206.14	481.26	79627.28	30487.72
207	0 0	273.27	207.99	481.26	79900.56	30279.74
208	0 0	271.41	209.85	481.26	80171.97	30069.89
209	0 0	269.53	211.73	481.26	80441.49	29858.15
210	0 0	267.63	213.63	481.26	80709.12	29644.52
211	0 0	265.72	215.54	481.26	80974.84	29428.98
212	0 0	263.78	217.48	481.26	81238.62	29211.50
213	0 0	261.83	219.43	481.26	81500.46	28992.08
214	0 0	259.87	221.39	481.26	81760.33	28770.69
215	0 0	257.88	223.38	481.26	82018.21	28547.31
216	0 0	255.88	225.38	481.26	82274.09	28321.93

This schedule has been processed with interest calculated not in advance.

Table 15.4   (continued)

Loan	$28321.93		Rate %11.0000		Compounded Semi-Annually		Term 300
Payment	$ 481.26		Paid Monthly		Factor 0.0089633939		

No.	Due Date		Interest	Principal	Payment	Accumulated Interest	Balance
217	0	0	253.86	227.40	481.26	82527.95	28094.53
218	0	0	251.82	229.44	481.26	82779.77	27865.09
219	0	0	249.77	231.49	481.26	83029.54	27633.60
220	0	0	247.69	233.57	481.26	83277.23	27400.03
221	0	0	245.60	235.66	481.26	83522.83	27164.37
222	0	0	243.48	237.78	481.26	83766.31	26926.59
223	0	0	241.35	239.91	481.26	84007.66	26686.68
224	0	0	239.20	242.06	481.26	84246.87	26444.63
225	0	0	237.03	244.23	481.26	84483.90	26200.40
226	0	0	234.84	246.42	481.26	84718.75	25953.99
227	0	0	232.64	248.62	481.26	84951.38	25705.36
228	0	0	230.41	250.85	481.26	85181.79	25454.51
229	0	0	228.16	253.10	481.26	85409.95	25201.41
230	0	0	225.89	255.37	481.26	85635.84	24946.04
231	0	0	223.60	257.66	481.26	85859.44	24688.38
232	0	0	221.29	259.97	481.26	86080.73	24428.41
233	0	0	218.96	262.30	481.26	86299.69	24166.11
234	0	0	216.61	264.65	481.26	86516.30	23901.46
235	0	0	214.24	267.02	481.26	86730.54	23634.44
236	0	0	211.84	269.42	481.26	86942.39	23365.03
237	0	0	209.43	271.83	481.26	87151.82	23093.20
238	0	0	206.99	274.27	481.26	87358.81	22818.93
239	0	0	204.54	276.72	481.26	87563.34	22542.20
240	0	0	202.05	279.21	481.26	87765.40	22263.00
241	0	0	199.55	281.71	481.26	87964.95	21981.29
242	0	0	197.03	284.23	481.26	88161.98	21697.06
243	0	0	194.48	286.78	481.26	88356.46	21410.28
244	0	0	191.91	289.35	481.26	88548.37	21120.93
245	0	0	189.32	291.94	481.26	88737.68	20828.98
246	0	0	186.70	294.56	481.26	88924.38	20534.42
247	0	0	184.06	297.20	481.26	89108.44	20237.22
248	0	0	181.39	299.87	481.26	89289.83	19937.35
249	0	0	178.71	302.55	481.26	89468.54	19634.80
250	0	0	175.99	305.27	481.26	89644.53	19329.53
251	0	0	173.26	308.00	481.26	89817.79	19021.53
252	0	0	170.50	310.76	481.26	89988.29	18710.77

This schedule has been processed with interest calculated not in advance.

Table 15.4   (continued)

No.	Due Date		Interest	Principal	Payment	Accumulated Interest	Balance

Loan Payment: $18710.77 / $ 481.26 — Rate %11.0000 / Paid Monthly — Compounded Semi-Annually / Factor 0.0089633939 — Term 300

No.	Due Date		Interest	Principal	Payment	Accumulated Interest	Balance
253	0	0	167.71	313.55	481.26	90156.00	18397.22
254	0	0	164.90	316.36	481.26	90320.90	18080.86
255	0	0	162.07	319.19	481.26	90482.97	17761.67
256	0	0	159.20	322.06	481.26	90642.17	17439.61
257	0	0	156.32	324.94	481.26	90798.49	17114.67
258	0	0	153.41	327.85	481.26	90951.90	16786.82
259	0	0	150.47	330.79	481.26	91102.36	16456.02
260	0	0	147.50	333.76	481.26	91249.86	16122.26
261	0	0	144.51	336.75	481.26	91394.37	15785.51
262	0	0	141.49	339.77	481.26	91535.87	15445.75
263	0	0	138.45	342.81	481.26	91674.31	15102.93
264	0	0	135.37	345.89	481.26	91809.69	14757.05
265	0	0	132.27	348.99	481.26	91941.96	14408.06
266	0	0	129.15	352.11	481.26	92071.10	14055.94
267	0	0	125.99	355.27	481.26	92197.09	13700.67
268	0	0	122.80	358.46	481.26	92319.90	13342.22
269	0	0	119.59	361.67	481.26	92439.49	12980.55
270	0	0	116.35	364.91	481.26	92555.84	12615.64
271	0	0	113.08	368.18	481.26	92668.92	12247.46
272	0	0	109.78	371.48	481.26	92778.70	11875.98
273	0	0	106.45	374.81	481.26	92885.15	11501.17
274	0	0	103.09	378.17	481.26	92988.24	11123.00
275	0	0	99.70	381.56	481.26	93087.94	10741.44
276	0	0	96.28	384.98	481.26	93184.22	10356.46
277	0	0	92.83	388.43	481.26	93277.04	9968.02
278	0	0	89.35	391.91	481.26	93366.39	9576.11
279	0	0	85.83	395.43	481.26	93452.23	9180.69
280	0	0	82.29	398.97	481.26	93534.52	8781.72
281	0	0	78.71	402.55	481.26	93613.23	8379.17
282	0	0	75.11	406.15	481.26	93688.34	7973.02
283	0	0	71.47	409.79	481.26	93759.80	7563.22
284	0	0	67.79	413.47	481.26	93827.59	7149.75
285	0	0	64.09	417.17	481.26	93891.68	6732.58
286	0	0	60.35	420.91	481.26	93952.03	6311.67
287	0	0	56.57	424.69	481.26	94008.60	5886.98
288	0	0	52.77	428.49	481.26	94061.37	5458.49

This schedule has been processed with interest calculated not in advance.

Table 15.4   (continued)

| Loan | $5458.49 | Rate %11.0000 | | Compounded Semi-Annually | Term 300 |
| Payment | $ 481.26 | Paid Monthly | | Factor 0.0089633939 | |

No.	Due Date		Interest	Principal	Payment	Accumulated Interest	Balance
289	0	0	48.93	432.33	481.26	94110.29	5026.15
290	0	0	45.05	436.21	481.26	94155.35	4589.95
291	0	0	41.14	440.12	481.26	94196.49	4149.83
292	0	0	37.20	444.06	481.26	94233.68	3705.76
293	0	0	33.22	448.04	481.26	94266.90	3257.72
294	0	0	29.20	452.06	481.26	94296.10	2805.66
295	0	0	25.15	456.11	481.26	94321.25	2349.55
296	0	0	21.06	460.20	481.26	94342.31	1889.35
297	0	0	16.93	464.33	481.26	94359.24	1425.02
298	0	0	12.77	468.49	481.26	94372.02	956.54
299	0	0	8.57	472.69	481.26	94380.59	483.85
300	0	0	4.34	476.92	481.26	94384.93	6.93

Daily Factor = .00029342   Balance Remaining on Loan   6.93

This schedule has been processed with interest calculated not in advance.

INDEX